让法律被信仰

美国《统一商法典》案例

Cases on Uniform Commercial Code

（中英文对照本）

潘琪 编·译

法律出版社
LAW PRESS·CHINA
北京

图书在版编目(CIP)数据

美国《统一商法典》案例：中英文对照本 / 潘琪编译. -- 北京：法律出版社, 2022
ISBN 978-7-5197-6369-5

Ⅰ. ①美… Ⅱ. ①潘… Ⅲ. ①商法-法典-案例-美国-汉、英 Ⅳ. ①D971.222.9

中国版本图书馆 CIP 数据核字(2022)第 008631 号

美国《统一商法典》案例(中英文对照本)
MEIGUO《TONGYI SHANGFADIAN》ANLI
(ZHONGYINGWEN DUIZHAOBEN)

潘 琪 编译

策划编辑 沈小英
责任编辑 陈 妮 毛镜澄
装帧设计 李 瞻

出版发行 法律出版社
编辑统筹 法治与经济出版分社
责任校对 王晓萍 王语童
责任印制 吕亚莉
经 销 新华书店

开本 710 毫米×1000 毫米 1/16
印张 51.25 字数 746 千
版本 2022 年 7 月第 1 版
印次 2022 年 7 月第 1 次印刷
印刷 北京中科印刷有限公司

地址：北京市丰台区莲花池西里 7 号(100073)
网址：www.lawpress.com.cn
投稿邮箱：info@lawpress.com.cn
举报盗版邮箱：jbwq@lawpress.com.cn

销售电话：010-83938349
客服电话：010-83938350
咨询电话：010-63939796

书号：ISBN 978-7-5197-6369-5
定价：480.00 元

凡购买本社图书，如有印装错误，我社负责退换。电话：010-83938349

编译者简介

潘琪

1957 年生，北京市人。1982 年春毕业于北京大学国际政治系，获法学学士学位。在对外经济贸易大学师从沈达明教授、冯大同教授，获法学硕士学位。后赴美国学习法律，获耶鲁大学法学硕士学位（LL.M）及华盛顿大学（Washington University）法律博士学位（JD）。1988 年取得中国律师资格，1994 年取得美国律师资格（宾夕法尼亚州）。曾任教于对外经济贸易大学法律系，后长期在国际律师事务所（O' Melveny & Myers；White & Case）及通用汽车公司（General Motors）、强生公司（Johnson & Johnson）的法律部从事律师工作。分别于 1990 年和 2018 年出版美国《统一商法典》中译本（中国对外经济贸易出版社 1990 年版、法律出版社 2018 年版）。著有《美国破产法》（法律出版社 1999 年版）、《美国〈统一商法典〉解读》（法律出版社 2020 年版）。

经验的意义

法律出版社近年分别出版了美国《统一商法典》（以下简称法典）的中译本（2018年版，2020年再版）和解读（2020年版）。本书以中英文对照本的形式，收集了法典的45个实际案例，算是法典三部曲中的最后一部。3本书可以独立使用，也可以配合使用。从法典译文，可以完整地看到法典的全部条文。从法典解读，可以方便地理解法典主要条文的结构、含义和逻辑，感受法典为有效解决实际商业问题而采用的理念、角度、原则和方法。从法典案例，可以直观地看到法典在实际争议中的适用，体会在美国判例法制度下制定法与判例法之间的关联和互动。3本书为研究和了解法典提供了不同视角。结合起来，可使读者对法典获得较全面的认识。

谈到案例，一个很自然的问题是，案件、案例和判例有什么区别？从英文的角度，实际上都是使用“case”这个词。所以，主要是中文的表达角度问题。大体上，案件是指正在审理的案子，案例是指法院已经作出判决的案件，判例则是指对后来案件具有一定法律约束力的案例。判例法的特点，就是某些案例对后来的案件具有判例效力。任何具体案例是否具有判例效力，以及在何种意义上和何种程度上具有判例效力，是相对复杂和微妙的问题，并且很难脱离具体案件和具体环境而谈。通常在谈及判例或判例制度时，更多是从整体制度上看。本书收集的绝大多数案例，都是美国联邦上诉法院、州上诉法院以及州最高法院的案例，具有较强的判例效力。

与美国那些缺乏制定法的法律领域相比，法典领域的判例稍有不同。在合同法或侵权法这些传统法律领域，只在特定问题上存在少量制定法。因此，在很大程度上，判例就是法律，法律就是判例。比较而言，在法典覆盖的领域，不仅存在法典这部制定法，而且法典的规定比较全面和具体。法官在面对法典领域内的商业争议时，必须以法典的规定为准。但是，如果因此而忽视或低估了判例的效力和作用，并以大陆法的思维方式看待法典，就是对美国法律体制、理念和方法的误解。

首先，法典的很多基本原则都是对长期积累的判例的总结和归纳，是对判例所确立的法律原则的继承和确认。从这个意义上讲，不是先有法典后有判例，而是相反。法官在适用法典条文时，经常参考和引用法典之前的判例，因为它们在很大程度上体现了法典条文的渊源、意图和含义。其次，法官在判案时，经常同时引用法典条文和判例，甚至仅仅引用判例。在法官眼中，两者几乎具有同等效力，甚至判例的效力可能更直接、更具体和更相关，因为判例通常具有与当事案件接近的事实背景，能够较好地将法律原则与具体事实相结合。最后，有限的法典条文不可能具体涵盖无限的现实组合。理论是单纯而天真的，现实是复杂和狡猾的。看似丰满的法典，在现实面前常常显得十分单薄和无奈，很多问题都缺乏直接的解决方法，只觉“书到用时方恨少”。此时，多年积累起来的数量庞大的案例，则能起到很好的参考作用。通常说“阳光之下无新事”（there is nothing new under the sun），就是指绝大多数问题都曾以某种形式出现过，都有一定的处理原则和应对方法。

总之，虽然法官在判案时首先要看法典的规定，但法典与判例的关系，不是简单的主次或先后关系。理论上，两者都是法律；实践中，两者相辅相成。特别是当法典条文无法简单地提供答案或可能导致不合理结果时，美国法官的判例法传统、理念和方法就会更加显现和活跃。法官会充分发挥自由裁量权，通过灵活的解释方式，来获得自己认为合理的结果。从本书的案例中也许可以感受到，在有些情况下，法官很可能是先得出了自己认为合理的结果，然后再为该结果寻找适当根据。理查德·波斯纳（Richard A. Posner）法官在其所著的《法官如何思考》（北京大学出版社2009年版，苏力译）一书中，就讨论了法官的“实用主义”（pragmatism）理念和方法。本书的案例，鲜明地体现了美国法官在判例法制度下，是如何通过发挥自己的高度自由裁量权来解释和适用法典这部制定法的。

法官的自由裁量权看似与制定法的理念存在冲突，但在美国的法律体制中，这是非常自然和必要的。法典本身就允许、鼓励甚至要求法官这样做。法典第1.103条（a）款开宗明义地说，“必须灵活地解释和适用本法，以促进本法之基本宗旨的实现”。这项规定不仅允许和鼓励法官“灵活”（liberally）运用法典，而且要求“必须”这样做。法典第1.305条（a）款进一步规定，“必须灵活提供本法规定的救济，以使受损方尽可能地达到另一方充分履行义务时受损方本应达到的状态”。因此，如果法典条文本身无法适当地向受损方提供充分和合理的救济，法官就有权为了获得公平结果而“灵活”判案。法典第1.103条（b）款还规定，除非被法典特别排除，其他法律（包括普通法和衡平法）的各项原则，均应作为法典的“补充”。

法典的上述规定，为法官行使自由裁量权几乎提供了无限可能。并且，这些规定在法典中具有最高地位。仅凭这些规定，法官就可以运用各种方法去追求其认为的公平，而不必拘泥于在具体案件中可能会导致不公的具体条文，也不会因法典对某个问题缺乏具体规定或存在模糊之处而无所适从。摒弃死板规则和脱离具体规则而追求和实现最终结果的公平合理，是法典起草者和美国法律界都深信不疑的宗旨、目标和方法。因此，法典虽然是一部制定法，但无论其立法起源、指导思想，还是实际应用，都与判例法的传统、理念和方法高度吻合、密不可分。

在这种体制下，即便对于法典这样的制定法，无论是法官还是律师，在处理具体案件时，都离不开判例。但是，谈论判例制度易，适用具体判例难。对于任何具体案件，要在经年累月堆积起来的浩如烟海、杂乱无序和五花八门的案例中寻找合适的判例，不是一件易事。如何找到相关判例，并准确判断和表述其效力，是律师和法官专业能力的重要体现。即使是表面类似的判例，也不可能毫无差别，而看似微小的差别，有时会导致结论的完全不同。这是甄别、提炼、归纳和总结的过程，是当事方各自律师之间的博弈，是对法官的知识、经验和判断力的考验。

尽管与制定法相比，判例法总体上比较模糊和杂乱，但判例是美国法律体制的根基和支柱，并且，判例法不仅是制度，更是理念。法官和法学家奥利弗·温德尔·霍姆斯（Oliver Wendell Holmes Jr.，1841–1935）有一句名言："法律的生命一直都不在于逻辑，而在于经验。"（The life of the law has not been logic: it has been experience.）这是他在 1881 年出版的《普通法》（*The Common Law*）一书中，针对美国的判例法制度所作的评论。霍姆斯从 1902~1931 年担任美国联邦最高法院法官，是美国历史上最有思想性和影响力的法学家之一。霍姆斯上述评论所要表达的主要观点是：一方面，法律是经验的总结；另一方面，法律的应用要以经验为基础。经验决定了法律的内容、应用和发展，是法律的生命，而逻辑只是辅助工具。

普通法或判例法的起源和发展也正是这样。总体而言，不是先有法律后有判决，而是先有判决后有法律。法官早期在处理商业争议时，常常依据"商人法"（law merchant）。商人法不是法，而只是商界的做法和惯例。某项做法或惯例被法院以实际案例肯定后，法律就产生了。法官判案时，也必然动用自己对社会规范和行为准则的理解，并代入自己的公平感和正义感。这些做法、惯例、规范和认知，都可以称为经验。过去的经验总和，决定了目前案件的结果；目前案件的结果，则构成未来经验的一部分，并有可能构成今后的法律。循环往复，就形成了目前我们所看到的判例和判例制度。法官对案件的判决，既是用法过程，也是造法过程。在判例法的早期阶段，已积累的判例数量有限，因此更多的是造法。那些经受住了时间考验的案例，最终就成为后世遵循的判例。英国 1854 年的"Hadley v. Baxendale 案"所确立的间接损失赔偿原则，至今仍是英美合同法的基本原则之一。该案法官在判案时，虽然也引用了之前的一些判例，但更多的是依赖自己的看法和分析。

关于经验对造法和用法的意义，霍姆斯在《普通法》一书中说："无论是公开宣称的还是潜意识中存在的，那些自我感知的时代需要、占据主流的道德观念和政治理论，以及源于直觉的公共政策，在决定人民应受何种规则约束时所起的作用，一直远比三段论逻辑推理要大。前者甚至包括法官与民众共享的偏见。"霍姆斯这段话中所举的例子，都属于他所说的经验，都是影响判例法制度下法律原则的形成和应用的主要因素。这些因素的作用，远比抽象的理论或机械的逻辑重要。并且，霍姆斯并非认为法律应该基于经验，而是认为法律实际上"一直"（has been）就是基于经验而形成、应用和发展的。也就是说，他不是在表达主观理念，而是在描述客观事实。

这是霍姆斯对判例法制度下法官判案情况进行观察和思考后得出的结论。法官不是机器，因此其判案时无法脱离个人经验。法官自然要考虑各种相关因素，包括法条或判例的目的、原则和含义，以及法条或判例对当事案件的应用等。但无论中间经过多少过程或存在多少因素，法官最终都要基于个人的经验和理解，将纷繁复杂的外部因素综合在一起，来形成自己的个人结论。法官对案件所作结论，不仅受到客观因素的影响，也受到主观因素的影响，包括法官自己的公平感和正义感。按照霍姆斯的说法，法官的公平感和正义感，大概也属于法官的"偏见"（prejudices）。"偏见"通常是贬义词，但霍姆斯没有贬低法官的意思，而只是试图说明，法官的知识、经历、判断、情感和立场，无论多寡对错，实际上都属于经验的一部分，都会影响案件的判决，也就是影响法律的形成、应用与发展。

虽然判例法制度下的法官在判案时实际上拥有较大的裁量权和造法权，但从原则上讲，法官不能自行其是，而是必须依法判案。那么，这里的"法"到底是指什么？在判例法的早期阶段，很多问题没有先例，因此很可能没有直接可用的判例。经过长时间的积累，各法律领域目前都已存在大量判例，但面对纷繁复杂和日新月异的实际问题，常常还是缺乏直接可用的依据。同样，对于法典这样的制定法来说，尽管法典条文已相对完备，但从本书的案例可以看出，凡是能成为案例的，争议问题基本上都无法通过直接引用法典条文来解决。

美国法学会于1923年成立时，其首任会长威廉·路易斯(William D. Lewis)教授曾说，“在大街上遇到的普通人会认为，每个问题都有现成的法律规则，但作为律师，我们当然知道这个观点不正确。不可能每个问题都已存在适用的法条或判例”。那么，遇到法条或判例不能提供现成答案的案件时，法官依据什么来判案？在美国的法律体制中，法官的判案依据包括所谓的“一手依据”(primary sources)和“二手依据”(secondary sources)。

所谓一手依据，大体上就是我们通常理解的“法律”。这既包括法典这样的制定法，也包括对当事案件有约束力的判例。制定法的条文可直接阅读，但判例的应用则复杂和模糊得多。一个判例可达几千字，甚至数万字，其中哪一句是法律？实际上，与其说判例是法律，不如说判例包含了需要由当事方(包括律师和法官)进一步甄别、加工、提炼和定性的法律原则，即所谓的“判例原则”(holding)。判例实际上是法律的“原材料”，而不是法律的“制成品”。将原材料加工为制成品，不是简单劳动。这个过程需要高超的技巧，且充满未知。这就是判例法的模糊之处。但无论如何，从理论上讲，制定法和判例法都属于判案时有法律效力的一手依据。

所谓二手依据，主要是指声誉较高的学者的著作和文章，特别是诸如美国法学会所编撰的《合同法重述》(*Restatement of the Law: Contracts*)和《侵权法重述》(*Restatement of the Law: Torts*)这类具有高度学术权威性的著述。法典的“正式评论”(Official Comments)大体上也属于这类。对当事案件没有法律约束力的其他州或其他法院的案例，也可以算作二手依据。理论上，这些依据都不是“法律”。但是，从本书的案例可以清楚地看到，法官经常将二手依据作为判案依据。根据美国法学会的统计，其法律重述系列著作已在20多万个案件中被法官引用。在有关法典的案件中，法典的正式评论几乎被当作法典条文使用。法典领域的权威著作，例如，詹姆斯·怀特(James J. White)教授和罗伯特·萨莫斯(Robert S. Summers)教授的著作，也被大量引用。

实际情况是，法官的判案依据与其说是法律，不如说是法律原则；而所谓的法律原则，在很多情况下只是学者或法官的理解。背后的理念似乎是，关键在于道理能否成立，而不在于道理来自何处。这种“英雄不问出处”的方法，似乎颠覆了有关依法判案的基本认知。但在很大程度上，判例法就是这样发展起来的，因此可以说这就是判例法的基本特征。尽管二手依据严格地讲不是法律，但其主要来自相关法律领域广受尊敬的专家。相对于他们对法律原则和内在逻辑的理解和表述，真的还有更值得信赖的其他依据吗？法官自己长期从事法律争议的处理，自然也会积累相当丰富的知识和经验。

也许会有担心，即法官的自由裁量权过大后，容易导致司法腐败。但是，最好的遏制方法，也许就是公开透明。法院判决是公共信息，而判决又必须说明道理，因此，每个法官都必须做好接受社会和业内监督和质疑的心理准备。所有的案例都有可能被研究，包括与其他案例的对比研究，因此法官不能抱有侥幸心理，寄希望于自己缺乏道理的判决不被注意到。此外，由于存在多人同审和上诉制度，任何单一法官都无法单独操控判决结果。

所以，在判例法制度下，判案所依据的“法律”，与我们通常理解的法律未必是同一个概念。即使是像法典这样白纸黑字的制定法，其真实含义也需要通过判例来体现。在判例法制度中，无论纸面如何表述法律原则，也无论存在何种学术观点，只有实际案例所体现和确认的法律原则，才是最终影响当事方权利和义务的真实意义上的法律。假如纸面的某种原则或学者的某种观点在实际案件中得不到体现和确认，那么该原则或观点就不代表真实的法律。

1897 年霍姆斯法官在名为《法律的道路》（The Path of the Law）的演讲中说，学习法律不是探索“未知奥秘”（unknown mystery），而是掌握“已知技艺”（known profession）。霍姆斯认为，所谓学习法律，既不是宏观地探讨某种学说，也不是简单地记住某些原则，而是要通过研究之前判例所体现的原理、原则、思路和逻辑，来尽可能地准确理解和预测法官可能会如何判决下一个案件。这是律师为客户争取尽可能有利判决的关键。律师面对的是具体的案件，而不是抽象的学说。对律师来说，法律主要不是纸面如何说，也不是学者如何想，而是法院过去如何判以及今后可能会如何判。因此，在美国的法律体制中，无论一个领域是否存在制定法，研究判例都是学习法律的主要方法。判例的结论固然重要，但引向结论的理由更重要。每个案件都有独特性。只有理解判例的思维和逻辑，才能较准确地把握影响最终结论的关键因素。对于包括法典在内的任何一部制定法来说，法律条文都必然带有相当的原则性、抽象性和孤立性。只有基于具体判例所提供的具体事实，才能综合地进行分析、判断和权衡，公平地区分对错、善恶和轻重。

具体环境下的分析和判断，永远是最重要的能力。这种能力的培养，只能通过研究判例来实现。这就是为什么美国的法学院要采用案例教学方法，并辅之以苏格拉底式的究问。这种方法主要不是教授法律规定，而是培养法律思维。不是授之以鱼，而是授之以渔。其教育理念是，所有从事法律工作的人，都必须学会"像律师一样思考"（think like a lawyer）。这不是说每个人都要从事律师职业，也不是说律师比其他人的思考能力更强，而只是说，法律的本质在于对抗性思辨，而律师基于其工作性质，通常处于对抗性思辨的最前沿。

目前，国内有一种称为"法律人"的表述。这个词似乎最初是从英文"lawyer"翻译过来的，目前已泛指任何从事法律工作的人。但在美国法律界，"lawyer"基本上专指执业律师。法官或教授都不是"lawyer"，尽管他们通常都有律师资格。主要区别在于，律师与法官或教授的工作性质不同。法官是站在中立的立场上，相对被动地判断当事方的对错。教授可以不谈他人的观点而只谈自己的观点。对于律师来说，则必须在与对手的对抗环境中胜出。律师思维方式的独特性，就在于对抗性。

尽管如此，所有从事法律工作的人都不能抱有自说自话和自娱自乐的心态，而是要有在对抗环境中以理服人的思维方式。律师要在法庭上向法官和对手讲理。法官要在判决书中向当事方和公众讲理。教授不需要反驳或质疑他人，但需要经得起他人的反驳或质疑。律师、法官和教授的专业能力和声誉，最终都建立在讲理能力上。本书中的每一份判决书，都代表了法官的讲理过程和能力。判决书的表述是否清晰，逻辑是否严谨，论证是否充分，结论是否合理，虽然对外行人来说不能说一目了然，但对内行人来说，应该说自有公论。

由于判例法的关键在于讲理，而不在于结论，因此本书的主要目的，也不是用案例来说明法典对具体问题的规定，而是要展现法官在判案过程中的分析和思考。重要的不是结论，而是通往结论的过程。案件具体情况不同，社会实践不断发展，法律原则随时变化，解释方法灵活多变。案件的最终结论，通常都是各种因素综合作用的结果。永远不应假定，某个案例的实际结果就是其唯一可能的结果。从本书的案例可以看到，大部分问题都不是简单引用法典条文就可以解决的，都需要分析、判断和权衡，有时甚至需要另辟蹊径。

读者在阅读本书时，应注意案例的特点和局限。案例的作用，有点像在高倍放大镜下观察物体。通常看不到的情况，现在可以看到；通常理解的情况，现在显得有些不同；通常可以看到宏观情况，现在只能看到微观情况。案例既可以展现法典条文无法展现的问题，也可以使本来看上去清晰明了的法典条文瞬间变得扑朔迷离。这对于激发法律想象、学习法律逻辑、培养法律思维和锻炼法律能力，都有极大好处。但是，每个案例通常只涉及非常狭隘的具体问题，且判决结果高度依赖具体事实环境。同时，法官在判决书中的分析和表述，不可避免地要受到法官本人知识、经验、能力、判断、好恶等因素的影响和制约，几乎不可能做到在各个方面都无懈可击。这也正好说明，判案是艺术，而不是科学。1000 个人的眼中，就有 1000 个哈姆雷特。

此外，对于像法典这样的制定法，法典条文本身的庄严感，有时会掩盖或淡化一个事实，即制定法也是由人起草的，也必然受到人的经验和知识的限制，因此也完全有可能存在瑕疵。对于法典范围内的案例，很多判决困难实际上是由法典自身的不足而引起的。本书第 10 个案例的判决书由著名的波斯纳法官撰写。他在花费了很大精力解读法典第 2.209 条的含义后抱怨说，该条文“本来可以写得更清楚一些”，但同时又说，“人类的哪些产品能做到无可挑剔”？同时，对于波斯纳法官的该案判决，同院的另一位著名法官弗兰克·伊斯布鲁克（Frank H. Easterbrook）提出了长篇异议意见，不同意波斯纳对法典第 2.209 条的分析。撰写本书第 1 个案例判决书的法官也认为，波斯纳法官对法典该条的解读并不准确。无论这些法官谁对谁错，此种分歧本身就说明，不能期待制定法的条文或法官的解读在任何情况下都是完美无瑕的。

从本书的案例，还可以看到美国法官判案的其他一些特点。比如，判决书中常常体现出两种不同的，甚至可以说相互对立的精神。一方面是分析的技术化。法官通常从技术角度入手，尊重和依赖法典条文，尊重和依赖判例原则，同时讲求细致严谨和令人信服的说理和推理过程。另一方面是目标的理想化。法官的最终目标，仍然是追求最终结果的公平合理（尽管有时只是其自己认为的公平合理）。因此，除直接相关的制定法和判例法外，法官还要考虑公共政策、立法目标和价值取向，考虑商业现实、通常做法和合理期待，并考虑当事方的实力对比、处境差异和善意程度。法官力争将技术分析与公平理念结合起来。两种精神结合起来，就形成了美国法官较普遍的重技术分析但不唯技术分析的判案风格。此外，法官在判决书中的某些阐述，有时不是作出判决的必要表述，而只是法官专业思考和法律理念的发挥。这类阐述有时被称为“附带意见”（dicta），即不具有法律约束力的看法。同时，在有些案例（如上述提到的本书第10个案例）中，还可以看到同一法院其他法官的“异议意见”（dissenting opinion）。这种异议也有很好的研究价值，因为其通常从另一个角度对案件作出很有说服力的表述。

相信读者在阅读本书案例后，不仅会对法典的相关原理、原则和方法获得更真切的理解，同时也会对美国的法律体制、理念、方法和逻辑获得更直观的感受。刻板的法典条文必须结合生动的实际案例，才能显出法典的真实本色。源于真实生活的案件，是法律的“试金石”。无论是法典还是任何其他法律，还是任何理论或概念，还是任何观点或方法，都必须经受实践的检验。既中看又中用，才是硬道理。

2022年1月于北京

编译说明

货物买卖、流通票据和担保交易是法典最主要的内容，因此本书的案例集中在这 3 个领域。货物买卖的案例更多一些，因为货物买卖是法典的核心，相关法律原则对日常商业活动的影响更广泛、更明显，具有较强的代表性。本书案例采用中英文对照本的形式。这是考虑到，一方面，美国法律中的很多表述和概念，无法准确地体现在译文中，因此读者可能希望参看英文原文，以便更好地理解判决书的分析和推理过程；另一方面，判决书属于较难阅读的法律文件，因此这些案例正好可以作为高阶法律英语的理想参考读物。

本书每个案例均由 3 个部分组成。第一部分是标题，包括当事方、审理法院以及案例索引号。标注当事方的通常格式为“甲诉乙”，表明甲是原告而乙是被告。在破产案件中，则通常标为“甲案”（“In Re”或“In the Matter of”），说明甲是破产债务人。审理法院既有联邦法院，也有州法院。美国的法院采用两个相互独立的系统，即联邦系统和州系统。每个系统大体上都分为初审法院、上诉法院和最高法院。

联邦初审法院称为“地区法院”（District Court），上诉法院称为“联邦上诉法院”（U. S. Court of Appeals）并附有编号。例如，位于纽约市的联邦上诉法院称为“联邦第二巡回上诉法院”（U. S. Court of Appeals for the Second Circuit），而位于芝加哥市的则称为“联邦第七巡回上诉法院”。州法院的名称缺乏统一规则。州的最高法院通常都称为“Supreme Court”，但纽约州的“Supreme Court”是初审法院，其中的上诉庭是上诉法院，而纽约州的最高法院是“纽约州上诉法院”(New York Court of Appeals)。

无论是联邦法院还是州法院，绝大部分案件的初审都是由最低级的初审法院进行的。如果当事方不服判决，可以上诉至上诉法院。如果再次不服判决，可以请求最高法院复审。最高法院可以同意复审，也可以拒绝复审。本书的大部分案例，来自联邦上诉法院以及州最高法院或州上诉法院。破产案件的最低级法院为联邦破产法院。如果不服判决，可以上诉至联邦地区法院，并可以再上诉至联邦上诉法院。

法典是州法，因此有关法典的争议似乎应该由州法院审理。但实际上，如果案件的当事方来自不同的州，联邦法院就有管辖权，以避免州法院偏袒本州的当事方。在联邦民事诉讼法中，这类案件称为“州际案件”(diversity case)。但是，无论是州法院还是联邦法院，在审理有关法典的案件时，适用的实体法都是州法。例如，如果案件的适用法是纽约州法律，那么，无论是州法院还是联邦法院，在审理时都要以纽约州法律为准，包括纽约州所采纳的法典和纽约州的相关判例。

案例的“索引号”(citation)是查找案例时最重要的信息。美国法院判决的每一个案例都带有按规定方式编排的索引号。编排方式规定在一本称为“蓝皮书”(bluebook)的工具书里。这本书为各个种类的法律文献都规定了索引标注方式。案例索引号采用“卷号+法院或地区或领域等内容+页数”的方式。卷号和页数很简单。卷号就是案例装订成册后的卷号，而页数就是该卷中该案例的开始页数。稍难判断的是索引号中间内容的含义，因为可能需要查阅蓝皮书后才能知道。例如，“US”或“S. Ct.”说明，审理法院是美国联邦最高法院，而“F”则说明，审理法院是联邦巡回上诉法院。如果是“F.2d”，则是指“F”案例中的第二系列，因为第一系列的册数太多，需要重新开始编排。如果是“P.2d”，则是指由美国西部几个州所组成的太平洋(Pacific)地区第二系列。各州不同层级的法院可能也有各自的代号。“UCC Rep.Serv.”则是指专门为法典所编的案例集。此外，一个案例也可以有两个或多个索引号，说明该案例被同时收入不同的案卷。

只要知道案例的索引号，即使不理解索引号中间那部分内容的含义，也不影响查找该案例。美国主要的法律信息服务商，如“Westlaw”和“LexisNexis”，都向付费客户提供高度完善的案例检索服务。使用者可以根据不同的检索方式，搜索到几乎所有的案例。此外，由于案例属于公共信息，因此有大量网站提供免费搜索服务。比较主要的网站有：courtlistener.com、openjurist.com、leagle.com、caselaw.findlaw.com、law.justia.com、www.ecases.us、www.casemine.com等。从联邦法院系统主办的pacer.com网站，可以获取联邦法院几乎全部的案例，但该网站可能要收取费用。对于州法院的案例，通常也可以直接到州政府或州法院设立的网站中搜索。

本书每个案例的第二部分称为“简介”。这是为了方便读者理解案例，由本书编译者所撰写。简介包括案件的当事方、基本事实、争议问题、法律问题以及法院的结论和主要理由等。案例的第三部分是法院的判决书，包括英文原文和中文译文。判决书的分析和说理部分是全文翻译。为了方便读者阅读，编译者已将判决书中原有的事实叙述和案件历史等内容，用中文简化和归纳后放入案例简介中。对判决书英文原文的处理还包括：（1）删除了与法典无关的其他法律问题的讨论；（2）删除了制定法、判例、著作、文章等的详细引用信息，只保留了基本信息；（3）删除了引文和注释；（4）作了少量方便阅读的技术性改动。如果读者希望查阅未经处理的英文原文，可在上述提到的网站搜索，也可在“Bing”国际版上搜索。对译文的处理主要包括：（1）对于原文引用的判例或著作等，译文只简单注明而不翻译；（2）对于原文中当事方的名字或称谓等，译文适当改为当事方的实际身份；（3）译文的大部分段落开头部分，增加了提示性的黑体标题。

读者在阅读本书案例时，应适当注意其中包含的程序问题，因为这些问题会影响当事方的实体权利。关于程序规则，比较经常遇到的概念包括：事实问题（matter of fact）与法律问题（matter of law）的区别；陪审团（jury）

的地位和作用，以及法官对陪审团的指示；法官的无审判决（summary judgment）；法官排除陪审团审理的直接判决（directed verdict）；法官推翻陪审团裁定的判决（judgment notwithstanding verdict）。

在美国法律体制中，事实问题与法律问题的区分，对案件的审理和判决具有重大意义和影响。如果案件的审理使用陪审团，则陪审团负责裁定事实问题。因此，法官必须首先确定哪些问题属于应由陪审团裁定的事实问题，然后将其提交给陪审团，并向陪审团作出必要的解释和说明（指示）。对于陪审团的裁定，法官即使有不同意见，原则上也必须服从。如果法官在向陪审团提交问题或作出指示时出现错误，这种错误本身就有可能导致其判决被上级法院推翻。在上诉程序中，上诉法院主要凭借书面材料进行审理，不举行庭审，也不使用陪审团。

初审法院的有些判决，是基于特定程序规则作出的，例如，无审判决、排除陪审团审理的直接判决、推翻陪审团裁定的判决等。所谓“无审判决”，就是法院基于任何当事方的动议，不进行法庭审理而直接判决非动议方败诉。这是因为法官认为案件不存在“重大事实的真实争议”（genuine issue of material fact），且即使按最有利于非动议方的情况分析，也应判其败诉。所谓“排除陪审团审理的直接判决”，就是对于本应提交给陪审团裁定的事实问题，法官认为事实已足够清楚，无须再提交给陪审团裁定，因此直接基于自己认定的事实而作出判决。这相当于法官代替陪审团就事实问题作出了裁定。无审判决和排除陪审团审理的直接判决，都是为了提高审理效率。所谓“推翻陪审团裁定的判决”，就是在事实问题被提交给陪审团并收到其裁定后，法官认为陪审团的裁定与案件证据明显不符，因此无视陪审团的裁定而根据自己的判断作出判决。这是程序法赋予法官的一项权力，因为陪审团成员毕竟是普通市民，难免在一定情况下作出与实际证据不符的裁定。在这种情况下，法官需要予以纠正。

初审法院与上诉法院有较明确的分工和权限。初审法院的任务包括认定案件事实和得出法律结论。上诉法院对事实问题的审理权限比较小。只有在初审法院的事实认定不存在“大量证据”（substantial evidence）支持，因而属于“明显错误”（clearly erroneous）时，上诉法院才能推翻初审法院的认定。在通常情况下，即使初审法院的认定存在一定问题，或即使上诉法院本来会作出不同认定，上诉法院也必须尊重初审法院的认定。这样规定的道理在于，事实认定经常带有很大的主观性、微妙性和模糊性，需要在庭审中综合判断。例如，当事方或证人的说辞或人品是否可信，可能只有在看到其回答问题时的表情、态度或方式后，才能更好地判断。初审法院负责庭审，因此最有能力和资格作出判断。所以，初审法院的审理有时也称为事实审，尽管初审法院实际上也必须同时作出法律结论。

上诉法院的主要任务是审查初审法院的法律结论。也就是说，当初审法院所认定的事实不存在明显错误时，或在当事方对事实本来就不存在争议时，上诉法院要在此种事实的基础上，审查初审法院的法律结论是否适当。在此种审查中，上诉法院有权彻底重审（de novo），而不限于明显错误。如果上诉法院认为初审法院在适用法律时存在错误，则无论其性质和程度，上诉法院都有权推翻初审法院的判决。所以，上诉法院的审理有时也称为法律审。

需要说明的另一个问题是，本书案例来自不同时期，且适用法来自不同的州，因此，案例中提到的法典条文的内容和编号，有时可能与目前最新的标准法典文本不同。在有些情况下，案例所引用的旧版法典条文编号可从本书编译者 1990 年 5 月版的法典中译本中找到。但通常而言，判决书本身都会对其引用的法典条文进行描述和说明，因此，不同法典版本在内容和编号上的差异，基本上不影响案例的阅读和理解。此外，本书虽然可以作为独立读物，但最好能与法典的译文和解读两本书结合起来阅读。法官在判案时，总体上不可能在判决书中系统地讲解相关概念和背景知识。因此，如果对法典本身和相关法律问题缺乏较好的了解，就难以真正跟上法官的思路和分析，也难以充分理解法官的观点和立场。

目　　录

货物买卖

流通票据

担保交易

货 物 买 卖

案例1　如何区别货物合同与服务合同?

BMC Industries, Inc. v. Barth Industries, Inc.
比姆斯工业公司诉巴斯工业公司案

联邦第十一巡回上诉法院1998年；160 F.3d 1322, 37 UCC Rep.Serv.2d 63

简　介

本案涉及一套用于生产眼镜片的复杂设备的设计、制造、安装、调试和买卖。本案被告供应方（Barth）和原告受供方（BMC）于1986年订立了设备合同，其中规定，供应方“将对设备进行设计、制造和调试，并监督设备的安装和启动”。合同价格为515,200美元。合同规定的交付日期为1987年10月，同时规定该时间具有关键意义。在生产过程中，供应方持续遭遇设计和制造困难，造成严重超期。但是，当事方未明确提出对原始交付日期进行延期；相反，双方都显示愿意继续履行合同。1989年5月，供应方表示已可交付设备，但受供方拒绝接受，并于1989年6月提起诉讼。

本案主要涉及两个问题。第一个问题是，合同到底属于出售货物的合同，还是提供服务的合同？如果是货物合同，就应适用《统一商法典》（以下简称法典）第2篇，并根据该篇解决当事方争议。如果是服务合同，就应适用法典以外的普通法。这个问题之所以重要，是因为对于当事方争议的实质问题，包括受供方是否作出过弃权，以及供应方应在何时交付设备等问题，法典第 2 篇和普通法的规定有所不同。受供方为了争取对自己有利的判决，主张本案合同为服务合同。初审法院支持了受供方的主张。上诉法院基于“主要内容”（predominant factor）原则推翻了初审法院的判决，判定本案合同属于法典第 2 篇范围内的货物合同。根据主要内容原则，合同的性质要根据合同的主要内容来决定，而何为主要内容，则需要综合判断。需要考虑的因素包括合同所使用的语言、当事方的行为、合同的相关规定等。

第二个问题是，受供方是否已放弃了合同约定的 1987 年 10 月的交付日期？如果没有弃权，则供应方明显已经违反合同，因为实际交付日期比合同日期晚了 18 个月。如果已经弃权，就相当于合同未规定交付日期，因此根据法典规定，供应方应在合理时间内作出交付。确定受供方是否已经弃权的关键，在于如何理解法典第 2.209 条有关弃权的规定，而其中的主要问题是，法典是否要求弃权必须存在“损害性依赖”（detrimental reliance）？

损害性依赖是普通法中的概念。根据普通法原则，如果一方作出弃权，但另一方未就此支付对价，则弃权没有约束力。作为该原则的例外，即使另一方没有支付对价，但只要依赖该弃权而受到了损失，弃权就有约束力。也就是说，依赖方的损失就相当于其支付的对价，而此种依赖就称为损害性依赖。在本案中，供应方未支付对价，也没有明显的依赖损失。因此，如果弃权必须伴随损害性依赖，则即使受供方已经明示或默示地作出了弃权，该弃权对其也没有约束力。

关于法典第 2.209 条中的弃权是否要求存在损害性依赖的问题，不同法院的判决存在分歧。本案判决特别提到了著名的波斯纳法官的一个判例（本书第 10 个案例），因为波斯纳法官认为，法典要求存在损害性依赖。但是，本案法官不同意波斯纳法官的观点，并说明为什么法典中没有这个要求。随后，本案法官在分析后认定，受供方已通过其行为，放弃了合同约定的 1987 年 10 月的交付日期。

基于上述理由，上诉法院推翻了原判并发回重审。上诉法院认定，由于受供方已经放弃了 1987 年 10 月的交付日期，因此根据法典规定，供应方必须在合理时间内作出交付。在本案中，卖方实际于 1989 年 5 月作出了提示交付。

考虑到双方在此之前的交往活动,上诉法院要求初审法院通过重新审理来确定,供应方 1989 年 5 月的提示交付，是否属于合理时间内的交付。在确定这个问题后，初审法院应重新作出相应判决。

判　决

本案的主要问题和基本结论 我们在本判决中将分析，本案合同主要是（受法典管辖的）货物合同，还是（受普通法管辖的）服务合同？我们的结论是，本案合同是货物合同。我们随后在本判决中将分析，在交付日期已经超过之后，受供方是否已通过其行为，放弃了 1987 年 10 月的交付日期？我们的结论是，作为法律问题，受供方对交付日期作出了弃权，但仍然存在需要审理的事实问题，即根据当时情况，供应方是否在合理时间内对（被受供方拒收的）设备作出了提示交付？因此，我们推翻初审法院有关供应方败诉的判决并将案件发回重审，以便对合理时间问题作出认定。

In this opinion, we consider whether the Contract was predominantly a transaction in goods （and thus governed by the UCC） or in services （and thus governed by the common law）, and conclude that it was a transaction in goods. We ［next］ examine whether BMC waived the October 1987 delivery date through its conduct after the delivery date had passed. We conclude that BMC waived the delivery date as a matter of law, but that a triable issue of fact remains as to whether Barth tendered the equipment （which BMC rejected） within a reasonable time under the circumstances. We therefore vacate the judgment entered against Barth, and remand the case for a new trial on the reasonableness issue.

法典第 2 篇的适用范围 法典第 2 篇仅适用于“货物交易”

The UCC’s Article 2 only applies to “transactions in goods”. Fla. Stat. 2-102.

（法典第 2.102 条）。根据法典的定义，货物是指“在特定于买卖合同项下时可以移动的所有物品（包括特别制造的货物），但不包括用于支付价款的金钱，也不包括投资证券（第 8 篇）或诉权物”[法典第 2.105 条（1）款]。因此，纯粹的服务合同不受法典第 2 篇的管辖。但是，法院经常需要面对同时包含货物和服务的合同，即所谓的“混合”合同。大多数法院采用“主要内容”的检验标准，用于确定此种混合合同到底是受法典管辖的货物合同，还是不受其管辖的服务合同（参见 B 诉 C 案）。

Goods are defined as “all things（including specially manufactured goods）which are movable at the time of identification to the contract for sale other than the money in which the price is to be paid, investment securities（chapter 8）and things in action”. Fla. Stat. 2.105（1）. A contract that is exclusively for services, therefore, is not governed by Article 2. Courts are frequently faced, however, with contracts involving both goods and services--so-called “hybrid” contracts. Most courts follow the “predominant factor” test to determine whether such hybrid contracts are transactions in goods, and therefore covered by the UCC, or transactions in services, and therefore excluded. See Bonebrake v. Cox.

主要内容的检验标准 根据上述检验标准，法院需要确定，“如果以合理方式描述合同，其主要内容、本质或目的是否系提供服务，因而所涉及的货物只是附带内容（如画家的画作合同）？还是货物交易，因而所涉及的劳务只是附带内容（如浴室里安装热水器的合同）？”（B 诉 C 案）佛罗里达州至少有一个法院默示

Under this test, the court determines “whether their predominant factor, their thrust, their purpose, reasonably stated, is the rendition of service, with goods incidentally involved（e.g., contract with artist for painting）or is a transaction of sale, with labor incidentally involved（e.g., installation of a water heater in a bathroom）”. Id. At least one Florida court has implicitly adopted the predominant factor test. See

采纳了“主要内容”的检验标准［参见U诉N案（“由于交易的主要性质是提供产品，而不是提供服务，因此我们认为，本案的预制管件应被视为货物”）］。

United States Fidelity & Guar. Co. v. North Am. Steel Corp. （“Since the predominate nature of the transaction was the furnishing of a product rather than services, we believe that the fabricated pipe could properly be characterized as goods.”）

合同用词 一般而言，法院尚未找到任何单一因素，用于确定混合合同到底是货物合同还是服务合同，但法院认为，合同的几个方面具有特别重要的意义。合同文字本身可以提供一定线索，用于说明当事方自认为协议的主要内容是货物还是服务。例如，合同中将交易称为“采购”的用语，或将当事方称为“买方”和“卖方”的用语，可以显示该交易为货物交易，而不是服务［参见B诉C案（提及“设备”的用语，专指货物而不是服务）；B诉M案（合同将交易称为“采购”，并将其中一个当事方称为“客户”，说明该交易属于货物交易）；M诉H案（合同将当事方称为“卖方”和“采购方”，说明其为货物合同）］。

Although courts generally have not found any single factor determinative in classifying a hybrid contract as one for goods or services, courts find several aspects of a contract particularly significant. First, the language of the contract itself provides insight into whether the parties believed the goods or services were the more important element of their agreement. Contractual language that refers to the transaction as a “purchase”, for example, or identifies the parties as the “buyer” and “seller”, indicates that the transaction is for goods rather than services. See Bonebrake （stating that language referring to “equipment” is peculiar to goods rather than services）; Bailey v. Montgomery Ward & Co. （holding that a contract that identifies the transaction as a “purchase” and one of the parties as the “customer” signals a transaction in goods）; Meeker v. Hamilton Grain

Elevator Co. (stating that a contract that calls the parties "seller" and "purchaser" indicates a contract for goods).

计费方式 法院还会审查交易的计费方式。如果合同价格不包括服务的成本，或货物的费用超过服务的费用，合同就更有可能是货物合同[参见T诉H案(如果账单不包括服务，就显示合同是货物合同)；L诉D案(该案合同为服务合同，因为可以看到，账单没有给服务和货物分别计费，且证据显示，货物的成本不足合同价格的一半)]。

Courts also examine the manner in which the transaction was billed; when the contract price does not include the cost of services, or the charge for goods exceeds that for services, the contract is more likely to be for goods. See Triangle Underwriters, Inc. v. Honeywell, Inc. (stating that a bill that does not include services indicates a contract for goods); Lincoln Pulp & Paper Co. v. Dravo Corp. (holding that the contract at issue was for services after noting that the bill did not allocate costs between services and goods, and the evidence showed that the cost of the goods was less than half of the contract price).

可移动的货物 可以移动的货物也是一个标志，说明是货物合同，而不是服务合同。在确定一项合同是否为货物合同时，法典对货物的定义明确强调了移动性问题。法典规定，货物是指"在特定于合同项下时可以移动的所有物品(包括特别制造的货物)"[法典第2.105条(1)款]。在涉及一份印刷材料的编辑和出

Movable goods is another hallmark of a contract for goods rather than services. The UCC's definition of goods makes clear the importance of mobility in determining whether a contract is for goods; the UCC states that goods are "all things (including specially manufactured goods) which are movable at the time of identification to the contract for sale". Fla. Stat. 2.105 (1). Noting the importance of mobility, one Florida court

版合同时，佛罗里达州一家法院强调了移动的重要性，并基于该理由判定合同为货物合同。法院说明，“上诉人声称的其已提供的物品，是专门生产或制造的，并且可以移动”［L 诉 F 案；另参见 S 诉 U 案（提供材料和劳务来安装房屋屋顶的合同属于货物合同，因为“将要安装的材料，在特定于合同项下时是可以移动的”）］。

held that a contract to edit and publish printed materials was a contract for goods after stating that "[t] he items allegedly furnished by the appellant were specially produced or manufactured and were movable". Lake Wales Publ' g Co. v. Florida Visitor, Inc.; see also Smith v. Union Supply Co. (holding that a contract to provide the materials and labor for installation of a new roof was a contract for goods because "[t] he materials to be installed ... were movable at the time of identification to the contract for sale").

初审法院的结论　在本案中，初审法院主要依据 L 诉 D 案而得出结论，认定本案合同是服务合同而不是货物合同。在 L 诉 D 案中，合同涉及为纸浆工厂设计和建造一台热力和化工回收设备。初审法院认为，本案与 L 诉 D 案类似，因为在本案合同中，供应方有义务设计、制造、检测和安装设备，并且合同的价款未区分服务费用和材料费用。初审法院的结论是，本案与 L 诉 D 案有足够的相似度，因此应该得出同样的结论，即合同是服务合同而不是货物合同。

In this case, the district court relied primarily on Lincoln Pulp & Paper for its conclusion that the contract was for services rather than goods. The contract at issue in Lincoln Pulp & Paper involved the design and construction of a heat and chemical recovery unit in a pulp mill. The district court noted that, similar to Lincoln Pulp & Paper, the Contract obligated Barth to design, manufacture, test, and construct equipment, and also that the Contract's price did not allocate expenses between services and materials. The district court concluded that this case was sufficiently analogous to Lincoln Pulp & Paper to warrant the same result:

a determination that the Contract was for services rather than goods.

事实问题与法律问题 一项合同的主要内容是货物还是服务，通常属于事实问题（参见A诉H案）。但是，如果当事方对有关合同条款的重大事实不存在真实争议，法院也可将其作为法律问题进行判定（参见A诉H案）。在本案中，初审法院认定不存在有关合同条款的重大事实问题。因此，初审法院判定，作为法律问题，本案合同为服务合同。对于法律问题，在上诉审查时，我们可以彻底地重新审阅（参见P诉U案）。

The question whether a contract is predominantly for goods or services is generally one of fact. See Allmand Assocs., Inc. v. Hercules Inc. When there is no genuine issue of material fact concerning the contract's provisions, however, a court may determine the issue as a matter of law. See id. Concluding that there are no material issues of fact as to the terms of the contract, the district court decided as a matter of law that the contract was for services. We review questions of law de novo. See Preserve Endangered Areas of Cobb's History, Inc. v. United States Army Corps of Eng'rs.

本案采用主要内容标准 根据“主要内容”的检验标准来检验本案合同，我们的结论是，合同主要是货物交易。我们是基于合同用语、合同相关情况以及货物性质得出这个结论的。

Applying the "predominant factor" test to the Contract, we conclude that it was predominantly a transaction in goods. We reach this conclusion based on the contractual language, the circumstances surrounding the Contract, and the nature of the goods at issue.

合同文字 我们的起始点是合同文字本身，因为该文字提供了一系列线索，说明当事方将合同视为货物合同，而不是服务合同。首先，合同的标题是“采

Our starting point is the language of the Contract itself, which provides a number of indicia that the parties intended a contract for goods rather than services. First, the Contract is titled "PURCHASE ORDER",

购订单”，且这个用法在文件中多次重复。这个标题能够说明问题，因为当事方在称呼他们的协议时，如果使用这个标题，则几乎都是用于货物交易。其次，在合同里，当事方称他们自己为“买方”和“卖方”。最后，合同说明，该合同是“制造和安装自动设备”的采购订单。所有这些合同文字，都“特指货物，而不是服务”（B 诉 C 案），并说明当事方自己将合同视为货物合同。

a reference that is used repeatedly throughout the document. This title is most instructive, as the parties have chosen to identify their agreement with a name that is almost exclusively used for transactions in goods. Second, the parties refer to themselves in the Contract as the “Buyer” and “Seller”. Third, the Contract states that it is a purchase order “for the fabrication and installation of automated equipment”. All of this contractual language is “peculiar to goods, not services”, Bonebrake, and indicates that the parties had a contract for goods in mind.

可移动的货物　本案合同涉及可移动的货物。供应方在其自己的场地设计和制造了自动设备，并计划只有在设备完成之后，才将其移至受供方的工厂。在随后被写入合同的供应方原始要约中，包含了“运输工具上交货 / 供应方泊位”的字样，说明只要设备被交付至供应方的装载泊位，就被视为已提示交付给受供方。因此，虽然供应方仍有义务对设备进行安装和调试，但显然，设备在特定合同项下的当时，是可以移动的。

Additionally, the Contract involves movable goods. Barth designed and fabricated the automated equipment in its own facilities, and planned to move the equipment to BMC’s plant only once it was completed. Barth’s original offer, which was incorporated into the Contract, included the term “F.O.B. Barth dock”, meaning that the equipment was tendered to BMC once it was delivered to Barth’s loading dock. Consequently, although Barth was still obligated to install and debug the equipment, it was clearly movable at the time it was identified to the Contract.

付款与交货之间的联系　L诉P案与本案有所区别。本案的初审法院认为，与L诉P案相同，本案合同的价格没有区分服务价格与货物价格。但是，初审法院未能注意到，本案合同的各次付款，都取决于自动设备的交付。根据合同的付款日程表，每交付和接受一条自动设备生产线，受供方就需要支付70,050美元。假设合同价格主要用于供应方的设计服务和工程服务，则当事方本来会将付款与施工和设计进度挂钩，而不是设备的交付。此外，在L诉D案中，服务费用超过合同价格的一半，但在本案中看上去正好相反。与设备交付而挂钩的付款数额达到280,200美元，超过了合同价格的一半。

Lincoln Pulp & Paper is distinguishable from this case. The district court stated that the Contract price, similar to Lincoln Pulp & Paper, does not allocate costs between services and goods. The district court failed to note, however, that the Contract allocates payments according to delivery of automated equipment; the Contract's payment schedule calls for the delivery and acceptance of each automated equipment line to be met by a $70,050 payment from BMC. If the Contract price were being paid predominantly for Barth's design and engineering services as BMC claims, then the parties would have pegged payments to completion of the engineering and design services, not to the delivery of equipment. Furthermore, while the cost of services made up over half of the contract price in Lincoln Pulp & Paper, the opposite appears to be true in this case. A total of $280,200, which is over half of the contract price, is pegged to the delivery of equipment.

货物合同也可以包含服务　我们最后要说明的是，在L诉D案中，法院的判决说，"即使在供应商交付或安装设备之前，该设备需要专门设计和制造，也

Finally, we note that the court in Lincoln Pulp & Paper stated that "[a] sale of equipment is not removed from the scope of Article 2 merely because the equipment was specially designed and manufactured before

不能仅因这个事实，就认为设备的销售不属于法典第 2 篇的管辖范围”。事实上，虽然本案合同包含了大量服务内容（如设计和制造），但这种情况并不令人意外，因为之前从未有其他公司成功地对眼镜片的生产实现过自动化，因此本案的供应方必须花费大量时间来设计这台首次生产的机器。但是，此种必要的服务内容，并不意味着本案合同不再属于法典第 2 篇所适用的特别设计和制造的设备的合同。

delivery or installed by the supplier”. In fact, it is not surprising that the Barth-BMC Contract included such a significant services element （i.e., design and manufacturing）. Because no other company had successfully automated its eyeglass lens production, Barth had to spend considerable time designing this first-of-its-kind machinery. This necessary services element, however, does not remove the Contract from the category of agreements for specially designed and manufactured equipment to which Article 2 applies.

不适用的判例 受供方所引用的两个其他判例也同样不适用。在这两个判例中，很明显，当事方所设想的就是服务合同。第一个判例，即 W 诉 M 案，涉及狩猎服装的生产。但在该案中，买方提供了制造商为生产该服装所需要的（除缝纫线外）全部材料。因此，制造商并未销售货物，只是提供了将原料转化为制成品的服务。

The other two cases on which BMC relies are also inapposite. Both cases involved parties that clearly contemplated a contract for services. The first case, Wells v. 10-X Mfg. Co., involved the production of cloth hunting shirts. In that case, however, the buyer provided all of the materials （except thread） that the manufacturer used to produce the clothing. Consequently, the manufacturer did not sell goods, only the service of turning the materials into a finished product.

受供方引用的另一个判例，即 I 诉 G 案，涉及一套固体废物

The other case BMC cites, Inhabitants of the City of Saco v. General Elec. Co.,

处理设施的设计和建造合同。该案也与本案有所区别，因为该案所涉及的是典型的建造合同，即建造不可移动的处理设施。唯一可以移动的，是用于建造不可移动结构的那些材料。更重要的是，该案的合同文字明确将该合同称为服务交易。合同规定，其目的是“在一期项目中提供服务，以便建立必要的前提条件，使承包商在该基础上提出二期服务的建议”。不仅合同文字说明其系服务合同，而且合同将一方称为“承包商”，而这个词通常都是用在服务交易中。

involved a contract for the design and construction of a solid waste disposal facility. That case is also distinguishable because it involved a typical construction contract for a non-movable product--the disposal facility. The only movable goods were the materials that were used to construct the immobile structure. Even more significantly, the contractual language in that case clearly identified the contract as a transaction in services. The contract stated that its purpose was “for the furnishing of services in Phase I of the project, and to establish the conditions on which Contractor ［GE］ will propose to furnish services under Phase Ⅱ”. Not only did the language state that the contract was for services, it also referred to one of the parties as the “Contractor”, a term typically used in services transactions.

受供方的弃权问题 在确定法典适用于本案后，我们下面必须将法典第2篇的弃权条款适用于本案合同。法典有关弃权的相关条款规定：“（2）如果已签署的协议规定，必须签署书面文件才能修改或取消该协议，则该协议不得用其他方法修改或取

Having determined that the UCC governs this case, we must next apply Article 2’s waiver provision to the Contract. The UCC waiver provision states in relevant part: （2） A signed agreement which excludes modification or rescission except by a signed writing cannot be otherwise modified or rescinded... （4） Although an attempt at

消……（4）意图作出修改或取消的行为，即使不满足（2）款或（3）款的要求，仍可构成弃权。（5）一方作出影响合同尚未履行之部分的弃权后，可以撤回该弃权，但应使另一方收到合理通知，说明另一方应严格履行弃权所涉及的条款。但是，如果另一方依赖该弃权已严重改变了处境，致使该撤回导致不公平，则不得撤回。”（法典第2.209条）

modification or rescission does not satisfy the requirements of subsection （2） or （3） it can operate as a waiver. （5） A party who has made a waiver affecting an executory portion of the contract may retract the waiver by reasonable notification received by the other party that strict performance will be required of any term waived, unless the retraction would be unjust in view of a material change of position in reliance on the waiver. Fla. Stat. 2.209.

弃权的要素　虽然法典并未具体列出构成弃权的要素，但我们曾说过，弃权需要具有如下要素：“（1）在弃权的当时，存在可以被放弃的权利，包括特权、优势或利益；（2）弃权人实际知道或被视为知道该权利；以及（3）弃权人具有放弃该权利的意图。”（D诉W案）一项行为也可以构成对合同条款的默示弃权，但此种弃权必须通过明确证据表现出来（参见A诉T案）。如果当事方的行为与继续保留权利的意图相矛盾，则该行为有可能被视为默示弃权（参见F诉O案）。

Although the UCC does not specifically lay out the elements of waiver, we have stated that waiver requires “（1） the existence at the time of the waiver a right, privilege, advantage, or benefit which may be waived;（2） the actual or constructive knowledge thereof; and （3） an intention to relinquish such right, privilege, advantage, or benefit” . Dooley v. Weil. Conduct may constitute waiver of a contract term, but such an implied waiver must be demonstrated by clear evidence. See American Somax Ventures v. Touma. Waiver may be implied when a party’s actions are inconsistent with continued retention of the right. See First Pa. Bank, N.A. v. Oreck.

不需要存在损害性依赖 我们首先必须分析的问题是，根据法典，是否必须伴随损害性依赖，才有可能认定存在弃权。在佛罗里达州的普通法里，已经确定的原则是，只有伴随有效对价或损害性依赖，才有可能存在弃权（参见M诉L案），但是，对于法典是否保留了这一要求，法院有不同意见。我们的结论是，对合同条款的弃权，法典不要求必须存在对价或损害性依赖。

As an initial matter, we must determine whether, under the UCC, waiver must be accompanied by detrimental reliance. Although it is settled that waiver under Florida common law must be supported by valid consideration or detrimental reliance, see Masser v. London Operating Co., courts disagree on whether the UCC retains this requirement. We conclude, however, that the UCC does not require consideration or detrimental reliance for waiver of a contract term.

法典文字 我们是从法典第2.209条（4）款和（5）款的直白文字本身中得出这个结论的。该条（4）款说明，试图作出的修改，即使不能构成修改，也仍有可能构成弃权，而该条（5）款规定，弃权可以撤回，除非另一方已对该弃权产生依赖。因此，法典承认，在不存在损害性依赖［该条（5）款所提到的可被撤回的弃权］的情况下，仍然可以存在弃权。只有采用这种解释，该条（5）款才具有意义。如果将（4）款解释为，所有的弃权

Our conclusion follows from the plain language of subsections 2.209（4） and （5）. While subsection （4） states that an attempted modification that fails may still constitute a waiver, subsection （5） provides that the waiver may be retracted unless the non-waiving party relies on the waiver. Consequently, the statute recognizes that waivers may exist in the absence of detrimental reliance--these are the retractable waivers referred to in subsection （5）. Only this interpretation renders meaning to subsection （5）, because reading subsection （4） to require detrimental reliance for all

都必须伴随损害性依赖，那就意味着没有任何弃权是可以被撤回的｛参见 W 诉 N 案［该案异议法官认为，如果认为法典要求必须存在损害性依赖，那就等于否定第 2.209 条（4）款和（5）款有任何区别］｝。在这种情况下，该条（5）款将没有任何意义。

waivers means that waivers would never be retractable. See Wisconsin Knife Works v. National Metal Crafters (dissenting) (noting that reading a detrimental reliance requirement into the UCC would eliminate the distinction between subsections (4) and (5)). Subsection (5) would therefore be meaningless.

相关判例　佛罗里达州至少有一个法院默示同意上述结论。在 L 诉 S 案中，法院判定，虽然没有任何事实可以说明存在损害性依赖，但仍然存在对合同条款的弃权。法院在该案中面对的是制造商与电子安保器材零售商之间的合同。合同的一项条款规定，对于零售商无法销售的器材，制造商不会再回购。合同的另一项条款规定，合同的修改必须以书面形式作出。虽然存在这些合同规定，零售商仍然提起诉讼，声称制造商随后曾作出回购器材的口头承诺，但未履行该承诺。

At least one Florida court implicitly agrees with this conclusion; in Linear Corp. v. Standard Hardware Co., the court held that a contract term had been waived despite the absence of any facts showing detrimental reliance. The court in Linear addressed a contract between a manufacturer and a retailer for the sale of electronic security devices. The contract included a provision stating that the manufacturer would not repurchase any devices the retailer was unable to sell, and another term providing that contract modifications must be in writing. Despite this contractual language, the retailer filed suit claiming that the manufacturer subsequently made an oral agreement to repurchase unsold devices, but failed to adhere to this oral agreement.

该案法院在得出其结论时，

Citing chapter 2.209 (4), the

引用了法典第 2.209 条（4）款的规定。法院认为，当事方的行为表明，他们已放弃了必须以书面形式修改合同的要求。因此，法院承认了口头修改的效力。在该案中，虽然看上去并不存在损害性依赖，但法院仍然承认了该弃权的效力。实际上，该案法院甚至从未提出，损害性依赖是法典对弃权的一项要求。因此，法院默示判定，即使非弃权方不存在损害性依赖，合同条款也可以被放弃。

相反判例　虽然其他法院也曾判定，在弃权时，法典要求必须存在依赖，但是，这些法院都忽视了法典的直白文字。对弃权持此种观点的主要判例是 W 诉 N 案。在该案中，联邦第七巡回上诉法院所面对的合同，包含了禁止口头修改的条款。法院需要分析，试图作出的口头修改，即使不能构成修改，是否仍然可以构成弃权？波斯纳法官代表多数派法官撰写了判决书。其结论是，如果不存在损害性依赖也可以对合同条款作出弃权，那么法典第

court concluded that the parties’ conduct demonstrated that they had waived the requirement that modifications be in writing, and therefore gave effect to the oral modification. The court recognized this waiver despite the apparent absence of any detrimental reliance by the retailer--in fact the court never even mentioned any reliance requirement for waiver under the UCC. Consequently, the court implicitly held that a contract term could be waived without the existence of detrimental reliance by the non-waiving party.

Although other courts have held that waiver requires reliance under the UCC, those courts have ignored the UCC’s plain language. The leading case espousing this view of waiver is Wisconsin Knife Works v. National Metal Crafters, in which a panel of the Seventh Circuit addressed a contract that included a term prohibiting oral modifications, and considered whether an attempted oral modification could instead constitute a waiver. Writing for the majority, Judge Posner concluded that the UCC’s subsection （2）, which gives effect to “no oral modification” provisions, would become superfluous if

2.209 条（2）款就是多余的，因为法典该款承认，“禁止口头修改”的合同条款具有效力。

contract terms could be waived without detrimental reliance.

波斯纳法官的理由　波斯纳法官的理由是，对于试图作出的口头修改，如果根据法典该条（2）款不可强制履行，但根据该条（4）款却构成可以强制履行的弃权，那么，该条（2）款“基本上就成为废纸”。波斯纳法官认为，只有在修改和弃权之间存在某种区别时，该条（2）款和（4）款才能同时具有意义，而此种区别，就是弃权需要存在损害性依赖。

Judge Posner reasoned that if attempted oral modifications that were unenforceable because of subsection（2）were nevertheless enforced as waivers under subsection（4）, then subsection（2）is “very nearly a dead letter”. According to Judge Posner, there must be some difference between modification and waiver in order for both subsections（2）and（4）to have meaning. This difference is waiver’s detrimental reliance requirement.

但是，波斯纳法官忽视了修改和弃权之间的下列根本区别：一个当事方如果同意了另一方对合同的修改，就不能再撤回该同意，除非另行就该撤回支付对价；但是，一个当事方即使已同意对合同条款作出弃权，仍可在给予另一方合理通知后，单方撤回该弃权。弃权可以被单方撤回的情况，使法典第 2.209 条（2）款和（4）款有所区别，并使两项条款同时具有意义。因此，我们的结论是，法典中的弃权不取决于

Judge Posner, however, ignores a fundamental difference between modifications and waivers：while a party that has agreed to a contract modification cannot cancel the modification without giving consideration for the cancellation, a party may unilaterally retract its waiver of a contract term provided it gives reasonable notice. The fact that waivers may unilaterally be retracted provides the difference between subsections（2）and（4）that allows both to have meaning. We therefore conclude that waiver under the UCC does not require detrimental reliance.

是否存在损害性依赖。因此，我们不再考虑本案中是否存在损害性依赖，而只考虑受供方是否对合同规定的1987年10月的交付日期作出了弃权。

Consequently, without reaching the issue of detrimental reliance, we consider whether BMC waived the Contract's October 1987 delivery date.

受供方通过行为作出弃权 在将弃权的要素应用于本案事实后，我们判定，作为法律问题，受供方放弃了1987年10月的交付日期。1987年10月的交付日期属于可以被放弃的权利，且受供方实际知道该权利。我们的进一步结论是，受供方的行为，默示地表明了其放弃该权利的意图。

Applying the elements of waiver to the facts before us, we hold as a matter of law that BMC waived the October 1987 delivery date. The October 1987 delivery date was a waivable contract right, of which BMC had actual knowledge. We also conclude that BMC's conduct impliedly demonstrated an intent to relinquish that right.

本案的具体事实 受供方弃权的最有力证据，是受供方自己表述的其与供应方母公司的关系。受供方在本诉讼全部过程中一直声称，从1988年8月起，母公司“开始介入并承诺完成该项目。在该过程中，母公司明确表示，其全部资源都将被投入该项目，并指示受供方只与母公司交往”。因此，根据受供方的说法，母公司在1988年秋天主动承担了代替供应方完成该项目

The most cogent evidence of this waiver is BMC's own representation of its relationship with Nesco. Throughout this litigation, BMC has maintained that Nesco, beginning in August 1988, “stepped in and promised to complete the project. In doing so, Nesco expressly represented that all of its resources were committed to the project, and instructed BMC to deal solely with Nesco”. According to BMC, therefore, Nesco voluntarily became liable, in the fall of 1988, for Barth's completion of the project. By that

的责任。当时，1987年10月的交付日期已经过期。如果按受供方所称，当时已经发生了合同违约，那么，母公司本来没有可能履行其义务，因为在作出履约承诺的同时，母公司已经处于违约状态，因此受供方第二天就可以起诉母公司。为了使母公司的承诺具有意义，受供方一定是给予了供应方和母公司额外的时间来履约。也就是说，受供方一定是已经放弃了1987年10月的交付日期。

time, however, the October 1987 delivery date had already passed. If, as BMC claims, the contract was already breached, then Nesco could never have performed its obligations; Nesco was in breach of its promise as soon as that promise was made, and could have been sued by BMC the next day. For Nesco's promise to have meaning, BMC must have given Barth and Nesco additional time to perform--in other words, BMC must have waived the October 1987 delivery date.

受供方的理由不能成立　受供方辩称，虽然为了换取母公司的承诺，自己同意推迟强制履行对供应方的权利，但并未放弃该权利。受供方的此种争辩不合逻辑。根据这个理论，受供方可以随时起诉供应方和母公司。这会导致非常奇怪的现象，因为母公司即使在承诺后的第二天就完成该项目，也仍要对供应方承担违约的全部责任。此种协议对母公司来说有百弊而无一利。

BMC argues, however, that while it agreed to delay enforcing its rights against Barth in return for Nesco's promise, it did not waive those rights. BMC's argument defies logic. According to this theory, BMC could sue Barth and Nesco at its whim. Consequently, Nesco miraculously could have completed the project the day after its promise, and still have been fully liable to BMC for Barth's breach of contract. Nesco had nothing to gain and everything to lose from such an agreement.

受供方自己的起诉书，也支持我们有关受供方已放弃了

BMC's own complaint buttresses our conclusion that BMC waived the October 1987

1987年10月的交付日期的结论。根据受供方的起诉书，母公司承诺，“供应方将会遵守修改后的协议所规定的日期、性能和可靠度标准”，并且母公司将“保证设备及时完工并被送至受供方”。但是，当时已超过了1987年10月的交付日期，因此，除非交付日期已被延长，否则供应方不可能“遵守”日期，或“及时”完成设备的制造。

双方的交易过程 受供方与供应方的交易过程，也证明受供方已放弃1987年10月的交货日期，因为受供方未及时要求供应方遵守合同条款，也没有终止合同并提起诉讼。在交付日期已过而卖方未能交付时，买方必须在合理时间内提出异议，并警告卖方其已违约［参见K诉E案；另参见H诉C案（法官说，“我不承认这样的原则，即合同一方在另一方违反合同后，前者可以一方面继续接受该合同，另一方面拖到未来某个时间才要求就之前的违约取消合同”）］。

delivery date. According to BMC's complaint, Nesco promised "that Barth would meet dates, performance and reliability criteria under the agreement, as amended", and that Nesco "ensure［d］ that the equipment was timely completed and delivered to BMC". Because the October 1987 delivery date had already passed, however, Barth could not "meet dates" or "timely" complete the equipment unless the delivery date had been extended.

Furthermore, BMC's course of dealing with Barth evidenced BMC's waiver of the October 1987 delivery date, because BMC failed timely to demand compliance with that contract term or terminate the Contract and file suit. When a delivery date passes without the seller's delivery, the buyer must object within a reasonable time and warn the seller that it is in breach. See KLT Indus., Inc. v. Eaton Corp.; see also Harrison v. City of Tampa（"I do not recognize any principle by which one party to a contract, after a breach by the other party, may continue acting under such contract to some future time, and then abrogate the contract by reason of such former breach"）.

虽然受供方在初审中声称，供应方从 1987 年 10 月开始违反合同，但直到 1989 年 5 月，受供方才告知供应方，其打算终止合同，并要求供应方承担责任。实际上，受供方最早在 1988 年 8 月才提出，其会考虑终止合同。当时受供方高层管理人员会见了供应方高层管理人员，寻求其就供应方的履约提供保证。但是，该会议的结果，就是受供方放弃了 1987 年 10 月的交货日期，而不是及时行使了受供方终止合同的权利。直到 1989 年 2 月，受供方才严肃地警告供应方，其打算终止合同。当时，受供方向供应方发出一封信，其中包含 100,000 美元的付款。这是 1988 年 8 月会议上供应方高层管理人员所要求的 250,000 美元的一部分。这封信警告供应方说，对于供应方未能遵守合同交付日期的行为，受供方并未放弃其权利和救济。受供方 3 月再次发信给供应方，警告说其打算“就供应方的初始违约，以及未能遵守所有随后承诺的日期，追究供应方的

Although BMC maintained at trial that Barth breached the contract as of October 1987, BMC did not tell Barth it intended to terminate the contract and hold Barth liable for the breach until May 1989. In fact, the earliest indication from BMC that it was considering termination was August 1988, when BMC executives met with Tomsich to seek assurance that Barth would perform. However, the result of that meeting was a waiver of the October 1987 delivery date, not a timely exercise of BMC's right to terminate the Contract. BMC did not warn Barth in earnest of its intent to terminate until February 1989, when BMC sent Barth a letter along with $100,000 of the $250,000 payment Tomsich had requested at the August 1988 meeting. This letter warned Barth that BMC was not waiving its rights and remedies for Barth's failure to meet contractual delivery dates. BMC warned Barth again in March when it sent a letter advising of its intent to "hold [Barth] responsible, both for the initial breach and for all failures to meet subsequently promised dates".

责任”。

但是，在1989年之前，受供方的所作所为，一直就如同双方仍受到合同约束且供应方并未违约一样。在1987年10月的交付日期过后，受供方未有任何表示。受供方的工程师仍然经常向供应方人员提供建议或帮助，协助后者克服技术困难。受供方的高层管理人员仍然经常访问供应方工厂设施，并鼓励供应方继续努力完成设备制造。受供方甚至继续为项目支付费用。1987年12月，即1987年10月的交付日期过期1个多月后，受供方花费71,075美元购买了机器用的弹簧和工具。总之，受供方继续按合同仍然有效的方式作为，而不是终止合同，或至少警告供应方说，在1987年10月的交付日期过期后，供应方已处于违约状态。

Until 1989, however, BMC continued to act as though both parties were bound by the Contract and that Barth was not in default of its obligations: the October 1987 delivery date passed without comment from BMC; engineers from BMC frequently provided advice or assistance to help Barth personnel overcome technical problems; BMC executives frequently visited Barth's production facilities and encouraged Barth to continue working to complete the equipment; BMC even continued to spend money on the project--in December 1987, over one month after the October 1987 delivery date had passed, BMC purchased an additional $71,075 worth of springs and tooling for the machines. In sum, rather than terminating the Contract, or at least warning Barth that it was in breach after the October 1987 delivery date had passed, BMC continued to act as though the Contract remained in effect.

抱怨不构成违约通知 这并不是说，受供方从未就超期问题向供应方提出过抱怨。对于项目严重超期问题，受供方的高层管理人员经常表示担心和失望。例

This is not to say that BMC never complained that Barth had missed deadlines; BMC executives frequently expressed their concern and disappointment that the project was so far behind schedule. On April 5, 1988,

如，1988 年 4 月 5 日，受供方的董事长、总裁兼首席执行官向供应方发出信件说："项目已严重超期，而每超期一天都意味着我们的损失。我希望供应方尽一切努力，确保设备的迅速完工和安装，并避免进一步延迟。"虽然受供方对超期提出抱怨，但其从未声明供应方已经违约，也从未终止合同。反之，受供方告诉供应方继续工作。但是，在供应方又花费了 18 个月的时间和费用之后，且根据供应方的说法，在其已准备好交付机器时，受供方突然决定终止合同。受供方是无权这么做的。

for example, the Chairman, President, and CEO of BMC sent a letter to Barth in which he stated: "[T] he project is well behind schedule, and each day of delay represents [our loss]. I hope that Barth will exert every effort to ensure the speedy completion and installation of the equipment and avoid any further delay." But while BMC complained of delays, it never declared Barth in default or terminated the contract--instead, BMC told Barth to keep working. After Barth had spent an additional eighteen months of time and money and, according to Barth, was prepared to deliver the machines, however, BMC suddenly decided to terminate the Contract. This BMC could not do.

是否在合理时间内作出提示交付　根据法典规定，如果合同约定的交付日期已被放弃，交付就必须在合理时间内作出［参见法典第 2.309 条（1）款；K 诉 E 案］。由于受供方已对 1987 年 10 月的交付日期作出弃权，因此，供应方的义务仅仅是在合理时间内交付机器。我们将本案发回初审法院重审，以确定供应方是否已在合理时间内就机器作出

The UCC states that when a contractual delivery date is waived, delivery must be made within a reasonable time. See Fla. Stat. 2.309 (1); KLT Indus., Inc. v. Eaton Corp. Consequently, because BMC waived the October 1987 delivery date, Barth was only obligated to deliver the machines within a reasonable time period. We remand this case to the district court for a new trial on the question of whether Barth tendered the machines within a reasonable time period.

了提示交付。

结论 基于以上理由，我们判定，初审法院有关法典不适用于本合同的判决是错误的。我们还判定，受供方放弃了 1987 年 10 月的交付日期。因此，我们推翻初审法院作出的供应方败诉的判决，并将本案发回重审。初审法院应根据法典的规定，重审受供方对供应方的索赔，以及供应方的反诉。

For the foregoing reasons, we hold that the district court erred in concluding that the UCC did not apply to the Contract. Furthermore, we conclude that BMC waived the October 1987 delivery date. We therefore VACATE the district court's judgment against Barth and REMAND the case to the district court for retrial of BMC's claims against Barth as well as Barth's counterclaims in accordance with the UCC.

案例 2　买方是否属于正常业务中的买方?

Porter v. Wertz
波特诉沃斯案

纽约州高等法院上诉庭 1979 年；68 A.D.2d 141, 26 UCC Rep.Serv. 876

简　介

本案涉及一幅称为“大海”(作者为 Utrillo) 的名贵画作的争议。本案原告是画作的主人 (Porter)，从事名贵画作的买卖。画作主人曾多次与一位使用假名 (Von Maker) 的骗子进行画作交易，但不知其是骗子，而以为其是艺术品中介。1973 年，画作主人曾出售给假中介另一幅画作，而假中介则出具了本票作为付款。在本票尚未到期时，假中介表示有意购买“大海”画作。为此，画作主人同意假中介先把画作拿回家观看一段时间，然后再决定是否购买。假中介在拿到“大海”画作后，偷偷将其出售给一家画廊 (Feigen)。画廊随后将画作出售给一个买家 (Brenner)。该买家再度将画作出售给国外客户。画作主人随后发现画作被假中介卖掉，但此时画作已被多次转手，不知所踪。假中介 (出售画作给画廊的卖方，真名叫 Wertz) 因诈骗罪和其他罪名被捕入狱。画作主人唯一有可能追究责任的主体，就是从假中介购买画作的画廊。

画作主人称，假中介不是画作所有权人，也不持有出售画作的授权，没有权利或权力向画廊转让画作所有权，因此画廊不可能取得画作所有权。在这种情况下，画廊留持和再出售画作的行为构成了对画作主人财产的侵占，因此必须退回画作或支付画作价值。画廊提出两项“禁止自相矛盾”(estoppel) 的抗辩。第一项抗辩包含在法典第 2.403 条中，第二项抗辩是衡平法中的原则。这两项抗辩源于不同法律，但核心原则都是一样的，即如果画作主人由于自己的行为，导致假中介以看上去正常的方式将画作出售给画廊，画作主人就无权向画廊索赔，因为其之前的行为与之后的索赔自相矛盾。或者说，是画作主人自己的疏忽导致假中介将画作出售给画廊，因而画廊不承担责任。

纽约州高等法院初审庭判定，画廊无权引用法典第 2.403 条的抗辩，但可以引用衡平法的抗辩。由于后一项抗辩成立，画廊被判无须向画作主人承担责任。纽约州高等法院上诉庭判定，画廊的两项抗辩均不成立，因为画廊不属于法典第 2.403 条规定的以“善意”作为的“正常业务中的买方”；同时，画廊也不属于衡平法规定的善意购买人。上诉庭因此推翻了初审庭的判决，判定画廊必须向画作主人承担责任。

判　决

法典中禁止自相矛盾的原则

我们同意初审法院的判决，即法典中的禁止自相矛盾原则，不妨碍本案画作主人取得赔偿。法典禁止自相矛盾的原则，规定在法典第 2.403 条中。该条（2）款规定，“如果将货物委托给从事该类货物经营的商人占有，该商人即有权力将委托人的全部权利转让给正常业务中的买方”。

We agree with the conclusion of the trial court that statutory estoppel does not bar recovery. The provisions of statutory estoppel are found in section 2-403 of the Uniform Commercial Code. Subdivision (2) thereof provides that “[a]ny entrusting of possession of goods to a merchant who deals in goods of that kind gives him power to transfer all rights of the entruster to a buyer in the ordinary course of business”.

正常业务中的买方　法典第1.201条（9）款将“正常业务中的买方”定义为：“在不了解向其所作的出售侵犯了第三方对货物之所有权或担保权益的情况下，在正常业务过程中，以善意向从事该类货物销售业务的卖方买进货物的人。”

Subdivision （9） of section 1-201 of the Uniform Commercial Code defines a “buyer in the ordinary course of business” as “a person who in good faith and without knowledge that the sale to him is in violation of the ownership rights or security interest of a third party in the goods buys in ordinary course from a person in the business of selling goods of that kind”.

为了判断本案画廊是否持有法典禁止自相矛盾原则的抗辩，我们必须首先判断，画廊是否符合“正常业务中的买方”的定义［法典第1.201条（9）款］。基于两个原因，画廊不符合该定义。

In order to determine whether the defense of statutory estoppel is available to Feigen, we must begin by ascertaining whether Feigen fits the definition of “a buyer in the ordinary course of business”.（Uniform Commercial Code, § 1- 201, subd ［9］.） Feigen does not fit that definition, for two reasons.

卖方不是从事该类货物经营的人　首先，向画廊出售“大海”画作的假中介卖方不是艺术品经销商，即他不是“从事该类货物销售业务的人”［法典第1.201条（9）款］。如果他可以算作从事某种业务的人，那也只是一家熟食店的雇员。卖方也从未自称是经销商。尽管画廊在庭审中作证说，在其从卖方购进“大海”画作之前，将卖方介绍给自己的

First, Wertz, from whom Feigen bought the Utrillo, was not an art dealer--he was not “a person in the business of selling goods of that kind”.（Uniform Commercial Code, § 1-201, subd ［9］.） If anything, he was a delicatessen employee. Wertz never held himself out as a dealer. Although Feigen testified at trial that before he （Feigen） purchased the Utrillo from Wertz, Sloan, who introduced Wertz to Feigen told him （Feigen） that Wertz was an art dealer, this

艺术品经纪人曾告诉自己说，该卖方是艺术品中介，但这个证词不可信。该证词与画廊在庭审前取证时的证词是相矛盾的，因为画廊主人当时说，他不记得该艺术品经纪人是否曾这样对他说。

testimony was questionable. It conflicted with Feigen's testimony at his examination before trial where he stated he did not recall whether Sloan said that to him.

画廊未以善意作为 其次，画廊在与假中介卖方的交易中，不属于以“善意”作为的人［法典第 1.201 条（9）款］。根据法典第 2.103 条（1）（b）款的定义，涉及商人时，“善意”是指“事实上的诚实，以及遵守公平交易的合理商业准则”。这项规定中包含了“公平交易的合理商业准则”的表述，但这句话中的商业准则不应被解释为，也不可能被解释为，那些允许、鼓励或容忍奸猾商业手段的准则和做法，以及对于货物“来历”（艺术品的所有权历史，以及持有和出售艺术品的权利）的无视。而此种做法和无视，正是本案所展现的情况。

Second, Feigen was not “a person ... in good faith”（Uniform Commercial Code, § 1-201, subd［9］）in the transaction with Wertz. Section 2-103（subd［1］, par［b］）of the Uniform Commercial Code defines “good faith” in the case of a merchant as “honesty in fact and the observance of reasonable commercial standards of fair dealing in the trade”. Although this definition by its terms embraces the “reasonable commercial standards of fair dealing in the trade”, it should not--and cannot--be interpreted to permit, countenance or condone commercial standards of sharp trade practice or indifference as to the “provenance”, i.e., history of ownership or the right to possess or sell an object d' art, such as is present in the case before us.

我们注意到，无论是画廊的雇员女士，还是她的雇主画廊，均未对假中介卖方的身份进行过

We note that neither Ms. Drew-Bear nor her employer Feigen made any investigation to determine the status of Wertz, i.e., whether

任何调查，以确认其是否为艺术品经销商，即“从事该类货物销售业务的人”[法典第1.201条(9)款]。只要雇员女士进行稍许调查，如使用卖方留下的两个电话号码中的任何一个给他打个电话，本来就会发现，卖方只是一家熟食店的雇员，而不是艺术品经销商。雇员女士或画廊没有作出任何努力，来核实卖方是否为“大海”画作的所有权人，或是否被所有权人授权出售该画作。

he was an art merchant, “a person in the business of selling goods of that kind”. (Uniform Commercial Code, § 1-201, subd [9].) Had Ms. Drew-Bear done so much as call either of the telephone numbers Wertz had left, she would have learned that Wertz was employed by a delicatessen and was not an art dealer. Nor did Ms. Drew-Bear or Feigen make an effort to verify whether Wertz was the owner or authorized by the owner to sell the painting he was offering.

画廊本应引起警觉 雇员女士当时可以看到画册作者所编撰的有关“大海”画家的书籍，而书的目录中就包括该著名画家的这幅“大海”画作。尽管这个事实本身可能不足以构成对画廊的通知，即在交易的当时，卖方可能不是该画作的真正所有权人，但是，画廊本来应基于该情况而对卖方是否有权占有该画作的问题产生警觉，并在完成购买前作出进一步的核实。因此，我们认为，法典第2.403条（2）款所规定的禁止自相矛盾的原则，如同初审法院所准确判定的，不能

Ms. Drew-Bear had available to her the Petrides volume on Utrillo which included “Chateau de Lion-sur-Mer” in its catalogue of the master’s work. Although this knowledge alone might not have been enough to put Feigen on notice that Wertz was not the true owner at the time of the transaction, it could have raised a doubt as to Wertz’ right of possession, calling for further verification before the purchase by Feigen was consummated. Thus, it appears that statutory estoppel provided by subdivision (2) of section 2-403 of the Uniform Commercial Code was not, as Trial Term correctly concluded, available as a defense to Feigen.

成为画廊可以使用的抗辩。

衡平法中禁止自相矛盾的原则 我们不同意初审法院的另一个结论，即画廊所引用的衡平法中的禁止自相矛盾原则（参见Z诉H案），可以作为画廊拒绝赔偿的抗辩。

We disagree with the conclusion of the trial court that the defense of equitable estoppel （see Zendman v. Harry Winston, Inc.） raised by Feigen bars recovery.

善意购买人 我们首先说明，一个人即使不是法典所定义的正常业务中的买方，也仍然有可能属于支付了价值的善意购买人，并可以享受法典制定之前所确立的禁止自相矛盾原则的保护（参见T诉A案；法典第1.103条）。下面我们讨论，在本案中，衡平法中禁止自相矛盾的抗辩条件是否得到满足。

We pause to observe that although one may not be a buyer in the ordinary course of business as defined in the Uniform Commercial Code, he may be a good- faith purchaser for value and enjoy the protection of precode estoppel （see Tumber v. Automation Design & Mfg. Corp.; Uniform Commercial Code, § 1-103）. We now reach the question whether the defense of equitable estoppel has been established here.

禁止自相矛盾 总体而言："衡平法中的禁止自相矛盾原则，即禁止行为上的自相矛盾，是指对于某项重要事实，法律和衡平原则均绝对禁止当事方否认该事实，或主张与该事实相反的证据，只要该当事方通过其言语或行为（包括主动或被动作出的，也包括故意作出或严重疏忽引起的），诱使另一方在不了解且有合理理

In general terms："Equitable estoppel or estoppel in pais is the principle by which a party is absolutely precluded, both at law and in equity, from denying, or asserting the contrary of, any material fact which, by his words or conduct, affirmative or negative, intentionally or through culpable negligence, he has induced another, who was excusably ignorant of the true facts and who had a right to rely upon such words or conduct, to believe

由无法了解真相的情况下，且在有权依赖该言语或行为的情况下，相信了该事实，并依赖该言语或行为采取了行动，且作为可以合理期待的后果，该另一方的状况因此发生变化，且如果允许前者否认该言语或行为，或允许其主张相反的证据，后者就要因为此种改变而受到损害。只有在一个人通过其言语或行为诱使另一人以特定方式作为时，禁止自相矛盾的原则才适用。基于诚信以及公平和公开交易的原则，上述衡平原则禁止前者强制履行其权利，以防止其作为或不作为导致欺诈或不公。”（引用著作）

and act upon them thereby, as a consequence reasonably to be anticipated, changing his position in such a way that he would suffer injury if such denial or contrary assertion were allowed. An estoppel in pais can arise only when a person, either by his declarations or conduct, has induced another person to act in a particular manner. The doctrine prohibits a person, upon principles of honesty and fair and open dealing, from asserting rights the enforcement of which would, through his omissions or commissions, work fraud and injustice.” （NY Jur, Estoppel）

相关判例 如本州上诉法院在 Z 诉 H 案中所强调，“如果货物的所有权人使卖方占有货物，并使卖方看上去是货物的所有权人，则在对抗支付了价值的善意买方时，货物所有权人即被禁止证明自己拥有货物所有权，并被禁止证明卖方不拥有所有权”（引用著作）。确实，“正当的所有权人也可因自己的行为而被禁止主张所有权。如果他向另一人

As the Court of Appeals reiterated in Zendman v Harry Winston, Inc., an “owner may be estopped from setting up his own title and the lack of title in the vendor as against a bona fide purchaser for value where the owner has clothed the vendor with possession and other indicia of title, Am. Jur., Sales” . Indeed “[t] he rightful owner may be estopped by his own acts from asserting his title. If he has invested another with the usual evidence of title, or an apparent authority to dispose

交付了代表所有权的通常表象证据，或提供了处置所有权的表见授权，那么，该所有权人就不能对抗依赖此种表见证据或授权而作为的无辜购买人”(S诉C案)。

在Z诉H案中，纽约市的一个钻石商人将一枚戒指送到一家拍卖公司。该公司在新泽西州大西洋城的马路边上从事拍卖生意。商人在将戒指交给拍卖公司时附有一份备忘录，其中说明，该戒指仅供拍卖公司查看，因此，只有在拍卖公司愿意进行拍卖，同意支付商人开出的要价，且商人对拍卖公司的同意表示接受并出具销售合同后，戒指的所有权才能转移。

该戒指随后被放在拍卖公司营业地的一个公共展示窗内展示。戒指在那里展示1个多月后，在一次公共拍卖中被出售给案件的买方。由于有证据证明，商人也同时允许拍卖公司将商人的其他珠宝在那里展示，并允许拍卖公司将其他珠宝出售，因此，法院判定，商人由于自己的行为，而被禁止从买方追回该戒指。

of it, he will not be allowed to make claim against an innocent purchaser dealing on the faith of such apparent ownership” (Smith v. Clews) .

In Zendman v Harry Winston, Inc., a diamond merchant in New York City sent a ring to Brand, Inc., a corporation which conducted auctions on the boardwalk in Atlantic City, New Jersey, with a memorandum reciting that the ring was for examination only and that title was not to pass until the auctioneer had made his selection, and had notified the sender of his agreement to pay the indicated price and the sender had indicated acceptance thereof by issuing a bill of sale.

The ring was placed in a public show window at the auctioneer’s place of business, remaining there for more than a month, before being sold to the plaintiff at a public auction. Under circumstances where it was demonstrated that the defendant had permitted other pieces of jewelry it owned to be exhibited and sold by the auctioneer, it was held that the defendant by his conduct was estopped from recovering the ring from the plaintiff.

画作主人不存在过错 在本案中，画作主人的行为无可指责。当假中介的第一张本票被拒付后，他聘请了毕晓普调查公司进行调查，并将涉及多张本票的财务交易通知了联邦调查局。他的律师则安排签署了有关几幅画的详细协议，其中包含了当时使用冒名的假中介的保证（尽管现在证实，该保证是虚假的），即假中介仍然掌握着“大海”画作。尽管画作主人允许假中介占有画作，但他没有向其提供画作所有权的其他证明。仅仅占有而没有其他更多因素，不足以引起禁止自相矛盾原则的适用(Z诉H案)。

In the case at bar, Porter's conduct was not blameworthy. When the first promissory note was dishonored, he retained Bishop's investigative service and informed the FBI of the financial transactions concerning the series of notes. His attorney obtained a comprehensive agreement covering several paintings, within which was the assurance （now proven false） by Von Maker that he still controlled the Utrillo. Although Porter had permitted Von Maker to possess the painting, he conferred upon Von Maker no other indicia of ownership. Possession without more is insufficient to create an estoppel（Zendman v. Harry Winston, Inc.）.

画作主人不知情且以善意作为 我们认定，画作主人与假中介之前进行的艺术品交易，足以支持初审法院的结论，即画作主人认为假中介是艺术品经销商。尽管如此，当事方的证词亦毫无疑义地显示，“大海”画作不是为了商业目的而被寄售给假中介的，而是仅供假中介在其家里展示（Z诉H案）。在这种情况下，

We find that the prior art transactions between Porter and Von Maker justified the conclusion of the trial court that Porter knew that Von Maker was a dealer in art. Nevertheless, the testimony remains uncontradicted, that the Utrillo was not consigned to Von Maker for business purposes, but rather for display only in Von Maker's home （Zendman v. Harry Winston, Inc.）. In these circumstances, it cannot be said that

不能说画作主人的行为在任何意义上助推了假中介卖方向画廊作出的欺诈行为。

Porter's conduct in any way contributed to the deception practiced on Feigen by Von Maker and Wertz.

画廊未以善意作为 最后，我们必须再看一下画廊的状况，以确定其是否属于善意购买人。在购买“大海”画作时，画廊没有依赖卖方对画作的任何所有权证明。画廊的交易对象，是本案的假中介卖方，而后者没有合法权利占有“大海”画作。即使从画廊的角度，我们将卖方视为假中介的代理人，或将卖方与假中介视为一体，画廊仍然不属于善意购买人。如我们已经评论过的，无论是雇员女士还是画廊，在当时情况下都没有作出或试图作出进一步的了解。

Finally, we must examine again the position of Feigen to determine whether Feigen was a purchaser in good faith. In purchasing the Utrillo, Feigen did not rely on any indicia of ownership in Von Maker. Feigen dealt with Wertz, who did not have the legal right to possession of the painting. Even were we to consider Wertz as the agent of Von Maker or merge the identities of Von Maker and Wertz insofar as Feigen was concerned, Feigen was not a purchaser in good faith. As we have commented, neither Ms. Drew-Bear nor Feigen made, or attempted to make, the inquiry which the circumstances demanded.

漠视画作来历 画廊声称，虽然其没有调查卖方出售“大海”画作的授权，但这个做法符合行业惯例。但是，这不能成为原谅该做法的理由。这个说法正好证实了初审法院的看法，即“在这个行业中，本来非常需要核实交易物品的所有权，但是，提问却被视为不妥做法”。确实，商界

The Feigen claim that the failure to look into Wertz' authority to sell the painting was consistent with the practice of the trade does not excuse such conduct. This claim merely confirms the observation of the trial court that "in an industry whose transactions cry out for verification of ... title ... it is deemed poor practice to probe". Indeed, commercial indifference to ownership or the right to

对所有权或出售权的不闻不问，助长了被盗艺术品的流通。商界的不闻不问，使本已冷漠的商人更加放松操守、胆大妄为。在这种背景下，我们不可能再去聆听画廊的抱怨。

sell facilitates traffic in stolen works of art. Commercial indifference diminishes the integrity and increases the culpability of the apathetic merchant. In such posture, Feigen cannot be heard to complain.

结论　根据上面描述的情况，本案画作主人的起诉本来不应被驳回。此外，我们认为，画作主人是“大海”画作的真正所有权人，有权取得该画作的占有权，而画廊不正当地留持了该画作，因而有义务归还该画作，或支付该画作在本案初审时所具有的价值。基于以上理由，纽约州高等法院初审庭于 1978 年 6 月 22 日作出的判决，应从法律和事实双重角度被推翻，并被认定无效，而画作主人的指控则被恢复效力。

In the circumstances outlined, the complaint should not have been dismissed. Moreover, we find that plaintiffs-appellants are the true owners of the Utrillo painting and are entitled to possession thereof, that defendants-respondents wrongfully detained that painting and are obligated to return it or pay for its value at the time of trial. Accordingly, the judgment of the Supreme Court, New York County, entered June 22, 1978, should be reversed and vacated, on the law and the facts, ［and］ the complaint reinstated.

案例3　简单的手写记录是否可以构成书面合同？

Southwest Engineering Co., Inc. v. Martin Tractor Co.

西南工程公司诉马丁设备公司案

堪萨斯州最高法院 1970 年；473 P.2d 18

简　介

本案涉及机电设备的买卖。买方（Southwest）为了承包一项工程，计划从卖方（Martin）购买机电设备。双方通过电话沟通，大体确定了设备的型号、数量和价格。买方随后向发包商提交了投标文件，其中将此种设备列为买方将会使用的设备。买方中标后，为了落实相关机电设备的采购，与卖方约定面谈。买方代表（Cloepfil）与卖方代表（Hurt）在一家机场餐厅见面。卖方代表将双方在餐厅商定的主要内容写在一张纸上，包括设备的型号、数量和价格，以及买方可以获得的折扣，然后在纸上写上了自己的名字、公司的名字以及公司的地址。买方代表没有在纸上添加任何内容。两人离开餐厅前，卖方代表将这张纸交给了买方代表。

几天以后（1966 年 5 月 2 日），买方给卖方写了一封信，主要目的是请卖方准备招标文件，其中也提到对卖方付款条件的不同意见。大约 3 个星期后（1966 年 5 月 24 日），卖方给买方写信，表示“撤回所有的口头报价”，并拒绝向买方出售所讨论的机电设备。买方最终从另一家供应商购买了所需的机电设备，随后以卖方违约为由起诉卖方。初审法院判决合同成立且卖方违约，并判决买方可就直接损失取得赔偿，但无权就间接损失取得赔偿。买方没有提起上诉，但卖方提起上诉，认为双方之间根本不存在有效合同。

本案的主要争议是，双方是否已经达成法典所要求的书面合同？根据法典第 2.201 条的规定，价款达到或超过 500 美元的货物买卖合同，必须存在适当的书面文件，且被要求强制履行的一方已在文件上签名，且文件规定了货物数量。在本案中，双方最主要的书面文件就是卖方代表在机场餐厅写的那张纸，其中虽然记录了双方约定的主要内容，但非常简单，基本上只是列出了主要设备的型号、数量和价格，而没有任何其他条款。卖方代表虽然在纸上写下了自己的名字等，但看上去更像是名片内容，而不是代表卖方所作的合同签名。同时，买方代表没有在纸上写任何内容。初审法院认定，虽然这张纸的内容非常简单，但已经可以满足法典对书面文件的要求，因此合同已经成立。堪萨斯州最高法院同意初审法院的认定，维持了该判决，但认为初审法院对买方 1966 年 5 月 2 日信件的分析存在模糊之处，应明确认定该信件没有任何法律效力。

判　决

法典对书面合同的要求　法典第 2.201 条（1）款规定：“除本条另有规定外，价款达到或超过 500 美元的货物买卖合同，只有存在足以表明当事方已达成买卖合同的书面文件，且被要求强制履行的当事方或其授权代理人或经纪人已在该书面文件上签名，才可通过诉讼或抗辩强制履

K.S.A. 2-201（1）provides:“Except as otherwise provided in this section a contract for the sale of goods for the price of $500 or more is not enforceable by way of action or defense unless there is some writing sufficient to indicate that a contract for sale has been made between the parties and signed by the party against whom enforcement is sought or by his authorized agent or broker. A writing is

行。一份书面文件，即使漏写或错写任何已约定的条款，也并非不足以表明合同的达成，但在本款意义上，合同只能在不超出该书面文件显示的货物数量的范围内强制履行。”

not insufficient because it omits or incorrectly states a term agreed upon but the contract is not enforceable under this paragraph beyond the quantity of goods shown in such writing.”

买方的主张 买方的立场是，卖方代表在机场餐厅所准备的备忘录，已包含了法典上述规定中所要求的实质构成因素，因为该备忘录:（1）系由被要求强制履行的一方所签署，（2）系用于货物买卖，且（3）显示了数量。此外，读者可以注意到，该备忘录还列出了几项货物的价格。

Southwest takes the position that the memorandum prepared by Hurt at [airfield restaurant] supplies the essential elements of a contract required by the foregoing statute, i.e., that it is （1） a writing signed by the party sought to be charged, （2） that it is for the sale of goods and （3） that quantity is shown. In addition, the reader will have noted that the memorandum sets forth the prices of the several items listed.

法典的要求非常宽松 不可否认，对于如何订立有强制履行力的合同，法典对之前法律作出了近乎根本性的改变。本法院和其他法院都曾就此进行过阐述。法典第 2.201 条的堪萨斯州正式评论有下述解释:“本条（1）款比很多法院之前的解释都更加宽松。根据该款，所要求的书面文件，并非必须包含所有重大条款，而重大条款也并非必须加以准确

It cannot be gainsaid that the Uniform Commercial Code has effected a somewhat radical change in the law relating to the formation of enforceable contracts as such has been expounded by this and other courts. In the Kansas Comment to 2-201, the following explanation is given: “Subsection （1） relaxes the interpretations of many courts in providing that the required writing need not contain all the material terms and that they need not be stated precisely. All that is

表述。唯一需要的，就是该文件能够提供一个理由使人相信，在文件之外提供的任何口头证据，均确有真实的交易基础。本款只包含了3项绝对必须和不可改变的要求。第一，必须证明存在货物买卖合同；第二，必须存在‘签名’，而这个词包含了任何形式的认证，只要其指明了被要求强制履行的一方；第三，必须规定数量。有关价格、时间、付款或交货地点、货物的总体质量，以及任何特定担保的条款，都可以被省略。”

required is that the writing afford a basis for believing that the offered oral evidence rests on a real transaction. Only three definite and invariable requirements as to the writing are made by this subsection. First, it must evidence a contract for the sale of goods; second, it must be ‘signed,’ a word which includes any authentication which identifies the party to be charged; and third, it must specify quantity. Terms relating to price, time, and place of payment or delivery, the general quality of goods, or any particular warranties may all be omitted.”

专家的阐述　我们还可以从相关法律著作中知道，法典第2.201条规定的可以强制履行的书面文件，应满足3项必须具备的要求：能够证明货物买卖；包含了签名或认证；规定了数量。在堪萨斯州法典评注中（引用著作），作者明确写道:“在法典中，书面文件无须包含交易的全部条款，条款的表述也无须非常准确，但法典确实要求，书面文件的含义必须足够宽泛，能够证明当事方之间的买卖合同，且被要求履

From legal treatises, as well, we learn that the three invariable requirements of an enforceable written memorandum under 2-201 are that it evidence a sale of goods, that it be signed or authenticated and that it specify quantity. In Vernon’s Kansas Statutes Annotated, Uniform Commercial Code, Howe and Navin, the writers make this clear: “Under the Code the writing does not need to incorporate all the terms of the transaction, nor do the terms need to be stated precisely. The Code does require that the writing be broad enough to indicate a contract of sale

行合同的一方或其代理人必须在文件上签名，且该文件必须说明相关货物的数量。”

卖方的主张 关于权威作者和学者对法典条款的解释，本案卖方未提出真正质疑，但卖方声称，本案中的书面文件尚不足以构成法典所要求的那种已经签署的备忘录，且该文件仅仅列出口头报价，目的是在随后的谈判中进一步考虑。

初审法院认定合同成立 但是，关于这个问题，初审法院已经认定，卖方代表和买方代表在机场餐厅确实已经达成了协议，并认定法典第2.201条的形式要求已经得到满足。初审法院还认定，卖方代表所准备的备忘录，包含了法典所要求的3项必要条件，即证明了货物买卖，得到了卖方代表的认证，并注明了数量。此外，初审法院还特别认定，卖方代表具有订立协议的表见授权，且买方和卖方均属于法典第2.104条所定义的“商人”，且

between the parties; that the party against whom enforcement is sought, or his agent, must have signed the writing; and that the quantity dealt with must be stated.”

The defendant does not seriously question the interpretation accorded the statute by eminent scriveners and scholars, but maintains, nonetheless, that the writing in question does not measure up to the stature of a signed memorandum within the purview of the Code; that the instrument simply sets forth verbal quotations for future consideration in continuing negotiations.

But on this point the trial court found there was an agreement reached between Hurt and Cloepfil at [airfield restaurant]; that the formal requirements of K.S.A. 2-201 were satisfied; and that the memorandum prepared by Hurt contains the three essentials of the statute in that it evidences a sale of goods, was authenticated by Hurt and specifies quantity. Beyond that, the court specifically found that Hurt had apparent authority to make the agreement; that both Southwest and Martin were “merchants” as defined in K.S.A. 2-104; that the agreement reached at [airfield restaurant] included additional terms not

在机场餐厅达成的“协议”还包含了未反映在该书面文件中的其他条款，包括：（1）买方负责设备安装；（2）卖方负责将设备交付至施工工地；（3）卖方将在3个星期内收集和提供投标文件。初审法院还认定，卖方1966年5月24日的信件，构成了对合同的预前毁约。

noted in the writing:（1）Southwest was to install the equipment;（2）Martin was to deliver the equipment to Wichita and（3）Martin was to assemble and supply submittal documents within three weeks; and that Martin's letter of May 24, 1966, constituted an anticipatory breach of the contract.

存在证据支持　我们相信，本案的证据材料能够支持初审法院的上述所有认定。下述证据与书面备忘录的制备过程和完备程度直接有关：买方代表作证说，他和卖方代表在餐桌前坐下，并摊开了卖方代表带给他的规划材料。他们逐一讨论了每个部件的规格，且卖方代表写下了每个部件并标明了价格。虽然招标文件要求承包商使用D353发电机，但卖方代表认为D343型号作为替代型号，应该也可以被接受，因此同时标明了两个型号的价格，并允许买方采用发包商所批准的任何一个型号。卖方代表将备忘录交给买方代表后说，“这是我们已完成事项的记录，是我们在

We believe the record supports all the above findings. With particular reference to the preparation and sufficiency of the written memorandum, the following evidence is pertinent: Mr. Cloepfil testified that he and Hurt sat down at a restaurant table and spread out the plans which Hurt had brought with him; that they went through the specifications item by item and Hurt wrote each item down, together with the price thereof; that while the specifications called for a D353 generator, Hurt thought the D343 model might be an acceptable substitute, so he gave prices on both of them and Southwest could take either one of the two which USCE would approve; that Hurt gave him（Cloepfil）the memorandum “as a record of what we had done, the agreement we had arrived at at

机场餐厅会面中所达成的协议”。

卖方的书写构成签名 我们暂且搁置上述讨论，先来回复卖方的辩称，即备忘录没有按法典第2.201条的规定进行签署。备忘录上的唯一认证，是其左上角的下列手写文字：卖方代表的名字；卖方公司名字；卖方地点。初审法院认定，这足以构成卖方签名，而我们认为这个结论是正确的。

法典第1.201条（37）款规定：“签名”包括使用或采纳任何符号，只要当时具有对书面文件作出认证的意图。法典正式评论的相关部分说明：“在‘签名’的定义中包含了认证这个概念。这是为了说明，在法典中，签名无须是完整的签字。认证的形式包括印刷、盖章或手写。认证可以出现在文件上的任何部位。在适当情况下，文件或信件的抬头也可以构成认证。需要考虑的问题永远是，当事方在使用或采用该符号时，是否具有对书面文件作出认证的意图。”应该承认的是，卖方代表准备了备忘录，且

our meeting in the restaurant at the airport”.

We digress at this point to note Martin’s contention that the memorandum is not signed within the meaning of 2-201. The sole authentication appears in handprinted form at the top left-hand corner in these words: “Ken Hurt, Martin Tractor, Topeka, Caterpillar.” The court found this sufficient, and we believe correctly so.

K.S.A. 1-201 (37) provides as follows: “Signed” includes any symbol executed or adopted by a party with present intention to authenticate a writing. The official U.C.C. Comment states in part: “The inclusion of authentication in the definition of ‘signed’ is to make clear that as the term is used in this Act a complete signature is not necessary. Authentication may be printed, stamped or written ... It may be on any part of the document and in appropriate cases may be found in a billhead or letterhead.... The question always is whether the symbol was executed or adopted by the party with present intention to authenticate the writing.” Hurt admittedly prepared the memorandum and

没有否认其在上面留下了自己的名字。我们认为，此种认证足以满足法典的要求。

has not denied affixing his name thereto. We believe the authentication sufficiently complies with the statute.

双方证词　上述引用的证据，已经足以支持初审法院的认定，即在机场餐厅，卖方代表与买方代表已经达成了协议。但是，买方代表的证词，并不是支持该认定的唯一证据。在审前采证时，卖方代表自己在回答质询时说，“对于我要报价的那些内容，我们达成了约定，并且，对于主要货物，我们达成了总体约定”。在庭审中，卖方代表作证说，他无意改变审前的陈述。

The evidence already cited would be ample to sustain the trial court's finding that an agreement was reached between Hurt and Cloepfil ［at airfield restaurant］. However, Cloepfil's testimony is not the only evidence in support of that finding. In a pretrial deposition, Mr. Hurt, himself, deposed that "we agreed on the section that I would be quoting on, and we come to some over-all general agreement on the major items". At the trial Hurt testified he did not wish to change that statement in any way.

付款条件缺失　卖方代表进一步作证说，其个人看法是，阻碍当事方最终成交的因素，是卖方规定的付款条件。也就是说，假设买方当时同意了卖方的付款条件，他本人就会认为，双方已最终成交。在法庭作证时，卖方代表承认，他自己写下了该备忘录，并且，如备忘录所记，对于两个可供选择的发电机，买方均被给予 10% 的折扣。两个发电机的通用附件均按净价计算，卖

Hurt further testified that in his opinion the thing which stood in the way of a firm deal was Martin's terms of payment— that had Southwest agreed with those terms of payment, so far as he was concerned, he would have considered a firm deal was made. Mr. Hurt acknowledged while on the stand that he penned the memorandum and that as disclosed therein a 10 per cent discount was given Southwest on the price of either of the generators listed, and that the accessories common to both generators were to be net —

方没有任何利润。

如初审法院所认定的，双方在机场餐厅的会面中，确实未能就付款条件达成协议。卖方代表作证说，在准备备忘录时，卖方希望订单出具时支付10%，货物交付时支付50%，货物接受时支付余款，但他记不清买方代表是如何回复的。买方代表的作证稍有不同。他作证说，在双方准备离开时，他们在大堂握手，当时卖方代表说，他们的条件通常是20%的定金，而余款在货物交付时支付，而买方代表说，自己公司的通常付款方式是，货物交付后的下一个月10日支付90%的货款，而余款在最终接收货物时支付。很明显，当事方对此未能达成协议。

法典可以补充付款条款 虽然卖方和买方未能约定付款条件，但如果双方在其他方面已达成有效的协议，则未能约定付款条件本身并不导致该协议无效。法典第2.204条（3）款规定："即使买卖合同的一项或多项条款存在空缺，只要当事方有意订立合

that is, sold without profit.

It is quite true, as the trial court found, that terms of payment were not agreed upon at [airfield restaurant] meeting. Hurt testified that as the memorandum was being made out, he said they wanted 10 per cent with the order, 50 per cent on delivery and the balance on acceptance, but he did not recall Cloepfil's response. Cloepfil's version was somewhat different. He stated that after the two had shaken hands in the lobby preparing to leave, Hurt said their terms usually were 20 per cent down and the balance on delivery; while he (Cloepfil) said the way they generally paid was 90 per cent on the tenth of the month following delivery and the balance on final acceptance. It is obvious the parties reached no agreement on this point.

However, a failure on the part of Messrs. Hurt and Cloepfil to agree on terms of payment would not, of itself, defeat an otherwise valid agreement reached by them. K.S.A. 2-204 (3) reads: "Even though one or more terms are left open a contract for sale does not fail for indefiniteness if the parties have intended to make a contract and there

同，且存在比较确定的方法用以提供适当救济，合同即不因缺乏确定性而不能成立。”

is a reasonably certain basis for giving an appropriate remedy.”

合同的确定性问题　法典的正式评论对此具有指导意义：“对于本篇后述条款所涉及的‘空缺条款’，本条（3）款陈述了相关原则。如果当事方意图达成具有约束力的协议，则本条（3）款承认，只要存在比较确定的基础来提供救济，则即使缺失某些条款，协议仍具有法律效力。不应将确定性作为检验标准。也就是说，无须确切地知道当事方要做什么，也无须确切地判断受损方的赔偿数额。此外，即使一项或多项条款需要随后约定，致使本来可以成立的协议可能因缺乏该条款而无法成立，这也不构成检验标准。相反，对于‘不确定性’问题，本法希望按商业标准加以解决，即本法其他条款将会提供缺失的条款，包括履约、价格、救济和其他类似条款。当事方缺失的条款越多，他们意图达成一项有约束力协议的可能性就越小，但是，即使存在这些缺失，

The official U.C.C. Comment is enlightening: “Subsection (3) states the principle as to ‘open terms’ underlying later sections of the Article. If the parties intend to enter into a binding agreement, this subsection recognizes that agreement as valid in law, despite missing terms, if there is any reasonably certain basis for granting a remedy. The test is not certainty as to what the parties were to do nor as to the exact amount of damages due the plaintiff. Nor is the fact that one or more terms are left to be agreed upon enough of itself to defeat an otherwise adequate agreement. Rather, commercial standards on the point of ‘indefiniteness’ are intended to be applied, this Act making provision elsewhere for missing terms needed for performance, open price, remedies and the like. The more terms the parties leave open, the less likely it is that they have intended to conclude a binding agreement, but their actions may be frequently conclusive on the matter despite the omissions.”

他们的行为往往会为此问题提供最终答案。”

在P诉W案中，法院引用了法典的上述规定和正式评论。法院的看法是：“对于这项具有约束力但新近制定的法典条款，似乎还没有相关法院判例作出解释。在法典制定之前所发表的一篇文章中（引用文章），威利斯通教授认为，应该仅允许缺失那些‘次要’条款。他认为，如果‘重要条款’存在缺失，那就应该仅以‘商人自尊’作为唯一的强制力。但是，在法典起草时，他的建议被拒绝了。这表明，法典起草者的意图是，即使一项重要条款存在缺失，仍然可以根据法典的规定，来认定当事方具有订立合同的意图。”

The above Code provision and accompanying Comment were quoted in Pennsylvania Co. v. Wilmington Trust Co., where the court made this observation: “There appears to be no pertinent court authority interpreting this rather recent but controlling statute. In an article entitled ‘The Law of Sales In the Proposed Uniform Commercial Code’, Harv. Law Rev., Mr. Williston wanted to limit omissions to ‘minor’ terms. He wanted ‘business honor’ to be the only compulsion where ‘important terms’ are left open. Nevertheless, his recommendation was rejected. This shows that those drafting the statute intended that the omission of even an important term does not prevent the finding under the statute that the parties intended to make a contract.”

本案应根据法典规定付款

对于本案来说，法典第2.310条提供了缺失的条款。该条相关部分规定：“除另有协议外，（a）价款应在买方预定收到货物的时间和地点支付，即使发运地同时为交付地。”

So far as the present case is concerned, K.S.A. 2-310 supplies the omitted term. This statute provides in pertinent part: “Unless otherwise agreed, (a) payment is due at the time and place at which the buyer is to receive the goods even though the place of shipment is the place of delivery.”

我们的看法是，法典两项条款的文字是清晰和确定的。将两项条款放在一起分析，我们的结论是，如果当事方已经达成了可强制履行的货物买卖协议，但缺少了付款条款，法律就会默示认为，作为协议的条款之一，货款将在交付地支付。在这个问题上，法律的规定与本院多年以前确定的原则相比，并没有很大区别。

之前的判例　在T诉S案中，当事方按约定价格就玉米买卖达成一项书面协议，规定交货地点为买方粮仓。协议没有提到付款条件。在卖方交货时，买方无法支付现金，因此提议用支票付款，但卖方拒绝了该建议，并取消了合同。买方因此起诉卖方违反合同。本院的判决如下："玉米的书面买卖合同规定，将在买方粮仓交货。这个规定默示表明，应以现金付款。卖方作出了提示交付，但买方只同意以支票付款。由于当时银行不能立即将支票兑现，因此，买方无权就卖方未能交付货物而寻求赔偿。"

In our view, the language of the two Code provisions is clear and positive. Considered together, we take the two sections to mean that where parties have reached an enforceable agreement for the sale of goods, but omit therefrom the terms of payment, the law will imply, as part of the agreement, that payment is to be made at time of delivery. In this respect the law does not greatly differ from the rule this court laid down years ago.

In Thompson v. Seek, the parties entered into a written agreement for the sale of corn at a stated price to be delivered at Thompson's elevator. Terms of payment were not mentioned. Thompson was unable to pay cash on delivery but proposed to pay by check instead. Seek refused this tender and rescinded the contract, whereupon Thompson sued for breach of contract. The decision of the court is ［as follows］："A written contract for the purchase of corn to be delivered at the buyer's elevator implies payment in cash, and upon offer to deliver, and refusal to pay except by check, at a time when banks are not honoring checks by paying cash, the buyer is not entitled to damages for failure to deliver."

付款条件在本案不具重要性 我们的意思并不是说，在很多情况下，付款条件并不重要，也不是说，当事方无权将付款条件作为合同的前提条件。但是，根据我们看到的本案事实，卖方和买方并没有重视付款条件，也没有多想此事。卖方代表作证说，他不记得在他说明付款条件时，买方代表的回复是什么。买方代表作证说，在两人将要离开餐厅时，各自说明了自己公司通常的付款条件，但仅此而已。初审法院认定，关于付款条件问题，当事方只进行过短暂和随意的商谈。我们认为，这是对当时情况的适当总结。

We do not mean to infer that terms of payment are not of importance under many circumstances, or that parties may not condition an agreement on their being included. However, the facts before us hardly indicate that Hurt and Cloepfil considered the terms of payment to be significant, or of more than passing interest. Hurt testified that while he stated his terms he did not recall Cloepfil's response, while Cloepfil stated that as the two were on the point of leaving, each stated their usual terms and that was as far as it went. The trial court found that only a brief and casual conversation ensued as to payment, and we think that is a valid summation of what took place.

付款问题是卖方的借口 此外，值得说明的是，卖方律师在1966年9月15日的信中，才第一次提到缺失付款条件的问题，并将其作为取消合同的合理理由，而这距离卖方代表写下备忘录的时间，已有4个多月。在此之前的多个场合，对于为什么要取消双方在机场餐厅的约定，卖方给出的都是其他理由。对于为

Moreover, it is worthy of note that Martin first mentioned the omission of the terms of payment, as justifying its breach, in a letter written by counsel on September 15, 1966, more than four months after the memorandum was prepared by Hurt. On prior occasions Martin attributed its cancellation of the ［airfield restaurant］ understanding to other causes. In its May 24 letter, Martin ascribed its withdrawal of "all verbal quotations" to

什么取消“全部口头报价”，卖方5月24日的信件解释说，这是因为“供应商产品和零部件商受到限制”。卖方在向买方澄清其信件的含义时说，卖方当时在堪萨斯城和其他地区为本案发包商承担了另外一些工程，因此不想同时再承担额外的工程。

“restrictions placed on Caterpillar products［and］accessory suppliers”. In explaining the meaning of the letter to Cloepfil, Hurt said that Martin was doing work for the USCE in the Kansas City and Tulsa districts and did not want to take on additional work with them at this time.

所有这些情况都使我们完全有理由怀疑，卖方现在的说法，即当时还计划就付款条件作进一步谈判，主要是事后才想到的用于逃避责任的借口。毫无疑问，初审法院在就本案事实作出认定时，就是这样看待卖方借口的。

The entire circumstances may well give rise to a suspicion that Martin's present insistence that future negotiations were contemplated concerning terms of payment, is primarily an afterthought, for use as an escape hatch. Doubtless the trial court so considered the excuse in arriving at its findings.

买方5月2日信件问题　我们也注意到卖方的辩称，即买方1966年5月2日的信件提到此次买卖交易，并可证明双方尚未最终达成合同。虽然也许可以对信件使用的某些措辞作此解释，但初审法院认定，当事方确实在机场餐厅达成了协议。我们认为，该认定所依赖的证据具有足够的数量和效力。根据我们的一贯原则，在上诉中，即使存在某些相反证据，初审法院的认定，仍对

We are aware of Martin's argument that Southwest's letter of May 2, 1966, referring to the sale is evidence that no firm contract had been concluded. Granted that some of the language employed might be subject to that interpretation, the trial court found, on what we deem to be substantial, competent evidence, that an agreement of sale was concluded at［airfield restaurant］. Under our invariable rule those findings are binding upon this court on appeal even though there may have been evidence to the contrary.（See

我们具有约束力（引用著作）。

信件包含卖方未曾同意的内容 卖方特别指出了买方5月2日信件的一部分内容，认为该内容说明，对于在机场餐厅达成的协议，买方随后又增加了一项新的和不可接受的条款。信件内容如下："对于在出具本订单时支付部分货款的付款条件，我们不能接受。但是，在发电机交付后，我们在第一次付款中，可以包含发电机100%的货款，并只留持总价的10%至接收货物后支付。通常，这意味着供应商可以期待在交货后30日内获得90%的付款。"

新的内容没有法律效力 必须承认，买方信件所建议的付款条件，之前未得到过卖方的接受。但我们认为，这项建议不影响本案的结果。虽然双方之前未就付款条件达成协议，但法典第2.310条提供了缺失的条款，即交货时付款，且对于已经成立的协议，该条款构成协议的组成部分。从法律效力的角度看，买方的上述建议只是要改变法律所默示提供的付款条件。由于卖方未接受该

cases in Hatcher's Kansas Digest.)

The defendant points particularly to the following portion of the May 2 letter, as interjecting a new and unacceptable term in the agreement made at [airfield restaurant].

"... We are not prepared to make a partial payment at the time of placing of this order. However, we will be able to include 100% of the engine generator price in our first payment estimate after it is delivered, and only 10% will have to be withheld pending acceptance. Ordinarily this means that suppliers can expect payment of 90% within about thirty days after delivery."

It must be conceded that the terms of payment proposed in Southwest's letter had not been agreed to by Martin. However, we view the proposal as irrelevant. Although terms of payment had not been mutually agreed upon, K.S.A. 2-310 supplied the missing terms, i.e., payment on delivery, which thus became part of the agreement already concluded. In legal effect the proposal was no more than one to change the terms of payment implied by law. Since Martin did not accept the change, the proposal had no effect,

改变，因此该建议没有任何效力，不能改变或终止在机场餐厅达成的协议。

either as altering or terminating the agreement reached at ［airfield restaurant］.

不得单方改变协议内容　如同密歇根州上诉法院在 A 诉 A 案中所说，“……毫无疑问，任何当事方在订立协议后，都不能简单地通过发送一封包含额外条款或不同条款的书面‘确认’来改变该协议……”。也许我们还可以补充说，任何当事方也都不能自行添加严重改变原始协议的额外建议，除非另一方表示同意。

As the Michigan Court of Appeals said in American Parts v. Arbitration Assn.: “... Surely a party who has entered into an agreement cannot change that agreement by the simple expedient of sending a written ‘confirmation’ containing additional or different terms ...” Neither, may we add, will an extraneous proposal which materially alters the original agreement, be included unless agreed to by the other party.

在本案双方的书面陈述中，很多讨论都集中于法典第 2.207 条规定的含义和效力。联邦第一巡回上诉法院在 R 诉 F 案中，将法典这项条款中扑朔迷离的文字称为“不太令人愉快的文笔”。这项条款带来了大量诉讼，并引起了法律专家的激烈学术讨论。

Substantial parts of the briefs filed by both parties are devoted to discussions of the meaning and effect of K.S.A. 2-207. This murky bit of prose, which the United States Court of Appeals, First Circuit, characterized in Roto-Lith, Ltd. v. F.P. Bartlett & Co. as “not too happily drafted” has given rise to a good deal of litigation and has prompted a spate of learned articles from legal savants.

法典的文本冲突规定　法典该条的（1）款和（2）款规定：“（1）确定且及时的承诺表示，或合理时间内发送的书面确认，即使与要约条款或与已同意的条

Section （1）and（2）of this statute read:“（1）A definite and seasonable expression of acceptance or a written confirmation which is sent within a reasonable time operates as an acceptance even though

款相比，包含了不同条款或补充条款，亦构成承诺，除非其明确规定，以要约人同意这些不同条款或补充条款作为承诺生效的条件。（2）补充条款应被解释为对合同进行补充的建议。在商人之间，这些条款构成合同的组成部分，除非：（a）要约明确规定，承诺限于要约条款，（b）补充条款严重改变了要约，或（c）已对补充条款作出过拒绝通知，或在收到补充条款通知后的合理时间内作出了拒绝通知。”

it states terms additional to or different from those offered or agreed upon, unless acceptance is expressly made conditional on assent to the additional or different terms. （2） The additional terms are to be construed as proposals for addition to the contract. Between merchants such terms become part of the contract unless:（a） the offer expressly limits acceptance to the terms of the offer; （b） they materially alter it; or （c） notification of objection to them has already been given or is given within a reasonable time after notice of them is received.”

买方信件不构成文本冲突问题 在本案中，对法典这项条款的讨论起源于初审法院的认定，即买方5月2日的信件，同时构成了法典该款项下的“承诺”和“确认”；并且，无论是作为“承诺”还是“确认”，相比已经约定的条款，该信件都包含了额外条款，并构成对协议的重大改变。由于初审法院之前已经认定，双方在机场餐厅已经达成了有效的合同，因此我们认为，初审法院有关买方信件的上述认定实属多余，并无必要。

The discussions centering on this section of the Code are occasioned by findings of the trial court that Southwest's letter of May 2 is both an “acceptance” and a “confirmation” within the purview thereof; that as either an “acceptance” or “confirmation” the letter stated additional terms which were different from those agreed upon and which constituted a material alteration of the agreement. In view of the court's previous findings that a viable contract had already been concluded at ［airfield restaurant］, we deem these findings superfluous and extraneous.

我们不打算对法典第 2.207 条的目的和含义撰写一份长篇论文。我们的看法是，该条与本案事实无关。我们认为，按法典的设计，该条适用的情况是，通过一项“承诺表示”（我们假设其为书面表示）来接受一项之前尚未被接受的要约，或者以随后的书面文件来确认之前的口头协议。本案不存在上述任何一种情况。

We do not propose to engage in an extended dissertation upon the purpose or meaning of 2-207. In our view the statute is not germane to the facts of this case; we think it designed for situations where an open offer is accepted by "an expression of acceptance" (we presume in writing) or where an oral agreement is later confirmed in writing. Neither situation is presented in the case now before us.

初审法院认定，双方在机场餐厅已经达成了具有强制履行力的协议，且用书面形式将协议记录下来。这项认定默示表明，要约和承诺都已具备，且两者已融合成最终合同。在买方书写 1966 年 5 月 2 日的信件时，已经不存在尚待接受的要约，无论是附条件要约还是其他要约。也不存在需要确认的口头协议，因为协议已经于 4 月 28 日以书面备忘录的形式被记录下来了。

The trial court found that an enforceable agreement, memorialized in writing, had been reached [at airfield restaurant]. This finding implies both offer and acceptance, the two being merged into the resulting contract. When the letter of May 2, 1966, was written there was no outstanding offer to accept — conditionally or otherwise. Neither was there an oral agreement to confirm — the agreement having previously been memorialized in the written memorandum of April 28.

双方律师引用了相关判例，试图向本院解释法典第 2.207 条的含义。但在我们看来，其中没有任何判例与本案特征相似。所引用的判例全都涉及两种情况：

As we read the authorities pointed out by counsel on both sides, as they have attempted to divine for us the sense of 2-207, none of them appear to fit the pattern of the present action. The cited cases involve either

对于尚待接受的要约，在承诺时使用了包含不同条款或额外条款的书面文件；对口头协议作出书面确认，但确认文件包含了新的或额外的条款。

an outstanding offer, accepted by written instrument containing different or added terms, or an oral agreement later confirmed by a writing which states new or additional terms.

在这个问题上，我们承认，“确认”这个词可以有很多种含义，但我们认为，在法典第2.207条的使用中，这个词是指“书面订单或协议，目的是对之前以口头方式达成的协议作出确认或证明”（引用词典）。对于在机场餐厅达成的协议，不需要买方在5月2日的信中，通过作出确认或承诺而使该协议获得生命力，因为在达成该协议时，已经用书面形式将其记录下来。我们认定初审法院对本案的判决不存在错误，因此维持原判。

In this connection, while we recognize that the term “confirmation” may be employed in a variety of meanings, we think it is used in 2-207 in the sense of “a written order or agreement that verifies or substantiates an agreement previously concluded orally”.（Webster's Third New International Dictionary, Unabridged.）Neither confirmation nor acceptance by Southwest was needed on May 2 to breathe life into the agreement previously concluded at [airfield restaurant], for it was memorialized in writing at the time of making. We find no error in this case and the judgment of the trial court is affirmed.

案例 4　合同的一体化条款是否有效？

ARB, Inc. v. E-Systems, Inc.
埃博公司诉电子系统公司案

联邦哥伦比亚特区巡回上诉法院 1980 年；663 F.2d 189, 30 UCC Rep.Serv. 949

简　介

本案涉及设备买卖合同的纠纷。买方（ARB）从事电视受众调研业务，通过在家庭内安装收视监测设备，来统计大众的收视习惯和收视率。卖方（E-Systems）是电子系统的设计和制造公司，产品包括安装在家庭内的监测设备。买卖双方于 1973 年 10 月订立了监测设备买卖合同。合同共有 53 页，由双方经验丰富的谈判人员经过长时间的仔细谈判而制定。

试生产的第一台设备于 1973 年年底交付，但测试显示，设备存在较明显的性能问题。随后交付的试生产样机经过进一步测试，也均显示存在明显问题。但卖方向买方保证，到正式生产时，这些问题都会解决。基于此种保证，买方允许卖方开始正式生产。在此期间，卖方交付了部分设备，由买方安装在取样家庭内收集受众数据。但是，已安装的设备多数都不能正常工作，致使买方丧失对卖方产品的信心，并不得不另行寻找供应商。随后，买方起诉卖方。买方认为，卖方设计和制造的设备不符合合同规定，且卖方违反了明示担保，并违反了货物商销性和适用性的默示担保。而卖方则认为，买方违反了合同中的多项条款。

在初审中，由于本案涉及复杂的电子设备，初审法院在当事方的同意下，根据联邦民事诉讼法的相关规定，任命了一名有相关知识的特聘审判员(special master)，由其对案件进行审理并提出判决意见。特聘审判员在向法院提交的“意见备忘录”中说，卖方的设备存在严重瑕疵，构成卖方对合同及担保的违反，因此，卖方应向买方支付直接和间接损失赔偿。但是，特聘审判员不允许买方取得“补进”(cover)赔偿，认为买方在订立合同前的谈判中，已放弃了获得此种赔偿的权利。初审法院基于特聘审判员的意见作出了判决。

特聘审判员所说的弃权，是指在订立合同前的谈判期间，买方建议在合同中加入“转购”(reprocurement)条款。该条款规定，如果卖方违约致使买方另行从第三方采购设备，则对于该采购中高出合同价格的部分，卖方应承担责任。这实际上就是法典第2.712条所提供的“补进”救济，也就是买方另行购买替代货物的权利，以及就原始合同价格与补进价格的差额取得赔偿的权利。对于买方建议的转购条款，卖方没有同意。因此，在正式签订的书面合同中，没有提到转购问题。特聘审判员认为，这显示买方已放弃了补进的救济。由于买方实际上已为另行采购设备和重建监测系统花费了大量费用，特聘审判员的这项认定意味着，买方可能无法就全部损失从卖方取得赔偿。同时，在买卖双方正式签署的书面合同中，还包含了“一体化”(integration)条款。该条款规定，所签署的书面合同代表了双方的全部约定，因此，除书面合同条款外，双方不存在任何其他约定。

在上诉中，上诉法院需要解决双方提出的多个问题。卖方提出的问题包括，虽然设备存在一定问题，但买方已认可该设备并要求卖方开始正式生产；买方已经接受了设备；买方无权拒绝付款；买方无权提起诉讼。买方提出的主要问题是，虽然在谈判时买方所建议的转购条款未能进入合同，但买方仍然享有法典第2.712条提供的补进救济。对此，法院首先讨论了卖方和买方违约的问题，因为如果卖方根本没有违约，买方自然就无权作出转购或补进，也无权拒绝付款等；而如果买方违约，买方不仅不能转购，还要就自己的违约向卖方作出赔偿。上诉法院的结论是，卖方确实存在违约，而买方并未违约。

上诉法院随后需要解决的最重要的问题是，在卖方违约而买方实际上已另行采购了替代设备后，买方是否可就合同价格与替代设备价格的差额，寻求法典所规定的“补进”救济？在较大程度上，这涉及买方是否实际上已放弃了该救济。卖方认为，买方已放弃了该救济，因为在合同谈判时，卖方拒绝了买方的“转购”方案，而买方也接受了卖方立场。买方认为，卖方引用的谈判过程，属于法典第 2.202 条所说的“口头证据或外部证据”，不应被法院采纳。

上诉法院认定，合同中包含了一体化条款，因此原则上应以合同书面条款本身为准。法典虽然也允许补充外部证据，但条件是该证据必须与书面条款的内容相协调，而卖方提出的证据不符合此种要求。在这种情况下，卖方提出的证据不应被采纳。而如果不采纳卖方的证据，就意味着“合同”不仅包含其中所书写的内容，而且还包含法律提供的任何其他补充内容，包括“补进”的救济。虽然合同的书面条款没有提到买方享有补进救济，但这是法典提供给买方的天然权利。因此，只要未被书面条款明确排除，买方就享有这项权利。

判　决

双方上诉的问题　卖方上诉至本院的问题是：初审法院有关设备未能达到合同规定的认定，是否存在明显错误？初审法院有关买方停止向卖方付款的行为不构成违约的判定，是否存在错误？初审法院有关买方提起诉讼的行为不构成违反合同的判定，是否存在错误？初审法院有关买

E-Systems appeals to this court on the following issues： whether the trial court's finding that the equipment failed to meet contract specifications was clearly erroneous; whether the trial court erred in holding that the cessation of payments to E-Systems did not breach the contract； whether the trial court erred in holding that the filing of the law suit by ARB did not breach the contract；

方未接受货物，或即使接受了亦已及时撤销了接受的判定，是否存在错误？初审法院是否正确地计算了附带损失和间接损失数额？买方上诉的问题是：初审法院拒绝买方取得“补进”赔偿的判定，是否存在错误？

whether the trial court erred in holding that ARB did not accept or, alternatively, that it made a timely revocation of acceptance; and whether the trial court properly calculated incidental and consequential damages. ARB appeals on the basis of [this issue]: whether the trial court erred in denying ARB damages for cover.

卖方设备存在严重瑕疵 特聘审判员在其1978年11月15日“意见备忘录”中认定，设备存在“严重的设计和组件瑕疵”，且该情况“构成了严重违约，致使该设备不适合买方的用途，也不适合商业使用的一般用途”。他的结论主要基于买方和卖方雇员在同一时期作出的报告，以及在诉讼开始后，各个专家对设备进行测试后提出的报告和证词。对于卖方所聘专家提交的报告，特聘审判员基本没有采纳，认为测试环境条件不足，削弱了测试结果的证明效力。

In his Memorandum Opinion of November 15, 1978, the special master found that the equipment had “substantial design and component defects” which “amounted to material breaches of the contract, (and) rendered the equipment unfit for ARB’s purposes and unfit for commercial application generally”. He based his conclusions on contemporary field reports made by employees of both ARB and E-Systems, and on the reports and testimony of experts based on tests carried out after the litigation began. He assigned little weight to the report of the expert retained by E-Systems, finding that the conditions under which the tests were made weakened their probative worth.

买方没有继续付款的义务 特聘审判员随后驳回了卖方提出的全部抗辩和反诉。卖方声称，

The master next rejected each of the affirmative defenses and counterclaims raised by E-Systems. Regarding E-Systems’s claim

买方停止向卖方付款的行为构成买方违约，但特聘审判员认定，“合同中不存在此种继续付款的义务”。他还认定，根据法典第2.609 条的规定，买方拒绝付款存在合理依据，因为法典该条规定，如果当事一方要求对方提供充分保证，即后者保证将根据合同规定履行义务，那么，当后者未能提供保证时，前者可以暂时中止自己的履约。特聘审判员还驳回了卖方有关买方行为存在恶意的指控，认定该指控缺乏足够证据。

that ARB breached the contract by halting payments to E-Systems, he found that there was “no such obligation ... imposed by the contract”. He further held that ARB's nonperformance was justified under Md.Com. Law § 2-609, which authorizes a party to suspend his performance if he demands, and fails to receive, adequate assurance from the other party that said party will fulfill its part of the bargain. He also rejected the argument that ARB had acted in bad faith, holding that there was insufficient evidence to establish this claim.

随后，基于“对于主要因卖方违约而给买方带来的损失，买方有权获得充分和公平的赔偿”的理由，特聘审判员确定了卖方应支付的损害赔偿。

The master then awarded damages based on the proposition that “ARB is entitled to recover full and fair compensation for the damages proximately resulting from these breaches”.

买方有权获得损害赔偿　首先，特聘审判员判定，买方有权收回根据合同已向卖方支付的款项。其次，他判定，买方可就卖方违约造成的附带损失和间接损失，获得 195 万美元赔偿。他对买方的附带损失和间接损失描述如下：为了终止与卖方的关系，

First, he determined that ARB was entitled to the return of payments it had made to E-Systems on the contract. Second, he decided that ARB could recover $1.95 million for incidental and consequential damages suffered as a result of the breach. He described ARB's incidental and consequential damages as follows: ARB incurred extensive expenses

并为了完成与记录仪服务有关的必要工作，买方支出了大量费用。最后，他判定，买方在“谈判时已放弃”其根据法典第2.712条而获得“补进”赔偿的权利。根据该条，对于货物的合同价格与善意购买替代货物（补进）的价格的差额，买方原本有权取得赔偿。

买方已放弃补进救济 关于“补进”赔偿，特聘审判员认定，在合同谈判中，在卖方的要求下，双方从合同较早的草稿中删去了下面这段话：如果卖方出现违约，致使合同全部或部分终止，并致使买方需从其他途径采购合同项下的任何产品或服务，则相对于卖方圆满完成订单时买方本应支付的费用，卖方将对超出的采购费用承担责任。

特聘审判员认定，上述转购条款相当于法典的补进条款，因此，买方在“谈判时已放弃”补进救济。作为该结论的依据，他引用了法典第2.303条：当本篇以“除另有协议外”为条件而将

in terminating its relationship with E-Systems and performing again those activities essential to establishment of a successful meter service. Third, he held that ARB had "bargained away" its right under Md.Com.Law § 2-712 to recover as damages the difference in price between the contract goods and a good faith purchase of substitute goods (cover).

He based this decision upon the deletion at E-Systems's request, during negotiations on an earlier contract draft, of the following sentence: If, as a result of default of performance by the Seller, this contract is terminated in whole or in part and it is necessary to procure any of the specified products or services elsewhere, then Seller will be liable for any re-procurement charges which exceed the amount which would have been due the Seller if he had satisfactorily completed this order.

He found that this reprocurement provision was the equivalent of cover, and that ARB had thus "bargained away" its cover remedy. The master quoted Md.Com.Law § 2-303 to justify his decision. This section provides: Where this title allocates a risk

风险或责任划给一方时，当事方不仅可以通过协议将风险或责任转给另一方，还可以将风险或责任在当事方之间划分。

or a burden as between the parties "unless otherwise agreed", the agreement may not only shift the allocation but may also divide the risk or burden.

买方声称，根据有关口头证据的法典第2.202条，在解释合同时，不应将已被删除的草稿作为考虑因素。特聘审判员驳回了该辩称，认为限制补进的约定与合同其他条款并不冲突。

ARB contended that Md.Com.Law § 2-202, the parol evidence rule, barred consideration of the deleted sentence in interpreting the contract. The master rejected this argument, concluding that the agreement limiting cover is not inconsistent with any of the terms of the contract.

初审法院的判决　在考虑了双方以书面和口头形式对特聘审判员"意见备忘录"提出的异议后，初审法院完全采纳了特聘审判员的结论，判决买方胜诉。初审法院简单地回顾了特聘审判员对两个事项的结论，即补进问题及附带损失和间接损失问题。

After considering written and oral objections of both parties to the master's Memorandum Opinion, the district court issued a Memorandum and Order, adopting the opinion of the master in full and ordering judgment for plaintiff. The district court reviewed briefly the master's decision in [two] matters: cover, [and] incidental and consequential damages.

关于补进，初审法院表示，买方引用的合同一体化条款，不能明确起到该作用，且特聘审判员有关该条款作用不足的结论，是经过"冗长审理后"得出的。在该期间，"他有机会看到和听到证人作证，并审阅书面证据"。

As to cover, it indicated that the clauses pointed to by ARB as integration clauses do not clearly serve that purpose, and that the master's conclusion that they were insufficient was reached "after a lengthy trial in which he had the opportunity to see and hear witnesses as well as review the

关于附带损失和间接损失，卖方称，特聘审判员已就补进问题作出结论，但其判定的附带和间接损害赔偿数额包含了本来不应被包含的补进赔偿数额。初审法院驳回了卖方的辩称。

卖方提出的两项主张 特聘审判员认定，卖方的设备不符合合同规定，且卖方违反了明示担保，并违反了适用性和商销性的默示担保。卖方称，基于两个理由，特聘审判员的认定存在明显错误。首先，特聘审判员错误地拒绝了卖方所聘专家的报告和证言，并错误地采纳了买方所聘专家的证言。其次，初审法院错误地排除了某些有利于卖方，且产生时间与合同订立时间同步的证据。

有合理理由忽略卖方检测结果 本院认为，卖方上述两项主张均缺乏合理基础。第一项主张不能成立的原因是，案件材料实际上足以支持特聘审判员“不认可”卖方测试结果的决定。该测试由卖方组织，并由一位外聘

documentary evidence”. As to incidental and consequential damages, the district court rejected the contention of E-Systems that damages awarded by the master under this heading included amounts that should have been barred by his conclusion as to cover.

E-Systems claims that the master's finding that the equipment did not conform to contract specifications, and that E-Systems breached express warranties and the implied warranties of fitness and merchantability, was clearly erroneous. It bases this claim on two contentions: first, that the master improperly disregarded the reports and testimony of the expert retained by E-Systems and improperly credited the testimony of the experts retained by ARB; and, second, that the trial court erroneously ignored evidence contemporary with the contract which was favorable to E-Systems.

Neither contention is well-founded. The first fails because the record adequately supports the master's decision to “discount” the results of the testing commissioned by E-Systems under the direction of Mr. Popkin-Clurman. Mr. Popkin-Clurman testified that he gave E-Systems “carte blanche” to do

专家负责指导。该专家作证说，他曾允许卖方在将设备提交测试前，对设备“全权”采取任何行动。在这种情况下，所测试的设备相比 1974 年春夏交付给买方的设备，并非处于同等状况；在有些方面，甚至不是同样的技术配置。此外，测试没有充分模拟该设备的实际使用环境。

anything it wanted to the equipment before turning it over for testing. Thus the equipment tested was not in the same condition, or, in some respects, even of the same technical make-up, as the equipment delivered to ARB in the spring and summer of 1974. Moreover, the testing did not adequately simulate the environment in which the equipment was required to perform.

关于该测试未充分反映设备原定实际使用环境的问题，特聘审判员列出了该测试的 9 个重大不足。卖方未能对列出的这些不足作出有说服力的反驳。因此，卖方关于特聘审判员的结论存在明显错误的说法，很难被认可。但这并不是说，买方所聘专家的测试就无懈可击。例如，他们在测试中使用的设备，看上去不一定是两三年以前交付给买方时的状态，因为设备在这个期间经历了运输和存储。

The master listed nine material respects in which the tests did not adequately reflect the actual conditions in which the equipment was contracted to perform. E-Systems did not persuasively refute these findings. Its claim that the master's conclusion is somehow clearly in error is therefore difficult to credit. This is not to say, however, that the testing carried out by experts retained by ARB is beyond criticism. For example, it appears that the equipment they tested may not have been in the condition in which it had been delivered two or three years earlier, due to the effects of shipment and storage.

但无论如何，特聘审判员对买方专家证言的采纳，不属于明显错误。有两个事实可以支持这个结论。首先，在买方 3 个专家

That the master did not clearly err in crediting the testimony of the ARB experts, however, is established by two facts: first, much of the testimony of the three

的证词中，很大一部分证词涉及设备和设备内部组件的设计，而不涉及测试的结果。其次，两位专家进行的相互独立的测试，结果有高度相似性，且都显示出设备性能远未达到合同规格。数据相似程度之高，偏离合同程度之大，足以抵消卖方对该测试的个别指责。

有合理理由排除卖方证据

卖方的第二项主张同样不具有说服力。卖方认为，特聘审判员错误地排除了同时期的其他证据，主要包括档案中的设备性能报告。卖方希望特聘审判员采纳的证据，主要涉及买方在使用监视系统中的非卖方设备时所遇到的问题，如通信设备和计算机设备的问题。但是，本案不涉及买方设备的效率问题。本案的问题是，卖方提供的设备是否违反了合同规格，以及是否违反了担保。我们认定，特聘审判员基于专家证词和同时期的其他证据而对此问题作出的结论，不存在明显错误。

ARB experts was based on the design of the equipment and of the components used therein, not on the results of the testing; second, the results of the tests carried out independently by two of the experts resembled each other so closely, and fell so far short of the contract specifications, as to reduce the weight of the limited criticisms of the tests made by E-Systems.

E-Systems's second contention, that the master erroneously ignored pertinent contemporary evidence-consisting mainly of filed reports on the equipment's performance-is also unpersuasive. Much of the evidence that E-Systems would like the master to have relied upon relates to the problems that ARB suffered in connection with the non-E-Systems part of the monitoring system, for example, with the telecommunications and computer equipment. The efficiency of ARB's equipment is not at issue, however; the question is whether the equipment supplied by E-Systems was in breach of contract specifications and warranties. We find that the master's decision on this point, based upon expert testimony and contemporary evidence, was not clearly in error.

买方有权暂停付款 卖方与买方之间的合同附有付款日程表，其中规定了买方的付款日期，并大体上对应卖方“交付内容”的日期。1974年夏，买方停止了该日程表项下的付款。卖方声称，其获得付款的权利不取决于买方是否接受相关设备；由于买方未能按日程表的时间付款，因此买方违反了合同。

The contract between E-Systems and ARB included a schedule for payments by ARB, integrated, for the most part, with the schedule of “Deliverables” due from E-Systems. In the summer of 1974, ARB ceased payments under this schedule. E-Systems contends that its right to payment existed independently of acceptance by ARB of the equipment in question, and thus that ARB breached the contract by failing to maintain the payments according to schedule.

特聘审判员认定，合同未要求买方在收到不符合合同规格的设备后仍必须支付货款。卖方引用了明确将付款与“设备交付”挂钩的合同条款。但该条款的假定是，所交付的“设备”符合合同。也许通常可以假定所交付的货物符合合同，但在本案中，基于设备交付之前所发生的一切，包括试验型号所出现的问题，此种假定已不复存在。

The master found that the contract did not require ARB to pay upon delivery for equipment which failed to conform to contract specifications. E-Systems cites a contract provision expressly tying payment to “delivery of units”. This assumes, however, that the “units” conform to the contract. Here, the events leading up to delivery, including the problems experienced with the pre-production models, dispelled any presumption of conformance that might otherwise have existed.

合同第6.8条规定，“买方订购的所有‘交付内容’，交付后均须经买方检验和批准，无论之前是否已经作出付款。双方明

Paragraph 6.8, which provides that “(a)ll Deliverables ordered will be subject to final inspection and approval by Buyer after delivery, notwithstanding prior payment, it

确同意，付款不代表对设备的最终接受”。合同的这项条款，只适用于货物交付后已经实际作出的付款。如果货物在交付时就存在本案的情况，该条款未规定买方仍有义务先付款。

合同第 6.11 条为上述结论提供了另一个依据。该款在引用了有关质量和性能的明示担保后规定，“所有的担保均被视为前提条件，并同时被视为担保”。根据这项规定，买方的履约(付款)系以卖方交付符合该担保之设备为前提条件。由于卖方未交付此种设备，买方的付款义务尚未到期。

买方有权要求卖方提供履约保证 还有另外一个独立理由，即法典第 2.609 条，也可以用于驳回卖方的主张。法典该条相关部分规定：“一方如果有合理理由担心另一方不能正常履约，可书面要求另一方提供正常履约的充分保证。不安全的一方在收到此种保证之前，只要商业上合理，即可针对另一方尚未履约的

being expressly agreed that payment shall not constitute final acceptance”, applies only where the goods are, in fact, paid for upon delivery. It imposes no obligation of prior payment under the circumstances that existed at the time of delivery in this case.

An alternative ground for this conclusion is found in contract paragraph 6.11, which, after reciting certain express warranties of quality and performance, states “(a)ll warranties shall be construed as conditions as well as warranties ...” This paragraph makes ARB’s performance, i. e., payment, conditional upon delivery by E-Systems of equipment that conforms to these warranties. Since such equipment was not delivered, ARB’s obligation to pay did not mature.

A second, independent ground for the rejection of this contention is provided by Md.Com.Law § 2-609. This section provides in relevant part that: “When reasonable grounds for insecurity arise with respect to the performance of either party the other may in writing demand adequate assurance of due performance and until he receives such assurance may if commercially reasonable suspend any performance for which he has not

部分，暂停履行自己相应部分的义务。”

already received the agreed return.”

卖方辩称，初审法院和买方都处于自相矛盾的状态，因为在涉及某些问题时，他们称买方从卖方收到的保证是充分的；但在涉及另外一些问题时，他们又说不充分。事实上，这仅是初审法院的立场，且并不存在矛盾。在设备的试生产样机被证实达不到合同要求后，买方没有取消合同，而是决定继续进入正式生产，因为卖方保证问题可以解决。但是，买方虽然允许卖方正式生产，但并未因此放弃收到合格货物的权利。

E-Systems argues that the district court and ARB are each caught in a web of inconsistencies, arguing for some purposes that the assurances ARB received from E-Systems were adequate, and for other purposes that they were inadequate. In fact, this is the position of the district court, but it is not inconsistent. ARB, rather than cancel the contract when the pre-production models proved inadequate, decided to go ahead with production on the basis of assurances that the problems could be remedied. In giving E-Systems the go-ahead, however, ARB was not waiving its right to conforming goods.

买方的行为是合理的　这些事实与法典第 2.609 条所规定的原则完全吻合。在 1974 年整个夏季，买方的行为在商业上都是合理的。当情况显示卖方很可能无法按合同规定履约时，没有任何合同条款要求买方仍然必须完全履行自己的义务。为了证明法典第 2.609 条不适用于本案事实，卖方引用了 S 诉 V 案作为依据。但是，该判例不能帮助卖方。在

These facts fit comfortably within the framework of section 2-609. ARB acted in a commercially reasonable manner throughout the summer of 1974. Nothing in the contract required ARB to perform fully once it became apparent that E-Systems's conforming performance was unlikely. E-Systems relies upon Stewart-Decatur Security Systems, Inc. v. Von Weise Gear Co., as authority for the proposition that section 2-609 does not apply to these facts. This reliance is misplaced. In

S诉V案中，买方“对样品的性能表示满意”。在本案中，大量证据表明，对于试生产的样机，买方向卖方表示了担忧。在卖方保证问题将得到纠正后，买方才允许卖方继续生产。

Stewart-Decatur, buyer "was satisfied with the performance of the prototype". Here the weight of the evidence establishes that ARB had communicated its reservations about the pre-production model to E-Systems, and had authorized continuing production only on the basis of E-Systems's assurances that the problems would be corrected.

如特聘审判员所认定的，A诉M案是更合适的判例。该案涉及计算机化的收银机。买方对样机的性能表示不满，因此要求合同项下的生产暂停，直至找到双方可以接受的性能标准。双方随后一直未能就该标准达成协议，买方因此取消了合同，而卖方提起诉讼。法院判定，由于卖方未能提供充分保证，因此，根据法典第2.609条的规定，买方有权取消合同。A诉M案与本案的唯一区别是，在本案中，卖方的保证一度更令人可信。但是，当卖方交付的产品不符合合同时，此种可信度本身不能给卖方提供依合同条款取得付款的权利。

As the master found, AMF, Inc. v. McDonald's Corp., is more helpful. There McDonald's, dissatisfied with the performance of a prototype unit of a computerized cash register, asked that production under the contract be held up until mutually acceptable standards of performance could be found. The standards were never agreed upon, McDonald's cancelled the contract, and AMF sued. The court held that AMF's failure to provide adequate assurances justified McDonald's action under section 2-609. The only difference between AMF and this case is that E-Systems's assurances were, for a while, more persuasive. This persuasiveness did not entitle E-Systems to payment, on contract terms, for delivery of a non-conforming product.

买方有权起诉　卖方声称，

E-Systems claims that ARB breached

买方提起诉讼的行为违反了合同规定，因为合同规定，对于“无效家庭”，卖方有权更换或调整设备。无效家庭是指所安装的设备不能进行正常记录的那些家庭。但是，我们在审阅了合同相关条款后认为，只有当合同在其他方面都正常履行时，这项规定才能作为合同的补救措施而适用于无效家庭。如果争议中的违约具有整体性。也就是说，如果设备的基本设计和组件都被认为不符合合同，该条款即不适用。因此，该条款不限制买方的违约救济。

卖方还辩称，即使设备不符合合同，买方也无权就违约起诉，因为买方既没有拒收货物，也没有撤销接受。但特聘审判员的认定是，买方拒收了货物，或者即使接受了，也撤销了接受。

买方已拒收设备　法典第 2.602 条涉及对货物的拒收。该条相关部分规定：“拒收货物必须在交付或提示交付后的合理时

the contract by instituting this suit in contravention of a contract provision giving E-Systems the right to replace or modify equipment in “failed homes”; that is, homes in which an installation of equipment had not resulted in a functioning metering system. Review of the relevant contract provision reveals, however, that it applies only to the contractual treatment of “failed” homes under an otherwise unimpaired contract. The provision has no application where the breach alleged is a generic one; i. e., where the basic design and components of the equipment are claimed to be non-conforming. It did not limit ARB's remedies for breach of contract.

E-Systems also argues that, even if the equipment was non-conforming, ARB has no action for breach of contract because it neither rejected nor revoked an acceptance of the goods. The master found that ARB rejected the goods or, alternatively, revoked its acceptance of them.

The relevant statutory provision on the rejection question is Md.Com.Law § 2-602, which reads in part: “Rejection of goods must be within a reasonable time after their

间内作出。如果买方未能及时通知卖方，则拒收无效。”

delivery or tender. It is ineffective unless the buyer seasonably notifies the seller.”

卖方对此辩称，买方反复告知卖方可以开始后续生产，并以其他方式对设备表示满意。之前，当卖方声称，买方未能付款属于违约行为时，也是这样辩称的。但是，此处辩称与之前辩称一样，都不具有说服力。特聘审判员认定，“买方及时地，实际上是反复地告知卖方，所交付的设备不可接受”。这种认定达到了法典第 2.602 条的要求。

E-Systems argues here, as it did in connection with its argument that ARB breached the contract by withholding payment, that ARB consistently gave the go-ahead for further production and otherwise demonstrated its satisfaction with the equipment. This argument is no more convincing in this context than it was in the former. As the master found, “ARB seasonably, and indeed repeatedly, notified E-Systems that the equipment as delivered was unacceptable”. This finding meets the requirements of section 2-602.

买方已将拒收通知卖方 虽然买方允许卖方开始生产，并在有限范围内安装记录仪，但这种允许的基础是，卖方曾作出保证说，设备将会符合合同且能够符合合同。买方从未接受过所交付的设备，并且，基于本案情况，在合理时间内拒收了设备。买方与卖方始于 1974 年 1 月的沟通，足以构成法典第 1.201 条（26）款所定义的“通知”（“采取正常情况下为告知另一方所合理需要

ARB’s authorizations of the production run and limited installation of the meters were made on the basis of assurances by E-Systems that the equipment would and could be made conforming. ARB never accepted the equipment as delivered, and rejected it within a reasonable time under the circumstances. The communications from ARB to E-Systems beginning in January 1974 constituted sufficient “notification” within the meaning of Md.Com.Law § 1-201（26）（“taking such steps as may be reasonably required to

的步骤”）。

无论如何买方也已撤销接受　特聘审判员认定，作为替代理由，即使买方已接受了设备，买方随后也根据法典第 2.608 条的规定，撤销了该接受。法典该条相关部分规定：“（1）如果已被接受的一批或一个商业单位的货物不符合合同，致使其对买方的价值严重降低，买方可以撤销接受，只要原来作出的接受系因：（a）有合理理由假定不符合合同之处将得到补救，但未得到及时补救……（2）撤销接受必须在买方发现或应该发现撤销理由后的合理时间内作出，并在货物状况发生重大改变前作出，除非该改变系因货物自身瑕疵造成。在买方通知卖方之前，买方的撤销不发生效力。”

卖方的理由　卖方基于两点理由对上述认定提出异议。首先，不存在通知；其次，即使有通知，也不可能存在撤销接受，因为“货物状况已发生重大改变，且该改变非因货物本身瑕疵导致”。由于上文所述原因，即特聘审判员

inform the other in ordinary course”).

The master found alternatively that, even if ARB accepted the equipment, it later revoked this acceptance under Md.Com.Law § 2-608. This section provides in relevant part:（1） The buyer may revoke his acceptance of a lot or commercial unit whose nonconformity substantially impairs its value to him if he has accepted it （a） On the reasonable assumption that its nonconformity would be cured and it has not been seasonably cured ... （2） Revocation of acceptance must occur within a reasonable time after the buyer discovers or should have discovered the ground for it and before any substantial change in condition of the goods which is not caused by their own defects. It is not effective until the buyer notifies the seller of it.

E-Systems challenges this finding on two grounds: first, there was no notification, and second, revocation would have been impossible even had notification been given because of “substantial change in condition of the goods which （was） not caused by their own defects”. The first contention fails for

认定，买方已向卖方作出了满足法典第2.608条和第1.201条(26)款之要求的通知，因此，卖方的第一项理由不能成立。

the reasons set out immediately above: the master's finding that ARB notified E-Systems within the meaning of sections 2-608 and 1-201 (26) was not clearly erroneous.

不构成对卖方所有权的侵犯

第二项理由涉及卖方另外提出的一项独立理由，即根据法典第2.606条（1）（c）款，买方应被视为已接受了货物，因为买方损坏了设备，构成了"与卖方所有权不符"的行为。所以，需要将卖方的这两个说法一起讨论。假如卖方所声称的"损坏"，是指在尝试让设备正常工作的过程中自然形成的损坏，那么该情况既不与卖方所有权相冲突，也不属于法典第2.608条所说的重大改变。

The second contention is related to and should be discussed together with E-Systems's independent argument that ARB accepted the goods under section 2-606 (1) (c) by damaging the equipment, in that such damage was "inconsistent with the seller's ownership". To the extent that the "damage" E-Systems is alleging here is damage naturally flowing from the attempts to make the equipment work, it was neither inconsistent with the seller's ownership nor a substantial change within the meaning of section 2-608.

善意努力不属于侵犯所有权

怀特教授和萨莫斯教授对法典上述条款在类似情况下的适用进行了讨论，"最难处理的情况是，买方在对货物作出拒收前知道货物存在瑕疵，但仍在业务中使用了货物。涉及复杂的机器设备时，这种情况经常发生，因为买方和卖方可能会试图一边使用机器，另一边解决机器中的问题。在这

White and Summers discuss the application of these provisions in a similar situation: "The most difficult case is that in which the buyer uses the goods in his business with the knowledge that they are defective but before he has attempted to reject. Such circumstances will often arise as the buyer and seller are attempting to work the bug out of a complex piece of machinery. In such circumstances courts should be hesitant to find

种情况下，法院不应急于作出结论，认为买方的行为与卖方的所有权不符。应该鼓励当事方作出此类妥协、迁就和调整，而买方不应为曾作出此种努力而受到惩罚”。（引用著作）

货物状况未发生重大改变

上述理由同样适用于“状况发生重大改变”的辩称。在本案情况下，为使设备能够正常工作而进行的善意尝试，虽然引起了“改变”，但不属于第 2.608 条（2）款所说的“状况发生重大改变”。假设卖方所声称的损伤，系来自买方对设备的其他不当处置，那么，卖方提供的证据也过于零碎和稀少，不足为证。

买方对放弃补进救济的异议

对于初审法院的结论，即买方在“谈判时已放弃”法典第 2.712 条提供的“补进”权利，买方提出异议。买方的主要理由是，特聘审判员作出该结论所依赖的证据，本应被法典有关口头证据的第 2.202 条所排除。如下所述，

that the acts are inconsistent with the seller's ownership. The parties should be encouraged to engage in this kind of bargaining and adjustment, and the buyer should not be made to engage in it at his peril." J. White & R. Summers, Handbook of the Law of the Uniform Commercial Code.

The same reasoning applies to the "substantial change in condition" argument: under the circumstances of this contract, "changes" occurring in the process of a good faith attempt to make the equipment work are not "substantial changes in condition" within the meaning of section 2-608（2）. To the extent that the damage E-Systems claims is damage caused by ARB's mistreatment of the equipment stemming from other causes, E-Systems's evidence is spotty and inadequate.

ARB challenges the district court's conclusion that it "bargained away" its right to cover under section 2-712. It contends primarily that the evidence relied upon by the master in reaching this conclusion should have been excluded under Md.Com. Law § 2-202, the statutory parol evidence rule. As discussed below, ARB's contention on this point is well-

买方的此项异议存在合理理由。因此,本案将被发回,以便就“补进”赔偿进行重新审理。

口头证据和外部证据规则

法典第2.202条全文如下:“当事方在确认性备忘录中同意的条款,或当事方以其他方式记录在书面文件中作为当事方协议之最终表示的条款,不得以任何之前达成的协议或同时达成的口头协议作为证据加以否认,但可以用下列内容加以解释或补充:(a)交易过程或行业惯例(第1.205条),或履约过程(第2.208条);以及(b)与上述条款相和谐的补充条款证据,除非法院认定,当事方的意图是将上述书面文件作为协议条款之完整和排他的表述。”

书面合同是否为最终表述

将上述规定适用于本案事实时,存在两个问题。首先,当事方是否意图将书面合同“作为协议条款之完整和排他的表述”,因此不允许引入任何证据对其进行解释或补充?其次,如果没有此种意图,且合同条款系属“当事方

founded, and this case will be remanded to the district court for the calculation of “cover” damages.

Section 2-202 provides in its entirety: “Terms with respect to which the confirmatory memoranda of the parties agree or which are otherwise set forth in a writing intended by the parties as a final expression of their agreement with respect to such terms as are included therein may not be contradicted by evidence of any prior agreement or of a contemporaneous oral agreement but may be explained or supplemented (a) By course of dealing or usage of trade (§ 1-205) or by course of performance (§ 2-208); and (b) By evidence of consistent additional terms unless the court finds the writing to have been intended also as a complete and exclusive statement of the terms of the agreement.”

Two issues are raised by the application of this provision to the present facts: first, was the written contract “intended ... as a complete and exclusive statement of the terms of the agreement”, such that no evidence is admissible to explain or supplement it? Second, if not, and the contract was the “final expression of their agreement with respect to

协议之最终表示的条款”。那么，特聘审判员所考虑过的那些具体证据，是否应被视为“否认”合同，或不属于“相和谐的补充条款”，因而不应被采纳?

一体化条款　我们认为，本案的书面合同，确实被当事方作为“协议条款之完整和排他的表述”。两个因素可以支持该结论。首先且最重要的是，书面合同包含了一体化条款。通常，在适用第 2.202 条时，应承认一体化条款的效力（参见 F 诉 P 案；U 诉 H 案）。本案的一体化条款不存在其他合理解释。该条款规定：“本合同构成买方和卖方之间的全部协议。”合同的另一项条款则明确保留了“法律或衡平原则所提供的其他救济或进一步救济”。还有一项条款规定，对于“法律或衡平原则所提供的全部救济”，买方保留“叠加”寻求这些救济的权利。将合同一体化条款与上述两项条款结合后可以看到，如果以一项补充性的非书面条款来排除“法律提供的其他救济”，将属于错误做法。

such terms as are included therein”, should the specific evidence considered by the master have been barred as “contradict (ory)” or as not constituting a “consistent additional term”?

We believe that the written contract was “intended ... as a complete and exclusive statement of the terms of the agreement”. Two factors support this conclusion: first and most important is that the written contract contains an integration clause, and integration clauses are generally to be given effect under section 2-202. See Franz Chemical Corp. v. Philadelphia Quartz Co.; United States v. Haas & Haynie Corp. The integration clause in question here is not susceptible of any other reasonable interpretation; it states: “This Contract ... constitutes the entire agreement between Buyer and Seller.” When combined with two other clauses in the contract, explicitly preserving “other or further remedies provided in law or in equity”, and a clause reserving to ARB the power “to avail itself cumulatively of all remedies provided in law or in equity”, it makes the addition of a non-written term eliminating an “other ... remedy provided in law” an error.

当事方的意图 本判决对一体化条款效力的承认，也符合法典以外的马里兰州法律。根据该州法律，一体化条款虽然不具有“绝对的决定意义”，但“体现了当事方的意图，即以书面合同最终记录他们之间的全部谅解，或者说，在书面合同之外，不存在之前作出的或同时作出的其他协议”(P诉K案)。但是，马里兰州法律也进一步要求，为了确定相关的一体化条款是否事实上构成了当事方将书面合同作为他们之间协议的完整和最终表达的真实意图，法院必须同时考虑合同订立时的其他相关情况(S诉R案；R诉B案)。因此，如果当事方在订立书面合同之前删除了草稿中的某项条款，那么，关键问题不在于当事方是否对被删除的事项达成了某种约定，而在于当事方在采纳一体化条款时，是否真的具有一体化意图。

This decision to give effect to the integration clause is consistent with non-U.C.C. Maryland law, which holds that integration clauses, although not “absolutely conclusive”, are “indicative of the intention of the parties to finalize their complete understanding in the written contract... that there was no other prior or contemporaneous agreement not included in the written contract”. Pumphrey v. Kehoe. Maryland law further requires, however, that the circumstances surrounding the making of the contract be considered to discover whether the integration clause in question does, in fact, express the genuine intention of the parties to make the written contract the complete and exclusive statement of their agreement. Shoreham Developers, Inc. v. Randolph Hills, Inc.; Rinaudo v. Bloom. Thus, the issue is not whether the deletion of a given sentence antecedent to the making of the written contract was an agreement as to the matter deleted, but whether the integration clause, at the time it was agreed upon, represented the intentions of the parties.

本案大量证据表明，当事方意图将书面合同作为他们之间协

Here, the bulk of the evidence suggests that the parties intended the written contract

议条款的完整和排他的表述。将合同的长篇大论、条款的细致入微以及签字之前的漫长谈判结合起来后，可以得出上述结论。与此同时，卖方并未提出有说服力的证据来支持其主张，即在订立合同时，当事方的意图是，未进入书面合同的其他内容，也构成了整体协议的一部分。

不和谐的检验标准　即使当事方并未意图将书面合同“作为协议条款的完整和排他的表述”，我们仍然相信，法典第 2.202 条也不会允许将被删除的转购条款作为证据，因为该转购条款不属于第 2.202 条（b）款所述的“相和谐的补充条款”。马里兰州法律采用的是“一致性”检验标准，而我们的上述结论，是在适用该标准后得出的。该标准的基础，并不是特聘审判员所使用的外部证据不能与合同明示条款相冲突的简单方法，而是有更严格的要求，即书面合同与外部补充条款必须具备更高程度的一致性。

并非只有否定或冲突才属于

to be the complete and exclusive statement of the terms of their agreement. The length of the contract, its exhaustive detail, and the prolonged period of negotiation preceding its signing, collectively considered, support this conclusion. At the same time, E-Systems has offered no persuasive evidence supporting a determination that the parties intended, at the time of contracting, that non-written terms be part of the overall agreement.

Even if the written contract had not been “intended ... as a complete and exclusive statement of the terms of the agreement”, however, we believe that section 2-202 would bar evidence of the deletion of the reprocurement provision on the grounds that this evidence is not a “consistent additional term” within the meaning of section 2-202（b）. We reach this conclusion by applying the appropriate test of consistency under Maryland law. This test is based not on the standard of simple non-contradiction of an express term of the contract applied by the master, but on a stricter standard requiring a substantially greater agreement between the contract and the proffered additional terms.

The Court of Special Appeals explained

不和谐 马里兰州特别上诉法院在S诉H案中对此解释说：我们判定，上诉方所提供的补充条款与合同本身并不和谐。我们在作出这个结论时，拒绝有关和谐性的狭隘观点。该观点认为，只有当“补充条款”排除或否定协议的明示条款时，补充条款才属于不和谐。

对法典第2.202条整体解读后可以看到，对不和谐的含义作出狭隘解释，本身就与法典不和谐。直接与合同明示条款冲突的补充条款，已被法典第2.202条的开始一段所禁止。因此，必须避免狭隘解释，否则将会使法典该条的整段内容失去意义。因此我们认为，第2.202条（b）款所说的不和谐，是指相关文字与当事方各自义务之间缺乏合理的协调性。

本案的补充证据属于不和谐

将上述和谐标准适用于本案合同争议条款后，我们认为，很明显，争议中的“补充条款”，也就是排除补进的条款，将会打破书面合同为当事方“各自的义务”建立起来的平衡与协调。

it this way in Snyder v. Herbert Greenbaum & Assoc., Inc.: we hold that the additional terms offered by appellants are inconsistent with the contract itself. In doing so we reject the narrow view of inconsistency ... that to be inconsistent the “additional terms” must negate or contradict express terms of the agreement.

This interpretation of “inconsistent” is itself inconsistent with a reading of the whole of § 2-202. Direct contradiction of express terms is forbidden in the initial paragraph of § 2-202. The (narrow) interpretation renders that passage a nullity, a result which is to be avoided...Rather we believe “inconsistency” as used in § 2-202 (b) means the absence of reasonable harmony in terms of the language and respective obligations of the parties...

We think that application of this test to the term here disputed indicates clearly that consideration of this “additional term” - the no-cover provision-would disrupt the delicate balance, the harmony, that the written contract establishes among the “respective obligations” of the parties.

此外，法典第 2.202 条正式评论 3 所述的标准也可以支持上述结论，且该标准得到了马里兰州法院的明确认可（参见 S 诉 H 案）。该评论的相关部分说：“涉及补充条款时，如果法院认为，假设当事方实际上同意该条款，其本来无疑会被纳入书面合同，此时，即使任何当事方声称存在该条款，也不应将其作为证据提交给事实审的审理人。”

Moreover, this conclusion is reinforced by application of the standard set out in Official Comment 3 to section 2-202 and expressly endorsed by the Maryland courts. See, e. g., Snyder v. Herbert Greenbaum & Assoc., Inc. It states in relevant part: “If the additional terms are such that, if agreed upon, they would certainly have been included in the document in the view of the court, then evidence of their alleged making must be kept from the trier of fact.”

结论　关于书面合同是否构成了当事方协议的完整和排他的表述，基于以上理由，并考虑到本案的全部情况，我们相信，假设当事方曾同意对补进救济作出限制，该条款无疑会被纳入书面合同。作为该结论的支持，我们还注意到，补进救济在法典的救济体系中占据中心位置。如同怀特教授和萨莫斯教授所说，在法典第 2.711 条向买方提供的各种救济中，补进属于“主要”救济。

We believe, for the reasons set out above in our discussion of the contract as a complete and exclusive statement of the agreement, that under all the circumstances of this case a term limiting the cover remedy, if agreed upon, would certainly have been included in the contract. In support, we note further that cover-referred to by White and Summers as “chief” among the general remedies of the buyer set out in section 2-711-occupies the central place in the U.C.C. remedy scheme.

本案将被发回初审法院重审，以便确定损害赔偿数额问题，包括根据法典第 2.712 条计算的“补进”赔偿。初审法院必须确认，

This case will now return to the district court for a redetermination of damages, including “cover” damages under Md.Com. Law section 2-712. The district court will

在买方为建立新的记录仪系统所实际花费的费用中，有多少费用属于第2.712条（1）款所说的“合理购买替代货物”的费用。

我们今天的判决，不对上述需要重审的问题本身发表任何意见。但是，我们的判决确立了两项主要原则。首先，法典第2.202条以及马里兰州其他法律所确立的原则是，对于经过深入谈判的商业合同，不应轻易排除其中的一体化条款。其次，在任何州（如马里兰州），如果第2.202条中的“相和谐的条款”被解释为，书面合同与外部补充条款之间必须存在“合理的协调”，那么，当补充条款严重限制了当事方本可享有的合同权利时，则只有整体合同明确打算限制该通常本可享有的权利，才可添加该补充条款。据此，部分地推翻本案的原判，并发回初审法院根据本判决意见重新审理。

have to decide how much of the costs actually incurred by ARB in setting up its new metering system fall within the “reasonable purchase of ... goods in substitution” provision of section 2-712（1）.

Our decision today expresses no opinion on this question. It does, however, stand for two main propositions: first, that section 2-202 and other relevant Maryland law establish that integration clauses in extensively negotiated commercial contracts should not be lightly disregarded; second, that where, as in Maryland, the “consistent term” provision of section 2-202 is interpreted to require a “reasonable harmony” between the written contract and the terms sought to be added, terms severely limiting otherwise available contract rights should be added only where the clear import of the contract, taken as a whole, is to limit usually available remedies. This case is hereby reversed in part and remanded to the district court for proceedings consistent with this opinion.

案例5　多年前的陈述可否构成目前合同的明示担保?

Belden, Inc. v. American Electr. Components
拜尔登公司诉美国电子器件公司案

印第安纳州上诉法院 2008 年；885 N.E.2d 751

简　介

本案买方（AEC）和卖方（Belden）从 1996 年到 2004 年保持了多年的合作关系，由卖方供应电子产品的某种电线。双方的交易形式是，对于每一批电线，都是由买方发出采购订单，然后由卖方发出订单确认书。每个订单构成单独一项合同。双方合作期间内的交易总数超过 100 次。

本案的起因是，从 2003 年 10 月起，即诉讼发生前的一段时间，卖方更换了电线绝缘材料的供应商，由原来的 QU（Quantum）公司改为 DO（Dow）公司。随后，由于 DO 公司绝缘材料的物理性能不同，致使买方向自己的汽车制造商客户提供的电子产品出现问题。汽车制造商不得不召回大约 14,000 辆已经售出的装有该电子产品的汽车，并对另外 4000 辆尚未出厂的汽车更换相关部件。为此，买方赔偿了汽车制造商的损失。之后，买方转而就此种赔偿向卖方提出索赔。

卖方拒绝赔偿，理由是其订单确认书中包含了赔偿限制条款。根据该条款，买方无权就此种损失索赔。卖方同时认为，自己未就电线的绝缘材料提供担保，且双方的订单和确认书中也不包含绝缘材料的规定，因此，不存在卖方违反担保的问题。最终，双方的争议集中于两个问题。第一，合同是否包含了赔偿限制条款？第二，合同是否包含了有关电线绝缘材料的明示担保？

第一个问题涉及法典第 2.207 条中的“文本冲突”（battle of forms）问题。本案的实际情况是，在双方交往的初期，对于每一笔订单，买方都会寄出自己的订单。订单背面包含了采购条件，且未免除卖方的责任。随后，卖方会寄回订单确认书。确认书背面包含了固定格式条款，包括赔偿限制条款。到后期，买方的订单只用传真发送正面，其中包括电线的规格和数量等，但不再传真背面的采购条件。引起本案争议的是买方 2003 年 10 月 17 日的订单。卖方于 10 月 22 日发出确认书，其中包含了背面的赔偿限制条款。确认书还说明，如果确认书被认定构成对买方要约的承诺，则该承诺明确规定，以买方完全同意确认书的条款作为该承诺生效的前提条件。并且，买方对卖方产品的接受，将被视为买方对确认书条款的同意。

关于这个问题，法院认为，卖方的订单确认书虽然包含了赔偿限制条款，但买方未作答复，不能认为买方已同意该条款。卖方认为，买方接收货物的行为构成了对卖方条款的接受，而卖方的确认书也是这样规定的。但法院认为，卖方无权通过此种方式，单方将自己的条款施加于买方。并且，卖方的确认书明确规定，以买方同意其内容为前提条件，而买方并未同意。因此，合同不能成立。法院认为，在这种情况下，本案应根据法典第 2.207 条（3）款的规定处理。根据该款，如果当事方交换的文件不足以导致合同成立，但当事方随后以行为承认合同的存在，则合同可以成立，但合同条款以当事方已明确同意的条款为准，再加上法典所补充的“填补条款”（gap-fillers）。在本案中，双方没有明确同意赔偿限制条款，所交换的文件也不足以使合同成立，但双方已经履行了合同。因此，合同成立，但赔偿限制条款不进入合同。在这种情况下，买方有权按法典的规定取得损害赔偿。

第二个问题的起因是，在买方选定卖方作为电线供应商时，卖方为了满足买方的质量控制规范，曾于 1996 年和 1997 年说明，电线将使用 QU 公司的绝缘材料。之后，双方没有再讨论过绝缘材料的问题，但卖方一直在使用 QU 公司的绝缘材料。从 2003 年 6 月起，卖方更换了供应商，开始使用 DO 公司的绝缘材料，但未将该情况告诉买方。卖方认为，有关绝缘材料的说明是多年以前作出的，不能成为 2003 年订立的合同中的担保，并且，所有合同均没有包含对绝缘材料的说明或保证。

关于这个问题，法院认为，卖方早期有关绝缘材料的陈述并没有时间限制，因此原来的明示担保没有失效期，可以被视为存在于后续的合同中。另外，从双方的交易情况看，买方一直订购同一型号的电线，而卖方多年也一直使用 QU 公司的绝缘材料，因此可以认为双方已存在“交易过程”（course of dealing）。在这种情况下，买方有合理理由期待并要求卖方继续使用该绝缘材料。因此，卖方违反了合同中的明示担保。

判　决

卖方上诉的两个问题　我们将卖方提出的 4 个问题归纳和重述为两个问题：第一，卖方订单确认书背面所包含的赔偿限制条款是否适用于当事方的合同？第二，卖方之前向买方作出的某些陈述是否构成卖方的明示担保？

Belden raises four issues, which we consolidate and restate as：Ⅰ. whether the limitation on damages on the back of Belden's order acknowledgment applies to the parties' contract； and Ⅱ. whether Belden created an express warranty based on its prior assertions to AEC.

法典有关文本冲突的规定　基于当事方之间的文件交换，他们争议的问题是，他们之间的协议是否包含赔偿限制条款。我们的分析从法典第 2.207 条开始。

Based on these exchanges, the parties dispute whether the limitation on damages is a term of their agreement. We start our analysis with Section 2-207 of the Uniform Commercial Code （“UCC”），which

该条规定:“(1)确定且及时的承诺表示,或合理时间内发送的书面确认,即使与要约条款或与已同意的条款相比,包含不同条款或补充条款,亦构成承诺,除非其明确规定,以要约人同意这些不同条款或补充条款作为承诺生效的条件。(2)补充条款应被解释为对合同进行补充的建议。在商人之间,这些条款构成合同的组成部分,除非:(a)要约明确规定,承诺限于要约条款;(b)补充条款严重改变了要约;或(c)已对补充条款作出拒绝通知,或在收到补充条款通知后的合理时间内作出了拒绝通知。(3)双方承认合同存在的行为,足以使买卖合同成立,即使双方的书面文件原本不足以证明合同的成立。此时,该特定合同的条款,系当事方在书面文件中同意的条款,再加上根据本法任何其他规定而进入合同的填补条款。”

provides: “(1) A definite and seasonable expression of acceptance or a written confirmation which is sent within a reasonable time operates as an acceptance even though it states terms additional to or different from those offered or agreed upon, unless acceptance is expressly made conditional on assent to the additional or different terms. (2) The additional terms are to be construed as proposals for addition to the contract. Between merchants such terms become part of the contract unless: (a) the offer expressly limits acceptance to the terms of the offer; (b) they materially alter it; or (c) notification of objection to them has already been given or is given within a reasonable time after notice of them is received. (3) Conduct by both parties which recognizes the existence of a contract is sufficient to establish a contract for sale although the writings of the parties do not otherwise establish a contract. In such case the terms of the particular contract consist of those terms on which the writings of the parties agree, together with any supplementary terms incorporated under any other provisions of this Act.”

相关判例　对于本案到底应适用第2.207条(2)款还是(3)款,当事方存在分歧。在U诉C案中,我们处理过惊人相似的问题。在该案中,买方向卖方邮寄出一份垫圈采购订单,其中规定了数量、价格和发运日期。卖方回复了一份“订单确认书”,其中的相关部分说明:“我们对订单要约的承诺,以买方接受本确认书背面的销售条件为前提条件。如果买方不接受此种销售条件,买方应在收到本确认书7日内以书面形式通知本卖方。”在卖方确认书的销售条件中,包含了赔偿限制条款。事后确认,垫圈存在瑕疵。买方寻求从卖方取得赔偿,而初审法院以无审判决形式,判决买方胜诉。

The parties disagree as to whether Section 2-207(2) or Section 2-207(3) applies. In Uniroyal, Inc., v. Chambers Gasket and Manufacturing Co., we addressed a strikingly similar issue. In that case, Chambers mailed a purchase order for gaskets to Uniroyal, specifying the quantity, price, and date for shipment. Uniroyal responded with and "Order Acknowledgment" stating in part, "Our Acceptance of the order is conditional on the Buyer's acceptance of the conditions of sale printed on the reverse side hereof. If buyer does not accept these conditions of sale, he shall notify seller in writing within seven days after receipt of this acknowledgment". Included in the conditions of sale was a limitation on damages. The gaskets were later determined to be defective. Chambers sought indemnification from Uniroyal, and the trial court entered summary judgment in favor of Chambers.

普通法与法典的区别　在该案的上诉中,本院讨论了普通法有关合同成立的规则,以及法典对这些规则的修改。在普通法中,如果通过要约与承诺订立合同,承诺必须在所有方面均与要

On appeal, we discussed the common law rules of contract formation and the UCC's modification of those rules: At common-law, for an offer and an acceptance to constitute a contract, the acceptance must meet and correspond with the offer in every respect,

约相符与对应。与要约条款相比，承诺不能少也不能多，而是必须在所有方面均与要约条款完全相等，并完全接受要约条款。改变了要约条款的承诺，被视为对要约的拒绝，并构成反要约。原始要约方可对反要约作出承诺，但同样不能对反要约的条款提出异议。

neither falling within nor going beyond the terms proposed, but exactly meeting （those terms） at all points and closing with them just as they stand. An acceptance which varies the terms of the offer is considered a rejection and operates as a counter-offer, which may be accepted by the original offeror by performing without objection under the terms contained in the counter-offer.

法典的原则和目标 法典第2.207条的设计，就是为了改变普通法的上述“镜像”原则。法典起草者承认，在商业实践中，特别是随着印刷格式文件的使用，“要约”条款与“承诺”条款几乎不会完全相同。法典起草者还承认，商业交易的当事方也很少注意到他们交换的印刷格式文件中的冲突条款和条件。因此，第2.207条的设计目标，就是在要约与承诺存在分歧的情况下，允许对协议强制履行，只要此种强制履行不致使任何一方受到其未曾同意的重要条款的约束（U诉C案）。

§ 2-207 was specifically designed to alter the common-law “mirror-image” rule. The drafters recognized that in commercial practice, especially with the advent of printed forms, the terms of the “offer” and “acceptance” were seldom the same. They further recognized that the parties to a commercial transaction seldom were aware of the conflicting terms and conditions contained in the printed forms they exchanged. § 2-207 was therefore designed to allow enforcement of an agreement despite discrepancies between offer and acceptance, if enforcement could be required without either party being bound to a material term to which he has not agreed. Id.

法典对文本冲突的处理 根据法典第2.207条，如果合同系

Pursuant to Section 2-207, if a contract is formed under Section 2-207（1）, the

根据第 2.207 条（1）款成立，则承诺中的补充条款被视为建议条款，并且，除非其根据第 2.207 条（2）款不发生效力，否则，补充条款将成为合同的组成部分。“但是，如果承诺明确规定以要约人同意新条款为前提条件，而要约人未作出同意，则整个交易都不能成立。”（U 诉 C 案，其中引用 D 诉 C 案）也就是说，如果承诺规定，该承诺以要约人同意承诺中的补充条款或不同条款作为承诺生效的前提条件，则现有书面文件不能构成合同（U 诉 C 案）。“但是，如果当事方通过履约行为承认合同的存在，则买卖合同即可成立。”（U 诉 C 案）。在这种情况下，合同条款是当事方在书面文件中同意的条款，“再加上基于本法任何其他条款而被结合进合同的填补条款”[第 2.207 条（3）款；U 诉 C 案]。

additional terms in the acceptance are considered proposals and become part of the contract unless Section 2-207（2） renders the proposed terms inoperative. “However, if an acceptance is expressly conditioned on the offeror's assent to the new terms, and no assent is forthcoming, the entire transaction aborts.” Id. （quoting Dorton v. Collins & Aikman Corp.）. In other words, if an acceptance contains a clause conditioning the acceptance on assent to the additional or different terms, the writings do not form a contract. Id. “Yet if the parties' conduct recognizes the existence of a contract by performance it is sufficient to establish a contract for sale.” Id. The terms of such a contract are those on which the writings of the parties agree, “together with any supplementary terms incorporated under any other provisions of this act”. § 2-207（3）; see also Uniroyal.

应遵循法典原则而放弃普通法原则　在 U 诉 C 案中，我们采用了法典上述原则框架，而拒绝了某些判例的方法。根据这些

We applied this framework in Uniroyal and rejected a line of cases suggesting Uniroyal's order acknowledgement was a counter-offer that Chambers accepted by

判例，在U诉C案中，卖方确认书本来会被视为反要约，而买方在接受了卖方交付的货物且未对新条款提出异议后，等于接受了卖方的反要约。我们认为，这些判例(要约人仅因接受了货物，就要受补充条款的约束）等于复原了普通法“镜像”原则中的“最后一枪”规则，而法典第2.207条的目的，正是要废除该规则。我们还说明，如果允许受要约人在回复文件中包含补充条款或不同条款，但同时规定，只要要约人未作出反应，就等于接受该条款，那么法典第2.207条的目的就很难实现，因为法典假定商业人士不阅读所交换的印制格式文件，并假定要约人不知道该补充条款。

taking the delivery of the goods and failing to object to the new terms. We reasoned that such an application revives the "last-shot" doctrine under the common law "mirror-image" rule, the very rule that Section 2-207 was intended to avoid, by binding the offeror to additional terms upon the mere acceptance of goods. Further, we observed that the purpose of Section 2-207 would not be well-served by allowing an offeree's responsive document to state additional or different terms, and provide that the terms will be deemed accepted by the offeror's inaction, because Section 2-207 presumes that business people do not read exchanged preprinted forms and assumes that the offeror would not learn of such terms.

在U诉C案中，我们还认为，如果要求原始要约人对另一方的回复主动提出异议，这种要求本身就是对要约的修改，因此要约人首先必须同意该要求；如果要约人未同意，则货物的发运或接受，就应被视为合同已根据第2.207条（3）款而成立。

We also reasoned: the clause placing the burden of affirmative objection on the original offeror is itself a modification of the offer to which the offeror should first have to assent, and absent its assent, any shipping and acceptance of the goods should be deemed to constitute the consummation of the contract under Section 2-207（3）.

书面文件不足的情况　在U诉C案中，我们的结论是，买方和卖方所交换的文件未导致合同成立，但当事方履行了合同义务，因此，合同根据第2.207条(3)款得以成立[另参见C诉F案(根据第2.207条及U诉C案原则，当事方的文件和行为未导致合同成立)]。在上述情况下，合同条款包括当事方书面文件中所同意的条款，再加上法典的填补条款[U诉C案；第2.207条(3)款]。

We concluded that the writings exchanged by Chambers and Uniroyal did not create a contract but that the parties performed their contractual obligations so as to create a contract under Section 2-207 (3). see also Continental Grain Co., v. Followell (applying Section 2-207 and Uniroyal to conclude that no contract was formed by the parties' writings or actions). Therefore, the terms of the contract consisted of the terms upon which the parties' writings agreed and the supplementary terms of the UCC. Uniroyal; see also § 2-207 (3).

本案当事方的行为承认了合同的存在　如同U诉C案一样，我们同意，在本案中，卖方的补充条款明确要求以买方同意为条件，在这种情况下，卖方无权单方添加该条款。因此，当事方的文件没有导致合同的成立。尽管如此，我们的结论是，当事方的行为已构成对合同存在的承认，并足以导致电线买卖合同的成立。此时，合同的条款包括当事方所同意的书面条款，以及“根据法典其他条款而被结合进合同的填补条款”[法典第2.207条(3)款]。

As in Uniroyal, we agree here that Belden could not unilaterally include terms that were expressly conditional on AEC's assent. Thus, the parties' writings did not create a contract. Nevertheless, we conclude that the parties' actions were in recognition of the existence of a contract and were sufficient to establish a contract for the sale of wire. The terms of the contract are the written terms on which the parties agreed and the "supplementary terms incorporated under any other provisions of [the UCC]". § 2-207 (3).

卖方主张适用第2.207条（2）款 但是，对于到底法典的哪项填补条款被结合进入合同，本案当事方存在争议。我们必须讨论的第一个问题是卖方的辩称，即基于法典第2.207条正式评论6，该条（2）款所要求的条款被结合进入合同。该评论写道："提出补充条款的建议后，如果合理时间内未收到答复，则从公平角度，且从商业合理性角度，应假设该建议已被接受。但是，如果当事双方发送的确认文件中存在条款冲突，就应假设每一方都反对另一方确认文件中与自己条款相冲突的条款。其结果是，应认为已发出（2）款所要求的异议通知，因此冲突条款不能成为合同的一部分。"

在上述情况下，合同条款包括：原已明确同意的条款；确认书同意的条款；法典［包括第2.207条（2）款］提供的填补条款。书面确认书还受第2.201条的约束。根据法典该条，如果未答复，即可强制履行之前的口头协议；根据第2.207条，如果未

The parties dispute, however, what supplementary terms are incorporated into their contract. The first question we must address is Belden's argument that the terms called for in Section 2-207（2） are included in the parties contract based on Comment 6, which provides： "If no answer is received within a reasonable time after additional terms are proposed, it is both fair and commercially sound to assume that their inclusion has been assented to. Where clauses on confirming forms sent by both parties conflict each party must be assumed to object to a clause of the other conflicting with one on the confirmation sent by himself. As a result the requirement that there be notice of objection which is found in subsection （2） is satisfied and the conflicting terms do not become a part of the contract."

The contract then consists of the terms originally expressly agreed to, terms on which the confirmations agree, and terms supplied by this Act, including subsection （2）. The written confirmation is also subject to Section 2-201. Under that section a failure to respond permits enforcement of a prior oral agreement； under this section a failure to

答复，补充条款即可成为协议的一部分（第2.207条正式评论6）。

卖方请求本院根据第2.207条（2）款来确定，卖方订单确认书中的条款是否已被结合进入合同。卖方辩称，根据法典第2.207条（2）款，其补充条款应该成为合同的一部分，除非该条款严重改变了合同。在本案事实背景下，严重改变合同是第2.207条（2）款所允许的唯一例外。卖方辩称，对损害赔偿作出限制，并未严重改变合同。

第2.207条（2）款不适用

我们无须认定对损害赔偿的限制是否严重改变了合同，因为我们相信，卖方对法典正式评论6的解读过于宽泛。正如马萨诸塞州最高法院曾说过的，正式评论6仅适用于条款存在冲突的情况（C诉B案）。在本案中，只有卖方自己的确认书包含了对损害赔偿的限制，因此不存在可以适用正式评论6的冲突条款（参见C诉B案）。

应适用第2.207条（3）款

此外，法典第2.207条（2）款

respond permits additional terms to become part of the agreement. § 2-207 cmt. 6.

Belden urges that we look to Section 2-207（2） to determine whether the terms in the order acknowledgement are included in the contract. Pursuant to Section 2-207（2）, Belden contends that its additional terms became part of the contract unless they materially altered the contract — the only exclusionary provision of Section 2-207（2） that is relevant under these facts. Belden claims that the limitation on damages does not materially alter the contract.

We need not determine whether the limitation on damages is a material alteration because we believe that Belden's reading of Comment 6 is overbroad. As the Supreme Judicial Court of Massachusetts has observed, Comment 6 only applies where the terms conflict. Commerce & Industry Ins. Co. v. Bayer Corp. Because only Belden's order acknowledgment contained a limitation on damages, there are no conflicting terms to implicate Comment 6. See id.

Further: the criteria in [§ 2-207（2）] determine what "additional or different

的标准是用于确定，对于已通过交换书面文件而成立的合同，到底哪些“补充条款或不同条款”应成为合同的组成部分。在书面文件不足以导致合同成立时，第2.207条（3）款提供了自己的标准——“书面文件所同意的条款”，再加上法典其他条款提供的填补条款。当（2）款明确规定不适用于一项交易时，不能将（2）款本身用作提供填补条款的法典其他条款{C诉B案；另参见C诉E案［当合同系根据法典第2.207条(3)款而成立时，当事方不能利用第2.207条（2）款来提供填补条款］}。

我们同意上述推理。在当事方书面文件不足以导致合同成立的情况下，假如我们根据第2.207条（2）款来确定合同的条款，那么第2.207条（3）款将变得毫无意义。我们不能这样做［参见C诉S案（“为了实现立法意图，我们要把法律的不同条款结合起来解读。只要法律的某项条款有可能与其他条款和谐相处，我们就不能让前者失去意义”）］。

terms” will or will not be part of a contract that is formed by the exchange of writings. Where the writings do not form a contract, ［§ 2-207（3）］ states its own criteria — “those terms on which the writings agree” plus any terms that would be provided by other Code sections. One cannot turn to subsection （2） as another Code section that would supply a term when, by its express provisions, subsection （2） simply does not apply to the transaction. Id.; see also Coastal & Native Plant Specialties, Inc. v. Engineered Textile Prod., Inc. （“［A］ party cannot utilize section 2-207（2） to provide additional terms once a contract is formed pursuant to section 2-207（3）”）.

We agree with this reasoning. If we turned to Section 2-207（2） to determine the terms where the parties’ writings did not create a contract, then Section 2-207 （3） would be rendered meaningless. We will not do this. See City of Carmel v. Steele （“To effectuate legislative intent, we read the sections of an act together in order that no part is rendered meaningless if it can be harmonized with the remainder of the statute”）. Thus, we rely solely on Section

因此，我们将完全依赖第 2.207 条（3）款来确定，到底哪些条款进入了合同。

不存在赔偿限制条款的交易过程　卖方还辩称，根据第 2.207 条(3)款进入合同的“填补条款”，也包括当事方的交易过程。卖方声称，当事方的交易过程已经承认了损害赔偿限制，因此，该条款已成为合同条款。

填补条款的来源范围存在分歧　法典第 2.207 条（3）款提到的“填补条款”是包括了第 1.205 条所定义的履约过程、交易过程和行业惯例，还是仅包括了法典第 2 篇所列出的标准“填补条款”？对于这个问题，法院判例存在分歧。在 C 诉 H 案中，法院认为，“当合同(如本案合同)系根据第 2.207 条（3）款而成立时，合同条款既包括法典提供的标准‘填补条款’，也包括法典其他条款规定的履约过程、交易过程和行业惯例”。在 D 诉 G 案中，法院判定，根据威斯康星州法典，法院不仅可适用第 2 篇的标准“填补条款”，还可适

2-207（3） to determine what terms are included in the contract.

Belden also argues that the parties’ course of dealing is a “supplementary term” to be included by Section 2-207（3）. Belden contends that the parties’ course of dealing acknowledges the limitation on damages and that it is therefore included as a term of the contract.

There is a split in authorities as to whether Section 2-207（3）’s reference to “supplementary terms” includes course of performance, course of dealing, and usage of trade as defined in Section 1-205 or just the standard “gap fillers” contained in the Article 2 of the UCC. Compare Coastal & Native Plant Specialties（“When a contract is formed pursuant to section 2-207（3）, as here, the contract terms consist of the standard gap-filler provisions of the UCC as well as those sections relating to course of performance and course of dealing and usage of trade”）, and Dresser Industries, Inc., Waukesha Engine Div. v. Gradall Co.（concluding that under the Wisconsin UCC, a court is not limited to the standardized gap-

用根据法典规定而产生的合同条款，包括基于履约过程、交易过程和行业惯例而产生的条款。但在C诉J案中，法院的结论正相反："我们认定，第2.207条（3）款所设想的'填补条款'，仅限于根据第2篇标准'填补条款'而产生的合同条款。"仅仅为本案讨论目的，我们假设（但并不作出此种结论），当事方的交易过程确实属于第2.207条（3）款所提到的填补条款。

fillers of Article 2, but may utilize any terms arising under the entire UCC, including course of performance, course of dealing, and usage of trade), with C. Itoh & Co. (America) Inc. v. Jordan Int'l Co. ("We find that the 'supplementary terms' contemplated by Section 2-207 (3) are limited to those supplied by the standardized 'gap-filler' provisions of Article Two"). For the sake of argument, we assume, without deciding, that the parties' course of dealing is in fact a supplementary term for purposes of Section 2-207 (3).

卖方的主张 卖方声称，1998~2003年当事方之间的交易超过100笔，而在这些交易中，买方从未对赔偿限制条款提出过异议。因此，当事方的该交易过程，使赔偿限制条款进入了合同。买方回复称，"毫无争议的是，在双方15年的关系中，买方从未在任何交易中对卖方该条款给予明确同意，因此，作为法律问题，卖方未能证明存在交易过程"。

Belden asserts that during the more than 100 transactions between the parties from 1998 to 2003, AEC never objected to the limitation on damages and, therefore, the parties' course of dealing incorporates the limitation on damages into the contract. AEC responds, "since it is undisputed that AEC never gave its express assent to Belden's terms in any prior transaction throughout the parties' fifteen-year relationship, Belden has not established a course of dealing between the parties as a matter of law".

交易过程指主动行为 根据法典第1.205条（1）款的规定，

Pursuant to Section 1-205 (1), "A course of dealing is a sequence of previous

"交易过程指特定交易当事方之间在先前交易中的系列行为，且从合理角度，该等行为应被视为已构成共同理解基础，用于解释他们的表达和其他行为"。我们查明的是，涉及反复交换的格式文件时，大多数判例不认为此种交换本身就构成了当事方之间的交易过程，因此，这些格式文件中的条款，并不因此根据第 2.207 条（3）款进入当事方的合同［参见 S 诉 W 案（"虽然有一个法院曾判定，当多份书面确认书反复地重申某些条款时，尽管任何一方均未就该条款中的问题采取过任何行动，该等条款仍最终成为合同的组成部分，但是，大多数法院拒绝了此种推理"）；另参见 P 诉 C 案（"此外，虽然一方将自己的客户确认书反复发送给另一方，但这个事实本身不能构成交易过程；多次发出的格式文件，仅仅表明前者希望让仲裁条款成为合同条款"）］。

conduct between the parties to a particular transaction which is fairly to be regarded as establishing a common basis of understanding for interpreting their expressions and other conduct". Our research shows that most cases involving the repeated exchange of forms does not in and of itself establish a course of dealing between the parties that incorporates the terms of those forms into the parties' contract under Section 2-207 (3). See Step-Saver Data Sys., Inc. v. Wyse Tech. ("While one court has concluded that terms repeated in a number of written confirmations eventually become part of the contract even though neither party ever takes any action with respect to the issue addressed by those terms, most courts have rejected such reasoning"); see also PCS Nitrogen Fertilizer, L.P. v. Christy Refractories, L.L.C. ("Moreover, the fact that Christy repeatedly sent its customer acknowledgment form to PCS does not establish a course of dealing; the multiple forms merely demonstrated Christy's desire to include the arbitration clause as a term of the contract.").

单方反复发送文件不构成交易过程　我们同意 S 诉 W 案中

We agree with the reasoning set forth in Step-Saver: "For two reasons, we hold

的下述分析:“我们基于两个理由判定,虽然反复发出了包含某些标准条款的书面文件,但如果缺乏针对该条款所涉及之问题的任何行动,则该发送不能构成交易过程。因此,如果书面文件中的条款已被第2.207条排除,该条款不能通过文件的此种发送进入合同。”

that the repeated sending of a writing which contains certain standard terms, without any action with respect to the issues addressed by those terms, cannot constitute a course of dealing which would incorporate a term of the writing otherwise excluded under § 2-207."

该院认为:“首先,当事方反复交换的格式文件只是告知买方,卖方希望采纳某些条款。由于卖方在发送软件时并未事先征得买方对该条款的明确同意,因此买方可以合理相信,虽然卖方希望采纳该条款,但买方只同意按另外条款,也就是当事方已明确同意的那些条款,来进行他们的交易。因此,虽然买方对于卖方希望采纳该许可条款的愿望不会感到吃惊,但如果说,该许可条款已进入当事方协议,买方很可能会感到吃惊。”

"First, the repeated exchange of forms by the parties only tells Step-Saver that TSL desires certain terms. Given TSL's failure to obtain Step-Saver's express assent to these terms before it will ship the program, Step-Saver can reasonably believe that, while TSL desires certain terms, it has agreed to do business on other terms-those terms expressly agreed upon by the parties. Thus, even though Step-Saver would not be surprised to learn that TSL desires the terms of the license, Step-Saver might well be surprised to learn that the terms of the license have been incorporated into the parties' agreement."

“其次,在当事方多次交易的情况下,卖方通常有机会就当事方协议的详细条款进行谈判,就如同本案卖方所试图做的。如

"Second, the seller in these multiple transaction cases will typically have the opportunity to negotiate the precise terms of the parties' agreement, as TSL sought

果卖方不愿或无力通过商谈来获得包含其条款的合同，这本身就有力地证明，尽管卖方希望在发生争议时法院能够承认这些条款，但该条款实际上不构成当事方商业交易的组成部分。由于这些原因，我们不认为有充分理由说明，卖方反复发送其产品许可协议的单方行为，在卖方和买方之间构成了交易过程，并导致该许可条款被采纳。”

to do in this case. The seller's unwillingness or inability to obtain a negotiated agreement reflecting its terms strongly suggests that, while the seller would like a court to incorporate its terms if a dispute were to arise, those terms are not a part of the parties' commercial bargain. For these reasons, we are not convinced that TSL's unilateral act of repeatedly sending copies of the license with its product can establish a course of dealing between TSL and Step-Saver that resulted in the adoption of the terms of the license."

本案情况　在本案中，卖方反复发送订单确认书，其中包含了内容相同的条款，即损害赔偿限制，并要求买方作出同意。但此种发送本身不构成当事方之间的交易过程，不代表当事方已经同意了卖方的销售条款和条件。这最多只表明卖方希望买方同意卖方的条款和条件，但实际上买方从未同意过。

Belden's repeated sending of the order acknowledgement containing the same limitation on damages and same requirement of assent by AEC does not in and of itself establish a course of dealing between the parties showing that the parties agreed to the Belden's terms and conditions of sale. At best, it shows that Belden wanted AEC to assent to its terms and conditions, which AEC never did.

有关索赔问题的交易过程　卖方还声称，买方以前认为货物存在瑕疵时，曾接受过卖方的退款，而这构成了当事方之间关于损害赔偿问题的交易过程。也就

Belden also asserts that AEC's acceptance of a credit or refund in other instances of alleged non-conformity establishes the parties' course of dealing regarding damages. In other words, Belden argues that by foregoing

是说，卖方主张，由于买方过去曾放弃了间接损失索赔，因此该情况构成了交易过程，使买方无权在本次违约中就间接损失寻求赔偿。

consequential damages in the past, the parties have established a course of dealing in which AEC is precluded from seeking consequential damages for this alleged breach.

交易过程仅限于“当事方之间在先前交易中的行为”［第1.205条（1）款］。因此，对于2003年10月那项交易，不能用当事方在该时间之后的行为，来证明之前交易的过程。明确这点之后，我们看一下卖方所提到的买方向其发出的5份“重大退货通知”。这些文件列出了退还的货物、拒收的原因以及买方的退款要求。

A course of dealing is limited to “previous conduct between the parties”. § 1-205（1）. Thus, the parties’ conduct after the October 2003 transaction is not relevant to establish their course of dealing for purposes of the October 2003 transaction. With this in mind, we refer to the five “material return notices” from AEC to Belden cited by Belden. These forms state the material being rejected, the reason for rejection, and AEC’s request for a credit.

可以看出，这些文件不能明确证明买方已放弃寻求进一步赔偿的权利，而仅表明买方要求就瑕疵电线取得退款。此外，即使买方过去未曾就利润损失或间接损失提出过索赔，该情况本身也不能最终证明买方已同意在未来放弃此种权利。卖方未能证明，作为法律问题，买方已通过双方的交易过程，同意了卖方对救济的限制。

These forms do not expressly establish that AEC has forfeited its right to seek additional damages. They simply show that AEC requested a credit for non-conforming wire. Further, that AEC did not previously claim lost profits or consequential damages does not conclusively show that AEC agreed to forego such remedies in the future. Belden has not established a course of dealing in which AEC agreed to Belden’s limitation on remedies as a matter of law.

文本冲突的结论　归纳而言，我们同意初审法院的结论，即法典第 2.207 条（3）款适用于本案；并且，第 2.207 条（3）款，而不是第 2.207 条（2）款，决定了当事方协议的条款。我们还判定，不存在根据第 1.205 条建立的交易过程，因此，买方未对损害赔偿的限制给予同意。对于卖方的赔偿限制条款的适用效力问题，初审法院作出买方胜诉的无审判决是适当的。

In sum, we agree with the trial court's conclusion that Section 2-207（3） applies to this case and that Section 2-207（3）, not Section 2-207（2）, controls the terms of the parties' agreement. We also conclude that Section 1-205 does not establish a course of dealing in which AEC agreed to the limitation on damages. The trial court properly granted summary judgment in favor of AEC as to the issue of the applicability of Belden's limitation on damages.

明示担保的问题　卖方还辩称，初审法院错误地判定，卖方设立了一项明示担保，承诺遵守自己制定的质量控制规范。"当一项协议完全由书面文件构成时，其是否设立了明示担保，应完全由法院认定。"（M 诉 H 案）。具体而言，如果当事方所依赖的全部陈述均以书面形式作出，那么，是否存在明示担保，属于法律问题（M 诉 H 案）。本案中所主张的担保，源于所交换的书面文件，因此，该书面文件是否足以导致明示担保的产生，属于无审判决可以判定的法律问题。

Belden also argues that the trial court erroneously concluded that Belden created an express warranty regarding compliance with its quality control program. "Where an agreement is entirely in writing, the question of whether express warranties were made is one for the court." Martin Rispens & Son v. Hall Farms, Inc. More specifically, if all of the representations upon which the parties rely were in writing, the existence of express warranties is a question of law. See id. Because the alleged warranty is based on written exchanges, whether the writings are sufficient to create an express warranty is a question of law appropriate for summary judgment.

背景情况　买方于1994年向自己的供应商表示，为了满足自己客户(汽车制造商)的要求，买方正在制订质量控制规范。为此,买方举办了一次“供应商日”，就该控制规范作出解释。卖方的两位代表参加了会议。对于认证供应商所必须做到的事情，买方作出了解释，并说明认证供应商的产品可以享受“直接入库”的免检待遇。

为了符合买方的质量控制规范，卖方于1996年填写了买方发出的问询表，并就卖方的国际ISO 9000认证提供了详细信息。卖方1997年向买方发出信件说明：“如我们已说，卖方全部电子工厂均已获得ISO认证。信件附件所显示的文件和体系，包括了卖方为生产买方YR29803产品所采用的控制和检验程序。”此外，信的附件还说明，卖方使用QU公司提供的材料。1997年，买方批准了卖方提交的质量控制规范。

明示担保的产生　卖方称，

In 1994, AEC indicated to its suppliers that it was adopting a quality control program to satisfy the requirements of AEC's purchasers, automobile manufacturers. AEC held a "supplier day" meeting explaining its quality control program. Two Belden representatives attended the meeting. AEC explained what its suppliers needed to do to become certified by AEC and that a certified supplier's product receives "ship-to-stock" status, bypassing inspection.

In 1996, in an attempt to comply with AEC's quality control program, Belden completed a survey by AEC and provided detailed information regarding its ISO 9000 certification, an international accreditation. In 1997, Belden sent a letter to AEC stating in part: "As I mentioned, all of the Belden electronic plants are ISO certified. The attached documents are the documents and system by which Belden controls and inspects the process to manufacture YR29803." Among other things, the attached documents indicated that Belden used materials supplied by Quantum. In 1997, AEC approved Belden's PPAP.

Belden claims that these 1996 and 1997

1996年和1997年的沟通材料，不足以构成2003年10月所订立之合同的明示担保。法典第2.313条规定："（1）卖方通过下列方式作出明示担保：（a）如果卖方就货物向买方确认的事实或作出的许诺，构成交易之基础的一部分，卖方即明示担保，货物将符合此种确认或许诺。（b）如果对货物的任何描述构成交易之基础的一部分，卖方即明示担保，货物将符合此种描述。（c）如果任何样品或模型构成交易之基础的一部分，卖方即明示担保，全部货物都将符合此种样品或模型。（2）明示担保的产生，不取决于卖方是否使用'担保'或'保证'这类正式用语，也不取决于卖方是否具有提供担保的具体意图。但是，卖方仅确认货物的价值，或仅表明自己对货物的看法或赞扬，并不构成担保。"

communications did not amount to an express warranty for purposes of the October 2003 contract. Section 2-313 of the UCC provides: "（1） Express warranties by the seller are created as follows:（a） any affirmation of fact or promise made by the seller to the buyer which relates to the goods and becomes part of the basis of the bargain creates an express warranty that the goods shall conform to the affirmation or promise. （b） any description of the goods which is made part of the basis of the bargain creates an express warranty that the goods shall conform to the description. （c） any sample or model which is made part of the basis of the bargain creates an express warranty that the whole of the goods shall conform to the sample or model. （2）It is not necessary to the creation of an express warranty that the seller use formal words such as 'warrant' or 'guarantee' or that he have a specific intention to make a warranty, but an affirmation merely of the value of the goods or a statement purporting to be merely the seller's opinion or commendation of the goods does not create a warranty."

争议的问题　根据M诉H案的原则，"明示担保必须来源

"An express warranty requires some representation, term or statement as to how the

于某种陈述、条款或声明，说明如何对产品进行担保”。在本案中，双方似乎对此并无争议，即在1996年和1997年，卖方就电线提供了明示担保。争议在于，卖方于1996年和1997年就其ISO认证所提供的说明，是否构成了伸延至2003年10月合同的明示担保。

product is warranted." Martin. There does not seem to be a dispute that in 1996 and 1997 Belden made express warranties regarding its wire. Instead, the issue is whether the 1996 and 1997 statements by Belden regarding certification created an express warranty that extended to the October 2003 contract.

陈述的时间无关紧要 基于双方已承认的证据，我们认为，卖方遵守买方的质量控制规范，对双方之间的合同具有至关重要的意义，且卖方的意图是将该遵守伸延至双方随后多次订立的合同。首先，法典第2.313条正式评论7说，“作出文字描述或确认的确切时间，或展示样品的确切时间，本身并不重要。唯一的问题是，从公平的角度，是否应将该文字或样品视为合同的组成部分”。虽然本案卖方的初始陈述是1996年和1997年作出的，但没有证据表明，这些陈述具有时间上的限制，或卖方随后表示不再遵守买方的质量控制规范，或买方改变了这些规范。如初审

Based on the designated evidence, we believe Belden's compliance with AEC's quality control program was essential to its contracts with AEC and was intended to extend to the parties' repeated contracts. First, Comment 7 to Section 2-313 provides in part, "The precise time when words of description or affirmation are made or samples are shown is not material. The sole question is whether the language or samples or models are fairly to be regarded as part of the contract". Thus, although Belden made its initial representations in 1996 and 1997, there is no indication that those representations were limited in time, that Belden subsequently disclaimed its compliance with AEC's quality control standards, or that AEC changed those standards. As the trial court observed, "it is

法院所说，“如果认为买方的意图是，仅仅在电线的一次发货中依赖卖方的这些表述，而对于随后的发货，卖方可以任意采用任何质量规范，则这种看法完全不合逻辑”。

illogical to believe that [AEC] intended to rely in this representation for only one (1) shipment of Wire and then to understand that Belden would follow whatever quality procedures it wanted as to future shipments".

交易过程可以引起明示担保 其次，法典第 2.213 条正式评论 5 说，“有可能通过交易过程，使过去的交货构成对货物质量的明示或默示描述”。卖方主张，如果当事方的交易过程不足以使赔偿限制条款进入当事方的合同，那么，该交易过程也不足以引起明示担保。我们不同意此说法。无论交易过程是否可证明买方已同意了卖方所建议的赔偿限制条款，当事方的交易过程都可以证明，对于遵守买方的质量控制规范，卖方作出了明示担保。赔偿限制条款和明示担保是两个毫无关联的问题，在两者之间没有联动关系。

Further, Comment 5 of Section 2-213 provides in part, "Past deliveries may set the description of quality, either expressly or impliedly by course of dealing". Belden claims that if the parties' course of dealing was insufficient to incorporate the limitation on damages into the parties' contract, then the course of dealing is also insufficient to establish an express warranty. We disagree. Irrespective of whether the course of dealing established that AEC assented to Belden's proposed limitation on damages, the parties' course of dealing established that Belden made an express warranty regarding its compliance with the quality control standards. The limitation on damages and the express warranty are unrelated issues--there is no correlation between the two.

实际使用的绝缘材料构成交易过程 交易过程是一种行为，且“从公平的角度，该行为应被

A course of dealing is conduct "fairly to be regarded as establishing a common basis of understanding for interpreting their

视为已构成共同理解的基础，用于解释他们的表达和其他行为”［第1.205条（1）款］。毫无争议的是，在当事方之间100多次的交易中，卖方的电线均符合买方的质量控制要求，而只是从2003年10月起才不再符合，因为卖方从QU公司绝缘材料转至DO公司材料，且未将该变化通知买方。卖方在1996年和1997年曾就遵守买方质量控制规范作出了陈述，且在反复多次的生产中一直使用QU公司材料，因此，卖方已明示担保其将遵守买方的质量控制规范。

不需要反复沟通 虽然卖方和买方并未反复或经常就卖方继续使用QU公司材料的问题进行“沟通”，但这种情况并不削弱当事方的交易过程。交易过程的核心是，允许将当事方过去的行为视为共同理解的基础。卖方1996年和1997年的陈述，再加上其继续使用QU公司绝缘材料的行为，就具有此种作用。

买方提供的规格不影响担保 虽然电线的技术规格系由买方工

expressions and other conduct”. § 1-205 (1). It is undisputed that Belden's wire complied with the AEC's quality control requirements for the parties' more than 100 transactions, until October 2003, when Belden switched from Quantum insulation to the Dow insulation without informing AEC of the changes. Based on Belden's 1996 and 1997 assertions regarding its compliance with AEC's quality control program and Belden's repeated production of wire containing Quantum insulation, Belden expressly warranted its compliance with AEC's quality control program.

That Belden and AEC did not repeatedly or routinely “communicate” regarding Belden's continued use of Quantum insulation does not undermine the parties' course of dealing. The very point of a course of dealing is to allow the parties' prior actions create a basis of common understanding. This is exactly what Belden's 1996 and 1997 assertions taken with its continued use of Quantum insulation did.

The fact that AEC provided technical specifications prepared by an engineer that did

程师提供，且未涉及电线的物理品质，但这种情况不能否定卖方的明示担保。买方 2003 年 10 月的采购订单指明 YR29803，而这正是卖方 1997 年信件和材料清单中所提到的电线型号。虽然买方的具体需求在每次采购订单中有所变化，但卖方对 YR29803 型号电线的规格作出了担保，而买方购买的正是该型号的电线。

not include the physical qualities of the wire does not negate Belden's express warranty. AEC's October 2003 purchase order refers to YR29803; this is the type of wire referred to in Belden's 1997 letter and the materials list. Although AEC's specific needs may have varied from order to order, Belden warranted the specifications of the YR29803 wire and AEC purchased YR29803 wire.

卖方称，买方每一次采购订单都对规格作出改变。但是，“这些变化均未涉及物理性能、抗拉强度、延伸率、绝缘材料类型等”。这表明，买方并不希望改变这些已经存在的规格要求。买方采购单中的声明也强调了这个事实，即“材料必须取得认证”。卖方并未提出任何确定证据证明，买方已不再要求卖方的材料符合其质量控制规范，或证明卖方已通知买方说，其将不再遵守该规范。

Belden points out that AEC changed its specifications with each of its orders, yet "none of these changes relate to the physical properties, tensile strength and elongation or the type of insulation compound ...". This shows that AEC did not want to change any of these pre-existing requirements. This fact is bolstered by AEC's statement on its order form, "Material Certification Required". Belden does not point to any designated evidence showing that AEC no longer required that Belden's materials comply with its quality control program or that Belden informed AEC that it was no longer complying with such.

知情问题　最后，本案卖方声称，只有当一个卖方对买方所

Finally, Belden contends that an express warranty can only be created when a seller

不知道的事实作出说明时,该说明才引起担保,而本案买方是专业商人,因此,明示担保的说法,“表面上就不能成立”。即使假设卖方在初审时曾提出过这个问题,我们也不同意其对M诉H案的解读。在完整阅读卖方所引用的M诉H案判决词后可以看到,该判决说:“明示担保必须源于某种陈述、条款或声明,说明如何对产品进行担保。换言之,如果卖方对买方所不知道的事实作出声称,这可以构成担保;但是,如果卖方只是对其没有特别知识的事项阐明意见,且可以期待买方同样有自己的意见或判断,则卖方的声称就不构成担保。因此,如果卖方作出事实性的声称,说一台机器装有新马达,该声称即构成明示担保。如果卖方保证,一年内出现瑕疵的地毯将会被更换,这也足以构成明示担保。”(M诉H案)

买方对更换绝缘材料不知情 我们不认为M诉H案上述文字的含义是,只有买方并不专业或基本无知时,才有可能存在

states a fact of which the buyer is ignorant and claims that because AEC was a sophisticated merchant “the proposition is at once facially implausible”. Assuming Belden raised this issue before the trial court, we disagree with its reading of Martin. A complete reading of the language upon which Belden relies shows: “An express warranty requires some representation, term or statement as to how the product is warranted. Stated another way, an express warranty may be created if the seller asserts a fact of which the buyer is ignorant, but not if the seller merely states an opinion on a matter on which the seller has no special knowledge and on which the buyer may be expected also to have an opinion and to exercise his judgment. Thus, a seller's factual statement that a machine had a new engine constituted an express warranty. Assurances by a seller that carpet would be replaced if any defects surfaced within one year of purchase was sufficient to create an express warranty.” Martin.

We do not take this language to mean that a buyer has to be unsophisticated or generally ignorant before an express warranty can be created. Instead, we believe this language

明示担保。反之，我们认为其含义是，只要卖方声称一项情况是事实，而买方并不知道该情况不是事实，卖方就设立了明示担保。在本案中，没有证据表明，买方实际上知道，卖方所提供的电线将不具有其在 1996 年和 1997 年信中所称的物理特性。因此，卖方的声称不能成立，而初审法院对此问题作出的买方胜诉的无审判决是正确的。

means that if a seller asserts a fact about which the buyer does not have knowledge to the contrary, then the seller creates an express warranty. There is no indication that AEC knew that Belden would supply wire with physical properties other than what it asserted in its 1996 and 1997 letters. This argument is without merit, and the trial court properly granted summary judgment in favor of AEC on this issue.

判决　卖方的赔偿限制条款不构成当事方合同的条款；并且，通过遵守买方的质量控制规范，卖方明示担保其会继续遵守该规范，包括继续使用 QU 公司的绝缘材料。初审法院对买方无审判决动议的批准和对卖方无审判决动议的驳回是正确的。本院维持原判。

Belden's limitation on damages is not a term of the parties' contract and, by complying with AEC's quality control program, Belden expressly warranted its compliance with AEC's quality control program, which included the use of Quantum insulation. The trial court properly granted AEC's motion for summary judgment and denied Belden's motion for summary judgment. We affirm.

案例6　如何确定合同的担保条款？

Northrop Corporation v. Litronic Industries
诺斯洛普公司诉莱托尼克工业公司案

联邦第七巡回上诉法院 1994 年；29 F.3d 1173, 24 UCC Rep.Serv.2d 407

简　介

本案判决书由著名的联邦第七巡回上诉法院首席法官波斯纳撰写。判决书体现了典型的波斯纳风格，思辨清晰、构思巧妙、文辞精练。同时，又带有浓郁的法律经济学味道。本案争议涉及“文本冲突”（battle of forms）问题，需要由法院根据法典第 2.207 条对当事方的合同条款作出适当解释。

本案买方（Northrop）是一家制造商，需要采购某种印刷线路板。为此，买方向多家供应商发出投标邀请，包括本案卖方（Litronic）。买卖双方经过沟通，基本达成了交易意向。随后，卖方就自己生产的型号为“1714”的印刷线路板，使用自己的格式文本，向买方发出了出售线路板的要约。该文本规定，卖方对线路板提供为期 90 天的担保。买方未直接回复，但在随后与卖方的电话沟通中，说明买方将发出自己的标准采购订单。买方随后发出了自己的订单，其中规定卖方对线路板的担保没有失效期。卖方对此没有回复。

尽管双方的文本不同，且相互没有直接确认，但卖方显然认为双方已订立合同，因此开始了线路板的生产，并在约定时间内交付了线路板。买方收下了线路板，但出于种种原因，直到 6 个月以后才告诉卖方，线路板存在瑕疵，不能正常工作，因此拒收线路板。卖方则认为，90 天的担保期已过，因此自己不再对线路板的问题承担责任。买方则认为，自己的采购订单已规定担保没有失效期，因此卖方必须承担责任，并因此起诉卖方。

本案主要涉及两个问题。首先，双方是否已达成合同？这个问题相对简单，因为无论买卖双方交换的格式文件本身是否足以使合同成立，双方随后的行为，包括卖方的生产和交货，以及买方对货物的接收和付款，都属于法典第 2.207 条（3）款所说的承认合同成立的行为，因此合同已经成立。其次，合同包含了何种担保条款？在卖方发出出售要约后，买方随后发出的采购订单可被视为承诺，但买方承诺中的永久担保条款与卖方要约中的 90 天担保条款有所不同，属于法典第 2.207 条（1）款所说的“不同条款”（different term）。在这种情况下，应该以谁的担保条款为准？

第二个问题是法院在本案中需要解决的主要问题。由于法典第 2.207 条对“不同条款”的规定不够清晰，因此，各个法院对该条的解释存在很大分歧。根据波斯纳法官的总结，法院对这个问题有 3 种不同立场，即多数派立场、少数派立场和加州立场。波斯纳法官自己认为加利福尼亚州的立场更有道理，但由于本案合同受伊利诺伊州法律管辖，他必须服从该州法院的立场，而该州法院的通常做法是采纳多数派立场。

多数派的立场是，当承诺条款与要约条款不同时，承诺中和要约中的相关条款均被排除出合同，然后由法典的填补条款（gap-fillers）来代替。在这种情况下，由于本案买方的永久担保与卖方的 90 天担保不同，因此两者均被排除出合同。在这种情况下，必须根据法典的规定，来重新确定担保的期限。根据法典第 2.309 条的规定，该期限为“合理”期限。初审法院所采纳的立场就是上述多数派立场。上诉法院维持了该判决。同时，初审法院判定，考虑到线路板的复杂性，虽然买方在交货 6 个月后才提出拒收，但该拒收没有超过“合理”时间，因此买方有权退货。由于卖方在初审阶段没有对 6 个月时间的合理性问题提出适当反驳，因此上诉法院在这个问题上也维持了初审法院的判决。

判　决

文本冲突问题　“文本冲突”是一种并不少见的情况，指一家公司使用格式合同发出一项要约，而受要约人使用自己的格式合同作出答复。在普通法中，如果格式合同之间存在分歧，则受要约人的回复不能构成一项承诺（参见P诉B案）。在这种情况下，也就不可能产生合同。

法典的规定　这就是法典第2篇所抛弃的“镜像”原则。取代该原则的法典规定是，“确定且及时的承诺表示，或合理时间内发送的书面确认，即使与要约条款或与已同意的条款相比，包含不同条款或补充条款，亦构成承诺，除非其明确规定，以要约人同意这些不同条款或补充条款作为承诺生效的条件”［第2.207条（1）款；参见U诉O案］。但是，“补充条款或不同条款”这个用语，潜藏很多问题。

“Battle of the forms” refers to the not uncommon situation in which one business firm makes an offer in the form of a preprinted form contract and the offeree responds with its own form contract. At common law, any discrepancy between the forms would prevent the offeree’s response from operating as an acceptance. See Poel v. Brunswick-Balke-Collender Co. So there would be no contract in such a case.

This was the “mirror image” rule, which Article 2 of the Uniform Commercial Code jettisoned by providing that “a definite and seasonable expression of acceptance or a written confirmation which is sent within a reasonable time operates as an acceptance even though it states terms additional to or different from those offered or agreed upon, unless acceptance is made conditional on assent to the additional or different terms”. UCC Sec. 2-207（1）. See Union Carbide Corp. v. Oscar Mayer Foods Corp. Mischief lurks in the words “additional to or different from”.

承诺中的补充条款　法典第 2.207 条下一款的规定是，如果承诺中的补充条款与要约中的条款不存在严重不同，则除去某些限制，补充条款将成为合同的组成部分［第 2.207 条（2）款］，但如果存在严重不同，这些条款则属于建议。在后一种情况下，除非要约人同意这些条款，否则这些条款不具有任何效力（第 2.207 条正式评论 3）。在要约人没有给予同意的情况下，合同条款仍然为原要约的条款。通常不被视为重大补充条款的类型包括：对过期账单规定按正常利率收取利息的条款；在货物瑕疵处于商业惯例所允许的误差范围内时，对拒收权利进行限制的条款等。即使要约人从未对这些条款表示过同意，这些条款也会成为合同的组成部分（第 2.207 条正式评论 5）。

The next subsection of 2-207 provides that if additional terms in the acceptance are not materially different from those in the offer, then, subject to certain other qualifications, they become part of the contract, Sec. 2-207（2）, while if the additional terms are materially different they operate as proposals and so have no effect unless the offeror agrees to them, UCC Sec. 2-207, comment 3； if the offeror does not agree to them, therefore, the terms of the contract are those in the offer. A clause providing for interest at normal rates on overdue invoices, or limiting the right to reject goods because of defects falling within customary trade tolerances for acceptance, would be the sort of additional term that is not deemed material, and hence it would become a part of the contract even if the offeror never signified acceptance of it. Id., comment 5.

承诺中的不同条款　但是，当受要约人的回复包含了法典第 2.207 条（1）款所述的不同条款（而不是补充条款）时，到底会发生什么，法典并未解释。对于

The Code does not explain, however, what happens if the offeree's response contains different terms （rather than additional ones） within the meaning of section 2-207（1）. There is no consensus on

这个问题，不存在共识（引用著作；引用文章）。我们知道，合同已经存在了，因为虽然承诺包含了不同条款,但承诺是有效的。但是，要约和承诺到底为合同带来了什么条款？

that question. See James J. White & Robert S. Summers, Uniform Commercial Code; John E. Murray, Jr., "The Chaos of the 'Battle of the Forms': Solutions", Vand. L.Rev. We know there is a contract because an acceptance is effective even though it contains different terms; but what are the terms of the contract that is brought into being by the offer and acceptance?

两种观点 一种观点认为，不一致的冲突条款，包括要约中和承诺中的相关条款，全部被排除出合同，而法典其他条款提供的填补条款则被用来填补合同的空白。另一种观点认为，受要约人的不同条款被排除出合同，而要约人的原始条款则成为合同的组成部分。

One view is that the discrepant terms in both the nonidentical offer and the acceptance drop out, and default terms found elsewhere in the Code fill the resulting gap. Another view is that the offeree's discrepant terms drop out and the offeror's become part of the contract.

第三种观点 但是，最有道理的也许是第三种观点。该观点认为，"不同"条款与"补充"条款应被平等对待，因此，新条款的结局如何，取决于其与要约中的条款是否存在重大不同。如果存在重大不同，新条款就只是建议。此时，除非要约人对这些条款表示同意，否则将以要约人

A third view, possibly the most sensible, equates "different" with "additional" and makes the outcome turn on whether the new terms in the acceptance are materially different from the terms in the offer--in which event they operate as proposals, so that the offeror's terms prevail unless he agrees to the variant terms in the acceptance--or not materially different from the terms in the

的条款为准。如果不存在重大不同，新条款将成为合同的组成部分（引用文章）。

法典历史支持第三种观点

法典该条的起草历史，可以支持将“不同”条款与“补充”条款平等对待的解释方式，因为起草历史显示，第 2.207 条（2）款中之所以没有包含“不同条款”，是由于起草中的笔误（引用文章）。基于此种解释，就可以采用比较容易应用的“重大”标准，来代替几乎无法分辨的另一个标准，即辨别“不同”与“补充”之间的区别(U 诉 O 案; S 诉 T 案; 引用文章）。之所以说“不同”与“补充”几乎无法分辨（有人从贬义角度称此区别为“故弄玄虚”、“诡辩”或“文字游戏”），是因为所有的不同条款都是用于补充的，而所有的补充条款都是不同的。

伊利诺伊州的立场　在这项州际案件中，当事方约定将伊利诺伊州法律作为适用法，因此该

offer, in which event they become part of the contract. John L. Utz, “More on the Battle of the Forms: The Treatment of ‘Different’ Terms Under the Uniform Commercial Code”, U.C.C.L.J.

This interpretation equating “different” to “additional”, bolstered by drafting history which shows that the omission of “or different” from section 2-207（2） was a drafting error, Utz, U.C.C.L.J.; Murray, Vand.L.Rev., substitutes a manageable inquiry into materiality, Union Carbide Corp. v. Oscar Mayer Foods Corp.; Schulze & Burch Biscuit Co. v. Tree Top, Inc.; Douglas G. Baird & Robert Weisberg, “Rules, Standards, and the Battle of the Forms: A Reassessment of Section 2-207”, Va.L.Rev., for a hair-splitting inquiry into the difference between “different” and “additional”. It is hair-splitting（“metaphysical”, “casuistic”, “semantic”, in the pejorative senses of these words） because all different terms are additional and all additional terms are different.

Unfortunately, the Illinois courts--whose understanding of Article 2 of the UCC is binding on us because this is a diversity

州法院对法典第2篇的解释，对本院具有约束力。不幸的是，该州法院尚未有机会就下述问题从上述不同立场中作出选择：包含了不同于要约条款的承诺到底具有何种效力？因此，我们只能自己作出选择。

suit governed, all agree, by Illinois law--have had no occasion to choose among the different positions on the consequences of an acceptance that contains "different" terms from the offer. We shall have to choose.

本来也许属于合理拒收时间问题 作为初始问题，也许有一个疑问，即这项争议也许不是质量担保的期限问题，而是买方在拒收不符合合同的货物时，是否已超过了法典所允许的“合理时间”[第2.602条(1)款]。如我们下面将要看到的，这实际上正是初审法官认定需要解决的问题。但是，当事方继续将其视为“担保”问题。他们暗含的立场是，如果卖方的90天担保期限构成合同条款，那么，对于交付90天之后才出现的线路板瑕疵，买方不仅无权抱怨，而且买方基于线路板中不符合合同的瑕疵而拒收的权利，也将被限制在90天之内。在此上诉案中，为解决本案争议，我们接受了当事方的这个观点。

As an original matter one might suppose that this dispute is not over the terms of the warranty but over whether Northrop waited more than the "reasonable time" that the Uniform Commercial Code allows the buyer of nonconforming goods to reject them. UCC Sec. 2-602 (1). That in fact is how the magistrate judge framed the issue, as we shall see. But the parties continue to treat it as a "warranty" case. Their implicit view is that Litronic's 90-day warranty, if a term of the contract, not only barred Northrop from complaining about defects that showed up more than 90 days after the delivery of the boards but also limited to 90 days the time within which Northrop was permitted to reject the boards because of defects that rendered them nonconforming. We accept this view for purposes of deciding these appeals.

本案的要约 卖方的上诉涉及1714线路板违反担保的问题。如果担保确实于 90 天后失效，卖方即可获得胜诉。当事方同意，在买方邀请制造商就 1714 线路板投标后，卖方向买方出售产品的要约，构成了本案中的要约。如果买方的采购经理在电话中接受了该要约，当事方即在当时当地达成了合同。即便如此，仍然存在合同条款到底是什么的问题。

Litronic's appeal concerns the breach of its warranty on the No. 1714 boards. It wins if the warranty really did expire after only 90 days. The parties agree that Litronic's offer to sell the No. 1714 boards to Northrop, the offer made in response to Northrop's request for bids, was--the offer. If Northrop's Mr. Lynch accepted the offer over the phone, the parties had a contract then and there, but the question would still be on what terms.

合同是否已经成立 关于第一个问题，即合同是否已经成立，我们暂可假定买方的承诺足够“确定”，能够满足第 2.207 条（1）款对确定性的要求，因为该承诺毕竟已使卖方立即开始了生产，且无人声称卖方系鲁莽从事。我们并不知道，在与卖方的电话中，买方采购经理是否曾明确说明，对完整合同的接受要以其上级的批准为前提条件。我们知道，他的最高订约权限为 24,999 美元，但我们不知道，他是否向卖方说明了自己权限的准确限额，或虽然没告知，但卖方已知道该限额。但这些都无关紧要。如果确实存

Regarding the first question, whether there was a contract, we may assume to begin with that the acceptance was sufficiently "definite" to satisfy the requirement of definiteness in section 2-207（1）; after all, it impelled Litronic to begin production immediately, and there is no suggestion that it acted precipitately in doing so. We do not know whether Lynch in his conversation with Lair made acceptance of the complete contract expressly conditional on approval by Lynch's superiors at Northrop. We know that he had authority to contract only up to $24,999, but we do not know whether he told Lair what the exact limitation on his authority was or whether Litronic knew it without being told.

在买方上级批准的前提条件，该条件也已满足，不再成为问题。

买方的承诺不属于附条件

我们不认为，买方通过采购经理作出的对卖方要约的接受(承诺)，应被视为附有前提条件，即卖方必须遵守买方提出的永久担保。虽然买方提到了自己的采购订单，因此也许已经提醒了卖方，即买方希望担保的期限不局限于90天，但是，买方并没有试图将期限更长的担保作为买方接受卖方要约的前提条件。因此，即使存在该条件，其也不构成明示条件，而之前的判例都要求此种条件必须是明示条件(参见M诉V案；C诉C案；D诉C案；引用著作)。

主要问题在于确定担保条款 因此，我们认定合同已成立。并且，如我们将会谈到的，合同成立的进一步确切证据是，当事方已按合同成立的情况作为，因为卖方发运了线路板，而买方作出了付款。所以，下一步的问题在于，合同中的担保条款到底是什么？买方采购经理在电话中提

It does not matter. The condition, if it was a condition, was satisfied and so drops out.

We do not think that Northrop's acceptance, via Lynch, of Litronic's offer could be thought conditional on Litronic's yielding to Northrop's demand for an open-ended warranty. For while Lynch's reference to the purchase order might have alerted Litronic to Northrop's desire for a warranty not limited to 90 days, Lynch did not purport to make the more extensive warranty a condition of acceptance. So the condition, if there was one, was not an express condition, as the cases insist it be. See, e.g., McCarty v. Verson Allsteel Press Co.; Clifford-Jacobs Forging Co. v. Capital Engineering & Mfg. Co.; Dorton v. Collins & Aikman Corp.; White & Summers.

There was a contract, therefore; further, and, as we shall note, decisive, evidence being that the parties acted as if they had a contract--the boards were shipped and paid for. The question is then what the terms of the warranty in the contract were. Lynch's reference in the phone conversation to the forthcoming purchase order shows that Northrop's acceptance contained different terms from

到，买方很快就会发出采购订单。这表明，买方的承诺包含了与要约不同的条款，即采购订单中的不同条款，特别是担保条款。很明显，买方意图采用的担保条款是没有失效期的。因此，要约中对担保期限的限制，属于重大不同条款。至少，当行业惯例对缺乏失效期的担保不存在任何限制时（参见第 2.207 条正式评论 4 和 5），对担保有效期进行限制的条款，属于重大不同条款（D 诉 P 案；参见 O 诉 S 案）。但是，当事方并未提出行业惯例的问题。

the offer, namely the discrepant terms in the purchase order, in particular the warranty--for it is plain that the Northrop warranty was intended to be indefinite in length, so that, at least in the absence of some industry custom setting a limit on warranties that do not specify a duration （cf. UCC Sec. 2-207, comments 4 and 5）, a point not raised, any limitation on the length of the warranty in the offer would be a materially different term. Daitom, Inc. v. Pennwalt Corp.; cf. Owens-Corning Fiberglas Corp. v. Sonic Development Corp.

买方的订单包含不同条款

当然，即使买方希望获得比卖方所提供的期限更长的担保期，这个事实本身也不能证明买方的承诺确实包含了不同条款。但是，买方采购经理实际上没有接受卖方的要约，而是暂停下来。他说，将会发出买方自己的采购订单，而且他和卖方销售经理都知道（至少应该知道），买方的采购订单格式包含了不同于卖方销售订单格式的担保条款。我们前文已述及，虽然买方采购经理口头

Of course the fact that Northrop preferred a longer warranty than Litronic was offering does not by itself establish that Northrop's acceptance contained different terms. But Lynch did not accept Litronic's offer and leave it at that. He said that he would issue a Northrop purchase order, and both he and Lair knew （or at least should have known） that the Northrop purchase order form contained a different warranty from Litronic's sale order form. And we have already said that Lynch did not, by his oral reference to the purchase order, condition Northrop's purchase on

提到了采购订单，但其并未将卖方同意遵守该采购订单中的所有条款作为买方采购的前提条件，而法院都坚持要求，此种条件必须是明示条件（法官不太相信商人会阅读标准格式条款，所以无论法官的做法是否正确，他们不太愿意仅仅基于格式合同中印制的某个条件，就宣布合同无效）。但在本案中，对于承诺条款将与要约不同这一点，买方已清楚地告知卖方。

Litronic's agreeing to comply with all the terms in the purchase order form, given the courts' insistence that any such condition be explicit. (Judges are skeptical that even businesspeople read boilerplate, so they are reluctant, rightly or wrongly, to make a contract fail on the basis of a printed condition in a form contract.) But Lynch said enough to make clear to Lair that the acceptance contained different terms from the offer.

多数法院对不同条款的立场 如同我们前文所述，与承诺中仅仅包含补充条款时的情况不同，当要约与承诺的条款不同时，法典并没有说明合同的条款到底是什么。多数法院的立场是，冲突的条款全部被排除出合同，并由法典中适用的填补条款来代替（参见D诉P案；S诉A案；C诉M案）。本案的初审法官采纳了这个立场，并因此引用了法典第2.309条。该条规定，拒收不符合合同的货物，应该在“合理时间”内作出[另参见第2.601条（1）款]。初审法官进一步

The Uniform Commercial Code, as we have said, does not say what the terms of the contract are if the offer and acceptance contain different terms, as distinct from cases in which the acceptance merely contains additional terms to those in the offer. The majority view is that the discrepant terms fall out and are replaced by a suitable UCC gap-filler. E.g., Daitom, Inc. v. Pennwalt Corp.; St. Paul Structural Steel Co. v. ABI Contracting, Inc.; Challenge Machinery Co. v. Mattison Machine Works. The magistrate judge followed this approach and proceeded to section 2-309, which provides that nonconforming goods may be rejected within

认定，由于线路板所需的检测十分复杂，因此，买方在 6 个月之后才对卖方的线路板作出拒收，并未超出合理时间。

少数法院和加州的立场　在少数法院中，主流的观点是，承诺中的不同条款应该被排除（V 诉 G 案；R 诉 G 案）。这种立场将意味着本案卖方的胜诉。我们更愿意采纳的立场是，把“不同”与“补充”一视同仁，因此，只有当承诺中的条款与要约条款存在重大不同时，才以要约中的条款为准。但是，到目前为止，这种观点只在加利福尼亚州的法院中得到过采纳（S 诉 M 案）。根据这种观点，以及根据少数法院中的“主流”观点，卖方要约中的担保条款，也就是为期 90 天的担保，构成了合同的担保条款，因为买方承诺中的永久担保属于重大不同条款。

伊利诺伊州遵循多数法院的立场　伊利诺伊州法院对于其他的法典案件，倾向采纳多数法院的立场（参见 R 诉 F 案）。同时，

a “reasonable” time（see also Sec. 2-601（1））, and she held that the six months that Northrop took to reject Litronic’s boards was a reasonable time because of the complexity of the required testing.

The leading minority view is that the discrepant terms in the acceptance are to be ignored, Valtrol, Inc. v. General Connectors Corp.; Reaction Molding Technologies, Inc. v. General Electric Co., and that would give the palm to Litronic. Our own preferred view--the view that assimilates “different” to “additional”, so that the terms in the offer prevail over the different terms in the acceptance only if the latter are materially different, has as yet been adopted by only one state, California. Steiner v. Mobil Oil Corp. Under that view, as under what we are calling the “leading” minority view, the warranty in Litronic’s offer, the 90-day warranty, was the contractual warranty, because the unlimited warranty contained in Northrop’s acceptance was materially different.

Because Illinois in other UCC cases has tended to adopt majority rules, e.g., Rebaque v. Forsythe Racing, Inc., and because the interest in the uniform nationwide application

尽管多数法院的立场并不完美（但也并非一无是处），为了使法典的应用在全国保持一致（法典本身也强调这一点）（参见第1.102条），应尽量将多数法院的立场推向统一化。对于本案，由于我们必须预测伊利诺伊州法院的立场，我们将假定其会采纳多数法院的立场。

of the Code--an interest asserted in the Code itself（see Sec. 1-102）--argues for nudging majority views, even if imperfect （but not downright bad）, toward unanimity, we start with a presumption that Illinois, whose position we are trying to predict, would adopt the majority view.

多数法院立场的理由 我们不认为存在否定上述假定的理由。多数法院立场的理由是，当承诺存在不同条款时，说明受要约人未接受要约人的条款，但双方又都愿订立合同；此时，为什么不能找一个中立条款来解决他们的分歧？当然，对于要约人的条款，受要约人也有可能在订约时本不持有强烈异议，而只是在寄出包含自己标准条款的格式文件时并未考虑其中的条款，或未考虑该条款对特定合同的适当性。

We do not find the presumption rebutted. The idea behind the majority view is that the presence of different terms in the acceptance suggests that the offeree didn't really accede to the offeror's terms, yet both parties wanted to contract, so why not find a neutral term to govern the dispute that has arisen between them? Of course the offeree may not have had any serious objection to the terms in the offer at the time of contracting; he may have mailed a boilerplated form without giving any thought to its contents or to its suitability for the particular contract in question.

其他因素 但是，要约中的冲突条款，本身也同样有可能未认真考虑合同订约的情况，而只是使用了标准格式条款。并且，如果要约人真的只想按自己的要

But it is just as likely that the discrepant terms in the offer itself were the product of a thoughtless use of a boilerplate form rather than a considered condition of contracting. And if the offeror doesn't want to do

约条款进行交易，他为了保护自己，本来完全可以在要约中规定，只有受要约人接受全部要约条款，合同才成立［第 2.207 条（2）（a）款；T 诉 C 案］。本案的实际情况是，卖方确实在要约中说明，要约中的条款“优于买方的条款和条件，除非另有特别商定”。但是，出于我们不了解也无须了解的原因，卖方在诉讼中并未辩称，要约中的这段文字构成合同存在的前提条件，即买方必须接受卖方要约中的 90 天担保期限。因此，卖方被视为已放弃提出这项辩称的权利。

不同方法的分析　毫无疑问，受要约人为了保护自己，同样可以规定前提条件，即只有要约人接受承诺中的不同条款，该承诺才有效。但是，如同本案情况一样，很多承诺都是职务较低的雇员通过电话作出的，因此，期待受要约人按上述方式保护自己，也许不太现实。要约人是首先提出要约的，因此有更多时间去仔细设定合同中其愿意接受的条款。

business other than on the terms in the offer, he can protect himself by specifying that the offeree must accept all those terms for the parties to have a contract. UCC Sec. 2-207(2)(a); Tecumseh International Corp. v. City of Springfield. Now as it happens Litronic did state in its offer that the terms in the offer “take precedence over terms and conditions of the buyer, unless specifically negotiated otherwise”. But, for reasons that we do not and need not fathom, Litronic does not argue that this language conditioned the existence of the contract on Northrop’s acceding to the 90-day warranty in the offer; any such argument is therefore waived.

It is true that the offeree likewise can protect himself by making his acceptance of the offer conditional on the offeror’s acceding to any different terms in the acceptance. But so many acceptances are made over the phone by relatively junior employees, as in this case, that it may be unrealistic to expect offerees to protect themselves in this way. The offeror goes first and therefore has a little more time for careful specification of the terms on which he is willing to make a contract.

我们所称的少数派主流观点，也许会诱使要约人对受要约人发起突然“袭击”，并期望后者不会阅读那些细琐条款。而在多数派观点下，如果受要约人打算对要约人发起突然袭击（要约人不可能这样做，因为只要受要约人的条款不同，要约人就会失败），当事方会被移至中立场地；因此我们认为，要约人比受要约人更容易免受突然“袭击”。加利福尼亚州规则可以解决所有这些问题，但由于缺乏其他州的支持，不适合作为伊利诺伊州的参照。至少，我们猜测伊利诺伊州法院不会将其作为参照。

What we are calling the leading minority view may tempt the offeror to spring a surprise on the offeree, hoping the latter won't read the fine print. Under the majority view, if the offeree tries to spring a surprise (the offeror can't, since his terms won't prevail if the acceptance contains different terms), the parties move to neutral ground; and the offeror can, we have suggested, more easily protect himself against being surprised than the offeree can protect himself against being surprised. The California rule dissolves all these problems, but has too little support to make it a plausible candidate for Illinois, or at least a plausible candidate for our guess as to Illinois's position.

第 2.207 条（3）款会得出同样结论 还有另外一个问题需要考虑。法典第 2.207 条（3）款规定，即使合同未能根据该条前两款而成立，“当事方的行为”仍可导致合同的成立。在这种情况下，正如（3）款所明确规定的，冲突条款被全部排除，并由法典的填补条款所代替。看上去，即使要约规定承诺必须严格对应要约，上述规定似乎也会使要约人

There is a further wrinkle, however. The third subsection of section 2-207 provides that even if no contract is established under either of the first two subsections, it may be established by the "conduct of the parties", and in that event (as subsection (3) expressly provides) the discrepant terms vanish and are replaced by UCC gap fillers. This may seem to make it impossible for the offeror to protect himself from being contractually bound by specifying that

无法保护自己，因为在承诺不对应的情况下，要约人仍有可能受到合同约束。但是，只有当事方用行为证明合同已经存在时，上述（3）款才适用。例如，要约人虽然规定承诺必须严格对应要约，但在收到与要约不一致的承诺后却开始履约，如同合同已经订立一样。这就属于（3）款适用的情况。对于本案发生的情况，这是一种解释方法。但是，这种解释所得出的结果，与采用多数派观点解释（2）款后得出的结果是一样的，因此我们此处不作单独分析。

the acceptance must mirror his offer. But subsection （3） comes into play only when the parties have by their conduct manifested the existence of a contract, as where the offeror, having specified that the acceptance must mirror the offer yet having received an acceptance that deviates from the offer, nonetheless goes ahead and performs as if there were a contract. That is one way to interpret what happened here but it leads to the same result as applying subsection （2） interpreted as the majority of states do, so we need not consider it separately.

双方实力对比问题　考虑到1714线路板的复杂性，买方原本也不太可能同意对担保设置90天的期限。卖方在辩称时强调，其公司规模比买方小得多，因此自然不愿意承担过重的担保责任。但是，假如说规模不同的公司谈判时，小公司比大公司更有可能按自己的意愿订合同，这个说法是很奇怪的。

Given the intricacy of the No. 1714 boards, it is unlikely that Northrop would have acceded to a 90-day limitation on its warranty protection. Litronic at argument stressed that it is a much smaller firm, hence presumably unwilling to assume burdensome warranty obligations； but it is a curious suggestion that little fellows are more likely than big ones to get their way in negotiations between firms of disparate size.

结论　在本案中，买方虽然实际上仅实现了其一半愿望，但

And Northrop actually got only half its way, though enough for victory here；

已算是取得了胜利。由于买方在接受卖方要约时，没有明确规定前提条件，即卖方必须接受自己的条款，因此，买方没有获得其采购订单上所述的永久担保。但是，在初审法院的帮助下［根据多数派理解的法典第2.207条(2)款的规定］，买方获得了具有“合理期限”的担保。如果根据本案特殊情况，90天的担保期就属于合理期限，则卖方本来有权在初审中说明其理由。

for by virtue of accepting Litronic's offer without expressly conditioning its acceptance on Litronic's acceding to Northrop's terms, Northrop got not a warranty unlimited in duration, as its purchase order provides, but (pursuant to the majority understanding of UCC Sec. 2-207 (2)) a warranty of "reasonable" duration, courtesy the court. If special circumstances made a 90-day warranty reasonable, Litronic was free to argue for it in the district court.

我们的观点是，买方的采购订单仅显示，买方的承诺包含(尽管是以引用的方式包含)了不同条款。此外，该订单没有其他效力。另外两个事实对本案也没有意义，即卖方从未签署过该采购订单，且买方从未就此情况提醒过卖方。此外，也无须讨论买方的辩称，即如果强制履行卖方的90天担保期，将构成显失公平。但是，作为未来案件的参考，我们愿提醒本案买方以及类似公司，“显失公平”这个概念的发明，不是用来保护那些大公司，并使他们不受雇员犯错的影响。实际

On the view we take, the purchase order has no significance beyond showing that Northrop's acceptance contained (albeit by reference) different terms. The fact that Litronic never signed the order, and the fact that Northrop never called this omission to Litronic's attention, also drop out of the case, along with Northrop's argument that to enforce the 90-day limitation in Litronic's warranty would be unconscionable. But for future reference we remind Northrop and companies like it that the defense of unconscionability was not invented to protect multi-billion dollar corporations against mistakes committed by their employees,

上，显失公平主要是为了保护合同项下的消费者（O诉R案；S诉W案；引用著作）。维持原判。

and indeed has rarely succeeded outside the area of consumer contracts. Original Great American Chocolate Chip Cookie Co. v. River Valley Cookies, Ltd.; Salt River Project Agricultural Improvement & Power District v. Westinghouse Electric Corp.; White & Summers. AFFIRMED.

案例7　合同的数量条款是否足够确定?

Riegel Fiber Corp. v. Anderson Gin Company, Ellis Brothers et al.
瑞格尔纺织品公司诉安得森棉加工公司案

联邦第五巡回上诉法院 1975 年；512 F.2d 784, 16 UCC Rep.Serv. 1207

简　介

本案涉及两个层级的棉花买卖合同。一个层级是本案买方（Riegel）与卖方（“Anderson Gin” 等，即 “ginners”）之间的合同，即主合同（master contracts）。另一个层级是卖方与棉花独立种植主（farmers）之间的合同，即个体合同（individual contracts）。本案买方是纺织品生产商，是棉花真正的买家。本案卖方大体上是中间商。卖方一方面自己种植和轧制部分棉花，并将其出售给买方；另一方面通过与棉花独立种植主订立的个体合同，从后者收购棉花，然后再与自己的棉花一起转售给买方。主合同中的棉花既包括了卖方自己的棉花，也包括了卖方通过个体合同从种植主收购的棉花。

1973年3月，买方与卖方订立了若干远期棉花合同，价格为每磅0.32美元。合同中的棉花小部分来自卖方自己的预计产量，大部分来自卖方将从种植主采购的棉花。在主合同订立之前，卖方已经和种植主订立了个体合同。根据个体合同，种植主出售给卖方的价格也是每磅 0.32 美元。也就是说，对于从种植主收购的棉花，卖方没有收取任何差价，等于无偿向买方提供了中间商服务。这是当地棉花行业的通行做法，包含了一定的商业逻辑，并得到了买方、卖方和种植主的共同认可。在这种情况下，种植主实际上知道，个体合同项下棉花的真正买家是本案买方。个体合同和主合同的格式是一样的，都是由买方提供的格式合同。

总体而言，两类合同的数量条款都比较模糊。在主合同中，只说明了棉花的英亩总数，并说明每英亩预计产量为 500 磅，还说明卖方将把英亩总数的所有产量都出售给买方。在英亩总数中，没有说明卖方自己的田地有多少，更没有说明每个种植主的田地有多少，甚至也没有列出每个种植主。也就是说，根据主合同本身的描述，无法把英亩总数与任何特定田地或特定种植主对应起来。在每个种植主的个体合同中，有田地的英亩数，但没有田地的描述。由于种植主的田地数量通常都超过这个英亩数，因此，无法从个体合同中确定其到底指的是哪片田地。

到了 1973 年 10 月，棉花的市场价格大幅上升，达到每磅 0.81 美元，远高于合同价格。买方担心卖方违约，因此与卖方和种植主提前进行了沟通。在感到这种沟通无法阻止卖方和种植主另行出售棉花的想法后，买方提起了针对卖方的诉讼，要求法院确认其与卖方的主合同的有效性，并寻求合同的实际履行。同时，买方将独立种植主也列为被告，以个体合同的第三方受益人的身份，要求法院确认其受益权。卖方则要求法院认定合同不满足法典第 2.201 条的反欺诈法，因而不具有强制履行力。

在初审中，初审法院驳回了买方的起诉，而批准了卖方的动议。初审法院认为，对于主合同来说，数量条款过于模糊，不能满足法典第 2.201 条的要求，因此不具有强制履行力。对于个体合同，初审法院则认为，其中没有任何文字能将买方与种植主具体联系起来，因此不能证明个体合同的意图是将买方作为第三方受益人。并且，个体合同的数量条款同样模糊，因此大概也不能满足第 2.201 条的规定。但是，在买方提起上诉后，在买方的要求下，初审法院根据相关的法律规定作出初步履行令，指令卖方暂且将合同项下的全部棉花交付给买方，但买方必须支付将近200万美元的保证金，以便在上诉被驳回后，用于赔偿卖方的相关损失和费用。

上诉法院认为，关于买方是否为个体合同第三方受益人的问题，不能仅看合同文字，而是要考虑与合同有关的整体情况和全部证据。在本案中，所有的种植主都知道他们的棉花是为了出售给买方，而卖方仅仅是提供中间服务的中间人。因此，完全可以认定买方的第三方受益人身份。关于数量条款问题，上诉法院认为，法典第2.201条仅仅要求书面文件中包含数量条款，而不涉及条款的明确性或确定性。对于模糊的数量条款，要根据法典的其他规定，像解释合同的任何其他条款一样，通过各种不同方式进行解释，而不能仅看合同文字本身。特别是，数量条款是否可行，要以棉花种植业的商业标准来判断。上诉法院认为，数量条款符合当地棉花行业的惯例，且在订立合同时，当事方自己并不认为数量条款不清晰。上诉法院最终认定，主合同与个体合同的数量条款足够清楚，不影响合同的效力。

判　决

本案的基本问题　初审法院经过未使用陪审团的审理，批准了卖方有关驳回买方起诉的动议。初审法院判决，买方起诉所涉及的若干合同未能满足亚拉巴马州反欺诈法的要求。本院面临的问题是，该判决是否正确？本院认定该判决存在错误。因此，我们推翻原判并发回重审。

This appeal comes from a judgment entered pursuant to an order of the district court, sitting without a jury, granting appellees' motion for involuntary dismissal of appellant's case. The question presented [is], did the court correctly hold that certain contracts on which appellant brought suit failed to satisfy the Alabama statute of frauds. We answer no to [the] question and accordingly reverse and remand.

初审法院的具体判决　初审

The district judge held (1) that the

法院判定，（1）买方与卖方之间的合同（主合同）未包含能够满足亚拉巴马州反欺诈法的数量条款；（2）主合同中的一体化条款使法院无权用外部证据来解释合同，并证明合同的有效性和可强制履行性；（3）买方没有合法依据来强制履行卖方与种植主之间的合同（个体合同）。买方辩称，初审法院的上述每一项判定均属错误。我们同意买方的立场。

Riegel-ginner contracts （the "master" contracts） did not contain a quantity term sufficient to satisfy the Alabama statute of frauds;（2） that integration clauses in the master contracts prohibited the court from looking at extrinsic evidence to aid in interpreting the contracts so as to render them valid and enforceable; and （3） that Riegel had no standing to enforce the contracts between the ginners and the farmers （the "individual" contracts）. Appellant argues, and we agree, that each of these holdings is incorrect.

买方的 3 个理论　为了清晰起见，我们首先考虑买方与个体合同的关系。买方为了证明其对个体合同的权益，提出了 3 个不同理论：转让；第三方受益人；法典第 2.501 条（1）款和第 2.722 条（a）款规定的可强制履行的"特别财产权"。对于这 3 个理论，初审法院全部予以驳回。我们认为，买方作为第三方受益人而强制履行个体合同的权利，无疑可以得到本案证据的支持。因此，我们不再考虑和分析买方提出的另外两个理论。

For the sake of clarity we will first consider Riegel's status with regard to the "individual" contracts. The district court rejected all three theories put forward by Riegel to establish its interest in those contracts: assignment, third party beneficiary, and enforceable "special property interest" as granted by U.C.C. § 2-501（1） and § 2-722（a）. Because we think the evidence conclusively supports appellant's right to enforce the individual contracts as a third party beneficiary, we do not pause to consider the merits of Riegel's other theories.

第三方受益人的基本原则 本院在U诉F案的判决中说，根据亚拉巴马州法律，如果要判定一项合同系以第三方为受益人而订立的，“该合同在订立时的意图，就必须是以该第三方为直接受益人，而不是仅仅附带地使其受益”（A诉H案）。此外，一旦任何当事方被确认属于第三方受益人，该当事方即有充分的权利，强制履行使自己受益的许诺（A诉H案）。

初审法院的理由 初审法院在驳回本案买方的第三方受益人主张时，提供了下列理由：“不存在认定买方为个体合同第三方受益人的法律依据。个体合同规定，独立种植主将把棉花出售给本案卖方，并由卖方最终交付给买方。但是，该合同的其他条款规定得非常清楚，即必须将棉花出售和交付给卖方。至少从卖方与种植主之间的个体合同看，没有任何合同条款显示，卖方本来完全没有权利将棉花出售给买方之外的其他制造商。”

In United States Pipe v. Foundry Co., we noted that: Under Alabama law ... for a contract to be considered made for the benefit of a third person “the contract must have been intended for the direct benefit of the third person, as distinguished from a mere incidental benefit to him”. Anderson v. Howard Hall Co. Moreover, once it is established that a party is a third party beneficiary, he is fully entitled to enforce the promise made for his benefit. Anderson v. Howard Hall Co.

The district court disposed of Riegel’s third party beneficiary argument with the following reasoning: “There is no basis for concluding that the plaintiff was a third party beneficiary of the individual contracts. They provide that the individual farmers were to sell to the ginner defendants with ultimate delivery to Riegel Fiber Corporation, but by other terms of the same agreement it is made clear that that was to be a sale and a delivery to the ginner defendants. There is nothing that indicates in the contract that the ginner defendants would not have been free so far as the individual contracts with the farmers are concerned to have sold to some other manufacturer other than Reigel.”

书面合同文字不是唯一的判断标准 上述判决的文字，说明了初审法院判决错误的根源。在亚拉巴马州，法院在确定当事方是否意图使第三方直接受益时，不局限于书面文件的表面规定，而是可以听取与合同订立有关的其他背景证据（A 诉 H 案；M 诉 B 案）。在本案中，无论从个体合同的表面可以获得或不可以获得哪些信息，从诉辩文件和订立合同相关情况的证据中，都可以确切无疑地得出结论说，买方本质上系从种植主直接购买棉花，而卖方仅仅是为此种交易提供某种方便的融通方。

The [above] language discloses the source of the lower court's error. In Alabama, courts are not limited to the face of the writing when deciding whether the parties intended directly to benefit a third party; they may also hear evidence on the circumstances surrounding the making of the contract. Anderson v. Howard Hall Co.; Mutual Benefit Health & Acc. Ass'n of Omaha v. Bullard. Whatever information may or may not be derivable from the face of the individual contracts here, the pleadings and the evidence concerning the circumstances of the execution of these contracts leave no possible doubt that in substance Riegel was making a direct purchase from the farmers, with the ginners acting only as a form of accommodation party.

合同是否符合反欺诈法 基于以上理由，我们判决，买方有权作为第三方受益人而强制履行种植主的个体合同。但是，本案仍然存在另一个问题，即此种强制履行的权利是否具有任何价值？因为初审法院还判定，主合同未能满足亚拉巴马州反欺诈法的要求。初审法院还强烈暗示，

Accordingly, we hold that appellant is entitled to enforce the individual contracts as a third party beneficiary thereof. The question remains, however, whether this right is of any value, since the district judge held that the master contracts failed to satisfy the Alabama statute of frauds and strongly implied that if necessary he would have reached the same conclusion concerning the individual

如果需要，对于个体合同，其原本也可以作出同样的判决。

法典反欺诈法的规定 如同初审法院一样，我们的分析从有关货物买卖交易反欺诈法的法典第2.201条入手。第2.201条（1）款规定："除本条另有规定外，价款达到或超过500美元的货物买卖合同，只有存在足以表明当事方已达成买卖合同的书面文件，且被要求强制履行的当事方或其授权代理人或经纪人已在该书面文件上签名，才可通过诉讼或抗辩强制履行。一份书面文件，即使漏写或错写任何已约定的条款，也并非不足以表明合同的达成；但在本款意义上，合同只能在不超出书面文件所标明的货物数量的范围内强制履行。"

根据法典第2.201条正式评论1，对于该条（1）款来说，只有3个要求是书面备忘录所必须具备且不可改变的。首先，必须证明存在货物买卖合同；其次，必须存在签名，包括任何可以指明被强制履行之当事方的认证；最后，必须规定货物的数量。

contracts.

Our analysis begins, as did the district court's, with Code of Alabama § 2-201, the UCC's statute of frauds for the sale of goods. Section 2-201（1） provides： "Except as otherwise provided in this section a contract for the sale of goods for the price of $500 or more is not enforceable by way of action or defense unless there is some writing sufficient to indicate that a contract for sale has been made between the parties and signed by the party against whom enforcement is sought or by his authorized agent or broker. A writing is not insufficient because it omits or incorrectly states a term agreed upon but the contract is not enforceable under this paragraph beyond the quantity of goods shown in such writing."

As Official Comment 1 to § 2-201 notes： Only three definite and invariable requirements as to the memorandum are made by this subsection. First, it must evidence a contract for the sale of goods； second, it must be "signed", a word which includes any authentication which identifies the party to be charged； and third, it must specify a quantity.

数量条款的模糊性问题　本案卖方并不质疑，本案中条款详细且业经签名的书面合同，已满足法典上述正式评论中提到的前两项要求。卖方也很难真正否认书面文件包含了数量条款，因为其中确实包含了此种条款。但卖方显然是在辩称，格式合同中的数量条款过于模糊，不足以使该书面文件具有强制履行力。因此，该文件的法律效力是，文件并不包含任何数量条款（参见 D 诉 S 案）。卖方因此辩称，初审法院的判决是正确的，即根据法典第 2.201 条，合同不可强制履行。

Appellees do not question that the detailed and signed written contracts involved in this case satisfy the first two requirements set out in the comment. Nor can they well deny that the writings contain a quantity term, since they plainly do. Instead, appellees apparently argue that because the quantity terms included in the written forms are allegedly too indefinite to support enforcement of the underlying agreement, the writings in legal effect have no quantity term at all. Cf. Doral Hosiery Corp. v. Sav-A-Stop, Inc. Accordingly, appellees contend, the district judge correctly held that § 2-201 barred enforcement of the contracts.

数量条款的解释属于另一个问题　我们的看法正相反。我们认为初审法院对法典第 2.201 条的引用是错误的。在导致协议不能强制履行的所有障碍之中，反欺诈法只是其中之一。如同第 2.201 的文字所显示，该条款的最终目的是，“表明当事方之间确已订立了货物买卖合同”。该规定只是工具，目的是在实际上不存在合同时，避免以欺诈或虚

To the contrary, we think that the lower court erred in relying on § 2-201. The statute of frauds is only one of many potential barriers to the enforcement of agreements. As the language of § 2-201 reveals, the statute's overriding purpose is "to indicate that a contract for sale has been made between the parties". It is a device to prevent fraudulent and perjurious assertions of a contract where none in fact existed; the writing evidencing the parties' contractual status need not,

假方式声称存在合同。但是，证明当事方之间合同关系的书面文件，不需要且经常也不会列出协议的全部条款。

and often does not, state all the terms of the agreement.

反欺诈法的要求已满足 在本案中，案件证据强有力且毫无争议地显示，当事方意图订立合同，且确实订立了合同。并且，他们将合同转化为书面形式；实际上，初审法院的认定是，他们将全部协议内容都纳入了书面文件。书面文件经过了签署和认证，并包含了数量条款。更重要的是，如果仅仅是为了在形式上满足法典第 2.201 条反欺诈法的要求，数量条款的准确度并不重要（参见 W 诉 B 案）。

In the instant case the evidence is overwhelming and uncontradicted that the parties intended to and did enter into a contract. They reduced their agreement-in fact, as the district judge found, they reduced their entire agreement-to written form： the writings were signed, attested, and contained a quantity term. Moreover, for the limited purposes of meeting the technical statute of frauds requirement embodied in § 2-201 the accuracy of the quantity term is immaterial. Cf. West Point-Pepperell, Inc. v. Bradshaw.

应适用合同解释的一般原则 很明显，本案的真正问题不在于合同是否满足了第 2.201 条的要求，因为正如已签署的书面文件所显示的，无可否认的是，当事方已经达成协议。真正的问题在于，协议的数量条款是否过于模糊，致使法院无法强制履行该数量条款。第 2.201 条本身并未试图解决这个问题。该条暗含的假

Plainly, the real issue in this case is not whether these contracts satisfy § 2-201, but whether the quantity term in the agreement the parties undeniably made-as reflected in the signed writings-is too indefinite to support judicial enforcement. Section 2-201 itself does not purport to address this question. The unspoken assumption in that section is that when court and litigants turn to the writing for the quantity term, no dispute will remain

定是，当法院和诉讼当事方开始关注书面文件的数量条款时，他们一定是认为反欺诈法的要求已经满足，不再存有争议。此时，这项协议与法典范围内的任何其他合同是一样的。因此，对于合同条款的确定性问题，我们必须离开第 2.201 条，从法典其他条款中寻找适用标准。

that the statute of frauds has been satisfied; hence, the agreement is no different from any other contract to which the Code applies. Thus, for the applicable standards of definiteness in contract provisions we must have recourse to Code sections other than § 2-201.

无须考虑法典第 2.306 条　买方所依赖的主要条款是法典第 2.306 条。该条以卖方产出量或买方需求量作为合同的数量条款，是法典有关数量问题的主要填补条款。但是，我们无须讨论本案合同是否属于第 2.306 条范围内的合同，因为我们认为，买方已就主合同和个体合同中的数量条款（规定了交付不同磅数的棉花）提供了足够证据，且这些证据已经满足了法典的确定性标准，使合同可以强制履行。

Appellant places principal reliance on U.C.C. § 2-306, which relates to output and requirements contracts and is the primary "gap-filler" in the Code for quantity terms. We need not reach the question whether these contracts fall within the reach of § 2-306, however, because we think appellant presented ample evidence that the quantity terms in the master and individual contracts-viewed as requiring delivery of various pounds of cotton-meet the standards of definiteness required by the Code for enforceability.

有关确定性的一般原则　法典第 2.204 条（3）款规定了一般原则："即使买卖合同的一项或多项条款存在空缺，只要当事方有意订立合同，且存在比较确

Section2-204（3） states the general rule: "Even though one or more terms are left open a contract for sale does not fail for indefiniteness if the parties have intended to make a contract and there is a reasonably

定的方法用以提供适当救济，合同即不因缺乏确定性而不能成立。"该条的正式评论补充说,"法典的意图是，'确定性'问题应按商业标准衡量"。因此，我们认为，我们的分析应局限于这个问题，即本案合同所包含的数量条款，对于棉花行业具备相关知识的大多数买家和卖家来说，是否属于可以接受的数量条款?

certain basis for giving an appropriate remedy." The official comment to this section adds that "commercial standards on the point of 'indefiniteness' are intended to be applied". Thus, we view our inquiry as limited to the question whether these contracts contained quantity terms acceptable to the majority of buyers and sellers knowledgeable in the cotton trade.

商业背景同样重要 不幸的是，当事方在庭审辩论时，更多地集中于从技术角度讨论合同法原则，而不是关注这些合同在规定数量时所使用的方法是否具有商业合理性。但是，在审阅了案件记录、当事方陈述和律师意见后，我们确信，合同中所包含的数量条款，可以满足法典对确定性的要求。

Unfortunately, the parties directed their arguments more to technical contract doctrine than to the commercial reasonableness of the method used in these agreements to designate quantity. A review of the record, briefs, and argument of counsel convinces us, however, that the quantity terms as stated in the contracts can meet the Code's test for definiteness.

当事方认为数量条款足够清晰 很重要的一点是，案件证据清楚地显示，合同中的实际数量条款，是卖方自己在买方提供的格式合同上填写的。独立种植主提供了个体合同的农场编号和英亩数量，而卖方则把所有个体合

Significantly, the record is clear that appellees themselves supplied the actual quantity provisions on the forms tendered by Riegel. The individual farmers provided the farm numbers and the acres to be covered by their contracts. The ginner defendants totalled the acreage in the individual contracts,

同相加后得出他们的英亩总数，再加上自己的英亩数量，然后把两者相加后填入主合同。证据显示，在订立主合同时，卖方对格式合同没有提出任何异议。同样，证据显示，尽管卖方现在辩称，数量条款应该更加明确，但卖方当时并未试图使用他们现在所称的更明确的条款，尽管其当时无疑有机会这样做。此外，还有一个我们不认为具有决定意义但也不应忽视的因素。在初审法院之前签发履行令时，卖方曾根据法院要求，准确无误地区分出了合同项下的棉花和非合同项下的棉花。

added their personal acreage, and inserted the resulting total acreage into the master contracts. The evidence shows no objections made by any appellee to the forms at the time the contracts were entered into; likewise, it reveals no attempt by appellees to insert what they now argue would be more definite terms, even though they clearly had the opportunity to do so. Moreover, although we do not give controlling weight to this factor, it cannot be ignored that appellees successfully identified and allocated contract and non-contract cotton when required to do so by the lower court's injunction.

符合习惯做法和行业惯例

从主合同表面，无法区分出该合同所包含的具体种植田地。这是初审法院在作出其判决时的重要依据。同样，初审法院还认为，在确定主合同中每个种植田地的准确英亩数时，个体合同也没有很大的帮助作用。但我们认为，本案证据显示，没有任何当事方认为此种具体区分在商业上是必要的，甚至不认为具体区分更加

The district court relied heavily on the impossibility of determining from the face of the master contracts the specific fields covered by the agreements. The judge likewise expressed doubt that the individual contracts would help much in locating this precise acreage. Yet we find no evidence that any of the parties believe that such specificity is commercially necessary or even desirable. For its part, Riegel is apparently willing to rely to a large extent on the farmers' good faith and

有利。从买方的角度，对于种植主到底将他们田地中的哪一部分田地用来种植合同项下的棉花，在很大程度上，买方似乎更愿意依赖种植主的善意和商业合理性。同样，没有任何案件材料显示，独立种植主和卖方本来会更愿意对相关的具体田地作出严格规定，并以此作为合同的正常做法。我们认为，买方提交的材料明确构成了初步证据，即主合同和个体合同中的数量条款，符合棉花行业的行业惯例（参见R诉Y案；T诉A案；M诉L案）。初审法院的判决批准了卖方有关驳回买方起诉的动议。基于上述理由，该判决是错误的（参见I诉W案）。推翻原判，发回初审法院根据本判决意见重新审理。

commercial reasonableness in choosing which of their acres are to be used to grow contract cotton. Likewise, the record contains no hint of why the individual farmers or the ginners might prefer as a normal practice to contract as to rigidly specified fields. We think Riegel's evidence clearly makes out a prima facie case that the quantity terms in the master contracts, as well as in the individual contracts, conform to acceptable practice in the cotton trade. Cf. R. N. Kelly Cotton Merchant, Inc. v. York; Taunton v. Allenberg Cotton Co., Inc.; Mitchell-Huntley Cotton Co., Inc. v. Lawson. Consequently, the district judge erred in granting appellees' motion for involuntary dismissal. See Ingraham v. Wright. Reversed and remanded for proceedings consistent with this opinion.

案例8　排除卖方担保和赔偿责任的条款是否显失公平？

A&M Produce Co. v. FMC Corp.
埃姆农产品公司诉弗姆斯公司案

加利福尼亚州上诉法院 1982 年；135 Cal. App. 3d 478

简　介

本案涉及一台西红柿称重分拣机的买卖。买方（A&M）是一家农业公司，其总经理（Abatti）是其唯一的股东。买方总经理一生从事农业种植，但从未种植过西红柿。1973 年年底，买方决定开始种植西红柿。西红柿收获后，需要根据大小进行分拣，以便分级出售。为此，买方需要购买一台分拣机。买方总经理没有使用过分拣机，不熟悉这种设备。1974 年 1 月，买方联系了本案卖方（FMC）。卖方销售代表接待了买方，并推荐了自己公司的设备。设备的最终价格为 32,000 美元。之前，买方曾联系过另一家设备公司，其分拣机的报价超过 60,000 美元。本案卖方说，自己的设备不需要降温器，因此价格较低。随后，双方签署了卖方提供的标准格式合同。

当年 5 月下旬，买方开始第一次收获西红柿，但在使用卖方设备时遇到巨大困难。西红柿在分拣机履带上出现堆积，造成了西红柿的混乱和损坏。同时，由于分拣机没有降温器，因此西红柿在破损时非常容易变质。最终，由于设备存在的问题无法解决，也无法在短期内取得替代设备，买方只好用手工方式进行分拣，但速度太慢且成本太高。6月中旬，买方只好关闭了分拣车间，并结束了公司运营，而剩余的西红柿也基本被浪费了。买方随后起诉卖方违反合同。

卖方辩称，合同中包含了排除所有担保和排除间接损失赔偿的两项条款，因此卖方既不存在违反担保的问题，也不对买方的间接损失承担责任。初审法院认定，卖方的两项条款均属于显失公平，因此不可强制履行。在此基础上，初审法院判决卖方支付225,000美元的直接损失和间接损失赔偿，远高于32,000美元的合同价格。上诉法院维持了初审法院的判决，并就显失公平问题从程序和实质两个角度进行了详细分析。

判　决

初审法院的判决　初审法院判决，卖方应向买方净支付损害赔偿共计225,000美元，再加45,000美元的律师费。卖方提起上诉。案件的起因很普通，只是一项简单的商业交易，即卖方在1974年以32,000美元的价格向买方出售了一台农用称重分拣机。但本案涉及的问题，却需要我们仔细梳理一下法典错综复杂的规定，而加利福尼亚州本身的判例比较有限。

Defendant FMC Corporation (FMC) appeals from the judgment entered in favor of plaintiff A&M Produce Co. (A&M) in the net sum of $225,000 plus $45,000 attorney's fees. Although this case has a rather humble origin arising from the simple business transaction in 1974 when FMC sold A&M an agricultural weight-sizing machine for $32,000, the issues now require our traversing the labyrinthine complexities of the Uniform Commercial Code, only partially illuminated by California precedent.

排除担保和间接损失赔偿的条款　本案主要涉及排除担保和限制救济的条款的效力问题。这

The major issues in this case involve the validity of FMC's purported disclaimer of warranties and limitation on the buyer's

些条款试图排除卖方的担保，并在卖方违反担保而导致买方受到损失时，限制买方取得间接损失赔偿的权利。这两个问题的解决，在很大程度上取决于如何正确适用显失公平的原则。在初审中，法院基于显失公平的原则，拒绝强制履行排除担保和限制间接损失赔偿的条款。

ability to recover consequential damages resulting from a breach of warranty. Resolution of both these issues turns largely on the proper application of the doctrine of unconscionability, which the trial court utilized in precluding enforcement of the warranty disclaimer and the consequential damage limitation.

排除担保的条款是否适用显失公平原则　卖方承认，在适当情况下，法典第 2.719 条允许法院将限制间接损失的条款认定为显失公平，但卖方辩称，对于排除担保的条款，显失公平的原则并不适用，因为法典第 2.316 条是有关担保排除条款的具体监管条款，并在此问题上取代了第 2.719 条。

Although FMC concedes that California Uniform Commercial Code section 2-719 allows a court under proper circumstances to declare a consequential damage limitation unconscionable, it argues that unconscionability is inapplicable to disclaimers of warranty, being supplanted by the more specific policing provisions of section 2-316.

显失公平的分析方法　但是，我们的结论正相反。关于显失公平这个常常难以捉摸的法律原则，我们需要分析其性质。为此，首先需要划定分析框架，用于确定特定合同条款是否属于显失公平。然后我们使用这个框架来得出我们对本案的结论。在本

We conclude otherwise, however, and turn our attention to the nature of this often-amorphous legal doctrine, outlining the analytic framework to be used in determining whether a particular contractual provision is unconscionable. That framework is then utilized in finding that the facts of this case, involving a preprinted form sales contract,

案中，买卖合同是事先印刷的格式合同。案件事实可以支持初审法院的结论，即排除担保和限制间接损失的两项条款均属显失公平。我们同时驳回卖方的辩称，即买方所声称的间接损失具有过度的猜测性，因此不能成为判决损害赔偿的基础。

support the trial court's conclusion that both the disclaimer of warranties and the limitation on consequential damages were unconscionable. We also reject FMC's argument that the consequential damages alleged by A&M were too speculative to be the basis for any damage award.

卖方诉权是否受到不当损害 卖方对初审判决首先提出的异议是，初审法院存在损害卖方诉权的错误，因为法院不允许陪审团看书面协议的背面。协议背面印有两项条款：一项条款排除了全部的担保；另一项条款则规定，如果卖方已经作出担保，则在卖方违反担保时，买方无权就间接损失取得赔偿。

FMC's initial attack on the judgment alleges prejudicial error by the trial court in not allowing the jury to see the reverse side of the written agreement which contained both a disclaimer of all warranties as well as a provision stating that in the event a warranty was made, the buyer was precluded from recovering consequential damages resulting from a breach of the warranty.

可以不向陪审团提交显失公平的证据 初审法院之所以将协议背面的内容作为应该排除的证据，是因为法院认定，排除担保和限制间接损失的条款属于显失公平，因此不可强制履行。如果这项认定是正确的。也就是说，如果初审法院确实将显失公平原则恰当地适用到了本案事实，那

The trial court's decision to exclude evidence of the contents of the agreement's reverse side was based on its determination that the warranty disclaimer and the consequential damage exclusions were unconscionable and therefore unenforceable. If this determination was correct--that is, if the trial court properly applied the unconscionability doctrine to the facts of this

么，不向陪审团展示合同背面，就是正确的决定。

卖方称排除担保不存在显失公平问题　卖方承认，限制间接损失的条款有可能构成显失公平［法典第 2.719 条（3）款］，但卖方辩称，初审法院错误地将该原则也适用于排除担保的条款。卖方辩称，显失公平的原则与排除担保的条款完全无关，因为法典第 2.316 条本身的具体规定，已经排除了显失公平的原则（引用著作；引用文章）。作为替代理由，卖方辩称，加利福尼亚州立法机构在将法典采纳为加利福尼亚州法律时，没有采纳其中有关显失公平的第 2.302 条。在这种情况下，初审法院在本案中无权适用显失公平的原则。

应灵活适用法典　虽然卖方的辩称并非完全没有道理，但我们的结论是，即使排除担保的条款从技术角度已经满足了法典第 2.316 条的规定，法院仍然可以拒绝强制履行显失公平的担保排除条款（参见 F 诉 M 案）。显

case--then the reverse side of the contract was appropriately withheld from the jury.

Acknowledging that a limitation on consequential damages may be unconscionable （§ 2-719, subd.（3））, FMC asserts the trial court erred in applying that doctrine to the disclaimer of warranties. It contends unconscionability is irrelevant to warranty disclaimer provisions, having been eliminated by the specific statutory requirements of section 2-316.（See White and Summers; Leff, Unconscionability and the Code--The Emperor's New Clause, U.Pa.L.Rev.）Alternatively, FMC suggests the California Legislature's failure to adopt the general Uniform Commercial Code section on unconscionability（§ 2-302）as part of California's Uniform Commercial Code precludes the trial court's reliance on the doctrine in this instance.

While FMC's argument is not without force, we conclude that an unconscionable disclaimer of warranty may be denied enforcement despite technical compliance with the requirements of section 2-316.（See FMC Finance Corp. v. Murphree）Unconscionability is a flexible doctrine

失公平是一项灵活的原则，目的是使法院能够直接考虑订约过程中的各种不良因素。法典第2.302条规定，“合同的任何条款”都有可能被视为显失公平。

designed to allow courts to directly consider numerous factors which may adulterate the contractual process. Uniform Commercial Code section 2-302 specifies that “any clause of the contract” may be unconscionable.

法典第2.316条的局限 法典第2.316条的监管条款仅被用来应对某些问题，即排除条款的醒目程度，以及排除条款与明示担保的冲突。但是，显失公平原则的主要针对目标，是源于其他不良商业做法的欺压和不公平突袭。

The policing provisions of section 2-316 are limited to problems involving the visibility of disclaimers and conflicts with express warranties. But oppression and unfair surprise, the principal targets of the unconscionability doctrine, may result from other types of questionable commercial practices.

此外，对于在谈判中处于弱势的当事方，“默示”与“明示”担保之间的差别过于微妙，因此，这种区别对保护弱势方免受强势方的欺压没有太大帮助。一项担保只要可以被视为“默示”，第2.316条的监管条款就无能为力。

Moreover, the subtle distinction between an “implied” warranty and an “express” warranty may do precious little to mitigate the exploitation of a party with inferior bargaining power. Yet as long as the warranty remains “implied”, section 2-316’s policing provisions are ineffective.

加利福尼亚州法院承认显失公平原则 关于显失公平原则在加利福尼亚州的地位，卖方的辩称同样不具有说服力。显失公平原则长久以来一直都是普通法的原则，且在制定法专门就该原

FMC’s contention regarding the status of the unconscionability doctrine in California is similarly unpersuasive. Unconscionability has long been recognized as a common law doctrine which has been consistently applied by California courts in the absence

则作出规定前，加利福尼亚州法院一直都在应用该原则（参见 G 诉 S 案；S 诉 F 案）。虽然加利福尼亚州立法机构在采纳法典时没有采纳其中的第 2.302 条，但是，与法典相同的文字和相关评论，近期被作为加利福尼亚州民法典第 1670.5 条而纳入法律。该条的标题是“非法合同”。该条与法典第 2.302 条唯一的重要区别是，该条适用于所有类型的合同，而不仅仅是法典范围内的货物交易。我们认为，初审法院对买方主张的支持是正确的，即限制间接损失和排除担保的两项条款均属于显失公平。

of specific statutory authorization. (See Graham v. Scissor-Tail, Inc.; Steven v. Fidelity & Casualty Co.) And although the Legislature did not adopt section 2-302 as part of California's version of the Uniform Commercial Code, the identical language, complete with accompanying commentary, was recently enacted as section 1670.5 of the Civil Code. The only significant difference is that section 1670.5, placed under the "Unlawful Contracts" heading, applies to all contracts rather than being limited to those sales transactions governed by the Commercial Code. We think the trial court properly entertained A&M's arguments directed at the unconscionability of both the consequential damage exclusion and the warranty disclaimer.

本次上诉的主要问题　现在我们讨论本次上诉的主要问题。初审法院的结论是，卖方试图排除担保并限制间接损失赔偿的做法属于显失公平，因此不可强制履行。初审法院的这个结论是否存在错误？在我们回答这个问题之前，必须首先分析一下显失公平原则的性质。

We now turn to the principal question involved in this appeal: Whether the trial court erred in concluding that FMC's attempted disclaimer of warranties and exclusion of consequential damages was unconscionable and therefore unenforceable. Before we can answer that question however, we must first concern ourselves with the nature of the unconscionability doctrine.

显失公平包括程序和实质两个方面 法典并未试图就“显失公平”是什么或不是什么作出精确定义（参见K诉R案）。但是，“普遍承认的标准是，显失公平包含两个因素：首先，一个当事方没有真正的其他选择；其次，合同条款对另一个当事方的偏袒超过了合理限度”（W诉W案）。从另一个角度说，显失公平这个概念，包含了“程序”和“实体”两个方面（I诉R案；引用文章；引用著作）。

The Uniform Commercial Code does not attempt to precisely define what is or is not “unconscionable”.（See Kugler v. Romain）Nevertheless, “[u] nconscionability has generally been recognized to include an absence of meaningful choice on the part of one of the parties together with contract terms which are unreasonably favorable to the other party.”（Williams v. Walker-Thomas Furniture Company）Phrased another way, unconscionability has both a “procedural” and a “substantive” element.（Industralease Automated & Scientific Eq. Corp. v. R.M.B. Enterprises, Inc.; see also Leff, U.Pa.L.Rev.; White and Summers）

程序方面的两个因素 程序方面主要涉及两个因素，即“欺压”与“突袭”（参见法典第2.302条正式评论1；G诉L案）。欺压的来源是，双方议价的能力差距过大，致使一方无法与另一方进行真正的谈判，即“没有真正的选择”（W诉W案；F诉D案；引用文章）。突袭主要涉及隐蔽程度问题。假如寻求强制履行格式合同中争议条款的一方，正是

The procedural element focuses on two factors: “oppression” and “surprise”.（See U. Com. Code com. No. 1, § 2-302; Geldermann and Company, Inc. v. Lane Processing, Inc.）“Oppression” arises from an inequality of bargaining power which results in no real negotiation and “an absence of meaningful choice”.（Williams v. Walker-Thomas Furniture Company; Fleischmann Distilling Corp. v. Distillers Co. Ltd.; see Spanogle, Analyzing Unconscionability Problems, U.Pa.

起草该合同的那一方，并且，其所称的双方已通过谈判而约定的条款，就隐藏在冗长乏味的格式文件中，则只要相关条款的隐蔽性达到了一定程度，该情况就构成“突袭”（引用文章）。典型的情况是，格式合同是由具有优势谈判地位的一方制定的（引用著作）。

L.Rev.） “Surprise” involves the extent to which the supposedly agreed-upon terms of the bargain are hidden in a prolix printed form drafted by the party seeking to enforce the disputed terms. （See Ellinghaus, In Defense of Unconscionability, Yale L.J.; Eddy, On the “Essential” Purposes of Limited Remedies: The Metaphysics of UCC Section 2-719 （2）, Cal.L.Rev.; Spanogle, U.Pa. L.Rev.） Characteristically, the form contract is drafted by the party with the superior bargaining position. （See Calamari and Perillo, Contracts）

显失公平的实质方面　当然，即使未参与合同起草的另一方没有阅读或没有理解合同，或即使合同的起草方占有优势谈判地位，这些事实本身也不允许法院拒绝强制履行该合同。虽然可以辩称，没有经过当事方真正商谈过的合同条款，不属于“约定内容”，因此不构成实际达成的协议（引用文章），但是，从商业实践的角度考虑，即使是未经商谈的合同条款，也只有在实质内容不合理的情况下，才能拒绝强制履行（引用文章；引用著

Of course the mere fact that a contract term is not read or understood by the nondrafting party or that the drafting party occupies a superior bargaining position will not authorize a court to refuse to enforce the contract. Although an argument can be made that contract terms not actively negotiated between the parties fall outside the “circle of assent” which constitutes the actual agreement （see Eddy, Cal. L.Rev.）, commercial practicalities dictate that unbargained-for terms only be denied enforcement where they are also substantively unreasonable. （Ellinghaus, Yale L.J.;

作)。至于什么是实质显失公平，不可能作出精确定义。不同判例使用过不同的形容词，例如，合同的结果“过于苛刻”或“一边倒”(参见S诉F案；W诉A案)。但是，一位评论家曾指出，“显失公平并不完全是由于存在‘一边倒’的结果，而是由于该结果还缺乏‘合理理由’”(引用文章)。这个评论只是希望说明，对于实质显失公平，必须基于合同订立当时的情况来进行分析(参见法典第2.302条)。

Murray on Contracts) No precise definition of substantive unconscionability can be proffered. Cases have talked in terms of “overly harsh” or “one-sided” results. (See, e.g., Schroeder v. Fageol Motors, Inc.; Weaver v. American Oil Company) One commentator has pointed out, however, that “... unconscionability turns not only on a ‘one-sided’ result, but also on an absence of ‘justification’ for it”. (Eddy, Cal. L.Rev.), which is only to say that substantive unconscionability must be evaluated as of the time the contract was made. (See U. Com. Code, § 2-302.)

风险划分问题 对此问题作出最详细和最具体评论的文章则认为，在很大程度上，任何合同都是将风险在当事方之间进行划分。如果按客观标准判断，一项合同条款将风险以不合理或出乎意料的方式分配给一方，则从实质显失公平的角度，该条款就会引起疑问(引用文章；G诉L案)。

The most detailed and specific commentaries observe that a contract is largely an allocation of risks between the parties, and therefore that a contractual term is substantively suspect if it reallocates the risks of the bargain in an objectively unreasonable or unexpected manner. (Murray, Unconscionability, U.Pitt.L.Rev.; see also Eddy, Cal.L.Rev.; Geldermann and Company, Inc. v. Lane Processing, Inc.)

但是，并非所有的不合理风险分配都构成显失公平。实际上，此种条款是否可以强制履行，还

But not all unreasonable risk reallocations are unconscionable; rather, enforceability of the clause is tied to the procedural aspects

取决于显失公平的程序因素。不公平突袭越明显，或谈判地位差距越悬殊，就越不能容忍不合理的风险分配（引用文章）。

of unconscionability such that the greater the unfair surprise or inequality of bargaining power, the less unreasonable the risk reallocation which will be tolerated.（See Spanogle, U.Pa.L.Rev.）

加利福尼亚州可供参考的判例　虽然基本上不存在直接涉及这个问题的加利福尼亚州判例，但是，加利福尼亚州最高法院最近的 G 诉 S 案，就显失公平中需要同时考虑程序因素和实质因素的重要性，提供了可供类比的支持。在该案中，某音乐推广人为一家由音乐家组成的公司预定了音乐会。双方之间的合同是音乐家工会制定的标准格式合同。合同规定，在有关合同争议的所有仲裁中，仲裁员应由音乐家工会选定。该推广人对该条款的强制履行力提出异议，声称按这种方式选出的仲裁员，可以推定必然偏向音乐家。

Although there is little California precedent directly on point, the importance of both the procedural and substantive elements of unconscionability finds support by analogy in the recent decision by the Supreme Court in Graham v. Scissor-Tail, Inc. Graham, a music promoter, booked concerts for a group of musicians incorporated under the name of “Scissor-Tail”. A standard form contract drafted by the musicians’ union provided that the arbitrator for all contract disputes was to be selected by the union. Graham challenged enforcement of the clause, arguing that an arbitrator so selected was presumptively biased in favor of the musicians.

加利福尼亚州最高法院首先认定，该合同属于“附意合同”（另一方不能谈判而只能签或不签的合同）。虽然该推广人是摇

The court first determined that the contract was one of adhesion, noting that although Graham was a prominent and successful rock music promoter, the union--which represented

滚乐领域很成功的著名推广人，但工会代表了几乎所有的知名音乐家，并坚持要求所有的推广协议都必须基于工会的标准格式合同进行“谈判”。法院的结论是，该推广人“作为音乐会推广人，迫于其行业的商业现实，对于其希望签约的任何音乐家，都不得不签订工会的格式合同”。法院的这个表述，与显失公平程序因素中的“不平等谈判地位”非常接近。

法院随后对该案的讨论，涉及了显失公平程序因素中的“不公平突袭”。法院认定，合同中包含的仲裁条款不属于对该推广人的突袭。考虑到当事方之间的交易过程，以及该音乐推广人在音乐行业中的丰富经验，法院的结论是，无论是合同中包含了仲裁条款这个事实本身，还是该仲裁条款的含义，都没有超出他的“合理期待”。

最后，加利福尼亚州最高法院在该案中表示，“对于合同这架机器，其运行必须满足最低合理性”(G 诉 S 案，其中引用联

nearly all significant musicians--mandated that promotion agreements be “negotiated” pursuant to standard union-prepared contracts. In language closely approximating the “unequal bargaining power” prong of the procedural unconscionability factor, the court concluded that Graham “... was required by the realities of his business as a concert promoter to sign [union] form contracts with any concert artist with whom he wished to do business ...”.

Moving next to a discussion paralleling the “unfair surprise” prong of procedural unconscionability, the court determined that Graham was not surprised by the inclusion of the arbitration clause. It relied on the course of dealing between the parties as well as Graham’s vast experience in the music industry in concluding that neither the inclusion of the arbitration clause nor its effect were outside of Graham’s “reasonable expectations”.

Finally, in a discourse resembling substantive unconscionability analysis, the court indicated that “contractual machinery [must] operate within some minimal levels

邦最高法院在 H 诉 A 案中的表述）。这个表述接近显失公平中的实质因素。加利福尼亚州最高法院认为，该案的合同没有达到这个“最低”要求，因为在发生争议时，作为对合同作出“附意”的一方，该推广人根本没有任何真正的和公平的机会在仲裁中获胜。

of integrity”.（Graham, quoting Hines v. Anchor Motor Freight）The contract in Graham did not attain this “minimal level” because the arbitration clause left the “adhering” party without any real and fair opportunity to prevail in the event of a contractual dispute.

如果以实质显失公平的语言进行表述。也就是说，所有的风险都被分配给了该推广人，而其只能在无法谈判的情况下接受该合同。加利福尼亚州最高法院以显失公平为由，拒绝强制履行该仲裁条款。毫不意外的是，该院将程序因素和实质因素联系在了一起。该院在判决中说，“我们认为，对于需要通过非司法方式解决争议的合同来说，本案合同未达到‘最低合理性’的要求，因为合同规定，在双方雇佣关系出现争议时，一方的工会将成为争议的仲裁员。特别是，本案合同属于附意合同，而上述问题对这类合同而言就更加严重”。

In the language of substantive unconscionability, all the risks were allocated to Graham who was forced to accept the contract without negotiation. Not surprisingly, the court’s conclusion denying enforcement to the arbitration clause on unconscionability grounds ties procedural and substantive elements together:“[W] e are of the view that the ‘minimum levels of integrity’ which are requisite to a contractual arrangement for the nonjudicial resolution of disputes are not achieved by an arrangement which designates the union of one of the parties as the arbitrator of disputes arising out of employment--especially when, as here, the arrangement is the product of circumstances indicative of adhesion.”

对本案的分析 在考虑了上述情况后，我们现在必须确定，

With these considerations in mind, we must now determine whether the trial court

本案初审法院的结论是否正确？初审法院判定，卖方格式合同中的排除全部担保的条款，以及排除间接损失赔偿的条款，均属于显失公平。我们在进行分析时必须注意，虽然显失公平最终属于法律问题，但是，各种事实情况都会影响该问题的答案（参见R诉W案；Z诉J案）。

合同订立当时的商业状况，直接影响当事方的相对议价能力、合理期待以及书面协议所规定的风险分配的商业合理性。如果对证据存在争议，或对从证据中得出的事实性结论存在争议，我们就必须假定，相关事实的实际情况，就是初审法院在认定显失公平时所依据的那些事实，只要此种假定可以得到大量证据的支持。

本案的程序因素 我们先对显失公平的程序因素进行分析。我们首先注意到，本案合同的商业背景是，卖方是一家规模巨大的多元化公司，而买方是一家相对较小但对农业生产具有丰富经

in this case was correct in concluding that the clauses in the FMC form contract disclaiming all warranties and excluding consequential damages were unconscionable. In doing so, we keep in mind that while unconscionability is ultimately a question of law, numerous factual inquiries bear upon that question.（See Royal Indemnity Co. v. Westinghouse Electric Corp.; Zicari v. Joseph Harris Co.）

The business conditions under which the contract was formed directly affect the parties' relative bargaining power, reasonable expectations, and the commercial reasonableness of the risk allocation as provided in the written agreement. To the extent there are conflicts in the evidence or in the factual inferences which may be drawn therefrom, we must assume a set of facts consistent with the court's finding of unconscionability if such an assumption is supported by substantial evidence.

Turning first to the procedural aspects of unconscionability, we note at the outset that this contract arises in a commercial context between an enormous diversified corporation（FMC）and a relatively small but experienced farming company

验的公司。通常而言，“法院对商人之间的显失公平问题并不十分关心”（引用著作；另参见 F 诉 D 案）。这也许是因为，法院认为，相对于普通消费者，商人对商业问题的知识更丰富，且经济实力更强大。因此，如果商人想借助“不公平突袭”或“不平等议价能力”等理由来证明存在程序显失公平，通常难以得到法院支持。

（A&M）. Generally, “... courts have not been solicitous of businessmen in the name of unconscionability”.（White and Summers; see also, e.g., Fleischmann Distilling Corp. v. Distillers Co. Ltd.） This is probably because courts view businessmen as possessed of a greater degree of commercial understanding and substantially more economic muscle than the ordinary consumer. Hence, a businessman usually has a more difficult time establishing procedural unconscionability in the sense of either “unfair surprise” or “unequal bargaining power”.

商人之间的交易也有可能存在程序不公　但是，所有的通常情况都有例外。因此，概念化的结论很少能代替具体的分析。法院已开始越来越多地承认，经验丰富但法律知识不足的商人，也有可能受到显失公平的合同条款的“突袭”（参见 W 诉 A 案；S 诉 F 案）。并且，取决于合同另一方的身份和协议的商业环境，即使是大型的商业公司，也有可能存在缺乏议价能力的情况（参见 G 诉 S 案；A 诉 M 案）。此种承认背后的理念是，如果情况

Nevertheless, generalizations are always subject to exceptions and categorization is rarely an adequate substitute for analysis. With increasing frequency, courts have begun to recognize that experienced but legally unsophisticated businessmen may be unfairly surprised by unconscionable contract terms（see, e.g.,Weaver v. American Oil Company; Schroeder v. Fageol Motors, Inc.）, and that even large business entities may have relatively little bargaining power, depending on the identity of the other contracting party and the commercial circumstances surrounding the agreement.

表明，尽管当事方已经“同意”一项合同条款，但假如其真的了解该条款，或假如其真的可以作出选择，该当事方本来是永远不会同意该条款的，那么，在这种情况下，契约自由所带来的社会效益，实际上已被严重削弱（参见K诉R案）。

（See, e.g.,Graham v. Scissor-Tail, Inc.; Allen v. Michigan Bell Telephone Company）This recognition rests on the conviction that the social benefits associated with freedom of contract are severely skewed where it appears that had the party actually been aware of the term to which he “agreed” or had he any real choice in the matter, he would never have assented to inclusion of the term.（See Kugler v. Romain）

本案存在程序显失公平 本案的具体事实显示，程序显失公平的两个因素都存在。虽然从印刷角度看，排除担保的条款属于醒目，但排除间接损失赔偿的条款并不很明显，因为其只比其他合同字体稍大。两项条款的位置，都处于事先印制好的冗长格式合同背面的文字中间，并且卖方只是随意地让买方总经理看了一下合同。卖方从未以口头形式或书面形式提醒买方总经理看一下合同的背面。买方总经理作证说，他从未看过合同背面的条款。因此，有足够的证据来支持初审法院的结论，即对于排除担保的条款，以及排除间接损失赔偿的条

Both aspects of procedural unconscionability appear to be present on the facts of this case. Although the printing used on the warranty disclaimer was conspicuous, the terms of the consequential damage exclusion are not particularly apparent, being only slightly larger than most of the other contract text. Both provisions appear in the middle of the back page of a long preprinted form contract which was only casually shown to Abatti. It was never suggested to him, either verbally or in writing, that he read the back of the form. Abatti testified he never read the reverse side terms. There was thus sufficient evidence before the trial court to conclude that Abatti was in fact surprised by the warranty disclaimer and the consequential damage

款，从事实的角度看，买方感到吃惊。

exclusion.

至于买方的吃惊在多大程度上属于“不公平”，则属于有争议的问题。他当然有机会阅读合同的背面，也有机会寻求律师的建议。但作为一个事实问题，考虑到条款的复杂性，以及卖方并未让其注意这些条款，那么，买方总经理的省略，也不能算是完全不合理。关于这点，印第安纳州最高法院在 W 诉 A 案中的评论非常恰当：“涉及预先印制的标准格式合同时，对于其中非同寻常或显失公平的条款，提供此种合同的当事方要承担举证责任，证明另一方对这些条款已经有所了解。这与涉及默示担保时所适用的原则是相同的，即除非另有说明，否则，向购买者销售的货物必须适用于预定目的，且不包含有害材料。”（另参见 S 诉 J 案）。

How “unfair” his surprise was is subject to some dispute. He certainly had the opportunity to read the back of the contract or to seek the advice of a lawyer. Yet as a factual matter, given the complexity of the terms and FMC’s failure to direct his attention to them, Abatti’s omission may not be totally unreasonable. In this regard, the comments of the Indiana Supreme Court in Weaver v. American Oil Company are apposite: “The burden should be on the party submitting ［a standard contract］ in printed form to show that the other party had knowledge of any unusual or unconscionable terms contained therein. The principle should be the same as that applicable to implied warranties, namely that a package of goods sold to a purchaser is fit for the purposes intended and contains no harmful materials other than that represented.” （See also Steele v. J. I. Case Company）

在本案中，卖方未就排除担保或排除赔偿的条款采取任何措施，以使买方对该条款获得必要信息。事实上，我们相信，大多

Here, FMC made no attempt to provide A&M with the requisite knowledge of the disclaimer or the exclusion. In fact, one suspects that the length, complexity and

数格式合同的冗长、繁复和隐晦，至少在一定程度上代表了卖方的内心希望，即对于其声称买方已经同意的这些条款，该格式会阻碍买方的阅读。这个过程几乎毫无例外地导致“一边倒”的“合同”（参见K诉A案）。

即使我们抛开“不公平突袭”这个说法，本案也有大量证据表明，双方议价能力存在差距，并缺乏对合同条款的真正谈判。我们承认，根据当地标准，买方算是一家大规模农业企业，因为其日常雇用5名工人，并在收获季节雇用多达50名的季节工人。买方1974年的耕种面积达到8000英亩。尽管如此，卖方仍然完全是另一个级别的企业。仅农业机械一个部门，1974年的营业额即达4000万美元。更重要的是，卖方的格式合同是标准合同。对于事先印制在合同背面的条款，卖方销售员没有谈判权限。虽然卖方声称，在特殊情况下，个别合同也可谈判，但其从未将这个选项告诉买方。将所有这些情况加起来后得出的结论

obtuseness of most form contracts may be due at least in part to the seller's preference that the buyer will be dissuaded from reading that to which he is supposedly agreeing. This process almost inevitably results in a one-sided “contract”.（See Klein v. Asgrow Seed Co.）

Even if we ignore any suggestion of unfair surprise, there is ample evidence of unequal bargaining power here and a lack of any real negotiation over the terms of the contract. Although it was conceded that A&M was a large-scale farming enterprise by [local] standards, employing 5 persons on a regular basis and up to 50 seasonal employees at harvest time, and that Abatti was farming some 8000 acres in 1974, FMC Corporation is in an entirely different category. The 1974 gross sales of the Agriculture Machinery Division alone amounted to $40 million. More importantly, the terms on the FMC form contract were standard. FMC salesmen were not authorized to negotiate any of the terms appearing on the reverse side of the preprinted contract. Although FMC contends that in some special instances, individual contracts are negotiated, A&M was never

是，只有对“约定”这个词作出最宽泛的解释，本案合同才属于当事方的约定（S 诉 J 案）。

made aware of that option. The sum total of these circumstances leads to the conclusion that this contract was a “bargain” only in the most general sense of the word. (Steele v. J. I. Case Company)

本案存在实质显失公平　虽然本案存在程序显失公平的问题，但我们相信，对于初审法院的最终结论，排除担保和排除赔偿条款中的实质显失公平，也产生了同样重要的影响。关于排除担保的条款，本案事实可以支持初审法院的结论，即此种排除从商业上是不合理的。买方指控卖方所违反的这项担保，涉及产品的基本运行功能。卖方在排除了这项担保和其他担保以后，本质上就是不对其产品的功能作任何保证。

Although the procedural aspects of unconscionability are present in this case, we suspect the substantive unconscionability of the disclaimer and exclusion provisions contributed equally to the trial court’s ultimate conclusion. As to the disclaimer of warranties, the facts of this case support the trial court’s conclusion that such disclaimer was commercially unreasonable. The warranty allegedly breached by FMC went to the basic performance characteristics of the product. In attempting to disclaim this and all other warranties, FMC was in essence guarantying nothing about what the product would do.

产品的功能属于货物买卖合同的核心基础。当卖方从事工业化生产，并出售标准化和大规模生产的产品时，假如说买方在购买这样一件产品后，却不存在可以强制履行的任何性能标准，那这种情况是完全不合理的。从社会的角度看，最有能力防止损失

Since a product’s performance forms the fundamental basis for a sales contract, it is patently unreasonable to assume that a buyer would purchase a standardized mass-produced product from an industry seller without any enforceable performance standards. From a social perspective, risk of loss is most appropriately borne by the party best able

发生的当事方，最应该承担该损失的风险（E诉C案；R诉K案；引用著作）。几乎在所有情况下，作为制造商的卖方都比买方更有能力评估一台机器的运行功能。

to prevent its occurrence. （Escola v. Coca Cola Bottling Co.； Rodgers v. Kemper Constr. Co.； Holmes, The Common Law） Rarely would the buyer be in a better position than the manufacturer-seller to evaluate the performance characteristics of a machine.

此外，本案证据表明，买方之前对称重分拣设备没有经验，因此不得不依赖卖方的推荐来采购合适的设备。卖方完全了解这个情况。本案陪审团一定是作出了这样的裁定，即卖方明示或默示地对设备的性能作出了保证，但该设备并未达到此种性能。特别是在涉及没有经验的买方时，为了促使买方从不同的竞争产品中作出有意识的购买选择，卖方对产品性能的说明，是绝对必要的。

In this case, moreover, the evidence establishes that A&M had no previous experience with weight-sizing machines and was forced to rely on the expertise of FMC in recommending the necessary equipment. FMC was abundantly aware of this fact. The jury here necessarily found that FMC either expressly or impliedly guaranteed a performance level which the machine was unable to meet. Especially where an inexperienced buyer is concerned, the seller's performance representations are absolutely necessary to allow the buyer to make an intelligent choice among the competitive options available.

在这种情况下，如果卖方试图以排除担保的条款，来否定买方对该说明的合理依赖，这种做法就使该协议的商业合理性产生很大疑问，且完全有可能构成实质显失公平。案件存在大量证据，

A seller's attempt, through the use of a disclaimer, to prevent the buyer from reasonably relying on such representations calls into question the commercial reasonableness of the agreement and may well be substantively unconscionable. The

可以支持初审法院的此种结论。

trial court's conclusion to that effect is amply supported by the record before us.

关于排除间接损失赔偿的条款，基于本案的事实，将多项因素结合起来看，该排除是不合理的。由于卖方的违约，买方实际上受到了间接损失，而此类间接损失在商业中是得到承认的。一方“应该有权认为，其可就此种损失获得赔偿，除非已被告知不存在此种赔偿”（S 诉 F 案）。考虑到本案合同签订时的商业现实，这个因素就更加重要。

As to the exclusion of consequential damages, several factors combine to suggest that the exclusion was unreasonable on the facts of this case. Consequential damages are a commercially recognized type of damage actually suffered by A & M due to FMC's breach. A party " ...should be able to rely on their existence in the absence of being informed to the contrary ..." . （Schroeder v. Fageol Motors, Inc.） This factor is particularly important given the commercial realities under which the contract was executed.

当本案卖方违反担保时，买方的间接损失不仅可以“合理预见”，而且非常显而易见。所有的当事方都知道，当西红柿开始成熟时，必须在相对较短的时间内全部进行采摘和包装（参见 S 诉 J 案；另见 W 诉 S 案）。

If the seller's warranty was breached, consequential damages were not merely "reasonably foreseeable" ; they were explicitly obvious. All parties were aware that once the tomatoes began to ripen, they all had to be harvested and packed within a relatively short period of time. （See Steele v. J.I. Case Company； see also Wille v. Southwestern Bell Telephone Company）

另一个因素也可以支持初审法院的认定。这个因素涉及损失是否可以避免的问题，并直接涉

Another factor supporting the trial court's determination involves the avoidability of the damages and relates directly to the allocation

及风险如何分配的问题，而风险分配是合同交易的基础。有一种观点认为，“转嫁风险的社会成本很高，因此，在没有适当理由的情况下，不应这样做。对于自由谈判后订立的合同，如果无视合同的约定来转嫁风险，就需要更好的理由”(S诉S案)。但是，如同我们前面说过的,在本案中，卖方是唯一可以合理避免损失的一方，因为如果设备本来无法达到买方所表述的需求，卖方可以选择不向买方出售该设备。“如果说，哪一类风险分配应该受到特别严格的审核，那么，也许就是那类只有一方可以避免却转嫁给另一方的风险。”(引用文章)

of risks which lies at the foundation of the contractual bargain. It has been suggested that "[r] isk shifting is socially expensive and should not be undertaken in the absence of a good reason. An even better reason is required when to so shift is contrary to a contract freely negotiated". (S. M. Wilson & Co. v. Smith Intern., Inc.) But as we noted previously, FMC was the only party reasonably able to prevent this loss by not selling A&M a machine inadequate to meet its expressed needs. "If there is a type of risk allocation that should be subjected to special scrutiny, it is probably the shifting to one party of a risk that only the other party can avoid." (Eddy, Cal.L.Rev.)

显失公平问题的总结 归纳而言，在对本案的全部情况进行综合分析后，包括合同订立时的商业环境，我们支持初审法院的认定，即卖方格式合同中排除担保和排除间接损失赔偿的条款属于显失公平,因此不可强制履行。在本案中，预制格式合同的条款没有谈判余地，且双方的议价能

In summary, our review of the totality of circumstances in this case, including the business environment within which the contract was executed, supports the trial court's determination that the disclaimer of warranties and the exclusion of consequential damages in FMC's form contract were unconscionable and therefore unenforceable. When nonnegotiable terms

力存在巨大差距。从社会和经济的角度，如果这种情况导致了不合理的商业风险分配，那么，法典第 2.302 条和第 2.719 条（3）款所规定的显失公平的原则就提供了相应法律依据，可以拒绝强制履行其所带来的不良后果。

on preprinted form agreements combine with disparate bargaining power, resulting in the allocation of commercial risks in a socially or economically unreasonable manner, the concept of unconscionability as codified in Uniform Commercial Code sections 2-302 and 2-719, subdivision （3）, furnishes legal justification for refusing enforcement of the offensive result.

利润损失的确定性问题 卖方辩称，即使排除间接损失赔偿的条款无效，初审法院有关损害赔偿的判决也应被推翻，因为该损失具有猜测性。加利福尼亚州民法典第 3301 条规定，“对于违反合同所造成的损失，如果不能明确界定损失的性质和来源，就无权取得损害赔偿”。该民法典的一般原则是，“如果业务尚不稳固的一家企业受到干扰而中断经营，则即使该企业在未受干扰时本来有可能获得利润，该企业也不能就未来利润取得损害赔偿，因为该利润带有不确定性、或然性或猜测性”（G 诉 G 案）。但是，卖方所引用的 G 诉 G 案还提供了该规则的例外，即“当

FMC claims that even if the disclaimer of consequential damages is invalid, the damage award should be set aside because it is speculative. Civil Code section 3301 provides that “[n] o damages can be recovered for a breach of contract which are not clearly ascertainable in both their nature and origin”. The general rule under this statute is that “... where the operation of an unestablished business is prevented or interrupted, damages for prospective profits that might otherwise have been made from its operation are not recoverable for the reason that their occurrence is uncertain, contingent and speculative”. （Grupe v. Glick） However, Grupe, which FMC cites, also stands for the exception to the rule：“[A] nticipated profits dependent upon future events are allowed where their nature

预期利润取决于未来事件时，如果可以证明该利润的性质和发生具有合理确定性，则可以就该利润取得赔偿”。

and occurrence can be shown by evidence of reasonable reliability.”

对于初审法院就利润损失而听取的证据，卖方在上诉中并未称该证据本身具有猜测性。该证据包括农作物的规模，以及买方所种植的西红柿品种的市场价格。虽然买方公司之前从未种植过西红柿，但买方总经理本身是经验丰富的种植主。此外，在收获季节当时，西红柿处于良好状态。没有证据显示，已经收获的西红柿在收获过程中受到了损害，也没有证据显示西红柿运输有可能成为问题。这些情况说明，应该适用上述一般原则的例外，且该情况足以支持初审法院有关间接损失赔偿的判决。维持原判。

FMC does not argue on appeal that the evidence the trial court heard on the issue was itself speculative. That evidence included size of the crop and market price of the type of tomato A&M grew. Although A&M had never grown tomatoes before, Abatti was an experienced farmer. Moreover, the crop itself was in good condition at harvest time. There was no evidence of crop damage from harvesting to those tomatoes actually picked, nor was there any evidence that transportation of the crop would have posed a problem. These circumstances make the exception to the rule applicable and provide ample support for the trial court's decision to allow the award of consequential damages. The judgment is affirmed.

案例9　买方是否对货物作出了正当和有效拒收?

Integrated Circuits Unlimited, Inc. v. E. F. Johnson Company
无限集成电路公司诉约翰逊公司案

纽约东区联邦地区法院 1988 年；691 F. Supp. 630

简　介

本案卖方（ICU）是电子部件制造商和经销商，买方（Johnson）是小型电子设备制造商，主要生产出租车使用的双向对讲机。为了组装对讲机，买方需要采购特定型号的微处理器。1984 年，由于微处理器供应短缺，买方无法从自己通常的供应商取得供货，因此转而与本案卖方订立了合同。合同涉及 3 份订单：（1）4746 号订单的 2500 个微处理器；（2）4747 号订单的 2500 个微处理器；（3）4750 号订单的 1100 个微处理器。1984 年 4 月 7 日，买方收到了 4750 号订单的全部 1100 个微处理器。至 4 月 13 日止，买方分批收到了 4746 号订单 1709 个微处理器，大约相当于该订单数量的 70%。两个订单所收到的微处理器共计 2809 个。

1984 年 4 月 24 日，买方致信卖方，拒收 4746 号订单的 130 个微处理器，理由是根据买方检验，产品质量有问题。信中说，买方的最低质量标准是，如果一批交货中瑕疵微处理器超过 1%，整批货物即不可接受。信中随附了一份实验室检验结果，其中显示130个微处理器中有6个不合格，占总数的4.6%。4月25日，买方就4750号订单发给卖方一封类似的信。信中说，所检验的115个微处理器中，113个都不合格。检测结果显示，对于113个不合格的部件，检测温度超过了商业标准的最高值，并高于买方自己的采购规格；但其中3个在标准温度环境下也不合格，不合格率为2.6%。所有的检测都是由外部的独立实验室进行的。5月8日，买方发给卖方一份清单，逐个列明了根据实验室检测结果而希望退货的1973个微处理器。这些部件并非每一个都单独测试过，而是由实验室进行了抽样检测。

在随后3个月里，买方反复给卖方写信和打电话，要求退还被拒收的微处理器。但卖方一直拒绝接受退货，同时继续要求买方支付剩余货款。5月21日，买方给卖方出具了一张支票，作为4月11日收到的一批829个微处理器的货款。买方于8月15日通知卖方，再次要求退回被拒收的部件，并随后自行将部件发运回卖方。卖方拒绝收取被运回的部件，因此货物又被退还给买方。卖方随后起诉买方，要求买方支付剩余货款。

法院审理后作出如下判定：(1)买方的拒收属于正当拒收，因此既无须支付价款，也不承担其他责任。合同本身没有对微处理器的瑕疵率作出规定，但在审阅了专家证言、行业出版物和其他证据后，法院认定瑕疵率不应超过1%，而卖方产品的瑕疵率已远高于此。(2)即使买方的拒收是错误拒收，但只要拒收是有效的，买方仍然没有义务支付价款，而只有义务支付损害赔偿。法院认为，买方遵守了法典规定的拒收程序，因此即使拒收本身没有合理理由，从程序上拒收也是有效的。因此无论如何，卖方无权提起价款诉讼。(3)即使买方的拒收属于错误拒收，因而买方有义务向卖方支付损害赔偿，在本案的事实背景下，卖方也不可能得到赔偿。根据法典规定，在买方错误拒收的情况下，卖方可就交付货物时的合同价格和市场价格的差额取得赔偿。在本案中，在交付货物时，市场价格高于合同价格。因此，按这种方法计算，卖方没有受到损失。(4)到本案诉讼时，虽然微处理器的市场价格已回落至低于合同价格，但这是卖方自己造成的，因为卖方未能及时接受退货，因而未能及时采取措施来减少自己的损失。

判　决

本院的结论　根据法典规定，买方有权拒收不符合合同的货物（法典第 2.601 条）。基于本案证据材料，本院起初认定，买方对 1973 个部件的拒收是错误的，因为在每份订单中，只有不到 5% 的微处理器通过检测被证实不符合合同。但是，在进一步分析相关证据后，本院最终认定，对于包含瑕疵部件的任何批次来说，该瑕疵均导致整个批次不符合合同。

A buyer is entitled under the U.C.C. to reject goods which fail to conform to the contract. U.C.C. § 2-601. The court concluded preliminarily on the trial record that Johnson's rejection of 1973 parts was wrongful because less than five percent of the microprocessors from each order, proportional to the percent which had proven defective during testing, were nonconforming. Upon further consideration of the relevant testimony, however, the court finds that the defects rendered the shipments which contained defective parts nonconforming in their entirety.

瑕疵率问题　本院起初所作认定的主要依据是，卖方在审理中提供专家证言说，在微处理器行业，电子器件可接受的瑕疵率为 5%。根据这个标准，如果拒收不超过 5% 瑕疵率的部件，就属于不合理拒收。

The court's preliminary finding was primarily based on the testimony at trial of ICU's expert witness that the acceptable defect rate for electronic parts in the microprocessor industry is five percent. Under this standard, rejection of the parts based on a defect rate of less than five percent would be unjustified.

卖方证词不可信　尽管本院

Although the court initially credited

最初认可了上述证词，但本院在案件档案中注明，该证人的证言与我们的直觉不符，且表述令人困惑。并且，该证言与业内出版物的表述相矛盾，也与卖方雇员的证言相矛盾。卖方雇员给法院的印象是，尽管他们对整体行业缺乏经验，但他们是合格且诚实的技术人员。基于卖方证人的资历、在法庭上的表现以及证词结论的后果，我们重新考虑了他的证词，并决定对该证词不予采纳。

货物瑕疵率过高 像买方这样的制造商，需要将很多部件组装在对讲机中。如果每个部件都有 5% 的概率存在瑕疵，买方就不可能生产出可靠的产品。例如，假设对讲机只有 5 个部件，且每个部件的瑕疵率是 5%，那么从概率上讲，在每 4 个对讲机中，就会有 1 个对讲机的至少 1 个部件存在瑕疵，因为单独的概率会叠加起来。买方在与卖方沟通中所主张的最低标准是 1%，但实际上，基于可信的证词和证物，该行业所要求的瑕疵率远低于 1%。

this testimony, it noted on the record that the witness's conclusion was counterintuitive and his presentation confusing. It was also contrary to industry publications and to the testimony of defendant's employees who impressed the court as sound and honest technicians even though they did not have industry-wide experience. Having reconsidered the testimony of plaintiff 's expert in light of the witness's qualifications, his demeanor on the stand, and the implications of his conclusions, we decline to credit it.

Manufacturers such as Johnson which incorporate many component parts into their radios could not produce a reliable product if each of those parts had a five percent chance of being defective. Even if a radio contained only five component parts, for example, a five percent failure rate for each part would result in a probability that one in four such radios had at least one inadequate component, since the independent probabilities would be multiplied. In fact, the credible testimony and exhibits suggest that the industry requires a failure rate much lower than one percent, the lowest standard claimed by Johnson in its correspondence.

检测条件问题　虽然买方在检验某些部件时，使用了稍高于商业标准所要求的承受温度，但这个事实不具有决定意义。无论在较高温度时发生了什么，检测显示，在约定的温度下，部件不能正常工作的比例仍然是不可接受的。

The fact that Johnson tested some of the parts at somewhat higher temperatures than they were required to withstand by commercial standards is not decisive. Regardless of what happened at the higher temperatures, the tests showed that an unacceptable percentage of the parts failed to perform adequately at the agreed-upon temperature.

检测样品的代表性　买方在决定拒收微处理器前，对足够数量的样品进行了检测。买方对 4746 号订单中被拒收的产品的 8%（1709 个中的 130 个）进行了检测，并对 4750 号订单中所有被拒收的产品进行了检测。关于前者，130 个被送至实验室检测的产品，与根据该检测而被拒收的其余产品是一样的。虽然样品并非按科学方法随机挑选，但挑选过程不存在偏见。在用于本商业案的货物拒收时，此种检验足以作为根据。

Johnson tested an adequate sample of the microprocessors before deciding to reject them. It tested eight percent （130 out of 1709） of the rejected WO4746 devices, and all of the rejected WO4750 devices. In the case of the former, the 130 devices which were sent to the laboratory were identical to the devices rejected based on the test results. While the sampling was not scientifically randomized, selection for testing was made without bias. It sufficed as a basis for commercial rejection in this case.

虽然买方没有将剩余的全部部件均送至实验室进行昂贵的检测，但买方得出的结论是合理的，即未经检验的部件也存在同样瑕疵［参见 U 诉 D 案（在该案中，

It was reasonable for Johnson to conclude that the remaining untested devices were similarly defective without sending all of them to the laboratory for expensive tests. See Union Paint & Varnish Co. v. Dean （in

当事方称一桶未开封的油漆存在瑕疵，并因此要求取得退款。法院认定，同一品牌且从同一销售员于5个月前购进的油漆曾对房屋屋顶造成损害，而该油漆可以作为证据，证明未开封的油漆是否存在瑕疵）；引用著作；引用另一本著作（对事实的认定，可以基于统计概率作出，只要统计的取样数量足够大，能够保证概率的准确）；引用另一本著作］。

an action for the price of an unopened drum of paint, evidence that paint of the same brand, bought from the same salesman five months earlier, had caused damage to a roof could be used to determine whether the unopened drum was also defective). See also James, Relevancy, Probability and the Law; Cohen, Conceptualizing Proof and Calculating Probabilities: A Response to Professor Kaye (factual determinations can be premised on statistical probability if the statistical sample is large enough to ensure probability of accuracy); Kaye, Apples and Oranges: Confidence Coefficients and the Burden of Persuasion.

两位教授的上述著作虽然在某些具体方面存在分歧，但将他们的著作与另一位教授的著作加起来看，足以支持这个结论，即本案中的统计概率已经足够高且足够可靠，可以作为买方拒收这些部件的合理理由。

The work of professors Kaye and Cohen, while disagreeing in some particulars, along with that of James, support the conclusion that the statistical probabilities here were high enough and sufficiently reliable to warrant rejection by a manufacturer of these electronic devices.

错误拒收亦可构成有效拒收

基于买方拒收情况的不同，卖方的救济也不同。如果买方拒收时未能遵守适当程序，则拒收“无效”。如果买方缺乏合理的拒收

The seller's remedies for a rejection of goods which is "ineffective" because the buyer failed to follow proper procedures are distinct from the remedies for a rejection which is "wrongful" because it was

理由，则拒收“错误”。在本案中，如果买方是错误拒收，但属于有效拒收，卖方就无权提起货物的价款诉讼。

unjustified. If Johnson’s rejection had been wrongful but nevertheless effective, ICU would not be entitled to maintain an action for the price.

法典对价款诉讼的要求　根据法典第 2.709 条的规定，只有货物已被买方“接受”（或货物发生丢失或损坏，或无法转售，但本案不存在这些情况），卖方才可提起价款诉讼。第 2.606 条则将“接受”定义为“未能作出有效拒收”。该款通过交叉索引又关联至第 2.602 条（1）款，即拒收必须在“交付或提示交付后的合理时间内作出”，且“除非买方及时通知卖方，否则拒收无效”。因此，对于第 2.602 条（1）款所述的因程序瑕疵而无效的拒收，卖方的救济是价款诉讼。

Section 2-709 allows an action for the price only if the goods have been “accepted” （or are lost, damaged, or non-resalable, none of which are true in this case）. Section 2-606, in turn, defines acceptance as “failure to make an effective rejection”. It is cross-referenced to § 2-602（1）, which provides that a rejection of goods must be made “within a reasonable time after their delivery or tender”, and is “ineffective unless the buyer seasonably notifies the seller”. Thus, the remedy for an ineffective rejection which is procedurally defective under § 2-602（1）is an action for the price.

错误拒收的效力　相比而言，错误拒收仍然有可能构成有效拒收，因此本身不使卖方有权取得价款。由于无效拒收构成对货物的接受，其反面含义就是，只要拒收是有效的，则无论是否存在合理理由，该拒收都意味着买方不可能再接受货物，因

By contrast, a wrongful rejection may still be an effective rejection, and does not in itself entitle the seller to the price. Since an ineffective rejection constitutes an acceptance, by negative inference any effective rejection whether or not it is justified bars acceptance and protects the buyer from § 2-709 damages.

此也没有义务根据第2.709条支付价款。

法典第2.606条规定，接受货物就意味着拒收无效。第2.602条(3)款虽然没有通过交叉索引关联到第2.606条，但另外提到了“错误”拒收。该款规定，错误拒收的救济，包含在标题为“卖方救济的一般规定”的第2.703条中。

Subsection (3) of § 2-602, which is not cross-referenced to the § 2-606 definition of acceptance as ineffective rejection, makes separate mention of goods "wrongfully" rejected. It provides that the remedies in cases of wrongful rejection are contained in § 2-703, entitled "Seller's Remedies in General".

错误拒收时的损害赔偿计算

法典第2.703条(e)款规定，当货物被错误拒收时，损害赔偿数额为合同价格与市场价格(第2.708条)的差额，或“在适当情况下”为第2.709条规定的“价款”。因此，如果货物被错误拒收，只有当价款可以“适当”地作为损害赔偿救济时，卖方才有权根据第2.709条取得价款。而“适当”情况，就是指拒收因程序瑕疵而无效。

Subsection (e) of § 2-703 states that the measure of damages for goods wrongfully rejected is the difference between the contract price and the market price (§ 2-708), or "in a proper case the price" under § 2-709. Thus, a seller whose goods have been wrongfully rejected will be entitled to the price only if that measure of damages is "proper" under § 2-709 because the rejection was also procedurally ineffective.

上述解释可以得到法典相关评论和相关判例的支持。法典第2.602条规定了有效拒收的程序，而其正式评论说，本条(3)款对错误拒收的规定，只是为了强

This interpretation is supported by both the U.C.C. commentaries and by the authorities. The official commentary to § 2-602, the section setting forth procedures for an effective rejection, states that Subsection

调两套规则的“截然不同”。一套规则涉及合法有效的拒收，另一套规则涉及“构成违约的不接受”，即程序上有效但属于错误拒收的拒收（不接受）。

（3） on wrongful rejections was included only to emphasize the “sharp distinction” between the rules governing procedures for making an effective rightful rejection and those governing “non-acceptance which is a breach” i.e., procedurally effective rejection （non-acceptance） which is wrongful.

怀特教授和萨莫斯教授在他们的著作中对该问题作出如下分析：“所有评论家都同意，法典起草者已经考虑到，有效的拒收有可能在本质上是错误的，因此起草者的意图是，即使拒收在本质上是错误的，此种拒收仍然排除了买方对货物的接受。”霍纳德教授代表纽约法律修订委员会写道：“买方的拒收即使属于违约，并使买方必须承担支付赔偿的责任，买方可能仍有权力作出‘有效’的拒收。”

Professors White and Summers, in their treatise on the U.C.C., analyze the issue as follows：“All commentators agree that the Code drafters contemplated effective rejections which might be substantively wrongful and intended that all such rejections forestall acceptance without regard to their substantive wrongfulness.” Writing for the New York Law Revision Commission, Professor Honnold stated： “buyer may have the power to make an ‘effective’ rejection even though his action is in breach of contract and subjects buyer to liability for damages.”

区别两种拒收的判断标准

因此，关键在于区别“错误”拒收和“无效”拒收。当我们使用“拒收”这个词时，如果拒收了符合合同的提示交付，就属于错误拒收。我们相信，法典起草者也认为该词是这个意思。但无论

It is important to distinguish between “wrongful” rejections and “ineffective” rejections. As we use the term （and as we believe the drafters intended the term to be used）, a rejection of a conforming tender would be a wrongful rejection. Nevertheless if timely notice was sent and if the buyer

如何,只要买方及时发出了通知,且遵守了第 2.602 条规定的拒收后的义务和其他随后义务,则即使该拒收是“错误”的,亦属“有效”。因此,买方不被视为已接受了货物,且买方也没有义务根据第 2.709 条(1)(a)款支付价款(引用著作)。

lived up to his post rejection obligations under section 2-602 and those following, the rejection though "wrongful" would be "effective" and would so preclude his acceptance of the goods and foreclose a consequent liability for the price under 2-709(1)(a). J. White & R. Summers, Uniform Commercial Code.

一家法院曾在判决中特别指出:“初审法院在审理中的这个表述是错误的,即‘错误的拒收将构成对货物的接受’。法典在其他条款中规定了错误拒收的救济,且法典不将错误拒收视为对货物的接受。无效的拒收才有可能构成接受。”(B 诉 N 案)。

One court has specifically held: "The trial court's statement during trial that 'a wrongful rejection ... would constitute an acceptance' is not correct. The remedies for wrongful rejection are separately set out and do not include treating that action as an acceptance. An ineffective rejection may be an acceptance." Blue Sky Forest Products, Inc. v. New Hampshire Doors Co.

买方的拒收是有效的 在本案中,买方对微处理器的拒收是有效的。该拒收符合法典第 2.602 条的要求,即拒收必须在交付或提示交付后的合理时间内作出,且买方必须及时通知卖方。

Johnson's rejection of the microprocessors was effective. It met the requirement in § 2-602 that a rejection be made within a reasonable time after delivery or tender, and that the buyer seasonably notify the seller.

检测时间问题 必须要为测试复杂电子部件留出时间。在本案中,买方所聘请的独立实验室进行了快速和充分的检测。当测

Time to test complex electronic parts must be afforded. Here testing by the independent laboratory retained by Johnson was prompt and thorough. Immediately after

试结果显示微处理器瑕疵率过高后，买方马上就将该结果以及拒收该部件的意图通知给卖方。一个多星期后，对于被拒收的部件，买方向卖方发送了一份逐件列明的清单。买方5月8日的信件满足了第2.605条的要求，即买方必须以足够详细的程度说明瑕疵的性质，使卖方能够进行补救。

learning that the test results had revealed excessive flaws in the microprocessors, Johnson notified ICU of these results and of its intent to reject the parts. Less than two weeks later, it sent ICU an itemized list of parts being rejected. Its letter of May 8 satisfied the requirement of § 2-605 that the buyer set forth the nature of the defect with sufficient particularity to allow the seller to cure it.

检测期间的占有和使用问题

虽然买方对微处理器保持了暂时的实际占有，甚至在拒收前使用了其中的一部分，但这个事实不说明买方已接受货物。这些行为是在完成检测所需的期间内发生的。法典第2.606条规定，在买方已有“合理机会检验货物”之前，不存在对货物的接受［参见B诉U案（本案中为了检验货物，需要较长时间和特定条件，因此，对货物的使用是否构成对货物的接受，属于事实问题）；参见S诉E案（在检验货物后仍然使用货物，构成法典所规定的对货物的接受）］。

The fact that Johnson took temporary physical possession of the microprocessors and even used some of them before rejecting them does not mean that it accepted them. Those actions were taken during the time required to complete the tests. Section 2-606 provides that acceptance of goods does not occur until the buyer has had a “reasonable opportunity to inspect them”. See Barrett Paving Materials, Inc. v. United States Fidelity and Guaranty Company （whether use of product constituted acceptance was a question of fact because of the substantial time and special conditions needed to test it）. Cf. Shokai Far East Ltd. v. Energy Conservation Systems, Inc. （use of goods subsequent to testing them constituted acceptance under the U.C.C.）.

支付货款的问题 此外，虽然买方在拒收微处理器之后仍然支付了货款，但这同样不说明买方放弃了任何权利。该付款代表了买方友好解决争议的努力［参见B诉U案（对于货物是否已被接受，支付货款本身不具有决定意义）］。

Nor did Johnson waive any rights by paying for the microprocessors after it had rejected them. The payments represented an effort on the part of Johnson to resolve the dispute amicably. See Barrett Paving Materials, Inc. v. United States Fidelity and Guaranty Company （payment for goods is not dispositive of whether they were accepted）.

因此，即使买方对微处理器的拒收在本质上是错误的，卖方也无权提起价款诉讼。确定损害赔偿数额的合理标准，应为合同价格与交付货物时的市场价格的差额，再加上附带损失（法典第2.708条）。

Thus, even if Johnson's rejection of the microprocessors were substantively wrongful, ICU would not be entitled to maintain an action for the price. The proper measure of damages would be the difference between the contract price and market price at the time of delivery plus incidental damages. U.C.C. § 2-708.

卖方不可能取得损害赔偿 根据上述计算方法，卖方无法获得损害赔偿。在交付当时，相关微处理器的市场价格上升，因为对该产品的需求超过了供给。买方所支付的价格，是之前的通行市场价格。卖方辩称，虽然证人作证说，30美元是“标准成本”，但实际意思是说，30美元是市场价格。卖方的这种辩称不能成

ICU would receive no damages under this measure. At the time of delivery, the market price of the microprocessors in question was inflated because demand for them had outstripped supply. The price paid by Johnson was the then current market price. There is no merit to ICU's argument that the witness who testified that $30 was the “standard cost” actually meant that $30 was the market price. If the parts were available on

立。如果当时可以用该价格在市场上买到相关部件，买方本来就不会花费大约 3 倍的价格从不熟悉的供应商购买。对于本案中那些无瑕疵的部件，卖方本来可以在市场上售出，价格与买方支付的价格相同。

the market for that price, Johnson would not have had to pay nearly three times that much to an unfamiliar supplier. ICU could have sold those units which were not defective for the same price it was charging Johnson.

买方拒收后的行为是适当的　法典第 2.602 条要求，买方必须以合理谨慎的方式持有被拒收的货物，并服从卖方对货物的处置，直至卖方有足够时间将货物取走。买方履行了该义务。买方将微处理器在仓库中存放了 3 个月。在该期间，货物保持了良好状态，没有因为检测或搁置而出现物理损伤。在这几个月中，买方一直请卖方允许将货物运回给卖方，但没有得到卖方同意。当买方试图在未获得授权的情况下运回货物时，卖方又将货物退回。因此，虽然货物价格从 1984 年 9 月开始下降，但对于此种随后的价格波动给卖方带来的损失，买方不承担责任。

Section 2-602 requires that a buyer hold rejected goods with reasonable care at the seller's disposition for a time sufficient to permit the seller to remove them. Johnson fulfilled this duty. It held the microprocessors in storage for three months, during which time they remained in good condition, without physical deterioration as a result of the testing or the passage of shelf time. Throughout those months it unsuccessfully sought authorization from ICU for return of the microprocessors. When it attempted to ship them back without such authorization, ICU sent them back. Thus, although the market price of the parts began to fall in September of 1984, Johnson is not liable to ICU for any damages incurred as a result of that subsequent price fluctuation.

买方没有义务出售被拒收的货物　买方没有义务根据第

Johnson was not required under § 2-603 to resell the rejected parts. Since Johnson

2.603条转售被拒收的货物。买方在向卖方发出拒收通知后，没有从卖方获得处置货物的指示，因此，买方没有义务采取任何进一步的行动。该部件不属于“易腐”物品，且在争议发生的当时，不存在“价值迅速降低的危险”。卖方是微处理器经销商，因此本来远比买方可以更方便地将其转售。买方是制造商和组装商，接触不到卖方所拥有的该部件的市场。

买方试图退回部件的行为是及时的。假如卖方当时就接受退货并将其转售，卖方本来不会受到任何损失。卖方不合理地拒绝降低损失，对此，买方不应承担责任。判决卖方向买方支付4638.73美元，并从1984年8月15日支付利息。

received no instructions from ICU with respect to disposition of the parts after it gave notice of rejection, it was not required to take any further action. The parts were not “perishable” and did not, when the dispute arose, “threaten to decline in value speedily” . ICU is a dealer in microprocessors and would have been able to sell them far more readily than Johnson. Johnson is a manufacturer and assembler; it had no ready access to the seller’s market for these components.

Had ICU accepted Johnson’s timely attempts to return the parts and resold them, it would not have suffered any loss. Johnson cannot now be held responsible for ICU’s unjustified refusal to mitigate damages. Johnson is ordered to pay ICU the sum of $4,638.73, with interest from August 15, 1984.

案例 10　如何解读有关合同修改和弃权的法典第 2.209 条?

Wisconsin Knife Works v. National Metal Crafters
威斯康星刀具公司诉国民金属工艺公司案

联邦第七巡回上诉法院 1986 年；781 F.2d 1280, 42 UCC Rep.Serv. 83

简　介

本案买方（Wisconsin Knife Works）是金属工具配件的制造商，从卖方（National Metal Crafters）订购了一批刀头工具钢，目的是用该工具钢生产刀头，然后向自己的客户（Black & Decker）出售。双方共签订了 6 份订单，所有订单的格式和内容都一样。订单由买方发出。对于买方发出的前两份订单，卖方通过信件作出了确认。在买方发出的订单中，交货日期一栏是空白的。卖方的确认书列出了交货日期。买方收到卖方的确认书后，在自己保存的订单上填上了卖方确认书中提供的交货日期。对于买方发出的后 4 份订单，卖方没有再发出确认书，而是在收到订单后向买方口头告知了交货日期。买方将该日期填入了自己保存的订单。

根据卖方提供并被买方填入订单的交货日期，卖方本应于 1981 年 10 月和 11 月交货，但实际未能交货。但买方没有指责卖方违约，也没有取消合同或对卖方提出索赔。1982 年 7 月 1 日，买方又发出一份订单，但随后因某些原因取消，所以订单仍为6份。直到超过约定的交货日期1年多之后，即直到1982年12月，卖方才基本完成了刀头工具钢的生产。但是，买方于1983年1月13日通知卖方取消合同。6份订单的工具钢总数为281,000件。到1月13日为止，卖方已实际交付144,000件。买方随后起诉卖方违约，称卖方延迟1年多才交货，违反了合同的交货条款。卖方答辩说，当事方并未将订单中的交货日期作为确定的交货日期，且买方实际上随后也同意了推迟交货日期。

本案争议的主要问题是，双方是否已修改了合同原来约定的交货日期？买方订单中的一项条款规定，对合同的任何修改都必须使用书面文件，且该书面文件必须由买方签名。本案的实际情况是，不存在经过买方签名的书面修改文件。在初审中，初审法官认为，修改合同并非必须使用书面形式，而是也可以采用口头形式或行为形式等，并将合同是否已被修改作为一个事实问题提交陪审团裁定。陪审团裁定，基于买卖双方的交往情况，合同原始交货日期已通过当事方的行为被修改，因此卖方的交货虽然晚于原始交货日期，但符合修改后的日期，不存在违约。买方随后提起上诉。

本案的判决书由著名的波斯纳（Richard A. Posner）法官撰写。他认为，本案的主要问题是如何解释法典第2.209条。他通过大量论述说明了自己的困惑、观点和理解。他认为，合同中包含了仅允许书面修改的条款，而该条款的效力应该得到承认。初审法官给陪审团的指示存在明显错误，因为该指示允许陪审团裁定，合同是否已通过其他形式被修改。但他同时认为，虽然初审法官无视合同条款的做法是错误的，且该法官在指示中使用的"修改"一词也是错误的，但从指示的内容看，也许该法官实际上不是指"修改"（modification），而是指"弃权"（waiver）。根据法典第2.209条，弃权并非必须采用书面形式。为此，波斯纳法官需要对法典该条中的"弃权"概念作出适当分析和解释。

法典第2.209条的规定如下："（1）修改本篇项下合同的协议，即使不存在对价，亦可具有约束力。（2）如果已签署的协议规定，必须签署书面文件才能修改或解除该协议，则该协议不得用其他方法修改或取消；但除在商人之间外，如果此种规定载于商人一方提供的表格上，另一方必须在此规定处另加签名。(3)如果修改后的合同属于本篇反欺诈条款(第 2.201 条)范围内的合同，则必须遵守该条的规定。(4)意图作出修改或取消的行为，即使不满足(2)款或(3)款的要求，仍可构成弃权。(5)一方作出影响合同待履行部分的弃权后，可以撤回弃权，但应使另一方收到合理通知，说明另一方应严格履行弃权所涉及的条款。但是，如果另一方依赖该弃权已严重改变了处境，致使该撤回导致不公平，则不得撤回。"

波斯纳法官经过分析后认为，上述第 2.209 条(4)款中的"弃权"，应该也包含了"依赖"(reliance)的因素。在本案中，如果买方对原始交货日期已经弃权，且卖方依赖了该弃权，那么卖方就不存在违约。在这种情况下，虽然初审法官给陪审团的指示是错的，但最终的结果是一样的，即卖方获得胜诉。从程序法的角度，如果法官给陪审团的指示存在错误，就必须重审，除非该错误无害。波斯纳法官认为，自己不想说该指示无害，但确有可能无害，因为上述"弃权"和"依赖"有可能导致卖方最终胜诉。有可能导致卖方最终胜诉的另一个理由是，卖方的延迟交货与买方的损失不存在因果关系，因此，虽然卖方违约，但无须实际作出赔偿。但无论如何，这需要由初审法院重审后作出认定。据此，上诉法院推翻了初审法院的原判。

波斯纳法官代表多数派作出的判决，引起了该院另一位著名法官伊斯特布鲁克(Frank H. Easterbrook)的强烈反对。后者为此撰写了长篇异议意见。伊斯特布鲁克曾经是波斯纳的学生，比波斯纳稍晚几年成为第七巡回上诉法院的法官，后担任首席法官。在此案中，伊斯特布鲁克法官认为，波斯纳法官对第 2.209 条的解释是错误的，因为波斯纳法官认为"弃权"的概念包含了"依赖"的因素。伊斯特布鲁克法官认为，第 2.209 条相关条款并没提到"依赖"的概念，也根本没有必要引入该概念。也就是说，即使不存在依赖，仍然可以认定弃权有效。在本案中，买方确有弃权行为，因此应该维持原判。虽然初审法官给陪审团的指示是错误的，但该错误无害，不构成推翻原判的理由。

判 决

合同中仅允许书面修改的条款 我们现在讨论本次上诉的实质问题。经过一番谈判，买方向卖方发出了一系列采购订单。每份采购订单背面都写着：“接受本订单后，无论以确认书还是以履约接受，该接受均构成对下列内容的无条件同意。”这些内容包括“采购条件”清单，其中第一项是：“对本合同的任何修改都必须采用书面形式，并经买方授权代表签名，否则该修改对买方没有约束力。买方有权向卖方发出书面通知而修改订单。”

We come, then, to the merits of the appeal. After some negotiating, Wisconsin Knife Works sent National Metal Crafters a series of purchase orders on the back of each of which was printed, “Acceptance of this Order, either by acknowledgment or performance, constitutes an unqualified agreement to the following”. A list of “Conditions of Purchase” follows, of which the first is, “No modification of this contract, shall be binding upon Buyer [Wisconsin Knife Works] unless made in writing and signed by Buyer’s authorized representative. Buyer shall have the right to make changes in the Order by a notice, in writing, to Seller.”

初审法院的判决 初审法官认定合同已经成立，但将其余问题留给陪审团裁定，即合同是否已被修改，以及如果已被修改，卖方是否违反了修改后的合同。陪审团裁定，合同已被修改，且卖方没有违反修改后的合同。初审法官据此作出判决，驳回买方的起诉。买方因此提起上诉。

The judge ruled that there had been a contract but left to the jury to decide whether the contract had been modified and, if so, whether the modified contract had been broken. The jury found that the contract had been modified and not broken. Judgment was entered dismissing Wisconsin Knife Works’ suit. Wisconsin Knife Works has appealed from the dismissal of its suit.

上诉的主要问题　上诉的主要问题，是采购订单相关条款的效力问题。该条款规定，合同的修改必须以书面形式作出，且必须经买方授权代表签名，否则对买方没有约束力。初审法官把合同修改问题提交给陪审团裁定的理由是，合同修改可以采用口头或行为形式，也可以采用签署书面文件的形式。卖方之前提供证据说，买方已接受了延迟交付的刀头工具钢，且买方并非因延迟交付而取消合同，而是因为无法以其客户能接受的价格生产刀头。

The principal issue is the effect of the provision in the purchase orders that forbids the contract to be modified other than by a writing signed by an authorized representative of the buyer. The theory on which the judge sent the issue of modification to the jury was that the contract could be modified orally or by conduct as well as by a signed writing. National Metal Crafters had presented evidence that Wisconsin Knife Works had accepted late delivery of the spade bit blanks and had cancelled the contract not because of the delays in delivery but because it could not produce spade bits at a price acceptable to Black & Decker.

法典第 2.209 条（2）款的规定　法典第 2.209 条（2）款规定，“如果已签署的协议规定，必须签署书面文件才能修改或取消该协议，则该协议不得用其他方法修改或取消；但除在商人之间外，如果此种规定载于商人一方提供的表格上，另一方必须在此规定处另加签名”。这项规定的含义和例外，并非水晶般清澈，且几乎没有相关判例。人们也许会认为，如果协议规定只能通过签名

Section 2-209（2） of the Uniform Commercial Code provides that “a signed agreement which excludes modification or rescission except by a signed writing cannot be otherwise modified or rescinded, but except as between merchants such a requirement on a form supplied by the merchant must be separately signed by the other party”. The meaning of this provision and its proviso is not crystalline and there is little pertinent case law. One might think that an agreement to exclude modification except by a signed

的书面文件来修改，那么在任何情况下，被强制履行该条款的一方都必须签名（本案卖方），而不是由寻求强制履行该条款的一方签名。

上述（2）款的模糊之处不影响本案 但如果真是这样，那么，例外条款（“除在商人之间外……”)的效力就变得模糊了，因为该条款设想，在商人之间，被要求遵守该条款的当事方并不需要另加签名。对此，存在一个可能的折中解释，尽管我们并不需要采纳该解释来判决本案。根据该解释，法典的要求是，对于禁止口头修改的条款，以及包含该条款的合同本身，都必须另加签名或首字母签。本案不存在此种签名，但这无关紧要，因为本案合同是“商人之间”的合同。制造商在日常用语中不属于商人，但在法典中，“商人之间”具有专门含义，是指双方都富有商业经验［法典第2.104条（1）款；引用著作］。本案当事方就是这种情况。

本案存在卖方签名的书面文

writing must be signed in any event by the party against whom the requirement is sought to be enforced, that is, by National Metal Crafters, rather than by the party imposing the requirement.

But if so the force of the proviso （“but except as between merchants ...”） becomes unclear, for it contemplates that between merchants no separate signature by the party sought to be bound by the requirement is necessary. A possible reconciliation, though not one we need embrace in order to decide this case, is to read the statute to require a separate signing or initialing of the clause forbidding oral modifications, as well as of the contract in which the clause appears. There was no such signature here; but it doesn't matter; this was a contract “between merchants”. Although in ordinary language a manufacturer is not a merchant, “between merchants” is a term of art in the Uniform Commercial Code. It means between commercially sophisticated parties （see UCC Sec. 2-104（1）; White & Summers, Handbook of the Law Under the Uniform Commercial Code）, which these were.

Of course there must still be a “signed

件　当然，仍然必须有一项“已签署的协议”，且该协议包含一项条款，禁止用书面以外其他形式修改协议。但是，本案已有此种协议［参见法典第 1.201 条（3）款和（39）款对“协议”和“签名”的定义］。对于前两份采购订单,卖方发出过签名的确认书。这表明卖方同意了买方订单中印制的合同条件，并且很自然、合理地使买方相信,卖方的意思是,如果随后的订单中包含同样的条件，那么只要卖方接受了订单，就表示同意了该条件。这些随后的订单确实被接受了，因此构成了与之前订单条件相同的新合同。随后的订单是以履约方式被接受的，因为卖方已开始制造订单中的刀头工具钢［第 2.207 条（3）款］。因此，所有的订单都存在经卖方签名的协议。当卖方收到订单时，订单中尚缺少交货日期，但卖方对此无可抱怨，因为这相当于给予卖方完全的自由，可以随意填写交货日期。

货物规格的修改和项目进度表　当卖方在制造中遇到困难，

agreement” containing the clause forbidding modification other than by a signed writing, but there was that（see definition of “agreement” and of “signed” in UCC Secs. 1-201（3），（39））. National Metal Crafters’ signed acknowledgments of the first two purchase orders signified its assent to the printed conditions and naturally and reasonably led Wisconsin Knife Works to believe that National Metal Crafters meant also to assent to the same conditions should they appear in any subsequent purchase orders that it accepted. Those subsequent orders were accepted, forming new contracts on the same conditions as the old, by performance--that is, by National Metal Crafters’ beginning the manufacture of the spade bit blanks called for by the orders. See UCC Sec. 2-207（3）. So there was an agreement, signed by National Metal Crafters, covering all the purchase orders. The fact that the delivery dates were not on the purchase orders when received by National Metal Crafters is nothing of which it may complain； it was given carte blanche to set those dates.

When National Metal Crafters had difficulty complying with the original

无法满足原来规定的刀头工具钢规格时，买方修改了规格。卖方声称，包含了这些修改的工程图纸，属于法典第 2.209 条（2）款（如果该款适用）所说的书面修改。但实际上，这些特定修改，似乎属于合同条款中允许买方以通知方式作出的有关规格问题的修改。该项合同条款的上下文清楚地显示，此种通知不属于合同前一句所指的书面修改。但是，无论如何，对于交货日期，从未作出过修改。卖方提供给买方的“项目进度表”虽然标示了力争实现的新交货日期，但并未试图修改合同，且没有经过买方签名。

specifications for the spade bit blanks, Wisconsin Knife Works modified them; and National Metal Crafters argues that the engineering drawings containing those modifications are the written modification that section 2-209（2）, if applicable, calls for. In fact these particular modifications seem to fall within the clause of the contract that allows the buyer （Wisconsin Knife Works） to modify the specifications by notice. The context of this clause makes clear that such notice is not the written modification to which the previous sentence refers. But in any event there was no modification of the delivery dates. The “pert charts” which National Metal Crafters supplied Wisconsin Knife Works, and which showed new target dates for delivery, do not purport to modify the contract and were not signed by Wisconsin Knife Works.

对陪审团的指示存在错误但可能无害 我们的结论是，禁止用书面以外其他形式修改合同的条款，是有效和适用的，因此本来不应允许陪审团来裁定合同是否已通过其他形式被修改。但初审法官的这个错误可能是无害

We conclude that the clause forbidding modifications other than in writing was valid and applicable and that the jury should not have been allowed to consider whether the contract had been modified in some other way. This may, however, have been a harmless error. Section 2-209（4） of the Uniform

的。法典第 2.209 条（4）款规定，“试图作出的修改”，如果不满足合同规定的书面修改要求，仍“可以构成弃权”。初审法官在对陪审团就修改问题作出指示时，虽没有使用“弃权”这个词，但他的指示也许本质上就是指弃权，且陪审团也许本来裁定的就是“弃权”，而只是将其称为“修改”。

初审法官给陪审团的指示

初审法官的相关指示如下：“当事方是否修改了合同？对于这个问题，卖方应承担举证责任。只有在你们有合理把握确信当事方已经修改了合同，你们才可以对这个问题作出肯定回答。如果你们认定，卖方的履约方式未能严格符合合同的义务，但买方以行为或其他表达方式诱使卖方合理地相信，买方不坚持要求卖方严格履行合同，且修改后的履约令人满意，可以作为等同于原始履约的替代履约被接受，那么，你们就可以得出结论说，当事方已经同意修改原始合同的条款，且当事方已经同意，替代的履约方

Commercial Code provides that an “attempt at modification” which does not satisfy a contractual requirement that modifications be in writing nevertheless “can operate as a waiver”. Although in instructing the jury on modification the judge did not use the word “waiver”, maybe he gave the substance of a waiver instruction and maybe therefore the jury found waiver but called it modification.

Here is the relevant instruction: “Did the parties modify the contract? The defendant bears the burden of proof on this one. You shall answer this question yes only if you are convinced to a reasonable certainty that the parties modified the contract. If you determine that the defendant had performed in a manner different from the strict obligations imposed on it by the contract, and the plaintiff by conduct or other means of expression induced a reasonable belief by the defendant that strict enforcement was not insisted upon, but that the modified performance was satisfactory and acceptable as equivalent, then you may conclude that the parties have assented to a modification of the original terms of the contract and that the parties have agreed that the different mode of performance will satisfy

式可以满足合同加赋给当事方的义务。”

合同法的目的是保护交易

为了确定上述指示是否本质上构成有关弃权问题的指示，我们必须考虑法典有关合同修改和弃权问题的第2.209条的背景。合同当事方的履约通常不是同步进行，因此，合同的一方可能会发现，如果合同法不保护自己，自己就只能依赖另一方的仁慈。实际上，合同法最重要的作用，就是帮助当事方完成非同步发生的履约交换。其帮助方式是，对于因履约时间差引起的脆弱之处，合同法保护一方不会让另一方占便宜。如果甲约定为乙建造一栋高度个性化的小亭子，且完工后付款，那么，如果完工后乙拒绝付款，则除非甲有权就货款起诉乙，否则甲的处境就会非常尴尬，因为小亭子的转售价值可能大大低于甲的成本。即使甲有权就乙的违约起诉，这对甲也不完全构成充分救济，因为诉讼的成本很高。此时，乙也许会对甲说，“如果你不降价，我就拒绝付款，并

the obligations imposed on the parties by the contract.”

To determine whether this was in substance an instruction on waiver we shall have to consider the background of section 2-209, the Code provision on modification and waiver. Because the performance of the parties to a contract is typically not simultaneous, one party may find himself at the mercy of the other unless the law of contracts protects him. Indeed, the most important thing which that law does is to facilitate exchanges that are not simultaneous by preventing either party from taking advantage of the vulnerabilities to which sequential performance may give rise. If A contracts to build a highly idiosyncratic gazebo for B, payment due on completion, and when A completes the gazebo B refuses to pay, A may be in a bind--since the resale value of the gazebo may be much less than A’s cost--except for his right to sue B for the price. Even then, a right to sue for breach of contract, being costly to enforce, is not a completely adequate remedy. B might therefore go to A and say, “If you don’t reduce your price I’ll refuse to pay and put you to the expense of suit”; and A might

让你承担诉讼成本”，而甲也许会屈服。如果允许对合同进行此类修改，类似乙这样的人就会很难再订立合同，同时每个人都会受损。

knuckle under. If such modifications are allowed, people in B's position will find it harder to make such contracts in the future, and everyone will be worse off.

普通法对价原则的缺陷　在普通法中，对应上述问题的方法是，如果修改没有新对价的支持，法律就不予承认（参见 S 诉 B 案中对 A 诉 D 案的讨论）。因此，在上述假想案件中，即使甲同意降价，乙也无法强制履行该降价许诺。但这种解决方法，一方面保护过度，另一方面又保护不足。说其过度，是因为大多数修改都不是强迫性的，因此无论是否存在新对价，都应该能够强制履行。说其不足，是因为在普通法中，法院仅考虑是否存在对价，而不考虑对价是否充分。因此，所谓的新对价只是没牙的老虎。在上述例子中，乙可以给甲一粒胡椒、一只小猫或一件浴衣，用来换取甲对降低合同价格的同意。此时，合同修改就可以强制履行，而甲就无法再起诉要求获得原始价款（引用著作）。

The common law dealt with this problem by refusing to enforce modifications unsupported by fresh consideration. See, e.g., Alaska Packers' Ass'n v. Domenico, discussed in Selmer Co. v. Blakeslee-Midwest Co. Thus in the hypothetical case just put B could not have enforced A's promise to accept a lower price. But this solution is at once overinclusive and underinclusive--the former because most modifications are not coercive and should be enforceable whether or not there is fresh consideration, the latter because, since common law courts inquire only into the existence and not the adequacy of consideration, a requirement of fresh consideration has little bite. B might give A a peppercorn, a kitten, or a robe in exchange for A's agreeing to reduce the contract price, and then the modification would be enforceable and A could no longer sue for the original price. See White & Summers; Farnsworth, Contracts.

法典的合同修改原则 对于这个问题，法典起草者采取了全新的方法。法典规定，没有对价支持的修改，也可以强制履行［参见第2.209条（1）款］，同时，依据有关胁迫或恶意的法律原则，来防止具有剥削性质或投机性质的修改企图，如上述例子中的这类企图（参见第2.209条正式评论2）。但是，法典起草者还完成了另外一项工作，即根据法典第2.209条（2）款，当事方可以禁止口头修改。本案卖方辩称，法典该条在相隔两款之后又收回了该禁止，因为其允许非书面修改具有弃权的效力。

The draftsmen of the Uniform Commercial Code took a fresh approach, by making modifications enforceable even if not supported by consideration (see section 2-209 (1)) and looking to the doctrines of duress and bad faith for the main protection against exploitive or opportunistic attempts at modification, as in our hypothetical case. See UCC Sec. 2-209, official comment 2. But they did another thing as well. In section 2-209 (2) they allowed the parties to exclude oral modifications. National Metal Crafters argues that two subsections later they took back this grant of power by allowing an unwritten modification to operate as a waiver.

仅允许书面修改的条款不被普通法承认 第2.209条（2）款允许强制履行的那类协议，在普通法中不允许强制履行。普通法的“理由”是，当事方在任何情况下都有权以口头形式取消他们之间的合同，而如果他们口头取消了合同，那么，禁止非书面修改的条款也将随着合同的消失而消失。“只要口头修改有足够证据支持，该修改就像乙炔割刀，

The common law did not enforce agreements such as section 2-209 (2) authorizes. The "reasoning" was that the parties were always free to agree orally to cancel their contract and the clause forbidding modifications not in writing would disappear with the rest of the contract when it was cancelled. "The most ironclad written contract can always be cut into by the acetylene torch of parol modification supported by adequate proof." Wagner v.

可以切开任何铜墙铁壁的书面合同。”（W 诉 G 案）

Graziano Construction Co.

但这并不是说理，而只是用比喻掩盖的结论。这或许是一种担心，即对于经验不足的人，隐藏在格式合同细琐文字中的这类条款就是个陷阱。或许是一种感觉，即这些条款并没有必要，因为只有存在对价支持的修改，才可以强制履行。或许是一种反对，即不愿让当事方事实上扩大反欺诈法的范围，因为该法只要求某些合同必须采用书面形式。

This is not reasoning; it is a conclusion disguised as a metaphor. It may have reflected a fear that such clauses, buried in the fine print of form contracts, were traps for the unwary; a sense that they were unnecessary because only modifications supported by consideration were enforceable; and a disinclination to allow parties in effect to extend the reach of the Statute of Frauds, which requires only some types of contract to be in writing.

法典以书面形式代替了普通法原则　但法典制定者在废除合同修改所要求的对价时，作为该废除的必然组成部分，一定也同时抛弃了传统观念，并且一定是相信，对于敲竹杠式的合同修改，也许还需要加强有关胁迫和恶意的法律原则所提供的制约。但也许不是从对价的角度加强，因为这已被证明无效；而是从另一个角度，即允许当事方的合同规定，必须以签字的书面文件作出修改。

But the framers of the Uniform Commercial Code, as part and parcel of rejecting the requirement of consideration for modifications, must have rejected the traditional view; must have believed that the protection which the doctrines of duress and bad faith give against extortionate modifications might need reinforcement--if not from a requirement of consideration, which had proved ineffective, then from a grant of power to include a clause requiring modifications to be in writing and signed.

另一个同样重要的问题是，

An equally important point is that

如果合同修改不再需要对价，那么很自然就需要给当事方提供某种方法，来代替对价的提醒和证据作用；而所提供的方式就是，允许他们禁止口头修改。

with consideration no longer required for modification, it was natural to give the parties some means of providing a substitute for the cautionary and evidentiary function that the requirement of consideration provides; and the means chosen was to allow them to exclude oral modifications.

法典第2.209条(4)款对(2)款的冲击 如我们所说，第2.209条(4)款规定，试图作出的修改，即使不符合该条(2)款的要求，仍可构成"弃权"。如果对该条(4)款作出过于宽泛的解释，使任何口头修改都可不顾该条(2)款的规定而构成弃权，那么，法典的这两款规定都将成为多余，而我们将重回普通法；区别只是，现在甚至不再需要借助对价来减少虚称的或无意的口头修改。

If section 2-209 (4), which as we said provides that an attempted modification which does not comply with subsection (2) can nevertheless operate as a "waiver", is interpreted so broadly that any oral modification is effective as a waiver notwithstanding section 2-209 (2), both provisions become superfluous and we are back in the common law--only with not even a requirement of consideration to reduce the likelihood of fabricated or unintended oral modifications.

区别(2)款和(4)款的一种可能的方法 有一个并不理想但可破解上述难题的方法。这就是把情况分为两种：一种是用新条款代替旧条款的"修改"；另一种是仅去掉旧条款的"弃权"。这种解释方法使本案卖方无法强

A conceivable but unsatisfactory way around this result is to distinguish between a modification that substitutes a new term for an old, and a waiver, which merely removes an old term. On this interpretation National Metal Crafters could not enforce an oral term of the allegedly modified contract but could

制履行声称已被修改的合同中的口头条款，但有可能被解除某项书面条款的义务。

be excused from one of the written terms.

上述方法可以解决诸如 A 诉 D 案中面临的问题。该案对合同的修改是增加工资，而海员试图强制履行该修改。但是，假设同样是该案情况，只是海员试图取得约定的工资，但不愿承担约定的工作，则上述方法就不可行。实际上，当一方声称合同已被修改时，其究竟是寻求将苛刻的新条款强加给对方，还是寻求摆脱原合同给自己套上的苛刻的旧条款，进行该区分是没有意义的。从本案情况出发，就可以看出这一点。

This would take care of a case such as Alaska Packers, where seamen attempted to enforce a contract modification that raised their wages, but would not take care of the functionally identical case where seamen sought to collect the agreed-on wages without doing the agreed-on work. Whether the party claiming modification is seeking to impose an onerous new term on the other party or to wriggle out of an onerous term that the original contract imposed on it is a distinction without a difference. We can see that in this case.

修改或弃权对本案买方均不利　本案卖方虽然声称，合同经口头修改后延长了交货时间，且买方违反了修改后的合同，但实际并未追究买方的违约责任。但是，买方也高兴不起来，因为买方认为，包含固定交货日期的原合同有约束力。无论将其称为修改还是弃权，卖方所寻求的，都是在缺乏签名的书面文件的情况

National Metal Crafters, while claiming that Wisconsin Knife Works broke their contract as orally modified to extend the delivery date, is not seeking damages for that breach. But this is small comfort to Wisconsin Knife Works, which thought it had a binding contract with fixed delivery dates. Whether called modification or waiver, what National Metal Crafters is seeking to do is to nullify a key term other than by a signed writing. If it

下，废除合同的一项关键条款。如果卖方仅凭口头修改的证据即可废除合同的关键条款，法典第2.209条（2）款基本上就成为废纸。

can get away with this merely by testimony about an oral modification, section 2-209（2） becomes very nearly a dead letter.

弃权需要加入依赖因素 要想将法典第2.209条（2）款与（4）款相协调，就需要仔细分析（4）款的文字。该款并没有说试图作出的修改"是"弃权，而只是说"可以构成弃权"。该款也没有说修改在何种情况下可以构成弃权。但如果只有存在"依赖"时，试图作出的修改才具有弃权效力，那么，第2.209条（2）款和（4）款就可以同时具备各自的效力。

The path of reconciliation with subsection （4） is found by attending to the precise wording of （4）. It does not say that an attempted modification "is" a waiver; it says that "it can operate as a waiver". It does not say in what circumstances it can operate as a waiver; but if an attempted modification is effective as a waiver only if there is reliance, then both sections 2-209（2） and 2-209（4） can be given effect.

依赖的概念 为使许诺具有法律约束力，经常用"依赖"这个概念来代替对价，但条件是许诺方的引诱合理地引起了被许诺方的合理依赖。关于此种代替，部分原因是，相对于被许诺方的单纯口头说辞，"依赖"可为该方增加可信度。禁止口头修改的主要原因，在于防止一方虚假声称已对合同作出修改，以逃避合同义务。如果要求声称方必须实际上已付出成本（已作出"依

Reliance, if reasonably induced and reasonable in extent, is a common substitute for consideration in making a promise legally enforceable, in part because it adds something in the way of credibility to the mere say-so of one party. The main purpose of forbidding oral modifications is to prevent the promisor from fabricating a modification that will let him escape his obligations under the contract; and the danger of successful fabrication is less if the promisor has actually incurred a cost, has relied. There is of course a

赖”），则成功伪造合同修改的可能性就会降低。当然，还会存在投机取巧的风险，即为了证明合同确已被修改，而故意产生某种成本。但这条路比较危险，因此，相对于仅仅提供口头证词，试图走这条路的可能性较低，因为要付出真金白银。

danger of bootstrapping--of incurring a cost in order to make the case for a modification. But it is a risky course and is therefore less likely to be attempted than merely testifying to a conversation； it makes one put one's money where one's mouth is.

专家的意见分歧　某些专家著述也支持按上述建议的方式，对第 2.209 条（2）款和（4）款进行协调（引用文章；引用著作）。但是，确实也有其他专家认为（引用著作），试图作出的修改即使不存在“依赖”，也可以构成弃权。但是，该专家并未对其结论作出解释，也没有提供可以支持该结论的原因或判例。另一位专家评论说（引用著作），“如果除单纯的口头证据外，还存在明确的其他事实证据，并可以得出结论说，已经达成了修改合同条款的口头协议，那么，就可以认定存在弃权。但在通常情况下，法院还是应该小心，不应让那些有争议的口头证据来摧毁第 2.209 条（2）款和（3）款提

We find support for our proposed reconciliation of subsections （2） and （4） in the secondary literature. See Eisler, Oral Modification of Sales Contracts Under the Uniform Commercial Code： The Statute of Frauds Problem, Wash. U.L.Q.； Farnsworth； Corbin on Contracts. It is true that Anderson on the Uniform Commercial Code opines that reliance is not necessary for an attempted modification to operate as a waiver, but he does not explain his conclusion or provide any reason or authority to support it. Hawkland, Uniform Commercial Code Series, remarks, “if clear factual evidence other than mere parol points to that conclusion ［that an oral agreement was made altering a term of the contract］, a waiver may be found. In the normal case, however, courts should be careful not to allow the protective

供的保护功能”。在本案中，初审法官给陪审团的指示未能符合这个标准，但无论如何，我们认为，相对于“除单纯的口头证据外，还存在明确的其他事实证据”这个要求，“依赖”是一个更加明确的要求。

features of sections 2-209（2） and （3） to be nullified by contested parol evidence”. The instruction given by the judge in this case did not comply with this test, but in any event we think a requirement of reliance is clearer than a requirement of “clear factual evidence other than mere parol”.

第 2.209 条（5）款与（4）款的区别 我们的上述方法，与第 2.209 条（5）款并不冲突。在合同处于尚待履行的状态时，该款允许撤销已作出的弃权，只要不存在“依赖该弃权已严重改变了处境”的情况。不言而喻，“依赖”问题在（5）款中完全不存在，因为该款的实质就是，除非存在依赖，否则可以撤销弃权。但该款的适用范围不同于（4）款，因为前者不局限于试图作出的但被（2）款或（3）款视为无效的修改，而是也可以适用于诸如以签名的书面形式作出的明示弃权，只要合同处于尚待履行状态。

Our approach is not inconsistent with section 2-209（5）, which allows a waiver to be withdrawn while the contract is executory, provided there is no “material change of position in reliance on the waiver”. Granted, in（5） there can be no tincture of reliance; the whole point of the section is that a waiver may be withdrawn unless there is reliance. But the section has a different domain from section 2-209（4）. It is not limited to attempted modifications invalid under subsections （2） or （3）； it applies, for example, to an express written and signed waiver, provided only that the contract is still executory.

举例而言，假设在合同尚待履行时，一个买方向卖方发出签名的信件，放弃合同的某项条款，

Suppose that while the contract is still executory the buyer writes the seller a signed letter waiving some term in the contract and

但第二天，在卖方尚未作出依赖之前，买方又书面撤回弃权。此时，我们没有理由认为这项撤回不满足第 2.209 条（5）款的要求。但这并不是我们今天必须解决的问题。无论如何，我们不是说“弃权”在（4）款和（5）款中不是同一含义。它们确实是同一含义，但在（4）款中，试图作出的修改是否构成弃权，部分地要根据（2）款来确定，因为（4）款对（2）款作出限定，但（5）款则没有此种限定。在很多情况下，弃权与禁止自相矛盾（其有效性取决于是否存在依赖）被归为一类（参见 C 诉 M 案；H 诉 M 案）。

then, the next day, before the seller has relied, retracts it in writing; we have no reason to think that such a retraction would not satisfy section 2-209 (5), though this is not an issue we need definitively resolve today. In any event we are not suggesting that "waiver" means different things in (4) and (5); it means the same thing; but the effect of an attempted modification as a waiver under (4) depends in part on (2), which (4) (but not (5)) qualifies. Waiver and estoppel (which requires reliance to be effective) are frequently bracketed. See, e.g., Chemetron Corp. v. McLouth Steel Corp.; Hirsch Rolling Mill Co. v. Milwaukee & Fox River Valley Ry.

条文可能存在模糊之处　法典本来可以写得更清楚一些，但起草者在起草（1）款和（2）款时，目的是大刀阔斧地打破普通法，但很自然地未能预见到其所带来的全部后果。法典第 9 篇的革新过于新颖，以至不得不在制定 10 年后就全面修订（参见法典 1978 年正式文本附件 2）。第 2 篇没有那么多革新，但起草水平当然也未达到无可挑剔。但

The statute could be clearer; but the draftsmen were making a big break with the common law in subsections (1) and (2), and naturally failed to foresee all the ramifications of the break. The innovations made in Article 9 of the UCC were so novel that the article had to be comprehensively revised only ten years after its promulgation. See Appendix Ⅱ to the 1978 Official Text of the Uniform Commercial Code. Article 2 was less innovative, but of course its draftsmanship

是，人类的哪些产品能做到无可挑剔？就在几个月前，在涉及法典第2篇另一条文时，面对其中明显出于不小心而神秘失踪的关键文字，我们不得不绞尽脑汁[J诉P案，涉及第2.509条（2）款]。怀特和萨莫斯教授在其著作中讨论了有关法典第2篇填补条款的另一个案件[引用著作，涉及第2.316条（3）（a）款]。但实际上，关于为什么要对法典第2篇的空缺作出填补，只需看一下第2.209条（5）款即可。

联邦第三巡回法院在D诉G案中判决，如果对反欺诈法作出弃权，第2.209条（5）款允许撤回该弃权。判决中说，"对于法典起草中因疏忽而留下的缝隙，我们有必要进行修补"。

判例法存在分歧 我们知道，法典第2.209条的起草人意图允许当事方以一定方式来禁止口头修改。起草人的目的不是要给"修改"另起一个"弃权"的名字。我们的上述解释使他们的意图能够实现。这种解释与判例法并不矛盾，尽管判例法也并不

was not flawless--what human product is? Just a few months ago we wrestled with the mysterious and apparently inadvertent omission of key words in the middle subsection of another section of Article 2. See Jason's Foods, Inc. v. Peter Eckrich & Sons, Inc. (section 2-509 (2)). Another case of gap-filling in Article 2 is discussed in White & Summers (section 2-316 (3) (a)). But as a matter of fact we need go no further than section 2-209 (5) to illustrate the need for filling gaps in Article 2.

In holding that that section allows the retraction of a waiver of the Statute of Frauds, the Third Circuit said in Double-E Sportswear Corp. v. Girard Trust Bank, "We have found it necessary to fill the interstices of the code", because of "a drafting oversight".

We know that the draftmen of section 2-209 wanted to make it possible for parties to exclude oral modifications. They did not just want to give "modification" another name-- "waiver". Our interpretation gives effect to this purpose. It is also consistent with though not compelled by the case law. There are no Wisconsin cases on point. Cases from other

必然导致这种解释。威斯康星州没有这个问题的相关判例，其他州判例的立场也不一致。有些州对口头弃权采取坚决反对态度，不允许通过口头弃权来否定禁止口头修改的合同条款（S 诉 S 案；U 诉 P 案）。其他州则允许通过口头弃权来放弃这些条款；但很明显，在多数判例中，主张另一方弃权有效的一方，都因依赖该弃权而受到了损害（G 诉 P 案；L 诉 S 案；R 诉 S 案）。

在法典以外的判例中，威斯康星州遵循普通法的原则，允许（在反欺诈法不禁止时）对合同作出口头弃权，即使合同规定只能通过书面形式进行修改（参见 S 诉 B 案）。当然，对于法典范围内的合同，法典原本的意图是改变普通法的上述原则。

已完成的修改不需要存在依赖　在本案初审法官就修改问题给陪审团的指示中，未提到依赖问题。法官没有提到，买方曾安慰卖方说，延迟交付可以接受，而卖方合理依赖了该保证并因此

jurisdictions are diverse in outlook. Some take a very hard line against allowing an oral waiver to undo a clause forbidding oral modification. See, e.g., South Hampton Co. v. Stinnes Corp.; U.S. Fibres, Inc. v. Proctor & Schwartz, Inc. Others allow oral waivers to override such clauses, but in most of these cases it is clear that the party claiming waiver had relied to his detriment. See, e.g., Gold Kist, Inc. v. Pillow; Linear Corp. v. Standard Hardware Co.; cf. Rose v. Spa Realty Associates.

In cases not governed by the Uniform Commercial Code, Wisconsin follows the common law rule that allows a contract to be waived orally (unless within the Statute of Frauds) even though the contract provides that it can be modified only in writing. See, e.g., S&M Rotogravure Service, Inc. v. Baer. But of course the Code was intended to change this rule for contracts subject to it.

Missing from the jury instruction on "modification" in this case is any reference to reliance, that is, to the incurring of costs by National Metal Crafters in reasonable reliance on assurances by Wisconsin Knife Works that late delivery would be acceptable. And

产生了费用。虽然本案存在此种依赖的证据，但很自然，这不是本案的关键，因为本案当事方认为修改已经完成，而不是试图作出修改。对于已完成的修改，即使不存在依赖，也可强制履行。

although there is evidence of such reliance, it naturally was not a focus of the case, since the issue was cast as one of completed （not attempted） modification, which does not require reliance to be enforceable.

与依赖可能无关的因素 原始交货日期过期后，卖方肯定为生产刀头工具钢发生了费用。但这些费用是否属于“依赖”费用，则是另一个问题。也许卖方本来也会继续生产刀头工具钢，因为其希望出售给其他人。当事方在初审中有关卖方反诉的约定也许有重要意义。双方约定，如果反诉成立，就按双方约定的数额进行赔偿，但该赔偿似乎仅涉及另一项口头协议的违约问题。根据该口头协议，卖方为了履行合同而对设备进行了维护。

National Metal Crafters must have incurred expenses in producing spade bit blanks after the original delivery dates, but whether these were reliance expenses is a separate question. Maybe National Metal Crafters would have continued to manufacture spade bit blanks anyway, in the hope of selling them to someone else. It may be significant that the stipulated counterclaim damages seem limited to the damages from the breach of a separate oral agreement regarding the maintenance of equipment used by National Metal Crafters in fulfilling the contract.

卖方的举证责任 我们不应将依赖问题过于扩大或缩小，并因此得出结论说，初审法官本来应该直接判决卖方胜诉，而无须提交陪审团裁定。卖方本来对此就应承担举证责任。实际上，卖方并未辩称，作为法律问题，已

The question of reliance cannot be considered so open and shut as to justify our concluding that the judge would have had to direct a verdict for National Metal Crafters, the party with the burden of proof on the issue. Nor, indeed, does National Metal Crafters argue that reliance was shown as a matter of law.

经证明存在依赖。

本案可能不是修改而是弃权　对于所称的初审中大多数其他错误，没有必要在此讨论，因为其在新的审理中不太可能再次出现。但我们确实要指出，将本案问题改称弃权问题后，买方对引入口头证据所提的异议就不能成立了。口头证据规则的目的是，防止以口头证据来改变已被当事方视为合同之最终和完整表述的书面文件的条款。因此，如果争议的问题是，一方是否随后已放弃要求对方严格履行这些条款，那么，口头证据规则就不适用。

买方可能本来也无权获得赔偿　值得讨论的最后一个问题是，买方声称，关于其制造刀头的高成本问题，初审法官本来不应引入这项证据，因为这与卖方是否违反了合同毫无关联。但实际上，两者确实有关联，只是关联到另一个问题。卖方辩称，自己虽然在交付刀头工具钢时出现延迟，但这实际上帮助了买方，因为买方的客户从自己当时现有供应商获得的价格，要远低于买

There is no need to discuss most of the other alleged errors in the conduct of the trial; they are unlikely to recur in a new trial. We do however point out that Wisconsin Knife Works' objections to the introduction of parol evidence have no merit once the issue is recast as one of waiver. The purpose of the parol evidence rule is to defeat efforts to vary by oral evidence the terms of a written instrument that the parties intended to be the fully integrated expression of their contract; it has no application when the issue is whether one of the parties later waived strict compliance with those terms.

The only other issue that merits discussion is Wisconsin Knife Works' contention that the judge should not have let in evidence about its high costs of manufacturing spade bits, which it says is irrelevant to whether National Metal Crafters broke the contract. But it is relevant, though to a different issue. National Metal Crafters argues that it did Wisconsin Knife Works a favor by its slow delivery of the spade bit blanks because Wisconsin Knife Works was unable to manufacture spade bits at anywhere near the

方制造该刀头的成本。如果卖方的这个辩称是正确的，那就只有两种可能。一种可能是，所称的卖方违约并未给买方带来任何损失；另一种可能是，所称的卖方违约与买方损失不存在因果关系。这两者带来的后果是相同的。如同在侵权法中一样，在合同法中，因果关系是产生责任的必要前提（参见L诉N案；S诉W案）。如果被许诺方所抱怨的损失，在许诺方没有违反许诺时本来也会发生，则许诺方即使违约，也无须支付赔偿。在本案中，如果无论卖方多么迅速地交付刀头工具钢，买方本来也不可能通过制造刀头来获得任何利润，那么，延迟交付就没有给买方造成法律所承认的损害。因此也就不能构成买方成功索赔的基础，即使延迟交付确实构成了违约。

结论 如果初审法官对陪审团的指示存在错误，则除非该错误无害，否则就必须重审。本案初审法官错误地指示陪审团说，陪审团有权裁定合同已被修改。

cost at which Black & Decker could buy them from its existing supplier. If the argument is correct, it shows either that Wisconsin Knife Works sustained no damage from the alleged breach of contract, or, what amounts to the same thing, that the alleged breach was not causally related to that damage. As in tort law, so in contract law, causation is an essential element of liability. See, e.g., Lincoln Nat’l Life Ins. Co. v. NCR Corp.; S.J. Groves & Sons Co. v. Warner Co. If the damage of which the promisee complains would not have been avoided by the promisor’s not breaking his promise, the breach cannot give rise to damages. If Wisconsin Knife Works couldn’t have made any money from manufacturing spade bits no matter how promptly National Metal Crafters delivered the blanks for them, the failure to make prompt delivery caused no legal injury and cannot provide the foundation for a successful damage suit even if the late delivery was a breach of the contract.

When a jury instruction is erroneous there must be a new trial unless the error is harmless. On the basis of the record before us we cannot say that the error in allowing the jury to find that the contract had been

基于本案情况，我们不能说该错误无害。但我们不想排除这种可能，即基于当事方的无审判决动议或其他动议，在不进行重审的情况下，也有可能认定该错误是无害的。基于两点理由，卖方显然有很大的胜诉可能性。关于交货截止期，卖方可辩称，买方已作出弃权，且卖方依赖该弃权。卖方还可辩称，卖方延迟交货与买方取消合同之间没有因果关系。我们只是不想基于现有材料说，因为卖方已有足够的胜诉基础，所以没必要将案件提交给陪审团。推翻原判，发回重审。

modified was harmless; but we do not want to exclude the possibility that it might be found to be so, on motion for summary judgment or otherwise, without the need for a new trial. Obviously National Metal Crafters has a strong case both that it relied on the waiver of the delivery deadlines and that there was no causal relationship between its late deliveries and the cancellation of the contract. We just are not prepared to say on the record before us that it is such a strong case as not to require submission to a jury. REVERSED AND REMANDED.

（异议法官的意见）　多数派法官已说明，本案合同中仅允许书面修改的条款是可以针对卖方强制履行的。在本案中，不存在以“签名的书面文件”所作的修改。但是，法典第 2.209 条（4）款规定，当合同要求修改采用书面形式时，“意图作出的修改”即使因不满足该条款而无效，该修改尝试“仍可构成弃权”。多数派法官判定，在第 2.209 条（4）款范围内，“修改尝试”不可能

［Dissenting Opinion］　The majority demonstrates that the clause of the contract requiring all modifications to be in writing is enforceable against National Metal Crafters. There was no modification by a “signed writing”. Yet Sec. 2-209（4）of the Uniform Commercial Code, provides that “an attempt at modification” that is ineffective because of a modification-only-in-writing clause “can operate as a waiver”. The majority holds that no “attempt at modification” may be a “waiver” within

构成“弃权”，除非寻求强制履行该弃权的一方因依赖该弃权而受到损失。但我不认为损害性依赖是第2.209条(4)款中弃权的关键因素。

弃权与依赖的关系 法典未定义“弃权”。在普通法中，“弃权”是指有意放弃已知权利。弃权可以采取不同形式，包括与权利相矛盾的行为，或口头或书面弃权声明。据我所知，任何法律(包括普通法、制定法或宪法)都不要求，只有一方依赖另一方的弃权并受到损失时，另一方对合法权利的放弃才有效。

法典中的对价问题 我承认，“对价”的法律包含了依赖原则。支付一个松仁(用特色烹饪，相当于胡椒粒)也属于小损失。有关对价的法律，通常正是将损失视为对价。但是，法典第2.209条(1)款规定，即使没有对价，合同的修改也可以生效。对于已经删除了对价原则的法律，又重新引入“依赖”原则，是一种新奇的做法。

依赖不是弃权的必要因素

the meaning of Sec. 2-209 (4) unless the party seeking to enforce the waiver has relied to its detriment. I do not think that detrimental reliance is an essential element of waiver under Sec. 2-209 (4).

"Waiver" is not a term the UCC defines. At common law "waiver" means an intentional relinquishment of a known right. A person may relinquish a right by engaging in conduct inconsistent with the right or by a verbal or written declaration. I do not know of any branch of the law--common, statutory, or constitutional--in which a renunciation of a legal entitlement is effective only if the other party relies to his detriment.

True, the law of "consideration" imposed something like a reliance rule; payment of a pine nut (the peppercorn of nouvelle cuisine) is a tiny bit of detriment, and often the law of consideration is expressed in terms of detriment. But Sec. 2-209 (1) of the UCC provides that consideration is unnecessary to make a modification effective. The introduction of a reliance requirement into a body of law from which the doctrine of consideration has been excised is novel.

Neither party suggested that reliance is

本案任何一方均未提出，依赖构成了弃权的关键因素。当事方在他们的陈述中，甚至没有提到这个问题，而是集中于“签名的协议”这个表述的含义。据我所知，至今没有任何一个法院曾判定，依赖是第 2.209 条（4）款所述之弃权的关键因素。反之，有一个法院曾说，依赖不是关键因素（D 诉 G 案，其中引用安德森教授著作）。安德森教授该著作的第 3 版同第 2 版一样，认为依赖不是必要因素［另引其他著作（其中说，如果弃权系采用履约过程的形式，弃权的效力与依赖无关）］。

essential to waiver. The parties did not even mention the question in their briefs, which concentrated on the meaning of “signed agreement”. So far as I can tell, no court has held that reliance is an essential element of waiver under Sec. 2-209（4）. One has intimated that reliance is not essential. Double-E Sportswear Corp. v. Girard Trust Bank, citing Anderson, Uniform Commercial Code. The third edition of Anderson, like the second, states that reliance is unnecessary. See also Hawkland, Uniform Commercial Code Series（suggesting that reliance on a waiver by course of performance is unnecessary）.

第 2.209 条的弃权与依赖是两个概念　新奇的东西并非都是错的，但法律中的新奇东西，如同生物变异，通常会很快消失。对于第 2.209 条本身，本案的新奇做法就会遇到障碍。第 2.209 条（5）款规定，“一方作出影响合同待履行部分的弃权后”，可向另一方发出合理通知后撤回弃权，除非“另一方依赖该弃权已严重改变了处境，致使该撤回导

Not all novel things are wrong, although legal novelties, like biological mutations, usually die out quickly. This novelty encounters an obstacle within Sec. 2-209. Section 2-209（5）states that a person who “has made a waiver affecting an executory portion of the contract may retract the waiver” on reasonable notice “unless the retraction would be unjust in view of a material change of position in reliance on the waiver”. Section 2-209 therefore treats

致不公平”。因此，第 2.209 条将“弃权”和“依赖”区别看待。根据（4）款，弃权可能有效；根据（5）款，只有同时也存在损害性依赖，弃权才可能会随后一直有效。

该条（4）款和（5）款具有同样适用范围 多数派法官为了尽可能将法典的两款规定协调起来，认为两款各有不同的适用范围。第 2.209 条（4）款涉及口头弃权，而（5）款“不局限于试图作出的但被（2）款或（3）款视为无效的修改，而是也可以适用于诸如以签名的书面形式作出的明示弃权，只要合同处于尚待履行状态”。

此种区分的言外之意是，该条（4）款所适用的情况，是（5）款适用情况的一个分支。实际上正好相反。该条（4）款规定，试图作出的修改，有可能构成“弃权”；（5）款对不存在依赖时该弃权的效力作出限制（参见第 2.209 条正式评论 4）。两项条款具有相同范围，即都适用于试图作出的修改，无论采用口头、

“waiver” and “reliance” as different. Under Sec. 2-209（4） a waiver may be effective; under Sec. 2-209（5） a waiver may be effective prospectively only if there was also detrimental reliance.

The majority tries to reconcile the two subsections by stating that they have different domains. Section 2-209（4） deals with oral waivers, while Sec. 2-209（5） “is not limited to attempted modifications invalid under subsections （2） or （3）; it applies, for example, to express written waivers, provided only that the contract is executory”.

This distinction implies that subsection （4） applies to a subset of the subjects of subsection （5）. Things are the other way around. Subsection （4） says that an attempt at modification may be a “waiver”, and subsection （5） qualifies the effectiveness of “waivers” in the absence of reliance. See comment 4 to Sec. 2-209. The two have the same domain--all attempts at modification, be they oral, written, or implied from conduct,

书面或行为形式，只要其不能满足反欺诈法的要求［第 2.209 条（3）款］，或第 2.209 条（2）款对“签名的书面文件”的要求。

that do not satisfy the Statute of Frauds, Sec. 2-209（3）, or a “signed writing” requirement of a clause permitted under Sec. 2-209（2）.

该条（5）款与（2）款无关　多数派法官认为，第 2.209 条（5）款也适用于签名的弃权。但这是一种倒退。根据第 2.209 条（2）款，“签名的书面文件”是有约束力的修改，因此无须引入“弃权”概念。第 2.209 条（1）款已去除了对价要求。因此，如果签名的书面文件承诺，不会强制履行合同某项条款，则根据第 2.209 条（5）款，该承诺不可撤回，除非承诺本身保留了撤回权。“弃权”是试图作出但不具效力的修改中的分支概念。因此，如果把有效修改（签名的书面文件）视为受（5）款约束的弃权，这不可能说得通。

The majority suggests that Sec. 2-209（5）also applies to signed waivers, but this gets things backward. A “signed writing” is binding as a modification under Sec. 2-209（2）without the need for “waiver”. Section 2-209（1）lifts the requirement of consideration, so a signed pledge not to enforce a term of a contract may not be revoked under Sec. 2-209（5）unless the pledge reserves the power of revocation. Because “waiver” is some subset of failed efforts to modify, it cannot be right to treat a successful effort to modify（a signed writing）as a “waiver” governed by subsection（5）.

弃权的含义　因此，在（4）款和（5）款中，“弃权”应具有同样含义。试图作出但不具效力的修改，可以构成第 2.209 条（4）款的弃权。第 2.209 条（5）款则涉及这些“弃权”中的一个

“Waiver” therefore ought to mean the same in subsections（4）and（5）. Unsuccessful attempts at modification may be waivers under Sec. 2-209（4）. Then Sec. 2-209（5）deals with a subset of these “waivers”, the subset that affects the executory portion

分支，即影响合同待履行部分的分支。此种弃权是否可以强制履行，取决于是否存在依赖。我们从第2.209条的文字和结构中知道，弃权分为两种：一种涉及合同待履行部分；另一种不涉及。但根据多数派法官的解读，此种区别并不存在，即如果不存在损害性依赖，任何弃权都是无效的。看上去，这像是多数派法官将第2.209条（4）款从法典中删除，然后将第2.209条（5）款的开头部分改写如下："一方尝试作出影响合同任何部分，但并不具效力的修改后，可以将其撤回"。

of the contract. Waivers affecting executory provisions are enforceable or not depending on reliance. We know from the language and structure of Sec. 2-209 that there is a difference between waivers that affect the executory portions of contracts and waivers that do not. Under the majority's reading, however, there is no difference. No waiver is effective without detrimental reliance. It is as if the majority has eliminated Sec. 2-209 （4） from the UCC and rewritten Sec. 2-209 （5） to begin: "A party who has made ［an ineffectual attempt at modification］ affecting ［any］ portion of the contract may retract."

条文是否模糊的问题 此类修补工作有时是必要的。立法机构人数众多。随着时间的推移，不同的人对于同一个词可能有不同使用方式。同样，由于参与制定一部复杂法典的人在不断更换，因此不同的人对同一个词也会赋予不同含义。特别是，起草中的妥协退让可能导致某些条款被删除，并代之以其他条款。此时，用词就更有可能存在歧义。

Repair work of this kind sometimes is necessary. A legislature has many minds, and as years pass these different people may use the same word in different ways; so, too, the shifting coalitions that create a complex statute may contribute to it multiple meanings of a single word, the more so because amendments may be added to a statute after other portions have been bargained out.

但法典第2.209条不是仓促

Section 2-209 of the UCC is not a

推出的产品，也不是具有竞争性质的不同小组各自为政的产品。法典是美国历史上最小心翼翼组装起来的制定法之一。法典的起草负责人只有很少几个，且都是严肃认真的起草者。法典由美国法学会和商业律师分会讨论了10 年才最终完成，并得到各州的整体采纳。法典当然存在模糊和不确定之处，因为无人能预见与法典条款有关的全部问题。在有些情况下，已预见的问题不是被解决，而是被绕过。但是，“弃权”这个问题没必要去绕过，且第 2.209 条是作为一个整体而起草和讨论的。第 2.209 条（4）款中的“弃权”与（5）款中的“弃权”仅相隔 6 个词。这不是很远的距离，不可能出现忘记其含义的问题。

slapdash production or the work of competing committees unaware of each other's words, however. The UCC is one of the most carefully assembled statutes in American history. It was written under the guidance of a few people, all careful drafters, debated for a decade by the American Law Institute and committees of commercial practitioners, and adopted en bloc by the states. Vague and uncertain in places the Code is; no one could see all of the problems that would come within its terms, and in some cases foreseen problems were finessed rather than solved. But “waiver” did not call for finesses, and Sec. 2-209 was drafted and discussed as a single unit. “Waiver” in Sec. 2-209（4）and “waiver” in Sec. 2-209（5） are six words apart, which is not so great a gap that the mind loses track of meaning.

该条（4）款和（5）款的解读并不困难　如果将两款中的弃权均解读为“有意放弃已知权利”，那么，两款放在一起就很容易读通。第 2.209 条（4）款说，不成功的修改尝试，仍有可能构成弃权，也就是放弃法律上享

The subsections read well together if waiver means “intentional relinquishment of a known right” in both. Section 2-209（4）says that a failed attempt at modification may be a waiver and so relinquish a legal entitlement（such as the entitlement to timely delivery）; Sec. 2-209（5） adds that a

有的权利(如按时取得交货的权利)。第2.209条(5)款补充说,如果弃权人撤回弃权,则弃权不影响合同的待履行部分(如未来交货时间),除非还存在损害性依赖。但是,对于第2.209条(2)款来说,即使不存在依赖,口头弃权也可以影响合同的待履行部分。要使法典每一部分均得到合理解释,并非必须改变"弃权"的含义。

waiver cannot affect the executory portion of the contract (the time of future deliveries, for example) if the waiving party retracts, unless there is also detrimental reliance. But for Sec. 2.209 (2) the oral waiver could affect the executory portion of the contract even without reliance. It is not necessary to vary the meaning of the word to make sense of each portion of the statute.

应对投机的问题 本案多数派法官之所以将依赖作为弃权的组成部分,不是因为法典结构要求作出此种解释,而是因为他们认为,不这样解释,法典就无法很好地应对投机行为。但是,为应对投机行为,法典起草者并未选择对"弃权"作出更严格的解读,而是依靠法典所要求的商业善意(参见第2.103条;第2.209条正式评论2)。要求以书面形式修改合同的条款,与投机行为毫无关系。如果一方用枪制伏了合同另一方,前者完全可以用书面形式记录后者的妥协。书面形式是前者最不担心的问题。在有

The majority makes reliance an ingredient of waiver not because the structure of the UCC demands this reading, but because it believes that otherwise the UCC would not deal adequately with the threat of opportunistic conduct. The drafters of the UCC chose to deal with opportunism not through a strict reading of waiver, however, but through a statutory requirement of commercial good faith. See Sec. 2-103 and comment 2 to Sec. 2-209. The modification-only-in-writing clause has nothing to do with opportunism. A person who has his contracting partner over a barrel, and therefore is able to obtain a concession, can get the concession in writing. The writing will be the least of his worries. In

关合同修改的几乎所有最著名判例中，当事方对于新达成的协议，都有书面文件。

法典的立法意图　要求以书面形式修改合同的条款，也许可使当事方强化对商业善意的要求，以对抗粗心的投机分子，但其主要功能是使商人更好地保护他们的协议，免受随后不经意言谈或故意陷害的影响。也就是说，强化了反欺诈法。尽管如此，法典并不允许该条款“刀枪不入”。第 2.209 条正式评论 4 说：“尽管有（2）款和（3）款的规定，本条（4）款的目的是，即使合同条款禁止以签名的书面文件以外的其他形式修改合同，也不应让该合同条款在其他方面限制当事方随后所实际采取之行为的法律效力。此种行为是否具有弃权的效力，由本条（5）款进一步规定。”

也就是说，对于以书面形式修改合同的条款，法典首次承认了该条款的效力，但起草者意图留下开口。多数派法官认为，对于第 2.209 条（2）款所允许

almost all of the famous cases of modification the parties reduced the new agreement to writing.

A modification-only-in-writing clause may permit the parties to strengthen the requirement of commercial good faith against the careless opportunist, but its principal function is to make it easier for business to protect their agreement against casual subsequent remarks and manufactured assertions of alteration. It strengthens the Statute of Frauds. Even so, the Code does not allow the clause to be airtight. Comment 4 to Sec. 2-209 states: “Subsection （4） is intended, despite the provisions of subsections （2） and （3）, to prevent contractual provisions excluding modification except by a signed writing from limiting in other respects the legal effect of the parties’ actual later conduct. The effect of such conduct as a waiver is further regulated in subsection（5）.”

In other words, the UCC made modification-only-in-writing clauses effective for the first time, but the drafters meant to leave loopholes. The majority’s observation that waiver under Sec. 2-209（4） could

的合同条款，该条（4）款中的弃权有可能抵消该合同条款的效力。这个看法是对的，但不构成给“弃权”这个概念增添新奇内容的理由。

nullify some benefits of clauses permitted under Sec. 2-209（2） is true, but it is not a reason for adding novel elements to “waiver”.

可以辅以履约过程 对声称的口头弃权持怀疑态度，并要求以履约过程来证明存在弃权，也许是合理的。如果发生延迟交货，但买方接受了交货且未提出抗议，或如果现有订单存在违约，但一方仍出具新订单（或改变旧订单的规格），这些情况就属于履约过程。以履约形式所证明的默示弃权较难虚构。以这种方式保护仅允许书面修改的合同条款，可使“弃权”在法典中有统一的含义，也不会帮助本案买方，因为对本案所称的弃权的证明，在很大程度上依赖履约过程。

It might be sensible to treat claims of oral waiver with suspicion and insist on waiver by course of performance--for example, accepting belated deliveries without protest, or issuing new orders （or changing the specifications of old orders） while existing ones are in default. Waiver implied from performance is less prone to manipulation. This method of protecting modification-only-in-writing clauses gives waiver the same meaning throughout the statute, but it does not help Wisconsin Knife, for the claim of waiver here is largely based on the course of performance.

本案定性的3种可能 对于仅允许书面修改的合同条款，我对“弃权”的解读方式可使该条款获得显著效力。为了说明这点，可以看一下对本案买方和卖方之间交往的3种定性。

The reading I give to waiver also affords substantial effect to modification-only-in-writing clauses. To see this, consider three characterizations of the dealings between Wisconsin Knife Works and National Metal Crafters.

不存在修改或修改尝试 第

The first, which Wisconsin Knife Works

一种定性是不存在修改，也不存在第 2.209 条（4）款所说的“修改尝试”。这是买方希望我们作出的定性。卖方承诺在 1981 年秋交付工具钢。在出现延迟后，买方不得不决定，是抛弃卖方（并寻求其可能有权获得的损害赔偿），还是要求卖方继续努力？卖方也许确实行动迟缓，但相对于有可能向买方提供工具钢的任何其他供应商而言，卖方还是提前起步了。买方希望一方面保留其权利，另一方面将损失降至最低。而买方降低损失的努力，并不意味其放弃了法律上的权利。因此，买方有权在 1983 年 1 月放弃努力，并就卖方的违约取得损害赔偿。

presses on us, is that there was no modification and no “attempt at modification” within the meaning of Sec. 2-209（4）. National Metal Crafters promised to deliver the blanks in the fall of 1981. When it fell behind, Wisconsin Knife Works had to decide whether to give up on National Metal Crafters （and collect any damages to which it may have been entitled） or ask National Metal Crafters to keep trying. National Metal Crafters may have been slow, but it had a head start on anyone else Wisconsin Knife Works might have asked to make the blanks. Wisconsin Knife Works wanted both to preserve its rights and to minimize its damages, and it did not surrender its legal remedies by trying to mitigate. It was entitled to throw up its hands in January 1983 and collect damages from National Metal Crafters for nonperformance.

买方的弃权　第二种定性是，当卖方的生产无法跟上原来规定的日程时，买方和卖方对该问题进行了讨论，并约定卖方可以获得更多的时间，以便圆满完成履约。这个说法的意思是，买方更看重的是优质的产品和良好的商业关系，而不是自己获得及

The second characterization is that when National Metal Crafters ran into trouble producing on schedule, National Metal Crafters and Wisconsin Knife Works discussed the problem and agreed that National Metal Crafters could have more time in order to get the job done right. On this story, Wisconsin Knife Works valued a high quality product

时履约的权利。也许买方甚至不希望卖方太快履约，因为对于将工具钢制成刀头的生产，买方尚未做好准备工作，因此不希望工具钢堆满自己的仓库。所以买方告诉卖方，可以多花一点时间把产品做好。

and a successful business relation more than it valued its legal right to prompt performance. Perhaps Wisconsin Knife Works did not even want performance so soon, for it was not ready to turn the blanks into spade bits and did not want blanks piling up in warehouses. So Wisconsin Knife Works told National Metal Crafters to take the time to do it right.

根据我的看法，这应该是第 2.209 条（4）款所说的弃权。在卖方所花费的时间超过了买方所能容忍的限度后，买方指责卖方太过分了，并收回了弃权。第 2.209 条（5）款正好允许买方这样做，除非卖方已经因依赖买方的语言和行为而受到损失。买方在收回其弃权后，可以宣布卖方违约，但是，由于该弃权已经原谅了卖方在 1983 年 1 月之前的履约状况，因此，买方不能就该延迟索取赔偿。当事方可以简单地宣布取消合同（参见 D 诉 M 案）。

On my view this would be a waiver under Sec. 2-209（4）. When National Metal Crafters took more time than Wisconsin Knife Works could stomach, Wisconsin Knife Works announced that too much is enough, and it retracted the waiver. Section 2-209（5）allowed it to do just this unless National Metal Crafters had relied to its detriment on Wisconsin Knife Works' words and conduct. Having retracted the waiver, Wisconsin Knife Works could declare National Metal Crafters in breach--but because the waiver excused National Metal Crafters' performance until January 1983, Wisconsin Knife Works could not collect damages for delay. The parties would simply walk away from the contract. See Dangerfield v. Markel.

订单未反映真实项目 对当事方交往的第三种定性，就是

The third characterization is the one National Metal Crafters presses here. National

卖方在上诉中希望我们采纳的定性。卖方告诉我们，采购订单从来就不是“真实”合同。反之，买方和卖方是在从事一项联合项目，以便找到制造刀头的新方法。采购订单只是更大合作项目的一部分，而该项目尚无正式条款。在项目进展过程中，当事方修改了他们的谅解并相互配合了对方的需求。最后一次修改是卖方向买方发出的“项目进度表”，其中标注了批量交货的实际可行日期，且买方人员说，这些日期和数量是可以接受的。

Metal Crafters tells us that the purchase orders never were the “real” contract. Instead Wisconsin Knife Works and National Metal Crafters embarked on joint operations to find a new way to make spade bits. The purchase orders were parts of a larger joint venture, which did not have formal terms. As the parties went along they modified their understandings and accommodated each other's needs. The latest modification occurred when National Metal Crafters gave Wisconsin Knife Works a “pert chart” indicating realistic dates for quantity shipments, and people at Wisconsin Knife Works said that these dates and quantities were acceptable.

这些日期已经排到了 1983 年 4 月。这意味着，当买方于 1983 年 1 月宣告双方关系终止时，买方违反了（修改后）的合同，因此卖方有权取得损害赔偿。至少，对于预计于 1983 年 4 月前交付的工具钢，卖方有权就利润损失取得赔偿。卖方甚至可能有权就双方商业关系未来较长期间的预期利润损失取得赔偿。

The dates ran into April 1983. This implies that when Wisconsin Knife Works declared the relationship at an end in January 1983, it breached the contract（as modified）, and National Metal Crafters is entitled to damages--at a minimum profits lost on blanks scheduled for delivery through April 1983, perhaps even profits National Metal Crafters anticipated through continuation of this relationship for a longer run.

弃权是最合理的解释　法典第 2.209 条（2）款使法院不

Section 2-209（2） puts this third position out of court. The third story would be

可能接受上述第三种定性。第三个说法涉及当事方义务的完全重构，而如果缺乏“签名的书面文件”，重构不可能发生。“项目进度表”不属于这种书面文件，因为被要求遵守该文件的是买方，但买方并未在文件上签名。当事方的讨论，最多可算作第2.209条（4）款所说的“修改尝试”，因此有可能构成弃权。根据第2.209条（5）款，买方可就未来履约撤回弃权，除非另一方“已严重改变了处境，致使该撤回导致不公平”。在本案中，假如证据表明，卖方已经制造了用于1983年4月交付的工具钢，或已经购买了没有其他用途的设备，撤回可能就属于不公平。

无须引入依赖的概念　卖方至今未辩称，由于其已产生依赖，因此有权对合同修改后的待履行部分进行强制履行。因此，买方有权于1983年1月取消并退出合同，且除去支付已交付的货物货款，并支付1983年1月之前卖方因依赖买方弃权而产生的费用，无须承担其他责任。对

a thoroughgoing reshaping of the obligations, which could not occur unless reflected in a “signed writing”. The “pert chart” is not such a writing because Wisconsin Knife Works, the party sought to be bound, did not sign it. The discussions could be at most “an attempt at modification” under Sec. 2-209（4）, and therefore could be a waiver. Under Sec. 2-209（5）Wisconsin Knife Works could rescind its waiver prospectively unless that “would be unjust in view of a material change of position in reliance on the waiver”--here, for example, proof that National Metal Crafters had already manufactured the blanks scheduled for delivery in April 1983, or had bought equipment with no alternative use.

National Metal Crafters has not argued that it had the sort of reliance that would enable it to enforce the executory portion of any modification, and therefore Wisconsin Knife Works was entitled to cancel the contract and walk away in January 1983 free from liability save for goods furnished or expenses incurred in reliance before January 1983. This treatment of Sec. 2-209

第 2.209 条（5）款进行此种处理，基本上可以解决虚假声称合同已被修改的问题。在这种情况下，“修改尝试”通常不能就未来履约强制履行，而如果存在商业上的恶意（投机行为），则该尝试就完全不能强制履行。因此，没有什么剩余的重大问题了，无须在“弃权”的定义中加入“依赖”这个因素予以解决。

（5） solves, for the most part, the problem of fabricated claims of modification. “Attempts at modification” generally are not enforceable prospectively--and if there is commercial bad faith （that is, opportunistic conduct）, they are not enforceable at all. There is no serious remaining problem to which a reliance element in the definition of waiver is a solution.

陪审团的裁定支持弃权的结论　由于第 2.209 条（2）款和（5）款否定了卖方的主要主张，我们只剩下前两种定性。一种定性是，买方保留了获得及时交付的权利，但为减少损失，维持了和卖方的关系。另一种定性是，买方放弃了对及时交货的要求，但在 1983 年 1 月，撤回了该弃权。陪审团裁定，买方和卖方“修改”了他们的合同。法官提交给陪审团的问题存在法律错误，但作为对该问题的答复，陪审团的裁定却解决了当事方的争议。

Because Sec. 2-209（2） and （5） eliminate National Metal Crafters’ principal position, we are left with the first two--either Wisconsin Knife Works stood on its entitlement to timely delivery but stuck with National Metal Crafters to mitigate damages, or Wisconsin Knife Works waived the requirement of timely delivery but in January 1983 rescinded the waiver. The jury’s finding that Wisconsin Knife Works and National Metal Crafters “modified” their contract, though an answer to a legally erroneous question, resolves this dispute.

只有买方弃权这种定性可以成立　买方在初审中强烈辩称，其在所有时间段里都一直坚持自

Wisconsin Knife Works vigorously argued at trial that at all times it stood on its rights but went along with delayed delivery as

己的权利，而对于延迟交货的容忍，只是不得已而为之。但陪审团裁定，买方和卖方修改了他们的合同，而修改的方式，按法官给陪审团的原话就是，“行为或其他表达方式”，且该修改“诱使卖方合理地相信，买方不坚持要求卖方严格履行合同，且修改后的履约令人满意，可以作为等同于原始履约的替代履约被接受”。该裁定自然否定了买方对事件进展的描述，且案件证据足以支持陪审团的否定。留给我们的只剩下可能构成弃权的“修改尝试”。买方可以撤销该弃权，且确实撤销了（参见C诉M案）。C诉M案对弃权因素的定义，与本案初审法官对合同修改所作的定义，基本上是一样的。

卖方并未索赔损失 假设卖方索赔利润损失，那本来就有必要确认，卖方是否依赖了买方的弃权并受到损失。但卖方并不想就1983年1月之后将要作出的履约寻求赔偿，而只想驳回买方就延迟交货提出的索赔（卖方还就1983年1月之前因依赖买

a second-best solution. The jury's finding that Wisconsin Knife Works and National Metal Crafters modified their contract--in the words of the instruction, that Wisconsin Knife Works "by conduct or other means of expression induced a reasonable belief by [National Metal Crafters] that strict enforcement was not insisted upon, but that the modified performance was satisfactory and acceptable as equivalent" --necessarily rejects Wisconsin Knife Works's version of events. The evidence was sufficient to permit the jury to reject this version. We are left with "an attempt at modification" that may operate as a waiver, which Wisconsin Knife Works may and did revoke. See also Chemetron Corp. v. McLouth Steel Corp., which defines the elements of waiver much as the district court's instruction defined modification.

If National Metal Crafters were claiming damages for lost profits, it would be necessary to determine whether National Metal Crafters detrimentally relied on Wisconsin Knife Works's waiver. But National Metal Crafters does not want damages for work to be performed after January 1983. It simply wants to defeat Wisconsin Knife Works's

方弃权而支出的费用提出索赔，并获得了 30,000 美元的赔偿。根据我对第 2.209 条的解读，这项赔偿不存在问题）。虽然法官对陪审团的指示不适当，但陪审团对事实的裁定提供了足够的证据，可以支持初审法院的判决，即卖方不对买方承担责任。在这种情况下，我们应该维持原判。

claim for damages for belated delivery.（It also sought and received $30,000 for reliance expenditures before January 1983, which is not problematic under my construction of Sec. 2-209.）The jury, although improperly instructed, has found enough to support a judgment discharging National Metal Crafters from liability to Wisconsin Knife Works. This requires us to affirm the judgment.

依赖问题对本案无影响　在很多情况下，即使引入“依赖”因素，对结果也没有影响。在本案中，则肯定没有影响。任何弃权，只要不是单纯对之前违约的宽恕，都会引起某种依赖。如果买方告诉出售种类物的卖方可延迟交货，则即使买方的弃权对货物生产不造成影响，也仍会使卖方作出依赖。当货物需要专门设计时，如本案中的刀头工具钢，“依赖”几乎是不可避免的。

A requirement of reliance will not make a difference very often--certainly not in this case. Any waiver that is more than a condonation of an existing default will induce some reliance. The buyer who asks a seller of fungible goods to defer delivery induces reliance even though the waiver of timely delivery will not affect the production of the goods. When the goods have a custom design, as the spade bit blanks do, some reliance is close to a certainty.

本案卖方无疑存在依赖　我认为，如果本案卖方未曾相信买方提出过相关要求，卖方就不会按同样的数量去生产同样的货物。多数派法官唯一需要知道的就是，当事方之间的多次讨论，

I doubt that National Metal Crafters would have produced the same goods in the same quantity but for a belief that Wisconsin Knife Works wanted to have them. A change of position in reliance on the frequent discussions is all the majority requires.

使他们的处境发生了变化。因此，初审中的无审判决应该没有大问题。但是，最好还是不过问那些并非必要的问题，即使已有现成答案。

Summary judgment cannot be far away. Still, it is better not to ask unnecessary questions even when the questions have ready answers.

专家可能不支持依赖因素

多数派法官为支持其立场而引用的典据并没有多少帮助。关于第2.209条（2）款，科宾教授的合同法著作认为，该款令人遗憾地削弱了灵活解释合同的原则（引用著作）。在科宾的讨论中，确实出现了“依赖”这个词，但我的解读是，这仅指第2.209条（5）款。科宾认为，第2.209条（4）款和（5）款可以防止该条（2）款造成“严重伤害”。但是，多数派法官在第2.209条（4）款中加入了“依赖”因素，来防止他们设想的对第2.209条（2）款的潜在严重伤害。

The sources the majority cites for the contrary position do not offer much support. Corbin's treatise on contracts views Sec. 2-209（2） as a regrettable inroad on the flexible construction of contracts. Corbin, Contracts. The word “reliance” does appear in Corbin's discussion, but I read it as a reference to Sec. 2-209（5）. Corbin's position is that Sec. 2-209（4） and （5） should prevent Sec. 2-209（2） from doing “serious damage;” the majority inserts a reliance requirement in Sec. 2-209（4） to prevent what it sees as potentially serious damage to Sec. 2-209（2）.

范斯沃斯教授与科宾教授一样，对第2.209条（2）款持敌视态度。他说，“完全有可能对这些条款中的‘弃权’一词赋予宽泛含义，并借此获得与基于普通法原则所判决的那些案件的同

Farnsworth, like Corbin, is hostile to Sec. 2-209（2）. He opines：“It would be possible to give an expansive meaning to the term waiver in these provisions and thereby reach results similar to those reached in cases decided under the common law rule. The

样结果。因此，只有不存在依赖时，第 2.209 条（2）款才有效力”（引用著作）。

clause, then, would be effective only if there had been no reliance.” Contracts.

上述说法似乎并不是建议弃权应该取决于依赖因素，而是建议，只有存在依赖因素，“该条款”（仅允许书面修改的合同条款）才具有效力。艾斯勒教授希望将“依赖”作为“弃权”的组成部分，因为她希望改变第 2.209 条。尽管有第 2.209 条（1）款的规定，但她认为，任何合同的口头修改都应该有对价，而依赖因素是往那个方向迈出了一步（引用文章）。

This does not look like a proposal to make waiver depend on reliance; it is a proposal to make “the clause” --the modification-only-in-writing clause--effective only if there has been reliance. Eisler would like to use reliance as part of a waiver because she wants to change Sec. 2-209. She thinks that oral modifications of any contract should require consideration, despite Sec. 2-209（1）, and a reliance rule is a step in that direction. Wash.U.L.Q.

案例 11　买方是否对所占有的货物承担损失风险？

United Air Lines, Inc. v. Conductron Corp.
联合航空公司诉康德龙公司案

伊利诺伊州上诉法院 1979 年；387 N.E.2d 1272

简　介

本案买方（United Air Lines）是一家航空公司，为了飞行训练的需要，从卖方（Conductron）订购了一台飞行模拟器。合同规定的交货日期为 1968 年 1 月 13 日。由于飞行模拟器系用于培训飞行员，因此合同规定，模拟器除要符合买方要求外，还必须获得联邦航空管理局（Federal Aviation Administration，FAA）的认证。合同规定，在模拟器被运往买方在科罗拉多州丹佛市的飞行培训中心之前，应由买方在卖方的工厂对模拟器进行检验和测试。卖方同意，将负责纠正此种检验中所发现的缺陷与不足。合同还规定，模拟器的所有权在交付时转移至买方，但此种交付不构成买方对模拟器的接受。只有买方对交付感到满意，且机器获得联邦航空管理局认证后，才构成买方对模拟器的接受。

在模拟器的生产过程中，买方人员经常到卖方工厂检查模拟器的情况，并发现机器存在大量问题。这些问题被记录下来并被报告给卖方。由于卖方未能在约定日期完成模拟器的制造，双方于 1969 年 2 月 20 日签署了“3 号修改文件”，对原始合同进行了修改。买方要求卖方先将模拟器交付至买方的丹佛培训中心，然后在那里完成验收检测程序。模拟器于 3 月被运至买方丹佛训练中心。1 个多月以后，模拟器失火，受到严重损毁。双方均未能找到起火原因。

买卖双方随后进行了一系列谈判，各自作出一些妥协，并达成一定协议。但是，买方最终决定起诉卖方违反合同，并认为模拟器的损失风险应由卖方承担。初审法院以无审判决的形式判决买方胜诉。卖方因此提起上诉。上诉法院维持了初审法院的原判，认定在模拟器失火时，损失风险尚未转移至买方。

判　决

初审法院的判决　买方起诉卖方等几名被告，指控卖方违反合同。本案涉及卖方向买方出售的一台飞行训练模拟器。机器在位于买方场地时失火烧毁。初审法院以无审判决形式判决买方胜诉，并判决买方有权从卖方取得 1,326,573.20 美元的赔偿。卖方提起上诉。

United Air Lines, Inc. (plaintiff), brought an action for breach of contract against Conductron Corporation [and others] (defendants). The case involves sale by defendants to plaintiff of an aircraft flight simulator. This machine was destroyed by fire while on plaintiff's property. The trial court entered summary judgment in favor of plaintiff for $1,326,573.20. Defendants appeal.

无审判决的条件　我们下面讨论初审法院有关买方胜诉的无审判决是否正确。该判决的理由是，在模拟器烧毁时，卖方应承担损失风险。任何法院都只有在下列情况下才可以作出无审判决，即“案件中的诉辩文件、质询记录、答复记录和证词材料全

We turn next to the merits of summary judgment in favor of plaintiff based on the theory that defendants should bear the risk of loss for the destruction of the simulator. Summary judgment should be entered "if the pleadings, depositions, and admissions on file, together with the affidavits, if any, show that there is no genuine issue as to any material

部结合在一起后显示，不存在对重要事实的真实争议，并且作为法律问题，无审判决的动议方有权获得胜诉判决”（C诉D案）。此外，根据之前的判例，“取得无审判决的权利，必须是清晰无疑的”（W诉A案），且“如果上诉法院认定，确实存在重大的事实争议，上诉法院就必须推翻下级法院的无审判决”（E诉N案）。

fact and that the moving party is entitled to a judgment as a matter of law”.（See Century Display Manufacturing Co. v. D.R. Wager Construction Co.）In addition it has been held that “the right to summary judgment must be clear beyond question”（Wright v. Adonis Compania Naviera, S.A.）, and that “[a] reviewing court must reverse an order granting summary judgment if it is determined that a material question of fact does exist”. Econo Lease, Inc. v. Noffsinger.

同时考虑合同和法典规定 在评估损失风险问题时，必须同时考虑法典的规定和合同的条款。法典第2.510条规定，“（1）如果提示交付或交付的货物不符合合同，致使买方有权拒收，则在卖方作出补救或买方接受货物前，损失风险仍由卖方承担”。

To evaluate the risk of loss issue, attention must be given to the impact of both the Uniform Commercial Code and the contract terms. Section 2-510 of the Code provides:“（1）Where a tender or delivery of goods so fails to conform to the contract as to give a right of rejection the risk of their loss remains on the seller until cure or acceptance.”

法典的正式评论 涉及法典这项条款的判例不是很多，而且这些判例也只是引用了法典的这项条款，而基本上没有作出解释（参见M诉B案；B诉A案；G诉S案；W诉C案）。法典的正式评论提供了一定指引，说

Few cases involve this section of the Code and those that do merely cite the Code with little explanation.（See McKnight v. Bellamy; Baumgold Bros., Inc. v. Allan M. Fox Co.; Graybar Electric Co. v. Shook; William F. Wilke, Inc. v. Cummins Diesel Engines, Inc.）The official Uniform

明第 2.510 条的目的在于提供清晰的规则，即“卖方不可能仅凭其单方行为而将损失风险转移至买方，除非卖方的行为满足了合同规定卖方必须满足的全部条件”。因此，本案最重要的问题是确定，模拟器与合同之间的不符程度，是否致使买方有权拒收，并确定买方是否已经接受了模拟器。

Commercial Code Comment provides some guidance by stating that the purpose of this section is to make clear that “the seller by his individual action cannot shift the risk of loss to the buyer unless his action conforms with all the conditions resting on him under the contract”. Of primary importance, then, is the determination of whether or not the simulator so failed to conform to the contract provisions as to vest the right of rejection in plaintiff and whether or not there was acceptance of the simulator by plaintiff.

买方接受模拟器的前提条件　采购协议的相关条款规定，模拟器应该“准确和严格地模拟”特定型号波音飞机的“配置和运行”，且买方最终接受模拟器的“前提条件”是，模拟器必须“令人满意地达到可靠性的演示要求”，并获得联邦航空管理局认证。买方有一位检测员，负责各种飞行模拟器的检验和评估，以确定模拟器是否符合买方和联邦航空管理局的规格。该检测员作证说，本案模拟器从未达到过这些要求，且买方从未有机会对模拟器进行验收检测。其证

The purchase agreement provided in part that the simulator would “accurately and faithfully simulate the configuration and performance of” a certain specified Boeing aircraft and that final acceptance of the simulator would be “subject to satisfactory completion of the reliability demonstration requirements” and to Federal Aviation Administration certification. The affidavit of John Darley, an employee of plaintiff who tests and evaluates flight simulators to determine whether they meet plaintiff's and the FAA specifications, states that the simulator at no time met those requirements and that plaintiff was never able to begin

词明确说明,“在买方准备对模拟器开始进行验收检测之前”,模拟器就被烧毁了。买方另一位模拟器技术助理员的证词再次确认,至少在1969年2月前,模拟器的运行还存在“诸多瑕疵”。卖方提出的反驳证词,未对买方的上述证词提出质疑。因此,买方的上述证词“应被法院采纳,且必须被认定属实”(H诉J案)。卖方的合同与定价部总监于1977年2月23日写信给买方律师说,模拟器“在最终被接受前损毁”。

买方是否放弃了异议权 卖方称,当事方的3号修改文件规定,模拟器应在买方丹佛培训中心交付,而这项规定构成了买方的弃权,即对于模拟器在交付前存在的瑕疵,买方放弃了异议权。我们不接受这个说法。根据原始协议,检测和验收应在卖方工厂进行,而修改文件只是说,检测和验收改在丹佛进行。原始

acceptance testing. His affidavit states clearly that the machine was destroyed by fire “before that time when United [plaintiff] was to begin acceptance testing”. The affidavit of Phil C. Christy, employed by plaintiff as a technical assistant regarding simulators, reaffirms that as late as February 1969 there were “numerous discrepancies” in the operation of the simulator. These affidavits stand uncontradicted by counteraffidavit. Therefore they “are admitted and must be taken as true”. (Heidelberger v. Jewel Companies, Inc.) On February 23, 1977, J.M. Gardner, director of contracts and pricing for defendants wrote a letter to plaintiff’s attorney in which he stated that the simulator was “destroyed prior to final acceptance”.

Defendants contend that Change Order Number 3, which provided for delivery of the simulator at plaintiff’s training center in Denver, resulted in waiver of plaintiff’s right to object to predelivery nonconformities. We reject this contention. The change order simply provides that the testing and inspection, which under the original agreement would have occurred at defendants’ plant, would take place in Denver. Sections of the original

协议规定，交付本身不构成对货物的接受，而 3 号修改文件没有改变这个规定。此外，修改文件的规定与弃权的说法存在矛盾。修改文件规定，检测和验收将在丹佛进行，且卖方将有权操作模拟器，以便向买方展示机器是否符合合同。这个规定说明，买方并未放弃对模拟器不合格之处的异议权。

agreement which provide that delivery does not constitute acceptance remain unchanged by this change order Number 3. Also, the language of the change order that testing and inspection would be completed in Denver and that the seller would have access to the simulator to demonstrate compliance are inconsistent with the idea that plaintiff had waived the right to object to nonconformity of the simulator.

卖方不否认模拟器存在技术困难的事实，因为买方雇员在测试期间，已将瑕疵问题记录在多达 645 份的问题报告中。但卖方强调，该机器具有复杂性。因此，尽管机器存在明显问题，卖方认定买方已接受了模拟器。

Defendants do not contest the fact that there were technical difficulties with the simulator, as evidenced by the hundreds of discrepancy reports, actually 645, prepared by plaintiff's employees during the testing period. Instead, defendants stress the complex nature of the device and urge that plaintiff accepted the simulator despite its manifest deficiencies.

法典的规定　卖方为了支持其上述主张，说明机器已在丹佛进行了 6 个星期的检验，并引用了法典第 2.606 条的规定："（1）下列情况代表货物已被接受：（a）买方在有合理机会检验货物后，向卖方表示货物符合合同，或表示尽管货物不符合合

In support of this contention defendants look to the six-week period of inspection of the simulator in Denver and cite Uniform Commercial Code section 2-606, which provides: "（1） Acceptance of goods occurs when the buyer （a） after a reasonable opportunity to inspect the goods signifies to the seller that the goods are

同，买方仍将收取或保留货物；或（b）买方未能作出有效拒收［第2.602条（1）款］，但是，此种接受只有在买方有合理机会检验货物后才能发生；或（c）买方作出任何与卖方对货物之所有权相抵触的行为。但是，如果该行为属于对卖方的不当行为，则只有卖方确认该行为构成接受，该行为才构成对货物的接受。”

conforming or that he will take or retain them in spite of their non-conformity; or (b) fails to make an effective rejection (subsection (1) of Section 2-602), but such acceptance does not occur until the buyer has had a reasonable opportunity to inspect them; or (c) does any act inconsistent with the seller's ownership; but if such act is wrongful as against the seller it is an acceptance only if ratified by him."

合同规定了接受模拟器的条件 因此，卖方希望本院判定，在模拟器发生损毁之前，买方已有合理机会检验和拒收模拟器。但是，这种说法完全忽视了合同条款。法典第1.102条说明了法典的目的。该条规定，当事方可以通过协议改变法典的规定。在F诉P案中，本院也说明了同样的原则，即“法典的目的，是给在本州进行的商业交易提供一般性的统一规则。但法典的目的，并不是让法院使用法典来得出与原始当事方明确意图所相反的结果”。

Defendants thus wish this court to hold that plaintiff had a reasonable opportunity to inspect the simulator and to reject it prior to its destruction. This approach completely ignores the terms of the contract. The purpose of the Uniform Commercial Code is set forth in section 1-102, which states that the provisions of the act may be varied by agreement. This court expressed the same principle in First Bank & Trust Co. v. Post, where we stated: "The Uniform Commercial Code was enacted to provide a general uniformity in commercial transactions conducted in this state and was never intended to be used by courts to create a result that is contrary to the clearly understood intentions of the original parties."

本案当事方的明显意图，已经规定在采购协议中。该意图是，卖方对模拟器的实际交付，以及卖方收到的买方付款，均不构成买方对模拟器的接受。买方接受模拟器的前提条件是，成功完成验收检测，并获得联邦航空管理局认证。毫无疑问，对于买方在此期间使用模拟器的问题，合同条款已经预见并认可。买方对模拟器的使用，是为了确认这台复杂昂贵的机器是否符合合同的要求。如果为了对货物作出适当评估而必须使用货物，此种使用不构成对货物的接受（参见 C 诉 B 案）。

The clear intent of the parties before this court, as stated in the purchase agreement, was that physical delivery of the simulator and payments received by the defendants were not to constitute acceptance of the simulator. Acceptance was to be predicated on successful completion of acceptance testing and also upon receipt of FAA certification. The contract terms definitely anticipated and sanctioned use of the simulator by plaintiff to enable it to determine whether this complex and expensive device met the contract specifications. If use of goods is necessary to allow proper evaluation of them, such use does not constitute acceptance. See Connor v. Borland-Grannis Co.

模拟器从未达到合同规定

本案证据显示，在任何时间节点，模拟器都不符合采购协议中约定的规格，并且直到损毁前，也仍然存在不合格之处。尽管买方在 6 个星期内一直使用并占有模拟器，但这项安排是合同所明确允许的，目的是对模拟器进行检测。为检测目的而留持模拟器，不构成对模拟器的接受，因而不导致

This record shows that the simulator at no time conformed to the specifications agreed to in the purchase agreement and it remained nonconforming until its destruction. Although plaintiff had use and possession of the simulator for six weeks that arrangement was expressly sanctioned by the contract to allow testing. Retention of the simulator for testing purposes did not constitute acceptance so as to shift the risk of loss to the plaintiff.

损失风险向买方的转移。

不存在重大事实的真实争议 模拟器的损毁发生在验收检测完成之前，以及收到联邦航空管理局认证之前。这两种情况，都是接受模拟器的前提条件。在这种情况下，损失风险继续由卖方承担。关于损失风险的问题，不存在对重大事实的真实争议。相反，我们认为，买方获得无审判决胜诉的权利是清晰无疑的。我们的结论是，作为法律问题，买方有权获得无审判决胜诉。

The simulator was destroyed before completion of acceptance testing and before receipt of FAA certification. Both were conditions precedent to acceptance of the simulator. In this situation the risk of loss remained on the defendants as seller. On the issue of risk of loss, there is no genuine issue regarding any material fact. On the contrary, in our opinion, plaintiff's right to summary judgment in this regard is clear beyond question. We conclude that the plaintiff is entitled to summary judgment as a matter of law.

失火原因和买方疏忽问题 卖方强调，初审法院判决买方胜诉的无审判决是错误的，因为导致模拟器损毁的“火灾原因”属于重大事实，且存在真实争议。卖方声称，只有在买方证明模拟器的损毁并非由于买方过错引起后，买方才能取消合同，并收回已作出的付款。卖方此种主张的理由似乎是，买方本应承担举证责任。也就是说，买方必须在主动证明自己不存在疏忽后，才有权取得赔偿。我们对此不能同意。

Defendants urge that the trial court erred in entering summary judgment for plaintiff because a genuine issue of material fact existed as to the "causation of the fire" that destroyed the simulator. Defendants contend that plaintiff may avoid the contract and recover payments made only if plaintiff can establish that the simulator was destroyed without its fault. By these contentions, defendants appear to take the position that the burden rested upon plaintiff of affirmatively proving absence of its own negligence as a prerequisite to recovery. We cannot agree.

卖方承担举证责任 确实，模拟器实际放置在买方的场地。但是，这台复杂的机器不仅最初是由卖方制造的，而且也是由卖方在自己场地拆卸后，自行运到科罗拉多州，并由自己员工在目的地重新组装的。在火灾之前以及火灾当天，卖方的员工就在机器上进行工作。事实上，案件证据显示，卖方的员工是在失火当天傍晚才离开买方场地的。此外，如上述已经说明的，损失风险本应完全由卖方承担。因此，如果买方的疏忽是火灾的本质原因，那么从逻辑上讲，此种疏忽应该属于卖方为了避免责任而主动提出的抗辩，且应由卖方承担举证责任。

It is true that the simulator was physically located on plaintiff's premises. However, not only was this complicated device initially constructed by defendants but also it was disassembled by defendants' personnel upon their premises, shipped to Colorado and there reassembled by defendants' employees. Defendants' employees were actually working on the machine prior to and on the very day of the fire. In fact, the record shows that defendants' personnel left plaintiff's premises during late afternoon on that day. In addition, in view of the fact that risk of loss rested squarely upon defendants, as above demonstrated, it would seem to follow logically that if negligence of plaintiff was the proximate cause of the fire that point constituted a matter of affirmative defense to be asserted and proved by defendants.

没有证据证明买方过错 在向本院提交的书面陈述中，卖方未能引用任何法律根据来支持其主张，即买方要取得赔偿，必须首先证明模拟器的损毁并非由于买方过错引起。并且，在书面陈述中，卖方实际上从上述立场有所退缩，因为陈述中说明，不能

Defendants cite no authority for the statement in their brief in this court that plaintiff could not recover unless it proved that the simulator was destroyed without its fault. Also defendants' brief recedes somewhat from this theory by making the statement that plaintiff as buyer should not be permitted to destroy the goods and still recover the

允许买方一方面毁坏货物，另一方面还收回货款。相对于卖方曾提出的问题，即买方的疏忽是失火的起源，上述陈述在性质上有很大不同。此外，卖方为此而引用的判例，不能推导出有关失火的本质原因的上述理论，也不能支持卖方的主张（O 诉 F 案；M 诉 B 案；W 诉 C 案）。

purchase price. That statement is far different from the issue raised by defendants to the effect that there was negligence by plaintiff with reference to the origin of the fire. Furthermore, the authorities cited in this regard by defendants advance no such theory concerning proximate cause of the fire and do not support defendants' contentions. Ozite Corp. v. F.C. Clothier & Sons Corp.; McKnight v. Bellamy; William F. Wilke, Inc. v. Cummins Diesel Engines, Inc.

在卖方的书面陈述中，有一个标题提到火灾的原因或来源，但卖方承认，没有证据表明，买方的任何行为或不行为，与火灾损失之间存在本质因果联系。卖方说，“模拟器的损毁，完全有可能本质上是因买方疏忽而引起的”。但是，在这个表述之后，卖方随后的讨论，与火灾的本质原因毫无联系。实际上，在这个问题上，卖方只是引用了从买方雇员的证词中看到的一些东西。卖方称，在发现电压表工作异常后，工作人员在没有将模拟器电源关闭的情况下就离开了。并且，起火之后，买方人员还允许一台

Although one of the headings in defendants' brief refers to the cause or origin of the fire, defendants concede that there is no proof of proximate connection between the fire loss and any act or omission by plaintiff. Defendants state that "loss of the simulator may well have been proximately caused by United's [plaintiff's] negligence". However, the discussion immediately following this statement has no relation whatsoever to the proximate cause of the fire. Rather, defendants cite in this regard only matters gleaned from the depositions of plaintiff's employees. Defendants urge that the simulator was left unattended with the power on after a malfunction of the voltmeter

排风机继续运行，而这种行为构成疏忽。并且，买方的许多灭火器都不能正常工作。

was discovered; plaintiff's personnel were negligent in permitting continued operation of an air blower after start of the fire; and many of plaintiff's fire extinguishers were inoperable.

但是，仔细审阅这些证词后，我们无法同意卖方的上述陈述。买方已经证明，无论电压表存在什么问题，该仪表与火灾原因都没有任何联系。并且，在所有的灭火器中，只有一个未能正常工作。并且，买方的一名员工在发现起火问题后，立即就关闭了排风系统的电源。

Careful examination of these depositions impels us to disagree with these statements. Plaintiff has shown that regardless of any defect in the voltmeter, this instrument had no connection whatsoever with the causation of the fire; only one of the fire extinguishers did not operate properly; and the exhaust system was shut down by an employee of plaintiff as soon as he became aware of the problem.

卖方最有能力查明火灾原因但未能查明　但是，从根本上讲，我们必须要驳回卖方的任何单项和全部主张。所有的这些主张，无论是单独看还是加在一起看，都不可能构成火灾的本质原因或来源。卖方在书面陈述中承认，“虽然经过大量调查，但一直未能令人满意地确定火灾的原因”。卖方在回答买方提出的质询时，也采用了同一立场。在被问到卖方是否已就火灾原因得出任何结论时，卖方的答复是否定的。卖

Basically, however, each and all of these contentions of defendants must be rejected for the reason that no one of them singly nor all of them together have any conceivable relation to the proximate cause or origin of the fire. Defendants concede in their brief that "despite an extensive investigation, the cause of the fire has never been satisfactorily determined". This same position was taken by defendants in response to an interrogatory served by plaintiff. Defendants responded negatively to the question as to whether they had reached any conclusion as to the cause of the fire. They

方还说明，自己没有雇请专家来帮助确定火灾的原因。案件证据显示，在火灾之后，机器被运回卖方场地。因此，卖方有能力调查火灾的原因。对于检查机器和确定起火原因，卖方似乎应该比任何其他机构都更有经验。

also stated that they had employed no expert to ascertain the cause. As the record shows, the machine was returned to defendants' premises after the fire. Therefore, defendants had the ability to investigate the origin of the blaze. Defendants would appear to be more skilled than any other agency in examining the machine and ascertaining the origin of the blaze.

买方同时强调，卖方在其反诉文件中并没有提出，火灾本质上是因买方疏忽而引起的。卖方的反诉文件及修改后的反诉文件仅声称，买方对其设施拥有“完全的和排他的控制”，并且，买方的雇员“在火灾发生时，掌控着该设施并位于设施现场”。但是，卖方的这些声称，都仅仅是为了就其支付的费用取得补偿而提出的，因为卖方为了取得机器的占有，且为了对机器进行保险和运输等支出了一些费用。关于买方的疏忽问题，这些声称都不够有力，甚至不够完整。在这些声称中，没有提到火灾的本质原因或来源。此外，在买方提出无审判决的动议后，卖方在答复该

Plaintiff also urges the failure of defendants to allege in their counterclaim that the fire loss was proximately caused by plaintiff's negligence. Defendants' counterclaim and amended counterclaim alleged simply that plaintiff had "sole and exclusive control" of the facility and that plaintiff's employees "controlled and were present at the facility at the time of the fire". However, these pleadings prayed only for a recovery of damages by defendants with reference to moneys expended in return of the machine to the possession of defendants and insurance, shipping and other costs in connection therewith. These allegations are not strong or even complete allegations of negligence. There is no allegation in these pleadings regarding the proximate cause

动议时，也从来没有提到火灾的本质原因（参见C诉B案）。

or reason for the fire. Also, the issue of proximate cause of the fire was never raised by defendants in response to plaintiff's motion for summary judgment. See Carruthers v. B.C. Christopher & Co.

结论　在审阅了全部案件材料以及当事方的全部主张后，我们的结论是，在无审判决程序中，关于模拟器的损失问题，没有提出有关重大事实的任何真实争议，因此，没有任何问题应通过审理来确定。我们进一步的结论是，初审法院所作的无审判决在各个方面都是适当的。维持原判。

Upon examination of the entire record and all contentions of the parties, we conclude that the summary judgment proceeding raised no genuine issues as to any material fact surrounding the loss of the machine which should properly have been the subject of a trial. We further conclude that the entry of summary judgment was proper in all respects. Judgment affirmed.

案例 12　买方对卖方陈述的依赖是否合理?

Royal Business Machines, Inc. v. Lorraine Corp.

皇家商用机器公司诉罗兰公司案

联邦第七巡回上诉法院 1980 年：633 F.2d 34, 30 UCC Rep.Serv. 462

简　介

本案卖方（Royal）是复印机制造商。在大约一年半的期间里，卖方通过一系列的货物买卖合同，陆续向作为经销商的买方（Lorraine）出售了两个型号（RBC Ⅰ和 RBC Ⅱ）总共大约 130 台普通纸复印机。买方随后将复印机出售给自己的客户。复印机在使用中出现了很多问题，包括复印质量不佳、严重卡纸、发生焦糊现象等，致使买方最终起诉卖方。买方的起诉理由是，复印机不符合卖方提供的明示担保和默示担保。由于买方早已接受了复印机，无权再提出拒收。因此，买方在提起本诉讼之后，主张撤销对复印机的接受（revocation of acceptance），即向卖方退还全部复印机并从卖方收回货款。买方同时称，卖方存在欺诈行为。欺诈行为一般属于侵权行为，但在合同纠纷中也可以作为索赔理由一并提出。

初审法院判定，卖方向买方作出了多项明示担保，且违反了这些担保；卖方必须承担货物具有商销性的默示担保责任，且卖方违反了这项担保；买方在起诉之后作出的撤销接受，没有超出法典规定的合理时间，因此买方有权就卖方的违反担保撤销对复印机的接受；卖方必须因欺诈行为向买方支付惩罚性赔偿。卖方为此提起上诉。

上诉法院对初审法院的判决进行了逐一分析。关于明示担保，上诉法院认为，必须对两种情况加以区分。一种情况是，对有关货物的事实作出确认，或就货物作出承诺。这种情况可以构成卖方的明示担保。另一种情况是，卖方仅仅表述自己的看法，包括销售中一般性的“自卖自夸”（puffing），而这不属于法典所说的担保。上诉法院认为，卖方的表述包含了这两种情况，但初审法院未能准确加以区别。

有关明示担保的另一个问题是，买方是否依赖卖方的陈述？根据法典规定，卖方的确认或承诺，只有在构成交易基础的组成部分（part of the basis of the bargain）时，才有可能构成明示担保。也就是说，如果买方在达成交易时，没有依赖卖方的确认或承诺，而是依靠了自己的判断，买方就不能指控卖方违反明示担保。在本案中，由于买卖双方之间的交易持续了一年半，且买方是复印机领域的专家，因此上诉法院认为，必须对每一笔购买交易进行独立分析，来确定买方是否依赖卖方的确认或承诺。上诉法院认为，即使在开始阶段买方依赖卖方的确认或承诺，但随着买方对复印机的了解，在随后的交易中，买方也完全有可能依靠自己的判断。因此，初审法院必须就此问题重新审理。

关于默示担保，由于卖方是复印机领域的商人，因此根据法典规定，卖方默示担保复印机具有商销性。但上诉法院认为，对于这个问题，买方必须承担举证责任，即必须证明货物不具有商销性，但在本案中，买方未完成此种举证。同时，默示担保也要求，买方必须是基于对卖方的依赖而购买了货物。上诉法院认为，这种认定也必须是对每一项购买交易单独认定，而初审法院仅作出了笼统认定。另外一个问题是，复印机所发生的问题，到底是由于复印机不具有商销性，还是由于买方使用或维护不当？上诉法院认为，根据相关法律规定，如果两者都有同等可能，就不能要求卖方承担责任，因为复印机的问题也完全有可能不是卖方造成的。

关于买方对复印机的撤销接受，上诉法院认为，即使卖方确实违反了明示担保或默示担保，且根据法典规定买方有权作出撤销接受，买方的撤销接受也必须在合理时间内作出。初审法院认定，买方的撤销是及时的，但上诉法院认为，根据本案的证据材料，该认定存在明显错误，因为买方拖延的时间明显过长，且在这段时间内，买方对复印机的瑕疵已有充分了解。

买方还指控卖方存在欺诈行为，而初审法院支持了买方的指控。上诉法院认为，初审法院的认定过于笼统，没有具体说明卖方的哪项行为构成了欺诈，而卖方的某些行为显然不可能构成欺诈。因此，初审法院必须重新审理。此外，初审法院还判决卖方支付惩罚性赔偿。上诉法院认为，惩罚性赔偿一般不适用于违反合同的案件，但如果违约方的行为同时构成侵权行为或具有侵权性质的行为，则可判决惩罚性赔偿，但初审法院没有具体说明判决惩罚性赔偿的理由，而不同理由所需的条件有所不同。为此，也必须进行重新审理。

判　决

是否存在并违反了明示担保　我们首先考虑的问题是，本案是否存在大量证据，可以支持初审法院的认定，即卖方向买方作出了明示担保，且违反了该担保。

We first address the question whether substantial evidence on the record supports the district court's findings that Royal made and breached express warranties to Booher.

初审法院的认定　初审法院判定，卖方作出了下列明示担保，且违反了该担保：（1）RBC Ⅰ型和Ⅱ型机器及其组件具有高品质；（2）使用和检测显示，此种机器过去的维修频率非常低，并会保持在此种低水平；

The trial judge found that Royal Business Machines made and breached the following express warranties: (1) that the RBC Model Ⅰ and Ⅱ machines and their component parts were of high quality; (2) that experience and testing had shown that frequency of repairs was very low on such machines and

（3）维修部件很容易获得；（4）维护RBC机器的费用，以及耗材的费用，过去处于低水平，并会保持在此种低水平，不超过每页纸0.5美分；（5）RBC机器经过了充分检测，随时可用于销售；（6）使用经验及合理预测表明，买方购买RBC机器并将该机器租赁给客户后，会使买方获得可观利润；（7）机器是安全的，不会发生火情；（8）平均计算，RBC Ⅱ型机器在复印7000页至9000页纸之后，才需要派人维护，包括预防性维护，且过去和将来都会是这种情况。

would remain so;（3） that replacement parts were readily available;（4） that the cost of maintenance for each RBC machine and cost of supplies was and would remain low, no more than 1/2 cent per copy;（5） that the RBC machines had been extensively tested and were ready to be marketed;（6） that experience and reasonable projections had shown that the purchase of the RBC machines by Mr. Booher and Lorraine Corporation and the leasing of the same to customers would return substantial profits to Booher and Lorraine;（7） that the machines were safe and could not cause fires; and （8） that service calls were and would be required for the RBC Model Ⅱ machine on the average of every 7000 to 9000 copies, including preventive maintenance calls.

初审法院的认定错误　初审法院对上述第（5）、（7）、（8）项的认定，以及对第（4）项中有关维护部分的认定，有大量证据予以支持。但是，上述第（1）、（2）、（3）、（6）项，以及第（4）项中有关耗材费用部分，作为法律问题，不能被视为明示

Substantial evidence supports the court's findings as to Numbers 5, 7, 8, and the maintenance aspect of Number 4, but, as a matter of law, Numbers 1, 2, 3, 6, and the cost of supplies portion of Number 4 cannot be considered express warranties.

担保。

明示担保的定义 根据印第安纳州法典第2.313条，明示担保包含下列因素：（a）确认了事实或作出了许诺，（b）该确认或许诺涉及货物，以及（c）该确认或许诺构成当事方交易之基础的组成部分。如果这3个因素全部存在，卖方就被视为设立了担保，保证货物将符合此种确认或许诺。

Paraphrasing U.C.C. § 2-313 as adopted in Indiana, an express warranty is made up of the following elements: (a) an affirmation of fact or promise, (b) that relates to the goods, and (c) becomes a part of the basis of the bargain between the parties. When each of these three elements is present, a warranty is created that the goods shall conform to the affirmation of fact or to the promise.

担保与看法的区别 一项陈述是担保还是仅为卖方看法，具有决定性的检验标准是，卖方是在声称一项买方所不知道的事实，还是仅就一个事项说明自己的看法或判断，且卖方对该事项并没有独特知识，且可以期待买方也对该事项有自己的看法并会作出自己的判断（W诉R案；G诉P案）。

The decisive test for whether a given representation is a warranty or merely an expression of the seller's opinion is whether the seller asserts a fact of which the buyer is ignorant or merely states an opinion or judgment on a matter of which the seller has no special knowledge and on which the buyer may be expected also to have an opinion and to exercise his judgment. Weiss v. Rockwell Mfg. Co., General Supply & Equipment Co. v. Phillips.

一般性的表述，如称货物为"最好"（T诉C案），或"优质"（O诉M案），或可以"终身使用"且处于"完美状态"（P诉A案），通常被视为卖方所表达的看法，

General statements to the effect that goods are "the best", Thompson Farms, Inc. v. Corno Feed Products, or are "of good quality", Olin-Mathieson Chemical Corp. v. Moushon, or will "last a lifetime" and be "in

或属于其“自卖自夸”，因此并不构成明示担保。

perfect condition”, Performance Motors, Inc. v. Allen, are generally regarded as expressions of the seller’s opinion or “the puffing of his wares” and do not create an express warranty.

因此，本案卖方关于两款RBC机器和组件均具有高品质的确认，不构成明示担保。这是卖方在表达自己的看法，是任何销售交易中都可以预期的“自卖自夸”，而不是对有关产品性能之事实的正面肯定。只有对事实的此种肯定才能构成明示担保（T诉C案；K诉F案）。

No express warranty was created by Royal’s affirmation that both RBC machine models and their component parts were of high quality. This was a statement of the seller’s opinion, the kind of “puffing” to be expected in any sales transaction, rather than a positive averment of fact describing a product’s capabilities to which an express warranty could attach. Thompson Farms, Inc. v. Corno Feed Products, supra; Keller v. Flynn, supra.

同样，虽然卖方表述说，过去的经验和检测表明，维修频率“非常低”，并且会保持在低水平，但是该表述不具有确认一项事实所需的具体性，因此不可能构成担保的基础。这些表述只是卖方的看法。

Similarly, the representations by Royal that experience and testing had shown that the frequency of repair was “very low” and would remain so lack the specificity of an affirmation of fact upon which a warranty could be predicated. These representations were statements of the seller’s opinion.

声称配件很容易获得的表述，确实是在声称一项事实，但该事实不是法典第2.313条（1）（a）款中有关所售货物的事实，

The statement that replacement parts were readily available is an assertion of fact, but it is not a fact that relates to the goods sold as required by Ind.Code § 2-313（1）

不属于货物必须满足的明示担保。关于每页纸的未来耗材成本为0.5美分的表述，同样不属于对所售货物之事实的说明，因此该表述亦不可能构成明示担保的基础。

（a） and is not an express warranty to which the goods were to conform. Neither is the statement about the future costs of supplies being 1/2 cent per copy an assertion of fact that relates to the goods sold, so the statement cannot constitute the basis of an express warranty.

卖方曾安抚买方说，买方所购买的RBC机器，可使买方获得可观利润。将此种表述视为明示担保，同样也是错误的。此种表述不是法典第2.313条（1）（b）款所说的对货物的描述，也不是第2.313条（1）（a）款所说的对货物相关事实的确认。这只是销售用语，只是卖方表达的看法［参见R诉B案（虽然卖方说，货物“随时可以卖出”且市场存在对该货物的需求，但法院判定该表述不构成担保）；另参见C诉T案；II诉II案］。

It was also erroneous to find that an express warranty was created by Royal's assurances to Booher that purchase of the RBC machines would bring him substantial profits. Such a representation does not describe the goods within the meaning of U.C.C. § 2-313（1）（b）, nor is the representation an affirmation of fact relating to the goods under U.C.C. § 2-313（1）（a）. It is merely sales talk and the expression of the seller's opinion. See Regal Motor Products v. Bender （representation that goods were "readily saleable" and that the demand for them would create a market was not a warranty）. See also Conant v. Terre Haute National State Bank; Harness v. Horne.

但另一方面，声称货物不会起火，是与货物事实有关的声称。本案存在大量证据，可以支持初审法院的认定，即卖方曾向

On the other hand, the assertion that the machines could not cause fires is an assertion of fact relating to the goods, and substantial evidence in the record supports the trial

买方作出了该声称。对于卖方向买方作出的机器已检测并可立即销售的声称，也可以得出同样的结论［参见 B 诉 C 案（卖方称，牛“已接种过运输发热疫苗，可立即放入农场”。法院判定，该陈述构成明示担保）；引用著作（如果卖方出售的产品带有第三方认证的标识，如检测实验室的标识，卖方即作出明示担保，保证该产品已得到该方的检测和认可。如果产品事实上未得到认证，卖方就要承担责任）］。本案材料可以支持初审法院的认定，即卖方曾作出过机器已通过检测的陈述。

judge's findings that the assertion was made by Royal to Booher. The same may be said for the assertion that the machines were tested and ready to be marketed. See Bemidji Sales Barn v. Chatfield (seller's representation that cattle "had been vaccinated for shipping fever and were ready for the farm" constituted an express warranty). See generally R. Anderson, Uniform Commercial Code (author asserts that seller who sells with seal of approval of a third person, e. g., a testing laboratory, makes an express warranty that the product has been tested and approved and is liable if the product was in fact not approved). The record supports the district court's finding that Royal represented that the machines had been tested.

关于上述第（8）项以及第（4）项中有关维修部分的认定，卖方辩称，这些陈述是未来预测，不可能构成担保。但是，此种辩称不具有说服力。对货物未来能力或性能的表述，完全可以构成明示担保。在 T 诉 S 案中，卖方说奶牛将会每天产 6 加仑奶。印第安纳州法院判定，这是卖方对货物事实的确认。这不是

As for findings 8 and the maintenance portion of Number 4, Royal's argument that those statements relate to predictions for the future and cannot qualify as warranties is unpersuasive. An expression of future capacity or performance can constitute an express warranty. In Teter v. Schultz, the Indiana courts held that a seller's statement that dairy cows would give six gallons of milk per day was an affirmation of fact by the seller relating

在表述价值判断，也不仅只是卖方看法。

to the goods. It was not a statement of value nor was it merely a statement of the seller's opinion.

印第安纳州法院还曾在一个案件中判定，该案卖方有关风力发电机的表述构成明示担保。卖方的表述是，发电机在中等风力的情况下，可以提供每小时研磨20~30蒲式耳粮食的电力，而在风力微弱的情况下，也可以提供大量抽水所需的电力。(S诉B案)

The Indiana courts have also found that an express warranty was created by a seller's representation that a windmill was capable of furnishing power to grind 20 to 30 bushels of grain per hour in a moderate wind and with a very light wind would pump an abundance of water. Smith v. Borden.

此外，在G诉P案中，得克萨斯州法院判定，该案卖方对房屋顶板的下列说明构成明示担保:(1)检测显示，在正常使用下，顶板在5年内不会受损;(2)即使多年使用之后，顶板也不会变黑或褪色;以及(3)顶板不会出现变色、腐坏、生锈或发霉。

Further, in General Supply and Equipment Co. v. Phillips, the Texas courts upheld the following express warranties made by a seller of roof panels: (1) that tests show no deterioration in 5 years of normal use; (2) that the roofing panels won't turn black or discolor ... even after years of exposure; and (3) that the panels will not burn, rot, rust, or mildew.

在S诉G案中，法院默示承认，在天然气设备安装之后，对未来天然气消耗的说明，有可能构成担保。佐治亚州法院虽然认定在该案中不存在担保，但同时说明:“卖方已表示自己的说

Snow's Laundry and Dry Cleaning v. Georgia Power Co. impliedly recognized that a warranty as to future gas consumption following installation of gas equipment was possible. In holding that no warranty was created in that particular case, the

明只是估计。他在任何地方都没有担保或保证天然气的消耗不会超过每月 230.50 美元。”（参见见 M 诉 B 案）

Georgia court noted: “The statements made by Spencer were denominated by him as estimates, nowhere did he warrant or guarantee that the gas consumption would not exceed $230.50 per month.” See Matlack, Inc. v. Butler Mfg. Co.

卖方是否通过确认事实或作出许诺而设立了担保，属于事实问题，需要由审理事实的审理人决定（G 诉 P 案）。本案存在大量证据，可以支持初审法院的认定，即卖方曾向买方声称，机器的维护费用为每页 0.5 美分，且该声称不属于估算，而是对机器运行能力所陈述的事实。

Whether a seller affirmed a fact or made a promise amounting to a warranty is a question of fact reserved for the trier of fact. General Supply and Equip. Co. v. Phillips. Substantial evidence in the record supports the finding that Royal made the assertion to Booher that maintenance cost for the machine would run 1/2 cent per copy and that this assertion was not an estimate but an assertion of a fact of performance capability.

关于第 8 项认定，即 RBC Ⅱ型机器在复印 7000 至 9000 页后才需要上门维护，也涉及机器的运行能力，因此有可能构成明示担保。本案存在大量证据，可以支持初审法院有关卖方曾作出过此种声称的认定。

Finding Number 8, that service calls on the RBC Ⅱ would be required every 7000 to 9000 copies, relates to performance capability and could constitute the basis of an express warranty. There is substantial evidence in the record to support the finding that this assertion was also made.

确认或许诺是否构成交易基础　虽然有大量证据支持初审法院的认定，即卖方曾作出过上述 4 项事实确认或许诺，但初审法

While substantial evidence supports the trial court’s findings as to the making of those four affirmations of fact or promises, the district court failed to make the further

院未能作出进一步认定，即该确认或许诺是否构成了交易基础的组成部分［法典第2.313条（1）款］。即使卖方确实向买方作出过此种确认，但买方的知识和对该确认的依赖是另一个问题。

依赖程度可能会发生变化 使本案复杂化的一个事实是，在大约18个月的期间内，相同当事方之间进行了涉及两种不同型号机器的一系列买卖交易。因此，可以预计，当事方的状况以及他们的知识和依赖程度，会随着他们在此期间内的经历而发生变化。即使卖方确认一项事实，但如果买方根据其经验已知该确认不属实，该确认就不可能构成交易的基础（C诉A案；引用著作）。

必须就每一次交易独立分析 因此，在确定卖方的陈述是否构成交易基础之组成部分时，必须要考虑到，每一次购买之后，买方对复印机性能的知识都在增长。对于系列交易来说，尽管有些陈述在初期的交易中可以构成明示担保，但在随后的交易中，

finding that they became part of the basis of the bargain. Ind.Code § 2-313（1）. While Royal may have made such affirmations to Booher, the question of his knowledge or reliance is another matter.

This case is complicated by the fact that it involved a series of sales transactions between the same parties over approximately an 18-month period and concerned two different machines. The situations of the parties, their knowledge and reliance, may be expected to change in light of their experience during that time. An affirmation of fact which the buyer from his experience knows to be untrue cannot form a part of the basis of the bargain. City Machine & Mfg. Co. v. A. & A. Machinery Corp. See generally R. Anderson, Uniform Commercial Code.

Therefore, as to each purchase, Booher's expanding knowledge of the capacities of the copying machines would have to be considered in deciding whether Royal's representations were part of the basis of the bargain. The same representations that could have constituted an express warranty early in the series of transactions might not

如果买方自己已对卖方所声称的事实拥有了相关知识，则同样的陈述也许就不再构成明示担保。

have qualified as an express warranty in a later transaction if the buyer had acquired independent knowledge as to the fact asserted.

对于本案的系列交易，我们没有看到初审法院的分析，即对于每项交易，卖方的担保是否可单独存在和适用，但此种分析是获得公正结论的关键。由于缺乏该分析，初审法院的认定不足以说明是否存在对明示担保的违反。

The trial court did not indicate that it considered whether the warranties could exist and apply to each transaction in the series. Such an analysis is crucial to a just determination. Its absence renders the district court's findings insufficient on the issue of the breach of express warranties.

明示担保需要考虑的因素

对于是否违反了明示担保的问题，以及损害赔偿数额的问题，初审法院必须重新审理。为此，我们提出若干意见。初审法院必须考虑机器在交付时是否存在缺陷。只有货物在交付时已经存在缺陷时，才属于违反担保。如果随后因滥用或维护不当而出现问题，则不属于违反担保（C 诉 J 案）。关于机器维护成本的许诺，初审法院在分析时需要确认，随着买方自身知识和经验的增长，其到哪个阶段后就不应再盲目依赖卖方的陈述了。关于 RBC Ⅰ

Since a retrial on the questions of the breach of express warranties and the extent of damages is necessary, we offer the following observations. The court must consider whether the machines were defective upon delivery. Breach occurs only if the goods are defective upon delivery and not if the goods later become defective through abuse or neglect. Chisholm v. J. R. Simplot Co. In considering the promise relating to the cost of maintenance, the district court should determine at what stage Booher's own knowledge and experience prevented him from blindly relying on the representations of Royal. A similar analysis is needed in

型机器起火问题的陈述，也需要作类似分析。初审法院还需要考虑，陈述是在哪个时间节点作出的。如果不是在1975年2月之前作出，则对于该日期之前的采购，该陈述就不可能构成交易基础的组成部分。

examining the representation concerning fire hazard in the RBC Ⅰ machines. The court also should determine when that representation was made. If not made until February 1975, the representation could not have been the basis for sales made prior to that date.

欺诈的问题 初审法院认定，从1974年4月或5月开始，且在1975年大多数时间里，卖方通过其代理人并通过其雇用并具有相应职权的雇员，故意作出重大口头不实陈述，以说服买方购买RBC Ⅰ型和RBC Ⅱ型复印机，且买方依赖了该陈述并因此受到损失。

The district court found that beginning in April or May of 1974 and continuing throughout most of 1975, Royal, by and through its agents and employees acting in the course and scope of their employment, persuaded Booher to buy RBC Ⅰ and RBC Ⅱ copiers by knowingly making material oral misrepresentations which were relied upon by Booher to his injury.

欺诈的构成因素 根据印第安纳州法律，可被诉的欺诈包含下列要件：陈述、虚假、故意、欺骗、损害。（M诉H案）欺诈诉讼所针对的，必须是有关现存事实的陈述，而不是未来履约的许诺（C诉T案）。并且，表述看法不构成欺诈性不实陈述。

Under Indiana law, the essential elements of actionable fraud are representations, falsity, scienter, deception, and injury. Middelkamp v. Hanewich. A fraud action must be predicated upon statements of existing facts, not promises to perform in the future. Conant v. Terre Haute Nat’l State Bank. Nor do expressions of opinion qualify as fraudulent misrepresentations.

未能具体区分 初审法院在认定本案存在欺诈时，没有特别

The district court made no specific findings as to which of the alleged

指明哪些陈述构成了欺诈。如果初审法院认定全部 8 项陈述都构成欺诈性不实陈述，则对第（1）、（2）、（6）项的认定就是错误的，因为如上所述，这些只是卖方表述的看法，而不是对重大事实的说明。欺诈诉讼只能针对后者提起。反之，第（3）、（4）、（5）、（7）、（8）项陈述很明显构成重大事实陈述。

representations it relied upon in finding fraud. If the court held all eight to be fraudulent misrepresentations, the court erred as to Numbers 1, 2, and 6 because, as discussed above, these were merely expressions of the seller's opinion rather than statements of material fact upon which a fraud action could be based. Numbers 3, 4, 5, 7, and 8, on the other hand, readily qualify as material factual representations.

关于第（3）、（4）、（5）（涉及 RBC Ⅱ型部分）、（7）、（8）项陈述，初审法院特别认定该陈述存在故意，且该认定有案件证据的支持。在可能的情况下，心理状态需要由审理事实的审理人确定。

The specific findings of the district court with regard to scienter connected to findings 3, 4, 5 （as it applied to the RBC Ⅱ）, 7, and 8 are upheld by the record. State of mind is a question to be determined, if at all possible, by the trier of fact.

买方是否存在依赖　但是，初审法院未涉及剩下的另一个问题，即对于卖方在各项交易中的陈述，买方是否受到欺骗或是否作出合理依赖（G 诉 S 案）。在上面讨论明示担保的理论时，我们要求初审法院就是否构成交易基础的问题进行重审。此处问题几乎相同。

The trial court, however, is silent on the remaining question, that of deception or reasonable reliance by Booher on the representations in the various transactions. Gonderman v. State Exchange Bank, Roann. This issue is virtually identical to the basis of the bargain question remanded under the express warranty theory.

基于上述原因，我们必须推

The district court's finding of fraud,

翻初审法院有关欺诈的认定。初审法院需要就买方在每一项交易中所依赖的具体陈述，以及该依赖的合理性问题,进行重新审理。

关于可否将撤销合同作为欺诈的救济，我们的看法是，只有对于那些受到欺诈影响的特定交易，才可以提供这项救济（W诉H案）。

默示担保的问题 初审法院认定，卖方违反了商销性和货物适用于特定用途的默示担保。我们认为，案件证据不支持初审法院的此种认定。

默示担保的定义 在任何货物买卖中，如果卖方是该类货物的商人，法律即默认卖方提供了商销性默示担保。货物要具有商销性，除去其他要求外，必须是根据合同描述可以在行业中不受异议地通过,拥有平均良好品质，且适用于该货物的通常用途（法典第2.314条）。货物必须“符合通常标准，且必须与类似情况下所销售的类似产品具有同样的平均等级、质量和价值”（J诉

therefore, must be set aside, and the cause remanded for retrial on the questions of the specific misrepresentations relied upon by Booher in each transaction and the reasonableness of that reliance.

With regard to rescission as a remedy for fraud, rescission would be available only for those specific sales to which fraud attached. Wolfeld v. Hanika.

The district court found that Royal breached the implied warranties of merchantability and of fitness for a particular purpose. We cannot agree that the record supports the court's findings.

A warranty of merchantability is implied by law in any sale where the seller is a merchant of the goods. To be merchantable, goods must, inter alia, pass without objection in the trade under the contract description, be of fair average quality, and be fit for the ordinary purposes for which such goods are used. Ind.Code § 2-314. They must “conform to ordinary standards, and ... be of the same average grade, quality and value as similar goods sold under similar circumstances” . Jones v. Abriani, citing Woodruff v. Clark

A 案，其中引用 W 诉 C 案）。

举证责任　在本案中，买方应当承担举证责任，证明复印机不具有商销性（M 诉 E 案；M 诉 G 案）。但是，买方并未完成举证，未能证明行业内有关 RBC Ⅰ型或 RBC Ⅱ型机器的标准。初审法院对违反商销性默示担保的认定，缺乏证据支持。

有理由知道用途　只要任何卖方有理由知道所需货物的特定用途，且有理由知道买方依赖卖方的技能或判断来选择或提供适用的货物，就存在适用于特定用途的默示担保（法典第 2.315 条）。初审法院认定，本案卖方知道所有 RBC 机器预计的特定使用目的，且事实上采取了积极步骤来说服买方成为其经销商，且卖方雇员有时甚至会陪同买方去拜访后者的客户（参见 T 诉 C 案）。

买方是否存在依赖　但是，对于 RBC Ⅰ型和 RBC Ⅱ型两种机型，以及每种机型的每一次交易，初审法院在讨论默示担保时，

County Farm Bureau Coop. Ass’n.

It was Booher’s burden to prove that the copying machines were not merchantable. Mullet v. Emme; McMeekin v. Gimble Bros. Inc. Booher failed to satisfy his burden of proof as to standards in the trade for either the RBC Ⅰ or RBC Ⅱ machine. No evidence supports the trial court’s findings of a breach of the implied warranty of merchantability.

An implied warranty of fitness for a particular purpose arises where a seller has reason to know a particular purpose for which the goods are required and the buyer relies on the seller’s skill or judgment to select or furnish suitable goods. Ind.Code § 2-315. The court found that Royal knew the particular purpose for which all the RBC machines were to be used and, in fact, that Royal had taken affirmative steps to persuade Booher to become its dealer and that occasionally its employees even accompanied Booher on calls to customers. See Thompson Farms, Inc. v. Corno Feed Products.

The district court, however, failed to distinguish between implied warranties on the RBC Ⅰ and on the RBC Ⅱ machines. Nor did the court differentiate among the different

未对不同情况作出区分。发回重审后，初审法院应进一步认定，买方在采购每一台 RBC Ⅰ型和 RBC Ⅱ型机器时，是否实际依赖卖方的技能和判断。买方作为经销商，现在承认自己是普通纸复印机领域的专家。我们的看法是，随着买方对该机器的经验的增长，在到达某个阶段后，买方几乎不可能不依赖自己的判断进行采购。

损害的因果关系 对初审法院认定的另一个方面，我们也感到困惑。根据法律，即使卖方违反明示担保或默示担保，买方在下列情况下也无权取得赔偿，即"事实证明，多个原因都有可能导致损害的发生，而卖方对其中至少一个或多个原因不承担责任；且此种原因与其他原因相比，同样有合理可能和概率会构成损害的原因……"（R 诉 P 案；C 诉 J 案）。

初审法院的理由不清 卖方辩称，证据显示，买方对机器的改装和疏于维护是机器损坏的原因。对两款机器，初审法院均认

transactions involving the two machines. On remand the district court should make further findings on Booher's actual reliance on Royal's skill or judgment in each purchase of the RBC Ⅰ and RBC Ⅱ machines. We view it as most unlikely that a dealer who now concedes himself to be an expert in the field of plain paper copiers did not at some point, as his experience with the machines increased, rely on his own judgment in making purchases.

We are troubled by one further aspect of the district court's rulings. It is the law that a plaintiff may not recover for breach of express or implied warranty "where the facts proven show that there are several possible causes of an injury, for one or more of which the defendant was not responsible and it is just as reasonable and probable that the injury was the result of one cause or the other ...". Republic Corp. v. Procedyne Corp., Chisholm v. J. R. Simplot Co.

Royal argues that the evidence demonstrates that Booher's modifications of the machines and lack of maintenance were the cause of the damages claimed. The

定，“买方对机器作出了某些改装，但这是因机器存在瑕疵或配件不足所导致的必要改装，且改装系在卖方建议下进行”。发回重审后，初审法院应对上述认定加以澄清。法院的认定是否意在说明，根据禁止自相矛盾原则，卖方无权以该改装作为抗辩？或者作为替代理由，法院认为违反担保是引起损害的唯一原因？

district court found as to both machines that “certain modifications were made which were necessitated by machine defects or by parts shortages all of which were suggested by representatives of Royal-Litton”. On remand, the district court should clarify its holding. Is the district court holding that Royal is estopped from arguing modification as a defense? Or, in the alternative, has the court found breach of warranties to be the sole cause of damages?

默示担保未被有效排除　我们拒绝卖方的这个辩称，即默示担保已被限制或排除。此种排除条款必须清晰、醒目、公平，且必须是主动谈判的结果。要排除适用于特定用途的默示担保，必须以书面形式作出排除［法典第 2.316 条（2）款；另参见法典第 2.317 条（c）款；W 诉 C 案］。

We reject Royal's argument that the implied warranties have been limited or disclaimed. Such a disclaimer must be clear, conspicuous, conscionable, and consciously bargained for, and, in the case of an implied warranty of fitness for a particular purpose, the disclaimer must be in writing. Ind.Code § 2-316（2）; See also Ind.Code § 2-317（c）; Woodruff v. Clark County Farm Bureau Coop. Ass’n.

撤销接受的问题　初审法院认定，对于 RBC Ⅰ型和 RBC Ⅱ型机器，买方及时撤销了接受。我们不同意这个认定。

The district court found that Booher made a timely revocation of acceptance of both the RBC Ⅰ and the RBC Ⅱ machines. We disagree.

撤销接受的条件　法典规定，买方在接收货物后还可以撤

The U.C.C. provides that a buyer who has accepted goods may revoke his acceptance

销接受，只要货物不符合合同，货物价值受到损害，且买方“在接收货物时不知道不符合合同，或在接受时合理假定该缺陷将得到补救”[法典第2.608条（1）款]。并且，“撤销接受是在合理时间内作出，且在货物发生实质改变之前”[第2.608条（2）款]。

when the goods are non-conforming and their value is impaired and "the goods were accepted without knowledge of the non-conformity or acceptance occurred with the reasonable assumption that the defect would be cured", Ind.Code § 2-608（1）, and "the revocation occurred within a reasonable time and before any substantial change in the condition of the goods", Ind.Code § 2-608（2）.

初审法院的认定 关于RBC Ⅰ型机器，初审法院认定，买方在接受机器时，没有发现其内在瑕疵，包括起火隐患，而这些瑕疵和隐患都是在机器使用之后才显现的。初审法院进一步认定:（1）卖方曾向买方作出保证，机器不存在瑕疵，且不会起火;（2）买方在发现RBC Ⅰ型机器确实有可能起火后的合理时间内，作出了撤销接受;（3）除去那些由于机器自身瑕疵以及配件短缺而引起的改变或必须作出的改变，撤销接受是在机器发生实质改变之前。

Regarding the RBC Ⅰ machines, the district court found that Booher accepted the machines without discovering the latent defects, including the fire hazard defect, which did not become apparent until the machines were in use. The district court further found （1） that Royal assured Booher that the machines were not defective and/or would not catch fire, （2） that Booher revoked acceptance of the RBC Ⅰ machines within a reasonable time after discovery was made that fires were indeed possible, and （3） that revocation took place before any substantial change had occurred to the machines except such changes as were caused or necessitated by defects in the equipment itself and by the shortages of Royal replacement parts.

撤销是否及时 买方在1974年6月购买了第一台RBC Ⅰ型机器。1975年12月之前，买方陆续购买了多台该型机器。初审法院认定，直到1976年秋，买方才获得了机器存在“明火”问题的第一手确认。1975年2月，买方曾就起火隐患问题询问卖方，但卖方保证，不存在起火风险。对货物的撤销接受，发生在1976年12月3日，即提起本诉讼3个月之后。

Booher purchased his first RBC Ⅰ in June 1974. He purchased additional machines through December of 1975. The district court found that it was not until the fall of 1976 that Booher received first-hand confirmation of “open flame” fires in the machines and that in February 1975, Booher had asked Royal about fire hazard and had been assured that there was no danger of fire. The revocation of acceptance of the goods occurred on December 3, 1976, three months after the commencement of this litigation.

买方早已知道机器的瑕疵 毫无争议的证据是，买方1975年2月4日之前就收到客户投诉，称RBC Ⅰ型机器发生“焦糊”问题。买方在运营连锁许可的两年期间内，一直收到客户的此种投诉。这无疑构成对买方的通知，即机器存在此类内在问题。买方所声称的其他功能性“瑕疵”，包括复印质量、电路瑕疵和严重卡纸问题，也都属于买方使用RBC Ⅰ型机器后熟知的问题。并且，如证据所显示，这些都是买方在成为连锁许可经营商之后很快就能看到的情况。

The evidence is uncontradicted that Booher had complaints from customers as early as February 4, 1975 that “burn jams” occurred in the RBC Ⅰ. Those complaints recurred during the two-year period Booher was operating the Royal franchise and must have put him on notice of a problem inherent in the RBC Ⅰ. The other “defects” in function claimed by Booher-copy quality, electrical defects, and gross jamming problems-were also well-known from his experience with the RBC Ⅰ and, as shown by the evidence, became apparent soon after Booher became the franchise operator.

事实认定的审核标准 联邦民事诉讼法规定，在上诉法院的审理中，初审法院“对事实的认定，除非存在明显错误，否则不得被推翻”。在U诉U案中，联邦最高法院说：“即使初审法院的认定有证据支持，但如果上诉法院在审阅全部证据之后，坚定无疑地相信该认定存在错误，该认定即属于‘明显错误’。”（引用著作）

在本案中，初审法院的认定看上去与证人的可信度无关，且基础事实不存在争议，且看不到有任何理由不相信这些事实。在这种情况下，上诉审查的范围就更加宽泛（A诉C案）。

初审法院的认定明显错误 关于撤销接受的及时性问题，在分析了本案全部证据后，我们“坚定无疑地相信”，初审法院的认定“是错误的”。初审法院认定，买方在合理时间内撤销了对RBC Ⅰ型机器的接受。这个认定明显是错误的，因为与确凿证据完全相反。证据表明，在撤

Federal Rules of Civil Procedure provides that upon appellate review a district court's "findings of fact shall not be set aside unless clearly erroneous". In United States v. United States Gypsum Co., the Supreme Court said: "A finding is 'clearly erroneous' when although there is evidence to support it, the reviewing court on the entire evidence is left with the definite and firm conviction that a mistake has been committed." See generally Moore's Federal Practice.

Where, as here, the decisions of the trial court do not appear to be based upon the credibility of the witnesses, and the underlying facts are uncontroverted, and no reason appears for not believing them, the scope of review becomes even broader. Apolskis v. Concord Life Ins. Co.

Considering all the evidence in the case bearing on timeliness of revocation, we are "left with the definite and firm conviction that a mistake has been committed". The district court's finding that Booher's revocation of acceptance of the RBC Ⅰ machines was reasonable in time is clearly erroneous. The finding is contrary to the clear weight of the evidence which reveals

销接受之前大约两年半时间里，买方在完全了解 RBC Ⅰ型机器性能瑕疵的情况下，一直在购买该机器。更有甚者，直到本诉讼开始 3 个半月之后，买方才作出撤销接受。

that, for some two and one-half years prior to revocation, Booher had been purchasing RBC Ⅰ machines with full knowledge of their operating deficiencies. Added to that, the revocation did not occur until three and one-half months after the inception of this litigation.

对于 RBC Ⅱ型机器，我们也可以得出同样结论。撤销对货物的接受的合理时间，取决于特定案件的性质、目的和客观情况。“合理时间”并不必然意味着“立即”（T 诉 J 案）。大约从 1974 年 8 月起，买方即对 RBC Ⅱ型机器的瑕疵有所了解。但证据显示，卖方一直作出保证，承诺补救 RBC Ⅱ型机器的瑕疵，并且于 1976 年 4 月用 9 台新的 RBC Ⅱ型机器更换了买方 9 台最旧的 RBC Ⅱ型机器。对于没有被更换的其余 5 台 RBC Ⅱ型机器，卖方于 1976 年 6 月 30 日进行了改装。

The same may be said for the RBC Ⅱ copiers. What is a reasonable time within which to revoke acceptance of goods depends upon the nature, purpose, and circumstances of the particular case. “Reasonable time” does not necessarily mean immediately. Trailmobile Div. of Pullman, Inc. v. Jones. Booher had known of the defects in the RBC Ⅱ machines since approximately August of 1974. The evidence reveals, however, that Royal continually made promises to cure the RBC Ⅱ defects and in April of 1976 replaced nine of Booher’s oldest RBC Ⅱ machines with nine new RBC Ⅱ machines. On June 30, 1976, Royal modified the remaining five RBC Ⅱ machines that had not been replaced.

如果任何卖方反复作出补救承诺，撤销接受的合理时间可以被延长。（J 诉 A 案）但在本案中，买方是在 9 台机器被更换大

A seller’s repeated assurances to cure can extend the time within which revocation is reasonable. Jones v. Abriani, supra. However, it was some seven months after

约7个月之后才撤销对RBC Ⅱ型机器的接受。假如机器的瑕疵本来未得到补救，那么买方肯定在1976年12月3日之前很久就已经知道。初审法院认定，买方对RBC Ⅱ型机器的撤销接受是及时的。这项认定是错误的（H诉U案）。

the replacement of the nine RBC Ⅱ machines that Booher finally revoked acceptance. If the defects had not been cured, that must have been known to Booher long before December 3, 1976. The trial court's finding that revocation of acceptance of the RBC Ⅱ machines was timely was in error. Heibel v. United States Air Conditioning Corp.

由于买方无权享有撤销接受的救济，初审法院在重审中可以恢复原先曾被推翻的无审判决。根据该判决，尚未支付的复印机价款为596,921.33美元，而卖方有权获得该付款。

Since the remedy of revocation is not available to Booher, on rehearing the district court may reinstitute the summary judgment, which was previously vacated, awarding Royal the $596,921.33 unpaid balance on the purchase price of the copying machines.

惩罚性赔偿的问题 初审法院判定，本案的一个买方有权获得83,512.80美元的惩罚性赔偿，而另一个买方有权获得376,492.32美元的惩罚性赔偿。两者总额为460,005.12美元。卖方强烈辩称，惩罚性赔偿缺乏任何法律和事实基础。

The district court awarded punitive damages in the sum of $83,512.80 to Booher and $376,492.32 to Lorraine Corp., for a total of $460,005.12. Royal argues strongly that no valid ground exists in law or in fact for the imposition of punitive damages.

符合侵权定义的行为 通常而言，在违反合同的案件中，印第安纳州的一般原则是不判决支付惩罚性赔偿（M诉W案）。但在V诉S案中，印第安纳州

Generally, Indiana follows the rule that punitive damages ordinarily are not awarded in cases involving a breach of contract. Monte Carlo, Inc. v. Wilcox. However, in Vernon Fire & Casualty Ins. Co. v. Sharp, the Indiana

最高法院判定，“如果违约一方的行为不仅构成对合同的违反，而且同时另外构成了诸如欺诈这样的普通法上的侵权行为”，则可以判决惩罚性赔偿。

Supreme Court held that punitive damages may be awarded “where the conduct of the breaching party not only amounts to a breach of the contract, but also independently establishes the elements of a common-law tort such as fraud”.

不符合侵权定义但具有类似性质的行为　印第安纳州最高法院在该案判决书中继续写道，作为替代的另一种情况是，“从证据的整体情况看，过错方的相关行为是具有侵权性质的严重过错，因此，虽然该行为无法简单地套入之前确立的侵权行为定义，但是，如果惩罚性赔偿有助于震慑该过错者以及处于类似情况的其他人，从而促进公共利益”，那么也可以判决惩罚性赔偿。在 V 诉 S 案后，上述原则被应用在一系列其他案件中（P 诉 F 案；F 诉 M 案；S 诉 F 案；U 诉 F 案；S 诉 S 案；H 诉 B 案；J 诉 C 案）。

Alternatively, the court continued, punitive damages may be awarded in the absence of an independent tort if “it appears from the evidence as a whole that a serious wrong, tortious in nature, has been committed, but the wrong does not conveniently fit the confines of a pre-determined tort ... (and) that the public interest will be served by the deterrent effect punitive damages will have upon future conduct of the wrongdoer and parties similarly situated”. This policy has been applied in a series of cases following Vernon Fire. Photovest Corp. v. Fotomat Corp.; First Fed. Sav. & Loan Ass’n of Indianapolis v. Mudgett; Sandock v. F. D. Borkholder Co.; United Farm Bureau Family Life Ins. v. Fultz; State Farm Mut. Auto. Ins. Co. v. Shuman; Hibschman Pontiac, Inc. v. Batchelor; Joseph Schlitz Co. v. Central Beverage Co.

初审法院未加区别　在本案

The district court does not specify which

中，初审法院没有说明，其在判决惩罚性赔偿时，到底适用了V诉S案所说的哪一种情况。初审法院判决卖方支付惩罚性赔偿的理由是，卖方存在“已证实的故意侵权不当行为”。如果惩罚性赔偿是基于欺诈，那么在作出该判决时，就必须重新考虑本院前面对欺诈问题提出的意见。在欺诈理论中，惩罚性赔偿只适用于与可被诉欺诈有联系的特定交易。

aspect of the Vernon Fire test the court relied upon in awarding punitive damages. The court awarded punitive damages against Royal “for the found willful tortious misconduct”. If the award of punitive damages was based on fraud, then the award must be reconsidered along with the issue of fraud as discussed earlier in this opinion. Under a fraud theory, punitive damages can be awarded only for those specific transactions which constitute actionable fraud.

但是，V诉S案也明确说明，除去可被诉欺诈，作为替代情况，惩罚性赔偿也可以用于具有侵权性质的行为（S诉S案）。在不存在欺诈时，如果要获得惩罚性赔偿，需要两个前提条件：（1）存在侵权性质的严重过错行为；并且（2）判决惩罚性赔偿可以维护公共利益。根据印第安纳州法院的解释，在无法证明可被诉欺诈全部要素的情况下，“侵权性质”的行为包括怀有欺诈心态的行为（F诉M案），或具有恶意的行为（J诉A案）。

Vernon Fire, however, makes it clear that, as an alternative, an award of punitive damages can be supported by tortious conduct other than actionable fraud. State Farm Mut. Auto. Ins. Co. v. Shuman. Absent fraud, there are two prerequisites to recovery：（1） the commission of a serious wrong, tortious in nature； and （2） the public interest must be served by the award. The Indiana courts have interpreted conduct “tortious in nature” to include an act committed with a fraudulent state of mind, First Fed. Sav. & Loan Ass’n of Indianapolis v. Mudgett, or in bad faith, Jones v. Abriani, even though all the elements of actionable fraud are not proved.

在上述情况下，违反合同的行为，有可能同时构成侵权性质的行为（M 诉 W 案），此时，判决惩罚性赔偿，可以通过震慑其他人的类似行为而促进公共利益。但是，亦请参见 O 诉 W 案（违约尚未达到压迫、欺诈或恶意的程度）。在本案中，如果初审法院在判决惩罚性赔偿时适用了 V 诉 S 案所说的第二种情况，那就必须结合本院前面讨论过的违反明示担保和默示担保的问题，重新考虑该判决。惩罚性赔偿只适用于那些违反合同的交易。

In this case, conduct which could constitute a breach of contract might also be tortious in nature, Monte Carlo, Inc. v. Wilcox, and an award of exemplary damages might serve the public interest by deterring others from like conduct. But see Owen Co. Farm Bureau Coop. v. Waeger（breach did not rise to level of oppression, fraud, or malice）. If the district court's award of punitive damages is based on the second aspect of Vernon Fire, the award must be reconsidered together with the issues of breach of express and implied warranties as discussed earlier in this opinion. Punitive damages could only be awarded for those transactions constituting a breach of contract.

律师费问题　卖方辩称，法典允许判决支付律师费（法典第 2.721 条），这说明其已否定了惩罚性赔偿。但是，卖方为支持该主张而引用的 J 诉 T 案和 S 诉 H 案，并不适用于本案。那些案件都已判定了法定的 3 倍赔偿。因此，如果再判决惩罚性赔偿，就会形成双重惩罚，因为 3 倍赔偿本身就具有惩罚性质。但是，律师费属于补偿性赔偿。法典第

Royal argues that a statutory authorization of attorneys' fees, Ind.Code § 2-721, precludes an award of punitive damages. Johnson v. Tyler, and Stoner v. Houston, cited by Royal to support its argument, are inapposite. They deal with situations providing for statutory treble damages where an additional allowance of punitive damages would work a double punishment. Treble damages are punitive in nature. Attorneys' fees are compensatory.

2.721 条正式评论说:"本条的目的是,在通常救济之外再增加法定救济。"很明显,在欺诈诉讼中,法典第 2.721 条并不排除普通法中获得惩罚性赔偿的权利。

The comments accompanying Ind.Code § 2-721 state:"The purpose of this section is to add the statutory remedies to the ordinary remedies." It seems evident that Ind.Code § 2-721 does not extinguish the common law right to recover punitive damages in a fraud action.

基于上述原因,特此推翻初审法院的判决,并将案件发回,根据本判决所列出的未决问题进行重新审理。

For the foregoing reasons the judgment of the district court is reversed, and the cause is remanded for a new trial on the remaining issues outlined herein.

案例 13　卖方的担保排除条款是否可有效对抗间接买方?

Patty Precision Products Co. v. Brown & Sharpe Mfc. Co., GE Co. et al
帕迪精密产品公司诉布沙制造公司案

联邦第十巡回上诉法院 1988 年；846 F.2d 1247, 6 UCC Rep.Serv.2d 692

简　介

本案涉及 3 个当事方，即制造数控组件的供应商（GE），购买该组件并用其制造机器的卖方（Brown & Sharpe），以及从卖方购买机器的买方（Patty Precision）。在本案中，供应商的数控组件存在瑕疵，致使卖方制造的机器也存在瑕疵，并导致买方在购买机器后受到损失。买方同时起诉卖方和供应商。

在供应商与卖方之间的合同中，存在一项担保排除条款。根据该条款，供应商排除了包括商销性在内的所有默示担保。当事方均同意，这项条款在供应商与卖方之间是有效的。争议的问题是，在供应商与买方没有"直接合同关系"（privity of contract）的情况下，且在供应商没有将这项排除条款通知给买方的情况下，该排除条款是否对买方也有效？下述判决书提到，俄克拉何马州的法律（本案的适用法）很明确，就是在没有直接合同关系的情况下，最终购买人也有权享受制造商提供的担保。但法律不够明确的是，如果制造商排除了担保，该排除是否对最终购买人也有效？

在初审中，法院允许供应商就担保内容和担保排除条款向陪审团作出说明。随后，法官向陪审团解释了担保和排除条款的含义。陪审团随后裁定，供应商没有违反对买方的明示担保或默示担保。基于陪审团的裁定，初审法院判决，供应商不对买方承担违反明示担保或默示担保的责任。买方认为，初审法官对供应商证据的采纳和对陪审团的指示存在错误，要求进行重新审理，但被初审法院驳回。买方因此提起上诉。

上诉法院认为，由于供应商没有将担保排除条款传达给买方，因此该排除条款对买方不具有效力。据此，上诉法院推翻了初审法院的判决。对于多数派法官的判决，上诉法院的一位法官提出了异议。该法官同意本案的判决结果，即供应商的排除条款对买方无效，但他认为，这是基于供应商与买方存在密切交往的特定背景而得出的结论。他认为，一般而言，既然最终购买人有权享受担保的好处，也就应该同时受到担保排除条款的限制。同时，在实际商业活动中，要求制造商将排除条款传达给最终购买人，常常是不合理或不实际的，特别是当制造商所生产的是用于产品内部的组件时。因此他认为，在本案中，假如供应商与买方不存在密切交往，供应商的排除条款本来应该是有效的。

判　决

本案基本情况　买方在本上诉中称，初审法院的判决存在错误，因为其允许将设备供应商对卖方的担保排除条款采纳为本案证据,并就此向陪审团作出指示。我们同意买方的立场。

On appeal, Patty Precision contends that the district court erred in permitting evidence of and instructing on any disclaimer from General Electric to Brown & Sharpe. We agree.

双方的主张　买方辩称，供应商仅将担保排除条款告知了卖方，因此，作为法律问题，不应

Patty Precision argues that General Electric's disclaimer was disclosed only to Brown & Sharpe and could not, as a matter

认为该条款对买方有效。买方声称，初审法院引入该证据并就其向陪审团作出指示的做法，构成对陪审团的误导，并损害了买方在本案中的利益。作为回复，供应商辩称，其针对卖方的担保排除条款对随后的购买人（本案买方）仍然有效，并构成法律上的有效抗辩。

of law, be considered effective against Patty Precision. Thus, Patty Precision contends that the introduction of evidence of and instructing on the disclaimer was misleading to the jury and prejudicial to its case. In response, General Electric argues that its disclaimer to Brown & Sharpe was effective as to Patty Precision as a subsequent purchaser and a valid defense as a matter of law.

基本事实、争议问题、上诉结论 当事方同意，本案关键问题在于，供应商的担保排除条款是否可以适用于买方？根据供应商提供的证据，该排除条款仅被提供给了卖方。买方在购买 3 台机器前，未被告知存在此种排除条款，也从未得到过该条款的书面文件。问题在于，在这种情况下，该条款是否仍然对买方具有约束力，并可被采纳为本案证据？根据我们对适用的俄克拉何马州法律的审阅，我们判定：供应商的排除条款对买方不具约束力，该排除条款与本案无关，初审法院将其采纳为证据并向陪审团作出指示的决定是错误的。

The parties agree that the dispositive issue is whether General Electric's disclaimer applies to Patty Precision. The disclaimer, according to General Electric's evidence, extended only to Brown & Sharpe. Patty Precision was not informed of the disclaimer prior to its purchases of the three machines, and the disclaimer was never expressed to Patty Precision in writing. The issue thus is whether the disclaimer of warranties can nonetheless be binding on Patty Precision and admissible herein. Based on our review of applicable Oklahoma law, we hold that General Electric's disclaimer to Brown & Sharpe was not binding on Patty Precision, that the disclaimer was irrelevant, and that the district court erred in admitting it in evidence and instructing on it.

两种默示担保的定义 在俄克拉何马州，货物至少要适用于其使用的通常用途，才能被视为具有商销性（P诉L案）。商销性是一个灵活概念，并不意味着货物必须具有最高品质或完美细节，但是货物必须能够正常用于其通常用途。并且，如果卖方违反了商销性的担保，就没有必要再去考虑其是否违反了适用于特定用途的担保（A诉W案）。

Goods are considered merchantable in Oklahoma when, at the least, they are fit for the ordinary purposes for which they are used. Perry v. Lawson Ford Tractor Company. Merchantability is a flexible concept which does not connote best quality or perfection in detail; merchantability does require, however, that goods operate for their ordinary purpose. Also, where there is a breach of warranty of merchantability, it is unnecessary to determine whether a seller is liable for breach of a warranty of fitness. American Fertilizer Specialists, Inc. v. Wood.

法典第2.314条规定，“如果货物买卖合同的卖方是该类货物的商人，合同即包含一项默示担保，即货物具有商销性，除非该担保被排除或修改（第2.316条）”。同样，法典第2.315条规定，“如果在订立合同时，卖方有理由知道货物系用于某种特定用途，且有理由知道买方依赖卖方的技能或判断来选择或提供适合的货物，卖方即默示担保，货物将适用于该用途，除非该担保被排除或修改(第2.316条)”。

Under Okla.Stat.Ann. Sec. 2-314, “Unless excluded or modified [under Sec. 2-316] ... a warranty that the goods shall be merchantable is implied in a contract for their sale if the seller is a merchant with respect to goods of that kind”. Similarly, Sec. 2-315 provides that “[w] hen the seller at the time of contracting has reason to know any particular purpose for which the goods are required and that buyer is relying on the seller's skill or judgment to select or furnish suitable goods, there is unless excluded or modified [under Sec. 2-316] ... an implied warranty that the goods shall be fit for such purpose”.

默示担保的排除　法典第 2.316 条的相关部分规定，“（1）引起明示担保的词句或行为，与具有否认或限制该担保之倾向的词句或行为，在合理的情况下，应作出互不矛盾的解释；但是，除本篇有关口头证据和外部证据的条款另有规定外（第 2.202 条），在此种解释不合理时，否认或限制无效。（2）除（3）款另有规定外，要排除或修改有关商销性的默示担保或其任何部分，用语必须提及商销性；如果使用书面形式，书写必须醒目。要排除或修改有关适用性的默示担保，必须使用书面形式，且书写必须醒目。要排除有关适用性的所有默示担保，可以使用诸如‘不存在超出此处描述的任何其他担保’一类的词句”。

Section 2-316 provides in part: “（1） Words or conduct relevant to the creation of an express warranty and words or conduct tending to negate or limit warranty shall be construed wherever reasonable as consistent with each other; but, subject to the provisions of this article on parol or extrinsic evidence （Section 2-202） negation or limitation is inoperative to the extent that such construction is unreasonable. （2） Subject to subsection （3）, to exclude or modify the implied warranty of merchantability or any part of it the language must mention merchantability and in case of a writing must be conspicuous, and to exclude or modify any implied warranty of fitness the exclusion must be by a writing and conspicuous. Language to exclude all implied warranties of fitness is sufficient if it states, for example, that ‘there are no warranties which extend beyond the description on the face hereof.’”

对排除条款的限制　根据法典第 2.316 条（1）款，文字或行为可以被解释为对明示担保的排除或限制，但是，如果此种解

Under Sec. 2-316（1）, words or conduct may be construed to negate or limit an express warranty, but negation or limitation of the warranty is inoperative to the extent that

释不合理，则对担保的排除或限制无效。根据法典第2.316条（2）款，对适用于特定用途的默示担保的排除，“必须以书面形式作出，且必须醒目”。根据法典第1.201条（10）款，醒目被定义为“条款的书写方式，使作为其受众且通情达理的人在阅读时，不致忽略该条款”。

such construction is unreasonable. Under Sec. 2-316（2）, the exclusion or modification of any implied warranty of fitness “must be by a writing and conspicuous”. Under Sec. 1-201（10）, conspicuous is defined as: “[a] term or clause is conspicuous when it is so written that a reasonable person against whom it is to operate ought to have noticed it.”

对间接买方的排除需要醒目的书面形式 涉及对法典第2.316条（2）款项下默示担保进行排除的条款时，俄克拉何马州法院一贯坚持，排除条款必须以书面形式作出且必须醒目，才具有效力（C诉B案；P诉O案）。我们判定，俄克拉何马州法院必然认为，本案供应商如果希望其排除条款得到第2.316条的承认，其对最终购买人的本案买方同样负有上述义务。上述判定与俄克拉何马州最高法院在E诉S案中的立场一致。在该案中，该院重审了O诉H案的判决原则。O诉H案承认，在最终消费者起诉建造商/供应商/制造商的诉讼中，对于违反担保的索赔，

In assessing the validity of a disclaimer of an implied warranty under Sec. 2-316（2）, the Oklahoma courts have consistently held that the disclaimer must be in writing and conspicuous. Collins Radio Company of Dallas v. Bell; P.E.A.C.E. Corporation v. Oklahoma Natural Gas Company. We hold that Oklahoma would impose this obligation upon General Electric to an ultimate purchaser such as Patty Precision before it would accord General Electric the benefits of Sec. 2-316. Our holding is consistent with Elden v. Simmons, in which the Supreme Court of Oklahoma reiterated its Old Albany Estates v. Highland Carpet Mills ruling recognizing that the U.C.C. eliminated the requirement of vertical privity in breach of warranty actions brought by ultimate consumers against

法典不再要求当事方必须存在纵向的合同关系。

不要求存在纵向合同关系

我们在本案第一次上诉中大量引用了 E 诉 S 案，包括其下述判词："当事方同意，O 诉 H 案废除了默示担保中的纵向合同关系的要求。在 E 诉 S 案中，俄克拉何马州最高法院再一次就纵向合同关系与默示担保的关系问题作出说明。"虽然并非作出该案判决所必需，但俄克拉何马州最高法院仍然作出如下说明："在作出我们今天这个判决的同时，我们希望说明，对于默示担保或明示担保的诉讼来说，在目前的市场体制下，将纵向合同关系作为诉讼的前提条件，无论是从法典的角度，还是从法典之外其他法律的角度，均已成为过时的概念。在产品经销的过程中，所生产的产品在最终到达消费者之前，要经过几十次中转。当产品存在瑕疵时，如果只允许最终消费者追究其直接卖方的责任，这完全不合情理。假设我们允许上述方法，则直接卖方为了维护自

builder-vendors or manufacturers.

We quoted Elden v. Simmons extensively in Patty Precision I as follows: "The parties are in agreement that Old Albany abolished the vertical privity requirement for implied warranties. In Elden v. Simmons, the Oklahoma Supreme Court again addressed the issue of vertical privity and implied warranties." While not necessary to reach its decision, the court made the following observation: "In reaching our holdings today, we note that the requirement of vertical privity as a prerequisite to suit on an implied or express warranty, both under the Uniform Commercial Code and outside the Code, is, given today's market structure, an antiquated notion. A manufactured product placed in the chain of distribution may literally pass through dozens of hands before it reaches the ultimate consumer. When the product is found to be defective, it makes little sense to allow the ultimate consumer redress against his immediate vendors only. If such were the case, the consumer's immediate vendor, if he were to have the full benefit of his bargain, would have to, in turn, sue his immediate

己在交易中应得的利益，只好再起诉自己的卖方。这样一级一级往上追究，直至找到那位将瑕疵产品投入市场的最终责任人。为了使最终责任人承担责任而进行这种无休止的连锁诉讼，是完全违背常理的。基于这个理由，本院在O诉H案中去除了纵向合同关系的要求，以便允许最终消费者对疑似瑕疵产品的制造商直接提起违反担保的诉讼。”

vendor, who would, in turn, have to sue his vendor, and so on up the chain, until the party ultimately responsible for placing a defective product in the market is reached. It defies common sense to require such an endless chain of litigation in order to hold the party at fault responsible. For this reason, this Court, in Old Albany Estates v. Highland Carpet Mills, eliminate the requirement of vertical privity, thus allowing ultimate consumers to bring direct breach of warranty actions against manufacturers of products which are allegedly defective.”

一般不适用于间接买方的经济损失 商销性的默示担保，一直被视为法典中最重要的担保（引用著作）。法典的主要目标之一是，废除对合同关系的要求。这与《侵权法重述》第402A条的原则是一致的，但“《侵权法重述》第402A条只废除了财产损害和人身伤害中的合同关系要求”。法典没有规定，即使买方与经销链条中的批发商或制造商没有直接合同关系，也可以就自己的直接或间接经济损失取得赔偿。大部分法院都判定，除非存

The implied warranty of merchantability has been referred to as the most important warranty in the UCC. See, White & Summers. One of the prime goals of the Code was to do away with the requirement of privity of contract consistent with “402A of the Restatement which abolishes the privity requirement only in cases of property damage and personal injury”. The Code does not state that a non-privity buyer may recover for direct or consequential economic losses against a wholesaler or manufacturer in the distribution chain. A majority of the courts, in the absence of reliance on express representations, hold a

在对明示表述的依赖，否则，不具有合同关系的买方不能就自己的直接或间接经济损失取得赔偿。

non-privity buyer cannot recover for direct or consequential economic loss.

俄克拉何马州法院的立场

但我们认为，俄克拉何马州最高法院在 O 诉 H 案中的具有广泛涵盖性的表述，以及 E 诉 S 案对该表述的重申和扩展，都说明该院拒绝了多数法院的上述立场，即不具有纵向合同关系的买方，也就是在经销链条中购买货物但并非从责任人直接采购的人，不能向责任人提起违反默示担保的诉讼。在 O 诉 H 案中和 E 诉 S 案中，买方均声称其经济损失来源于制造商 / 供应商对默示担保的违反。

In our view, the broad-sweeping language used by the Supreme Court of Oklahoma in Old Albany Estates v. Highland Carpet Mills, reiterated and enlarged upon in Elden v. Simmons, rejected the majority view that a "vertical" non-privity plaintiff, i.e., one who buys within the distribution chain but who does not buy directly from the defendant, cannot maintain an action for breach of implied warranty. In both Old Albany and Elden v. Simmons, the claimed economic losses were alleged to have resulted from a builder-vendor's breach of implied warranty.

我们曾在其他案件中判定，不具有合同关系的原告，在使用瑕疵产品并因此受到人身伤害时，可以根据俄克拉何马州法典的规定，以违反商销性默示担保为由获得赔偿（参见 W 诉 O 案；W 诉 F 案）。

We have held that a non-privity plaintiff can recover for personal injuries sustained as a result of use of defective goods based upon claimed breach of implied warranty of merchantability under the Oklahoma U.C.C. See Whiteley v. OKC Corp.; Wylie v. Ford Motor Co.

默示担保适用于间接买方

因此，在俄克拉何马州，经销链

Thus, an ultimate consumer in the distribution chain in Oklahoma can bring a

条中的最终消费者可以直接对制造商提起违反担保的诉讼，即使两者不存在直接合同关系。除非根据法典第2.316条予以排除，否则，就存在第2.314条的商销性默示担保和第2.315条的适用于特定用途的默示担保。本院判定，由于供应商未将针对卖方的排除条款告知买方，因此该条款与买方无关。初审法院采纳该证据并向陪审团作出指示的决定是错误的。

direct breach of warranty action against a manufacturer, notwithstanding his lack of privity. Since there is an implied warranty of merchantability under Sec. 2-314 and fitness for particular use under Sec. 2-315 unless excluded in accordance with Sec. 2-316, we hold that General Electric's disclaimer to Brown & Sharpe, undisclosed to Patty Precision, was irrelevant and that the district court erred in admitting it into evidence and instructing on it.

供应商了解情况并密切参与

此外，供应商完全了解其向卖方所售数控组件的预计使用用途，知道卖方会将该组件用于卖方的机器后再出售给买方。供应商的雇员参与了卖方机器在买方工厂的安装和测试。案件材料中没有任何证据显示，供应商所提供的数控组件是专门制造的。因此，虽然这些组件是买方在其加工制造中心所使用的零部件，但从商销性默示担保的角度，这些组件不因这种情况而与任何其他“货物”有所不同。案件材料显示，供应商知道买方对卖方机器的预

Furthermore, General Electric was fully aware of the use to be made of the numerical controls it sold to Brown & Sharpe, which were, in turn, sold to Patty Precision as part of the machines. General Electric employees participated in the installation and start-up of the machines at Patty Precision's plant. There is nothing in the record indicating that the numerical controls sold by General Electric were specially designed. Thus, the fact that they were components of a machining center used by Patty Precision does not distinguish them from any other "goods" insofar as implied warranty of merchantability is concerned. The record demonstrates that

定使用用途，也知道数控组件将被买方用于何种机器。在这种情况下，法典第 2.314 条规定的商销性默示担保将适用于该数控组件。推翻原判，并发回进行重新审理。

General Electric knew of the intended use of the machines by Patty Precision and the system for which the component was to be an integral part. Under these circumstances, the implied warranty of merchantability under Sec. 2-314 applied. REVERSED AND REMANDED for a new trial.

（异议法官的意见） 毫无争议的是，作为数控组件制造商的供应商，其针对卖方（第一个买方）的默示担保排除条款是有效的。卖方将该组件用于自己制造的机器中，然后出售给买方。在买方针对供应商的起诉中，关键问题是，买方在不了解供应商之担保排除条款的情况下，从卖方购买了机器并受到经济损失，那么，供应商是否可以依据该排除条款，使自己免于承担违反默示担保的责任？

［Dissenting Opinion］ There is no dispute that the disclaimer of implied warranties by the manufacturer of the component parts, General Electric Company（G.E.）, was effective against Brown & Sharpe Manufacturing Company, the first buyer, which incorporated the components into machines it fabricated and sold. The case against G.E. turns on whether the disclaimer was effective to protect G.E. from an implied warranty claim for economic loss by Patty Precision Products Company, a buyer from Brown & Sharpe unaware of the disclaimer.

同意结论但不同意推理 多数派法官判决，根据俄克拉何马州法律，该担保排除条款对买方无效，因为该条款没有被传达给买方。基于本案特定事实，我同意该条款无效，但我严重怀疑，假如在本案中不存在供应商和买

The majority holds that the disclaimer cannot be effective under Oklahoma law because it was not communicated to Patty Precision. Under the particular facts of this case I agree, but I have serious doubts that Oklahoma courts would deny validity to the disclaimer absent the extensive dealings

方之间的大量直接交往，俄克拉何马州法院是否仍会否定该排除条款的效力。为此，我单独发表我的意见。

between G.E. and Patty Precision. Therefore, I write separately.

引用的判例不支持相关推理

多数派法官将O诉H案和E诉S案视为与本案最相关的俄克拉何马州判例。我认为，这是正确的。但这两个判例都没有说明，如果未将有效的排除条款传达给后手买方，该条款对后手买方是否有效。

The majority correctly identifies Old Albany Estates, Ltd. v. Highland Carpet Mills, Inc., and Elden v. Simmons, as the Oklahoma cases most closely on point. But neither involved the effect of a valid disclaimer not disclosed to a subsequent purchaser.

不存在担保排除条款的判例

在O诉H案中，作为最终购买人的不动产开发商从室内装饰商购买地毯，而装饰商随后从制造商购买了该地毯。在两个合同(最终购买人和装饰商之间的合同，以及装饰商和制造商之间的合同)均已生效之前，最终购买人和制造商之间从未有过联系。在制造商与装饰商订立的合同中，制造商并未排除担保，但是，在制造商发给装饰商的书面发货单上，制造商醒目地注明了书面排除条款。装饰商随后将该发货单转发给最终购买人。俄克拉何马

In Old Albany, the ultimate purchaser, a real estate developer, contracted for the purchase of carpet from an interior decorator; the decorator then purchased the carpet from a manufacturer. The ultimate purchaser and the manufacturer never communicated until after both contracts--the contract between the purchaser and the decorator, and the one between the decorator and the manufacturer--had become binding. The manufacturer did not disclaim any warranties in its contract with the decorator. However, the manufacturer did include written and conspicuous disclaimers in its invoices sent to the decorator, who in turn forwarded the invoices to the ultimate

州法院判定，“因为在交付或收到发货单之前，地毯买卖合同已经存在”，因此，发货单中的排除条款，仅仅是具有要约性质的补充条款，而并未成为任何一项合同的组成部分。法院在该案中并没有明确判定，在涉及违反默示担保的诉讼中，最终购买人与制造商之间并不需要存在合同关系。

与 O 诉 H 案不同的是，在本案中，供应商与卖方（第一个买方）之间的担保排除条款确实构成了合同的组成部分。我认为，对 O 诉 H 案的正确解读是，该案并没有回答这个问题，即制造商和第一个购买人之间的排除担保和限制救济的条款，是否也有可能对第二个购买人和随后的购买人具有效力。

可能支持相反结论的判例　E 诉 S 案涉及一栋住宅的后手购买人。该案采纳了 O 诉 H 案中“无须存在合同关系”的原则，允许购买人就房屋违反宜居性的默示担保而起诉房屋建造商，并就房屋结构中使用的砖块，起诉砖块

purchaser. The Oklahoma court held that because “[t] here existed a contract for sale of carpet prior to delivery or receipt of the invoices”, the disclaimers in the invoice constituted merely an offer of additional terms that did not become part of any contract. The court did hold clearly that privity between the ultimate purchaser and the manufacturer was not necessary to permit suit on implied warranties.

In contrast to Old Albany, the disclaimer in the case before us between G.E., a manufacturer, and the first buyer, Brown & Sharpe, was part of their contract. I think the proper reading of Old Albany is that it leaves open the issue whether disclaimers of warranties and limitations of remedies effective between the manufacturer and the first purchaser also may be effective against the second and successive purchasers.

Elden applied the Old Albany “no privity” rule to a case involving a subsequent purchaser of a home, allowing that purchaser to sue the builder on an implied warranty of habitability and a manufacturer of bricks used in the home on an implied warranty of merchantability and fitness. As to the

制造商违反商销性和适用性的默示担保。关于制造商，法院说，“如果陪审团裁定，任何特定的瑕疵构件还在担保有效期内，则最终消费者(目前的房屋所有权人)可从该构件的建造商或制造商取得赔偿，只要可以证明存在违反担保”。但在该案中，并不存在担保排除条款。对于建造商或制造商的排除条款是否可以有效对抗购买人的问题，如果说该判决有所提及，那么其言外之意是，排除条款可能有效。

manufacturer the court said, “If a jury finds that a particular defective component is still under warranty, the ultimate consumer (the present owner) may recover against the builder and/or manufacturer of the component, if a breach of warranty is found to exist”. There was no disclaimer in Elden, but if the decision says anything about whether a disclaimer between the manufacturer and the builder would be effective against the purchaser, it implies that it might be valid.

其他州的判例 其他州的判例也许可以提供一些帮助。我所看到的判例都判定，对于制造商的产品，如果第一个买方将该产品添加至或组装进自己的另一个产品，或第一个买方对该产品作出改动或进行使用后再出售，则制造商的限制救济或排除担保的条款，均可有效对抗随后的买方(参见D诉I案；W诉C案；R诉C案；A诉W案；W诉S案；F诉W案；G诉H案)。

Looking to other jurisdictions for guidance, the cases I found hold that limitations of remedies and disclaimers of warranty are binding on subsequent buyers when the first buyer adds, assembles or incorporates the manufacturer's product into another item or when the first buyer modifies or uses the manufacturer's product before resale. See Datamatic v. International Business Machines Corp.; Wood Products, Inc. v. CMI Corp.; R & L Grain Co. v. Chicago Eastern Corp.; American Electric Power Co. v. Westinghouse Electric Corp.; Western Equipment Co. v. Sheridan Iron Works, Inc.;

Flintkote Co. v. W.W. Wilkinson, Inc.; General Motors Corp. v. Halco Instruments Inc.

将组件和成品相区别　反过来，当第一个买方是经销商或零售商时，如果其仅仅持有制造商的产品用于再出售，而并不改变产品的形式，则有些法院判定，排除担保的条款必须被传达给最终购买人后，才可以对抗该购买人［参见 P 诉 T 案；G 诉 U 案；P 诉 N 案；N 诉 F 案；另参见 F 诉 P 案（该案判定，根据佛罗里达州法律，将汽车出售给经销商用于再出售的汽车制造商，不得排除对最终购买人的担保）］。

Conversely, when the first purchaser was a dealer or retailer who merely held the manufacturer's product for resale without changing its form, several courts have held that, to be effective, a disclaimer must be communicated to the ultimate purchaser. See Pennington Grain and Seed, Inc. v. Tuten; Groppel Co. v. U.S. Gypsum Co.; Peterson v. North American Plant Breeders; Nakanishi v. Foster. Cf. Ford Motor Co. v. Pittman (holding that, under Florida law, automobile manufacturer who sells to retailer for resale may not disclaim warranties to ultimate purchaser).

商业合理性和可行性问题　对于类似本案这样的商业交易，上述区分合乎常理。如一个法院所说，"如果制造商希望（在商法所允许的范围内）排除担保，其唯一能做的，就是在与直接买方订立的合同文件中加入排除担保的条款。从商业的角度讲，要求制造商将排除条款通知给每一个最终购买人（在很多情况下，

This distinction makes sense in commercial transactions of the sort before us. As noted by one court: "A manufacturer who wishes to exclude warranties (to the extent permitted by the commercial law) can do so only by placing disclaiming language in the contract documents with his immediate buyer; it is commercially unreasonable to expect him to notify each ultimate purchaser (whose very identity is frequently unknown

制造商根本不知道谁是最终购买人），是不合理的”（W诉C案）。

当制造商生产的不是一件最终产品，而是一个组件时，就更难通知最终购买人。组件通常是埋藏在最终产品里面的。因此，组件制造商很难或不可能通过在组件上贴上排除条款的标签来通知最终购买人。此外，虽然本案供应商（制造商）有足够的经济优势来要求其直接买方向随后的所有购买人就担保排除条款作出通知，但是，典型的组件制造商通常是将产品出售给更大的公司，因此，期待前者可以控制后者，是不合理的想法。形成对照的是，如果制造商出售的是已完成的产品，而中间商仅仅是持有该产品并再出售，这个问题就没有那么困难，因为制造商通常可以通过在产品上贴上排除条款的标签来通知最终购买人（参见G诉U案）。

必要性问题 如果产品存在危险并造成人身伤害，我可以理解法院为什么要否定制造商的担保排除条款或救济排除条款。但

to him) of his disclaimers." Wood Products.

The difficulty of notifying ultimate purchasers is exacerbated if the manufacturer has produced a component rather than a finished product. Components are often hidden within the finished product, making it difficult or impossible for the manufacturer to notify ultimate purchasers by posting disclaimers on the product itself. Further, while the manufacturer before us, G.E., may be economically powerful enough to require someone like Brown & Sharpe to notify all purchasers of the warranty limitation, the typical component part manufacturer will be selling to a larger entity which it cannot reasonably be expected to control. In contrast, the problem of notice is less severe with a finished product which the middleman holds only for resale; the manufacturer frequently can notify the ultimate purchaser simply by affixing a copy of the disclaimer to the product. See Groppel Co.

I can see how a court might invalidate a manufacturer's warranty or remedy limitations for a product that is dangerous and causes personal injury. But for ordinary transactions

是，对于商业活动中的普通交易，如果产品的失效仅仅造成经济损失，则保护最终购买人的公共政策理由就不那么强烈。在大多数案件中，只要最终购买人可以起诉其直接卖方，购买人就可以获得充分保护。

一致性问题　法典承认，合同当事方之间的排除条款可以具有效力（参见法典第 2.316 条）。如果像 O 诉 H 案所判定的那样，一项担保所提供的保护，可以在没有合同关系的情况下传导下去，那么合理的结论是，在原始当事方之间有效的担保排除条款，也应该能够传导下去，至少是在仅涉及经济损失且不涉及消费品时。也就是说，"如果任何人在不存在排除条款时可以追究制造商的担保责任，那么，该人也要受到担保排除条款的约束"（引用著作）。

本案结论基于特定事实而得出　尽管我有上述意见，但在本案的特定事实背景下，我同意多数派法官的判决，即本案供应商的排除条款不能有效对抗买方，

in the stream of commerce, where failure of the product causes only economic loss, the policy objectives of protecting the ultimate purchaser are not as compelling. In most cases the ultimate purchaser's cause of action against his immediate seller should be sufficient protection.

The U.C.C. recognizes that disclaimers can be effective between contracting parties. See Okla.Stat.Ann. Sec. 2-316. If the benefits of warranties pass without regard to privity, as Old Albany and Elden hold, it seems reasonable--at least in cases involving only economic loss and not involving consumer goods--that disclaimers which are effective between the original parties should also bind "anyone asserting the liability of a defendant on a warranty that would exist but for the disclaimer". R. Anderson, Anderson on the Uniform Commercial Code.

Having said this, I nevertheless agree with the majority that under the particular circumstances of the instant case G.E.'s disclaimer should not be valid against Patty Precision because G.E. did not communicate

因为供应商没有将排除条款传达给买方。如同多数派法官在判决书中所说，虽然第一台机器的合同是在供应商与买方发生直接联系前订立的，但在安装该机器时，以及在随后几台机器的采购订单签订前，供应商与买方存在密切交往。供应商的一位售后工程师几乎全职在买方工地工作，且延长了给买方的明示担保。

the disclaimer to Patty Precision. As the majority opinion recites, the contract for the first machine was executed before G.E. commenced dealing directly with Patty Precision. But G.E. had extensive dealings with Patty Precision in the installation of that machine and before subsequent purchase orders were executed. It had a service engineer on the premises almost full time, and it extended express warranties to Patty Precision.

我相信，供应商对买方的参与，引起了买方对供应商之担保的依赖，并超出了仅协助自己客户（卖方）调整机器的范畴（参见N诉F案）。在这种情况下，期待供应商就默示担保的排除条款向买方作出明确和醒目说明，在商业上并非不合理（参见W诉C案）。我同意，由于供应商在与买方的全部交往中未向买方传达该排除条款，因此，供应商放弃了排除条款的抗辩，或根据禁止自相矛盾原则，无权再引用该条款。我同意推翻针对供应商的那部分初审判决。

Its participation, I believe, induced Patty Precision's reliance on warranties and went beyond mere aid in making adjustments to satisfy its customer, Brown & Sharpe. See Nakanishi. Under these circumstances, it is not commercially unreasonable to expect G.E. to communicate in clear and conspicuous language its disclaimer of implied warranties to Patty Precision. See Wood Products. I agree that by failing to communicate the disclaimer during all of these dealings with Patty Precision G.E. waived the disclaimer defense or is estopped from raising it. I agree with the reversal as to G.E.

案例 14　卖方是否享有补救权？

T. W. Oil v. Consolidated Edison Co. of N.Y.

迪塔石油公司诉纽约联合埃迪逊公司案

纽约州上诉法院 1982 年；57 N.Y.2d 574, 35 UCC Rep.Serv. 12

简　介

本案卖方（T.W. Oil）向买方（Con Edison）出售了载于卡辛号油轮（“Khamsin”，以下简称卡辛轮）上的一船燃料油。在订立合同之前，卡辛轮正在海上驶往美国的途中。卖方当时刚从该油料的炼油厂收到一份证书，说明油料的硫含量为 0.52%。随后，卖方于 1974 年 1 月 24 日与买方订立了出售该油料的书面合同，并约定油料的交付日期为 1 月 30 日之前。根据行业惯例，合同对硫含量按四舍五入的方式约定。由于卖方认为油料的硫含量为 0.52%，因此合同将卡辛轮油料的硫含量定为 0.5%。卖方在与买方谈判的过程中得知，买方可以使用的油料的最高硫含量为 1%。因此，买方在购买了较低硫含量的油料后，通常会将其与高硫含量的油料混合使用，以降低成本。

卡辛轮于 1 月 25 日抵达约定目的地新泽西州，并将油料卸载至买方的储油罐里。随后，根据独立检测机构的报告，油料的实际硫含量为 0.92%。对这份报告的准确性，双方没有争议。显然，炼油厂原来提供给卖方的报告存在错误。

无论如何，基于独立检测机构的报告，买方于2月14日拒收该船油料。双方都同意，拒收系在合理时间内作出，不存在争议。随后，双方就调整油料价格的问题进行谈判。2月20日，卖方提出减价建议，减价幅度大体上对应硫含量差异所引起的差价。尽管该油料的硫含量没有超出买方可以使用的范围，但买方拒绝了卖方的调价方案，而坚持认为油料价格不得超过当时的通行价格。由于市场供求发生变化，因此当时的市场通行价格大幅低于订立合同时的价格。实际上，这是买方不接受卖方按硫含量调整价格的主要原因。

在双方无法就卡辛轮油料价格的调整达成协议的情况下，2月21日，即买方拒绝卖方调价建议的第二天，卖方提出对原交付进行补救。当时，卖方还有另一艘阿波号油轮（“Appollonian”，以下简称阿波轮）正在开往美国，计划于2月28日抵达新泽西州，而其所载油料符合原始合同的规定。为此，卖方建议用阿波轮油料向买方作出替代交付。但第二天，即2月22日，买方又直接拒绝了该建议，因为买方实际上是希望利用市场价格大幅下跌的机会，迫使卖方作出更大让步。在双方谈判破裂后，卖方最终将卡辛轮油料以当时的市场价格出售给其他买家，所获得的价格大约相当于原始合同价格的60%。卖方随后起诉买方，要求就转售油料所受到的损失从买方取得赔偿。

在初审中，当事方同意不使用陪审团而由法院单独审理，但是，为了帮助法院作出判决，双方共同拟定了4个特别问题由陪审团进行裁定。双方同意，陪审团的裁定只供法院参考，而不具有约束力。这是一种比较特别的安排，但系诉讼法所允许。陪审团随后对这4个问题作出答复，其中只有一个问题最终引起双方的争议。该问题是，对于卖方交付替代货物（阿波轮油料）的建议，买方的拒绝是否合理？陪审团对此作出了“合理”的肯定答复。但初审法院在判决时，认为陪审团对于该问题的孤立答复毫无意义，因为该答复没有考虑到法典的相关规定。因此，初审法院无视该裁定而作出了卖方胜诉的判决。该判决得到初审法院上诉庭（相当于上诉法院）的确认。买方申诉至纽约州上诉法院（纽约州最高法院），并获得了再审的批准。

纽约州上诉法院认为，本案的关键问题是，卖方是否享有法典第2.508条（2）

款所规定的补救权？如果享有该权利，那么无论买方对卖方建议的拒绝是否合理，都不能阻止卖方行使补救权，因为这是卖方的权利。如果买方阻止，就属于违约。也就是说，陪审团的答复确实与第 2.508 条（2）款的适用没有关系。上诉法院认为，在这个问题上，初审法院对陪审团裁定的无视，从道理上是对的，并且也符合当事方自己的约定，即陪审团的裁定仅供法院参考。

但买方认为，无论如何，法典第 2.508 条（2）款只适用于卖方在交付货物时已知货物不符合合同的情况，而在本案中，卖方在交付货物时，独立检测机构的报告还不存在，因此卖方实际上不知道油料的硫含量超出合同规定，也就是不知道货物不符合合同。纽约州上诉法院认为，尽管个别学者认为，法典该款有关价格调整的文字似乎说明，卖方在交付货物时应该是已知其不符合合同，但合理的解释是，法典的重点不在于卖方交付时是否知道货物存在瑕疵，而在于卖方是否有合理理由相信，货物本来可以被买方接受，而在本案的具体情况下，卖方完全有理由这样认为。据此，法院判定卖方享有使用阿波轮油料作出替代交付的补救权，而买方拒绝此种补救的行为违反了法典规定。上诉法院最终维持了原判，即卖方有权按卡辛轮油料的合同价格与出售给其他买家的转售价格的差额取得赔偿。

判　决

本案的主要问题　本案面临的问题，是本院首次遇到。我们需要处理的主要问题是，当一个卖方所提示交付的货物不符合合同且买方正当地予以拒收时，如果卖方在交付时系以善意作为且对货物的瑕疵不知情，卖方是否有权引用法典第 2.508 条（2）

In the first case to wend its way through our appellate courts on this question, we are asked, in the main, to decide whether a seller who, acting in good faith and without knowledge of any defect, tenders nonconforming goods to a buyer who properly rejects them, may avail itself of the cure provision of subdivision （2） of section

款所规定的补救权？我们判定，只要卖方已向买方及时作出补救通知，且卖方系以善意作为，且合理期待原始货物本可被买方接受，卖方就有权要求在合同原始规定的履约期过后的合理时间内，对瑕疵进行补救。

2-508 of the Uniform Commercial Code. We hold that, if seasonable notice be given, such a seller may offer to cure the defect within a reasonable period beyond the time when the contract was to be performed so long as it has acted in good faith and with a reasonable expectation that the original goods would be acceptable to the buyer.

初审法院的判决 本次违约之诉的初审过程多少有些非同寻常，但初审法院最终在无陪审团审理的情况下作出判决，指令买方向卖方支付 1,385,512.83 美元，基本上相当于原始合同价格（3,360,667.14 美元）与卖方转售卡辛轮的油料所得价款的差额。转售价格是通过商谈确定的，但法院认定，作为事实问题，其属于当时公开市场上的合理价格。

This action for breach of contract, after a somewhat unconventional trial course, resulted in a nonjury decision for the plaintiff in the sum of $1,385,512.83, essentially the difference between the original contract price of $3,360,667.14 and the amount received by the plaintiff by way of resale of the Khamsin oil at what the court found as a matter of fact was a negotiated price which, under all the circumstances, was reasonably procured in the open market.

卖方的其他理论不成立 在得出上述结论的过程中，初审法院拒绝了卖方提出的其他责任理论，特别是卖方的指控，即买方未按照法典第 1.203 条的规定，以善意就卡辛轮油料与卖方进行价格调整的谈判。尽管如此，法院判定，作为法律问题，卖方有

To arrive at this result, the Trial Judge, while ruling against other liability theories advanced by the plaintiff, which, in particular, included one charging the defendant with having failed to act in good faith in the negotiations for a price adjustment on the Khamsin oil（Uniform Commercial Code, § 1-203）, decided as a matter of law that

权引用法典第 2.508 条（2）款规定的补救权，即使卖方之前对货物瑕疵并无了解。

交付时卖方不知货物不符合合同　初审法院认定，对于最终被证明硫含量为 0.92% 的油料，作为事实问题，卖方在交付货物时，并非认为该硫含量“处于可被买方接受的合理范围之内”。但法院同时认定，卖方及时作出了补救通知。法院随后判决，买方不适当地拒绝了卖方的“合理且及时的补救建议”。上诉庭一致同意维持原判。经本院许可后，本案被提交至本院审理。

买方的主张　买方为了支持其推翻原判的主张，声称初审法院存在如下错误：（a）陪审团就所收到的特定问题作出裁定后，法院错误地判定该裁定与本案结果无关；（b）法院错误地解释了法典第 2.508 条（2）款，因为其未能将该款解释为，如履约时间已过期，则卖方的补救权仅限于卖方已知货物存在瑕疵而仍然作出的交付；以及（c）法院对

subdivision （2） of section 2-508 of the Uniform Commercial Code was available to the plaintiff even if it had no prior knowledge of the nonconformity.

Finding that in fact plaintiff had no such belief at the time of the delivery, that what turned out to be a 0.92% sulfur content was “within the range of contemplation of reasonable acceptability” to Con Ed, and that seasonable notice of an intention to cure was given, the court went on to hold that plaintiff's “reasonable and timely offer to cure” was improperly rejected. The Appellate Division having unanimously affirmed the judgment entered on this decision, the case is now here by our leave.

In support of its quest for reversal, the defendant now asserts that the trial court erred （a） in ruling that the verdict on a special question submitted for determination by a jury was irrelevant to the decision of this case, （b） in failing to interpret subdivision （2） of section 2-508 of the Uniform Commercial Code to limit the availability of the right to cure after date of performance to cases in which the seller knowingly made a nonconforming tender, and （c） in

损害赔偿数额的计算存在错误，因为该计算系基于瑕疵货物的转售价格，而不是基于卖方建议用于替代瑕疵货物之货物的价格。基于下述说明的理由，我们驳回买方上述全部3项主张。

calculating damages on the basis of the resale of the nonconforming cargo rather than of the substitute offered to replace it. For the reasons which follow, we find all three unacceptable.

陪审团裁定的问题 我们首先看一下有关陪审团特别裁定的争议。这项裁定并不复杂，但如果初审法院的处理是错误的，就要推翻原判。此次陪审团的裁定源于庭审前的临时安排，属于民事诉讼中争议当事方自行掌控其诉讼进程的一种安排。对于此种安排，除非涉及公共政策，法律一般不予阻止（M诉C案）。

Initially, we deal with the threshold contention over the special verdict, which, though not complex, if erroneously decided below, would require reversal. A product of an ad hoc pretrial arrangement peculiar to this case, on analysis, however, it presents but another example of a decision by opposing parties in a civil case to chart their own litigation course, to which, unless public policy is affronted, the law ordinarily raises no obstacle（Martin v. City of Cohoes）.

当事方约定陪审团的裁定仅供参考 当事方自然有权彻底放弃陪审团审理。本案当事方约定使用陪审团，但是将陪审团的特别裁定实质上降格为咨询性裁定（如M诉M案）。如果不是这样，初审法院本来不可能仅因不同意该裁定而将其推翻（V诉C案）。

Here, by stipulation, the parties, who, of course, were free to waive a jury entirely, in effect relegated the special verdict, which otherwise could not be set aside merely because the court disagreed with it（Vaughn-Rees v. Connolly）, to a position tantamount to that of an advisory verdict（e.g., McKenna v. Meehan）.

实际约定 事情的起源是，当事方对大部分事实没有争议，

This came about when the parties, finding themselves in accord on most of the facts,

但共同约定，召集陪审团来回答 4 个特别拟定的问题。在证词的提交将要结束时，当事方对陪审团的任务范围作出进一步限制。他们在案件材料中记录了他们的如下谅解：“在将法律适用于事实以便作出最终判决的过程中，法院将考虑双方律师已书面确认的各项事实，并考虑陪审团对所收到的特定问题的答案。双方律师进一步约定，在将法律适当地适用于本案事实的过程中，如果还需要确认任何其他事实，但该事实未曾由当事方共同确认，也不属于陪审团已裁定的事实，则当事方特此授权法院，可以在无陪审团的情况下，作为适用法律的前提条件，对该事实作出确认，只要案件材料中存在可以支持该事实的证词，或存在可以确认该事实的任何其他种类的证据。”

mutually agreed that the jury only be called upon to answer four stipulated questions, and then, by the close of the testimony, went on to further limit the jury's scope by an understanding, as they read it into the record, "that in applying the law to the facts for an ultimate determination that the Court will consider the stipulated set of facts which have been presented in writing by counsel, the resolution of the specific questions by the jury as submitted to the jury, and counsel further stipulate that, if any other necessary fact is required to enable the proper application of the law to the facts of this case and such fact is not covered by either the stipulation of facts of the parties or the finding of the jury, and if further there is testimony in the record from which a finding could be made or in testimony or evidence of any kind from which a finding of such necessary fact can be made, the parties do hereby authorize the Court nonjury to make such determination as a prerequisite to the application of the law".

买方认为应采纳的裁定　初审法院随后无视陪审团的裁定而作出判决。从法院排除陪审团裁定时的说明看，法院明显是按上

That the court so understood its responsibility is clear from the language it employed in disregarding the verdict. For the only one of the four questions of which the

述方式理解其职责的。买方只就 4 个问题中一个问题的处理提出异议。该问题如下：“问：卖方 1974 年 2 月 21 日建议，作为替代油料，卖方将交付预计于 1974 年 2 月 28 日抵达的油料。买方对该建议的拒绝是否合理？陪审团答：合理。”

无视陪审团裁定的理由 法院在判决时，就上述裁定说明如下：“当事方基于他们的理解，共同制定了上述问题和其他问题，并提交给陪审团。他们的理解是，法院随后在适用法律时，应该对陪审团就事实问题作出的裁定给予适当重视。当事方明确理解并同意，提交给陪审团的问题，是他们共同制定且范围狭窄的事实问题，且未关联至法典的任何适用条款或要求；并且，法院随后需要将法典的法律原则适用于本案的全部事实。根据此种约定的程序，法院没有就当事方在法典项下的权利或义务向陪审团作出指示或提供信息。因此，陪审团的裁定，即买方对卖方建议的拒绝是合理的，在未与法典

appellant complains, reads as follows: “Q. Did Con Edison act reasonably in rejecting the substitute shipment which was offered by Joc Oil USA on February 21, 1974, for a scheduled February 28, 1974 arrival?” “Jury -- ‘Yes’” .

And the court’s words, in ruling, were: “The parties formed this and the other submission to the jury pursuant to their understanding that the factual verdicts would be afforded any appropriate significance when thereafter the court applied the applicable law. It was clearly understood and agreed that their mutually framed narrow factual questions would be submitted to the jury without any reference to applicable provisions or requirements of the Uniform Commercial Code, and that the court would thereafter apply the law as mandated by the code to all of the facts of the case. In accordance with this agreed procedure no instruction or information was given to the jury as to the rights or duties of the parties under the statute. The jury finding of reasonable rejection can have no meaning without the necessary absent

规定联系起来考虑的情况下，是毫无意义的。”

statutory frame of reference.”

补救权不取决于拒收是否合理　从初审法院的长篇判决中，可以很明显地看出，上述说明中所提到的法典条款是第 2.508 条（2）款。如同本判决下面将会解释的，在买方拒收不符合合同的货物后，卖方可以根据法典该条行使补救权；但是，买方是否已经作出了拒收，不取决于该拒收是合理还是不合理。实际上，只有当卖方根据法典的规定行使补救权时，才使用“合理”这个概念来规范卖方的行为。因此，陪审团的裁定，即买方的拒收行为是合理的，实际上与法典第 2.508 条的适用毫无关联。因此，初审法院无视陪审团对该问题答复的决定，并无错误。

The code reference in this statement, as made clear in the extensive writing in which the Trial Judge handed down his decision, was to subdivision （2） of section 2-508. As explained ［later in］ this opinion, while a buyer's rejection of a nonconforming tender provides the occasion for a seller's invocation of the statute, the buyer's rejection is not conditioned by any requirement that it have been a reasonable or unreasonable one. Rather, the word “reasonable” is employed only to qualify a seller's conduct once the seller invokes the statute. A finding by the jury, therefore, that the buyer's conduct was reasonable was irrelevant to the application of section 2-508. Consequently, it was not error to ignore the jury's answer to the question.

买方的弃权　对这个问题最后需要补充说明的是，买方现在似乎指责初审法院拒绝向陪审团就法典第 2.508 条（2）款进行宣读，但是，在卖方要求向陪审团宣读该条款时，买方律师并未支持该要求，事后也未对法院拒

As a final word on this issue, we also add that, to the extent that Con Ed now belabors the trial court for refusing to charge the provisions of subdivision（2）of section 2-508, suffice it to say that, since defense counsel did not join either in plaintiff's request that the statute be read to the jury or in the consequent

绝宣读的行为提出异议。因此，简单地说，我们现在已无权审查这个问题了（H诉B案）。

补救权的目的 我们现在讨论本次上诉的下述核心问题：如果我们公平地解释法典第2.508条（2）款，那么，法典该款是否要求买方必须接受卖方所建议的替代交货？在分析这个问题时，我们当然必须记住，卖方对有瑕疵的提示交付进行补救的权利，即法典第2.508条两项条款所提供的补救权，本意是对古老的完美提示交付原则的绝对性作出一定限制。完美提示交付原则对于提示交付的不完美之处，没有任何容忍余地。如一个法院所说，涉及商业义务时，该原则“没有为实质履行原则留下任何余地”（M诉A案；参见法典第2.508条正式评论；引用文章）。

灵活和善意的一般原则 形成对照的是，为了应对现今这种缺乏人情味的商业世界的现实，法典出于防止奸猾交易手段的目的，明确规定要对救济条款进行灵活解释（法典第1.102条），

exception to the court's refusal to do so, the matter was not preserved for our review (Hunt v. Bankers & Shippers Ins. Co. of N. Y.).

We turn then to the central issue on this appeal: Fairly interpreted, did subdivision (2) of section 2-508 of the Uniform Commercial Code require Con Ed to accept the substitute shipment plaintiff tendered? In approaching this question, we, of course, must remember that a seller's right to cure a defective tender, as allowed by both subdivisions of section 2-508, was intended to act as a meaningful limitation on the absolutism of the old perfect tender rule, under which, no leeway being allowed for any imperfections, there was, as one court put it, just "no room for the doctrine of substantial performance" of commercial obligations (Mitsubishi Goshi Kaisha v. Aron & Co.; see Note, Uniform Commercial Code, § 2-508; Seller's Right to Cure Non-Conforming Goods).

In contrast, to meet the realities of the more impersonal business world of our day, the code, to avoid sharp dealing, expressly provides for the liberal construction of its remedial provisions (§ 1-102) so that "good faith" and the "observance of reasonable

使“善意”和“遵守公平交易的合理商业准则”成为贸易的规则，而不是规则的例外［法典第 2.103 条（1）（b）款］。“善意”的定义是，“相关行为或交易中事实上的诚实”［法典第 1.201 条（19）款］。特别是对于法典第 2.508 条，法典正式评论说，该条的使命在于，保护卖方“不致因买方突然提出某种技术问题而形成令卖方吃惊的结果”（法典第 2.106 条正式评论 2；引用文章）。

commercial standards of fair dealing” be the rule rather than the exception in trade（see § 2-103, subd ［1］, par ［b］）, with “good faith” being defined as “honesty in fact in the conduct or transaction concerned”（Uniform Commercial Code, § 1-201, subd ［19］）. As to section 2-508 in particular, the code’s Official Comment advises that its mission is to safeguard the seller “against surprise as a result of sudden technicality on the buyer’s part”（Uniform Commercial Code, § 2-106, Comment 2; see, also, Peters, Remedies for Breach of Contracts Relating to the Sale of Goods under the Uniform Commercial Code）.

两种情况下的补救　法典第 2.508 条可以简单地细分为两部分。第一部分是“履约期限尚未过期”时的补救［第 2.508 条（1）款］。在本州，这是法典制定之前即已存在的概念（L 诉 N 案）。第二部分是履约期限已经过期的补救。这是新设立的一种方式，允许卖方获得“额外的合理时间，以便重新作出符合合同的提示交付，作为原始提示交付的替代”［第

Section 2-508 may be conveniently divided between provisions for cure offered when “the time for performance has not yet expired”（subd ［1］）, a precode concept in this State（Lowinson v. Newman）, and ones which, by newly introducing the possibility of a seller obtaining “a further reasonable time to substitute a conforming tender”（subd ［2］）, also permit cure beyond the date set for performance.

2.508 条（2）款］。

法典的规定 第 2.508 条的完整条文如下：“（1）如果卖方的提示交付或交付因不符合合同而被拒收，且履约期限尚未过期，卖方可将其准备进行补救的意图及时通知买方，然后可在合同规定的时间内作出符合合同的交付。（2）即使卖方所作的提示交付不符合合同，只要卖方原有合理理由相信，经过或不经过价格调整，买方本来可以接受该货物，此时，如果买方拒收，卖方应获得额外的合理时间，以便重新作出符合合同的提示交付，作为原始提示交付的替代，但卖方必须把此种意图及时通知买方。”

In its entirety the section reads as follows：“（1） Where any tender or delivery by the seller is rejected because non-conforming and the time for performance has not yet expired, the seller may seasonably notify the buyer of his intention to cure and may then within the contract time make a conforming delivery.（2） Where the buyer rejects a non-conforming tender which the seller had reasonable grounds to believe would be acceptable with or without money allowance the seller may if he seasonably notifies the buyer have a further reasonable time to substitute a conforming tender.”

原始履约期限已过期的补救 在本案中，卖方所建议的符合合同的货物，是在履约期限过期之后交付，因此，我们集中讨论上述（2）款。从该款表面看，该款所规定的适用条件按顺序为：（1）买方必须已经拒收了不符合合同的提示交付，（2）卖方必须有合理理由认为，该提示交付本可被接受（经过或不经过价

Since we here confront circumstances in which the conforming tender came after the time of performance, we focus on subdivision （2）. On its face, taking its conditions in the order in which they appear, for the statute to apply （1） a buyer must have rejected a nonconforming tender, （2） the seller must have had reasonable grounds to believe this tender would be acceptable （with or without money allowance）, and （3） the seller

格调整),并且(3)卖方必须“及时”通知买方,说明卖方有意在合理时间内作出符合合同的替代提示交付。

must have "seasonably" notified the buyer of the intention to substitute a conforming tender within a reasonable time.

本案的具体情况　在本案中,上述所列的 3 项条件没有任何一项会成为问题。第一项很容易满足,因为毫无疑问,卡辛轮油料的硫含量为 0.92%,不符合合同规定的 0.5%,且买方对该油料已作出拒收。第二项条件是,卖方是否有合理理由相信,原始提示交付本可被买方接受。证据毫无争议地显示,合同的 0.5% 与炼油厂证书所标明的 0.52% 在行业惯例中是相等指标。这可以构成卖方的合理理由。同时,根据证词,卖方在订立合同时知道,买方使用的燃油的硫含量可以高达 1%。因此,适当调整价格后,卡辛轮油料本来可以适合买方的用途。这也构成卖方的合理理由,尽管卖方对交付时 0.92% 的测试结果感到吃惊。此外,买方 2 月 20 日表示,愿意按降低后的市场价格收下油料,而这似乎证明了油料的适用性。无疑,基于案

In the present case, none of these presented a problem. The first one was easily met for it is unquestioned that, at 0.92%, the sulfur content of the Khamsin oil did not conform to the 0.5% specified in the contract and that it was rejected by Con Ed. The second, the reasonableness of the seller's belief that the original tender would be acceptable, was supported not only by unimpeached proof that the contract's 0.5% and the refinery certificate's 0.52% were trade equivalents, but by testimony that, by the time the contract was made, the plaintiff knew Con Ed burned fuel with a content of up to 1%, so that, with appropriate price adjustment, the Khamsin oil would have suited its needs even if, at delivery, it was, to the plaintiff's surprise, to test out at 0.92%. Further, the matter seems to have been put beyond dispute by the defendant's readiness to take the oil at the reduced market price on February 20. Surely, on such a record, the trial court cannot be faulted for having found as a fact that the

件上述证据，初审法院的认定，即法典规定的第二项条件也已得到满足，是无可指责的。

second condition too had been established.

关于第三项条件，毫无争议的是，阿波轮油料符合合同规定。并且，建议使用该油料作为替代提示交付的建议是在 2 月 21 日作出的，仅在买方最终拒绝卡辛轮油料的交付一天之后。并且，当时阿波轮的替代油料已经在驶往美国的路上，预计一星期后到达，且确实于 3 月 4 日到达，仅比预计的到达时间晚了 4 日。

As to the third, the conforming state of the Appollonian oil is undisputed, the offer to tender it took place on February 21, only a day after Con Ed finally had rejected the Khamsin delivery and the Appollonian substitute then already was en route to the United States, where it was expected in a week and did arrive on March 4, only four days later than expected.

特别是，由于买方没有主张自己受到损害（除非将油料价格下降视为一种损害），同时考虑到法典对“及时”与“合理”的定义的灵活性，因此几乎无法反驳这个认定，即法典规定的剩余条件也已满足。

Especially since Con Ed pleaded no prejudice（unless the drop in prices could be so regarded）, it is almost impossible, given the flexibility of the Uniform Commercial Code definitions of “seasonable” and “reasonable”, to quarrel with the finding that the remaining requirements of the statute also had been met.

买方所引用的学者观点 但买方仍力争将法典上述条款的适用局限于这类案件：卖方在已知货物不符合合同时仍然作出交付，且有理由相信买方会接受。严格地从法典文字看，此种主张

Thus lacking the support of the statute’s literal language, the defendant nonetheless would have us limit its application to cases in which a seller knowingly makes a nonconforming tender which it has reason to believe the buyer will accept. For this

得不到支持。买方的主张几乎完全依赖诺斯德姆教授的著作（引用著作）。该教授的评论和推理是，卖方如果相信自己的提示交付符合合同，就没有理由想到降低货物的价格。因此，允许此种卖方在履约期限已经过期的情况下作出补救，会使法典中有关价格调整的文字成为多余。

proposition, it relies almost entirely on a critique in Nordstrom, Law of Sales, which rationalizes that, since a seller who believes its tender is conforming would have no reason to think in terms of a reduction in the price of the goods, to allow such a seller to cure after the time for performance had passed would make the statutory reference to a money allowance redundant.

十分有趣的是，诺斯德姆教授认为，上述立场需要以某种有些悲观的预测作为支撑，即如果不将补救权局限于卖方已明知不符而仍作出的提示交付，卖方作出及时交付的动力就会被削弱。但是，该预测缺乏任何实证支持或其他证明。作为补充，诺斯德姆教授还有一项道德评判，即如果卖方对其货物的质量存在误解，其本来就不应该获得额外时间。

Nordstrom, interestingly enough, finds it useful to buttress this position by the somewhat dire prediction, though backed by no empirical or other confirmation, that, unless the right to cure is confined to those whose nonconforming tenders are knowing ones, the incentive of sellers to timely deliver will be undermined. To this it also adds the somewhat moralistic note that a seller who is mistaken as to the quality of its goods does not merit additional time.

判例不支持买方的主张　关于这个问题，目前仅有少数几个判例。但奇怪的是，虽然买方承认这些判例都与其立场相反，但买方仍将这些判例视为规则的例外，而不是规则本身［如 W 诉 S 案（卖方出售给买方的，是未

Curiously, recognizing that the few decisions extant on this subject have adopted a position opposed to the one for which it contends, Con Ed seeks to treat these as exceptions rather than exemplars of the rule（e.g., Wilson v. Scampoli［goods obtained by seller from their manufacturer in original

曾开封的制造商原始包装的货物。法院判定法典该款适用，尽管卖方没有理由相信货物存在瑕疵）；A诉L案（卖方不小心交付了错误品牌的缝纫机，但该缝纫机在其他方面与合同约定的缝纫机相同。法院判定卖方有权通过替换进行补救，尽管其原来不知道该错误）］。

carton resold unopened to purchaser; seller held within statute though it had no reason to believe the goods defective]; Appleton State Bank v. Lee [seller mistakenly delivered sewing machine of wrong brand but otherwise identical to one sold; held that seller, though it did not know of its mistake, had a right to cure by substitution]).

法典的关注点 无可否认的是，这些判例所体现的原则，远超这些判例自身的事实背景。这些判决表明，在适用法典第2.508条（2）款时，法院一贯考虑的问题是，当卖方相信货物可以被买方接受时，该相信是否具有合理性；而不是考虑，卖方在作出提示交付前，对瑕疵是否有所了解（W诉S案；请比较Z诉S案）。

That the principle for which these cases stand goes far beyond their particular facts cannot be gainsaid. These holdings demonstrate that, in dealing with the application of subdivision (2) of section 2-508, courts have been concerned with the reasonableness of the seller's belief that the goods would be acceptable rather than with the seller's pretender knowledge or lack of knowledge of the defect (Wilson v. Scampoli; compare Zabriskie Chevrolet v. Smith).

主流学者的观点 因此，毫不奇怪，上述提到的判例历史，也反映了主流学术评论对这个问题的看法。例如，怀特教授和萨莫斯教授对此就作出过精彩和坦率的评论。他们强调，法典的意

It also is no surprise then that the aforementioned decisional history is a reflection of the mainstream of scholarly commentary on the subject. White and Summers, for instance, put it well, and bluntly. Stressing that the code intended cure to be "a remedy

图是，将补救作为“应由法院精心培育和推进的救济”，因为其“提供了一定方法，使法律能与合理期待对接，并挫败奸猾者逃避不利交易的企图”。两位教授的结论是，只要卖方可以证明自己有合理理由相信，货物本来会被买方接受，且这种相信从客观角度可以证实，卖方就应享有法典第 2.508 条（2）款所提供的补救权。这也是我们对这个问题的结论。无须赘言的是，在这个问题上，“合理”的标准中必须包含“善意”和“公平交易的商业准则”的概念，因为这是贯穿整部法典的概念［法典第 1.201 条（19）款；第 1.203 条；第 2.103 条（1）（b）款］。

损害赔偿数额计算问题　关于买方提出的损害赔偿数额问题，我们直接维持原判，而不再讨论买方的主张是否具有合理性。在初审的全部阶段，对于卖方建议的计算方法，买方均未提出异议。卖方通过向法院提交的初步说明以及审前备忘录，已就该计算方法向买方作出了充分通

which should be carefully cultivated and developed by the courts” because it “offers the possibility of conforming the law to reasonable expectations and of thwarting the chiseler who seeks to escape from a bad bargain”, the authors conclude, as do we, that a seller should have recourse to the relief afforded by subdivision（2）of section 2-508 of the Uniform Commercial Code as long as it can establish that it had reasonable grounds, tested objectively, for its belief that the goods would be accepted. It goes without saying that the test of reasonableness, in this context, must encompass the concepts of “good faith” and “commercial standards of fair dealing” which permeate the code（Uniform Commercial Code, § 1-201, subd ［19］; § § 1-203, 2-103, subd ［1］, par ［b］).

As to the damages issue raised by the defendant, we affirm without reaching the merits. At no stage of the proceedings before the trial court did the defendant object to the plaintiff's proposed method for their calculation, and this though the plaintiff gave ample notice of that proposal by means of a preliminary statement and pretrial memorandum filed with the court.

知，而买方并未反对。

由于买方完全默认了卖方的计算方法，因此初审法院允许卖方仅就卡辛轮油料的转售价格提交证据，且买方并未提出异议。此外，在向陪审团提交的双方共同制定的4个咨询性问题中，有一个问题的文字涉及损害赔偿问题。该问题表明，当事双方的假设是，卡辛轮油料是法院应该考虑的。长久以来的法律原则是，在初审中对损害赔偿方法的同意，即使是默示同意，在上诉中也有约束力（参见M诉C案；H诉C案）。

So complete was defendant's acquiescence in the theory thus advanced that the plaintiff was permitted to introduce its proof of the Khamsin resale alone, and without opposition. Furthermore, in consensually submitting the four jointly framed advisory questions that went to the jury, the language of one of them, which was damages-related, indicates that both parties were acting on the assumption that the Khamsin oil was the one with which the court was to be concerned. It has long been the law that agreement on a theory of damages at trial, even if only implied, must control on appeal (see Martin v. City of Cohoes; Hartshorn v. Chaddock).

基于上述所有原因，上诉庭的判决应该得到维持，且买方应承担卖方的诉讼费用。维持原判。

For all these reasons, the order of the Appellate Division should be affirmed, with costs. Order affirmed.

案例 15　卖方是否有权选择计算损失的方法?

Tesoro Petroleum Corp. v. Holborn Oil Co.
特索罗石油公司诉霍尔邦石油公司案

纽约州高等法院 1989 年；547 N.Y.S.2d 1012, 10 UCC Rep.Serv.2d 814

简　介

本案卖方（Tesoro）与买方（Holborn）订立了出售 1000 万加仑汽油的合同。这批汽油被装载在一艘驶往纽约的油轮上，准备在纽约卸载后交付给买方。但随后买方提出拒绝收取该批汽油，理由是卖方未能对买方订立合同的要约及时作出承诺，因此双方之间不存在有效的合同。但是，买方的真实理由很可能与当时汽油的市场情况有关。由于油价大幅下跌，双方的合同价格远高于临近交货时的市场价格。

关于这 1000 万加仑汽油，卖方从供应商采购时的采购价格是每加仑 1.26 美元。卖方与买方的合同价格是每加仑 1.3 美元。也就是说，卖方预计每加仑赚取 4 美分。临近交货时，汽油的市场价格大跌至每加仑 80 美分，比合同价格低 50 美分。所以，买方不愿继续履行该合同。在双方谈判无果后，卖方将该 1000 万加仑汽油出售给了一家阿根廷公司（Esso Sapa）。出于种种原因，卖方在此次出售中获得的价格为每加仑 1.1 美元。这虽然低于 1.3 美元的原始合同价格，但比当时 80 美分的市场价格高出 30 美分。

随后，卖方起诉买方违反合同。尽管买方声称合同并未成立，但法院认定合同无疑已经成立，因此买方拒收货物的行为构成违约。最终，本案的争议集中于一个问题，即应该如何计算卖方有权获得的损害赔偿。根据法典规定，如买方发生毁约，卖方的损失可以根据法典第 2.706 条或第 2.708 条计算，但究竟在何种情况下应该使用何种方法，则存在一定的解释余地。根据第 2.706 条，当卖方将货物转售给第三方买家时，卖方的损失为原始合同价格与转售价格的差额。根据这种方法计算，本案卖方的损失为每加仑 20 美分（1.3–1.1=0.2）。根据第 2.708 条的规定，卖方的损失是原始合同价格与提示交付时的市场价格的差额。根据这种方法计算，本案卖方的损失为每加仑 50 美分（1.3–0.8=0.5）。自然，本案卖方主张，应根据第 2.708 条计算卖方的损失，因为这种方法可以使卖方获得更多赔偿。

在通常情况下，如果买方不收取货物，且卖方将货物转售给第三方买家，转售价格被假定等同于市场价格，因为通常的假定是，卖方只能按市场价格进行转售。在这种情况下，无论是适用第 2.706 条还是第 2.708 条，计算结果都是一样的。从法官的下述讨论看，法典起草者认为，转售价格实际上可能会低于市场价格，因为此种临时转售通常属于“慌不择路”，不一定能完全按市场价格售出。所以，第 2.706 条本来更多的是为了保护受损害的卖方。但在本案中，出于种种原因，卖方的转售价格远高于市场价格，而这通常是很难想象的。但正因如此，第 2.708 条的计算方式就对本案卖方更有利。卖方认为，较高的转售价格代表了自己的能力和努力，因此应该由自己享有其成果。如果按卖方主张的方法计算，其收益就要远高于买方履行合同时卖方本可获得的收益。

由于法典没有很明确地规定在何种情况下应该采用何种计算方法，本案法官不得不花费大量精力去讨论在本案的特定情况下，到底应该使用哪一种计算方法。法院最终判定，卖方无权根据第 2.708 条获得赔偿，而只能根据第 2.706 条获得赔偿。

判　决

本案的问题　本案唯一的问题是，在卖方已证明当事方订立了合同且买方违反了合同的情况下，为了计算卖方的损失数额，到底应适用法典第 2.706 条（合同价格和转售价格的差额），还是第 2.708 条（合同价格和提示交付时市场价格的差额）？

The sole issue presented is whether, in the event plaintiff establishes a contract between the parties and a breach thereof, the measure of damages should be governed by UCC 2-706 （difference between contract price and resale price） or UCC 2-708 （difference between contract price and market price at time of tender）.

本案的情况　卖方声称，其按每加仑 1.26 美元的价格购入 1000 万加仑汽油，并于几天后与买方订立了合同，约定按每加仑 1.30 美元的价格向买方出售该汽油。卖方随后将油轮名字通知给买方，因为油料将从该油轮交付。买方答复不会接受该汽油，称卖方对买方的要约所作的承诺不及时，因此双方不存在有约束力的协议。由于装载油料的油轮马上将抵达纽约，卖方经谈判后，按每加仑 1.10 美元的价格将船上油料转售给一家阿根廷公司。

Plaintiff asserts that it contracted to sell approximately 10 million gallons of gasoline to defendant at a price of $1.30 per gallon, having purchased it a few days earlier at $1.26 per gallon. After plaintiff sent notice of the name of the vessel to deliver the product, it was informed by defendant that the gasoline would not be accepted in view of the absence of a binding agreement resulting from the untimely acceptance of its offer. While the loaded vessel was proceeding to New York, plaintiff negotiated the sale of the cargo on board to Esso Sapa in Argentina for $1.10 per gallon.

卖方的主张　卖方声称，在买方违反合同的当时，汽油价格

Plaintiff claims that because of a sudden sharp drop in price, the value of the gasoline

出现突然的剧烈下跌，至每加仑75美分~80美分。因此，虽然其得以按每加仑1.10美元的价格将汽油转售，但其有权获得的损失赔偿数额，不应按买方违约导致的实际损失（每加仑20美分，再加附带损失）计算，而应按市场价格与合同价格的差额来计算。如果卖方的此种计算方式得到法院支持，则相比卖方的实际损失而言，卖方获得的赔偿额将再增加300万美元以上（1000万加仑乘以每加仑30美分，即1.10美元的转售价格与大约80美分的最高市场价格的差额30美分）。

at the time of defendant's breach was between 75 cents to 80 cents per gallon and that, although it resold the product for $1.10 per gallon, its recovery should not be limited to its actual loss resulting from the breach （20 cents per gallon plus incidentals）, but rather it is entitled to recover the difference between market price and contract price. If plaintiff were to prevail on this claim, it could recover at least $3,000,000 in excess of its actual contractual loss （10,000,000 gallons times difference of 30 cents per gallon between the resale price of $1.10 and highest market price discussed of approximately 80 cents per gallon）.

卖方认为效益属于自己 卖方认为，自己主张的计算方法是合理的，因为当自己有能力超出市场价格转售汽油时，其效益应属于自己，而不是违约的买方。虽然货物出售的实际价格通常是货物市场价格的证明，且在本案中未看到为什么阿根廷公司愿意按超出市场价格大约40%的价格购买该汽油的相关解释，但在上诉中，当事方未对所认定的实

Plaintiff justifies this recovery by asserting that it, rather than the defaulting buyer, is entitled to the benefit of its ability to resell the gasoline at above market price. Although the price for which one actually sells merchandise is evidence as to its market value, and there is no explanation as to why Esso Sapa was willing to pay a premium of about 40% above market to obtain this cargo, the question as to the actual market value is not raised for determination on this motion.

际市场价格提出质疑。

也可以视为利润损失　卖方主张，汽油属于种类物，因此，自己作为该种商品的经销商，不仅本来可以通过向买方出售获得一次利润，而且本来还可以在公开市场采购汽油后，通过向阿根廷公司出售而获得第二次利润。因此，除附带损失外，卖方主张，如果买方向卖方支付的损害赔偿数额按每加仑 50 美分计算（假定当时的市场价格为每加仑 80 美分），卖方将处于买方履行合同并按每加仑 1.30 美元支付货款时卖方本来可以达到的处境。

Plaintiff maintains that since gasoline is fungible, it, as a dealer in that commodity, could have made a profit not only on the sale to defendant, but also could have purchased gasoline on the open market and made a second profit on the resale to Esso Sapa. Hence it asserts （putting aside incidental damages） that by recovering damages of 50 cents per gallon （assuming a market price of 80 cents per gallon at the time） from defendant, it will be in the same position as if defendant had complied with its alleged contract and accepted the gasoline and paid $1.30 per gallon.

具体计算　上述计算方法是，从每加仑 50 美分的损害赔偿数额中，减去每加仑 16 美分的损失（每加仑 1.26 美元的卖方采购价格，与每加仑 1.10 美元的向阿根廷公司转售价格的差额），得出每加仑净利润为 34 美分。这等于买方履行合同时，卖方本可从原始合同获得的每加仑 4 美分的利润（1.26 美元采购价格，与 1.30 美元合同价格的差额），再加上其声称本可获得

This is calculated by deducting from such 50 cents per gallon damages, the loss of 16 cents per gallon （difference between purchase price of $1.26 and sales price to Esso Sapa of $1.10） with a resulting 34 cents per gallon net profit. This equals the total of the 4 cents per gallon profit it would earn on the alleged contract if performed （difference between purchase price of $1.26 and contract price of $1.30） and the 30 cents profit that allegedly could be earned if it purchased gasoline on the open market at 80 cents per

的另外 30 美分的利润，即以每加仑 80 美分的价格从公开市场采购汽油后，以 1.10 美元的价格出售给阿根廷公司后可以获得的利润。为了支持其主张，卖方声称，法典第 2.703 条允许其在起诉买方违约时，在第 2.706 条和第 2.708 条之间进行选择。

gallon and resold it to Esso Sapa at $1.10. To support its position, plaintiff relies on UCC 2-703 as giving it the option to proceed against a defaulting buyer under either UCC 2-706 or 2-708.

买方的主张和理由 买方则声称，假如能够证明买方违约，则支付卖方的损害赔偿数额，应限于买方违约所引起的实际损失（每加仑 20 美分），再加上附带损失。买方为此引用了法典第 1.106 条，称法典该条的宗旨是，应尽可能地使受损方恢复至另一方充分履约时受损方本可达到的状态。因此，如果按卖方主张的方式向其支付赔偿，卖方将获得一笔横财，与法典上述宗旨不符。此外，买方还声称，允许卖方为了获得最大赔偿数额而自由选择救济，不符合法典给当事方规定的降低损失的义务。

Defendant, on the other hand, asserts that if plaintiff establishes a breach, its damages should be limited to its actual loss resulting therefrom, which would be 20 cents per gallon plus incidental damages. In this regard defendant points to UCC 1-106, which it asserts sets forth the policy of the Code to place an aggrieved party in as good a position as if the other party had fully performed, and contends that granting plaintiff the profit it seeks would result in a windfall which would be inconsistent with such policy. Further, defendant maintains that permitting plaintiff to choose its remedy to maximize its damages would be inconsistent with the requirement that a party mitigate damages.

法典第 2.706 条的规定 法典第 2.706 条（1）款规定："卖方只要遵守有关卖方救济的第

Subdivision （1） of UCC 2-706 provides: "Under the conditions stated in Section 2-703 on seller's remedies, the

2.703 条规定的条件，就可转售有关的货物，或转售尚未交付的剩余货物。只要转售以善意和商业上合理的方式进行，卖方即有权就转售价格与合同价格的差额取得赔偿，加上本篇允许的任何附带损失（第 2.710 条），减去因买方违约致使卖方节省的费用。”

seller may resell the goods concerned or the undelivered balance thereof. Where the resale is made in good faith and in a commercially reasonable manner the seller may recover the difference between the resale price and contract price together with any incidental damages allowed under the provisions of this Article （Section 2-710）, but less expenses saved in consequence of the buyer's breach."

法典第 2.708 条的规定　法典第 2.708 条（1）款规定:“除（2）款和本篇涉及市场价格证明的条款另有规定外（第 2.723 条），买方拒收或毁约所造成的损失，是提示交付之时之地的市场价格与尚未支付之合同价格的差价，加上本篇规定的任何附带损失（第 2.710 条），减去因买方违约致使卖方节省的费用。”

Section 2-708（1）provides: "Subject to subsection （2） and to the provisions of this Article with respect to proof of market price （Section 2-723）, the measure of damages for non-acceptance or repudiation by the buyer is the difference between the market price at the time and place for tender and the unpaid contract price together with any incidental damages provided in this Article （Section 2-710）, but less expenses saved in consequence of the buyer's breach."

法典第 2.703 条的规定　法典第 2.703 条规定，如果“买方对货物作出错误拒收或错误撤销接受，或未能在交付之时或之前支付到期款项，则针对直接受到影响的货物，受损害的卖方可

Section 2-703 provides that if a "buyer wrongfully rejects or revokes acceptance of goods ... then with respect to any goods directly affected ... the aggrieved seller may ... （d） resell and recover damages as hereafter provided（Section 2-706）; [or]（e）recover

以……(d)根据后述规定(第2.706条),转售货物并取得损害赔偿;或(e)就拒收取得损害赔偿(第2.708条)”。

damages for non-acceptance (Section 2-708)”.

虽然法典第2.703条正式评论说,“法典第2篇的一项根本原则就是拒绝救济选择理论,因此,全部救济在本质上都是叠加的”,但其最终的结论是,“选择一项救济后,是否会导致另一项救济被排除,则完全取决于当事案件的事实”。

Although the Official Comment to section 2-703 states that the “Article rejects any doctrine of election of remedy as a fundamental policy and thus the remedies are essentially cumulative in nature”, it concludes that “[w]hether the pursuit of one remedy bars another depends entirely on the facts of the individual case”.

学者的解读和观点 著名的怀特教授和萨莫斯教授在他们的著作中说,法典及其正式评论对这个问题的规定“模棱两可”,并且,“不清楚法典起草者是否具有这个意图,即作出转售的卖方可根据第2.708条获得更高的损害赔偿数额”(引用著作)。关于这个问题,他们的结论是,“在货物已被适当特定于买方所违反的合同后,如果卖方的实际转售价格高于第2.708条(1)款中的市场价格,则应将卖方可得的赔偿限于合同价格与实际转售价格的差额。我们认为,这准

In White and Summers, Uniform Commercial Code, the distinguished authors indicate that the Code and Comments in this area are “equivocal”, and that “[w]hether the drafters intended a seller who has resold to recover more in damages under 2-708 ... is not clear”. On this question, White and Summers conclude that: “a seller who resells goods reasonably identified to the broken contract for a price above the 2-708 (1) market price should be limited to the difference between the contract price and his actual resale price. We believe that this is an exact measure of his expectation and that he should not recover more than that. As

确地反映了卖方的期待值，而卖方不应获得比这更高的赔偿。如上所述，买方要承担举证责任，证明卖方不是损失了销量的卖方，并且证明被转售的货物实际上就是本来预计给违约买方的货物”。

indicated above, the buyer bears the burden of showing that the seller was not a lost volume seller, and that the goods which in fact were resold were those that would have been delivered to him, the breaching buyer."

在作出上述结论时，两位教授也说明了应注意的问题：“上述所有讨论均假设，当买方希望将卖方获得的赔偿局限于合同价格与转售价格的差额时，买方有能力证明卖方所转售的货物实际上就是合同项下的货物。如果为了履行与买方的合同，卖方本来可以在市场上购买货物，或在不同的种类物中选择适当货物，买方就不能将卖方的损害赔偿局限于第 2.706 条规定的赔偿，因为在这些情况下，买方无法证明，转售的货物正是‘被适当特定于买方所违反之合同’的货物。也就是说，除非转售就是用来代替原始合同项下的那次出售，否则，合同价格与该次转售价格之间的差额，就不是衡量卖方期待值的适当方法。”

In so concluding the authors expressed the following caveat："All of the foregoing discussion assumes that the buyer who wishes to limit the seller to the difference between the contract and the resale price can show that the goods resold were in fact the goods contracted for. If the seller could have fulfilled the buyer's contract by buying on the market or by a choice among a variety of fungible goods, the buyer will be unable to limit the seller to 2-706 damages. The buyer will not be able to prove that the resale is 'reasonably identified as referring to the broken contract.' Put another way, the difference between the contract and a specific resale price is not the proper measure of the seller's expectation damages unless that resale is a substitute for the one actually conducted."

相关判例 上述立场也基本符合曾处理过这个问题的法院所阐明的立场。在N诉K案中，法院在说明不存在“与这个问题直接相关的法律”后，将违反化学品买卖合同后卖方的损害赔偿，限于第2.706条规定的赔偿。在该案中，法院主要依赖法典第1.106条（1）款所述的原则，即“应为使受损方尽可能恢复至另一方充分履行义务时受损方本应达到的状态而灵活提供本法规定的救济”。该法院的结论是：“没有人坚持说，而我们也不认为任何人可以说，为了就买方的违约向卖方提供补偿，必须采用已经降低了的市场价格与合同价格之间的差额。假设交易原本已经完成，那么，卖方的‘交易收益’本来不会受到市场价格降低的影响。因此，适用第2.708条（a）款中‘市场价格与合同价格差额’原则时给卖方带来的那笔横财，在原始交易顺利完成时，卖方本来是不可能得到的。”[N诉K案；H诉S案(在该案中，法典第1.106条的原则占了上风。法院认定，

The foregoing position has generally been that enunciated by the courts that have considered the issue. In Nobs Chem. v. Koppers Co., the court （after observing the lack of “any law directly on point”） limited damages on a breach of contract for the sale of chemicals to that provided in UCC 2-706. It heavily relied on the policy provision set forth in UCC 1-106（1） that “[t] he remedies provided by this Act shall be liberally administered to the end that the aggrieved party may be put in as good a position as if the other party had fully performed”, concluding that: “No one insists, and we do not think they could, that the difference between the fallen market price and the contract price is necessary to compensate the plaintiffs for the breach. Had the transaction been completed, their ‘benefit of the bargain’ would not have been affected by the fall in market price, and they would not have experienced the windfall they otherwise would receive if the market price-contract price rule contained in § 2.708（a） is followed.” （Supra; H-W-H Cattle Co. v. Schroeder [where the admonition of UCC 1-106 carried the day, the court finding that the section suggested

该条的意思是,“为了实现当事方在合同中所表述的期待,法院在必要时应透过交易的形式看本质”);C 诉 C 案;U 诉 C 案(法院认为,“如果第 2.708 条会导致卖方处于比买方履约时更好的处境,则法典该条并未允许法院判决此种赔偿”)。]在 U 诉 C 案中,法院适当地将该案与卖方所依赖的 W 诉 S 案进行了区别。法院认定,该案合同的当事方已自愿承担了价格变动的风险,因此,如果剥夺卖方从价格下降中获得的好处,就会不公平地剥夺卖方通过谈判而获得的交易收益。

本案的情况　本案中,从任何角度看,争议合同都不会受到所发生的价格急剧下降的影响,因为合同所买卖的,是价格固定且卖方已经采购到手的货物。因此,联邦第二巡回法院在 W 诉 S 案中所作的结论,不适用于本案。

纽约州立法历史　本案卖方声称,上述判例与本案无关,因为基于纽约州的立法过程,应该得出与上述判例不同的结论。卖

that it “should look through the form of a transaction to its substance when necessary to fulfill the parties’ expectations expressed in the contract”]; Coast Trading Co. v. Cudahy Co.; Union Carbide Corp. v. Consumers Power Co. [where it was stated that UCC 2-708 did “not authorize awards of damages which put the seller in a better position than performance would have put them”].) The Union Carbide case properly distinguished Trans World Metals v. Southwire Co., relied upon by plaintiff, as there it was found that the parties to the contract assumed the risks of price variations, and to deny plaintiff a gain from a drop in prices would unjustly deny it the benefit of its bargain.

Here the alleged contract would not in any way be affected by the sharp drop in prices that occurred, as the contract was for a fixed price of goods already purchased. Hence, the result reached by the Second Circuit in Trans World is not pertinent to the case at bar.

Plaintiff asserts that the foregoing cases are inapposite because New York legislative history calls for a different result. This argument is based on the 1956 New York

方这项主张的依据，是纽约州法律修订委员会1956年提出的一项建议，即删除法典草案中的第2.703条（e）款的文字，因为如果不删除，该款本来就会将第2.708条局限于“货物尚未被转售”的情况。显然，这项建议获得了统一法委员会的采纳，因此纽约州和其他州的法典均不包含该文字。但是，这种情况不足以让纽约州对法典的解释与其他州有所不同。

Law Revision Commission recommendation to delete language in the draft of UCC 2-703（e） that would have limited UCC 2-708 to situations where the “goods have not been resold”. This recommendation was apparently accepted by the Commissioners on Uniform State Laws, and hence the Code in New York, and elsewhere does not contain such language. This is hardly reason to call for an interpretation of the Code in New York different from that in other States.

在对该删除进行解释时，怀特教授和萨莫斯教授说：“纽约州法律修订委员会可能并未设想到，卖方会通过第2.708条（1）款的诉讼而获得横财。委员会可能只是希望澄清，卖方必须首先善意地根据第2.706条作出努力，且只有在该努力失败后，才能引用第2.708条（1）款。该报告没有任何地方显示，他们已考虑到这种情况，即在转售价非常接近合同价时，卖方根据第2.706条获得的赔偿会较少，而根据第2.708条的合同价与市场价差价方法获得的赔偿却很多。”

In explaining this deletion, White and Summers state：“It is possible that the New York Law Revision Commission had in mind the seller who would not receive a windfall by suing under 2-708 （1） and simply wanted to make it clear that a seller who makes a good faith attempt to comply with 2-706 but fails may then resort to 2-708（1）. Nothing in their report suggests that they considered the case in which 2-706 recovery would be small because the seller sold at a price very near to the contract price yet the contract-market differential under 2-708 would be large.”

法典本来设想第 2.706 条对卖方更有利　在 B 诉 R 案中，第 2.708 条被用于两位教授所设想的那类情况。在该案中，法院根据第 2.708 条计算了卖方应得的赔偿数额。法院认为，由于卖方未能就转售意图向买方作出必要通知，因此法典不允许根据第 2.706 条计算赔偿。但在该案中，无论采取哪一种方法，赔偿数额都是一样的，因为已经认定，市场价格与转售价格相同。

In B & R Textile Corp. v. Rothman Indus., UCC 2-708 was used in the type of situation contemplated by the authors. There damages were measured by that section because a UCC 2-706 recovery was not permissible due to the seller's failure to give the required notice of intention to resell. In that case, however, damages were the same under either measure as the market price was found to be the same as the resale price.

此外，第 2.706 条正式评论 2 说，“如果卖方未能根据本条采取适当行动，卖方即无权根据本条计算损害赔偿，而只能降格依据第 2.708 条获得赔偿”。这项评论的言外之意是，按法典设想，第 2.708 条所提供的赔偿数额，会少于采用合同价与转售价差额的第 2.706 条所提供的赔偿数额。

Further, Official Comment 2 under UCC 2-706 states that “[f] ailure to act properly under this section deprives the seller of the measure of damages here provided and relegates him to that provided in Section 2-708”, thus implying that it was contemplated that UCC 2-708 recoveries would be less than the contract-resale price differential authorized in UCC 2-706.

此外，如果因货物已被转售而不能适用第 2.708 条，且必须从违约买方本应支付的损害赔偿中减去货物转售给另一个买家后的价款，那么，出售库存货物的

Moreover, if UCC 2-708 could not be employed if the goods had been sold, a merchant who sells from inventory would lose his profit if required to reduce damages recoverable from a defaulting buyer by the

商人，就会丧失其本可获得的利润。因此，在N诉R案中，纽约州上诉法院在允许游艇零售商根据第2.708条（2）款就利润损失取得赔偿时，引用了霍克兰教授著作中提供的一个例子:“如果汽车经销商同意按2000美元的标准定价向买方出售一辆汽车，那么，在买方违反合同后，即使经销商有能力将该汽车按2000美元的价格出售给另一个买家，经销商仍然会受到损失。”因此很明显，删除法典草稿中第2.708条的适用条件，不意味着法典起草者所设想的是本案卖方所主张的这类损害赔偿。

amount of the sale price of the item when sold to another customer. Thus, in Neri v. Retail Mar. Corp., the Court of Appeals, in allowing a UCC 2-708（2） recovery of lost profits by a retailer of boats, quoted the following from an illustration contained in Hawkland, Sales and Bulk Sales: “Thus, if an automobile dealer agrees to sell a car to a buyer at the standard price of $2000, a breach by the buyer injures the dealer, even though he is able to sell the automobile to another for $2000.” Thus, it is clear that the deletion of the proposed condition for the use of UCC 2-708 does not mean that the drafters of the Code contemplated the type of recovery sought by plaintiff herein.

本案不存在本可完成的两次销售 本案卖方实质上是希望获得霍克兰教授上述例子中提到的汽车经销商的待遇。但是，我们不能向卖方提供这种待遇，因为本案与上述例子存在重大区别。在本案中，卖方向阿根廷公司销售的是特定船舶上的特定货物，因此，该船汽油可被视为已特定于争议合同的货物［参见法典第2.501条（1）（a）款］。

Plaintiff, in essence, wishes to be accorded the same treatment as the car dealer in Professor Hawkland’s illustration. However, there are significant differences that warrant the court declining such application. Here plaintiff was selling to Esso Sapa a specific cargo aboard a specific vessel, and thus the gasoline aboard that ship may be considered as goods identified (see, UCC 2-501（1）(a)) to a broken contract.

卖方在其初始法律陈述书第 2 页说:“在无法成功说服买方继续履行合同后,卖方费力找到了一个新买家。经过激烈、漫长和仔细的谈判后,卖方于 7 月 17 日完成了向阿根廷公司的出售。”卖方证人作证说,在将该汽油出售给阿根廷公司代表的过程中,“我恳请他购买该船货物”。

On page two of plaintiff's initial memorandum of law it is stated: "After unsuccessfully attempting to convince [defendant] to honor its contract, [plaintiff] scrambled to find a new buyer and, on July 17, after feverish, lengthy and deliberate negotiations, concluded a sale to Esso Sapa." Plaintiff's witness testified that, in seeking to sell the gasoline to a representative of Esso Sapa, "I asked him to buy the cargo".

这些声明都说明了一个事实,即虽然本案涉及的汽油品种属于种类物,因此,拥有交易资金的任何人(包括本案卖方这样的经销商)都可以在市场上购买该汽油,但是,向阿根廷公司出售的汽油,显然实际上就是卖方所称的原本出售给本案买方的同一批汽油。

These statements are illustrative of the fact that although gasoline of the type involved in the action is fungible, and thus may be purchased in the marketplace by anyone (including traders such as plaintiff) in a position to finance the transaction, the sale here to Esso Sapa was clearly a substitute for the one plaintiff claims it actually contracted for with defendant.

法典第 2.706 条的计算符合原始合同预期　如果根据法典第 2.706 条来计算卖方的损失,卖方所能获得的,就是其与买方订立本案合同时可以合理期待的收益。如果向卖方支付其所寻求的大约 300 万美元的额外赔偿,就会使卖方获得一笔横财,而不能

If plaintiff's damages are measured in accordance with UCC 2-706, it would be receiving the benefit reasonably to be expected when it entered into the alleged contract with defendant. Granting it the approximately $3,000,000 additional recovery that it seeks would result in a windfall which cannot be said to have been in the contemplation of the

说这笔收入是买卖双方在谈判时已经考虑在内的。并且，这也与法典第 1.106 条所表达的宗旨不符。

parties at the time of their negotiations, and would be inconsistent with the policy of the Code as expressed in UCC 1-106.

结论 基于上述理由，本院的结论是，法典第 2.706 条与第 2.708 条之间的关系，就是怀特教授和萨莫斯教授在上述著作中所总结的那种关系，且该原则已得到上述所引用判例的遵守。因此，在本案审理中，如果卖方可以成功证明买方存在违约，则卖方的损害赔偿数额应根据第 2.706 条进行计算。

Accordingly, the court concludes that the proper interrelationship of sections 2-706 and 2-708 is that summarized by White and Summers above and followed in the cases cited. Thus, in the event plaintiff prevails and establishes a breach of contract at trial, its damages will be measured in accordance with section 2-706.

如果实际情况不同，本案结果可能也不同 假设卖方向阿根廷公司出售的汽油原本来自其库存（此时，卖方将被视为上述例子中的汽车经销商），或在买方违约前卖方原本已约定向阿根廷公司出售汽油，或甚至卖方之前仅仅只是启动了该类汽油的贸易谈判，情况都会变得不同。但是，无人声称存在此类情况。卖方在答复买方的法律陈述书中说，“即使买方未出现违约，卖方也非常有可能与阿根廷公司谈成此次出

The situation would be different if plaintiff's sale were from its inventory (in which case it would be treated as the car dealer mentioned above), or if it had already contracted to sell the product to Esso Sapa, or perhaps even if it was then actually engaged in negotiations for trades in this type of gasoline. However, no such claim is made. The statement in plaintiff's reply memorandum of law that "in all likelihood, [plaintiff] would have negotiated such a sale [to Esso Sapa] even in the absence of [defendant's] breach" is not supported by any facts in the

售”。但是，此种说法得不到案件事实的支持，因为卖方并未主张其当时正与阿根廷公司或任何其他人就该类汽油的销售进行任何谈判。本案的实际情况很明显，即装载了一批已特定化的汽油的船舶当时正开往纽约，而卖方为了减少损失而四处寻找买家，并最终才将该汽油售出。

record, as there are no allegations that plaintiff had any negotiations then pending for the sale of this type of gasoline with Esso Sapa or any other party. This is simply a case where plaintiff, in an effort to mitigate its damages, went out and made a sale of a specific identified cargo of gasoline aboard a vessel then proceeding to New York.

与另一个判例的区别 F 诉 P 案的判决，不会使本案得出不同结果。在该案中，买方是“同时从事买进和卖出业务的肥料经销商”。在卖方因延迟交付而违反合同后，买方从第三方购进了替代货物。法院允许买方就此种采购所增加的成本从卖方取得赔偿，同时无须将卖方最终交付且由买方随后转售的货物的销售利润返还给卖方。

The decision in Fertico Belgium v. Phosphate Chems. Export Assn. does not require a different result. There a “trader in fertilizer who both buys and sells”, whose purchase contract was breached by late delivery, was allowed to recover damages for the increased cost to acquire product from a third party, without any deduction for profit realized on its subsequent sale of the untimely delivered goods.

该案法院认为，“本案的事实极为特殊”，因为在卖方出现延迟交货后，买方从第三方购买了替代肥料，以履行其对自己客户的出售义务。同时，在卖方迟交的货物到达后，买方取得了货物的占有，因为其已使用信用证

The court noted that “the facts here are exceptional” because the buyer who met its resale obligation by acquiring necessary fertilizer from a third party also had in its possession the late-delivered product which it had already paid for under a letter of credit, and “had no commercially reasonable

支付了货款，且“没有其他商业上合理的替代方法，而只能留持并转售该肥料”。

该案异议法官认为，按多数派法官的判决，完全未能交付货物的卖方反而会比延迟交付货物的卖方处境更好，因为前者可用自己占有的货物实现利润，而后者则不能，因为在买方将延迟交付的货物转售并获得利润后，卖方无法获得该利润。无论如何，该案买方在“极为特殊”的情况下所面临的“独特问题”，与本案情况并无相似之处。该案买方取得了延迟交付的货物的占有，且已经支付了货款。

最后，法典第2.703条正式评论1说，当事方可以获得何种救济，“完全取决于当事案件的事实”。这项评论虽然是针对卖方救济而言的，但F诉P案的判决，显示了在将法典原则适用于特定事实环境时，法典所具有的灵活性。

alternative but to retain and resell the fertilizer".

The dissent observed that under the majority view a seller who totally fails to deliver is in a better position than one who delivers late as in the former case the seller could make a profit from the goods in his possession, while the latter he gets no credit for the profit made by the buyer on the sale of the untimely delivered goods. In any event, the "particular problem" faced under the "exceptional" circumstances of a buyer having possession of untimely delivered goods which had been paid for is not analogous to the situation at bar.

Lastly, although Comment 1 to UCC 2-703, indicating that the remedies pursuable depend "entirely on the facts of the individual case", relates to seller's remedies, the decision in Fertico demonstrates the flexibility of the Code in the application of its rules to particular fact patterns.

案例 16　是否存在对协议具有修改或补充作用的行业惯例?

Western Industries, Inc. v. Newcor Canada Limited
西部工业公司诉加拿大纽克尔有限公司案

联邦第七巡回上诉法院 1984 年；739 F.2d 1198, 38 UCC Rep.Serv. 1458

简　介

本案买方（Western）与自己的客户日本夏普公司（Sharp）订立了一份合同，约定为夏普公司生产一批微波炉的外壳。夏普公司要求，微波炉外壳必须使用“凸焊”（projection welding）技术。这种方式与美国通常使用的“点焊”（spot welding）方式完全不同，因此所需的焊机也不同。为了履行与夏普公司的合同，买方需要重新购买用于凸焊的电焊机。为此，买方与本案卖方（Newcor）订立了购买 11 台此种焊机的合同。卖方虽然是特种焊机的专业厂家，但从未生产过这种凸焊机。但是，卖方最终还是同意接受这个合同，专门为买方设计和制造此种焊机。

但是，由于卖方缺乏制造凸焊机的经验，其所交付的产品最终都无法正常使用。这导致买方在生产夏普公司的微波炉外壳时，没有可以使用的焊机。买方最终只能使用手焊方式完成了与夏普公司的合同，并为此额外支出了大量费用。随后，买方以卖方违约为由起诉卖方，要求卖方赔偿自己的间接损失，也就是为了履行与夏普公司的合同而额外支出的费用。卖方则提起反诉，要求买方支付剩余货款。

初审法院基于陪审团的裁定，判决卖方向买方支付 130 万美元作为对买方间接损失的赔偿；同时，判决买方向卖方支付大约 65 万美元的剩余货款。也就是说，卖方最终需要向买方净支付大约 65 万美元。对于该判决，卖方提出异议并提起上诉，认为买方无权获得间接损失赔偿。基于卖方的上诉，买方也提起上诉，认为如果上诉法院推翻有关卖方间接损失赔偿的判决，则自己也没有义务支付剩余货款。

上诉法院的判决书由著名法官波斯纳主笔。波斯纳法官以经济分析著称，经常从经济合理性的角度来分析法律问题。同时，他的文笔简洁犀利，思辨性强，但有时稍显费解。本案判决书体现了他的这些特点。在上诉中，卖方主要提出两点理由，来说明为什么其没有义务向买方支付间接损失赔偿。第一个理由是卖方的主要理由，认为特种焊机的制造行业存在一项行业惯例，即卖方从来不对买方的间接损失承担责任。第二个理由是替代理由，认为合同的明示条款排除了卖方对间接损失的赔偿责任。第二个理由之所以是替代理由，是因为当事方的书面文件比较混乱，而且，包含了排除条款的书面文件，可能是在口头合同订立之后才发出的。因此，是否存在卖方所说的明示条款，存在很大疑问。

是否存在一项行业惯例，通常只能由证人提供证词来证明。卖方在初审中提供了 3 名证人，准备由他们作证说，特种焊机行业内存在不支付间接损失赔偿的惯例。但是，初审法官拒绝让这些证人作证，认为他们缺乏相应资格，且证词不可信。上诉法院认为，初审法官排除卖方证人的判决是错误的，因为这些证人实际上确实对行业具有丰富经验，可以就行业惯例提供他们的看法；同时，证词是否可信，主要应由陪审团判断，而初审法官不能仅仅因为自己不相信该证词就拒绝让证人作证。上诉法院对初审法官拒绝卖方举证的几个可能理由进行了分析，认为这些理由都不能成立。据此，上诉法院判决初审法院对案件进行重审，以便让卖方提交有关行业惯例的证据。

关于合同明示条款的问题，本案存在两个困难。首先，当事方可能最先在

1979 年 5 月 17 日的电话中，以口头讨论的方式达成了合同，而其中未涉及间接损失赔偿问题。当事方的书面文件，都是在口头讨论之后才交换的。因此，这些书面文件可能不构成合同的组成部分，因此也就不存在所谓的明示条款。其次，双方交换的格式文件存在矛盾，即存在所谓的“文本冲突”（battle of forms）。在卖方的格式文件中，排除了对买方的间接损失赔偿；在买方的格式文件中，则包含了获得间接损失赔偿的权利。双方都没有接受对方的格式文件。

初审法官认定，合同的订立时间是 1979 年 5 月 17 日，即当事方通过电话进行口头讨论的日期。双方该日的电话交谈非常简单，只约定了焊机的数量和交付日期，而没有就任何其他条款作出约定，甚至都没有约定价格。但初审法官认为，这个电话的时间就是合同订立的时间，而在订立合同时，卖方并未排除自己对间接损失的赔偿责任。双方随后交换的格式文件不具有任何效力，因为任何一方都没有对另一方的格式文件表示同意。陪审团的裁定，也是基于初审法官的这个认定而作出的。

上诉法院认为，明示条款问题的关键，首先在于合同是否确实于 5 月 17 日订立。如果确定于该日订立，那问题就简单了，因为 5 月 17 日的讨论没有排除间接损失责任，因此该责任自然就是存在的，除非被行业惯例排除。但是，合同是否成立，取决于当事方是否具有在该日订立合同的意愿。上诉法院认为，应将这个问题提交陪审团裁定。由于该电话讨论缺少很多细节，因此陪审团完全有可能裁定，当事方并没有在当日订立合同的意图。如果陪审团裁定合同没有在 5 月 17 日成立，而是在之后某个日期才成立的，那么，当事方所交换的矛盾的格式文件，就会在一定程度上构成合同的组成部分，而不是合同订立后对合同的事后修改。此时，就涉及哪一方的格式文件具有优先效力的问题。上诉法院认为，这个问题也应由陪审团裁定。

对于波斯纳法官代表多数派作出的判决，一位法官提出了异议。该法官同意多数派的这个意见，即初审法官本来应该允许卖方就行业惯例问题进行举证。但是，异议法官提出了两点不同意见。第一，他认为，在双方文本存在冲突的情况下，根据法典第 2.207 条（2）款或（3）款，双方的冲突条款应该同时从合同中被排除，而改由法典的填补条款(gap-fillers)或行业惯例补充。也就是说，不是谁的文本优先的问题，而是冲突条款全部被去除的问题。第二，他认为，对行业惯例应该采取更严格的认定标准，而多数派法官的认定标准过于宽泛。

判　决

本案基本情况和初审法院判决　本案买方从卖方购买了几台专门定制的焊机，准备用其制造微波炉外壳。因焊机不能正常工作，买方以卖方违反合同为由提起本诉讼。卖方则提起反诉，要求买方支付焊机的剩余货款。陪审团裁定，卖方应向买方支付 130 万美元的损害赔偿，而买方应就卖方的反诉，向卖方支付该数额的大约一半（相当于全部剩余货款）。初审法院分别就双方的索赔作出判决，而双方均提起上诉。本上诉涉及多项值得探讨的实体法和程序法问题。当事方同意，本案实体法为威斯康星州法律，包括其采纳的法典。

Western Industries purchased several custom-built welding machines from Newcor Canada for use in manufacturing microwave oven cavities. The machines did not work right and Western brought this breach of contract action against Newcor. Newcor counterclaimed for the unpaid portion of the purchase price of the machines. The jury awarded Western damages of $1.3 million dollars and Newcor about half that（the full unpaid balance of the purchase price of the machines） on its counterclaim. Separate judgments were entered on the two claims and both parties have appealed. The appeals raise a variety of interesting substantive and procedural issues, the former being controlled（the parties agree）by the law of Wisconsin, including the Uniform Commercial Code, which Wisconsin has adopted.

背景情况　买方与卖方之间

The contract between Western and

的合同，起源于买方与日本一家微波炉制造商夏普公司订立的合同。根据该合同，买方将向夏普公司提供微波炉外壳。夏普公司要求买方在焊接外壳时采用一种称为凸焊的工艺，因为在日本，微波炉外壳都是这样焊接。对此，买方表示同意。

5 月 17 日的电话讨论　美国不使用凸焊方法来焊接诸如微波炉外壳这样的薄金属材料，而是采用点焊。卖方是一家特种焊机的著名制造商。买方找到了卖方，探讨从卖方购买凸焊机用于履行夏普公司合同的可能性。基于与夏普公司的合同，买方不得不要求卖方设计和制造一种卖方并不熟悉的焊机。但是，卖方表示同意承接该项目。在进一步讨论后，买方的工程总监通过电话，于 1979 年 5 月 17 日向卖方的销售工程师发出了采购 8 台机器的订货要求。

随后交换的书面文件　根据两人所整理的电话交谈备忘录，双方只讨论了交付日期，而没有

Newcor grew out of Western's contract with a Japanese manufacturer of microwave ovens, Sharp, to supply Sharp with cavities for microwave ovens. Sharp wanted Western to weld the cavities by a process known as projection welding, because that is how microwave oven cavities are made in Japan; and Western agreed.

The projection method is not used in the United States to weld thin metal, such as the cavities of microwave ovens are made of; spot welding is the method used here. So when Western went to Newcor, a leading manufacturer of specialty welding machines, to explore the possibility of buying machines for use in fulfilling its contract with Sharp, it had to ask Newcor to design and build a type of welding machine that Newcor was unfamiliar with. Newcor agreed to do this, however, and after further discussions Western's director of engineering placed a purchase order by phone for eight machines with Newcor's sales engineer on May 17, 1979.

According to the memoranda that both men made of the conversation, no specific terms other than the date of delivery were

讨论其他具体条款，比如，双方并没有讨论价格。5 月 23 日，卖方向买方交付了一份正式的书面销售条件和报价文件，其中一页的背面印有若干标准合同条款，包括一项排除任何间接损失赔偿的条款。

买方没有立即回复。但在 7 月中旬，买方向卖方发送了一份正式采购订单，但采购订单注明的出具日期被神秘地提前至 5 月 15 日。该订单的背面包含了一系列印刷条款，其中一项说明，在卖方违反担保时，买方有权就一般损失和特殊损失取得赔偿。

7 月 20 日，卖方发给买方一份确认书，其中说“基于我们向你们发出的（5 月 23 日书面报价书中所载明的）销售条件，本确认书特此批准并接受你们的订单”。买方未作答复。双方对于他们所交换的格式合同中的印刷条款也从未进行过讨论。随后，在以类似方式交换格式合同后，买方又购买了 3 台机器。当事方将全部 11 台机器都视为一个买卖合同。我们也将这样认为。

discussed; price was not discussed, for example. On May 23 Newcor delivered to Western a formal written quotation of terms for the sale. On the back of one page a number of standard contract terms were printed, including one disclaiming all liability for consequential damages.

Western did not reply immediately, but in mid-July it sent Newcor a formal purchase order, mysteriously pre-dated to May 15, that included on the back a set of printed terms one of which stated that the buyer (Western) was entitled to general as well as special damages in the event of a breach of the seller's warranties.

On July 20 Newcor sent Western an acknowledgement form stating, “In conformity with our conditions of sale appearing in ［the written quotation of May 23］furnished to you by us, this approves and accepts your order”. Western did not respond. The parties never discussed any of the printed terms contained in the contract forms that they had exchanged. Three machines were bought later through a similar exchange of forms. The parties treat the sale of all 11 machines as one contract, as shall we.

焊机不符合合同　机器在完成制作后被交付给买方，但事实证明，机器无法用于微波炉外壳的制造。卖方将机器拿回，将其重新改造为点焊机，并在合同规定的交付日期 1 年之后才重新交付给买方。

The machines were built and delivered but turned out to be unusable for making microwave oven cavities. Newcor took the machines back and rebuilt them as spot welding machines, redelivering them to Western a year after the delivery date called for in the contract.

买方的损失　买方由于未能按时收到适合使用的机器，因此在履行其对夏普公司的承诺中支出了预料之外的费用。例如，买方不得不采用手工方法焊接外壳，而这相对于使用合适机器的情况，成本要高出很多。这些成本构成买方对卖方索赔的依据。

As a result of the delay in getting machines that it could use, Western incurred unforeseen expenses in fulfilling its commitment to Sharp; for example, it had to manufacture cavities manually at much higher cost than it would have incurred if it had had proper machines. These expenses are the basis of its damage claim against Newcor.

卖方希望提交的行业惯例证据　卖方在本上诉中提出的第一个理由是，初审法官不适当地排除了相关证据。该证据试图证明，特种焊机的行业惯例是，不向受损害的买方支付间接损失赔偿，而仅允许买方退回机器并取得退款，或在涉及延迟交付这类违约时，允许买方保留机器，同时减去部分货款作为延迟的损失补偿。

Newcor's first ground of appeal is that the district judge improperly excluded evidence that the custom of the specialty welding machine trade is not to give a disappointed buyer his consequential damages but just to allow him either to return the machines and get his money back or (for example if the breach consists in delivering them late) keep the machines and get the purchase price reduced to compensate for the costs of delay.

无须确认是否属于间接损失

Whether every penny of the damages

关于买方索赔的每一分钱是否都严格符合“间接”损失的定义，这一方面是非常困难的问题（参见M诉M案），另一方面对判决结果也没有影响。卖方声称，除去退还货款外，其不对买方的任何损失承担赔偿责任，无论以何种方式描述这些损失。如果这个说法可以成立，那么即使卖方违反了与买方的合同，卖方也没有责任支付所认定的买方损失。

that Western is claiming comes within a strict definition of “consequential” damages is a question at once difficult, see, e.g., Mead Corp. v. McNally-Pittsburg Mfg. Corp., and inconsequential. Newcor contends that it is not liable for any damages above the purchase price, however those damages are described; and if this is right, then even if Newcor had a contract with Western that it broke it is not liable for any of the damages that Western was awarded.

行业惯例证据被排除 尽管行业惯例属于事实问题［参见法典第1.205条（2）款；正式评论4和9；引用著作］，但初审法官拒绝让卖方的3名主要证人就所称的行业惯例作证，理由是这些证人没有足够的作证资格。在拒绝了卖方的证人之后，法官指示陪审团说，本案中不存在行业惯例的问题。

Although trade custom or usage is a question of fact, see UCC Sec. 1-205（2）and Official Comments 4 and 9; Wigmore, Evidence in Trials at Common Law, the district judge refused to allow Newcor's three principal witnesses on the existence of the alleged trade custom to testify, on the ground that they were incompetent to give such testimony; and having done this the judge later instructed the jury that there was no issue of trade custom in the case.

证词内容和证人资格 在卖方希望推出的3名证人中，有两人来自特种焊机的制造公司，是经验丰富的高级管理人员（其中一人还是此种制造商的行业协会

Two of the three witnesses whom Newcor wanted to call were experienced executives of companies that manufacture specialty welding machines（one of them was also the president of those manufacturers' trade

主席）。两人销售此种机器的经验加起来将近 75 年。第三名证人是买方的前高管，其对于此种机器的采购拥有丰富经验。

association), and between them the two had almost 75 years of experience in selling such machines. The third witness was a former executive of Western and had long experience in buying such machines.

这些证人本来预计作证说，在他们的行业中，从未听说过间接损失赔偿。在机器不能工作时，制造商会自行承担费用将其修复，或把机器收回并向买方退回货款，但不会就该瑕疵给买方业务带来的损害支付补偿。

These witnesses were prepared to testify that consequential damages were unheard of in their trade. When a machine did not work the manufacturer would spend his own money to fix it or would take it back and refund the purchase price to the buyer, but he would not compensate the buyer for the disruption to the buyer's business caused by the defect.

排除证词的理由　初审法官基于多项理由禁止了上述作证。他认为，其中一名证人的作证“必须在某种程度上被忽视”，因为该人是卖方高管。另一名证人本来预计作证说，该惯例在整个行业“无处不在”，但法官认为该证人没有足够的资历提供此种证词。

The district judge barred this testimony on a variety of grounds. He thought the testimony of one of the witnesses "had to be to some degree discounted" because he was an executive of Newcor. Another he thought was not competent to testify that the alleged trade custom was "pervasive" throughout the industry.

初审法官还说明，其不认为卖方或买方的单方作证具有足够说服力。他希望证人同时就交易的正反两面作证，即类似经纪人所能提供的那种证词。他还认为，

The judge also indicated that he did not think testimony by either sellers or buyers very probative; he wanted testimony about both sides of the transaction at once--for example, such testimony as a broker might give. And

卖方与行业协会立场一致并使用排除间接损失责任的格式合同的事实都说明，该惯例只是“单方”惯例，因此，除非买方也知道并接受了该惯例，否则该惯例不能被视为行业惯例。

单方惯例问题 对于初审法官的上述看法，存在 3 种可能的解读方法。第一种方法是，初审法官认为，即使陪审团相信证人所说的一切，卖方仍无法证明行业惯例的存在，因为证人并未打算就这个问题提供证词，即存在一种任何卖方和买方都知道并且都接受的惯例。但是，对于行业惯例来说，这个标准太过苛刻。实际上，法律并不要求买方必须知道惯例的存在，而是买方只要本应知道，就要受到约束［参见法典第 1.205 条（3）款，引用著作；引用文章（基于经济理由为上述原则辩护）］。因此，初审法官所称的“单方”惯例，确实有可能被用于排除卖方的责任。

证人资格问题 对初审法官

he thought that the fact that the sellers had gotten together in their trade association and adopted a form contract disclaiming liability for consequential damages was evidence of merely a “unilateral” custom; there could be no custom of the trade unless buyers knew about the form and accepted it.

There are three ways of taking these comments. The first is that the district judge thought that even if the jury believed everything the witnesses said, Newcor would have failed to establish the existence of a trade custom because the witnesses were not prepared to testify to the existence of a custom known to and accepted by all sellers and all buyers. But this would be too stringent a test of trade custom. It is not the law, for example, that the buyer must know of the custom; if he should have known, he is bound. See UCC Sec. 1-205（3）; Farnsworth, Contracts; and （for a defense of this principle on economic grounds） Warren, Trade Usage and Parties in the Trade: An Economic Rationale for an Inflexible Rule. Thus, what the judge called a “unilateral” custom could exonerate Newcor.

Another way to take the judge's

看法的另一种解读方式是，他认为这些证人打算提供的证词，本来也不具有说服力。但是，如果是这样，那么所涉及的问题就只是卖方关于行业惯例的证据的证明力度问题，而不是证据的可采纳性问题。在我们的系统里，法官没有权利仅仅因为其认为证据的证明力度不足，就不允许将该证据提交给陪审团（参见 J 诉 S 案）。

comments, however, is that he thought the evidence these witnesses would have given lacked persuasive force. But so viewed his comments went to the weight rather than admissibility of Newcor's evidence of trade custom, and a judge in our system does not have the right to prevent evidence from getting to the jury merely because he does not think it deserves to be given much weight. See, e.g., Joy Mfg. Co. v. Sola Basic Industries, Inc.

如果允许卖方证人就行业惯例提供证词，则买方本来可在交叉质询时，将初审法官对证人的批评性看法提交给陪审团考虑。但是，除去与本案无关的例外，在证人向陪审团作证之前，法官对于在交叉质询中听到的证词，即使认为证人不可信，也不能因此就不允许其作证。

The criticisms that the judge made of Newcor's trade-custom witnesses could have been put before the jury by Western in cross-examination if the witnesses had been allowed to testify. But a judge may not（with immaterial exceptions）, by listening to cross-examination before the witnesses go before the jury, decide that the witnesses are unworthy of belief, and forbid them to testify.

自然,对行业惯例进行作证，意味着对一个结论进行作证。虽然所有的证据，甚至包括目击者证词，都在一定程度上带有推理性质（引用文章），但是，当作证的事实涉及一种行业惯例是否存在时，相对于就被告头发颜色

Of course testimony of trade custom is testimony to a conclusion; and though all evidence, even eyewitness testimony, is inferential to a degree （see Hoffman, The Interpretation of Visual Illusions, Scientific American）, the chain of inference is longer when the fact testified to is the existence of

这样的问题进行作证，推理的链条就更长一些。如果要求本院法官在本案中作为证人回答这个问题，即在特种焊机行业中，不向受损害的买方支付间接损失赔偿是否属于行业惯例，我们是没有能力回答的。

a trade custom than when it is the color of the defendant's hair. If the members of this court had been called as witnesses in this case and asked whether it was the custom of the specialty welding machine trade not to give disappointed buyers consequential damages, we would not have been competent to answer.

但卖方证人都是行业中富有经验的高级管理人员，因此，对于是否存在所声称的行业惯例，他们可从自己的观察和经验中作出推断，因为他们每个人都经历了很多类似本案的买卖合同的谈判。《联邦证据法》可以打消任何对他们证词可采纳性的怀疑，因为该法规定，可以采纳类似本案中这样的外行人的意见(参见B诉P案)。此外,《联邦证据法》对“专家证人”的定义也非常灵活，因此本案所有这些证人，都无疑有资格成为可就行业惯例作证的专家证人。

But Newcor's witnesses were experienced executives in the trade, and the existence of the alleged custom was a matter they could infer from their own observations and experience, since each had negotiated many sale contracts such as the one in issue in this case. Any doubt about the admissibility of their testimony is dispelled by Rule 702 of Federal Rules of Evidence, which makes lay opinion evidence of the kind involved here admissible, see Bohannon v. Pegelow, and by the fact that under the liberal definition of “expert witness” in Rule 702 all of these witnesses could readily have been qualified as expert witnesses on the question of trade custom.

确凿程度问题 最后一种可能的解读是，初审法官在表述上述看法时，其脑海中可能想到了威斯康星州早在法典制定之前就存在的一些判例，而这些判例要

Finally, the judge may have had in the back of his mind a line of Wisconsin cases, long predating the Uniform Commercial Code, which require that proof of trade usage be “clear and explicit”. E.g., Knobel v. J.

求，对行业惯例的证明，需要“确凿和明确”（参见K诉J案，其中引用P诉K案）。我们可以不作结论地假定，上述标准属于实体法原则，因此假如该标准有效，则在州际案件中，联邦法院本应受其约束（参见B诉H案；H诉J案）。但实际上，不可能再认为上述标准具有任何约束力，因为法典对行业惯例的证明问题采取了非常宽松的态度［引用著作（其中说明，“法典对行业惯例的证据要求，比普通法的要求宽松很多”）］。

Bartel Co., quoting Power v. Kane. We can assume, without having to decide, that this standard expresses a substantive principle that, if it were still in force, would bind a federal court in a diversity suit. Cf. Breeland v. Hide-A-Way Lake, Inc.; Hardware Mutual Ins. Co. v. Jacob Hieb, Inc. But it cannot be considered authoritative any longer, in view of the hospitable approach that the Code（enacted into Wisconsin law） takes to evidence of trade custom. See White & Summers, Handbook of the Law Under the Uniform Commercial Code （“Code requirements for proof of trade usage are far less stringent” than common law requirements）.

有可能存在行业惯例　作为法官，我们没有能力确认卖方所声称的行业惯例是否确实存在。但是，该惯例的存在并非完全不可想象。因此，没有必要像排除与自然法则相矛盾的作证那样，排除对行业惯例的作证。

Although we are in no position to determine whether the custom alleged by Newcor actually exists, the hypothesis that it exists is certainly not so incredible that testimony on the subject could be excluded by analogy to the principle that excludes testimony in contradiction of the laws of nature.

本案的相关行业，就是专门定制特定种类的机器。专门定制的机器很容易出现一些问题，如不能按时交付或交付后不能工作

The relevant trade is the manufacture of a particular kind of custom-built machinery. A custom-built machine is quite likely either not to be delivered on time or not to work （not at

（至少在开始阶段可能会这样）。接受过房屋建造的人，都会知道定制的风险。

first, anyway） when it is delivered； anyone who has ever had a house built for him knows the perils of custom design.

一台定制机器如果出现延迟交付，或如果不能像买方希望和预期的那样使用，买方的业务很有可能受到不利影响，甚至可能被摧毁。这些焊机的买方都是大型制造商，且这些机器对其业务有关键影响。因此，当机器存在设计缺陷或出现延迟交付时，潜在成本都是天文数字。

If a custom-built machine is delivered late, or does not work as the buyer had hoped and expected it would, the buyer's business is quite likely to suffer, and may even be ruined； and as the buyers of these welding machines are substantial manufacturers to whose businesses the machines are essential, the potential costs of defective design or late delivery are astronomical.

间接损失的传统原则 当卖方未能及时交付具有关键作用的产品时，如H诉B案中的机轴，其给买方业务所带来的影响，属于典型的间接损失（参见E诉S案；M诉M案）。以H诉B案为代表的普通法的传统原则是，除非当事方通过谈判专门就间接损失作出约定，否则，在合同案件中，不能就间接损失取得赔偿（参见G诉L案）。

The effect on a buyer's business of the seller's failure to make timely delivery of some critical input, such as the mill shaft in Hadley v. Baxendale, is a classic example of consequential damages. See, e.g., Evra Corp. v. Swiss Bank Corp.； Mead Corp. v. McNally-Pittsburg Mfg. Corp. And the traditional rule of the common law, announced in Hadley v. Baxendale, was that consequential damages were not recoverable in contract cases unless specifically negotiated for. See Globe Refining Co. v. Landa Cotton Oil Co.

目前的原则更加灵活 但这项原则已经放宽。目前，大多数法院都会认为，只要间接损失是

The rule has been relaxed and today most courts would say that it was enough if the consequences were foreseeable, whether

可以预见的，就足以有权寻求赔偿，无论是否有证据表明，许诺方已就该损失的赔偿向被许诺方承担了义务（引用著作）。

or not there was evidence that the promisor had undertaken to insure the promisee against them. See, e.g., Farnsworth.

由于法典采取了非常灵活的标准，我们可以假设，只要未明确排除间接损失责任，或只要行业惯例不存在此种排除，本案买方就有权取得间接损失赔偿（参见法典第 2.713 条至第 2.715 条；第 2.715 条正式评论 3）。

Since the UCC adopts an especially liberal standard, we may assume that in the absence of an express disclaimer of liability for consequential damages, or of a disclaimer inferrable from a trade custom, they would be recoverable here. See UCC Secs. 2-713 to 2-715, and Official Comment 3 to 2-715.

陪审团有可能认定存在行业惯例　实际上，要确定卖方提供的行业惯例证据是否具有可采纳性，我们无须做其他事情，而只需要确信，具有正常思维的陪审团有可能得出下列结论：对于特种焊机制造商，行业惯例是不对间接损失承担责任。

But all we need find in order to conclude that Newcor's evidence of trade custom was admissible is that a rational jury could have concluded that, yes, it was the custom for manufacturers of specialty welding machines not to be liable for consequential damages.

在没有特别约定的情况下对间接损失承担合同责任，是相对近期的做法；很多违约情况并非源于自愿（如同本案情况）；如果机器是买方业务所必需，则对于机器卖方来说，该机器可能引起的间接损失完全没有上限；这些买方对于自己可能受到的潜在

That contractual liability for such damages （in the absence of special notice） is of relatively recent vintage, that many breaches of contract are （as here） involuntary, that only the sky would be the limit to the amount of consequential damages that manufacturers of machinery indispensable to their customers' businesses might run up,

伤害，不仅比卖方更加了解，而且比卖方更有能力去避免。考虑到上述所有因素，如果在这个行业中发展出一种惯例，不允许买方就卖方的违约获得间接损失赔偿,则该惯例并非完全不可思议。

行业惯例不意味着卖方逃避责任 即使存在上述惯例，该惯例也不会使特种焊机的制造商完全逃脱经济责任。当他们不得不将定制的机器拿回并重新销售时，他们将面临重大损失。根据某个买方的规格所定制设计的机器，也许无法适合其他厂家的规格。无疑，这就是为什么本案卖方花费了几十万美元，将机器重新改造为买方可使用的点焊机。

这也是我们拒绝了卖方辩称的原因。卖方辩称，根据禁止自相矛盾的原则，买方在诱使卖方改造机器后,就无权再寻求赔偿。但是，卖方的改造是为了其自己利益。在其不得不收回机器并退还货款的情况下，改造机器可以减少卖方本应承担的损失。卖方

that those customers not only have a better idea of what the potential injury to them might be but also might be able to avert it more easily than their supplier--all these things make it not at all incredible that a custom might have evolved in this industry against a buyer's getting consequential damages in the event of a breach.

If there was such a custom, it would not take the manufacturers of specialty welding machines off the financial hook completely. When they have to take back and resell custom-built machines they face the prospect of a heavy loss. A machine custom-designed to one manufacturer's specifications may not fit any other's. That is no doubt why Newcor spent hundreds of thousands of dollars to rebuild these machines as spot-welding machines that Western could use.

That is also why we reject Newcor's argument that Western should be estopped to claim damages because it induced Newcor to rebuild the machines. Newcor rebuilt them in its own interest, to mitigate the loss it would have incurred if it had had to take back the machines and refund the purchase price; if it had taken back the machines it would have

将机器收回后，要想重新售出，本来也要改造该机器。

行业惯例的另一个经济理由 尽管如此，对于特种焊机的制造商来说，在排除了间接损失的赔偿责任后，毕竟还是控制了责任的范围。同时，这也使买方不得不更加小心，防备机器不能使用时可能产生的灾难性后果，而买方的小心，也许具有很大作用（参见 E 诉 S 案）。

本案有很多证据表明，买方（看上去相当随意地）向夏普公司承诺使用凸焊方式制造微波炉外壳，是一个严重错误，因为最后发现，基于美国的安全标准，该焊接方法不切实际。假如买方原来已经明确知道，在机器无法工作时买方无权就间接损失取得赔偿，那么，买方本来就更有可能不会犯这个错误。

行业惯例的效力 到目前为止，如同初审法官一样，我们一直假设，如果行业惯例说，买方无权取得间接损失赔偿，那么该惯例就成为合同的一项条款。该条款虽然无形，但具有约束力，

had to rebuild them in order to be able to resell them.

But a disclaimer of liability for consequential damages would place some limit on the exposure of the manufacturers of specialty welding machines. It would also give buyers incentives to take their own precautions, which might be efficacious, against the disasters that might befall them if the machines did not work. See Evra Corp. v. Swiss Bank Corp.

There was much evidence that Western made a serious mistake in agreeing with Sharp（rather casually as it appears） to build microwave oven cavities by projection welding, a process which, it turned out, American safety standards made infeasible. Western would have been less likely to make such mistakes if it had known with certainty that it would not be able to get consequential damages if the machines didn't work.

Thus far we have assumed, as did the district judge, that if the custom of the trade is that the buyer shall not receive consequential damages, it is a binding though silent term of the contract and overrides the provisions in the UCC that, in the absence of a contrary

并取代法典的规定。法典的规定是，如果违反了买卖合同，且合同没有相反约定，救济通常包括间接损害赔偿。

provision in the contract, make consequential damages normally an available remedy for breach of a sales contract.

但买方反对上述假设。买方辩称，应维持初审法官对行业惯例证据的排除，因为根据第2.719条（1）（b）款的规定，行业惯例不能对责任进行限制。法典该款规定，“（合同）所提供的任何一项救济，均供自行选用，除非该项救济被明确约定具有排他性；此时，该救济为唯一的救济”。但买方的该辩称已被判例否定（参见T诉L案；P诉E案），且我们认为该否定是正确的。

But Western contests this premise and argues that the district judge's exclusion of evidence of trade custom can be upheld on the ground that a trade custom cannot limit liability, because section 2-719（1）（b） of the Uniform Commercial Code provides that "resort to a remedy as provided ［in the contract］ is optional unless the remedy is expressly agreed to be exclusive, in which case it is the sole remedy". The cases, rightly in our view, reject this argument. See, e.g., Transamerica Oil Corp. v. Lynes, Inc.; Posttape Associates v. Eastman Kodak Co.

合同解释曾有一项原则，即“明确规定一项原则，就相当于排除其他同类原则”。法典第2.719条（1）（b）款的作用，就是废除了上述原则。也就是说，即使合同规定了一项救济，也不等于排除了其他救济。这是完全合理的。但这并没有回答这个问题，即一项特定救济被排除，是否并非因为当事方在合同中未提

All section 2-719（1）（b） does is to repeal the rule expressio unius est exclusio alterius as a rule of contract interpretation. That is, the fact that a contract specifies one remedy is not to be taken to exclude others. This is perfectly sensible but does not answer the question whether a particular remedy is excluded not because the parties did not mention it in the contract but because the custom of the trade makes it unavailable.

到该救济，而是因为行业惯例排除了该救济?

卖方主张合同存在明示条款 卖方还有第二个上诉理由。卖方希望,不仅要向陪审团说明，行业惯例为合同补充了一项排除间接损失赔偿的默示条款，而且还要说明，合同的明示条款也排除了此种责任（但我们随后会看到，这两项说明并非完全相互独立）。卖方所说的明示条款，是5月23日卖方发给买方的正式书面报价书中的排除条款，以及卖方7月20日确认书中针对买方的冲突格式的用语。

Newcor has a second ground of appeal. It wanted to put before the jury not only the theory that trade custom had supplied a silent contractual term excluding liability for consequential damages, but also the theory that the explicit terms of the contract excluded such liability （though we shall see that these theories are not completely independent of each other）. The terms are the disclaimer in the formal written quotation that Newcor sent Western on May 23 and the language in which on July 20 it acknowledged Western's inconsistent form.

初审法官认定合同于5月17日订立 但初审法官的判定是,合同是在5月17日订立的,而5月23日的排除条款是对合同的重大改动，因此无效。由于初审法院错误地排除了卖方有关行业惯例的证据，因此本案必须重审。因此,我们同时需要决定,重审中是否应维持初审法官对卖方第二个理论的判决。

But the district court ruled that the contract was made on May 17 and that the disclaimer of May 23 was a material alteration of that contract and was therefore a nullity. Since the case must be tried again because of the erroneous exclusion of Newcor's evidence of trade custom, we must decide whether the judge's ruling on Newcor's alternative theory should be followed in the next round.

后续书面文件是否属于对合同的修改 初审法官认定合同是

If the judge was right that a contract was made on May 17, his conclusion followed. For

在5月17日订立的。如果该认定正确，则他的结论就正确，因为此时，卖方的正式书面报价书只是书面确认，而根据法典规定，该确认不能对口头合同作出重大改变［参见法典第2.207条（2）（b）款］。

then Newcor's formal written quotation was merely a written confirmation, which under the UCC could not alter the oral contract materially. See UCC Sec. 2-207（2）（b）.

如果报价书属于对口头合同的重大改变，那么，其无权改变的是，合同原本缺乏而由法典填补的无形条款，如允许间接损失索赔的条款（参见法典第2.207条正式评论6）。删除一项重要救济，属于重大改动。确认书随后（7月20日）对该排除条款再次进行确认，但这种确认对本案结果没有影响。

Among the terms that could not be changed if the effect was to alter the oral contract materially would be terms that the UCC reads into contracts when they are silent on a question, including remedy terms, such as that which allows consequential damages. See UCC Sec. 2-207, Official Comment 6. The deletion of a major remedy would be a material alteration. The fact that the disclaimer was repeated in a later confirmation （that of July 20） could make no difference.

关键问题 因此，卖方第二个理论能否成立的关键，在于合同是否于5月17日订立。如果合同于该日订立，该理论就不成立。而答案的关键则在于，当事方是否具有在该日订立合同的意图［参见法典第2.204条（3）款］？

Thus the question whether a contract was formed on May 17 was critical to Newcor's alternative theory; if it was formed then, the theory collapsed. The answer turned on whether the parties intended to make a contract then. See UCC Sec. 2-204（3）.

应交陪审团裁定 无疑，

This looks, of course, like a classic jury

这看上去是典型的应由陪审团裁定的问题。虽然书面文件的解释传统上由法官而不是陪审团进行，但在类似本案这样的合同案件中，我们已不再遵循该传统。这类案件包含多份矛盾的书面文件，而我们必须将它们与非文件证据放在一起，来确定合同是否已经成立，或于何时成立（参见M诉S案；引用《合同法重述》；引用著作）。

question; and though the interpretation of writings is traditionally the responsibility of the judge rather than the jury, tradition is no longer adhered to in contract cases such as the present where a series of mutually inconsistent writings must be put together with nondocumentary evidence to determine whether or when a contract was made. See Meyers v. Selznick Co.; Restatement (Second) of Contracts; Farnsworth.

陪审团有可能作出的裁定

因此，初审法官本来不应将合同成立时间的问题从陪审团那里拿走，除非从合理角度看，事实审的审理人不可能认为合同是5月17日之后才订立的。以合理方式工作的陪审团本来确有可能裁定，当事方5月17日的约定是，卖方将出售于1980年年初交付的凸焊机，但当事方必须在随后的谈判中，就协议细节达成相互可以接受的条款，包括价格条款，以及延迟救济或其他违约救济等重要条款，且买方必须满意地认为（买方当时计划去卖方工厂参观）卖方有能力按时制造出该机

Therefore the judge should not have taken the question when the contract was made from the jury unless no reasonable trier of fact could have found that it was made after May 17. A reasonable jury could have found--we do not say it would have had to find--that the parties on May 17 had agreed that Newcor would sell projection-welding machines for delivery early in 1980 only if mutually acceptable terms covering the details of the agreement, including such important details as the price and the remedies for delay or other breach, could be worked out by the parties in subsequent negotiations, and only if Western--which planned a visit to Newcor's plant--was satisfied that Newcor could manufacture the

器（现已证实卖方无法做到）。我们并不是说，陪审团本来必然会作出上述裁定，而只是说存在这个可能。

machines on time （which, as it turned out, Newcor could not do）.

假设陪审团确实作出上述裁定，则其本来还有可能得出结论说，当事方无意在5月17日订立具有法律强制履行力的合同，因为协议的关键内容仍然太模糊，因而当事方并不希望就所谓的违约承担法律责任。

The jury, having so found, could have concluded that the parties did not intend to make a legally enforceable contract on May 17, because essential elements of the agreement were still too vague for the parties to want legal consequences to attach to an alleged breach.

因此，陪审团本来也许有可能裁定，3个因素（卖方5月23日的书面报价书；卖方7月20日重申5月23日报价书条款的确认书；买方随后的沉默）共同构成了一份协议，且该协议已就初始订购的8台机器排除了间接损失，且可能也就随后通过交换类似格式文件而订购的3台机器作出了此种排除。

The jury might then have found that Newcor's May 23 written quotation, coupled with Newcor's July 20 acknowledgment reincorporating the terms of the May 23 quotation, followed by silence from Western, created an agreement to exclude consequential damages with respect to the eight machines initially ordered, and maybe also with respect to the three ordered subsequently through exchange of the same forms.

排除条款可以得到法典承认 法典并未假定不得作出上述排除［参见法典第2.207条（3）款］，只要在发生违约时，买方还继续享有其他合理救济。实际上，该假定也并不合理，因为法

The Code contains no presumption against such an exclusion, see section 2-207（3）, provided reasonable remedies remain to the buyer if there is a breach; such a presumption would not make sense in light of the liberality with which the Code allows

典本来就对间接损失赔偿采取灵活态度。并且，买方退还机器并取得退款的救济，远非微不足道的救济。

the award of consequential damages. And Western's option to return the machines and get its money back was not a trivial remedy.

卖方两个理论的区别　卖方最主要的理论是，行业惯例已排除了间接损失赔偿责任。从实际的角度看，卖方的第二个替代理论与其主要理论并无很大差别。由于当事方交换了矛盾的格式文件，因此卖方必须提供理由来说明，为什么其排除间接损失责任的格式文件应得到承认，而买方包含此种责任的格式文件就不应得到承认。该理由只能是行业惯例，因为对于卖方所主张的排除，这是卖方格式文件能够拥有优先效力的唯一重要理由。

As a practical matter, however, Newcor's alternative theory is not very different from its main theory--that the custom of the trade excluded liability for consequential damages. Given an exchange of inconsistent forms, Newcor would have to present a reason why its form disclaiming liability for consequential damages should be accepted over Western's form asserting such liability； and the reason would have to be the custom of the trade, as that is the only substantial ground that Newcor has for claiming precedence for its disclaimer.

因此，下列问题也许并不重要，即到底合同是 5 月 17 日订立的，且包含了行业惯例所补充的无形条款，还是随后订立的，且当事方接受了卖方的排除条款。我们重申，卖方要证明买方已接受其排除条款，就必须使陪审团相信存在行业惯例。但是，如果卖方确实希望向陪审团证

So it may not be important whether the contract was made on May 17 and contained a silent term created by trade custom, or was made later and the parties accepted Newcor's disclaimer. We repeat that to show acceptance Newcor must convince the jury of the existence of the trade custom. But we think Newcor is entitled to argue to the jury if it wants that the contract came into existence

明，合同是在5月17日之后才订立的，则我们认为卖方有权向陪审团提交其理由。

after May 17.

侵权责任问题 买方辩称，即使陪审团无论基于哪个理论本来有可能裁定卖方不就违反合同对买方承担间接损失赔偿责任，卖方仍然不能逃脱责任，因为陪审团已经裁定卖方存在疏忽，而疏忽是一种独立责任，不受买方合同权利的影响。

Western argues that even if the jury could, on whatever theory, have found that Newcor did not owe it consequential damages for breach of contract, Newcor would not be off the hook; the jury found Newcor negligent, and negligence is an independent basis for liability, unaffected by the plaintiff's contract rights.

在有些情况下，合同谈判中不当行为的受害方确实可就自己受到的损害提起侵权诉讼(参见A诉I案)。例如，假设本案卖方欺诈性地诱使本案买方放弃有关间接损失赔偿的全部权利，则除去违反合同的诉讼，买方本来还可以起诉卖方的欺诈侵权。或者，如果在合同履行中，本案卖方对买方的财产造成某种损害，例如，在焊机交付过程中将其掉落在买方工厂的地面上，买方也可以提起侵权诉讼。

Sometimes the victim of wrongdoing may indeed sue in tort for an injury growing out of contract negotiations. See, e.g., A/S Apothekernes Laboratorium v. I.M.C. Chem. Group, Inc. For example, if Newcor had fraudulently induced Western to disclaim all right to consequential damages, Western could have sued Newcor for the tort of deceit as well as for breach of contract. Or if in the course of performing the contract Newcor had done some physical damage to Western's property, maybe by dropping one of the welding machines on the floor of Western's plant during delivery, Western could have sued in tort.

一个人之财产不受损害的权

The right to be free from physical

利，与订立合同过程中不受欺诈性引诱的权利一样，不产生于合同，而是基于财产法和侵权法而享有的权利［参见 B 诉 L 案（“疏忽导致的责任，不是基于合同义务，而是基于其他独立义务”）］。

但是，如果合同权利是原告起诉的唯一基础，原告就必须证明合同确实提供了该权利（参见 G 诉 U 案）。从侵权法的角度看，买方不享有就其订购的机器获得迅捷和完美交付的权利。买方所享有的全部权利都基于与卖方的合同。买方要从卖方取得基于疏忽的损害赔偿，就必须证明，合同的原意是保证买方不受延迟交付或制造瑕疵的影响，且卖方违反了此种合同。

买方的反诉　现在我们看一下买方在上诉中的反诉。买方最主要的主张是，如果我们推翻对其有利的原判，那么，关于卖方反诉中提出的取得机器价款余额的主张，我们也必须推翻对卖方有利的原判。也就是说，将所有

damage to one’s property, like the right to be free from fraudulent inducements to contract, does not arise out of a contract. It is a right with which a person is endowed by property law and tort law. See, e.g., Berwind Corp. v. Litton Industries, Inc. （“the negligence liability was based upon independent duties and not upon contractual duties”）.

But where the only right upon which the plaintiff sues is a right created by a contract, proof that the contract created the right is indispensable. See, e.g., Gates Rubber Co. v. USM Corp. Western has no tort right to the prompt delivery of nondefective machines that it orders. Its rights if any are based on its contract with the vendor. Before it can recover damages for negligence it must show that there was a breach of a contract that had been intended to protect it from the consequences of delayed delivery or defective construction.

We turn now to Western’s cross-appeal, where the main contention is that if we reverse the judgment in its favor we should also reverse the judgment in favor of Newcor on its counterclaim for the unpaid balance of the purchase price of the machines, and thus remand for a new trial on all issues.

全部事项发回重审。

我们曾提到,卖方承认,针对其违反合同的可能救济之一,是降低合同价格。陪审团之所以裁定卖方有权获得货物的全部余款,无疑是因为其认为已向买方提供了间接损失的赔偿,因此没必要再从货物价款中减去任何部分。陪审团一定是已经假设,间接损失赔偿已充分补偿了买方的损失,因此,如果不向卖方支付货物余款,就会形成对买方的过度补偿。

在重新审理中,假设陪审团得出一个他们确有可能得出的结论,即从合同角度,买方无权获得间接损失赔偿,那么,陪审团可能会愿意向买方提供另一项救济,即降低合同价格,用以代替间接损失赔偿。为了使陪审团能够考虑这种可能,我们必须推翻初审法院有关卖方反诉的判决。推翻原判,发回重审。

(异议法官的意见) 我同意多数派法官的这个结论,即行业惯例有可能对救济产生限制,并且,本来也许应该允许就行业

Newcor concedes as we have said that a possible remedy for its breach of contract would be a reduction in the purchase price. The jury, which awarded Newcor the whole of the unpaid balance, no doubt thought that since it was giving Western consequential damages there was no need to give Western in addition some abatement of the purchase price. That would be overcompensation, assuming as the jury must have done that its award of consequential damages was fully compensatory.

If the jury should conclude in a new trial, as it may, that Western is not contractually entitled to consequential damages, it may then want to award Western an abatement of the purchase price in lieu of such damages. To enable the jury to consider this possibility we must reverse the judgment on the counterclaim. REVERSED AND REMANDED.

[Dissenting Opinion] I agree with the majority that a limitation of remedy might have been accomplished by trade custom or usage and that the evidence of trade

惯例举证。但我相信，多数派法官对于合同成立效力的讨论，以及对“文本冲突”的讨论，至少在一个问题上过于新奇。

custom should probably have been admitted. However, the majority's discussion of the significance of the contract formation issue and its analysis of the “battle of the forms” is, I believe, novel in at least one particular.

多数派法官似乎是说，如果当事方实际上没有在 5 月 17 日的电话交谈中订立合同，那么，应由陪审团裁定的问题是：假设存在禁止间接损失的行业惯例，那么根据该行业惯例，卖方（排除了间接损失）的格式文件是否优于买方（包含了间接损失）的格式文件？

Thus, the majority seems to be saying that, if the contract was not formed during the May 17 phone conversation, then the question to be put to the jury is whether the existence of a trade custom which denies consequential damages serves to give precedence to Newcor's form （excluding consequential damages） over Western's form （including consequential damages）.

文本冲突的结果　但在我看来，提交给陪审团的适当问题是：在根据第 2.207 条（2）款或第 2.207 条（3）款将双方格式文件中的冲突条款全部排除出合同后，是否存在足够确定的行业惯例，来为合同提供其原本缺乏的排除间接损失赔偿的条款？

Rather, it seems to me that the proper question for the jury is whether, once the conflicting terms in the Western and Newcor forms fall out of the contract （as they would under either a Sec. 2-207（2） or a Sec. 2-207（3） analysis）, a sufficiently established trade custom exists which supplements the otherwise-silent contract to supply a term excluding consequential damages.

我也不同意多数派法官对本案关键问题的界定。他们界定的问题是，在为合同补充缺失条款时，到底应适用法典的哪一条

I would also depart from the majority in its formulation of a critical issue in this case--that is, in supplying terms for such a silent contract, the question is which Code provision

款？是第 1.205 条和第 2.202 条吗？这两项条款允许用行业惯例来解释或补充合同条款。还是第 2.719 条？这项条款仅仅规定，合同可以排除间接损失赔偿。

法典第 2.715 条正式评论 3 说，“法典相关条款规定，在失去预想前提条件时，商人可以获得免责。但在不存在此种免责的情况下，只要卖方在订立合同时有理由知道买方的通常或特殊需求，卖方就要对间接损失承担赔偿责任”。

威斯康星州最高法院已对法典第 2.714 条和第 2.715 条作出过解释，认为这两款的本意是说明，“获得间接损失赔偿的潜在权利，是合同中默示存在的权利”（A 诉 F 案）。此外，对于法典所提供的损害赔偿救济，尽管第 2.719 条允许改变或排除此种救济，但法典“不鼓励对救济进行限制，并且，如果此种限制实际上剥夺了当事方就违约获得合理保护的情况，法典将否定该限制的效力”（M 诉 H 案）。

尽管如此，我们的看法是，

should govern: Secs. 1-205 and 2-202 invoking trade usage to explain or supplement contract terms or Sec. 2-719 providing only that the agreement may exclude consequential damages.

Comment 3 to Sec. 2-715 states that: “In the absence of excuse under the section on merchant's excuse by failure of presupposed conditions, the seller is liable for consequential damages in all cases where he had reason to know of the buyer's general or particular requirements at the time of contracting.”

The Wisconsin Supreme Court has interpreted Secs. 2-714 and 2-715 to mean “that a potential recovery for consequential loss is implicit in [a] contract”. Air Products & Chemicals, Inc. v. Fairbanks Morse, Inc. In addition, the UCC “disfavors limitations on remedies and provides for their deletion where they would effectively deprive a party of reasonable protection against breach”, despite the fact that Sec. 2-719 allows for the alteration or elimination of the damages remedies otherwise granted under the UCC. Murray v. Holiday Rambler, Inc.

Nevertheless, in my view, the policy of

法典的政策看上去是偏向扩大行业惯例在解释或补充合同条款中的作用，甚至到了忽视当事方明示协议而允许行业惯例对合同条款进行重要补充的程度（参见 C 诉 D 案）。一旦行业惯例构成了合同的组成部分，那么，就像明示条款一样，行业惯例就可以取代或改变那些通常由法典提供的填补条款（引用著作）。

the UCC may seem to favor an expansive use of trade custom in explaining or supplementing contract terms, even to the point of allowing, without regard to the parties' express agreement, trade custom to supply significant elements of a contract term. See, e.g., Columbus Milk Producers' Cooperative v. Department of Agriculture. Once trade usage becomes a part of the contract, then, like express terms, it may supersede or vary other provisions usually supplied by the Code. J. White & R. Summers, Handbook of the Law Under the Uniform Commercial Code.

行业惯例应该确凿和明晰

因此，应该允许就行业惯例举证，用以解释和补充合同条款，甚至用于排除间接损失赔偿。但是，行业惯例并非基于当事方的明示协议而产生。因此，“行业惯例的证据必须确凿和明晰。并且，惯例必须已稳固确立、业界通用和广为人知。如此，我们才可假定当事方已知该惯例，并在考虑到该惯例的情况下订立了合同”（K 诉 J 案；引用著作）。

Hence, evidence of trade usage may be admitted for the purpose of explaining and supplementing the terms of the contract to the extent of excluding consequential damages. Such a trade usage is not, however, something which arises by express agreement of the parties. "[T]he proof of such usage must be clear and explicit, and the usage so well established, uniform, and so notorious that the parties must be presumed to know it, and to have contracted in reference to it." Knobel v. J. Bartel Co. See also White & Summers.

虽然上面引用的威斯康星州

While this Wisconsin decision antedates

K诉J案产生于法典制定之前，但其明显与法典第1.205条（2）款中行业惯例之定义的精神是一致的。法典该条款规定："行业惯例指交易的任何做法或方法，其在一个地区、一个行业或一类贸易中已得到经常遵守，以至使人有理由相信其在现行交易中也会得到遵守。"

adoption of the Uniform Commercial Code, it finds a clear echo in the definition of trade usage provided by the Code itself, Sec. 1-205（2）："A usage of trade is any practice or method of dealing having such regularity of observance in a place, vocation or trade as to justify an expectation that it will be observed with respect to the transaction in question."

此外，与交易过程或履约过程的证明不同，对行业惯例的证明，通常需要邀请专家证人。公开出版的行业守则（本案卖方为了证明行业惯例所使用的材料）并不必然构成行业惯例。无论如何，惯例必须是对双方都有约束力的行业守则（引用著作）。

Further, proof of trade usage, unlike proof of course of dealing or course of performance, usually requires the calling of an expert witness. A published trade code（which Newcor attempted to use in establishing its trade usage） does not necessarily constitute a trade usage and, in any event, it must be a trade code binding on both parties. See White & Summer.

我们认为，应向陪审团说明并使他们理解有关行业惯例的这些原则。法典鼓励在适当情况下将行业惯例视为合同条款的组成部分。但是，排除间接损失赔偿责任是一个重大问题，因此，不应依据买方和卖方混乱交换的格式文件轻易地假定存在此种排除。

I believe the jury should be instructed with these principles of trade usage in mind. The Uniform Commercial Code favors the incorporation of trade custom into the contractual understanding where appropriate. But disclaimer of liability for consequential damages is certainly not something which may be lightly assumed from a flurry of forms between buyer and seller.

案例 17　卖方所售货物是否可用于计算转售损失？

Apex Oil Company v. The Belcher Company of New York, Inc.

埃派克斯石油公司诉纽约拜尔彻公司案

联邦第二巡回上诉法院 1988 年；855 F.2d 997, 6 UCC Rep.Serv.2d 1025

简　介

本案卖方（Apex）从事石油产品的经销业务，其产品包括本案所涉及的用于家庭取暖的“2 号加热器油”（No. 2 heating oil）。买方（Belcher）也是石油产品的经销商。1982 年 2 月，双方在纽约商品交易所达成了一项 2 号加热器油的期货合同。合同规定，卖方将于 2 月在纽约港交付 31.5 万桶符合纽商所规格的 2 号加热器油，每加仑价格为 89.7 美分。根据纽商所的规格，在纽约港交付的油料的硫含量不得超过 0.2%。卖方随后与买方约定，在波士顿港交付其中的 19 万桶油料，并将波士顿港的油料定为“实货交换”（exchange for physicals，EFP）合同，即卖方必须实际交付油料。卖方告知，在波士顿港卸载油料的船只为波尔多轮（Bordeaux）。本案的争议，涉及在波士顿交付的这 19 万桶油料。

波尔多轮于 2 月 9 日抵达波士顿港，10 日开始在买方码头卸载。10 日夜间，在大约 5 万至 6 万桶油料已被卸载后，一家独立石油检验机构告知买方，波尔多轮油料的硫含量为 0.28%，超过了合同规定。这个结果也立即被告知卖方。但买方继续卸货至11日上午11时。至此，约14.2万桶油料被卸入买方的储油罐。这时，买方又对油料进行了第二次检测，结果显示硫含量为 0.22%，处于 0.2% 硫含量油料允许的宽容度内。但买方并未将这个结果告诉卖方（卖方直到诉讼前不久才得知第二次检测结果）。11 日中午，买方拒绝进一步卸载，谎称油料不符合约定的 0.2% 的硫含量（尽管此时已有第二次检验结果）。买方要求波尔多轮载着剩余油料离开码头。在这种情况下，卖方立即联系了波士顿市政服务署（Cities Service）。卖方原本约定当月稍晚向市政服务署交付同一品种的加热器油，但市政服务署同意现在就接受波尔多轮剩余油料（约 4.8 万桶）的交付。因此，在买方拒收的第二天，即 2 月 12 日，卖方在波士顿港将剩余油料交付给市政服务署。卖方没有将这个情况通知买方。

与此同时，对于波尔多轮已卸载的油料（14.2 万桶），买卖双方展开谈判。买方谎称，油料因为硫含量高而不适用，只能以亏损方式售出，并产生了其他额外费用。但买方此时实际已将该油料正常出售给其他买家。买方以油料不符合合同为由拒绝支付已卸载油料的价款（约 530 万美元），并要求卖方继续交付合同项下剩余的约 4.8 万桶油料。2 月 17 日，卖方同意交付剩余的 4.8 万桶油料，但要求在双方继续谈判期间，买方先支付已卸载油料的大部分价款。买方向卖方出具了一张面额约为 500 万美元的支票，相当于合同价格中减去了每加仑 5 美分的折扣。支票包含了下列条件："接受并议付本支票即代表对全部索赔的充分付款和最终解决。"卖方因此拒绝接受该支票。买方告诉卖方，如果不接受该支票，就必须将已卸载的油料取走，并另行交付 19 万桶符合合同的油料。

卖方同意于 2 月 25 日将油料取走。但由于当时买方已将该油料出售给其他买家，所以实际上没有油料可以退还给卖方。买方只好虚称，暂时没有空余油轮码头可供卖方使用，并再次要求卖方同意接受每加仑 5 美分的折扣。双方最终达成和解协议，由买方按每加仑 2.5 美分的折扣收下已卸载的油料。之后，卖方多次询问买方如何交付剩余的 4.8 万桶油料，但买方 3 月 5 日告知卖方，说买方认为在订立和解协议后，其在原合同项下的义务已被全部解除，因此不再接受剩余的油料。卖方于 3 月 23 日向第三方买家（Gill & Duffus）出售了 4.8 万桶油料，价格为每加仑 76.25 美分，比原始合同价格每加仑低 13.45 美分。

1982 年 10 月 7 日，卖方起诉买方，称买方有欺诈行为，且违反了合同。欺诈问题主要涉及已卸载到买方储油罐中并被买方接受的 14.2 万桶油料。买方向卖方隐瞒了第二次检测结果，并隐瞒了油料已被出售给其他买家的情况。卖方认为，买方通过欺诈手段诱使卖方签订了和解协议，使卖方受到每加仑 2.5 美分的损失。初审法院根据陪审团的裁定，判决买方就欺诈行为向卖方支付损害赔偿。由于这个问题不涉及法典，所以相关讨论没有包括在下列节选的判决书中。

违反合同的问题，主要涉及未卸载至买方储油罐且买方最终没有接受的 4.8 万桶油料。初审法院认定，买方 2 月 11 日拒收油料的行为构成了违约，因为当时买方已经知道第二次检测的结果，而该结果没有超出合同约定的硫含量。对于买方违反合同的行为，初审法院根据陪审团的裁定，判决买方支付大约 28 万美元的赔偿。赔偿数额是以卖方出售给第三方买家的 4.8 万桶油料的价格为基础计算的。由于每桶油料等于 42 加仑，而出售给第三方买家的油料每加仑价格相对于原始合同价格减少了 13.45 美分，因此最终得出了 28 万美元的损失数额。买方认为这个计算存在错误，因此提起上诉。

从本案情况可以看出，卖方出售给第三方买家的 4.8 万桶油料，实际上不是原始合同项下的同一批油料。原始油料共 19 万桶，装载于波尔多轮。除去已卸载给买方的 14.2 万桶，船上其余的 4.8 万桶已被卖方于 2 月 12 日交付给市政服务署。卖方 3 月 23 日出售给第三方买家的 4.8 万桶油料，虽然也是 2 号加热器油，但与原始合同无关，而是卖方从其他来源取得的。并且，买方的违约是在 2 月 11 日，而卖方出售油料给第三方买家是在 3 月 23 日，即大约 6 个星期之后。

根据法典第 2.706 条（1）款的规定，在买方因错误拒收等原因毁约后，卖方可将合同货物“转售”（resell）给第三方买家，并根据原始合同价格与转售价格的差额来计算自己的损失数额。初审法院将卖方向本案第三方买家出售油料的价格，作为本案卖方的转售价格，并基于该转售价格计算买方应支付的赔偿数额。但如上面提到的，出售给第三方买家的油料，实际上与原始合同的油料没有关系。

初审法院之所以没有将卖方 2 月 12 日交付给市政服务署的那 4.8 万桶油料作为“转售”的油料，是因为虽然买方 2 月 11 日就发生了违约，但合同并未被取消，当事方也还在谈判。卖方当时并不知道买方违约。并且，买方（无论是真心还是假意）当时还要求卖方继续交付剩余的 4.8 万桶油料，而卖方也愿意作出交付（因为卖方有能力从其他来源取得 4.8 万桶油料）。因此，卖方虽然已将波尔多轮上的 4.8 万桶油料交付给市政服务署，但初审法院认为，这不属于法律意义上的转售。

在以上背景下，上诉法院需要解决两个问题。首先，卖方是否有权将出售给第三方买家的油料视为“转售”的油料？前面提到，给第三方买家的油料，本身与原始合同无关，而是卖方随后从其他来源取得的。上诉法院认为，本案 2 号加热器油属于“种类物”（fungible goods），因而卖方有较大自由度，可以使用其他货物来代替原始合同项下的货物。也就是说，即使卖方已将某批种类物（如波尔多轮油料）特定于合同项下，卖方也有权取消该特定化，并将其他一批种类物（如卖方随后取得并出售给第三方买家的油料）“再特定化”（reidentification）至合同项下。因此，本案卖方出售给第三方买家的油料，在是否属于被特定于原始合同项下的货物这个问题上，不存在绝对的法律障碍。

其次，虽然卖方有权作出“再特定化”，但本案卖方是否在其他方面遵守了法典对转售的规定？上诉法院认为，法典“转售”救济的本质是，通过转售行为来具体确定转售价格，从而确定卖方有权获得的损害赔偿。因此，卖方所主张的转售，必须能代表合理的转售价格。本案卖方所主张的转售，是在违约发生后 6 个星期才完成的。由于油料价格剧烈波动，耽延过久的转售明显使转售价格不能准确代表法典所要求的“转售价格”。同时，卖方未就耽延提供合理理由。上诉法院因此判定，虽然向第三方买家出售的油料理论上可以构成转售油料，但转售的耽延时间超出了合理限度，因此该次出售的价格不能作为确定“转售价格”的依据。据此，上诉法院推翻了初审法院的判决。

判　决

本案的问题　这个州际案件来自一起激烈的商业纠纷。本案的问题是，如果被特定于破裂合同的原始货物在违约后第二天即被售出，那么，卖方 6 个星期后另行作出的销售，是否可以合理地作为法典第 2.706 条项下转售损失赔偿的计算依据?

This diversity case, arising out of an acrimonious commercial dispute, presents the question whether a sale of goods six weeks after a breach of contract may properly be used to calculate resale damages under Section 2-706 of the Uniform Commercial Code, where goods originally identified to the broken contract were sold on the day following the breach.

初审法院的判决　本案的初审使用了陪审团。初审法院判决，在这起最终未能完成的加热器油交易中，买方违反了合同，并存在欺诈行为，因此必须向卖方支付 432,365.04 美元的损害赔偿。买方就该判决提起上诉。买方声称，初审法院允许卖方获得转售损失赔偿的判决是不适当的。我们同意买方的理由，并推翻原判。

Defendants The Belcher Company of New York, Inc. and Belcher New Jersey, Inc. (“Belcher”) appeal from a judgment, entered after a jury trial before Judge McLaughlin, awarding plaintiff Apex $432,365.04 in damages for breach of contract and fraud in connection with an uncompleted transaction for heating oil. Belcher claims that the district court improperly allowed Apex to recover resale damages. We agree and reverse.

有关卖方救济的一般规定　当买方违约时，纽约州 1964 年

The Uniform Commercial Code, adopted by New York in 1964, provides various

版法典向卖方提供了各种救济。例如，受损害的卖方可以留持货物不予交付，或取消合同，或就已被买方接受的货物取得价款，或基于市场价格就未被接受的或被毁约的货物取得损害赔偿（参见法典第2.703条）。此外，卖方还可以像本案卖方所试图做的那样，通过转售货物而固化其损失数额，然后就转售价格与合同价格的差额从买方取得赔偿。

remedies to sellers for default by buyers. An aggrieved seller may, for example, with hold delivery of goods, cancel the contract, recover the unpaid price of accepted goods, or recover damages for nonaccepted or repudiated goods based on their market price. See generally N.Y.U.C.C. Sec. 2-703. In addition, a seller may, as Apex seeks to do, fix its damages by reselling the goods and recovering from the buyer the difference between the resale price and the contract price.

法典有关转售的具体规定

具体而言，法典第2.706条相关部分规定："（1）卖方只要遵守有关卖方救济的第2.703条规定的条件，即可转售有关的货物，或转售尚未交付的剩余货物。只要转售以善意和商业上合理的方式进行，卖方即有权就转售价格与合同价格的差额取得赔偿，再加上本篇允许的任何附带损失（第2.710条），但须减去因买方违约致使卖方节省的费用。（2）除（3）款另有规定外，且除另有协议外，转售可以公开进行或私下进行，并可以订立一个或多个买卖合同，也可

Specifically, Section 2-706 of the Code provides in pertinent part："（1） Under the conditions stated in Section 2-703 on seller's remedies, the seller may resell the goods concerned or the undelivered balance thereof. Where the resale is made in good faith and in a commercially reasonable manner the seller may recover the difference between the resale price and the contract price together with any incidental damages allowed under the provisions of this Article （Section 2-710）, but less expenses saved in consequence of the buyer's breach. （2） Except as otherwise provided in subsection （3） or unless otherwise agreed resale may be at public or private sale including sale by way of one or

将货物特定于卖方任何现有合同的项下。货物出售可以整体或分批进行，可以在任何时间和地点以任何条件进行。但是，出售活动的各个方面，包括方法、方式、时间、地点和条件，都必须商业上合理。必须合理证明转售与被违反之合同存在联系，但并不要求在违约发生前货物已经存在，或已经部分或全部特定于合同项下。（3）如果转售是私下进行，卖方必须将转售的意图向买方作出合理的通知。”

more contracts to sell or of identification to an existing contract of the seller. Sale may be as a unit or in parcels and at any time and place and on any terms but every aspect of the sale including the method, manner, time, place and terms must be commercially reasonable. The resale must be reasonably identified as referring to the broken contract, but it is not necessary that the goods be in existence or that any or all of them have been identified to the contract before the breach. （3） Where the resale is at private sale the seller must give the buyer reasonable notification of his intention to resell.”

当事方的主张　买方上诉的主要辩称是，初审法院判决卖方可根据法典第 2.706 条的规定取得转售损失赔偿，但作为法律问题，该判决是错误的。具体而言，买方声称，卖方于 1982 年 3 月底向第三方买家出售的加热器油，不是被特定于本案破裂合同的油料。买方认为，特定到破裂合同项下的是波尔多轮的油料，即卖方在违约发生后第二天就出售给市政服务署的油料。作为回复，卖方辩称，加热器油是种类

Belcher's principal argument on appeal is that the district court erred as a matter of law in allowing Apex to recover resale damages under Section 2-706. Specifically, Belcher contends that the heating oil Apex sold to Gill & Duffus in late March of 1982 was not identified to the broken contract. According to Belcher, the oil identified to the contract was the oil aboard the Bordeaux --oil which Apex had sold to Cities Service on the day after the breach. In response, Apex argues that, because heating oil is a fungible commodity, the oil sold to Gill & Duffus was “reasonably

物，因此，出售给第三方买家的油料虽然不是装载于波尔多轮的同一批油料，但应属于“合理地被特定于”破裂合同项下。

identified” to the contract even though it was not the same oil that had been on board the Bordeaux.

种类物的特定化问题 我们同意卖方的这个说法，即至少对于种类物来说，为了转售目的而作出的特定化，不一定要求被转售的货物完全就是被拒收或被毁约的货物。尽管如此，我们的结论是，作为法律问题，3月出售给第三方买家的油料，并没有被合理地特定于2月11日被违反的破裂合同。并且，向第三方买家的出售，也不属于商业上合理。

We agree with Apex that, at least with respect to fungible goods, identification for the purposes of a resale transaction does not necessarily require that the resold goods be the exact goods that were rejected or repudiated. Nonetheless, we conclude that as a matter of law the oil sold to Gill & Duffus in March was not reasonably identified to the contract breached on February 11, and that the resale was not commercially reasonable.

法典有关特定化的规定 为了解决本案争议，我们有必要对法典的各项条款进行分析。首先需要分析的，是对“特定化”作出定义的第2.501条。该条相关部分规定：“（1）对于现实存在的货物，在其发生特定化并因此成为合同所指的货物后，买方即对货物取得特殊财产权和保险利益，即使特定化的货物不符合合同，致使买方有权退回或拒收。上述特定

Resolving the instant dispute requires us to survey various provisions of the Uniform Commercial Code. The first such provision is Section 2-501, which defines “identification” and states in pertinent part: “（1）The buyer obtains a special property and an insurable interest in goods by identification of existing goods as goods to which the contract refers even though the goods so identified are non-conforming and he has an option to return or reject them. Such identification can be made at any time and in any manner explicitly

化可根据当事方的明确协议，在任何时间以任何方式发生；如果没有明确协议，则：（a）当合同出售的是合同订立时现实存在且特定的货物时，特定化在订立合同时发生；（b）当合同出售的是（c）款（农作物和家畜）以外的待定货物时，特定化在卖方将货物发运、标注或以其他方式确定于合同项下时发生。”

agreed to by the parties. In the absence of explicit agreement identification occurs （a） when the contract is made if it is for the sale of goods already existing and identified; （b） if the contract is for the sale of future goods other than those described in paragraph （c） [crops and livestock], when goods are shipped, marked or otherwise designated by the seller as goods to which the contract refers."

特定化的准确含义　毫无疑问，波尔多轮的油料已根据法典第 2.501 条（1）（b）款特定于合同项下，且卖方对此不持异议。尽管如此，卖方辩称，“涉及第 2.706 条的转售救济时”，第 2.501 条并不适用，因为第 2.501 条对特定化的定义，仅用于确定买方取得对货物之“特殊财产权和保险利益”的时间点。

The Bordeaux oil was unquestionably identified to the contract under Section 2-501（1）（b）, and Apex does not assert otherwise. Nevertheless, Apex argues that Section 2-501 "has no application in the context of the Section 2-706 resale remedy", because Section 2-501 defines identification only for the purpose of establishing the point at which a buyer "obtains a special property and an insurable interest in goods".

上述辩称表面上具有一定说服力，但忽略了法典第 2.103 条，而该条包含了适用于法典第 2 篇整篇的各种定义和其他定义的索引。关于“特定化”，第 2.103 条（2）款规定，这个概念的定义列于第 2.501 条。

This argument has a facial plausibility but ignores Section 2-103, which contains various definitions, and an index of other definitions, of terms used throughout Article 2 of the Code. With regard to "[i]dentification", Section 2-103（2） provides that the definition is set forth in Section 2-501.

特定化不排除再特定化 因此，法典第2.501条告诉我们，波尔多轮的油料已被特定于合同项下。但是，我们的分析不能到此为止，因为作为法律问题，这并未排除另一个可能性，即卖方先将货物特定于合同项下，但随后以相等的其他货物特定于合同项下，用于取代之前已特定化的货物。

Section 2-501 thus informs us that the Bordeaux oil was identified to the contract. It does not end our inquiry, however, because it does not exclude as a matter of law the possibility that a seller may identify goods to a contract, but then substitute, for the identified goods, identical goods that are then identified to the contract.

相关判例 在M诉N案中，联邦第三巡回上诉法院认可存在上述可能性。在该案中，买方同意从卖方购买50,000吨黄沙。买方随后在卖方工厂的若干沙堆的旁边立起了牌子，上面写着“MM公司（买方）的财产”。由于卖方未对这些牌子提出异议，法院判定，特定化已经发生。但是，卖方的债权人辩称，该特定化随后已被撤销，因为卖方随后将已特定化的黄沙中的一部分另行出售给其他客户。

The Third Circuit recognized such a possibility in Martin Marietta Corp. v. New Jersey National Bank. In that case, plaintiff Martin Marietta agreed to buy 50,000 tons of sand from Hollander Sand Associates. Martin Marietta subsequently placed signs reading “Property of Martin Marietta” on piles of sand at Hollander’s plant. Because Hollander did not object to the signs, the court held that identification had occurred. Yet Hollander’s creditor argued that the identification had been negated because Hollander had nevertheless sold some of the identified sand to customers other than Marietta.

对种类物可以进行更新 在该案中，法院基于法典第2.501条的正式评论5驳回了卖方债权

The court rejected this argument, relying upon Official Comment 5 to Section 2-501: “We feel this argument does not overcome

人的主张。该法院说："我们认为，本案事实的说服力强于上述主张。如同法典正式评论所说，'可以出售已特定化的一批种类物中的未分割份额。对于已特定化的一批种类物，只要订立合同时指明其中的未分割份额即可'（第 2.501 条正式评论 5）。虽然这段评论针对的是订立合同时已经存在的货物，但该评论也说明，以本案卖方这样的方式对待种类物，与卖方将货物加以指定或特定的意图并不矛盾。该评论的核心是，如果卖方将种类物的一部分移走但随后再作出补充，这不会削弱法典鼓励特定化的宗旨。这很可能是因为，涉及种类物时，卖方的此种行为非常自然，因此不应认为卖方有意否定买方对货物的权益。简言之，本案中黄沙的出售和更换，不削弱支持特定化的事实或宗旨。"

the facts in this case. As already noted: 'Undivided shares in an identified fungible bulk ... can be sold. The mere making of a contract with reference to an undivided share in an identified bulk is enough.' UCC Sec. 2-501, comment 5. Although this passage deals with goods that exist when the contract is made, it demonstrates that treating fungibles as did Hollander here is consistent with an intent on the part of Hollander to identify or designate the goods. The crux of the passage is that if the seller removes some of the fungibles and later replaces them, that should not undercut the policy favoring identification, probably because such conduct is quite natural with fungibles and cannot be taken as an intent to negate the buyer's interest in the goods. In short, sale and replacement of the sand here does not overcome either the facts or the policy favoring identification."

所以，M 诉 N 案和法典正式评论 5 都说明，至少在涉及种类物时，卖方在作出特定化后，并非不可逆转地受到该特定化的约束。但是，M 诉 N 案和正式

Thus, Martin Marietta and Official Comment 5 suggest that, at least where fungible goods are concerned, a seller is not irrevocably bound to an identification once made. However, Martin Marietta

评论5均不涉及转售问题，因此它们并未告诉我们，哪些情况构成第2.706条项下可被视为“合理”的特定化。

本案买方的主张 尽管如此，当事方辩称，上述问题已由规定了卖方救济的法典相关条款所解决。具体而言，买方引用了第2.706条的规定，即“卖方可以出售相关货物”［第2.706条（1）款］，以及第2.704条的规定，即“受损害的卖方可以将尚未特定且符合合同的货物特定于合同项下，只要其得知违约时，货物在其占有或控制之下”［第2.704条（1）款］。买方辩称，这些规定完全否定了为转售目的而将货物重新特定化的可能性。

本案卖方的主张 另一方面，卖方则引用了法典第2.706条的规定，即“货物无须在违约前已经存在，或已经全部或部分被特定于合同项下”［第2.706条（2）款］。卖方认为，这段文字显示，“适用第2.706条时所应提出的相关问题是，货物在转售时是否已被合理地特定于破

and Comment 5 were not concerned with resales and thus do not inform us as to what constitutes “reasonable” identification under Section 2-706.

The parties nevertheless argue that this issue is resolved by the Code’s various provisions governing sellers’ remedies. In particular, Belcher relies upon Section 2-706’s statement that “the seller may resell the goods concerned”, N.Y.U.C.C. Sec. 2-706（1）, and upon Section 2-704, which states that “［a］n aggrieved seller ... may ... identify to the contract conforming goods not already identified if at the time he learned of the breach they are in his possession or control”. Sec. 2-704（1）. According to Belcher, these statements absolutely foreclose the possibility of reidentification for the purpose of a resale.

Apex, on the other hand, points to Section 2-706’s statement that “it is not necessary that the goods be in existence or that any or all of them have been identified to the contract before the breach”. Sec. 2-706（2）. According to Apex, this language shows that “［t］he relevant inquiry to be made under Section 2-706 is whether the resale transaction is reasonably identified to the breached

裂合同，而不是该货物是否原来就被特定于破裂合同”。

上述主张不能成立　但是，当事方所引用的上述法典条款，没有一项具有决定意义。首先，第 2.706 条（1）款所提到的“相关货物”的转售，对本案没有任何帮助，因为这是指已被特定于合同的货物，但本案要回答的问题是，到底哪些货物已被特定于合同。

其次，关于第 2.704 条，虽然受损害的卖方可以将“尚未特定”的货物进行特定化，但这本身并不意味着卖方不可以对之前已经特定的货物进行更换，重新将其他货物特定化。实际上，第 2.704 条看上去只单纯涉及上述第 2.706 条（2）款的情况，即货物尚不存在或尚未被特定于合同项下。因此，第 2.704 条或第 2.706 条（1）款并不能帮助买方。

最后，与此同时，第 2.706 条（2）款虽然提到了尚不存在或尚未特定的货物，但这并不像卖方所称的那样，意味着货物原来（违约前）发生的特定化已经

contract and not whether the goods resold were originally identified to that contract”.

None of the cited provisions are dispositive. First, Section 2-706（1）'s reference to reselling “the goods concerned” is unhelpful because those goods are the goods identified to the contract, but which goods are so identified is the question to be answered in the instant case.

Second, as to Section 2-704, the fact that an aggrieved seller may identify goods “not already identified” does not mean that the seller may not identify goods as substitutes for previously identified goods. Rather, Section 2-704 appears to deal simply with the situation described in Section 2-706（2）above, where the goods are not yet in existence or have not yet been identified to the contract. Belcher thus can draw no comfort from either Section 2-704 or Section 2-706（1）.

Third, at the same time, however, Section 2-706（2）'s reference to nonexistent and nonidentified goods does not mean, as Apex suggests, that the original（pre-breach）identification of goods is wholly irrelevant.

完全无关。实际上，法典有关尚不存在或尚未特定之货物的这款规定，所针对的是买方预前毁约这种特殊情况（第2.706条正式评论7）。在该情况下，除非允许卖方在买方违约后将货物特定于合同项下，否则自然就不可能存在转售救济。但本案明显不属于这种情况。

Rather, the provision regarding nonexistent and nonidentified goods deals with the special circumstances involving anticipatory repudiation by the buyer. See N.Y.U.C.C. Sec. 2-706 comment 7. Under such circumstances, there can of course be no resale remedy unless the seller is allowed to identify goods to the contract after the breach. That is obviously not the case here.

与转售有关的再特定化判例

由于我们无法从法典文字本身找到明确答案，因此，关于第2.706条项下种类物的特定化问题，我们将参考唯一有关这个问题的判例，即涉及肉类买卖合同的S诉E案。具体而言，在该案中，卖方与买方约定，卖方将向买方交付200,000磅含50%瘦肉的肉馅，作为买方生产罐装辣豆粥的原材料。交付方式是卖方向买方转让出货单和仓单。在约定的日期，卖方将该等文件交付给了买方，并在冷藏仓库现场将其中的某部分肉馅指定作为保留给买方的货物。但买方随后拒绝就该合同付款。并且，在卖方完成“交付”超过两个月之后，买方于5

Finding no clear guidance in the language of the Code, we turn to the only decision concerning the identification of fungible goods under Section 2-706, Servbest Foods, Inc. v. Emessee Industries, Inc. Servbest involved a contract for the sale of meat. Specifically, plaintiff Servbest and defendant Emessee agreed that Servbest would deliver to Emessee 200,000 pounds of fifty-percent lean navel trimmings, an ingredient used in making canned chili. Delivery was to be effected through the transfer of invoices and warehouse receipts. On the appointed day, Servbest delivered the papers to Emessee and physically designated certain navel trimmings in cold storage as reserved for Emessee. Emessee, however, refused to make payment on the contract. Instead it “redelivered”

月 3 日将该肉馅“重新交付”给卖方（大概是通过向卖方退还出货单和仓单），同时附上了一封信，宣布说买方认为合同和出货单已被取消。

the meat to Servbest on May 3, more than two months after it had been “delivered”,（presumably by returning the invoices and receipts） with a letter announcing that it considered the contract and invoices cancelled.

卖方因此起诉买方违反合同。初审法官判定肉馅属于种类物，并允许卖方“基于 1974 年 5 月 3 日之后所完成的，且总量达到 200,000 磅的肉馅的首次销售”，来计算损害赔偿数额。但是，该销售所售出的肉馅，实际上不是曾特定化给买方的肉馅，而是过期日最早的其他肉馅。

Servbest accordingly brought suit for breach of contract. The trial judge held that the navel trimmings were fungible and allowed Servbest to calculate its damages based “upon the first sales after the May 3, 1974 breach, which totalled 200,000 pounds of navel trimmings”. These sales were not, however, from the trimmings identified for Emessee, but rather the meat with the earliest storage expiration date.

上诉法院维持了该判决。法院驳回了该案买方提出的类似本案买方的辩称。该案买方辩称，根据法典第 2.706 条所转售的货物，必须是原来已经特定于合同项下的那些货物。但上诉法院说，必须对法典进行灵活解释，而不是机械地解释。法院认为，转售救济的目的，是使受损害的卖方恢复到未发生违约时其本来可以达到的处境。

The Appellate Court affirmed. It rejected Emessee’s argument--identical to that made by Belcher here--that the goods resold under Section 2-706 must be the very goods that were originally identified to the contract. The court noted that the Code must be construed liberally, not mechanically, and that the purpose of the resale remedy is to put the aggrieved seller in the position he would have occupied but for the breach.

该案上诉法院认为，在上述前提下，并考虑到肉馅属于种类物的事实，初审法院的转售损害赔偿理论是适当的。其结论是："按照买方的说法，从19,700仓位（包含已特定化肉馅的仓位）出售的任何200,000磅肉馅，都可以构成适当的转售，而从其他仓位出售的同等肉馅，就不足以构成该种性质的转售。我们不同意这个说法。根据我们对案件材料的分析，没有任何证据证明，从其他仓位售出的肉馅的市场价值，与19,700仓位肉馅的市场价值存在任何差别。此外，种类物的性质表明，在买方违反了涉及种类物的合同时，没有任何理由可以说，卖方不能根据法典第2.706条的规定，在原本特定于合同项下的货物之外，使用其他货物进行转售并就其损失取得赔偿，只要此种转售不会影响或改变货物在公开出售或私下出售中收到的价款。因此，我们判定，初审法院的判决并无错误，即违约发生后首次售出的总量为200,000磅肉馅，可以构成法典

Based upon these premises and the fact that navel trimmings are fungible, the court concluded that the trial court's resale-damage theory was proper: "Under Emessee's approach, a sale of any 200,000 pounds of meat from lot 19,700 （the lot containing the identified meat） would constitute a proper resale while identical meat from a different lot would be insufficient for that purpose. We do not agree. From our analysis of the record we find no basis upon which to conclude that the market value of the navel trimmings sold from outside of lot 19,700 was any different from the market value of the meat contained in lot 19,700. Moreover, the nature of fungible goods suggests no reason why, where a contract involving fungible goods is breached by the buyer, a seller could not recover a deficiency award under section 2-706 based upon a resale of goods other than those identified to the contract inasmuch as such a sale would not affect or alter the price received for the goods in either a private or public sale. Accordingly, we hold that the trial court's decision to employ the first sales of navel trimmings after the breach totalling 200,000 ［pounds］ as a mitigating resale

第 2.706 条项下的为减少损失而进行的转售。”

under 2-706 was not erroneous.”

该案上诉法院还说明，其结论与法典第 2.706 条的规定是一致的，即受损害的卖方可以转售在违约发生时尚不存在或尚未特定的货物。S 诉 E 案的法院认为，法典该条的规定表明，“在根据第 2.706 条取得赔偿时，特定化不是关键因素”。这也是本案卖方希望本院得出的结论。

The court also noted that its conclusion was consistent with Section 2-706's statement that aggrieved sellers may resell goods that were not in existence or identified at the time of the breach. As Apex asks us to do, the Servbest court viewed that statement as “suggest［ing］ that identification is not crucial to recovery under 2-706”.

当事方有关上述判例的主张 本案卖方认为，维持初审法院的本案判决，即卖方有权取得转售损失的赔偿，具有比 S 诉 E 案更强的理由。而买方的主要辩称是，S 诉 E 案的判决是“不正确”和反常的，因此不应为了保持判决结果一致而遵循该判例。我们不太同意 S 诉 E 案的很多推理，但我们认为其结论是正确的。尽管如此，我们仍然认为，法律支持本案买方的主张。

In Apex's view, affirmance of its resale-damage award follows a fortiori from Servbest. Belcher argues primarily that Servbest was an “incorrect” and aberrational decision that should not be followed in the name of uniformity. We think, however, that Servbest was rightly decided, although we do not agree with much of its reasoning. Nevertheless, our view of the law supports Belcher.

特定化并非不可逆 我们同意 S 诉 E 案的结论，即根据法典第 2.706 条的规定，虽然所转售的种类物必须是特定在合同项

We agree with Servbest that fungible goods resold pursuant to Section 2-706 must be goods identified to the contract, but need not always be those originally identified to

下的货物，但并非必须是原始特定于合同项下的货物。也就是说，至少在涉及种类物时，特定化并非必然是不可逆转的行为，因此不排除更换货物的可能性。

the contract. In other words, at least where fungible goods are concerned, identification is not always an irrevocable act and does not foreclose the possibility of substitution.

允许再特定化是合理的 假如M诉N案的判决本来是，在违约发生之前，已特定化的种类物不能被移走或更换，那么该判决将是毫无道理的。同样，假如本案判决，在违约发生之后，永远不能进行此种更换（重新特定化），则此种判决也是没有道理的。例如，假设法典要求受损害的卖方不能将原来特定于合同项下的货物与其他同类货物混合，而是必须分开，且这种要求会导致成本增加，那么法典的规定就没有道理。

Just as it would have made no sense in Martin Marietta to hold that the identified fungibles could not be removed and replaced before breach, here it would make no sense to hold that such replacement （that is, reidentification） can never occur after breach. For example, it serves no purpose of the Code to force an aggrieved seller to segregate goods originally identified to the contract when doing so is more costly than mixing them with other identical goods.

再特定化对本案的合理性 举一个具体的例子，假设本案买方拒收波尔多轮油料后，卖方原本未能立即找到任何人购买该油料，且在波士顿唯一可供卖方使用的储油罐中已存有半罐2号加热器油，此时，将波尔多轮的油料与该唯一储油罐中的油料进

To give a concrete example, suppose that Apex had been unable to find someone to take the Bordeaux oil immediately after the oil was rejected by Belcher and that the only storage tank available to Apex in Boston was already half-full of No. 2 heating oil. To mix the Bordeaux oil with the oil in the only available tank and to identify the first 48,000 barrels

行混合，并将首批出售的 48,000 桶特定于转售合同项下，就是唯一合理的方式。这样做之后，用于计算转售损害赔偿的油料，自然已不是原来特定于合同项下的油料，而是不同的油料。

sold to the contract is the only sensible thing to do. Doing so, of course, bases the damage award on resales of different oil from that previously identified to the contract.

假如规则禁止将货物重新特定于原始合同，那么在上述假想例子中，本案卖方只能选择放弃转售救济，而必须将波尔多轮进行昂贵的转港。但实际上，要计算转售救济，只需确定 48,000 桶 2 号油料种类物的价格，而转售任何同等数量的符合合同的油料，都可以完成该任务。

Under a rule that prevents any reidentification of goods to a contract, Apex would be forced in the hypothetical to choose between its resale remedy and a costly diversion of the Bordeaux. Yet for the purpose of the resale remedy--which is simply to fix the price of 48,000 barrels of fungible No. 2 oil--resale of any such quantity of conforming oil would do.

转售仍然必须合理 因此，不应将法典第 2.706 条解释为，在任何情况下都只能转售原始特定于破裂合同的货物，而不能转售任何其他货物。但是，尽管如此，如同该条所明确规定的，“转售必须合理指明与破裂合同的联系”，并且，“出售的各个方面，包括方法、方式、时间、地点和条件，都必须商业上合理”［第 2.706 条（2）款］。此外，法典之救济的目的是，使受损方恢复

Thus, Section 2-706 should not be construed as always proscribing the resale of goods other than those originally identified to the broken contract. Nevertheless, as that Section expressly states, “[t] he resale must be reasonably identified as referring to the broken contract”, and “every aspect of the sale including the method, manner, time, place and terms must be commercially reasonable”. N.Y.U.C.C. Sec. 2-706（2）. Moreover, because the purpose of remedies under the Code is to put “the aggrieved party ... in

至"另一方充分履约时受损方本可达到的处境"[第1.106条(1)款],因此,在确定特定化和转售的合理性时必须分析,所转售之货物的市场价值和所收到的转售货款,是否"准确地反映了原始合同项下之货物的市场价值"(S诉E案)。

合理性的判断 关于不合理的特定化和转售,最明显的一个例子也许是,所转售的货物不是与原始特定化之货物相同的种类物[参见S诉E案(该案判决说明,所转售的肉馅"在数量、质量和规格上",都与原始所指定之仓位的货物相同)]。

不合理特定化和转售的另一个例子是,与原始特定化的货物相比,转售货物所处的地理位置导致其价值显著偏低。例如,假设本案卖方在向波士顿市政服务署交付48,000桶2号油料的同时,试图将位于维尔京群岛的一个储油罐中同样数量的2号油料特定化于原始合同,并用其计算转售价格,那么该特定化和转售是不合理的,因为与波士顿地区

as good a position as if the other party had fully performed", Sec. 1-106(1), the reasonableness of the identification and of the resale must be determined by examining whether the market value of, and the price received for, the resold goods "accurately reflects the market value of the goods which are the subject of the contract". Servbest.

Perhaps the most obvious example of an unreasonable identification and resale would occur when the resold goods and the originally identified goods are not fungible. Cf. id. (noting that resold meat is "identical in quantity, quality and description" as that in lot originally identified).

Another example of an unreasonable identification and resale would be to claim as a resale the sale of goods located where they would have a significantly lower value than the originally identified goods. For example, had Apex purported to identify and resell 48,000 barrels of No. 2 oil contained in a storage tank in the Virgin Islands, where heating oil is presumably less useful and valuable than in Boston, while simultaneously delivering the same amount to Cities Service

相比，加热器油在维尔京群岛大概没有什么用处，因此价值较低。

转售中的时间因素　特定化和转售是否合理，其中最关键的因素是时间。一本专著作出如下解释："转售的目的，实际上就是准确地确定卖方的损失数额。原始合同价格与买方本应履约之时间和地点的市场价格的差额，就是卖方的损失数额。转售的目的，就是要确定实际市场价格是多少。除非作出转售的时间与本来的履约时间相差不多，否则，转售价格的参照意义就会损失很多，特别是对于价值快速波动的货物种类来说。如果在上述时间不存在合理的转售市场，则推延一段时间当然也有可能是适当的，且随后转售所提供的价格，也许是所能获得的卖方损失数额的最佳参照，但应该承认，该价格不是最理想的精确参照。"（引用著作；另参见 S 诉 E 案）

时间因素需要综合判断　关于从违约时间至转售时间这个期间的耽延问题，过去所遇到的情况只是，被特定于破裂合同的原

in Boston, the identification and resale would be unreasonable.

The most pertinent aspect of reasonableness with regard to identification and resale involves timing. As one treatise explains: "[T] he object of the resale is simply to determine exactly the seller's damages. These damages are the difference between the contract price and the market price at the time and place when performance should have been made by the buyer. The object of the resale ... is to determine what the market price in fact was. Unless the resale is made at about the time when performance was due it will be of slight probative value, especially if the goods are of a kind which fluctuate rapidly in value. If no reasonable market existed at this time, no doubt a delay may be proper and a subsequent sale may furnish the best test, though confessedly not a perfectly exact one, of the seller's damage." R. Anderson, Anderson on the Uniform Commercial Code; see also Servbest.

The issue of delay between breach and resale has previously been addressed only in the context of determining commercial reasonableness where the goods resold are

始货物在转售时，应如何确定转售是否具有商业合理性。但是，针对上述情况所确定的原则，也适用于本案，即转售时间是否合理，取决于货物性质、市场情况以及当事案件的其他情况。时间的长短，无法用法律尺子去衡量，也不可能被划分为不同刻度。例如，假如计划转售的卖方被告知，买方基于法典有关争议货物保存证据的规定，要求就相关货物进行检验，那么，自然就应将转售的时间推后（第2.706条正式评论5；B诉I案）。

the goods originally identified to the broken contract. However, the principles announced in that context apply here as well: What is ... a reasonable time [for resale] depends upon the nature of the goods, the condition of the market and other circumstances of the case; its length cannot be measured by any legal yardstick or divided into degrees. Where a seller contemplating resale receives a demand from the buyer for inspection under the section of [sic] preserving evidence of goods in dispute, the time for resale may be appropriately lengthened. N.Y.U.C.C. Sec. 2-706 comment 5; Bache & Co. v. International Controls Corp.

卖方所主张的转售不合理

在本案中，从1982年2月11日买方违约，到3月23日卖方试图转售，转售存在将近6个星期的延迟。即使卖方本来未曾向市政服务署出售，这个时间也明显不合理。卖方的专家证人在质询中作证说，在波尔多轮的油料于2月12日被交付给市政服务署时，2号加热器油的市场价格“是每加仑88美分或87美分左右”（本案实物交换合同的实际价格

Here, Apex's delay of nearly six weeks between the breach on February 11, 1982 and the purported resale on March 23 was clearly unreasonable, even if the transfer to Cities Service had not occurred. Steven Wirkus, of Apex, testified on cross-examination that the market price for No. 2 heating oil on February 12, when the Bordeaux oil was delivered to Cities Service, was "[p]robably somewhere around 88 cents a gallon or 87". (The EFP contract price, of course, was 89.70 cents per gallon.)

是每加仑 89.70 美分）。

在质询中，卖方专家证人提供证词说，市场价格在随后几个星期内不断波动。问：先生，虽然对 4 年前任何特定日期的油料价格你不一定记得，但如果说价格上下波动，这个说法适当吗？答：这个说法无疑是适当的。问：是每日有变化吗？答：是。问：价格在 2 月底是下降了吗？答：是这样的。问：价格在 3 月初又回升了？答：3 月初是回升了。问：应该是 3 月中旬左右又下降了，对吗？卖方律师：反对这个问题的提法。法官：反对成立。重新问：先生，价格在 3 月中旬是否下降了？答：根据我的记忆是下降了。问：价格在 3 月下旬发生了什么？答：市场又回暖了。

Wirkus also testified on redirect examination that the market price fluctuated throughout the next several weeks： Q. Sir, while you couldn't remember with particularity what the price of oil was on a given day four years ago, is it fair to say that prices went up and down? A. Definitely that's fair to say. Q. From day-to-day? A. Yes. Q. Towards the end of February prices went down? A. That's correct. Q. Then in early March it went back up? A. In early March, yes. Q. Then they went back down again towards the middle of March； isn't that correct? MR. GILBERT： I object to the form of this, your Honor, on redirect. THE COURT： Yes. Q. Did they go back down in mid March, Mr. Wirkus? A. My recollection, yes. Q. In late March what happened to the price? A. Market went back up.

此外，卖方的专家证人还作证说，在 3 月 23 日与本案转售无关的一项交易中，卖方购买了 25,000 桶定于 3 月交付的 2 号油料，价格是每加仑 80.50 美分，并出售了定于 4 月交付的同样数量的油料，价格是每加仑 77.25

Moreover, Wirkus testified that, on March 23, in a transaction unrelated to the resale, Apex purchased 25,000 barrels of No. 2 oil for March delivery at 80.50 cents per gallon, and sold an equivalent amount for April delivery at 77.25 cents per gallon. Other sales on March 22 and 23 for April delivery

美分。3月22日和23日发生的定于4月交付的其他油料交易的价格基本类似：以76.85美分的价格出售100,000桶，并以76.35美分的价格出售25,000桶。定于4月交付的向本案第三方买家出售的价格是每加仑76.25美分，比违约日的价格大约降低了12美分。

brought similar prices： 100,000 barrels were sold at 76.85 cents, and 25,000 barrels at 76.35 cents. The Gill & Duffus resale, which was also for April delivery, fetched a price of 76.25 cents per gallon--some eleven or twelve cents below the market price on the day of the breach.

考虑到转售的长期耽延和2号油料市场的明显波动，作为法律问题，本案卖方所主张的转售，不能满足法典第2.706条的要求。毫无疑问，此种耽延使该转售无法“准确地反映货物的市场价格”（S诉E案）。

In view of the long delay and the apparent volatility of the market for No. 2 oil, the purported resale failed to meet the requirements of Section 2-706 as a matter of law. The delay unquestionably prevented the resale from “accurately reflect［ing］ the market value of the goods”. Servbest.

时间问题的相关判例 实际上，在类似的证券市场环境下（大概可以说，按商品市场目前的集中程度和计算机化程度，其流动性和波动性已接近于证券市场），我们曾维持了地区法院的下述判决，即在一方违反收购要约后，另一方转售相关证券的商业上合理的时间，最多不超过30日（B诉I案）。此外，在该案中，原告是证券经纪人，系代表其客户

Indeed, in the analogous context of the securities markets （which are arguably not much more liquid or volatile than today's centralized and computerized commodities markets）, we have upheld a district court's conclusion that thirty days was a maximum time for the commercially-reasonable resale of securities after the breach of a tender offer. Bache & Co. v. International Controls Corp. In Bache, moreover, the plaintiff was a securities broker suing on behalf of its

起诉。地区法院考虑到其客户“分散在全国各地”的情况后，将转售的合理时间确定为 30 日。而在本案中，很明显，油料由卖方自己所有，并且只涉及卖方自己。

customers, and the district court considered “the distribution around the country” of those customers when it set the thirty-day limit on commercially-reasonable resales. In the instant case, of course, the oil was Apex's, and Apex's alone.

同时，我们也不认为卖方的延迟转售存在其他合理理由。例如，卖方并未主张“转售时间应被适当延长”，因为买方要求“检验货物，以便就争议货物保存证据”（第 2.706 条正式评论 5）。无疑，本案买方从未提出过此类要求。无论如何，卖方实际上很快就处置了波尔多轮的油料。

Nor do we find Apex's delay justified on any other ground. Apex does not assert, for example, that “the time for resale [should] be appropriately lengthened” because Belcher sought an “inspection ... [to] preserv[e] evidence of [the] goods in dispute”, N.Y.U.C.C. Sec. 2-706 comment 5; Belcher of course made no such request, and Apex immediately disposed of the Bordeaux oil in any event.

卖方的理由不能成立　卖方所主张的唯一理由是，与买方的持续谈判导致了耽延。初审法院接受了该理由，并据此驳回了买方的动议，即法院应该排除陪审团裁定而直接判决买方胜诉。我们认为，该判决与初审法院的立场存在矛盾，因为初审法院认为，如果买方确实存在违约，则违约的时间应为 2 月 11 日。

Apex's only asserted justification, which the district court accepted in denying Belcher's motion for judgment notwithstanding the verdict, was that the delay was caused by continuing negotiations with Belcher. We find that ruling to be inconsistent with the district court's view that Belcher's breach, if any, occurred on February 11.

转售的作用在于，通过确

The function of a resale was to put Apex

定被买方拒收之油料在转售日的价值，将卖方置于转售之日其本来可以达到的处境。油料在该日之后的价值已经无关紧要，因为无论是根据合同还是法典，卖方都没有义务在2月11日买方违约后仍为买方保留该48,000桶油料。实际上，这就是为什么卖方最初主张违约的发生时间为3月。初审法院拒绝了该主张，因此本上诉不再涉及这个问题。

结论 因此，在类似本案的案件中，即转售的货物已不是原始特定于合同项下的货物，应严格遵守这个原则，即“应在违约之后尽可能短的时间内作出转售”(B诉I案)。当然，这类情况也存在明显风险，即卖方有可能已在毫无亏损的情况下处置了原始货物，但为了获得尽可能多的损害赔偿，又将新的货物特定化并用于转售。

但S诉E案不属于上述情况。在该案中，违约之后的首次销售就是案件中的转售。形成对照的是，在本案中，原始特定于合同项下的油料在1982年2月

in the position it would have been on that date by determining the value of the oil Belcher refused. The value of the oil at a later date is irrelevant because Apex was in no way obligated by the contract or by the Uniform Commercial Code to reserve 48,000 barrels for Belcher after the February 11 breach. Indeed, that is why Apex's original theory, rejected by the district court and not before us on this appeal, was that the breach occurred in March.

The rule that a "resale should be made as soon as practicable after ... breach", Bache, should be stringently applied where, as here, the resold goods are not those originally identified to the contract. In such circumstances, of course, there is a significant risk that the seller, who may perhaps have already disposed of the original goods without suffering any loss, has identified new goods for resale in order to minimize the resale price and thus to maximize damages.

That was not the case in Servbest, for example, where the resale consisted of the first sales made after the breach. Here, by contrast, the oil originally identified to the contract was sold the day after the February 11,

11 日违约日的第二天就被售出，而卖方所声称的转售发生在 6 个星期之后。在此期间，卖方无疑还完成了多笔出售。

我们需要说明，卖方在其起诉书中以及在整个初审过程中均主张，其所称的买方违约，是在转售之前 3 日才发生的。考虑到 S 诉 E 案的判决、卖方耽延的时间，以及 2 号油料市场价格的回落，卖方的该主张并不令人意外。但是，如之前提到的，初审法院判决，唯一可供卖方使用的理论，就是违约发生于 2 月 11 日。卖方未就该项判决提出上诉。作为法律问题，在 2 月 11 日的第二天特定于合同项下并被出售给市政服务署的油料，已经确定了被拒收的货物的价值。因此，初审法院有关买方违反合同的判决必须被推翻。

1982 breach, and no doubt Apex sold ample amounts thereafter in the six weeks before the purported resale.

We note that in its complaint and throughout the trial Apex asserted that it was suing on a breach that occurred as late as three days before the resale. This is not surprising given Servbest, the length of Apex's delay, and the drop in the market price for No. 2 oil. But, as noted, the district court held, in a ruling not appealed from, that the only viable theory available to Apex was that involving a breach on February 11. Because the sale of the oil identified to the contract to Cities Service on the next day fixed the value of the goods refused as a matter of law, the judgment on the breach-of-contract claim must be reversed.

案例 18　买方是否有权获得补进和转售双重救济？

Fertico Belgium v. Phosphate Chems. Export Assn.

比利时弗提格公司诉磷酸盐化工出口联合公司案

纽约州上诉法院 1987 年；70 N.Y.2d 76, 3 UCC Rep.Serv.2d 1812

简　介

本案买方（Fertico）是一家经销肥料的国际贸易公司，卖方（Phosphate）是一家磷肥生产商。1978 年 10 月，双方订立了买卖两船磷肥的合同，均由卖方运至比利时安特卫普港交付。第一船 1.5 万吨将于 11 月 20 日前交付，第二船 2 万吨将于 11 月 30 日前交付。这 3.5 万吨磷肥将被买方用于出售给自己的已经订立了合同的下家客户伊拉克农业部（第三方买家）。卖方在与买方订立合同时已经知道该情况。

根据约定，买方为第一船货物出具了数额约为 170 万美元的信用证。但卖方 11 月上旬告知买方，第一船货物的交付日期将延至 12 月 4 日，而第二船的到达日期将会更迟一些，因为当时第二船货物还没有装船。买方立即回复卖方说，该延迟会给自己带来巨大的问题，因为货物将赶不上买方与伊拉克农业部约定的交付日期。此时，卖方已经兑付了第一船货物的信用证，且船只已经在驶往安特卫普港的途中。在这种情况下，买方一方面通知卖方取消第二船货物的合同，另一方面联系了另一家磷肥供应商（Unifert），并从该供应商购买了3.5 万吨磷肥，用于向伊拉克农业部交付。

根据卖方与买方之间的合同，3.5 万吨磷肥的总价是 4,025,000 美元，而根据买方与替代供应商之间的合同，总价是 4,725,000 美元，相差 70 万美元。买方在 11 月 15 日与替代供应商订立合同后，立即与伊拉克农业部商谈交付替代货物的问题。买方同意将交货地点从伊拉克的巴士拉海港改为内陆交付，而伊拉克农业部同意将交付时间推迟，并同意每吨货物比原合同价格多支付 20.50 美元的海港改内陆的运费，即总计支付了约 72 万美元的运费差价补贴。买方最终顺利完成了与伊拉克农业部的合同。

第一船货物实际于 12 月 7 日到达安特卫普港，12 月 17 日完成卸货。尽管货物延迟到达，但买方还是保留了货物。买方认为，卖方已经兑付了这船货物的信用证并取走了全部货款，因此买方除了保留货物，没有更好的选择。买方将这船 1.5 万吨货物存入仓库，并开始另寻买家。大约 3 个月之后，买方将这批肥料出售给第四方买家（Janssens）。这次转售的价格高于买方从卖方购买货物的合同价格，因此买方获得了 45.4 万美元的利润。

买方随后就卖方的违约起诉卖方。对于第一船货物延迟交付而构成卖方违约的问题，以及买方就第二船货物取消合同的问题，卖方不持异议。双方在本案中的争议，主要集中于如何计算买方损失的问题。本案涉及 3 笔大额争议金额：（1）在卖方发生延迟交货的违约后，买方从替代供应商购买了替代货物。法典将此种替代购买称为“补进”（cover）。买方为补进所额外支出的金额为 70 万美元，即原始合同价格和补进价格的差额。买方要求根据法典第 2.712 条的规定，就这笔差额取得赔偿。（2）对于买方向伊拉克农业部的交付，在双方同意下，交付地点从海港改为内陆，而伊拉克农业部为此支付给买方约 72 万美元。卖方认为，这笔款项属于法典第 2.712 条（2）款最后一句所说的“买方节省的费用”，因而买方应将这笔款项从卖方支付的损害赔偿中减去（相当于卖方有权获得这笔款项）。（3）关于买方向第四方买家出售第一船肥料后获得的 45.4 万美元利润，卖方认为，如果法院判决卖方支付买方的补进损失（70

万美元),那么买方就要将这45.4万美元的利润退还给卖方,因为买方在取得补进救济后,就被视为没有接受原始合同的货物。由于第一船肥料属于原始合同货物,因此货物本应属于卖方,而出售利润也应属于卖方。

本案经历了三级法院的审理,即纽约州初审法院、初审法院上诉庭和纽约州上诉法院(最高法院)。初审法院判定,卖方应向买方支付大约107万美元的赔偿,即70万美元的补进损失和其他费用支出。同时,买方有权保留伊拉克农业部支付的运费差价补贴,以及向第四方买家出售第一船肥料后获得的45.4万美元利润。卖方上诉后,上诉庭推翻了原判,认为伊拉克农业部支付的运费差价补贴,是法典第2.712条(2)款所说的卖方违约后导致买方节省的费用,因此这笔费用应该归卖方。同时,由于买方已经取得了70万美元的补进赔偿,即已经获得了法典规定的救济,因此无权再获得所谓的转售(向第四方买家的出售)救济。因此,这次出售的45.4万美元的利润也属于卖方。为此,买方向纽约州上诉法院申诉并得到上诉许可。

关于运费差价补贴问题,纽约州上诉法院认为,这不是节省的费用,而是属于本来应由卖方支付给买方的间接损失赔偿,但现在由于伊拉克农业部已经支付了这笔费用,因此买方没有间接损失,所以卖方不必支付这笔费用,但自然也无权要求买方将这笔费用退给卖方。

剩下的最主要问题,就是补进赔偿(70万美元)和转售利润(45.4万美元)之间的关系问题。这个问题的困难之处在于,根据法典的设计以及通常情况,在卖方发生违约时,对于某些救济,买方不能同时获得,而是需要进行选择。例如,在本案这种情况下,当卖方延迟交货时,买方的第一种选择是,拒收卖方的交付,然后另行购买替代货物(补进)。此时,买方可就合同价格与补进价格的差额(本案中的70万美元)取得赔偿。但在这种情况下,由于买方已经拒收,因此卖方所交付的货物(本案第一船肥料)将被视为卖方的货物。因此,如果买方出售这批货物并获得利润,就被视为代表卖方出售,而所得利润也属于卖方。买方的第二种选择是,接受延迟交付的货物。此时,买方无权再就这部分货物(本案第一船肥料)作出补进,因为买方已经得到了货物。买方只能寻求损害赔偿，也就是针对自己所能证明的因延迟交付而引起的损失，向卖方索赔。但在本案中，买方一方面接受了第一船货物，另一方面又另行补进了货物（补进的货物包含了第一船肥料的数量）。

纽约州上诉法院承认，本案的情况确实无法与法典的相关规定完全吻合，但同时认为，允许买方取得补进赔偿并同时保留转售利润，是在本案“极其特殊”的事实背景下最合理的处理。上诉法院的两位法官为此出具了长篇异议意见，因为他们认为，多数派法官的判决与法典的规定完全不符。单纯从法典的文字看，似乎异议法官的意见更有说服力。但是，从最终的整体结果上看，多数派法官的判决似乎更加合理。多数派法官的看法是，本案买方是受害方，其在卖方违约后所做的一切，都是正常商人在类似情况下为保护自己声誉和利益所采取的最自然的措施。因此，如果可以把向第四方买家转售所获得的利润称为“飞来横财”（windfall），那么，在受损方和违约方之间，宁可将其留给守约的买方，也不能留给违约的卖方。

判　决

本案的问题　卖方违反了合同，未能向身为经销商的买方按合同约定的时间交付货物。买方从另一家替代供应商作出了适当“补进”（在法典用语中，是指购买替代货物），以避免违反对自己客户伊拉克农业部（第三方买家）的义务。本案唯一的问题是，卖方违反合同后，应根据什么原则和方法来计算买方的损失数额？

A seller （Phoschem） breached its contract to timely deliver goods to a buyer-trader （Fertico） who properly sought cover （under the Uniform Commercial Code that means acquiring substitute goods） from another source （Unifert） in order to avoid breaching that buyer-trader’s obligation to a third-party buyer （Altawreed）. The sole issue involves the applicable principles and computation of damages for breach of the Phoschem-to-Fertico contract.

上诉法院的结论 我们判定，基于本案极其特殊的情况，身为经销商的买方有权从卖方获得的损害赔偿数额是：补进货物所增加的成本，加上间接损失和附带损失，减去买方节省的费用［法典第2.712条（2）款］。在本案中，卖方违约致使买方节省的费用，应局限于不存在违约时买方本来将会支出的费用。因此，就卖方所交付的不符合合同的货物而言，买方随后将该货物转售给第四方买家后，卖方无权要求买方归还该销售的利润。

买方的合理行为 由于卖方已向银行提示并兑付了买方出具的信用证，因此，根据本案具体事实，从商业角度看，买方没有合理的替代选择，只能保留并转售合同项下的肥料。尽管买方在第一轮交易中（卖方向买方的出售，以及买方向伊拉克农业部的转售）作出了补进，但买方仍有上述权利。但是，买方作出补进后，如果情况像本案这样，即买方的客户（第三方买家）向买方提供了额外补偿，用于抵消卖方

We hold that under the exceptional circumstances of this case plaintiff Fertico, as a buyer-trader, is entitled to damages from seller Phoschem equal to the increased cost of cover plus consequential and incidental damages minus expenses saved （UCC 2-712［2］）. In this case, expenses saved as a result of the breach are limited to costs or expenditures which would have arisen had there been no breach. Thus, the seller Phoschem is not entitled to a credit from the profits of a subsequent sale by the first buyer-trader Fertico to a fourth party （Janssens） of nonconforming goods from Phoschem.

Fertico's letter of credit had been presented by Phoschem and honored so, under the specific facts of this case, Fertico had no commercially reasonable alternative but to retain and resell the fertilizer. This is so despite Fertico's exercise of cover in connection with the first set of transactions, i.e., Phoschem to Fertico to Altawreed. The covering buyer-trader may not, however, as in this case, recover other consequential damages when the third party to which it made its sale provides increased compensation to offset additional costs arising as a consequence of

违约所引起的额外支出，买方就不能再寻求其他间接损失赔偿。

the breach.

初审法院的判决　买方于1981年起诉卖方，指控卖方违反了1978年10月的合同，并要求获得125万美元的损害赔偿。陪审团裁定卖方应支付107万美元。卖方要求初审法院无视该裁定而判决卖方胜诉，但法院拒绝推翻陪审团的裁定。

In 1981 Fertico commenced this action against Phoschem seeking $1.25 million in damages for Phoschem's breach of the October 1978 agreement. A jury returned a verdict of $1.07 million which the trial court refused to overturn on a motion for judgment notwithstanding the verdict.

上诉庭的判决　上诉庭推翻了初审法院有关损害赔偿的判决，并指令仅就损害赔偿问题进行重审。上诉庭认定，作为法律问题：（1）伊拉克农业部合同项下所增加的运输费用，不属于间接损失；（2）伊拉克农业部给买方提高的购买价格，属于卖方违约导致买方节省的费用；以及（3）必须从买方获得的损害赔偿数额中，减去将货物转售给第四方买家后获得的利润。

The Appellate Division vacated the damage award, ordered a new trial on the damages issue only and ruled, as a matter of law, （1） that the increased transportation costs on the Altawreed contract were not consequential damages; （2） that the higher purchase price paid by Altawreed to Fertico was an expense saved as a consequence of the Phoschem breach; and （3） that the Fertico damages had to be reduced by the profits from the Janssens' sale.

上诉法院的立场　买方向本院提起上诉。对于上诉庭的上述第2项和第3项认定，我们不能同意。我们的结论是，基于法典的规定和我们的分析，作为对当

Fertico appealed to this court. We disagree with propositions （2） and （3） in the Appellate Division ruling, and conclude that the Uniform Commercial Code and our analysis support a modification and

事方争议的最终判决，本院修改上诉庭的判决，恢复初审中向买方支付70万美元损害赔偿的判决。

买方的救济 应该承认，卖方未能在合同规定日期作出交付的行为，构成了对合同的违反（引用著作）。法典第2.711条向未违约方提供了两种可选救济。一种选择是，买方通过半自助方式，一方面作出补进，另一方面寻求损害赔偿（法典第2.712条）。另一种选择是，买方仅寻求损害赔偿。此时，赔偿数额为市场价格与合同价格的差额，加上附带损失和间接损失，减去节省的费用（法典第2.713条；另参见P诉F案）。在本案中，身为经销商的受损害买方行使了补进的权利，以便获得替代肥料，来履行其对伊拉克农业部的合同义务（参见法典第2.712条正式评论1）。

买方有权作出补进 假定补进价格高于原始合同价格，那么，作出补进的买方有权取得的损害赔偿数额是，补进价格和合同价格的差额，加上违约引起的附带

reinstatement of $700,000 of the damage award in a final judgment resolving this litigation between the parties.

Failure by Phoschem to make delivery on the contract dates concededly constituted a breach of the contract (White and Summers, Uniform Commercial Code). The Uniform Commercial Code § 2-711 gives the nonbreaching party the alternative of either seeking the partial self-help of cover along with recovery of damages (UCC 2-712), or of recovering damages only for the differential between the market price and the contract price, together with incidental and consequential damages less expenses saved (UCC 2-713; see also, Productora e Importadora de Papel, S.A. de C.V. v. Fleming). Fertico exercised its right as the wronged buyer-trader to cover in order to obtain the substitute fertilizer it required to meet its obligation under its Altawreed contract (see, UCC 2-712, comment 1).

A covering buyer's damages are equal to the difference between the presumably higher cost of cover and the contract price, plus incidental or consequential damages suffered on account of the breach, less

损失和间接损失，减去节省的费用［法典第 2.712 条（2）款］。因此，本案买方有权根据法典的该项规定取得损害赔偿，因为买方的补进系以善意作出，未出现不合理耽延，且替代供应商提供的肥料是卖方肥料的合理替代货物［法典第 2.712 条（1）款；R 诉 U 案］。

expenses saved （UCC 2-712［2］）. Fertico is thus entitled to a damage remedy under this section because its cover purchase was made in good faith, without unreasonable delay, and the Unifert fertilizer was a reasonable substitute for the Phoschem fertilizer （UCC 2-712［1］； Reynolds Sec. v. Underwriters Bank & Trust Co.）.

运费差价问题　买方把肥料的交付地点从海港改为内陆后，支出了额外费用。通常，这些费用可以构成间接损失，因为这些费用是卖方违约所引起的，且卖方知道买方会就下家客户的合同受到损失，且补进未能防止该损失［法典第 2.715 条（2）款］。

Fertico's additional costs for delivering the fertilizer inland rather than at a seaport would usually constitute consequential damages because they resulted from Phoschem's breach, because Phoschem knew that Fertico would incur damages under its separate contract obligation and because the damages were not prevented by the cover （UCC 2-715［2］）.

与伊拉克农业部合同相关的上述额外费用之所以属于间接损失，是因为其并非“直接基于卖方与买方之间的合同交易而产生，而是在买方与伊拉克农业部的交易中产生的损失，而这种损失主要是由于卖方违约引起的，且卖方在订立合同时可以合理预见该损失”。通常而言，对于

The increased costs attendant to the Altawreed contract are consequential damages because they did not “arise within the scope of the immediate ［Phoschem-Fertico］ transaction, but rather stem from losses incurred by ［Fertico］ in its dealings ［with Altawreed］ which were a proximate result of the breach, and which were reasonably foreseeable by the breaching party at the time

本案买方这样的经销商，必须就卖方违约所引起的间接损失取得赔偿，才能使自己恢复到卖方不存在违约时买方本可达到的处境（法典第 1.106 条；参见 N 诉 R 案；引用著作）。

of contracting". Ordinarily, an award for consequential damages occasioned by the seller's breach would be necessary to put a buyer like Fertico in as good a position as it would have been had there been no breach（UCC 1-106； see, Neri v. Retail Mar. Corp.； Hawkland, Uniform Commercial Code Series）.

但是，对于买方向伊拉克农业部交付货物时产生的上述额外费用，伊拉克农业部已向买方提供了补偿。因此，买方实际上未就此受到卖方违约的影响，因此不能寻求此种损害赔偿。上诉庭关于间接损失赔偿的判决是正确的。

Inasmuch as Altawreed compensated Fertico for the additional delivery costs, Fertico was insulated from any loss in that respect as a result of Phoschem's breach, thereby eliminating this category of potential damages. On this question of consequential damages, the Appellate Division was correct.

但是，伊拉克农业部向身为国际经销商的买方所支付的上述额外补偿，不属于因卖方违约而使买方节省的费用，因此，卖方无权要求买方将该补偿退给卖方［法典第 2.712 条（2）款］。在大多数案件中，特别是在本案中,法典所称的买方节省的费用，必须是在卖方不存在违约时买方本来预计支出的费用（P 诉 F 案）。例如，假设卖方本应向买

The additional compensation to Fertico, an international trader, from Altawreed is not, however, an expense saved as a consequence of the seller Phoschem's breach for which Phoschem is entitled to any credit（UCC 2-712 ［2］）. In most instances, and particularly in this case, saved expenses must be costs or expenditures which would be anticipated had there been no breach（see, Productora e Importadora de Papel, S.A. de C.V. v. Fleming）. For example, if

方交付未经包装的货物，且在卖方违约后,买方补进同样的货物，但货物已经包装完好，此时，买方本来需要支出的包装费用，就属于因卖方违约而使买方节省的费用（引用著作）。

a seller were to breach a contract to deliver an unpackaged product to the buyer and the buyer were to cover with the same product prepackaged, the cost of packaging which the buyer would have had to perform is an expense saved as a consequence of the breach （see, Hawkland, Uniform Commercial Code Series）.

伊拉克农业部所支付的额外补偿，是为了弥补买方交付货物时所增加的工作，而不是用于支付卖方未发生违约时买方本来预计支出的费用。因此，上诉庭对该补偿的定性和要求买方将该补偿退还给卖方的判决是错误的。

The increased remuneration from Altawreed was compensation for the additional shipment responsibilities incurred by Fertico, not a cost or expenditure anticipated in the absence of a breach, and therefore was erroneously analyzed and credited in Phoschem's favor by the Appellate Division.

向第四方买家出售的问题 对损害赔偿进行分析的第三个问题，涉及买方将卖方交付的肥料转售给第四方买家后获得的利润。上诉庭错误地认为，没有卖方违约，就没有该销售，并因此错误地判决，应以买方从该销售中获得的利润，抵销卖方应支付的损害赔偿。

The third prong of the damages analysis relates to the profit made from the independent sale of the Phoschem fertilizer to Janssens. The Appellate Division erred in offsetting this profit against the damages otherwise suffered since that court mistakenly concluded that the sale stemmed from and was dependent upon Phoschem's breach.

允许转售的理由 在本案独特的事实情况下，上述抵销将对

This offset, on these peculiar facts, would severely disadvantage Fertico, a trader

买方造成严重不公平。买方是肥料经销商，既有买进也有卖出。因此，即使没有卖方的此次违约，买方本来也会从事此类商业交易。如果认为在卖方不存在违约的情况下，买方本来不会继续从事其贸易业务，并基于此种推理，而用买方向第四方买家销售的利润来抵销卖方违约造成的损失，这种结论是有违常理的。

in fertilizer who both buys and sells, and who would have pursued such commercial transactions had there been no breach by Phoschem. It would be anomalous to conclude that had it not been for Phoschem's breach Fertico would not have continued its trade and upon such reasoning to counterpoise the profits from the Janssens' sale against the damages arising from Phoschem's breach.

本案的独特事实 本案的事实确实很特别。一方面，买方通过补进肥料，履行了向下家客户伊拉克农业部的出售义务；另一方面，对于卖方延迟交付的肥料，买方也取得了所有权和控制。因此，我们的判决，无法做到与法典提供的救济充分吻合，尽管异议法官希望我们能做到这点。异议法官希望，在判决本案时，能严格遵循N诉R案的原则和相关学者的评论（引用著作）。但如果那样做，就无法适当地解决本案所提出的独特问题。

Inasmuch as the facts here are exceptional because Fertico met its subsale obligations with the cover fertilizer and yet acquired title and control over the late-delivered fertilizer from Phoschem, our decision does not fit squarely within the available Uniform Commercial Code remedies urged by the dissent. Thus, strict reliance on Neri v. Retail Mar. Corp. and on Hawkland's commentary（Hawkland, Uniform Commercial Code Series）, as undertaken by the dissent, does not provide an adequate resolution to the particular problem presented in this case.

在买方得知卖方违约时，卖方已经议付了买方的170万美元的信用证，而该信用证是对第一

Fertico learned of Phoschem's breach after Phoschem had negotiated Fertico's $1.7 million letter of credit, which constituted

船货物的全额付款。由于没有其他商业上合理的替代方案，买方取得了对第一船货物的掌控，但在通知卖方其已违约后（法典第 2.607 条），取消了第二船货物的合同［法典第 2.601 条（c）款］。

买方虽然接受了延迟交付的那船肥料，但仍然必须作出补进。此种补进所引起的损失，仍然属于法典第 2.714 条（1）款项下可以索赔的损失（引用著作）。同时，法典第 1.106 条要求，必须灵活地提供法典所规定的救济，以使受损方尽可能地恢复到另一方充分履约时受损方本可达到的状态。假设卖方充分履行了合同，买方本可得到伊拉克农业部合同所带来的收益；并且，作为肥料经销商，买方本来还可另外得到向第四方买家出售所带来的利润。

专家观点　科宾教授认为，“发生违约后，受损方从其他交易中获得的利润，除非属于不存在违约时本来不可能获得的，否

complete payment for the first shipment. With no commercially reasonable alternative, Fertico took custody of the first shipment but canceled the second （UCC 2-601［c］）, having previously notified Phoschem of its breach （UCC 2-607）.

The loss resulting to Fertico by having to acquire cover, even in the face of its acceptance of a late-delivered portion of the fertilizer, is properly recoverable under section 2-714（1）（Hawkland, Uniform Commercial Code Series）. At the same time, Uniform Commercial Code § 1-106 directs that the remedies provided by the Uniform Commercial Code should be liberally administered so as to put the aggrieved party in as good a position as if the other party had fully performed. Had Phoschem fully performed, Fertico would have had the benefit of the Altawreed transaction and, as a trader of fertilizer, the profits from the Janssens’ sale as well.

“Gains made by the injured party on other transactions after the breach are never to be deducted from the damages that are otherwise recoverable, unless such gains

则，永远不应将该利润从本可索赔的损害赔偿数额中减去”（引用著作；另参见S诉R案）。肥料属于非独特产品，市场可以提供无限的供应，因此，买方从销售这种货物中获得的利润，不应从卖方应支付的损害赔偿数额中减去（引用著作；另参见N诉R案）。

could not have been made, had there been no breach”（Corbin, Contracts; see also, Steen Indus. v. Richer Communications）. Fertico's profit made on the sale of a nonspecific article such as fertilizer, of which the supply in the market is not limited, should not therefore be deducted from the damages recoverable from Phoschem（Corbin, Contracts; see also, Neri v. Retail Mar. Corp.）.

买方采取了合理措施 不能不承认，卖方的违约导致买方成为受害者，而买方则引用了法典提供的救济，且这些救济根植于我们所理解的市场现实。为了降低本案卖方所引起的风险，为了从商业角度想办法解决问题，买方所做的是任何通情达理的经销商都会做的和希望做的。也就是说，买方采取了措施来维护自己的业务、自己的客户、自己的信誉和自己的交易，并最终从过错方取得适当的损害赔偿。

Fertico was concededly wronged by Phoschem's breach and Fertico resorted to Uniform Commercial Code remedies which are rooted in what we perceive to be the realities of the marketplace. Fertico did what reasonable traders would do and would like to do in mitigating risks inflicted in this case by Phoschem and in exerting its commercial resourcefulness. That is, it took steps to save its business, its customers, its good will and its deals and ultimately to also recover appropriate damages from a wrongdoer.

尽可能维护受害者利益 对受损害的买方来说，上述处理并没有造成异议法官所说的“飞来横财”或“双重好处”。我们今天得出的结论，不是要鼓励这种

That did not produce a “windfall” or a “double benefit” to the aggrieved party as the dissenting opinion asserts. The result we reach today countenances no such thing. On the contrary, to deprive the buyer-trader

情况。恰好相反，对于身为经销商的买方，如果剥夺其正当应得的 70 万美元的差额损失赔偿，并将其从独立交易中获得的利润退还给卖方，就会以牺牲受害方为代价，违反常理地使加害方发财。这种结果会使商界人士无法理解，也不属于法典宽容救济原则所要求或允许的结果。

对于受损方就对方违反合同所取得的损害赔偿，异议法官将其称为“收益”。这种称呼是错误的，因为该称呼从效果上意味着，对于买方从其他交易中自行获得的收益，卖方享有某种留置权。

结论　上诉庭的判决是，维持初审法院对卖方违约责任的定性判决，但作为法律问题，推翻初审法院有关损害赔偿的判决并发回重审。当事方约定，本上诉仅涉及损害赔偿问题。据此，本院判定，修改上诉庭的判决，并指令其根据本意见，判决向买方支付 70 万美元的损害赔偿。特此修改上诉庭的判决，且在上诉庭根据本意见修改其判决后，维持上诉庭的判决。

Fertico of its rightful differential damages of $700,000 and to credit this transactionally independent profit to Phoschem would perversely enrich the wrongdoer at the expense of the wronged party, a result those in the marketplace would find perplexing and a result which the generous remedial purpose of the Uniform Commercial Code does not compel or authorize.

The dissent's characterization of the recovery by an injured party of damages for a breach of contract as a “benefit” is wrong, since that functionally attributes a kind of lien against the independently pursued benefit derived out of that separate transaction.

Accordingly, the order of the Appellate Division affirming liability but vacating, on the law, the damage award and remanding the matter for a new trial on the issue of damages, as appealed to this court on a stipulation for judgment absolute, should be modified and damages awarded to Fertico in the amount of $700,000 in accordance with this opinion. Order modified in accordance with the opinion herein and, as so modified, affirmed.

(异议法官的意见) 法典第2篇就卖方的违约向受损害的买方提供了各种救济。本上诉要解决的问题，是这些救济之间的关系。分析的关键是法典的这项原则，即“应灵活提供救济，以使受损方恢复到另一方充分履约时受损方本可达到的处境”[法典第1.106条(1)款]。

双重救济问题 本案多数派法官的结论是，受损害的买方可以一方面在作出补进后获得损害赔偿，另一方面在转售延迟交付的货物后保留其所获得的利润。也就是说，从效果上看，相当于从同一项交易中获得两次收益。这并不是法典宽容救济条款所要求的结果，甚至可以说与法典原则不符。因此，我必须表示异议。

补进相当于拒收 我的前提立场是，如果受损害的买方购买了替代货物，并根据法典第2.712条寻求“补进”的损害赔偿，就等于默示地拒绝了卖方所交付的不符合合同的货物。因此，货物此时属于卖方，而买方仅为担保

[Dissenting Opinion] At issue in this appeal is the relationship among the various remedies that article 2 of the Uniform Commercial Code provides for buyers aggrieved by sellers' defaults. Central to the analysis is the principle that the Code's remedies "shall be liberally administered to the end that the aggrieved party may be put in as good a position as if the other party had fully performed" (UCC 1-106 [1]).

Here, the majority has concluded that the aggrieved buyer may retain both cover damages and the profit from the resale of the late-delivered goods, in effect, securing the benefit of its bargain twice. Since that result is not required by, and indeed is not even consistent with, the purpose of Code's generous remedial provisions, I must respectfully dissent.

I begin with the premise that an aggrieved buyer who has purchased substitute goods and sued for "cover" damages under UCC 2-712 has impliedly rejected the seller's nonconforming performance and, consequently, holds the seller's goods only as security for any prepayments made to the

已付给卖方的预付款而持有该货物［法典第 2.706 条（6）款；第 2.711 条（3）款］。与上述相反的立场，即受损害的买方可以两全其美地一方面作出补进，另一方面将违约货物作为自己的财产而保留并转售，我认为在法律上缺乏支持，在经济上也不合理。

seller（see, UCC 2-706［6］；2-711［3］). I find the contrary position--that an aggrieved buyer may compatibly resort to cover and also retain and resell the nonconforming goods for its own account--to be legally insupportable and economically unsound.

补进可以充分补偿买方　补进这项救济代表了法典起草者的共识，即受到违约或毁约损害的买方，“可能无法仅通过取得损害赔偿获得充分补救，因为在卖方违约或毁约后，买方处于未得到所需货物的处境”（引用著作）。法典的“补进”条款允许买方在公开市场上购买相等货物，然后起诉卖方，就价格的差额取得损害赔偿（第 2.712 条）。该条款的目的是向买方提供一个切实可行的方法，使买方能够取得合理的替代货物，代替其在交易中争取到的但实际上未收到的货物。

The “cover” remedy represents a recognition by the Code’s drafters that a buyer aggrieved by a breach or repudiation “may not be made whole by the mere recovery of damages, because he is left, thereby, in a position in which he does not have the goods he wants”（Hawkland, Uniform Commercial Code Series）. The Code’s “cover” provision, which authorizes the buyer to purchase equivalent goods in the open market and then sue the breaching seller for any price differential（see, UCC 2-712）, was intended as a practical method of furnishing the buyer with a fair substitute for the goods it bargained for but did not receive.

因此，从经济角度看，买方根据第 2.712 条获得补进损害赔

Thus, from an economic standpoint, the buyer receives the full benefit of his bargain

偿后，就充分实现了其在原交易中争取到的收益。允许买方在此之外保留和转售货物，明显导致“飞来横财”，因为买方所得到的，超出了其在原交易中所争取到的收益。

when he obtains cover damages under UCC 2-712. Allowing the buyer to retain and resell the goods in addition obviously leads to a windfall, since the buyer is receiving more than the benefit of the transaction it bargained for.

法典文字明确否定双重救济 此外，法典的文字很明确，即买方不能一方面寻求补进赔偿，另一方面接受货物。第 2.712 条（1）款对“补进”的定义是，为“代替本应由卖方交付的货物”而购买货物。并且，只有在发生了“第 2.711 条（1）款所述的违约”后，受损害的买方才能行使补进的权利。而第 2.711 条（1）款特别规定，第 2.712 条（1）款项下的补进，只有在“卖方未能作出交付，或在买方正当拒收或正当撤销接受”时，才可以行使。最后，如果对第 2.711 条补进救济的适用范围还有疑问的话，该条正式评论 1 将打消此种疑问：“这里所列出的救济，是在买方没有接受货物或正当撤销了对货物的接受时，向买方提供的救济。”

Moreover, the language of the Code makes clear that the buyer cannot both sue for cover and accept the goods. UCC 2-712（1）defines “cover” as a purchase of goods “in substitution for those due from the seller” and authorizes an aggrieved buyer to resort to cover only “[a] fter a breach within [UCC 2-711（1）]”, which specifically states that cover “under [UCC 2-712（1）]” is available when “the seller fails to make delivery ... or the buyer rightfully rejects or justifiably revokes acceptance” （UCC 2-711 [1]）. Finally, any doubt about the applicability of the cover remedy referred to in UCC 2-711 is dispelled by comment 1. “The remedies listed here are those available to a buyer who has not accepted the goods or who has justifiably revoked his acceptance.”

补进的适用条件 简言之，

In short, consistent with its purpose, the

根据法典补进条款的规定和目的，只有在下列情况下才能使用补进救济：一种情况是，卖方未作出交付，因此买方未得到所需的货物；另一种情况是，货物无法使用，因为卖方的履约存在瑕疵。在所有其他情况下，受损害的买方必须使用第 2.714 条所提供的救济，因为该条适用于违约货物已被接受的情况（第 2.711 条正式评论 1）。

cover remedy is, by its terms, available only in situations where the buyer either does not have the needed goods because of nondelivery or cannot use the goods that were delivered because of a defect in the seller's performance. In all other situations, the aggrieved buyer must resort to the remedies provided in UCC 2-714, which concerns nonconforming goods that have been accepted （see, UCC 2-711, comment 1）.

虽然也存在这类情况，即接受了货物的买方仍可根据第 2.714 条（1）款寻求补进损害赔偿。但是，即使是本案多数派法官所引用的学者评论也明确说明，补进救济此时不是用于买方已经收到并接受了的那部分违约货物，而仅仅应该用于替补买方并未获得或并未收下的那部分货物（引用著作）。

While there are instances in which an accepting buyer may also seek cover damages under UCC 2-714 （1）, even the commentary the majority cites makes clear that the cover remedy is not intended to be used with respect to those nonconforming goods that the buyer has received and accepted; rather, the remedy is properly used only to replace the portion of needed goods the buyer either does not have or does not take （Hawkland）.

本案可以根据法典一般原则处理　在上述这些基本原则的框架范围内，类似本案的延迟交货的案件并不难以解决。如同那些根本就没有交付货物的案件

Viewed within the framework of these basic principles, cases such as this one involving late delivery are not difficult to resolve. As in cases where there has been a total failure to deliver, the buyer in late-

一样，在延迟交付的案件中，买方可以拒收延迟的交付，并补进替代货物。此外，与根本没有交付时的受损害的买方不同，延迟交付案件中的买方拥有另一种选择，就是可以接受那些延迟交付的货物，并自行保留从转售中获得的利润。

delivery cases may reject the untimely performance and cover with substitute goods. Additionally, unlike the buyer aggrieved by a total failure to deliver, the buyer aggrieved by a late delivery has the alternative option of accepting the belatedly delivered goods and retaining for itself any profit realized on resale.

但是，与买方的主张相反，受损害的买方不能同时寻求两种救济，因为这样做会使买方从一项交易中获得两次收益，而这种结果是法典第 1.106 条所不允许的［参见 M 诉 H 案（可以寻求法典的不同救济，但不得获得双重赔偿）］。

However, contrary to Fertico's claims, the aggrieved buyer may not pursue both courses simultaneously, since it would then benefit twice from what was a single bargain--a result that is unacceptable under UCC 1-106（see, Melby v. Hawkins Pontiac［alternative remedies may be pursued under UCC, but not where double recovery would result］）.

不应类比卖方利润损失救济

多数派法官为了使上述结果合理化，试图引用一项以前仅适用于受损害卖方的损害赔偿原则。根据该原则，卖方如果惯常经营某类货物，就可以要求违约买方赔偿卖方的利润损失，即使卖方已在无亏损情况下将买方不当拒收的货物转售给另一个买家。

The majority has attempted to rationalize that result here by relying on a damages rule that has previously been applied only to aggrieved sellers. The rule permits a seller who regularly deals in goods of a particular type to sue the breaching buyer for lost profit even though the wrongfully rejected goods have been sold to another buyer without loss.

但是，上述原则仅适用于卖方可以获得无限供应且价格标准

The rule applies only where the seller has an unlimited supply of standard-price

的货物的情况（参见 N 诉 R 案；引用著作）。在该情况下，“可以安全地假定”，假设买方未发生违约，卖方本来可以完成两次销售，而不是一次销售。因此，可以公平地说，买方的违约剥夺了卖方获得一次额外利润的机会（引用著作）。因此，诸如转售救济或市场差价救济这些传统的救济，“不足以使卖方恢复到买方履约时卖方本可达到的处境”，所以，卖方可就利润损失起诉［法典第 2.708 条（2）款］。

goods （see, Neri v. Retail Mar. Corp.; Hawkland）. In those situations, “it may safely be assumed that” the seller would have made two sales instead of one if the buyer had not breached, and, consequently, it can fairly be said that the buyer's breach deprived the seller of an opportunity for additional profit（Hawkland）. Thus, traditional remedies such as resale or market price differential are “ inadequate to put the seller in as good a position as performance would have done”, and the seller may sue for the lost profit（UCC 2-708［2］）.

买方的情况不同　但是，如果受损害的买方损失了销售机会，法典没有类似条款允许其获得利润损失赔偿。并且，缺乏此种类似条款，是存在合理原因的，因为适用于卖方利润损失救济的两个必要条件，对于受损害的买方来说均不存在。

The Code, however, does not contain an analogous provision allowing aggrieved buyers to recover profits from lost sales, and there is good reason for that omission, since neither of the conditions necessary for application of the sellers' lost-profit remedy may be satisfied in the case of an aggrieved buyer.

首先，基于“买方”这个概念的定义，不可能说处于买方地位的当事方拥有可以供其转售的无限供应的货物；即使货物是种类物，要转售货物的买方也必须先到市场上去获取该货物。其

First, a party in the position of a buyer cannot, by definition, be said to have an unlimited supply of the goods at his disposal for resale; even where the goods are fungible, the buyer who intends to resell must go into the marketplace to acquire the

次，必须到市场上去获取货物的买方，通常无法指望自己肯定可以获得“标准价格”。实际上，不同于库存中拥有无限供应且价格标准之货物的卖方，从事转售的买方必须承担批发市场上价格波动的风险。

goods in the first instance. Second, a buyer who must go into the market to obtain goods will ordinarily not be able to rely on the availability of a “standard price”; rather, unlike the seller who has an unlimited supply of standard-price goods in its inventory, the reselling buyer remains at the mercy of the wholesale market's price fluctuations.

由于上述区别，不可能“安全地假定”，如果卖方未发生违约，身为经销商的受损害买方本来可以在特定利润水平下完成第二项销售。正好相反，第二项交易能否发生以及能否从中获得利润，将取决于其他的不相关的可变因素，包括在买方从市场上获取货物时，货物的供应状况和批发价格等。因此，可以用于身为经销商的卖方的利润损失救济，从原理上无法适用于身为经销商的买方。

Because of these differences, it cannot “be safely assumed” that the aggrieved buyer-dealer would have made a second sale at a particular profit were it not for the seller's breach. To the contrary, the occurrence of and profit on a second transaction would depend on such other, unrelated variables as the availability and wholesale market price of the goods at the time the buyer-dealer went into the market to acquire them. Thus, the rationale for the seller-dealer's lost-profit remedy is simply inapplicable to buyer-dealers.

实际上，本案就显示了将卖方利润损失救济适用于受损害买方时所遇到的困难。假设卖方未发生违约，则对于从卖方购买的15,000吨肥料，买方本来会将其交付给伊拉克农业部；假设此时

Indeed, this case illustrates the difficulty of applying the seller's lost-profit remedy to aggrieved buyers. Were it not for Phoschem's breach, Fertico would have delivered the 15,000 tons of fertilizer it had purchased from Phoschem to Altawreed and would have had

买方打算向第四方买家作出第二项销售，买方本来必须从市场上另行购买 15,000 吨肥料。

从上述意义讲，本案买方的处境，与只有一份货物可以立即用于出售的受损害卖方相比，实际上没有什么不同。两者的处境都一样，即正是因为前一个协议出现了违约，才有了可以用于第二项销售的货物（引用著述）。并且，虽然从理论上讲，即使未发生违约，第二项销售本来也是有可能的，但是，由于买方 / 卖方需要重新从市场上获取额外的同类货物，其中所存在的不确定性就否定了本案多数派法官判决中所暗含的假定（N 诉 R 案），即在无违约的情况下，第二项销售以及其所带来的利润，本来也会以同等条件发生和存在。

to go into the marketplace again to acquire an additional 15,000 tons if it wished to make a second sale to Janssens.

In this respect, Fertico's position here is really no different in principle from that of an aggrieved seller which had only one set of goods at its immediate disposal. In both instances, the breach of a prior agreement is what has made the goods available for a second sale （cf., Corbin, Contracts）. And, while a second sale may have been theoretically possible even without the breach, the uncertainties occasioned by the buyer/seller's need to return to the marketplace for more goods of the same kind preclude the assumption, implicit in the majority's holding （see also, Neri v. Retail Mar. Corp.）, that the second sale and its accompanying profit would have been made on the same terms even if no breach had occurred.

特殊事实的理由不能成立

最后，我不同意多数派法官所依赖的理由，即本案似乎存在“极其特殊”的情况：买方“一方面用补进的肥料履行了向下家的出售义务，另一方面对延迟交付的

Finally, I cannot agree with the majority's reliance on the supposedly "exceptional" circumstance that Fertico both "met its subsale obligations with the cover fertilizer and acquired title and control over the late-delivered fertilizer".

肥料取得了所有权和控制”。

首先，多数派法官认定，买方取得了货物的所有权。但是，他们没有说清楚这个结论的理由和意义。买方已经支付了货款这个事实本身，无疑不具有决定意义，因为法典明确认为，支付货款和收到货物，不等于所有权的转移。恰好相反，法典明确预计到了此类情况的存在和应对，因此允许受损害的买方在拒收货物后，通过保留并转售处于其占有之下的货物来收回付款［第2.706条（6）款；第2.711条（3）款］。但法典同时要求，在此类情况下，买方要将其在转售中获得的额外利润交还给违约卖方［第2.706条（6）款］。多数派法官在判决中没有令人满意地解释，为什么这个救济对买方不够充分。

First, the basis for and significance of the majority's conclusion that Fertico acquired title to the goods is left unclear. Certainly, the fact that Fertico had already paid for the goods cannot be controlling, since the Code clearly does not equate payment and receipt of the goods with passage of title. To the contrary, the Code expressly contemplates and accounts for these situations by permitting a wronged buyer who has rejected to retain and resell the goods in its possession to recover any down payment （UCC 2-706［6］；2-711［3］）. The Code also requires in these situations, however, that the buyer account to the breaching seller for any additional profit it has made on the resale （UCC 2-706［6］）. Nothing in the majority opinion satisfactorily explains why this remedy is insufficient.

其次，多数派法官对所谓“极其特殊的事实”的强调并没有说服力，因为根据多数派法官的判决理由，对于任何一个特定案件来说，其结局在很大程度上将会取决于违约后碰巧哪一方占

Furthermore, the majority's emphasis on the asserted “exceptional facts” is unpersuasive because under the terms of the majority's holding the outcome in a given case would turn, in large measure, on the fortuity of which party had possession of

有货物。在普通的延迟交货案件中，违约发生后，通常是由买方占有货物。根据多数派法官的判决，买方此时可以一方面取得补进货物的损害赔偿，另一方面转售卖方的货物，并且自己保留所获得的利润。但是，在卖方根本未交付货物的情况下，违约发生后，通常是由卖方占有货物。根据法典，买方此时有两种选择，一种是取得补进损害赔偿，另一种是取得货物（只要货物已特定于合同项下），但不能两者兼得［法典第 2.716 条（3）款］。

the goods after the breach. In the case of a simple late delivery the buyer will ordinarily have possession after the breach. Under the majority's holding, that buyer may both obtain cover damages and resell the seller's goods, retaining any profit for itself. In the case of a complete failure to deliver, however, the seller will ordinarily have possession of the goods after the breach. Under the Code, the buyer in such a case may obtain either cover damages or the goods （if they have been specifically identified to the contract）, but not both（UCC 2-716［3］）.

因此，受到延迟交付损害的买方，处境将明显优于受到不交付损害的买方，但实际上，法律上或商业上没有合理理由将两者进行此种区分。更严重的是，彻底毁约的卖方，反而处于比延迟交付的卖方更有利的处境。虽然卖方在两种情况下都需要支付损害赔偿，但彻底毁约的卖方可将自己占有的尚未交付的货物作为自己的货物而转售，但已经交付了货物（虽然有些延迟）的卖方却不享有这一选择。我不能同意

Thus, the buyer aggrieved by a late delivery is placed in a substantially better position than a buyer aggrieved by a complete failure to deliver, although there is no apparent legal or commercial justification for the distinction. Even more seriously, a seller who completely repudiates is placed in a more advantageous position than one who merely delivers late. While both must pay cover damages, the repudiating seller may resell the undelivered goods in its possession for its own account-- an option unavailable to the seller who has delivered, albeit late. Since I

这样的法律规则，即对于两种类似的违约，较轻的违约最终反而要受到较重的惩罚。因此，我对本案判决提出异议，并主张维持上诉庭判决。

cannot agree with a rule of law that ultimately imposes a greater penalty on the less serious of two similar breaches, I dissent and vote to affirm.

案例 19　如何确定买方的直接损失数额？

Chatlos Systems, Inc. v. National Cash Register Corporation
查特莱斯系统公司诉全国现金柜台机公司案

联邦第三巡回上诉法院 1982 年；670 F.2d 1304

简　介

本案买方（Chatlos）从卖方（NCR）购买了一套型号为 NCR 399/656 的计算机系统，包括相关的硬件和软件，总价为 46,020 美元。卖方在合同中向买方担保，该计算机系统将具有双方约定的某些功能，包括运行相关软件的功能。但实际情况是，软件无法在该计算机系统中正常运行，因此计算机无法提供卖方所担保的功能。卖方多次努力进行调整和修复，但最终未能使计算机正常工作。因此，买方以卖方违反担保为由起诉卖方。

本案的审理一波三折。初审法院在第一次审理中，判定卖方违反了合同约定的担保，并判定卖方支付间接损失赔偿。卖方提起上诉。上诉法院认为，初审法院关于间接损失赔偿的判决有误，推翻原判并将案件发回初审法院重审，并特别指示初审法院唯一需要重审的问题，只是买方有权获得的直接损失赔偿数额。初审法院在重审中，将 NCR 399/656 系统被买方接收时本应具有的公平市场价值定为 207,826.5 美元。这个数额包括了硬件价值 131,250 美元和软件价值 76,576.5 美元。初审法院认定，被买方最终保留的硬件价值为 6000 美元，因此应从上述数额中减去。对于被买方保留的工资管理软件，法院则认定其没有任何价值。在减去硬件的 6000 美元后，初审法院判定卖方向买方支付 201,826.5 美元的损害赔偿，远高于双方的合同价格 46,020 美元。

为此，卖方第二次提起上诉。下述判决书就是上诉法院在第二次上诉中的判决意见。这次上诉基本上仅涉及一个问题，即如何计算买方因卖方违反担保而受到的直接损失。在本案中，由于买方已经接受了卖方交付的计算机且并未撤销接受，因此应该适用法典第 2.714 条的规定，即在买方已经接受了货物时买方损失的计算方法。根据第 2.714 条（2）款的规定，在卖方违反了担保但买方最终接受了货物的情况下，买方损失数额的计算方法是：损失数额 = 货物符合担保时本应具有的价值 – 被接受的货物的实际价值。在本案中，初审法院将货物的实际价值定为 6000 美元。对此，双方没有严重分歧。主要的争议是货物符合担保时本应具有的价值。

货物本应具有的价值，在通常情况下就是合同价格。在本案中，合同价格是 46,020 美元。但是，上诉法院在第一次上诉时判定，货物本应具有的价值不一定就是合同价格。例如，假设在订立合同时货物的价格较低，但在交付货物时货物的价格已经升高，此时，就应按照交付时的价格作为货物本应具有的价值。但是，本案的情况与市场价格波动没有关系。并且，初审法院所认定的应有价值大约相当于合同价格的 4.5 倍，差距巨大。

上述问题的关键，在于如何理解所谓的“本应具有的价值”。从本案的实际情况看，卖方出售的是一套低端计算机系统，因此大概本来就不可能具有卖方在合同中所许诺的功能，因为这些功能似乎只有在高端系统中才有可能实现。但出于种种原因，卖方作出了许诺。所以本案的困难问题就在于，合同货物本应具有的功能，到底是低端机的功能，还是高端机的功能？代表多数派法官意见的本案判决认为，卖方虽然描述了机器的型号，但许诺的是高端机的性能，因此买方所购买的，并不仅是特定型号的机器，而是拥有特定功能的机器。在这种情况下，买方有权按该性能来计算货物本应具有的价值。上诉法院最终将高端机的价值作为标准。

对于上述判决，上诉法院的另一位法官提出了强烈的异议意见。他认为，买方所购买的本来就是低端机，因此即使机器存在问题，也不能因此使用高端机的价值来计算赔偿。另外一个因素是，判决中作为参照的高端机实际上并不存在，而是买方专家证人所假想的一套系统。该证人认为，为了达到卖方所承诺的功能，可以使用不同组件拼凑出一套相应系统，并估算出该系统的成本。卖方认为，上诉法院的判决相当于说，虽然买方购买的是一辆福特汽车，但由于该汽车有问题，买方就有权获赔一辆劳斯莱斯汽车。

上诉法院的下述第二次判决是终审判决，因此卖方没有进一步上诉的权利。但是，根据《联邦民事诉讼法》，卖方有权申请由上诉法院全体法官（court in banc）共同对案件进行重审。案件通常只由一个或几个法官审理，而不会由法院的全体法官共同审理。全院共同审理的案件通常都是非常重要的案件。上诉法院对卖方的重审申请进行了法官投票表决。基于表决结果，卖方的重审申请被驳回。但是，赞成重审的 3 位法官又为重审申请撰写了异议意见。也就是说，上诉法院内部不仅对判决本身存在异议意见，而且对驳回重审的决定也存在异议意见。从这里也可以看出，上诉法院内部有关这个判决的争议非常大。但是，下述判决是终审判决，构成了美国货物买卖法中的一个重要判例。

判　决

本案基本情况　这个州际案件根据新泽西州法律审理。初审法院判定卖方违反担保并应支付损害赔偿。上诉的问题是，初审法院根据法典第 2.714 条（2）款计算的损害赔偿数额是否属于明显错误？我们的回答是否定

This appeal from a district court's award of damages for breach of warranty in a diversity case tried under New Jersey law presents [one] question: whether the district court's computation of damages under N.J.Stat.Ann. § 2-714 (2) was clearly erroneous. We answer [the]

的，因此维持原判。

初审法院的重审判决 初审法院上次重审时使用了第2.714条（2）款的“交易收益”公式，并据此计算出损害赔偿数额为201,826.50美元。卖方就该数额的计算再次上诉，称初审法院判决错误，因为所交付的计算机系统的合同价格为46,020美元，但初审法院不承认该价格是货物符合担保时本应具有的公平市场价格。卖方还认为，法院判决的赔偿数额缺乏证据支持。

卖方未提交新证据 在我们上次发回重审后，卖方放弃了就机器价值提交额外证据的机会，而选择依赖原始初审中的案件材料。对于计算机能够按照卖方担保的性能进行工作时本应具有的市场价值，卖方没有提供专家证言。

卖方的主张 我们上次判决已判定，合同价格并非一定等于市场价值。尽管如此，卖方仍然认为初审法官错误地拒绝了其主张。卖方的主张是，对于NCR

question in the negative and, therefore, we will affirm.

On remand, applying the “benefit of the bargain” formula of N.J.Stat.Ann. § 2-714（2）, the district court determined the damages to be $201,826.50. Defendant now appeals from these damage determinations, contending that the district court erred in failing to recognize the $46,020 contract price of the delivered NCR computer system as the fair market value of the goods as warranted, and that the award of damages is without support in the evidence presented.

Waiving the opportunity to submit additional evidence as to value on the remand which we directed, appellant chose to rely on the record of the original trial and submitted no expert testimony on the market value of a computer which would have performed the functions NCR had warranted.

Notwithstanding our previous holding that contract price was not necessarily the same as market value, appellant faults the district judge for rejecting its contention that the contract price for the NCR 399/656

399/656系统符合担保时的价值，该系统的合同价格是唯一的可靠证据。但是，初审法官宁愿相信买方专家证人的证词。该专家证人没有对NCR 399/656系统本身的价值进行估算，而是以如下方式作出估算：假设NCR 399/656系统具备卖方担保的所有运行功能，那么其本来应该具有多少价值。

was the only competent record evidence of the value of the system as warranted. The district court relied instead on the testimony of plaintiff-appellee's expert, Dick Brandon, who, without estimating the value of an NCR model 399/656, presented his estimate of the value of a computer system that would perform all of the functions that the NCR 399/656 had been warranted to perform.

买方专家证人的估值方法　买方专家证人在进行估算时，并没有局限于任何单一制造商的设备。他作证时所说的制造商，是指相对于卖方所担保的NCR 399/656机器所具有的功能，那些有能力制造同等功能机器的制造商。买方专家证人承认，其作证所涉及的那些设备，与NCR 399/656不处于同一个价格区间。卖方将此种作证比喻为，用劳斯莱斯汽车代替福特汽车。卖方的结论是，初审法院重新计算的损害赔偿数额，与公平市场价格存在明显矛盾。卖方的主张是，公平市场价格就是合同价格本身。

Brandon did not limit his estimate to equipment of any one manufacturer; he testified regarding manufacturers who could have made systems that would perform the functions that appellant had warranted the NCR 399/656 could perform. He acknowledged that the systems about which he testified were not in the same price range as the NCR 399/656. Appellant likens this testimony to substituting a Rolls Royce for a Ford, and concludes that the district court's recomputed damage award was therefore clearly contrary to the evidence of fair market value-which in NCR's view is the contract price itself.

估值的合理性　但问题在

Appellee did not order, nor was it

于，买方所购买和卖方所承诺提供的，并非仅仅是一台特定型号的 NCR 计算机系统，而是具有特定功能的 NCR 计算机系统。因此，根据法典第 2.714 条（2）款的规定，损害赔偿数额的正确计算方式是，所接受的货物的公平市场价值，与货物符合担保时本应具有的价值的差额。

promised, merely a specific NCR computer model, but an NCR computer system with specified capabilities. The correct measure of damages, under N.J.Stat.Ann. § 2-714（2）, is the difference between the fair market value of the goods accepted and the value they would have had if they had been as warranted.

按上述方式来计算赔偿数额，不局限于从订购至交付这个期间货物价值出现增长的情况，而是也可以包括合同价格带给买方的合同利益。无论卖方基于何种原因作出报价，只要该价格对买方特别有利，就属于合同利益。

Award of that sum is not confined to instances where there has been an increase in value between date of ordering and date of delivery. It may also include the benefit of a contract price which, for whatever reason quoted, was particularly favorable for the customer.

合同价格不等于市场价值

合同价格作为一项证据，也许可以用于证明公平市场价值，但不具有决定意义（M 诉 T 案）。卖方对公平市场价值的分析，仅局限于实际交付的计算机型号的合同价格。而买方提交的证据，则证明了卖方所承诺之性能的计算机所具有的价值。初审法院正确地采纳了后者的证据。

Evidence of the contract price may be relevant to the issue of fair market value, but it is not controlling. Mulvaney v. Tri State Truck & Auto Body, Inc. Appellant limited its fair market value analysis to the contract price of the computer model it actually delivered. Appellee developed evidence of the worth of a computer with the capabilities promised by NCR, and the trial court properly credited the evidence.

卖方承认需要性能更好的机

Appellee was aided, moreover, by the

器　此外，卖方计算机程序员的证词也帮助了买方。该程序员作证说，其曾向自己公司的管理人员提出，“目前的软件不足以支持买方所要求的程序。软件必须重新编排，或者必须向买方提供另一种系统”。该程序员建议，应向买方提供型号为 NCR 8200 的机器，但被公司告知，“那是不可能的”。

testimony of Frank Hicks, NCR’s programmer, who said that he told his company’s officials that the “current software was not sufficient in order to deliver the program that the customer（Chatlos）required. They would have to be rewritten or a different system would have to be given to the customer”. Hicks recommended that Chatlos be given an NCR 8200 but was told, “that will not be done.”

另一位卖方证人也承认，8200 型号比 399 型号在专业功能和价格方面高出两个档次。这个证词也支持了买方专家证人的证词，即如果要运行买方所要求的程序，所需硬件的价格大约在 10 万美元至 15 万美元。

Gerald Greenstein, another NCR witness, admitted that the 8200 series was two levels above the 399 in sophistication and price. This testimony supported Brandon’s statement that the price of the hardware needed to perform Chatlos’ requirements would be in the $100,000 to $150,000 range.

事实认定不存在明显错误　本质上，初审法官所面对的是当事方提交的互相矛盾的估值。买方专家的估值，在某种程度上被卖方证人所确认，而卖方自己则选择依赖合同价格。初审法官必须就证词的可信度作出结论。假设我们作为初审法官进行审理，我们本来也许有可能就机器符合

Essentially, then, the trial judge was confronted with the conflicting value estimates submitted by the parties. Chatlos’ expert’s estimates were corroborated to some extent by NCR’s supporters. NCR, on the other hand, chose to rely on contract price. Credibility determinations had to be made by the district judge. Although we might have come to a different conclusion on the

担保时本应具有的价值得出不同结论。但是，我们无权就可信度问题和事实问题作出认定。只有在初审法院对事实的认定存在明显错误时，我们才可以推翻其认定（K 诉 D 案）。在审阅了本案证据后，我们的结论是，对违反担保的损害赔偿数额的计算，初审法院不存在明显错误。因此，我们维持初审法院的原判。

（异议法官的意见） 在计算机系统的买卖交易中，卖方违反了担保，因此需要计算损害赔偿数额。本上诉的主要问题是，对于法典第 2 篇中有关损害赔偿数额的计算方法应如何适用？我对本院的上述判决持不同意见。初审法院就违反担保所判决支付的损害赔偿数额，几乎相当于合同采购价格的 5 倍。我相信，该数额缺乏可信证据的支持。同时，损害赔偿的计算方法也不适当，可能会给市场，特别是独特的新兴计算机市场，带来重大影响。

合同价格与市场价值的关

value of the equipment as warranted had we been sitting as trial judges, we are not free to make our own credibility and factual findings. We may reverse the district court only if its factual determinations were clearly erroneous. Krasnov v. Dinan. Upon reviewing the evidence of record, therefore, we conclude that the computation of damages for breach of warranty was not clearly erroneous. The judgment of the district court will be affirmed.

[Dissenting Opinion] The primary question in this appeal involves the application of Article 2 of the Uniform Commercial Code as adopted by New Jersey to the measure of damages for breach of warranty in the sale of a computer system. I respectfully dissent because I believe there is no probative evidence to support the district court's award of damages for the breach of warranty in a sum amounting to almost five times the purchase price of the goods. The measure of damages also has been misapplied and this could have a significant effect in the marketplace, especially for the unique and burgeoning computer industry.

Chatlos contends before this court, as it

系　本上诉中，买方的主张与重审时向初审法院提出的主张是一样的，即基于“交易收益”理论，本案货物在符合担保时本应具有的价值，相当于合同采购价格（46,020 美元）的数倍。

had before the district court on remand, that under its benefit of the bargain theory the fair market value of the goods as warranted was several times the purchase price of $46,020.

作为购买人，本案买方有义务对损失程度承担举证责任（C 诉 R 案）。在上次将本案发回初审法院重审时，我们并未拒绝将货物销售的合同价格作为适当标准来确认计算机符合担保时本应具有的价值。我们只是纠正了初审法院对法典文字的错误理解。我们认为，法典并没有禁止考虑公平市场价值。

As the purchaser, Chatlos had the burden of proving the extent of the loss. Council Brothers, Inc. v. Ray Burner Co. In remanding to the district court for a reassessment of the damages, we did not reject the contract price for the goods sold as the proper valuation of the computer as warranted. We merely corrected the district court's misconception that the language of the New Jersey statute precluded consideration of fair market value.

我们在上次的上诉中判定，法典第 2.714 条（2）款所规定的“价值”，必然是指货物被买方接受之当时、当地的公平市场价值。我们当时指出：“可以假定，在很多情况下，公平市场价值等于合同价格。因此，任何当事方如果希望说明两者不同，就要提供证据来证明两者确实不同。”

We held that “value” in section 2-714（2）must mean fair market value at the time and place of acceptance. We pointed out: “It may be assumed that in many cases fair market value and contract price are the same, and therefore, if a party wishes to show a difference between the two he should produce evidence to that effect.”

初审法院在重审中认定，计算机系统在 1975 年 8 月被买方

Thus, the sole issue before us now is whether the district court erred in fixing the

接受时，其符合担保时本应具有的价值为207,826.50美元。我们在本次上诉中所要解决的唯一问题是，该认定是否属于错误？

fair market value of the computer system as warranted at the time of the acceptance in August 1975 at $207,826.50.

事实问题与法律问题 我认为，初审法院存在法律问题的错误。多数派法官的结论是，对于初审法院在确定损害赔偿数额时对货物公平市场价值的认定，本院的审查标准是：初审法院的认定是否存在明显错误？对此，我持不同意见。假设初审法院仅仅错误计算了损害赔偿的数额，我也许会同意多数派法官的审查标准，因为在该情况下，我们担心的问题只涉及基本事实。但现在的问题是，买方根本没有提供证据来证明，所购买和所接受的特定货物在符合担保时本应具有何种市场价值。因此，我们面对的是法律问题的错误。此时，我们的标准是全面审查。但是，即使按照多数派法官所使用的审查标准，初审法院的判决仍然应被推翻，因为其对市场价值的认定缺乏可信事实的支持。

I believe that the district court committed legal error. The majority conclude that the standard of review of the district court's determination of the fair market value of the goods for the purpose of awarding damages is whether the trial judge's determination of market value is clearly erroneous. I disagree. Had the court merely miscalculated the amount of damages, I might agree with the majority's standard, for then our concern would be with basic facts. Here, however, no evidence was introduced as to the market value of the specific goods purchased and accepted had the system conformed to the warranty. Thus, the matter before us is one of legal error, and our standard of review is plenary. But even under the standard applied by the majority, the district court should be reversed because its determination of market value is not supported by probative evidence.

买方的理论不能成立 买方

There are a number of major flaws in

试图证明其损失数额超过合同价格，但该证明存在多项严重瑕疵。我先从买方的基本理论谈起。买方将其主张建立在这种理论上，即作为老练买家，其花费了几个月的时间讨价还价，最终选中了所需要的计算机系统，并按46,020美元的价格买下，但尽管如此，在卖方违反担保时，其有权获得的损害赔偿数额，却是昂贵许多的计算机的价值。也就是说，尽管买方讨价还价的标的是廉价系统，且低廉的价格反映的是低质，但由于该系统没有按照其所争取来的性能运行，买方就有权按照另一套系统的价值来确定损害赔偿数额，而该系统虽然有能力提供与NCR 399相同的功能，但质量明显更加优越，且相应更昂贵。

the plaintiff's attempt to prove damages in excess of the contract price. I commence with an analysis of plaintiff's basic theory. Chatlos presented its case under a theory that although, as a sophisticated purchaser, it bargained for several months before arriving at a decision on the computer system it required and the price of $46,020, it is entitled, because of the breach of warranty, to damages predicated on a considerably more expensive system. Stated another way, even if it bargained for a cheap system, i.e., one whose low cost reflects its inferior quality, because that system did not perform as bargained for, it is now entitled to damages measured by the value of a system which, although capable of performing the identical functions as the NCR 399, is of far superior quality and accordingly more expensive.

不能用假想货物作为估值基础　法典具体规定了违反担保时损害赔偿数额的计算方法。根据该方法计算的赔偿数额是，在买方接受货物的当时当地，"被接受的货物"的价值与"货物符合担保时本应具有的价值"的差额。

The statutory measure of damages for breach of warranty specifically provides that the measure is the difference at the time and place of acceptance between the value "of the goods accepted" and the "value they would have had if they had been as warranted" . The focus of the statute is

法典的关注点是“被接受的货物”，而不是假想中的具有相等功能的其他货物。“此外，作为衡量标准的价值，必须是所交付货物的合理市场价值，而不是该货物对特定购买人的价值，或适用于特定目的的价值。”（K诉V案）

upon “the goods accepted” --not other hypothetical goods which may perform equivalent functions. “Moreover, the value to be considered is the reasonable market value of the goods delivered, not the value of the goods to a particular purchaser or for a particular purpose.” KLPR-TV, Inc. v. Visual Electronics Corp.

但是，买方专家证人在对计算机系统的价值作证时，依据的是一台假想的于1978年12月组装的计算机系统的价值，且该证词被初审法院采纳。基于该专家证人的原始数据，法院在加入通货膨胀的因素后推算得出其判决的数额。买方在提出其主张时，使专家证词看上去像是在说，买方寻求的是第2.712条所说的“补进”赔偿，即购买替代计算机系统的成本。

The court, however, arrived at value on the basis of a hypothetical construction of a system as of December 1978 by the plaintiff's expert, Brandon. The court reached its value by working backward from Brandon's figures, adjusting for inflation. In presenting its case Chatlos developed its expert testimony as though it were seeking “cover” damages--the cost for the replacement of the computer system under section 2-712 of the statute.

买方估值的第一个问题 但对于本案来说，首先，按“补进”方式计算损害赔偿数额明显不当，因为初审法院和本院都在上次的审理中判决，必须根据法典第2.714条（2）款来计算损害赔偿数额。同时，本案买方并没

First, “cover” damages are obviously inappropriate here because both the district court and this court in its earlier decision held that the measure of damages is governed by section 2-714（2）. Furthermore, Chatlos did not “cover” in this case and, although there was testimony that it would use an IBM Series

有作出“补进”。虽然有证词提到，买方将使用其购买的 IBM 1 系微计算机来运行 NCR 399 的功能，但买方总经理亲自作证说，购买该机器的目的“不是用于取代 399 系统”。

估值的第二个问题 其次，买方未能提供证据来证明 IBM 1 系计算机的价格。但是，根据相关的法典第 2.714 条的规定，在计算损害赔偿数额时，必须局限于“被接受的货物的价值与其符合担保时本应具有的价值的差额”。法典的上述规定不包括第 2.712 条中“补进成本价格与货物合同价格的差额”。尽管卖方对设备性能作出过担保，但在设备不具备此种性能的情况下，应根据 NCR 399 的价值来确定公平市场价值。在缺乏该价值证据的情况下，不能将与所售货物毫无联系的系统的市场价值来作为计算基础。

但是，买方专家证人没有尽力就 NCR 399 符合担保时本应具有的公平市场价值作出估计，而是就另一套假想的机器作出此

1 mini-computer to perform the NCR 399 functions, the president of Chatlos personally testified that the IBM “wasn’t purchased with intent to replace the 399 system at the time of purchase”.

Second, Chatlos gave no evidence as to the cost of the IBM Series 1 computer system. However, under the applicable section of the statute, 2-714, the measure of damages is specifically confined to “the difference between the value of the goods accepted and the value they would have had if they had been as warranted” and does not include “the difference between the cost of cover and the contract price” as provided by section 2- 712. Although NCR warranted performance, the failure of its equipment to perform, absent any evidence of the value of any NCR 399 system on which to base fair market value, does not permit a market value based on systems wholly unrelated to the goods sold.

Yet, instead of addressing the fair market value of the NCR 399 had it been as warranted, Brandon addressed the fair market value of another system that he

种估值。他把IBM、BU和HO等公司生产的几种主流计算机系统的组件拼凑在一起而形成一套假想的机器，因为他认为此系统与买方所要购买的机器具有“相同性能”。他承认，这些其他公司的系统“也许与本案买方所购的系统不在同一个价格区间内”，并且,他没有指定特定软件程序。对于无法使用的NCR设备，买方专家证人本来可以很容易地确定其公平市场价值。但是，他却为一台假想的系统确定了一个价值，而不是假设当NCR设备可以运行时，其本来应该具有何种价值。

concocted by drawing on elements from other major computer systems manufactured by companies such as IBM, Burroughs, and Honeywell, which he considered would perform “functions identical to those contracted for” by Chatlos. He conceded that the systems were “[p]erhaps not within the same range of dollars that the bargain was involved with” and he did not identify specific packages of software. Brandon had no difficulty in arriving at the fair market value of the inoperable NCR equipment but instead of fixing a value on the system had it been operable attempted to fashion a hypothetical system on which he placed a value.

初审法院的错误 初审法院接着错误地采纳了上述估值，将其作为NCR 399系统可以正常使用时的公平市场价值。卖方对此作出正当反驳，认为买方专家证人用于估价的那些“可比”替代系统，都是技术性能更强的系统，因此不能作为第2.714条项下计算违反担保的赔偿数额的依据。此外，该专家所假想的系统并不存在，因此其价值在很大程

The district court, in turn, erroneously adopted that value as the fair market value for an operable NCR 399 system. NCR rightly contends that the “comparable” systems on which Brandon drew were substitute goods of greater technological power and capability and not acceptable in determining damages for breach of warranty under section 2-714. Furthermore, Brandon’s hypothetical system did not exist and its valuation was largely speculation.

度上只是猜测。

审阅买方专家证人的证词后可以看到，在法律上，该证词不足以确定买方从卖方所购买的系统的市场价值。该专家证人没有就下列问题提供任何证词：假设 NCR 399 系统能够提供卖方所担保的性能，其被买方接受时本应具有多少价值？甚至都没有人向他提出过这个问题。

A review of Brandon's testimony reveals its legal inadequacy for establishing the market value of the system Chatlos purchased from NCR. Brandon never testified to the fair market value which the NCR 399 system would have had had it met the warranty at the time of acceptance. He was not even asked the question.

买方证词的第一个问题　买方专家证人证词中的缺陷显示，该证词违反常理和市场现实。

Thus, the shortcomings in Brandon's testimony defy common sense and the realities of the marketplace.

第一，在通常情况下，公平市场价值的最佳证据，就是有意购买的人愿意向有意出售的人所支付的现金价格（V 诉 C 案；Y 诉 C 案）。我们在本案中看到的买方，明显“不是一个毫无经验的消费者”。本案买方花费了大量时间，与对计算机系统拥有丰富经验的制造商和供应商进行谈判并讨价还价。因此，他们就一套可运行系统约定的价格，通常就是该系统之价值的最好证据。

First, ordinarily, the best evidence of fair market value is what a willing purchaser would pay in cash to a willing seller. Vollmer v. City of Philadelphia; Yara Engineering Corp. v. City of Newark. In the instant case we have clearly "not ... an unsophisticated consumer", who for a considerable period of time negotiated and bargained with an experienced designer and vendor of computer systems. The price they agreed upon for an operable system would ordinarily be the best evidence of its value.

买方专家证人在其证词中所谈到的情况，不是我们在之前判

The testimony does not present us with the situation referred to in our previous

决中提到的情况，即“从合同订立到货物被接受的这个期间内，货物价值出现上升”。如果是这种情况，买方有权获得交易所带来的利益。正好相反，买方所依赖的专家证人纵情作出了最富有想象力的猜测。根据其证词，买方实际上是主张，一家高度专业化的跨国计算机设备公司，在经过几个月的谈判之后，竟不可思议地将实际上具有 207,000 美元公平市场价值的可用计算机系统，以 46,020 美元售出。

decision, where “the value of the goods rises between the time that the contract is executed and the time of acceptance”, in which event the buyer is entitled to the benefit of his bargain. On the contrary, Chatlos here relies on an expert who has indulged in the widest kind of speculation. Based on this testimony, Chatlos asserts in effect that a multi-national sophisticated vendor of computer equipment, despite months of negotiation, incredibly agreed to sell an operable computer system for $46,020 when, in fact, it had a fair market value of $207,000.

买方证词的第二个问题 第二，当然可以使用专家意见来证明市场价值，但是，该价值必须有合理基础。买方专家证人并没有就“被接受的货物”在符合担保时的公平市场价值提供证词。相反，他就自己内心假想的一套系统提供了证词。他忽视了这个因素，即在购买组合系统时，相对于从不同卖方购买“7 种不同应用组件的成本”，组合系统实际上具有成本优势。

Second, expert opinion may, of course, be utilized to prove market value but it must be reasonably grounded. Brandon did not testify to the fair market value “of the goods accepted” had they met the warranty. Instead, he testified about a hypothetical system that he mentally fashioned. He ignored the realistic cost advantage in purchasing a unified system as contrasted with the “cost of acquiring seven separate application components” from various vendors.

买方证词的第三个问题 第

Third, in arriving at his figure of $102,000

三，买方专家证人将软件价值估算为 102,000 美元，但是，在该估算中，专家证人不适当地将组装该系统时培训买方人员所需的时间和成本也包括在内。在庭审前提供的书面证词中，该专家说，他对软件的估价包括了培训买方人员使用该系统的必要时间。但在庭审的直接询问中，他作证说，为软件和编程所估算的 102,000 美元价值，不包括培训买方人员使用该系统的必要时间和成本，并说，培训客户和买方人员的成本“绝对”没有被包含在编程和软件的价格之中。当被询问到与之前作证的矛盾之处时，他承认在他的 102,000 美元的估价中，“我们包含了买方的时间”。

for the software, Brandon improperly included the time and cost of training the customer's personnel associated with the installation of the system. In a deposition prior to trial, Brandon testified that his valuation of the software included the time necessary to train Chatlos' personnel in the use of the system. On direct examination at trial, he testified that the $102,000 value fixed for software and programming did not include the time and cost necessary to train Chatlos' personnel in the use of the system, indicating that the cost of training a customer and his personnel is "definitely" not included in the price of programming and software. When confronted with his prior inconsistent deposition, he conceded that in his estimate of $102,000 "we included the Chatlos time".

买方证词的第四个问题　第四，从案件材料中包含的证词看，似乎无可置疑的情况是，计算机设备可以根据专业化程度分为多个层级。专业化程度更高的设备可以实现专业化程度更低的设备的功能，但专业化程度更低的设备无法实现更高等级设备的全部

Fourth, the record contains testimony which appears undisputed that computer equipment falls into one of several tiers, depending upon the degree of sophistication. The more sophisticated equipment has the capability of performing the functions of the least sophisticated equipment, but the less sophisticated equipment cannot perform all

功能。技术上更先进的设备显然会更昂贵。

毫无疑问，在1976年9月，对于带磁盘的NCR 399/656这种规格的设备，多家计算机供应商（包括IBM、PH和BU）都可以提供，价格在35,000~40,000美元，并且他们都可以提供买方所需要的软件程序。在1974年，正是这些公司于同一价格区间为销售本案这样的计算机而进行竞争。另外，“比399磁盘机器在价格和专业程度方面高3个等级”的计算机，也可以满足买方的需求。每高一个等级，就意味着更高的专业度、更强的功能以及更大的存储能力。卖方的专家证人作证说（该证词未受到反驳），BU、IBM和其他供应商所提供的价格在10万美元至15万美元的设备，可以满足买方的要求，但这些设备与399不是同一个等级，而是高出3个等级。这些设备与NCR 8400系列更接近。

买方证词的第五个问题 第

of the functions of those in higher levels. The price of the more technologically advanced equipment is obviously greater.

It is undisputed that in September 1976 there were vendors of computer equipment of the same general size as the NCR 399/656 with disc in the price range of $35,000 to $40,000 capable of providing the same programs as those required by Chatlos, including IBM, Phillips, and Burroughs. They were the very companies who competed for the sale of the computer in 1974 in the same price range. On the other hand, Chatlos' requirements could also be satisfied by computers available at “three levels higher in price and sophistication than the 399 disc”. Each level higher would mean more sophistication, greater capabilities, and more memory. Greenstein, NCR's expert, testified without contradiction that equipment of Burroughs, IBM, and other vendors in the price range of $100,000 to $150,000, capable of performing Chatlos' requirements, was not comparable to the 399 because it was three levels higher. Such equipment was more comparable to the NCR 8400 series.

Fifth, when it came to the valuation of the

五，在对硬件估值时，买方专家证人没有就其假想中的设备的市场价值给出具体估值。相反，他只给出了 10 万美元至 15 万美元的宽泛价格区间，认为这个价位的假想计算机可以满足买方的编程需求。这个宽泛区间本身就说明，该专家只是在猜测。

hardware, Brandon did not offer an opinion as to the market value of the hypothetical system he was proposing. Instead, he offered a wide ranging estimate of $100,000 to $150,000 for a hypothetical computer that would meet Chatlos' programming requirements. The range in itself suggests the speculation in which he indulged.

法典的基本原则是补偿　法典第 2.714 条的目的，是使买方恢复至卖方未违反担保时买方本可达到的处境［法典第 1.106 条（1）款］。违反担保的救济，目的是补偿买方的损失，而不是让买方发“横财”。买方不应获得高于原始买卖交易向其提供的收益。买方不应获得其本来并没有购买的更高等级的计算机的价值，即使这个系统可以提供较低级别的机器本来预计具备的全部功能。

The purpose of the N.J.S.A. 2-714 is to put the buyer in the same position he would have been in if there had been no breach. See Uniform Commercial Code 1-106（1）. The remedies for a breach of warranty were intended to compensate the buyer for his loss； they were not intended to give the purchaser a windfall or treasure trove. The buyer may not receive more than it bargained for； it may not obtain the value of a superior computer system which it did not purchase even though such a system can perform all of the functions the inferior system was designed to serve.

因此，在 M 诉 A 案中，法院判定，当买方购买的是二手的尚可使用的油加热系统时，如果产品被证明存在瑕疵，买方可以换成燃气系统（实际上买方确实

Thus, in Meyers v. Anton, the court held that where the buyers contracted for a properly functioning used oil heating system which proved defective, they were free to substitute a gas system （which they did）,

换了),可以改成热力强排系统,甚至也可以试一下光热力系统,但是,“他们不能基于这些调换系统的价值进行索赔。他们所约定购买的是二手的尚可使用的油加热系统,因此,他们不能获得高于原始交易的价值,也不能要求达到比合同充分履行时更好的处境”。

change over to forced air heating, or even experiment with a solar heating plant. “They could not, however, recover the cost of such systems. They contracted for a used oil system that would function properly, and can neither receive more than they bargained for nor be put in a better position than they would have been had the contract been fully performed.”

不应完全脱离合同价格 本院在之前的上诉中,曾指示初审法院将公平市场价值的分析作为确定损害赔偿数额的起点。在作出该指示时,本院注意到了买方的辩称,即如果单纯地采用合同价格作为标准,就会剥夺受损害的买方的“交易收益”。我们接受了“交易收益”这个概念,并就如何理解该概念解释如下:“如果从合同订立到货物被接受这个期间,货物的价值升高,则卖方的违反担保不应使买方失去有利合同带来的收益。反之,如果价值降低,卖方也有权按较低的价值计算。”

This court, in directing consideration of fair market value as the starting point in deciding damages noted Chatlos’ contention that exclusive use of contract price deprives the dissatisfied buyer of the “benefit of his bargain”. We accepted the concept of “benefit of the bargain” and explicated our understanding of the concept as follows: “If the value of the goods rises between the time the contract is executed and the time of acceptance, the buyer should not lose the advantage of a favorable contract price because of the seller’s breach of warranty. Conversely, if the value drops, the seller is entitled to the resulting lower computation.”

具有讽刺意味的是,这个有关“交易收益”的举例,其基础

Ironically, this example of benefit of the bargain is actually based on contract price.

正是合同价格。如果在买方接受货物的那天，货物的公平市场价值相对于合同价格出现了升高或降低，则在计算损害赔偿数额时，必须将该变动考虑在内。但是，目前的情况是，买方提供的且被初审法院在重审时接受了的市场价值，与合同价格没有任何形式的关联。

If on the date of acceptance the fair market value of the goods has risen or declined from the contract price, that variation must be taken into account in awarding damages. But here plaintiff's market value figures, accepted by the district court on remand, have no connection whatsoever with the contract price.

相关判例不支持买方　尽管可以说，“交易收益”的概念也适用于除市场价格周期波动外的其他情况，但买方所引用的判例只能证明，在证明货物的市场价值时，相关货物必须是已经被买方接受的货物。基于这个原因，在 M 诉 M 案中，当移动房屋的合同价格是 5300 美元时，根据法典第 2.714 条（2）款计算的违反担保时的损害赔偿数额是：所交付的房屋的 2000 美元实际价值与该特定房屋所能证明的 6000 美元市场价值的差额。

Although it may be that the “benefit of the bargain” concept is applicable to situations involving other than periodic fluctuations in market prices, the cases cited by Chatlos stand only for the premise that the proved market value of the goods in question must be accepted. Thus, in Melody Home Manufacturing Co. v. Morrison, where $5,300 was the price of a mobile home, the measure of damages for breach of warranty under U.C.C. § 2-714（2） was the difference between $2,000, the value of the delivered home, and $6,000 the proved market value of the particular home.

在涉及侵占家具的 M 诉 L 案中，家具买方与卖方和卖方的前夫产生争议。家具的所有权人是卖方的前夫，但卖方谎称自己

In Miles v. Lyons, the defendants （Lyons） sued for conversion of furniture, impleaded Anita Miles, former wife of the plaintiff, from whom they had purchased the

拥有家具，并以 100 美元的价格将其出售给买方。法官判决卖方的前夫有权获得 275 美元的赔偿,即家具被卖方侵占时的价值，但同时判决买方可以获得 100 美元的赔偿，即买方为家具支出的 100 美元。在上诉中，100 美元的判决被推翻，而被改判为 275 美元，即卖方因违反货物所有权担保而给买方造成的损失。上诉法院认定，买方有权根据法典第 2.714 条所规定的损害赔偿计算方法获得其“交易收益”。这里所说的交易，就是买方购买的特定家具的价值，而不是更时尚或更高档的假想家具的价值。

在本案中，即使假定我们接受买方的理论，即可以使用其他系统的价值来证明所购买的特定计算机系统的价值，买方为了支持其理论而引用的判例，也还是与本案情况不同。在 G 诉 J 案中，在地毯使用了 3 年以后，卖方以价格更高的地毯更换了违反担保的原有地毯，但买方拒绝支付超出的价格。初审法院支持了买方的主张，认定所更换的地毯

furniture. Mrs. Miles had sold it to the Lyons for $100, falsely asserting it belonged to her. The justice found for the plaintiff in the amount of $275, the value of the furniture at the time of conversion, but he found for the Lyons as third-party plaintiffs for $100. On appeal, the finding of $100 was vacated and judgment entered for $275, the loss resulting from the seller's breach of warranty of title. The Lyons were entitled, the court held, to the benefit of their bargain and the measure of damages under section 2-714. The bargain consisted of the value of the specific furniture they purchased-not other hypothetical furniture constructed in superior fashion or of superior materials.

Even if we were to accept plaintiff's theory that the value of other systems may be used to establish the value of the specific computer system purchased, the cases cited by Chatlos to support its theory are distinguishable. In Giant Food v. Jack I. Bender & Sons, when a seller, after three years, replaced carpet under warranty with new carpet of higher price, the buyer refused to pay the excess cost. The court agreed that the value of the replacement carpet

的价值代表了买方的损失数额。上诉法院维持了该判决，但明确解释说，“初审法院默示认定，新地毯的风格、货色和特点与买方原来购买的货物基本相似，因此才判定所更换的地毯是合理替代品”。

但是，本案不存在相关证词可以证明，假想中的系统除可提供相同功能这一点外，在其他方面与买方所购买的系统是相同的。此外，上述判例与本案的区别之处在于，该案的卖方实际上更换了货物。在法典制定之前的 H 诉 G 案中，烤箱的卖方声称，该烤箱比市场上任何烤箱的容量都大。在确定买方的损害赔偿数额时，法院拒绝以并不存在的其他烤箱作为参照，拒绝在合同价格以外确定损害赔偿数额。法院认为，购买人“无权以市场上并不存在的理想机器为参照，来获得猜测性的赔偿数额”。关于 NCR 399 被买方接受时的公平市场价值，由于买方专家证人的证词不能支持买方所提出的极度夸张的价值主张，因此，当事方通

represented the buyer's damages. However, the appellate court expressly noted that "（t）he trial court implicitly found that the replacement was a reasonable one-i.e., it was of substantially the same style, goods and character as that for which （the buyer） had originally contracted".

In the instant case, there was no testimony that the hypothetical system-apart from its ability to perform identical functions-was otherwise the same. Furthermore, as distinguished from this case, the goods were actually replaced by the seller. In Huyett-Smith Manufacturing Co. v. Gray, a pre-Code case, the vendor of a kiln represented that it had a capacity in excess of any kiln on the market. In measuring the damages claimed by the purchaser the court would not fix damages in excess of the contract by looking to a non-existent kiln stating that the purchaser "is not entitled to speculative damages for an ideal machine which was not on the market". Because Brandon's testimony does not support Chatlos' grossly extravagant claim of the fair market value of the NCR 399 at the time of its acceptance, the only evidence of the market value at the time is the price negotiated

过谈判而商定的NCR计算机系统符合担保时的价格，就是当时市场价值的唯一证明。

by the parties for the NCR computer system as warranted.

在很多案例中，货物的情况处于无可挽救或无法替代的情况，因此，无法采用修复成本或替代成本作为计算买方损失数额的方法。如果无法很方便地确定公平市场价值，那么，购买价格很可能反而就是证明货物符合担保时本应具有的价值的有力证据（引用著作；A诉A案）。

There are many cases in which the goods will be irreparable or not replaceable and therefore the costs of repair or replacement can not serve as a yardstick of the buyer's damages ... When fair market value cannot be easily determined ... the purchase price may turn out to be strong evidence of the value of the goods as warranted. J. White & R. Summers, Uniform Commercial Code. Auto-Teria, Inc. v. Ahern.

在L诉Q案中，法院依据法典第2.714条（2）款计算违反担保的损失赔偿数额。判决书说，在法典该条中，“价值”是指“公平市场价值”。该法院认为，“为货物所支付的现金价格，就是货物符合担保时的价值的表面证据”。怀特教授和萨莫斯教授的前述著作也提醒说，“货物符合担保时的价值很少成为争议问题，因为在该计算公式中，合同价格是强有力的衡量标准”。

In Long v. Quality Mobile Home Brokers, Inc., the court applied section 2-714（2） of the U.C.C. to arrive at a measure of damages for breach of warranty. Noting that “value” as used in that section meant “fair market value”, it asserted that “the cash price paid for goods is prima facie the value of the goods as warranted”. White & Summers, also remind us that “the value of goods as warranted will seldom be in dispute, for the contract price will be a powerful measure of that end of the formula”.

结论 因此，如果没有证据证明，货物价值与合同价格不同，

Thus, where there is no proof that market value of the goods differs from the contract

就应以合同价格为准｛参见G诉S案［“如果没有证据表明，所购买的货物的市场价格与合同价格有所不同”，当事方即无权根据法典第2.713条（1）款，基于交易收益，即合同价格与市场价格的差价，来计算损害赔偿］｝。而在本案中，赔偿数额应该就是46,020美元。本案买方保留了系统硬件，而初审法院认定该硬件在公开市场的现值为6000美元。初审法院将该数额从损害赔偿数额中减去的做法是正确的。

price, the contract price will govern, cf. Gulf Chemical & Metallurgical Corp. v. Sylvan Chemical Corp. （party not entitled under N.J.S.A. 2-713（1） to damages based on the benefit of his bargain, i.e., the difference between the contract price and the market price when “there is no proof ... that the market price for the goods purchased was any different than the price contracted for ...”）, and in this case that amounts to $46,020. Chatlos has retained the system hardware and the district court fixed its present value in the open market at $6000. The court properly deducted this sum from the damages awarded.

买方还购买了卖方的工资管理软件。买方在初审中承认，从1975年2月或3月至1978年10月（买方停用的时间），软件完全可以正常使用。初审法院认为不存在该软件公平市场价值的证据，因而认定该软件没有任何价值。但是，法律非常明确，即如果除合同价格外，没有其他证据可以证明价值，合同价格就应被视为工资管理软件的公平市场价值。当事方为该软件约定的合同

Chatlos purchased the NCR payroll program and acknowledged at trial that the program operated fully and satisfactorily beginning February or March 1975 until October 1978 when it discontinued its use. The district court assigned no value to it because there was no evidence of fair market value. However, the law is clear that without evidence of a value other than contract price, that price should be accepted as the fair market value of the payroll program. The parties agreed on a contract price of $1000

价格是1000美元，因此应从损害赔偿数额中减去该数额。

因此，基于本案证据，买方有权获得的损害赔偿数额为：46,020美元减去6000美元（买方所保留的硬件在初审时的公平市场价值），再减去1000美元（工资管理软件的公平市场价值）。最终的数额为39,020美元。基于以上理由，我的结论是应该推翻初审法院的判决。

（卖方申请上诉法院重审的请求被驳回） 关于卖方提出的由上诉法院重新审理本案的请求，由于对本院上述判决当时持赞成意见的法官无人同意重新考虑该判决，并且，投票同意由本院全体法官重新考虑本案的法官人数，没有达到本院所有在职法官人数的多数。因此，卖方提出的重新审理本案的请求被驳回。

（3位法官同意重审的意见） 通常而言，本院在州际案件中对州法的解释，不会产生非常重大的后果，因此无须本院全体法官

and that sum should be deducted from the measure of damages.

On this record, therefore, the damages to which plaintiff is entitled are $46,020 less $6000, the fair market value at time of trial of the retained hardware, and less $1000, the fair market value of the payroll program, or the net sum of $39,020. Accordingly, I would reverse the judgment of the district court.

[Sur Petition for Rehearing] The petition for rehearing filed by appellant in the above entitled case having been submitted to the judges who participated in the decision of this court and to all the other available circuit judges of the circuit in regular active service, and no judge who concurred in the decision having asked for rehearing, and a majority of the circuit judges of the circuit in regular active service not having voted for rehearing by the court in banc, the petition for rehearing is denied.

[Dissenting Opinion for Denial of Rehearing] Ordinarily, an interpretation of state law by this Court, sitting in diversity, is not of sufficient consequence to warrant

参与对本院判决的重新审理。其中一个原因是，如果任何联邦法院对州法作出了错误解释，该州法院将有机会在未来某个时间拒绝该联邦法院的解释（参见C诉P案）。

reconsideration by the Court sitting in banc. One reason is that if a federal court misconstrues the law of a state, the courts of that state have an opportunity, at some point, to reject the federal court's interpretation. See Chuy v. Philadelphia Eagles Football Club.

但在本案中，多数派法官所批准的计算损害赔偿数额的方法，看上去是基于对新泽西州商法（也就是对法典）的一种新型解释。由于法典在全国范围内都适用，因此，如果我们对该法典的解释存在错误，则与仅仅涉及新泽西州法的情况相比，纠正该错误的难度明显要高很多。

In this case, however, the majority's holding, which endorses a measure of damages that is based on what appears to be a new interpretation of New Jersey's commercial law, involves a construction of the Uniform Commercial Code as well. Rectification of any error in our interpretation is, because of the national application of the Uniform Commercial Code, significantly more difficult than it would be if New Jersey law alone were implicated.

特别是，本案所涉及的法典条款具有非同寻常的重要意义：本院所批准的损害赔偿数额计算标准，可能会在广泛的商业交易领域中形成巨大的经济风险和经济责任，特别是对本案所涉及的新兴计算机行业来说。本案异议法官的反对意见看上去很有说服力；并且，我们认为，本案多数

Moreover, the provision of the Uniform Commercial Code involved here is of unusual importance: the measure of damages approved by this Court may create large monetary risks and obligations in a wide range of commercial transactions, including specifically the present burgeoning computer industry. Because there would appear to be considerable force to the dissenting opinion of

派法官所阐述的原则在被最终采纳之前，应由本院全体法官加以审阅。据此，我们愿意批准卖方的请求，由全体法官重新考虑本案的判决。

Judge Rosenn and because I believe that the principle articulated by the majority should be reviewed by the entire Court before it is finally adopted, I would grant the petition for rehearing in banc.

案例 20　买方的有限救济是否已失去根本目的?

Milgard Tempering, Inc. v. Selas Corporation of America
密尔盖德钢化公司诉美洲赛莱思公司案

联邦第九巡回上诉法院 1990 年；902 F.2d 703, 11 UCC Rep.Serv.2d 558

简　介

本案买方（Milgard）是一家为住宅提供玻璃产品的公司，于 1979 年 6 月与身为锅炉制造商的卖方（Selas）订立了购买一台平置钢化炉的合同。锅炉系用于玻璃的钢化，价格为 145 万美元。锅炉本身高度复杂，且需要卖方专门为买方进行设计和制造。卖方设计和制造该锅炉的技术并不成熟，但在向买方推销该锅炉时，将其称为技术成熟的设备。锅炉的最晚交付日期为 1980 年 3 月 31 日，随后有几个月的试运行期。合同对锅炉的产量和转速作出了规定，但同时规定，如果卖方违反担保，卖方的责任仅限于修理或更换锅炉，且不就间接损失承担赔偿责任。

锅炉完成交付和安装后存在各种瑕疵，远达不到合同规定的运行指标。卖方在两年左右的期间里一直试图纠正这些问题，但直到 1982 年 1 月，仍然无法使锅炉达到约定指标。买方随后起诉卖方违反合同。买方起诉后，双方试图自行达成一项和解协议。虽然双方最终未能签署书面和解协议，但当时曾作出下述讨论：给卖方60天的锅炉运行管理权，以证明锅炉可以达到约定产量的90%；卖方支付买方在该期间的运营损失；之后，如果买方运行锅炉6个月而未出现事故，卖方将进一步使锅炉达到约定产量的95%。卖方随后按上述讨论内容开始了工作，而买方则在保留权利的条件下撤诉。

但是，在上述6个月期间内，锅炉既未达到合同指标，也未达到和解讨论中所说的指标。1983年3月，买方第二次起诉。此时，锅炉已在买方工厂运行了很长时间，并且，锅炉虽然达不到合同规定的指标，但基本上可以使用。因此，买方保留了锅炉并继续使用，但就锅炉不达标而产生的间接损失向卖方索赔。1984年6月，初审法院以无审判决的形式判决卖方胜诉。初审法院认定，本案双方都是富有专业经验的公司，并自愿约定了风险分担方式，因此，合同中限制间接损失责任的条款具有强制履行力。初审法院同时判定，当事方在1982年3月已经达成了有效的和解协议。

买方随后提起上诉，即下述判决中所称的第一次上诉。买方主要引用了法典第2.719条（2）款，该款规定，“如果客观情况导致唯一的或有限的救济失去其根本目的，可以根据本篇的规定提供救济”。买方主张，修理或更换是合同中的“唯一的或有限的救济”(exclusive or limited remedy)，但由于卖方无法完成修理，也不可能更换锅炉(因为卖方根本没有其他可更换的锅炉)，因此，合同规定的唯一救济已失去“根本目的”(essential purpose)。在这种情况下，法典第2.719条（2）款允许法院提供适当救济，包括赔偿间接损失的救济。本质上，这相当于彻底删除合同中原有的排除间接损失赔偿的条款。

在该上诉中，上诉法院支持了买方的主张，因此推翻了原判并发回重审。上诉法院认为，间接损失限制条款是否有效，自愿约定不是唯一的因素，还必须考虑卖方对锅炉的修理情况。在卖方完全无法修复锅炉的情况下，就应该考虑否定合同中的限制间接损失赔偿的条款。发回重审后，初审法院根据上诉法院的意见重审后判定，合同原有的救济条款，即修理或更换锅炉的条款，已经失去根本目的，因为卖方在两年半的时间里都未能将锅炉修好，且根据案件的实际情况，更换锅炉也不现实。初审法院判定，在合同原有的唯一救济不再存在的情况下，法院有权否定间接损失排除条款的效力。据此，初审法院判决卖方赔偿买方的间接损失。卖方随后提起上诉。下述判决是对第二次上诉的判决。

在第二次上诉中，上诉法院认为，即使有限的救济条款失去根本目的，也不意味着合同中原有的限制间接损失赔偿的条款自然失效，而是要进行更多的个案综合分析。因此，初审法院自动排除间接损失限制条款的做法是对相关法律的误解。但是，上诉法院同时认为，虽然初审法院对法律的理解不够准确，但其最终作出的结论是正确的，即应该否定本案合同中原有的间接损失限制条款，因为根据本案的实际情况，在个案综合分析后，应该允许买方在失去原有的唯一救济后，根据法典的一般规定取得救济，包括间接损失赔偿的救济。据此，上诉法院维持了初审法院重审后的判决。

判　决

本案的情况　本上诉意味着一场持续进行了将近 7 年的诉讼的结束。诉讼涉及买方大约 10 年前购买的一台玻璃钢化炉。初审法院判决，卖方未能修复锅炉的严重缺陷，因而买方有权获得损害赔偿。卖方提起上诉。我们维持原判。

This appeal marks the end of nearly seven years of litigation over a glass tempering furnace purchased over ten years ago. The seller, Selas Corporation of America （“Selas”） appeals the judgment of the district court awarding the buyer, Milgard Tempering, Inc. （“Milgard”）, damages resulting from its failure to repair serious defects in the furnace. We affirm.

第一次上诉　本案第一次上诉时，本院推翻了初审法院的判决并发回重审。我们当时判定，合同中的间接损失赔偿的限制条款是否具有强制履行力，不仅与

This court, in Milgard Tempering, Inc. v. Selas Corp. of America ［Milgard I］, reversed and remanded for trial. We held that the enforceability of the consequential damages limitation not only depended

该条款在起草时是否显失公平有关，还与卖方违约及无法修复锅炉的具体情况有关。由于后者存在争议，我们判定，无审判决是不适当的。我们进一步说明，所声称的和解存在严重事实争议，因此该事项也需要重审。由于需要通过重审来决定胜诉方，我们还推翻了有关律师费的判决。

upon the conscionability of the provision when drafted, but upon the circumstances surrounding Selas' breach and inability to repair. Because these circumstances were disputed, we found summary judgment inappropriate. We further noted that serious factual disputes surrounding the alleged accord and satisfaction required trial of that issue as well. We also vacated the award of attorneys' fees pending determination of the prevailing party at trial.

重审的情况 经过5个星期的无陪审团重审,初审法官认定，锅炉从未达到过合同标准。他判定，有限的维修救济已失去其根本目的,且卖方的违约过于严重，因此必须删除合同中的间接损失赔偿限制。他判决买方有权获得1,076,268美元的净赔偿额，但驳回了买方的律师费索赔。卖方就上述判决以及对更换法官重新审理之动议的否决提起上诉。买方则对驳回律师费索赔的判决提起上诉。本院维持原判。

On remand, after a five-week bench trial, Judge Bryan in the district court found that the furnace had never lived up to the specifications in the contract. He held that the limited repair remedy failed of its essential purpose and that Selas' default was sufficiently severe to expunge the cap on consequential damages. He awarded Milgard $1,076,268 in net damages. He also denied Milgard's claims for attorneys' fees. Selas appeals the judgment and denial of its motion for new trial and judge. Milgard cross-appeals the denial of attorneys' fees. We affirm.

第二次上诉 在本上诉中，卖方首先辩称，初审法官的判决

Selas first argues that the district court erred in ruling that the limited repair remedy

是错误的，即修复货物的有限救济已失去其“根本目的”，并因此导致合同对间接损失的限制被删除。合同第 28.5 条约定，卖方违反担保时，买方的救济限于卖方对缺陷设备的修理或更换。法典第 2.719 条（1）（a）款允许当事方对救济作出此种限制。

failed of its “essential purpose” and that such failure lifted the contractual cap on consequential damages. Section 28.5 of the contract limited Milgard’s remedies in the event of breach of warranty to repair or replacement of the defective equipment. Such limitations on a party’s remedies are permitted by Washington’s version of the U.C.C., Wash. Rev.Code Sec. 2-719（1）（a）.

整体审阅的原则　但是，必须根据法典第 2.719 条（2）款对唯一的或有限的救济作出解读。该款规定，“如果客观情况导致唯一的或有限的救济失去其根本目的，可以根据本篇规定提供救济”。法典该条要求，法院必须对合同进行整体审阅，并对救济条款进行专门审阅，以确定救济的根本目的，以及该目的是否已丧失。

An exclusive or limited remedy, however, must be viewed against the background of Sec. 2-719（2）, which provides：“Where circumstances cause an exclusive or limited remedy to fail of its essential purpose, remedy may be had as provided in this Title.” This section requires a court to examine the contract in general and the remedy provision in particular to determine what the remedy’s essential purpose is and whether it has failed.

有限救济已失去根本目的　有限的修理救济主要出于两个目的。首先，该救济给卖方提供一段时间，使其可以尽力将货物修理至符合合同规定的状况，而在这段时间里，卖方不承担其他责任。其次，该救济给买方提供一

A limited repair remedy serves two main purposes. First, it serves to shield the seller from liability during her attempt to make the goods conform. Second, it ensures that the buyer will receive goods conforming to the contract specifications within a reasonable period of time. See Chatlos Systems v.

种保证，使买方可以在合理时间内得到符合合同的货物［参见C诉N案；S诉S案（其中引用文章）］。如果合同条款将买方的救济局限于取得修理或取得缺陷部件的更换，但违约的制造商或卖方在合理时间内无法完成修理，则从第2.719条（2）款的角度看，该救济即失去根本目的（L诉S案）。此时，没有必要证明卖方存在疏忽或恶意，因为在卖方未能成功修理的情况下，无论卖方是勤奋还是拖延或疏忽，对买方造成的伤害都是一样的（参见S诉S案）。

在本案中，初审法院认定，锅炉从未达到过合同规定的标准。此外，法院认定，少数几次成功的改进，也未能在合理时间内完成，因为花费的时间总共长达两年半。我们同意，在这种情况下，不合理的耽延再加上最终的失败，已导致修理救济的失效。因此，该救济已失去根本目的。

是否自动排除间接损失限

National Cash Register Corp; S.M. Wilson & Co. v. Smith Int'l, Inc., citing Eddy, On the "Essential" Purposes of Limited Remedies. A contractual provision limiting the remedy to repair or replacement of defective parts fails of its essential purpose within the meaning of Sec. 2-719 (2) if the breaching manufacturer or seller is unable to make the repairs within a reasonable time period. Lidstrand v. Silvercrest Indus. It is not necessary to show negligence or bad faith on the part of the seller, for the detriment to the buyer is the same whether the seller's unsuccessful efforts were diligent, dilatory, or negligent. See Wilson.

The district court in this case found that the furnace had never lived up to the specifications of the contract. Moreover, the court found that the few successful improvements were not made within a reasonable period of time, taking over two and one-half years. We agree that under these circumstances, the unreasonable delay and ultimate failure in repair made the repair remedy ineffective; thus, the remedy failed of its essential purpose.

Washington courts have not addressed

制条款　在有限的修理救济失效后，该失效是否会使排除间接损失赔偿的条款失效？华盛顿州法院尚未处理过这个问题。因此，我们的责任是确定该州最高法院本来会如何处理这个问题。在完成这个任务时，我们可以参考公认的法律渊源，包括制定法、著述、法律重述以及已公布的案例（M 诉 U 案）。我们还可以参考“其他州的说理充分的判决”（T 诉 L 案）。我们要从头审查初审法院对华盛顿州法律的解释（参见 M 破产案）。

相关判例中的可分割理论　我们的分析从 F 诉 F 案开始。本院在该案中判定，根据华盛顿州法律，修理救济的失效并不自动删除限制间接损失赔偿的条款。我们曾预测，华盛顿州法院会采用个案处理的方式，通过审阅合同条款来确定：唯一救济和排除赔偿这两项条款，到底是属于“风险划分中各自独立的因素”，还是属于“风险划分一揽子交易中互不可分的因素”？

我们的推理是，如果排除条

the issue of whether failure of a limited repair remedy may serve to invalidate a consequential damages exclusion. Therefore, it is our responsibility to determine how the state’s supreme court would resolve it. In undertaking this task, we may draw upon recognized legal sources including statutes, treatises, restatements, and published opinions. Molsbergen v. United States. We may also look to “well-reasoned decisions from other jurisdictions”. Takahashi v. Loomis Armored Car Serv. We review the district court’s construction of Washington law de novo. See In re McLinn.

We begin our analysis with Fiorito Bros., Inc. v. Fruehauf Corp. In that case, we held that under Washington law, the failure of a repair remedy does not automatically remove a cap on consequential damages. We predicted that Washington courts would take a case-by-case approach and examine the contract provisions to determine whether the exclusive remedy and damage exclusions are either “separable elements of risk allocation” or “inseparable parts of a unitary package of risk-allocation”?

If the exclusions are inseparable, we

款属于不可分割的因素，那么，法院就应根据法典第2.719条（2）款的正式评论进行分析。该评论解释说，第2.719条（2）款“所针对的情况是，在客观情况发生变化后，合同的原有安排构成了欺压”。我们据此维持了初审法院对该案的判决，即在卖方专断且不合理地拒绝充分履行有限的修理义务后，“限制损害赔偿的条款已构成欺压并因此失去效力”。

reasoned, a court's analysis should track the Official Washington Comments to Sec. 2-719（2）, which explain that the subsection “relates to contractual arrangements which become oppressive by change of circumstances...”. We then affirmed the district court's ruling that the seller's arbitrary and unreasonable refusal to live up to the limited repair clause “rendered the damages limitation clause oppressive and invalid”.

F诉F案主要引用了本院在S诉S案中对法典第2.719条（2）款的分析。S诉S案涉及隧道挖掘机合同，当事双方均有丰富的商业经验。合同既包含有限的修理条款，也包含限制间接损失赔偿的条款。本院在该案中的结论是，尽管修理救济已失去第2.719条（2）款所述的根本目的，但限制间接损失赔偿的条款仍然有效。

Fiorito relied heavily on this circuit's analysis of Cal.Com.Code Sec. 2-719（2） in Wilson. Wilson involved a contract between commercially sophisticated parties for a tunnel boring machine. The contract contained both a limited repair clause and a cap on consequential damages. After concluding that the repair remedy failed of its essential purpose within Sec. 2-719（2）, this court held that the bar to consequential damages remained enforceable.

尽量避免由法院重新分配风险 我们在该案中作出如下解释：“本案中具有基本同等谈判实力的双方通过谈判确定了他们

We explained: “Parties of relatively equal bargaining power negotiated an allocation of their risks of loss. Consequential damages were assigned to the buyer, Wilson.

之间损失风险的分担方式。间接损失被分配给了买方。机器系专为买方目的设计的复杂设备。卖方并未无视其修理义务，而只是没有能力完成修理。这不足以导致由卖方承担买方原本明确同意承担的损失。重新转嫁风险的社会成本很高，因此，在缺乏适当理由时不应该这样做。对于自主谈判的合同，要以违背合同条款的方式重新转嫁风险，需要更加充分的理由。卖方的违约尚不构成完全的和根本的违约，未达到删除合同中限制间接损失赔偿条款的程度。”但是，本院在 S 诉 S 案中也及时指出，该判决只限于该案具体事实。该案绝对无意说明，在有限救济失效后，永远应该保留限制间接损失赔偿的条款。

The machine was a complex piece of equipment designed for the buyer's purposes. The seller Smith did not ignore his obligation to repair; he simply was unable to perform it. This is not enough to require that the seller absorb losses the buyer plainly agreed to bear. Risk shifting is socially expensive and should not be undertaken in the absence of a good reason. An even better reason is required when to so shift is contrary to a contract freely negotiated. The default of the seller is not so total and fundamental as to require that its consequential damage limitation be expunged from the contract." However this court in Wilson quickly pointed out that its holding was limited to the facts and was in no way intended to state that consequential damages caps always survive failure of limited repair remedies.

初审法院分析错误但结论正确　初审法院认定本案卖方的违约“属于根本违约，但不构成全面违约”。尽管如此，法院认定该根本违约的性质足够严重，因此必须删除限制间接损失赔偿的条款。卖方称，法院错误地理解

The district court in the instant case found Selas' default "fundamental, but not total". Nonetheless, it found the breach sufficiently fundamental to remove the cap on consequential damages. Selas claims that the court misunderstood the legal standard and that consequential damages may be allowed

了法律标准。卖方认为，只有在违约同时构成根本违约和全面违约后，才可以判决支付间接损失赔偿。

only when the seller's breach is both total and fundamental.

我们同意，初审法院对判例原则的总结存在错误。但法院的分析没有错误。在涉及法典第2.719条（2）款时，我们不认为“全面和根本违约”这个词有任何特别含义。我们在F诉F案中回避了标签式的死板分析，认为“每个案件应基于其自身事实进行分析”。我们对本案第一次上诉中的挡箭牌式分析表示了强烈反感。我们认为，F诉F案对“欺压”的分析，华盛顿州法典的正式评论，以及S诉S案对“全面和根本”违约的分析，实际上都是相互一致的。

We agree that the district court's characterization of the case law was flawed. However, the analysis it employed was not. This court has found nothing magical about the phrase "total and fundamental default" in relation to U.C.C. 2-719（2）. In Fiorito we eschewed such wooden analysis, leaving "[e] ach case [to] stand on its own facts". We further expressed our distaste for talismanic analysis in Milgard I, finding the "oppressive circumstances" analysis utilized by Fiorito and the Washington Comments and the "total and fundamental" default analysis in Wilson in accord with each other.

初审法院重审本案时的任务是，通过审阅合同救济条款来确定，卖方违约所造成的损失是否并不属于通过谈判已被分配给某方的损失｛参见F诉F案；参见W诉M案［其中解释了南卡罗来纳州的法典第2.719条（2）款］；K诉Y案；A诉J案｝。

The task before the district court was to examine the remedy provisions and determine whether Selas' default caused a loss which was not part of the bargained-for allocation of risk. See Fiorito. Cf. Waters v. Massey-Ferguson, Inc.（interpreting identical version of U.C.C. 2-719（2） enacted in South Carolina）; Kelynack v. Yamaha Motor

初审法院重审时所实际采用的分析方法就是上述的个案方法，并据此删除了限制间接损失赔偿的条款。我们同意该判决。

Corp.; Adams v. J.I. Case Co. This was the analysis that the district court actually employed. We agree with the district court's decision to lift the cap on consequential damages.

本案买方不是为参与一项科学实验而同意支付 145 万美元。买方同意购买的是，卖方所称的代表顶尖技术并在两个月试运行期结束后可以满足买方需求的玻璃锅炉。卖方虽然尽了力，但并未奏效。卖方两年半都未能完成修理，给买方造成了损失，而该损失不是当初作为谈判结果而被分配给买方的风险。因此，限制间接损失赔偿的条款不具有强制履行力。

Milgard did not agree to pay $1.45 million in order to participate in a science experiment. It agreed to purchase what Selas represented as a cutting-edge glass furnace that would accommodate its needs after two months of debugging. Selas' inability to effect repair despite 2.5 years of intense, albeit injudicious, effort caused Milgard losses not part of the bargained-for allocation of risk. Therefore, the cap on consequential damages is unenforceable.

赔偿数额的确定　卖方随后就初审法院对损害赔偿数额的计算提出异议。法院认定，锅炉在 21 个月里（1980 年 4 月 1 日至 1982 年 12 月 31 日）无法达到合同所列的任何产量指标。在之后的期间，锅炉能以某种稳定性达到其中少数几项指标。因此，法院为两个期间分别计算了损失数额。首先，计算了买方在 21 个

Next, Selas challenges the district court's determination of damages. The court had found that for 21 months （April 1, 1980 to December 31, 1982）, the furnace was incapable of reaching any of the yield rates outlined in the contract. Thereafter, the furnace could reach a few with some regularity. Accordingly, the district court calculated damages for two time periods. First, it calculated Milgard's lost profits during

月“损坏”期的利润损失；其次，计算了1982年12月31日之后实际受到和将会受到的损失。

初审法院的计算 在计算“损坏”期损失数额时，初审法院首先注意到买方在该期间内的实际利润为591,537美元。为了计算卖方违约致使买方在该期间内额外损失的利润，法院将买方在1983年1月1日至1984年9月30日的生产作为“对照”期。买方在对照期内获得了674,900美元的利润。法院将该数额乘以1.5，然后从乘积中扣除锅炉的折旧（按11年使用期计算），再扣除买方自己的低效在“损坏”期内导致的损失。法院最终认定，买方在“损坏”期的利润损失为860,497美元。

在计算1982年12月31日之后的损失数额时，法院依赖买方经济学家PF博士的专家证词。由于锅炉的转速和产量甚至一直都无法接近合同指标，PF博士估计，在上述日期之后，该状况给买方已实际带来并将会带来的利润损失超过300,000美

the 21-month “damage” period. Second, it calculated losses Milgard did and would incur after December 31, 1982.

In calculating the award for the damage period, the district court noted that Milgard earned an actual profit of $591,537 during that time. To determine what further profits Milgard lost during that period as a result of Selas’ breach, the court used Milgard’s production from January 1, 1983 to September 30, 1984 as a “benchmark” period. During that period, Milgard earned a net profit of $674,900. The court multiplied the benchmark figure by a factor of 1.5 and reduced the product to account for both depreciation of the furnace over its 11-year life span and losses caused by Milgard’s own inefficient operation during the damage period. The resulting award for lost profits was $860,497.

In determining damages incurred after December 31, 1982, the court drew upon testimony from Milgard’s expert economist, Dr. Peter Finch. Dr. Finch estimated that the furnace’s continued inability even to approach the specified cycle and yield rates did and would cause Milgard in excess of $300,000 in lost profits after that date. The court awarded

元。法院因此判决卖方另行支付252,608美元。

Milgard an additional $252,608.

卖方对上述两项数额提出异议，认为该数额缺乏证据支持，具有猜测性质。作为替代理论，卖方声称，初审法院在计算“损坏”期的利润损失时，存在数学计算错误。

Selas challenges both awards as speculative and unsupported by the evidence. Alternatively, it claims that the district court made a mathematical error in computing the lost profits for the damage period.

数额计算属于事实问题　损失数额的确定属于事实问题（V诉P案）。因此根据《联邦民事诉讼法》规则，本院不会干预有关损害赔偿数额计算的判决，除非其“明显缺乏证据支持”（R诉C案），或除非其“震惊良知”（B诉G案）。关于取得利润损失赔偿的基本原则，华盛顿州最高法院在其对后来案件具有重大影响的L诉W案中作出下列表述：“在下列情况下，可就利润损失获得赔偿：（1）在合同订立时，当事方可以预见到此种损失，（2）被告的违约是造成此种损失的主要原因，并且（3）能够以合理的确定性证明此种损失。”

The determination of damages is one of fact. V.C. Edwards Contracting Co. v. Port of Tacoma. Thus, in accordance with Federal Rule of Civil Procedure, this court will not disturb an award of damages unless it is “clearly unsupported by the evidence”, Roberts v. College of the Desert, or it “shocks the conscience”, Brady v. Gebbie. The basic test for recovery of lost profits was laid out in the seminal Washington Supreme Court opinion, Larsen v. Walton Plywood Co.: “[Lost profits] are properly recoverable as damages where (1) they are within the contemplation of the parties at the time the contract was made, (2) they are the proximate cause of defendant’s breach, and (3) they are proven with reasonable certainty.”

损失数额的确定性问题　上

The third element, dealing with certainty,

述有关确定性的第三项因素,“更多是针对损失是否存在的事实,而不是损失的程度或数额”[A诉G案(其中引用G诉H案)]。这与一直以来都承认的看法是一致的,即如果难以准确证明损失的数额,也不应因此让被告从该难题中受益,特别是当被告违约本身引起了该难题时[参见B诉G案(其中引用著作);B诉C案(主要依赖《合同法重述》中的原则)]。

"is concerned more with the fact of damage than with the extent or amount of damage". Alpine Indus., Inc. v. Gohl, quoting Gaasland Co. v. Hyak Lumber & Millwork, Inc. This comports with the long-held view that a defendant should not profit from the difficulty in proving exact damages, particularly if his breach contributes to that difficulty. See Butcher v. Garrett-Enumclaw Co., quoting Corbin on Contracts; Box v. Crowther, relying upon Restatement of Contracts.

在L诉W案之前,对于利润损失问题,华盛顿州法院严格遵循“新业务”的推理原则:如果索赔的一方在此次损失之前从未产生过利润,就无权取得赔偿,因为该损失的猜测性太强(参见I诉S案;H诉U案;L诉G案)。法院在L诉W案中认定,严格适用上述规则可能会导致不公,因此该案采用了下述原则:“如果存在可用来计算所称损失的实际数据,就不能仅因一项业务刚刚建立而禁止其获得利润损失赔偿。”

Until Larsen, Washington courts strictly applied the "new business" corollary to the lost profits rule: if the complaining party does not have a profit history prior to the period of damage, profits are denied as too speculative. See Ingersol v. Seattle-First Nat. Bank; Hole v. Unity Petroleum Corp.; Lockit Cap Co. v. Glove Mfg. Co. Concluding that strict adherence to this rule could produce unjust results, the Larsen court adopted the rule that "lost profits will not be denied merely because a business is new if factual data are available to furnish a basis for computation of probable losses".

专家证词作为证据 在计算

Expert testimony alone can provide a

利润损失数额时，单纯的专家证词也有可能构成足以依赖的事实基础（A 诉 G 案；B 诉 G 案）。只要专家意见包含了合理的推理，法院就脱离了“难以确定和随意猜测的范畴”（L 诉 W 案）。专家证词必须基于实际证据，而不能仅为揣测或假设。在此基础上，法院必须高度智慧地行使裁量权，来计算损失的具体数额［B 诉 C 案；参见 L 诉 T 案（在很难确定哪些损失数额是由被告引起时，事实审的审理人“必须极度负责和客观地行使自己的裁量权”）］。在确定利润损失时，存在某种不足的专家证词仍可作为证据支持。在证据不足以得出准确的损失数额时，事实审的审理人有权相应降低证词的证据力（A 诉 G 案）。

sufficient factual basis for an award of loss of profits. Alpine； Butcher. If the opinion of an expert provides a reasonable basis for inference, the court is freed from “the realm of uncertainty and speculation”. Larsen. Expert testimony must be based upon tangible evidence rather than mere speculation or hypotheses. The court then must exercise its sound discretion in determining the amount of damages. Barnard v. Compugraphic Corp. Cf. Long v. T-H Trucking Co. （where difficult to ascertain what amount of loss was caused by defendant, trier of fact “must exercise a large measure of responsible and informed discretion”）. Expert testimony with partial deficiencies may nevertheless support a finding of lost profits； the trier of fact is free to discount its weight accordingly, even if no evidence sustains the exact amount it awards. Alpine.

在本案中，利润损失的 3 个判断标准全部满足了。首先，初审法官认定的事实是，当事方曾预见到发生利润损失的可能。由于合同第 28.5 条提到了此种利润，因此法官的认定不存在明显错误。其次，初审法官认定，机

All three tests for loss of profits have been met in this case. First, the district judge made the factual finding that the parties contemplated the possibility of lost profits. Because Sec. 28.5 of the contract refers to such profits, this finding is not clearly erroneous. Second, the district court found

器不符合合同标准是引起买方利润损失的主要原因。卖方对此没有异议，因此我们不再讨论这个问题。最后，对于利润损失的计算，初审法官的结论有足够的事实基础。如同L诉W案及随后判例所预见的那样，买方利润损失的唯一证据就是买方专家证人PF博士的证词。虽然初审法官认为PF博士的某些数字难以理解，但同时说明并不否定这些数字。基于A诉G案确立的原则，初审法官降低了PF博士证词的证据力并降低了赔偿数额。对此，我们认为没有错误。

that the failure of the machine to conform to the contract specifications proximately caused Milgard to lose profits. Selas does not challenge this finding and we do not disturb it. Third, the district court had a sufficient factual basis upon which to make its computation of lost profits. As forecast by Larsen and its progeny, Milgard's sole source of evidence in this area was its expert witness, Dr. Finch. Although the district judge found some of Dr. Finch's figures difficult to swallow, he pointed out that that did not negate them. Consistent with Alpine, the court discounted the damage award in accordance with the weight of Finch's testimony. Therefore, we find no error.

卖方还就252,608美元的数额提出另一项异议理由，即书面合同未就机器转速提供具体保证。但是，该理由不具有说服力。初审法院的判决并非基于卖方违反了一项（明示或默示）保证，即锅炉实际上将按合同第2.5条约定的转速运行。实际上，法院所依赖的是买方经济学家PF博士的专家证词，即卖方所设计的锅炉根本不可能达到合同所说的转速，

Selas further challenges the award of $252,608 on the ground that the written contract contained no specific guarantees of cycle rates. This argument is unpersuasive. The district court did not base its award on a breach of a guarantee (express or implied), that the furnace would actually run at the cycle rates specified in Sec. 2.5 of the contract. Instead, the court relied upon the testimony of Milgard's expert economist, Dr. Finch, to conclude that Selas' failure to design

而这会给买方带来 252,608 美元的利润损失。买方也提交了书面证据（卖方未质疑），证明该设计失误将使买方受到 401,878.50 美元的损失。基于上述理由，我们认为初审法官的认定不存在错误。

净利润损失问题　最后，卖方称初审法官得出的 860,497 美元数额存在计算错误。具体而言，卖方称，法官因疏忽而未从上述数额中扣除买方在 21 个月“损坏”期内实际获得的利润（591,537 美元）。卖方的错误在于，其误认为 860,497 美元代表了买方在该期间内本可获得的全部利润，但实际上该数额所代表的是，在买方实际获得的 591,537 美元利润之外，买方在该期间内所额外损失的利润。

初审法官在 3 月 26 日的口头判决中，两次将该数额称为“所损失的利润”。案件第 120 项认定未明确如此区分，但口头判决已被收入案件“事实认定和法律结论”中。因此我们认为，初审法官仅指买方实际损失的利润。

a furnace capable of ever meeting those cycle rates would cost Milgard $252,608 in lost profits. Milgard also produced uncontroverted documentary evidence that such failure would cost it $401,878.50. For reasons expressed above, we find no error in the judge’s finding.

Finally, Selas contends the district court made a computational error in arriving at the $860,497 figure. Specifically, it argues that the court neglected to subtract the actual profit （$591,537） Milgard earned during the 21-month “damage period”. Selas errs by inferring that the court’s computation represented the total profit Milgard would have made during that period. Instead, the court referred to the profit Milgard lost during that period, over and above the $591,537 Milgard actually made.

In his March 26 Oral Ruling, Judge Bryan twice called this computation one of “lost profits”. Finding 120 does not make that distinction as clearly; however, because the Oral Ruling was incorporated into the Findings of Fact and Conclusions of Law, we believe the court referred only to profits

同时，初审中卖方曾提出“重新考虑损害赔偿和利润损失数额的动议”。初审法院直接驳回了上述动议。卖方当时提出的计算错误就是本次上诉中提出的问题。初审法院在驳回该动议时，要求双方注意这个事实，即法官的口头判决已被纳入案件的事实认定。因此，卖方有关数学计算错误的主张完全不能成立。

Milgard did not realize. Our conclusion finds further support in the district court's response to Selas' Motion to Reconsider Amount of Damages and Lost Profits. The court flatly rejected the very computational error argument now on appeal and directed both parties' attention to the fact that its Oral Rulings were incorporated into the Findings. Thus, Selas' claim of mathematical error simply does not add up.

和解协议问题 初审法院认定，当事方并未于1982年3月达成和解。卖方对该认定也提出异议。卖方辩称，当事方已达成和解，且买方已同意将其救济局限于解除合同和取得货物退款。

Selas further disputes the trial court's ruling that the parties did not enter into an accord and satisfaction in March, 1982. Selas maintains that the parties reached an accord whereby Milgard limited its remedies to rescission and return of the purchase price.

是否存在和解协议，通常是事实与法律相混合的问题。如果当事方对事实不存在争议，初审法院就要将该问题作为纯粹的法律问题解决（K诉F案）。无论是法律问题，还是法律与事实混合问题，上诉中都要重新审阅（U诉M案）。但是，如果基本上只涉及事实问题或历史事实的确认，则《联邦民事诉讼法》的上诉标准是审阅事实认定是否存在

Whether there has been an accord and satisfaction is generally a mixed question of law and fact. If the facts are not controverted by the parties, the question is purely one of law for the trial court. Kibler v. Frank L. Garrett & Sons, Inc. Both questions of law and mixed questions of law and fact are reviewed de novo. United States v. McConney. However, essentially factual inquiries or the establishment of historical facts are reviewed under the clearly erroneous standard of

明显错误。

Federal Rule of Civil Procedure.

一份和解协议包含3个因素：（1）存在真实争议；（2）已同意就该争议达成和解（达成协议）；（3）已订立和解协议（解除责任）（W诉R案）。这项新达成的协议必须按照通常的合同法原则来解释（参见P诉P案）。“和解协议的关键因素是当事方的意愿，而此种意愿原则上属于事实问题”[本案第一次上诉判决（其中引用B诉D案）]。事实审的审理人必须确定，当事方是否已就新协议所针对的事项达成一致意愿，以及是否具有作出真实妥协的意愿（P诉A案；J诉C案）。

An accord and satisfaction consists of three elements: （1）a bona fide dispute; （2）an agreement to settle that dispute （accord）; and （3） execution of that agreement （satisfaction）. Ward v. Richards & Rossano, Inc. The new agreement is interpreted according to ordinary contract principles. See Perez v. Pappas. “The key element of accord and satisfaction is the intention of the parties, which as a rule presents a question of fact.” Milgard I, quoting Black v. Denver United States Nat. Bank. The trier of fact must determine whether there was a meeting of minds as to the subject matter of the new agreement and an intention to reach a genuine compromise. Plywood Mktg. Assoc. v. Astoria Plywood Corp.; James S. Black & Co. v. Charron.

在本案中，初审法官认定，不存在此种一致意愿。特别是法官认定，协议在两个重要方面不完整：（1）买方是否保留了第二次起诉的权利；以及（2）当卖方有能力以90%的产出率将锅炉维持运营6个月时，买方对卖方承担何种义务。

In this case, the district judge found that there was no such meeting of the minds. In particular, he found that the agreement was incomplete in two important respects: （1） whether Milgard reserved the right to file a second lawsuit; and （2） the extent of Milgard’s obligations if Selas were able to operate the furnace for six months at a 90% yield rate.

卖方对上述认定提出异议，声称如果卖方未在上述事项上与买方达成协议，卖方本来就不可能同意去做那些后续工作。但是，该辩称只能证明，这是卖方对所声称的协议的理解。买方总经理GM先生的证词则描绘出另一幅场景。例如，关于买方在6个月期限后对卖方的义务，他的理解是，“我们（买方）的选择权仍然保留在我们手里。在6个月期限结束时，我们也许会说，虽然必须试一下，但现在只能处置掉这个锅炉；或者，我们也有可能留着它。但无论哪种情况，我们都要就自己的费用追讨损害赔偿”。

初审法院相信了买方的证词。在上诉中，不能轻易推翻初审法院就可信度问题作出的认定（参见S诉R案）。卖方未能提供理由说明为什么GM先生的证词不值得相信。因此，我们同意初审法官的结论，即当事方的意愿并不完全吻合，因此不存在和解协议。基于以上理由，我们维持初审法院的原判。

Selas disputes these findings, claiming that it never would have agreed to perform the work without reaching agreement on those issues. However, this argument proves only Selas’ understanding of the proposed agreement. The testimony of Milgard’s president, Gary Milgard, paints a different picture. For example, his understanding of his firm’s obligations to Selas after the six-month period was that “our [Milgard’s] options were still open to us. We could at the end of the six-month period determine that we were just going to go through this cycle and that we would have to get rid of [the furnace] or we could keep it--and under either condition, we were still going to go after those damages for expenses”.

The district court credited this testimony. Determinations of credibility are not lightly upset on appeal. See S.E.C. v. Roger. Because Selas provides no reason to disbelieve Mr. Milgard’s testimony, we agree with the district court that there was an incomplete meeting of the minds and therefore no accord. For these reasons, the judgment of the district court is Affirmed.

流 通 票 据

案例 21　执票人是否已得到抗辩通知?

Kaw Valley State Bank & Trust Co. v. Riddle
考瓦谷州民银行和信托公司诉瑞德尔案

堪萨斯州最高法院 1976 年；549 P.2d 927

简　介

本案涉及本票的付款责任问题。本案共有 3 个当事方，即设备买方兼本票制票人（Riddle），设备卖方兼本票受款人（Co-Mac），以及从受款人购买了本票并因此成为本票执票人的银行（Kaw Valley）。本案的这张争议本票，原本是制票人（买方）从受款人（卖方）购买设备后，作为分期付款的货款而出立给受款人的，并随后由受款人流通给银行。本诉讼的起因是，因未收到本票的后续付款，银行起诉制票人，要求制票人支付本票。制票人认为自己持有抗辩，即本票缺乏对价，因而拒绝支付。根据法典的规定，制票人所主张的缺乏对价的抗辩，可以对抗一般执票人，但不能对抗正当执票人。因此，银行是否有权取得付款，取决于银行是否具有正当执票人的身份。

本案的事实背景是，设备卖方（本票受款人）实际上从事了欺诈活动。卖方曾与买方订立一份合同，向买方出售某些机器设备。为了支付货款，买方出立了一张本票，并在卖方的诱导下，出具了一份已收到设备的确认书和其他相关文件，但实际上买方当时尚未收到设备。卖方随后提出无法向买方提供设备，双方因此同意取消合同。卖方向买方谎称，与设备有关的本票及相关文件已被销毁，因此买方不再承担该本票的义务。买方信以为真，未再过问此事。但卖方实际上没有将该本票销毁，而是将其流通给了银行。

在一段时间里，卖方继续为这张本票向银行进行分期付款。所以，从银行的角度，本票似乎一切正常。卖方随后宣布破产，并停止了本票付款。银行联系制票人（买方），要求其为本票付款，而后者此时才知道本票原来没有被销毁。由于卖方已经破产，因此所有问题现在都只能在制票人和银行之间解决。制票人认为，自己没有收到本票所购买的设备，因此本票不存在对价，而不存在对价是法典承认的抗辩之一。但是，这个抗辩不能对抗正当执票人，而银行认为自己是正当执票人。这成为本案的关键问题。

法院的分析主要集中于向银行转让本票的受款人（卖方）与银行的关系。法典第3.302条对正当执票人有3项要求（支付价值、以善意作为、未得到抗辩通知），而法院认为，银行主要是未能满足其中的第三项要求，因为银行在取得本票时，已得到其中存在抗辩的通知。在本案的具体事实背景下，此种通知不是指银行实际知道该特定本票存在问题，而是基于银行对受款人业务情况的了解，特别是对其中不规范之处的了解，以及双方长期的密切关系和某些特殊做法。据此，初审法院判决银行不属于正当执票人，而堪萨斯州最高法院维持了初审法院的判决。

判　决

本案基本情况　持有本票的银行起诉本票的制票人，要求制票人支付两张本票。本票的受款人（卖方）是建筑设备经销商，向制票人（买方）出售了建筑设

This action was brought by The Kaw Valley State Bank and Trust Company (Kaw Valley) to recover judgment against John H. Riddle (Riddle) on two notes. The two notes were given to purchase construction

备。制票人为了支付建筑设备的货款，向受款人出立了两张本票。受款人随后将本票转让给银行（执票人）。

初审法院的判决　初审未使用陪审团。对于两张本票中总额为 21,904.64 美元的一张，制票人以缺乏对价为抗辩并得到法院的支持。法院认定，银行不是该本票的正当执票人。初审时各方均承认，该本票系为采购建筑设备，但受款人从未交付过任何设备。银行就初审法院有关其不属于 1971 年 5 月 11 日之本票和担保协议的正当执票人的判决提起上诉。

缺乏对价的抗辩　法典第 3.306 条规定，如果票据的执票人不是正当执票人，其取得票据后，就要受制于票据中的下列抗辩：缺乏对价、票据前提条件未满足、票据未能交付、票据仅为特定目的的交付。在本案中，毫无疑问，制票人在出立本票后未收到任何对价，因为其从未收到过相关设备的交付，且受款人保证

equipment. Kaw Valley had acquired the two notes by assignment from Co-Mac, Inc.（Co-Mac）, a dealer, from whom Riddle purchased the construction equipment.

In a trial to the court Kaw Valley was found not to be a holder in due course of one of the notes. Its claim on said note, totaling $21,904.64, was successfully defended on the grounds of failure of consideration. It was stipulated at the trial that none of the construction equipment for which the note was given had ever been delivered by Co-Mac. Kaw Valley has appealed. The primary point on appeal questions the holding of the trial court that Kaw Valley was not a holder in due course of the note and security agreement dated May 11, 1971.

K.S.A. 3-306 provides that unless a holder of an instrument is a holder in due course he takes the instrument subject to the defenses of want or failure of consideration, nonperformance of any condition precedent, nondelivery or delivery for a special purpose. It was undisputed in this case that Riddle received no consideration after executing the note. The machinery was never delivered and he was assured by Co-Mac that the papers

将销毁本票文件。初审时，当事方已承认此事实。因此，只要银行不是正当执票人，就要受制于上述确凿抗辩，无权取得本票付款。

would be destroyed. The parties so stipulated. If Kaw Valley was not a holder in due course the proven defense was a bar to recovery by Kaw Valley.

正当执票人的条件 法典第 3.302 条规定，以下列方式取得票据的执票人是正当执票人：（1）支付了价值；（2）以善意作为；以及（3）未得到票据存在抗辩的通知。第一项条件已满足，因为当事方不质疑且法院也已认定银行支付了价值。但是，另外两项条件存在争议。

K.S.A. 3-302 states that a holder in due course is a holder who takes the instrument （1） for value, （2） in good faith and （3） without notice of any defense against it. It was not disputed and the court found that Kaw Valley took the note for value so the first requirement was satisfied. The other requirements were subject to dispute.

善意与抗辩通知 初审法院的结论是："银行不是 1971 年 5 月 11 日的本票和担保协议的正当执票人，因为银行未能在所有方面证明，其以善意取得该票据，且未得到制票人对票据持有抗辩或索赔的通知。因此，银行在取得该票据后，受制于其中存在的缺乏对价的抗辩。"因此，我们需要解决的问题是，执票人在取得票据时必须满足何种条件，才属于以"善意"作为，且"未得到抗辩通知"。

The trial court concluded: "Kaw Valley State Bank and Trust Company is not a holder in due course of the note and security agreement, dated May 11, 1971 for the reason that it did not establish in all respects that it took said instruments in good faith and without notice of any defense against or claimed to it on the part of John H. Riddle, and Kaw Valley State Bank and Trust Company therefor took said instruments subject to the defense of failure of consideration." So we are confronted with the question of what is required for a holder to take an instrument "in good faith" and "without notice of defense”.

善意的含义 法典第 1.201 条(19)款将“善意”定义为:“相关行为或交易中事实上的诚实。”在法典的首次建议稿中，不仅要求执票人的行为在事实上是诚实的，而且还要求其行为符合“合理的商业标准”。如果按上述要求，法院本来就必须分析，某项特定商业标准是否在事实上是合理的（引用法典第 1.201 条草稿）。但是，在所批准的法典最终版本中，合理的商业标准这个要求被删除了。这似乎意味着，在确定是否存在“善意”时，必须适用狭义的审查标准（引用著作）。从法典的历史看，似乎应该认为，“善意”的要求是，对于原始交易中的任何重大缺陷，执票人实际上并不知情，且没有参与。

“Good faith” is defined in K.S.A. 1-201 (19) as “honesty in fact in the conduct or transaction concerned.” The first draft of the Uniform Commercial Code (U.C.C.) as proposed required not only that the actions of a holder be honest in fact but in addition it required the actions to conform to reasonable commercial standards. This would have permitted the courts to inquire as to whether a particular commercial standard was in fact reasonable. (See Uniform Commercial Code, Proposed Final Draft § 1-201) However, when the final draft was approved the test of reasonable commercial standards was excised thus indicating that a more rigid standard must be applied for determining “good faith”. (See White and Summers, Uniform Commercial Code) From the history of the Uniform Commercial Code it would appear that “good faith” requires no actual knowledge of or participation in any material infirmity in the original transaction.

抗辩通知的问题 我们要考虑的第二个问题，是法典的另一个要求，即正当执票人在取得票据时，必须未得到票据存在抗辩

The second part of our question concerns the requirements of the U.C.C. that a holder in due course take the instrument without notice of any defense to the instrument. K.S.A. 1-201

的通知。法典第1.201条（25）款规定："一个人在下列情况下被视为得到一项事实的'通知'：(a)他实际已知道该事实；或(b)他已得到该事实的通知；或（c）根据当时他所了解的所有事实和情况，他有理由知道该事实的存在。一个人实际得到一项事实的信息后，即属于'知道'或'了解'。'发现'或'得知'或含义相似的其他词汇，是指知道而不是有理由知道。"

通知也包括应该知道 在审阅法典上述条文后可以看到，法典所阐述的标准，并不局限于狭义的标准，即实际上已经知道存在抗辩。"有理由知道"这个标准，似乎是指遵守合理商业标准（引用著作；C诉N案；U诉I案）。执票人在声称具有正当执票人的身份时，必须同时满足"善意"和"未得到抗辩通知"这两个条件。虽然两个标准对行为的要求可能不完全一样，但两者似乎并不冲突。

（25）provides: "A person has 'notice' of a fact when （a） he has actual knowledge of it; or （b） he has received a notice or notification of it; or （c） from all the facts and circumstances known to him at the time in question he has reason to know that it exists. A person 'knows' or has 'knowledge' of a fact when he has actual knowledge of it. 'Discover' or 'learn' or a word or phrase of similar import refers to knowledge rather than to reason to know."

As is apparent from reading the above statute the standard enunciated is not limited to the rigid standard of actual knowledge of the defense. Reason to know appears to be premised on the use of reasonable commercial practices. （See Bender's U.C.C. Service, Hart and Willier, Commercial Paper; Citizens Bank of Booneville v. National Bank of Commerce; and Universal C.I.T. Credit Corp. v. Ingel） Since "good faith" and "no notice of defense" are both required of a holder to claim the status of a holder in due course it would appear that the two standards are not in conflict even though the standards of conduct may be different.

银行有理由知道存在抗辩

在本案中，没有或基本没有证据表明，银行在购买 1971 年 5 月 11 日的本票时，系以不诚实方式作为，或“未以善意”作为。但是，关于“抗辩通知”，初审法院认定，从银行当时知道的所有事实和情况看，银行有理由知道本票存在抗辩。法院认定：“从 1960 年到 1971 年 5 月，银行从受款人购买了 250 张以上的本票，且在任何时间节点，都持有数额为 10 万美元至 25 万美元的此种债务。所有这些债务都由受款人提供担保，并由受款人的总经理个人担保。银行的一位职员代表银行处理了几乎所有这些交易。该职员知道，受款人就其出售的新设备和二手设备的适用性，向一些购买人作出了担保和陈述。该职员还知道，某些交易的实际情况与外表显示的情况不同，因为银行支付的款项本来应被受款人用于购买某些设备，但该设备正是受款人已经正在出售的设备。此外，向客户交付的设备，有时因维修或翻新而延迟

There is little or no evidence in the present case to indicate that Kaw Valley acted dishonestly or “not in good faith” when it purchased the note of May 11, 1971. However, as to “notice of defense” the court found from all the facts and circumstances known to Kaw Valley at the time in question it had reason to know a defense existed. The court found: “During the period 1960 to May, 1971, plaintiff purchased from Co-Mac over 250 notes and held at any given time between $100,000.00 and $250,000.00 of such obligations. All of which were guaranteed by Co-Mac and personally guaranteed by D.J. Wickern, its president. Conant Wait personally handled most if not all of such transactions for plaintiff. Mr. Wait was aware that Co-Mac was making warranties and representation as to fitness to some purchasers of new and used equipment. Mr. Wait further knew that some transactions were in fact not as they would appear to be in that the money from Kaw Valley would be used by Co-Mac to buy the equipment that was the subject matter of the sale. Further, that delivery to the customer of said purchased equipment was sometimes delayed 60 to 90 days for repairing and/or

60天至90天。很明显，在很多交易中，银行依赖受款人本身来确保本票得到付款；在本票付款出现延迟时，银行联系的是受款人。在多次交易中，受款人直接从本票义务人收取付款，然后再支付给银行。银行对于交易中的不正常之处并不关心，因为其明显依赖受款人为本票付款。”

初审法院还认定：“对于1971年5月11日那笔交易中的本票，本票付款凭单账册未被送至制票人；制票人从未作出过付款；在1972年1月25日之前，都是受款人在付款；在1972年3月初之前，制票人不知道银行从事了1971年5月11日的那笔担保交易；只有当银行职员于1972年3月12日联系制票人经理时，制票人才得知该交易；在之前不久，受款人进入破产程序；在1972年9月之前，银行从未要求制票人为该本票付款。”

此外，还有其他证据支持初审法院的判定，即银行有理由

overhauling of same. The plaintiff obviously on many transactions was relying on Co-Mac to insure payment of the obligations and contacted Co-Mac to collect delinquent payments. Co-Mac collected payments directly from debtors in various transactions and paid plaintiff. Plaintiff did not concern itself with known irregularities in the transactions as it clearly was relying on Co-Mac."

[The Court also found:] "The coupon book on the May 11, 1971 transaction was not sent to defendant Riddle; no payments on same were made by defendant Riddle; the payments were made by Co-Mac until January 25, 1972; prior to early March, 1972, defendant Riddle did not know plaintiff had the May 11, 1971 secured transaction; knowledge of said transaction came to defendant Riddle on March 12, 1972 when Mr. Wait contacted defendant Riddle's manager, that Co-Mac had shortly before been placed in receivership; that no demand for any payment on said transaction was made by plaintiff to defendant Riddle until September 1972."

To further support its holding that Kaw Valley had reason to know that the defense

知道本票存在抗辩。初审法院认定，1972 年 2 月 24 日银行、受款人和制票人见面，将制票人到当时为止的所有过期本票进行了整合。当时，银行承认受款人具有代表银行作为的授权。在之前的 8 项交易中，受款人有一次接受了设备退货，而银行承认受款人可代表银行接受该退货，且该设备的本票尚未付清的 5000 美元余额也被银行注销了。

existed the court found that when Kaw Valley, Co-Mac and Riddle met on February 24, 1972, to consolidate all of Riddle's past due notes Kaw Valley recognized Co-Mac's authority to act for it. Co-Mac had accepted return of the machinery on one of the eight transactions and Kaw Valley recognized its authority as their agent to do so and cancelled the $5,000.00 balance remaining due on the note held by the bank.

实际知道　关于“有理由知道存在抗辩”的问题，相关判例大体分为 4 类。在第一类判例中，有证据证明，执票人已从票据的转让人或义务人处获得了存在抗辩的信息。在这些判例中，很明显，如果执票人在取得票据之前或之时已得到抗辩的通知，该执票人就不属于正当执票人（B 诉 M 案）。本案不属于这一类，因为没有证据显示，在本票被流通给银行时，受款人或制票人曾将设备未交付的情况告知银行。

The cases dealing with the question of “reason to know a defense exists” seem to fall into four categories. The first includes those cases where it is established the holder had information from the transferor or the obligor which disclosed the existence of a defense. In those cases it is clear if the holder takes an instrument having received prior or contemporaneous notice of a defense he is not a holder in due course. （Billingsley v. Mackay） Our present case does not fall in that category for there is no evidence that Co-Mac or Riddle informed Kaw Valley that the machinery had not been delivered when the note was negotiated.

文件存在异常　在第二类判

The second group of cases are

例中，与本票一起被交付给执票人的文件已显示存在抗辩。例如，本票附有同时签署的担保协议，而该协议显示，本票的债务系用于购买在未来某个时间交付的设备。在这种情况下，可以认为票据文件在某些情况下已经作出披露，即本票可能会存在抗辩，如所购买的设备未被交付（其他举例另参见C诉D案；H诉S案）。本案也不属于这个类型，因为在向银行交付本票和担保协议时，制票人签署了设备接收的确认书，且该文件也一起被交付给银行。

those in which the defense appears in an accompanying document delivered to the holder with the note. For example, when a security agreement is executed concurrently with a note evidencing an indebtedness incurred for machinery to be delivered in the future. In such case the instrument may under certain circumstances disclose a defense to the note, such as nondelivery of the machinery purchased. （See also Commerce Trust Company v. Denson, and HIMC Investment Co. v. Siciliano, for other examples.） Our present case does not fall in this category because Riddle had signed a written delivery acceptance which was handed to Kaw Valley along with the note and security agreement.

其他异常信息　在第三类判例中，票据书面文件的表面信息就已经显示存在抗辩，例如，本票票面显示付款日期已过，或本票显示出涂改或伪造的痕迹，或本票明显不够完整（参见E诉S案；S诉K案；W诉P案）。在本案中，转让给银行的本票从表面上看没有任何不正常之处，且在所有方面都显得完整和适当。

A third group of cases are those in which information appears in the written instrument indicating the existence of a defense, such as when the note on its face shows that the due date has passed or the note bears visible evidence of alteration and forgery or the note is clearly incomplete.（See E.F. Corporation v. Smith； Srochi v. Kamensky； and Winter & Hirsch, Inc. v. Passarelli） In our present case the instrument assigned bore nothing unusual on its face and appeared complete and proper in all respects.

与票据转让人存在特殊关系

在第四类判例中，判例所确立的原则是，如果流通票据的执票人对票据转让人的业务做法有较多了解，或与转让人有较密切的利害关系，以至于有理由将转让人视为执票人的代理人，并将转让人的行为和所知视为执票人的行为和所知，那么上述情况有可能妨碍执票人成为正当执票人。

In the fourth category of cases it has been held that the holder of a negotiable instrument may be prevented from assuming holder in due course status because of knowledge of the business practices of his transferor or when he is so closely aligned with the transferor that transferor may be considered an agent of the holder and the transferee is charged with the actions and knowledge of the transferor.

本州早前的流通票据法包含了类似法典目前条文的规定，而本院曾根据该法拒绝承认一家设备公司正当执票人的身份，因为执票人系从自己一家经销商取得相关本票的转让，且执票人对该经销商的业务做法有所了解，且参与和受益于该经销商的业务（I 诉 W 案）。

Under our former negotiable instruments law containing provisions similar to the U.C.C. this court refused to accord holder in due course status to a machinery company receiving notes from one of its dealers because of its knowledge of the business practices of the dealer and the company's participation and alignment with the dealer who transferred the note.（International Harvester Co. v. Watkins）

在 U 诉 O 案中，新泽西州法院拒绝承认一家融资合伙企业的正当执票人身份，因为合伙企业与转让人关系密切，且合伙企业的成立就是为了给转让人和其他人的商业票据提供融资。对于

In Unico v. Owen, the New Jersey court refused to accord holder in due course status to a financing partnership which was closely connected with the transferor and had been organized to finance the commercial paper obtained by the transferor and others. The

转让人业务政策标准的制订，融资合伙企业有一定发言权。在该情况下，法院认定，必须将合伙企业视为票据交易的参与方，因此，其必须受制于票据受款人/转让人本来无权对抗的抗辩。

financing partnership had a voice in setting the policies and standards to be followed by the transferor. Under such circumstances the court found that the holder must be considered a participant in the transaction and subject to defenses available against the payee-transferor.

在U诉J案中，融资公司以本票面值50%的价格从本票的受款人购买了本票。法院判决，融资公司未能证明其正当执票人身份，因此必须受制于原始交易所包含的抗辩。

In United States Finance Company v. Jones, it was held that a finance company purchasing a note from a payee for fifty percent of its face value did not establish holder in due course status and must be held subject to defenses inherent in the original transaction.

其他州法院在拒绝承认执票人的正当执票人身份时，也遵循了U诉O案的理由。在A诉W案中，执票人向受款人提供了相关格式文件，设定了融资收费，并调查过本票制票人的信用状况，在C诉W案中，执票人完全控制了受款人的资金状况；在J诉A案中，执票人和受款人的所有权和管理权存在关联关系。

Other jurisdictions have followed the rationale of Unico. See American Plan Corp. v. Woods, where the holder supplied forms to the payee, established financing charges and investigated the credit of the maker of the note; Calvert Credit Corporation v. Williams, where the holder exerted total control over payee's financial affairs; and Jones v. Approved Bancredit Corp., where ownership and management of the holder and payee were connected.

本案属于第四类情况 在本案中，在超过10年的期间里，

In the present case Kaw Valley had worked closely with Co-Mac in over 250

银行与受款人在 250 多项融资交易中有密切交往。银行知道，在其中某些交易中，票据在交付时不存在适当对价，因为银行所提供的款项本来将被用于购买机器设备，但相应票据却注明，本票的制票人已经取得了该机器设备的占有。银行知道，受款人向其客户交付的设备有时会延迟 60 天至 90 天。银行一直依赖受款人来取得本票的付款，并且在付款出现延迟时，也是去联系受款人。在某些交易中，包括在本案的交易中，对于本票付款凭单账册，其应由本票义务人用于本票付款，但实际未这样使用。在本案中，银行未将自己是本票执票人的情况通知制票人，而是将本票付款凭单账册交给了受款人，相当于将受款人视为本票义务人，或授权受款人担任该交易的收款代理人。在 1971 年 5 月 11 日至 1972 年 2 月 25 日，银行收到了每月的付款并作出了贷记，但知道该付款来自受款人，而不是来自制票人。

在对制票人的欠款进行整合

financing transactions over a period of ten years. It knew that some of these transactions were not for valuable consideration at the time the paper was delivered since the bank's money was to be used in purchasing the machinery or equipment represented in the instruments as already in possession of the maker of the note. Kaw Valley had been advised that delivery to Co-Mac's customers was sometimes delayed from 60 to 90 days. Kaw Valley continued to rely on Co-Mac to assure payment of the obligations and contacted it to collect delinquent payments. Some of these transactions, including the one in question, involved the use of coupon books to be used by the debtor in making payment on the notes. In the present case Kaw Valley did not notify Riddle that it was the holder of the note. It delivered Riddle's coupon book to Co-Mac as if it were the obligor or was authorized as its collection agent for this transaction. Throughout the period from May 11, 1971, to February 25, 1972, Kaw Valley received and credited the monthly payments knowing that payments were being made by Co-Mac and not by Riddle.

Then when Riddle's loans were

时，银行出于疏忽或故意，未将1971年5月11日的交易列在制票人的债务之中。并且，受款人与银行保持密切关系，并在银行知情和同意的情况下，作为银行的代理人，就银行所持有的本票代为进行收款。

结论 法典第3.307条（3）款规定："如果表明存在抗辩，主张正当执票人权利的人就应承担举证责任，证明其自己或由其所代表的主张人，在所有方面都符合正当执票人的身份。"在本案中，基于银行所知道和所参与的事实和活动，我们不能说银行当时没有理由知道存在抗辩。这是应由事实审的审理人来裁定的事实问题。只要该审理人的裁定可以得到大量事实证据的支持，我们就必须维持该裁定。我们判定，1971年5月11日的本票必须受制于缺乏对价的确凿抗辩。因此，本案制票人对该本票的责任被解除。维持初审法院的原判。

consolidated, the May 11, 1971 transaction was not included by Kaw Valley, either by oversight or by intention, as an obligation of Riddle. Co-Mac occupied a close relationship with Kaw Valley and with its knowledge and consent acted as its agent in collecting payments on notes held by Kaw Valley.

K.S.A. 3-307（3） provides："After it is shown that a defense exists a person claiming the rights of a holder in due course has the burden of establishing that he or some person under whom he claims is in all respects a holder in due course." We cannot say under the facts and circumstances known and participated in by Kaw Valley in this transaction it did not at the time in question have reason to know that the defense existed. This was a question of fact to be determined by the trier of fact which if supported by substantial competent evidence must stand. Our holding that the May 11, 1971 note was subject to the proven defense of failure of consideration cancels the obligation of Riddle on the note. The judgment is affirmed.

案例22　如何判断执票人是否以善意作为?

Maine Family Federal Credit Union v. Sun Life Assurance Co. of Canada

缅因家庭联邦信贷联盟诉加拿大阳光人寿保险公司案

缅因州最高法院1999年；727 A.2d 335

简　介

本案的基本情况是，一位父亲（Elden Guerrette）有3名子女，即大儿子（Daniel）、小儿子（Joel）和女儿（Claire）。父亲生前购买了人寿保险。在父亲去世之后，保险公司（Sun Life）向3名子女（保险单的受益人）出具了3张保险理赔支票。保险公司的一名职员（Steven Hall，诈骗人甲）伙同另一名人员（Paul Richard，诈骗人乙）以欺诈方式，引诱3名子女将3张支票背书给诈骗人乙，因为2名诈骗人谎称可以帮助3名子女将该理赔款投入一家投资公司（HER）获取高收益。诈骗人乙在取得已背书的支票后，将其存入自己持有账户的信贷公司（Credit Union）。信贷公司向诈骗人乙提供了立即可用的贷记，而没有等待从付款银行（支票的受票人银行）收到支票的款项。诈骗人甲和乙在取到款项后立即挪作他用，且不知去向。

3名子女在将支票背书给诈骗人乙之后不久，就意识到可能受到了诈骗。他们随即通知保险公司停付支票，而保险公司随即通知支票的受票人银行（Chase Manhattan）停付支票。但是，保险公司和受票人银行此时都不知道支票实际在谁手中。很快，信贷公司将3张支票提示给受票人银行，而银行则根据保险公司的停付命令拒付了支票。由于受票人银行在承兑支票之前不对支票承担票据责任，因此信贷公司不能追究银行的责任，只能追究保险公司的出票人责任，以及3名子女的背书人责任。信贷公司随后通过各种方法从诈骗人乙追回大部分款项，但最终还有4万多美元无法追回。本案的争议问题是，信贷公司是否有权要求保险公司或3名子女支付该剩余数额？

3名子女是受到2名诈骗人的欺诈才对支票作出背书的，因此持有一定抗辩。但是，此种抗辩不能对抗正当执票人。因此，信贷公司是否有权要求3名子女付款，取决于信贷公司是否属于正当执票人。这是本案讨论的主要问题。缅因州最高法院在讨论这个问题时，说明了新版法典第3篇和旧版第3篇对“善意”这个概念的不同定义。在旧版中，只要求执票人具有主观善意；而在新版中，则要求同时具有主观善意和客观善意。法院的最终结论是，信贷公司立即向诈骗人乙支付资金的做法，未能满足善意的客观标准，因此属于未以善意作为，并因此不属于正当执票人。因此，3名子女不必对支票承担责任。

在本案中，保险公司作为支票的出票人，自己并不持有任何可以对抗信贷公司的抗辩。但是，保险公司试图以3名子女提出的欺诈作为自己的抗辩理由。根据法典第3.305条（3）款的规定，只有在涉及票据所有权或占有权的票据索赔时（第3.306条），一个当事方才可以引用另一个当事方的抗辩，而在本案中，3名子女并没有提出票据索赔。他们提出的欺诈问题，不是保险公司可以引用的抗辩。因此法院判决，保险公司不持有可以对抗信贷公司的抗辩，因而必须承担支票的付款责任。此时，虽然信贷公司不属于正当执票人，但这不妨碍其从保险公司取得付款，因为正当执票人与普通执票人的区别在于对抗抗辩的能力，但本案的保险公司没有任何可以使用的抗辩。

判　决

本案问题和基本结论　在本上诉中，我们需要解释新修订的缅因州法典流通票据篇所定义的“正当执票人”概念。在初审中，陪审团裁定信贷公司不属于正当执票人，因此初审法院作出相应判决。我们认为，根据修订后的法典，初审法院的该判决不存在错误。但我们认定，保险公司作为支票的出票人，无权通过引用第三方因受到欺诈而持有的抗辩，来免除自己的出票人责任。因此，对于初审法院有关此问题的判决，我们推翻原判中保险公司胜诉而信贷公司败诉的判决。

We are called upon here to address the concept of “holder in due course” as defined by recent amendments to the negotiable instruments provisions of the Maine Uniform Commercial Code. We conclude that, pursuant to those amendments, the Superior Court did not err when it entered a judgment based on the jury’s finding that the Maine Family Federal Credit Union was not a holder in due course. Because we find, however, that Sun Life Assurance Company was not entitled to raise a third party’s defense of fraud to its liability as drawer of the instruments, we vacate that portion of the judgment entered in favor of Sun Life and against the Credit Union.

陪审团的裁定　在初审中，提交给陪审团的唯一问题是，信贷公司就诈骗人乙存入的支票向其支付价值时，是否以“善意”作为，并因此属于正当执票人？陪审团裁定，信贷公司未以善意作为，因此不属于正当执票人。初审法院据此判决保险公司和3

At trial, the only issue presented to the jury was whether the Credit Union had acted in “good faith” when it gave value for the checks, thus entitling it to holder in due course status. The jury found that the Credit Union had not acted in good faith and therefore was not a holder in due course. Therefore, the Superior Court entered judgment in favor of

名子女胜诉，而信贷公司败诉。信贷公司提出上诉。

核心争议 本案的核心争议是，由于2名诈骗人看来已无力承担责任，因此，对于尚未追回的42,366.56美元的损失，应该如何在其余当事方之间分配？如同其他49个州一样，缅因州也采纳了法典。法典有关“流通票据”的第3篇和有关“银行存款和收款”的第4篇，适用于本案当事方之间的争议。

执票人的权利 根据法典第4篇，信贷公司作为存款银行，是票据的“执票人”[第4.205条（1）款]，并因此属于法典第3篇所说的“有权强制履行”票据的人[第3.301条（1）款]。对于有权强制履行票据的执票人来说，如果其出示了票据，且票据上包含了票据责任人的有效签名，执票人即有权获得票据付款，除非票据的责任人可以证明存在抗辩或扣减权[第3.308条（2）款]，或存在对票据本身占有权

Sun Life, Daniel, Joel, and Claire, and against the Credit Union. Credit Union filed this appeal.

At the heart of the controversy in this case is the allocation of responsibility for the loss of the unpaid $42,366.56, given the fact that Paul Richard and Steven Hall, the real wrongdoers, appear to be unable to pay. Maine, like the other forty-nine states, has adopted the Uniform Commercial Code. Under the Maine U.C.C., Articles 3 and 4 deal with “Negotiable Instruments” and “Bank Deposits and Collections”. It is these statutes that govern the parties’ dispute.

Pursuant to Article 4 of the Maine U.C.C., the Credit Union, as a depositary bank, is a “holder” of the instruments, see M.R.S.A. § 4-205（1）, making it a “person entitled to enforce” the instrument under Article 3. See M.R.S.A. § 3-301（1）. Upon producing an instrument containing the valid signature of a party liable on the instrument, a person entitled to enforce the instrument is entitled to payment, unless the party liable proves a defense or claim in recoupment, see M.R.S.A. § 3-308（2）, or a possessory claim to the instrument itself. See M.R.S.A.

的索赔主张（第 3.306 条）。

背书人的责任　本案支票的背面载有 3 名子女的签名，因此他们是支票的"背书人"[第 3.204 条（1）款和（2）款]。作为背书人，他们对每张被拒付的支票，均必须"根据票据背书时的条款"[第 3.415 条（1）(a）款]，承担票据应付数额的付款责任。此项义务的受益人是"有权强制履行票据的人，或根据本条规定支付了票据的后手背书人"[第 3.415 条（1）（a）款]。

出票人的责任　对于每张被拒付的支票，保险公司作为支票的出票人，均有义务"根据票据出立时的条款"支付该支票[第 3.414 条（2）（a）款]。同样，此项义务的受益人是有权强制履行票据的人，或根据第 3.415 条支付了票据的背书人[第 3.414 条（2）款]。受票人银行作为支票的受票人，没有义务接受支票和付款（第 3.408 条），因此未被列为本诉讼的当事方。

可以对抗非正当执票人的抗辩　除非信贷公司属于正当执票

§ 3-306.

Because their signatures appear on the backs of the checks, Daniel, Joel, and Claire are "indorsers" of the checks. See M.R.S.A. § 3-204 (1), (2). As indorsers, they are obligated to pay the amounts due on each dishonored instrument "[a]ccording to the terms of [each] instrument at the time it was indorsed". M.R.S.A. § 3-415(1)(a). This obligation is owed "to a person entitled to enforce the instrument or to a subsequent indorser who paid the instrument under this section". Id.

As drawer of the checks, Sun Life is obligated to pay each dishonored instrument "[a]ccording to its terms at the time it was issued". M.R.S.A. § 3-414 (2) (a). Again, this obligation is owed to a person entitled to enforce the instrument or to an indorser who paid the draft under section 3-415. See M.R.S.A. § 3-414 (2). Chase Manhattan, as drawee of these checks, was not obligated to accept them for payment, see M.R.S.A. § 3-408, and therefore has not been made a party to this action.

Unless the Credit Union is a holder in due course, its right to enforce the obligations

人，否则其强制支票出票人和背书人履行付款义务的权利，就要受制于各种抗辩，包括义务人的下列抗辩：有权强制履行票据的人在强制履行简式合同项下之付款义务时，该义务人本可引用的抗辩［第3.305条（1）（b）款］。此外，信贷公司的强制履行权还受制于扣减权［第3.305条（1）（c）款］或对票据本身的索赔权（第3.306条）。但信贷公司如能证明自己为"正当执票人"，则将只受制于第3.305条（1）（a）款所列的为数不多的抗辩［第3.305条（2）款］，而本案不存在该抗辩。信贷公司为此辩称，作为法律问题，其享有正当执票人身份，有权针对3名子女和保险公司强制履行相关支票。

of the drawer and indorsers of the instruments is subject to a variety of defenses, including all those defenses available "if the person entitled to enforce the instrument [s] were enforcing a right to payment under a simple contract". See M.R.S.A. § 3-305 (1) (b). In addition, its right to enforce is subject to any claims in recoupment, see M.R.S.A. § 3-305 (1) (c), or claims to the instruments themselves. See M.R.S.A. § 3-306. If, however, the Credit Union establishes that it is a "holder in due course", it is subject to only those few defenses listed in section 3-305 (1) (a). See M.R.S.A. § 3-305 (2). None of those specific defenses is applicable here. Thus, the Credit Union argues that because it is entitled as a matter of law to holder in due course status, it is entitled to enforce the instruments against the Guerrettes and Sun Life.

正当执票人的标准　执票人如果在取得票据时，以善意作为，支付了价值，且未得到任何票据索赔或抗辩的通知，即属于正当执票人［第3.302条（1）款］。对票据可能承担责任的人一旦提出法典承认的任何抗辩，执票人

A holder in due course is a holder who takes an instrument in good faith, for value, and without notice of any claims or defenses. See M.R.S.A. § 3-302 (1). Once the persons who may be liable on the instruments have raised a recognized defense to that liability, the burden is on the holder to prove

就要承担举证责任，通过提供优势证据来证明自己是正当执票人（参见 N 诉 G 案）。如果执票人未能完成举证，则票据的责任人只要能证明存在抗辩、扣减权或票据索赔，就可以不再对票据承担责任［第 3.305 条（1）（b）款；第 3.308 条（2）款］。

by a preponderance of the evidence that it is a holder in due course. See New Bedford Inst. for Sav. v. Gildroy. If it fails in that proof, the persons otherwise liable on the instruments may avoid liability if they prove a defense, claim in recoupment, or possessory claim to the instrument. See M.R.S.A. § § 3-305（1）（b）, 3-308（2）.

事实问题与法律问题　执票人是否属于正当执票人，通常是事实问题，但是，“如果相关事实不存争议且已得到确认，法院可将正当执票人身份作为法律问题来确定”（参见 T 诉 D 案）。在本案中，初审法院拒绝将正当执票人的问题作为法律问题自行确定，而是将该问题提交给陪审团。陪审团裁定，信贷公司不是正当执票人。这个裁定隐含的结论是，信贷公司在取得票据时，未以善意作为。

The issue of whether a party is a holder in due course is usually one of fact, although “where the facts are undisputed and conclusive, ［a court］ can determine holder in due course status as a matter of law”. See Triffin v. Dillabough. In this case, the Superior Court declined to decide the holder in due course issue as a matter of law, and submitted the question to the jury. The jury found that the Credit Union was not a holder in due course, implicitly because the Credit Union did not act in good faith.

作为法律问题审阅　信贷公司辩称，初审法院存在判决错误，因为其未作为法律问题而认定信贷公司属于正当执票人。L 诉 C 案的判决说：“下级法院驳回无审判决动议后，上诉法院必须将

The Credit Union argues that the court erred in failing to find, as a matter of law, that it was a holder in due course. “We review the denial of a motion for judgment as a matter of law to determine if any reasonable view of the evidence and those inferences

其作为法律问题审阅。在对案件证据及其合理推断进行合理审阅后，我们必须判断陪审团的裁定是否有证据支持”。因此，在本上诉中，我们的问题是，现有证据以及从中合理引申的推断，是否有任何可能会支持陪审团的裁定，即信贷公司未以善意作为，因此不是正当执票人？反过来说，我们要回答的问题是，根据现有证据，是否必须认定信贷公司是正当执票人？只要陪审团的裁定存在任何合理基础，我们就必须维持初审判决。

that are justifiably drawn from that evidence supports the jury verdict.” Larochelle v. Cyr. The question before us, therefore, is whether any reasonable view of the evidence, along with any justifiable inferences therefrom, can possibly support the jury's conclusion that the Credit Union did not act in good faith and therefore was not a holder in due course. Alternatively stated, the question is whether the evidence compelled a finding that the Credit Union was a holder in due course. If there is any rational basis for the jury's verdict, we must affirm the judgment.

善意的新旧定义 因此，我们需要看一下法典第3篇对“善意”的定义。1990年，统一州法全国委员会建议对法典进行重大修改。1993年，作为对该建议的响应，缅因州的立法机构采纳了新版法典第3篇，而该篇对“善意”有新的定义。旧版第3篇对“善意”的定义只要求执票人证明其行为方式属于“事实上的诚实”。而在新的定义中，“善意”是指事实上的诚实，以及对公平交易之合理商业准则的遵守

We therefore turn to the definition of “good faith” contained in Article 3 of the Maine U.C.C. In 1990, the National Conference of Commissioners on Uniform State Law recommended substantial changes in the U.C.C. The Maine Legislature responded to those recommendations in 1993 by enacting a new version of Article 3, which contains a new definition of “good faith”. While the previous version of the good faith definition only required holder to prove that it acted with “honesty in fact”, the new definition provides: “Good faith”

［第 3.103 条（1）（d）款］。由于在表述中使用连词将这两个标准联系在一起，因此，执票人现在必须同时满足“善意”的主观标准和客观标准。

means honesty in fact and the observance of reasonable commercial standards of fair dealing. M.R.S.A. § 3-103（1）（d）. Because the tests are presented in the conjunctive, a holder must now satisfy both a subjective and an objective test of “good faith”.

之前只要求主观善意　1993 年在缅因州立法机构采纳新版法典第 3 篇之前，在确定正当执票人时，仅以善意的主观标准为准。该标准通常称为“有心无脑”标准［引用文章；另参见 S 诉 C 案（其中说明，即使一个人按客观标准看是愚蠢的，只要其主观上是心地纯洁的，法典就会保护该人）］。该标准仅仅规定，只要执票人在取得票据时具有“事实上的诚实”，执票人就可以成为正当执票人。

Prior to the changes adopted by the Legislature in 1993, the holder in due course doctrine turned on a subjective standard of good faith and was often referred to as the “pure heart and empty head” standard. See Sinclair, Codification of Negotiable Instruments Law：A Tale of Reiterated Anachronism； see also Seinfeld v. Commercial Bank & Trust Co.（noting that the U.C.C. seem［s］ to protect the objectively stupid so long as he is subjectively pure at heart）. That standard merely required a holder to take an instrument with “honesty in fact” to become a holder in due course.

法院在对上述文字进行解释时通常认为，只要作为执票人的银行在取得票据时不了解其中的瑕疵、抗辩或停付命令，银行就属于正当执票人，即使银行未能进行相关调查（参见 U 诉 R 案；

Courts interpreting this language have routinely declared banks to be holders in due course, notwithstanding the failures of these banks to investigate, when they took the instruments with no knowledge of any defects, defenses, or stop payment orders. See, e.g.,

B诉A案)。一般的理解是，这个原则是为了促进票据(特别是支票)在商业活动中的流通性。

UAW-CIO Local #31 Credit Union v. Royal Ins. Co.; Bank of New York v. Asati, Inc. This approach has been understood to promote the negotiability of instruments, particularly checks, in the stream of commerce.

主观标准的理由 在说明为什么相反原则不可行时，某法院直白地说，“被告所主张的方式，会使银行系统的运作陷入停顿。如果支票的出票人向受票人发出停付命令，但参与收款的付款银行并不知道该命令，该命令对于付款银行就不具有任何法律上的阻止力；特别是，不能将收款银行的地位降格至票据普通受让人的地位，或不可流通票据执票人的地位，或流通票据普通执票人的地位”(M诉D案)。

Rejecting a contrary approach, one court put it bluntly: “The requirement urged by defendant would bring the banking system to a grinding halt. A stop payment order issued by the drawer to the drawee which is unknown to the paying-collecting bank cannot fasten upon the paying bank any legal disability; particularly it cannot reduce the status of the collecting bank to a mere assignee of the instrument or a holder of a non-negotiable instrument, or a mere holder of a negotiable instrument.” Mellon Bank, N.A. v. Donegal Mutual Ins. Co.

虽然经常有人敦促法院在“事实上的诚实”这个概念中融入具有客观合理标准的因素，但大多数法院拒绝这样做。他们拒绝的主要理由是：“支票是商业活动中资金支付的主要方式。支票的出票人、受款人和背书人很自然地期待支票能够迅速流通和收款。如果采纳客观标准，商业

Although courts were often urged to engraft an objective reasonableness standard onto the concept of “honesty in fact”, most refused to do so. Their refusals recognized that: “[T]he check is the major method for transfer of funds in commercial practice. The drawer, payee, and endorsers of a check naturally expect it will be rapidly negotiated and collected. The wheels of commerce would

的轮子就会陷入停顿。”（B 诉 S 案）

grind to a halt ［if an objective standard were adopted］.” Bowling Green, Inc. v. State St. Bank & Trust.

此外，在采用纯粹的主观标准时，对于客户新存入银行的支票，不要求银行必须等待支票资金实际进入客户账户后，才允许客户使用该资金。“在资金尚未收进账户前，即使银行已允许客户使用该资金，也不能否定银行的善意。”（B 诉 A 案；V 诉 J 案；F 诉 C 案；M 诉 D 案；C 诉 F 案；C 诉 F 案）

Moreover, under the purely subjective standard, a bank was not expected to require the presence of offsetting collected funds in the customers' account in order to give value on newly deposited checks: “A bank's permitting its customers to draw against uncollected funds does not negate its good faith.” Asati, Inc.; Vail Nat'l Bank v. J. Wheeler Constr. Corp.; Flagship Bank of Orlando v. Central Florida Coach Lines, Inc.; Mellon Bank; Central Bank & Trust Co. v. First Northwest Bank; Citizens Nat'l Bank of Englewood v. Fort Lee Sav. & Loan Ass'n.

信贷公司符合善意的主观标准　如果将“事实上的诚实”这个标准应用于本案信贷公司，就可以看出该原则的作用。毫无争议的是，信贷公司不知道诈骗人乙以欺诈方式取得保险公司出具的支票。信贷公司也不知道保险公司已就其出具的支票发出了停付命令。信贷公司迅速为支票支付了价值，而并不知道支票将会

Application of the “honesty in fact” standard to the Credit Union's conduct here demonstrates these principles at work. It is undisputed that the Credit Union had no knowledge that Richard obtained the Sun Life checks by fraud. Nor was the Credit Union aware that a stop payment order had been placed on the Sun Life checks. The Credit Union expeditiously gave value on the checks, having no knowledge that they would be

被拒付。从本质上说，信贷公司的做法，就是多年来一直允许银行采纳的做法，而银行不会因此而失去正当执票人的身份。信贷公司的做法属于事实上的诚实。

dishonored. In essence the Credit Union acted as banks have, for years, been allowed to act without risk to holder in due course status. The Credit Union acted with honesty in fact.

因此，假设本案争议在缅因州立法机构为“善意”这个概念增加客观标准之前判决，那么几乎没有疑问，信贷公司本来会被认定属于正当执票人。信贷公司在取得票据时，对于可能存在的拒付、瑕疵、欺诈或非法情况，都没有得到通知，因此，信贷公司可以一方面立即为票据支付价值，另一方面确知自己享有正当执票人身份（参见M诉D案；I诉L案；N诉G案；T诉D案）。但是，目前对正当执票人的要求，已经不仅是主观上的善意。

Thus, had the matter at bar been decided before the Legislature's addition of the objective component of “good faith”, there can be little question that the Credit Union would have been determined to have been a holder in due course. Because it took the instruments without notice of any possible dishonor, defect, fraud, or illegality, it could have given value immediately and yet have been assured of holder in due course status. See Mellon Bank; Industrial Nat’l Bank of Rhode Island v. Leo’s Used Car Exchange, Inc.; New Bedford Inst.; Triffin. Today, however, something more than mere subjective good faith is required of a holder in due course.

善意的客观标准 我们现在分析“善意”这个概念中的客观因素。根据法典新增加的文字，执票人必须证明其行为符合“公平交易的合理商业准则”。这标志“正当执票人”定义的重大变

We turn then to the objective prong of the good faith analysis. The addition of the language requiring the holder to prove conduct meeting “reasonable commercial standards of fair dealing” signals a significant change in the definition of a holder

化。对于如何解释这项新出现的客观要求，法院还没有很多时间积累相关法律原则，但毫无疑问，如果执票人仅凭善良之心而不动脑筋，就不可能再继续获得正当执票人的地位。现在，执票人的善良之心必须伴随必要的推理分析，以确保执票人的行为符合公平交易的合理商业准则。

in due course. While there has been little time for the development of a body of law interpreting this new objective requirement, there can be no mistaking the fact that a holder may no longer act with a pure heart and an empty head and still obtain holder in due course status. The pure heart of the holder must now be accompanied by reasoning that assures conduct comporting with reasonable commercial standards of fair dealing.

在“善意”的定义中加入客观因素，与其说是正当执票人定义演变中的新概念，不如说是在一定程度上回归到早期的原则［引用著作（其中讨论了英国法中“善意”这个概念的客观标准，而该标准首次被应用在 G 诉 C 案中）］。自从首次完成了法典的制定后，在有关正当执票人的讨论中，善意的客观因素一直就是其中一个问题［引用前述著作（其中说明，“有关善意的构成因素，从古至今一直就是争议问题”）］。

The addition of the objective element represents not so much a new concept in the doctrinal development of holder in due course status, but rather a return, in part, to an earlier approach to the doctrine. See James J. White & Robert S. Summers, Uniform Commercial Code（discussing the objective test of good faith in England, first applied by the King's Bench in Gill v. Cubitt）. The concept of an objective component of good faith has been part of the discussion regarding the holder in due course doctrine since the first enactment of the U.C.C. See id.（noting that “[t] he good faith requirement has been the source of a continuing and ancient dispute”）.

法典早期起草者对于包含客观因素的必要性和明智性一

The early drafters debated the need and wisdom of including such an objective

直进行辩论,但最终决定在善意的定义中不包含这个因素,因为其有可能冻结商业活动[引用前述文章(其中特别说明了银行界对善意定义中加入客观因素的反对)]。因此,善意定义中“新”加入的因素,即要求执票人的作为必须符合公平交易的合理商业准则,实际上是法典1962年版制定时,法典起草者曾考虑采纳但最终放弃了的“通情达理的人”这个概念的翻版,而仅仅是范围有所缩小。

component and ultimately determined not to include it in the definition of good faith because of its potential for freezing commercial practices. See Sinclair (noting, in particular, the objection by the banking industry to the addition of an objective good faith component). The “new” element of good faith requiring the holder to act according to reasonable commercial standards of fair dealing is actually a more narrow version of the “reasonable person” standard considered and rejected by the drafters of the 1962 Code.

客观标准不够清晰 但是,这个新的客观标准,不能算是条文清晰的典范。在“善意”的客观因素中使用“合理”这个措辞,虽然有可能触发“疏忽”的概念,但法典的起草者还是试图将“公平”交易的概念与“谨慎”交易的概念相区别。虽然“公平交易”是含义广泛的词,因此必须根据上下文予以定义,但很明显,这个词所关心的是行为的公平性,而不是采取行为时的谨慎性。在从事一项交易时,未能做到正常谨慎与未能公平地进行交易,是

The new objective standard, however, is not a model of drafting clarity. Although use of the word “reasonable” in the objective portion of the good faith test may evoke concepts of negligence, the drafters attempted to distinguish the concept of “fair” dealing from concepts of “careful” dealing. Although fair dealing is a broad term that must be defined in context, it is clear that it is concerned with the fairness of conduct rather than the care with which an act is performed. Failure to exercise ordinary care in conducting a transaction is an entirely different concept than failure to deal fairly in conducting the

两个完全不同的概念（第 3.103 条正式评论 4）。

transaction. U.C.C. § 3-103 cmt. 4.

不幸的是，虽然法典修订后的正式评论轻松地将“公平交易”和“谨慎交易”加以区分，但这种轻松只是假象，因为要将这些概念应用到任何具体案件的事实，或向陪审团解释这些概念，实际上非常困难。由于法典未定义“公平交易”，这种困难进一步加剧。在使用“公平”这个词时，最明显的问题是：到底对谁公平？

Unfortunately, the ease with which the distinction between “fair dealing” and “careful dealing” was set forth in the comments to the U.C.C. revisions belies the difficulty in applying these concepts to the facts of any particular case, or in conveying them to a jury. The difficulty is exacerbated by the lack of definition of the term “fair dealing” in the U.C.C. The most obvious question arising from the use of the term “fair” is： fairness to whom?

商业准则本身必须合理　对于流通票据交易，传统上一直要由法典对不同身份进行详细控制和定义。这恰恰是因为，任何一项交易都可能涉及非常多的当事方。如果要求执票人的行为对所有当事方都“公平”，执票人就必须对当事方的权利和权益进行平衡，而这几乎是不可能完成的任务。因此，法典起草者将公平交易的要求，局限于相关交易之商业背景下的合理行为。也就是说，基于商业准则，执票人的行为必须公平，而该商业准则本身

Transactions involving negotiable instruments have traditionally required the detailed level of control and definition of roles set out in the U.C.C. precisely because there are so many parties who may be involved in a single transaction. If a holder is required to act “fairly”, regarding all parties, it must engage in an almost impossible balancing of rights and interests. Accordingly, the drafters limited the requirement of fair dealing to conduct that is reasonable in the commercial context of the transaction at issue. In other words, the holder must act in a way that is fair according to commercial standards that are

也必须合理。

因此，事实审理人首先必须确定，执票人的行为是否符合适用于该交易的行业准则或“商业”准则，其次还必须确定，该准则是否属于旨在形成公平交易的合理准则。而每一项认定，都必须考虑当事交易的具体条件后作出。如果事实审理人对每一个问题的结论都是肯定的，执票人就被认定系以善意作为，即使在该交易中，最终的结果看上去并不合理。因此，只要执票人的行为符合公平交易的合理商业准则，则即使其存在疏忽，其仍有可能获得正当执票人的身份；反之，即使执票人的行为符合商业准则，但如果这些准则不能合理地导致公平交易的结果，执票人仍然会失去正当执票人的身份。

本案是否满足善意标准 因此，陪审团在本案中的任务是裁定，信贷公司在尚未收到票据资金时就向客户支付价值的行为，是否遵守了银行业相关商业准则；并且，如果遵守了此种准则，

themselves reasonable.

The factfinder must therefore determine, first, whether the conduct of the holder comported with industry or “commercial” standards applicable to the transaction and, second, whether those standards were reasonable standards intended to result in fair dealing. Each of those determinations must be made in the context of the specific transaction at hand. If the factfinder’s conclusion on each point is “yes”, the holder will be determined to have acted in good faith even if, in the individual transaction at issue, the result appears unreasonable. Thus a holder may be accorded holder in due course status where it acts pursuant to those reasonable commercial standards of fair dealing-even if it is negligent-but may lose that status, even where it complies with commercial standards, if those standards are not reasonably related to achieving fair dealing.

Therefore the jury’s task here was to decide whether the Credit Union observed the banking industries’ commercial standards relating to the giving of value on uncollected funds, and, if so, whether those standards are reasonably designed to result in fair dealing.

那么，该准则是否属于公平交易的合理准则。

信贷公司的理由 信贷公司为了证明自己的行为符合客观化的善意标准而提供了下列证据：信贷公司的内部政策是，任何客户存入支票后，公司将立即向客户提供临时贷记。在某些情况下，例如，支票数额很大，或受票人系外州银行，则公司政策允许在最长9天的期限内，对尚未收到的资金暂时冻结。信贷公司这方面的整体书面政策，每年都要由全国信贷公司管理局进行审阅，且每次都得到该机构的批准。该管理局属于联邦政府机构，专门负责管理联邦层级的信贷公司（引用联邦法典）。此外，信贷公司的上述政策也符合相关的银行法规，包括支票结算的法规（引用联邦条例）。

The evidence produced by the Credit Union in support of its position that it acted in accordance with objective good faith included the following: The Credit Union's internal policy was to make provisional credit available immediately upon the deposit of a check by one of its members. In certain circumstances-where the check was for a large amount and where it was drawn on an out-of-state bank-its policy allowed for a hold to be placed on the uncollected funds for up to nine days. The Credit Union's general written policy on this issue was reviewed annually-and had always been approved--by the National Credit Union Administration, the federal agency charged with the duty of regulating federal credit unions. See U.S.C.A. In addition, the policy complied with applicable banking laws, including Regulation CC. See C.F.R.

信贷公司还提供证据证明，无论是联邦有关支票结算的法规，还是信贷公司的内部政策，均不要求在提供临时贷记前，先留持支票或先调查支票的来源情况。信贷公司称，本案支票虽然

The Credit Union also presented evidence that neither Regulation CC nor the Credit Union's internal policy required it to hold the checks or to investigate the genesis of checks before extending provisional credit. It asserted that it acted exactly as its policy and

数额较大,且受票人系外州银行,但其立即提供临时贷记的行为,完全符合其内部政策和法律。最后,信贷公司还提供了专家证词,证明缅因州的大多数信贷公司都遵循类似政策。

保险公司和3名子女的主张 保险公司和3名子女则要求陪审团裁定,信贷公司未以善意作为。为此,保险公司和3名子女辩称,对于总额超过12万美元且受票人系外州银行的支票,信贷公司允许客户取得临时贷记的行为,不符合公平交易的合理商业准则,因为其没有:(1)作出进一步的调查,以保证受票人银行将会支付所存入的该支票;或(2)留持该支票,直至不正常之处自行浮现。

信贷公司的做法 相关联邦法规对本案信贷公司持有支票的最长期限设定了限制。虽然法律所规定的最长持有期限是陪审团需要考虑的证据,但是该规定本身不能证明公平交易的合理商业准则。事实审理人必须对交易

the law allowed when it immediately extended provisional credit on these checks, despite the fact that they were drawn for relatively large amounts on an out-of-state bank. Finally, the Credit Union presented expert testimony that most credit unions in Maine follow similar policies.

In urging the jury to find that the Credit Union had not acted in good faith, Sun Life and the Guerrettes argued that the Credit Union's conduct did not comport with reasonable commercial standards of fair dealing when it allowed its member access to provisional credit on checks totalling over $120,000 drawn on an out-of-state bank without either: (1) further investigation to assure that the deposited checks would be paid by the bank upon which they were drawn, or (2) holding the instruments to allow any irregularities to come to light.

The applicable federal regulations provide the outside limit on the Credit Union's ability to hold the checks. Although the limit on allowable holds established by law is evidence to be considered by the jury, it does not itself establish reasonable commercial standard of fair dealing. The factfinder

的所有相关情况进行考虑，而支票金额和付款银行的地理位置属于相关事实。因此，为了遵守公平交易的合理商业准则，银行在决定是否对账户内资金暂时留持时，需要考虑此种因素。

must consider all of the facts relevant to the transaction. The amount of the checks and the location of the payor bank, however, are relevant facts that a bank, observing reasonable commercial standards of fair dealing, takes into account when deciding whether to place such a hold on the account.

根据联邦政府有关支票结算的条例，如果存入账户的支票金额大于 5000 美元，或支票的付款银行不是本地银行，则任何信贷公司均有权对临时贷记设定比其他情况下更长的留持时间（引用联邦法规）。陪审团有权考虑上述因素。因此，根据善意的客观标准，支票金额和付款银行的地理位置，都是陪审团在确定存款银行是否系正当执票人时可以考虑的因素。

The jury was entitled to consider that, under Regulation CC, when a check in an amount greater than $5,000 is deposited, or when a check is payable by a nonlocal bank, a credit union is permitted to withhold provisional credit for longer periods of time than it is allowed in other circumstances. See C.F.R. Therefore, the size of the check and the location of the payor bank are, under the objective standard of good faith, factors which a jury may also consider when deciding whether a depositary bank is a holder in due course.

本案信贷公司的总经理承认，信贷公司的政策存在内在风险；并且，支票的付款银行通常只需要几天时间即可为支票付款，而自己公司对相关账户资金多留持几天，并非难以做到的事情。他承认本案支票的金额较大，

The Credit Union's President admitted the risks inherent in the Credit Union's policy and admitted that it would not have been difficult to place a hold on these funds for the few days that it would normally take for the payor bank to pay the checks. He conceded that the amount of the checks were relatively

且受票人系外州银行，因此该情况“也许本来会”使信贷公司有理由暂时对该账户进行留持。他还就自己的理解作证说，有些商业银行的政策是，对于外地支票，银行会在提供临时贷记前留持3个营业日。此外，本案信贷公司没有明确的书面政策，告知其员工对于尚未收到的资金如何留持。实际情况是，对于任何账户是否应临时留持，须由接受支票存入的柜台员工基于自己的“适宜感”来处理。毫无争议的是，根据本案信贷公司自己的政策，在支票金额超过5000美元时，员工有权自行决定是否留持，而本案3张支票的金额已远超该数额。

large, that they were drawn on an out-of-state bank, and that these circumstances “could have” presented the Credit Union with cause to place a hold on the account. He also testified to his understanding that some commercial banks followed a policy of holding nonlocal checks for three business days before giving provisional credit. Moreover, the Credit Union had no written policy explicitly guiding its staff regarding the placing of a hold on uncollected funds. Rather, the decision on whether to place a temporary hold on an account was left to the “comfort level” of the teller accepting the deposit. There was no dispute that the amount of the three checks far exceeded the $5,000 threshold for a discretionary hold established by the Credit Union’s own policy.

陪审团可能得出的结论 基于上述事实，陪审团本来完全有可能合理得出结论说，根据公平交易的合理商业准则，对于尚未收到的资金，应当留持一段合理时间；并且，根据本案情况，信贷公司为支票支付价值时所依据的商业准则，从结构上不能合理地实现公平交易的效果。

On these facts the jury could rationally have concluded that the reasonable commercial standard of fair dealing would require the placing of a hold on the uncollected funds for a reasonable period of time and that, in giving value under these circumstances, the Credit Union did not act according to commercial standards that were reasonably structured to result in fair dealing.

客观标准的理由　我们承认，立法机构为这个法律领域的行为增加了客观标准之后，“商业车轮”的运转很有可能会慢下来。一位评论家说：“历史上，一般的观点都认为，如果想让流通票据真正地流通起来，就不能要求后手执票人对票据背后的交易进行调查。因此，票据的流通性成为最重要的考虑因素，并主导了流通票据法的立法。大家都相信，汇票和本票必须能够自由转手，因此，除查看票据表面状况外，无须进一步调查，且除执票人的背书外，不存在其他要求。”（引用前述文章）

We recognize that the Legislature's addition of an objective standard of conduct in this area of law may well have the effect of slowing the "wheels of commerce". As one commentator noted: "Historically, it was always argued that if negotiable instruments were to be usefully negotiable a subsequent holder should not have to investigate the transaction giving rise to the paper. The paramount necessity of negotiability has dominated thinking and legislation on negotiable instruments law. Drafts and promissory notes, it has been believed, must be able to change hands freely, without investigation beyond the face of the instrument, and with no greater requirement than the indorsement of the holder." Sinclair.

尽管社会经常强调，必须考虑到商业交易的确定性和快捷性，但立法机构仍然在“善意”的定义中增加了客观因素的要求。立法机构一定是已经得出结论，此种增加具有重要意义。流通性这种无可置疑的最高需求，已经让位于或至少部分地让位于另一种需求，即流通票据的交易也需要具有合理的商业公平性。

Notwithstanding society's oft-cited need for certainty and speed in commercial transactions, however, the Legislature necessarily must have concluded that the addition of the objective requirement to the definition of "good faith" serves an important goal. The paramount necessity of unquestioned negotiability has given way, at least in part, to the desire for reasonable commercial fairness in negotiable transactions.

信贷公司不是正当执票人 在本案中，由于信贷公司未能说服陪审团将其认定为正当执票人，因此，信贷公司必须受制于3名子女或保险公司所持有的任何抗辩，只要“假设有权强制履行票据的人在强制履行简式合同项下的付款时”，该抗辩具有效力［第3.305条（1）（b）款］；或必须受制于“对票据或其收益具有财产权或占有权性质的索赔”（第3.306条）。本案2名诈骗人的欺诈行为通常有可能构成有效抗辩（参见S诉M案），并有可能构成对票据本身的索赔（参见B诉S案）。

Having failed to persuade the jury that it was a holder in due course, the Credit Union is subject to any defense of the Guerrettes or Sun Life "that would be available if the person entitled to enforce the instrument were enforcing a right to payment under a simple contract", M.R.S.A. § 3-305（1）（b）, or any "claim of a property or possessory right in the instrument or its proceeds". M.R.S.A. § 3-306. Generally, fraud, such as that perpetrated by Paul Richard and Steven Hall, may be the basis for both a valid defense, see Silber v. Muschel, and a valid claim to the instrument itself. See generally Bowling Green, Inc. v. State St. Bank & Trust Co.

诈骗已被证实 要将欺诈作为合同的抗辩，必须主动证明存在欺诈。因此，3名子女要想成功地引用欺诈抗辩，就必须以明确和有说服力的证据证明，他们向2名诈骗人转让其父亲寿险理赔款（保险公司的支票）的行为，受到了欺诈性不实陈述或重大不实陈述的引诱。此外，他们还必须证明，他们有合理理由依赖该欺诈性不实陈述（参见K诉E

Fraud is an affirmative defense to a contract. To prevail on their fraud defense, the Guerrettes were required to prove, by clear and convincing evidence, that a fraudulent or material misrepresentation induced them to transfer the proceeds of their father's life insurance policy, in the form of the Sun Life checks, to Steven Hall and Paul Richard. In addition, they were required to prove they were justified in relying on the fraudulent misrepresentation. See Kuperman v. Eiras.

案）。当事方均承认，2 名诈骗人欺诈性地引诱 3 名子女将支票投入其“投资公司”。基于此种承认，3 名子女的举证已经完成。因此，3 名子女虽在保险公司的支票上作出了背书，但不对该支票承担责任。

The parties' stipulation that Hall and Richard fraudulently induced the Guerrettes to invest the checks in their company, HER, Inc., is sufficient to satisfy the Guerrettes' burden on this issue. The Guerrettes are not liable to the Credit Union for their indorsement of the Sun Life checks.

欺诈不构成保险公司的抗辩 但是，本案保险公司无权以上述欺诈作为自己票据责任的抗辩。法典第 3.305 条（3）款的一般性规定是，在强制履行票据当事方的票据义务时，义务人不得引用另一个人对票据的抗辩、扣减权或票据索赔（第 3.306 条），来对抗强制履行票据的人［第 3.305 条（3）款］。

Sun Life, however, may not raise the fraud as a defense to its liability on the instrument. Section 3-305（3）provides generally that: in an action to enforce the obligation of a party to pay ［an］ instrument, the obligor may not assert against the person entitled to enforce the instrument a defense, claim in recoupment or claim to the instrument （section 3-306） of another person. M.R.S.A. § 3-305（3）.

不存在票据索赔问题 因此，诉讼中一个当事方就自己的票据责任提出的抗辩，如基础交易中的欺诈，不能被另一个当事方引用作为其票据责任的抗辩。但是，法典第 3.305 条（3）款规定，“票据义务人可以引用另一个当事方提出的票据索赔，只要该另一方加入了诉讼，并自行针对强制履行票据的人提出了该

Accordingly, a defense to liability on an instrument-such as fraud in the underlying transaction-raised by one party to an action may not be raised by another party to the action as its own defense to liability. Section 3-305（3） provides, however, that “the other person's claim to the instrument may be asserted by the obligor if the other person is joined in the action and personally asserts the claim against the person entitled to

索赔”。因此，只有在3名子女已经提出票据索赔且成为诉讼当事方之后，保险公司才可以将该欺诈作为自己责任的抗辩[参见第3.305条(3)款；F诉D案]。

enforce the instrument". Therefore, only if the Guerrettes have made a claim to the instrument and are parties to the proceeding may Sun Life assert the fraud in defense of its own liability. See M.R.S.A. 3-305(3); First Nat'l Bank of Nocona v. Duncan Sav. & Loan Ass'n.

但在本案中，对于信贷公司持有的支票，3名子女并没有主张他们自己有权取得该票据的占有。实际上，他们只是辩称，由于存在欺诈，因此，对于信贷公司持有的支票，他们不承担支票背书人的付款责任。因此，3名子女所提出的欺诈问题，只是用于抗辩他们对票据承担的背书人责任(参见L诉M案)。初审法院判决，3名子女将欺诈问题作为“票据索赔”问题提出。该判决是错误的。

The Guerrettes, however, made no claim that they were entitled to possession of the instruments held by the Credit Union. Instead, they merely argued that they were not liable as indorsers of the checks held by the Credit Union as a result of the fraud. The issue of fraud was therefore raised by the Guerrettes as a defense to their liability as indorsers of the instruments. See Louis Falcigno Enters., Inc. v. Massachusetts Bank & Trust Co. The Superior Court erred when it held that the issue of fraud had been raised as a "claim to the instruments".

保险公司应承担出票人的责任 因此，本案保险公司无权将欺诈问题作为其票据责任的抗辩。由于保险公司未能提出任何其他抗辩，因此保险公司作为支票的出票人，必须对信贷公司承担付款责任[参见第3.414条

Therefore, Sun Life may not raise the fraud against the Guerettes as a defense to its own liability. Because Sun Life raises no other relevant defenses, it is liable to the Credit Union as the drawer of the instruments, see M.R.S.A. § 3-414(2)(a), and we vacate that portion of the Superior Court's

（2）（a）款］。因此，对于初审法院关于保险公司无须对信贷公司承担责任的那部分判决，我们推翻原判。维持原判中有关 3 名子女不对信贷公司承担责任的判决。推翻原判中有关保险公司不对信贷公司承担责任的判决。将本案发回，由初审法院根据本判决意见进行重审。

judgment finding that Sun Life was not liable to the Credit Union. The entry is Judgment in favor of Daniel, Joel, and Claire Guerrette and against Maine Family Federal Credit Union affirmed. Judgment in favor of Sun Life Assurance Company of Canada and against Maine Family Federal Credit Union vacated and remanded for further proceedings consistent with the opinion herein.

案例 23　执票人是否为票据支付了价值?

European Asian Bank, A.G. v. G. Crohn & Company
欧亚银行诉格朗公司案

联邦第二巡回上诉法院 1985 年；769 F.2d 93, 41 UCC Rep.Serv. 850

简　介

本案涉及一张汇票的 3 个当事方，即作为汇票出票人（drawer）的出票公司（Kundamal），作为汇票受票人（drawee）并随后承兑了汇票的承兑公司（Crohn），以及作为受款人（payee）从出票公司取得汇票，从而成为执票人的持票银行（Eurasbank）。在本案中，承兑公司和出票公司都是经营钻石贸易的商业公司。身为买方的承兑公司，从身为卖方的出票公司购买了一批钻石。卖方为了收取货款，作为出票人出具了一张以自己持有账户的持票银行为受款人，以买方为受票人的汇票。买方随后对汇票作出了承兑，从而成为该汇票的承兑人（acceptor）。持票银行作为汇票的受款人而持有汇票。

本案卖方（出票公司）之所以将持票银行作为汇票的受款人，是希望将汇票项下的款项支付给持票银行，因为卖方在其他业务中（下述判决中提到的“信托收据”）欠银行一笔钱，而该债务存在于卖方在持票银行的账户上。在买方（承兑公司）承兑了汇票后，持票银行认为，汇票项下的收款已有一定保障，因此在卖方的账户上贷记了相应数额，用于清偿卖方在信托收据（trust receipts）业务中欠银行的钱。由于持票银行已就该汇票向卖方（出票公司）提供了贷记，并用该贷记清偿了出票公司的旧债。因此，一般而言，持票银行被视为已向卖方支付了价值。

随后，由于钻石交易本身出现问题，买卖双方之间产生争议，因而买方拒绝支付货款。由于货款就是买方已经承兑的汇票，所以买方（承兑公司）表示拒付该汇票。法典规定，汇票的受票人在对汇票作出承兑之后，即转变为承兑人，并对汇票承担直接的付款责任。本案卖方（出票公司）作为汇票的出票人，在作为承兑人的买方（承兑公司）拒付汇票时，也要对汇票承担责任。因此，在本案中，持票银行将承兑公司列为被告，将出票公司列为第三方被告。

在本案买方与卖方之间的交易中，也许买方拒绝支付货款的理由（如货物存在瑕疵或卖方存在欺诈等）存在一定的法律基础。如果买方的理由成立，买方作为汇票的承兑人，可能就对自己的汇票责任持有抗辩。但是，如果持票银行是正当执票人，买方的抗辩就不能对抗持票银行。因此，本案的关键在于，持票银行是否符合正当执票人的标准？当事方都承认，持票银行在取得汇票时，系以善意作为，并且不知道汇票上存在任何争议。因此，根据法典第 3.302 条的规定，剩下的唯一问题就是，持票银行是否为该汇票支付了价值？如果没有支付价值，持票银行就不属于正当执票人。

承兑公司（买方）的主张是，持票银行没有支付价值。具体理由在于，持票银行收到汇票后，确实贷记了出票公司的账户，并将该贷记用于抵销出票公司欠银行的一笔债务。从这个意义上讲，银行支付了价值。对此，承兑公司不予质疑。承兑公司所质疑的是，银行在贷记出票公司的账户时，同时又按同一金额借记了出票公司的另一个账户（下述判决中所说的“第二个账户”），并且这笔借记一直存在。承兑公司认为，这相当于银行一方面给了出票公司一笔钱，但另一方面又从出票公司拿走了另一笔数额相同的钱，因此等于没付钱，也就是没有为汇票支付价值。

关于这个问题，初审法院认定，持票银行对出票公司第二个账户的借记，并不构成真正的借记，而只是一种“入账需要”(book-keeping requirement)。也就是说，只是一种形式，而不是真正的借记，因此不影响第一个账户贷记的性质。上诉法院认为，虽然初审法院对这个问题的表述不十分清楚，但初审法院显然已经认真考虑了这个问题，并且该认定有优势证据的支持，因此应该维持该认定。上诉法院最终判定，持票银行已经为汇票支付了价值，成为正当执票人，因此，承兑了汇票的承兑公司即使持有可以对抗出票公司的抗辩，也不能使用此种抗辩对抗持票银行。

判　决

初审法院的判决和承兑公司的异议　在本次州际诉讼中，初审法院判决，作为原告的持票银行有权就其持有的汇票，从汇票的承兑公司取得292,445.42美元的赔偿以及利息。承兑公司提起本上诉并辩称：(1)初审法院的判决是错误的，因为其认定持票银行从第三方被告出票公司购买了汇票之后，成为该汇票的正当执票人，并且(2)承兑公司在承兑该汇票时，没有收到有效的对价，或者作为替代理由，由于出票公司违反了所承诺的履约义务，承兑公司无论如何也应被解除责任。

In this diversity case, G. Crohn & Company (“Crohn”) appeals from a judgment of the district court, granting plaintiff bank recovery of $292,445.42 plus interest on a bill of exchange. Crohn claims 1) that the district court erred in finding that European Asian Bank, A.G. (“Eurasbank”) had become a holder in due course when it purchased a bill of exchange from third-party defendant H. Khemchand Kundamal Enterprises (HK), Ltd. (“Kundamal”); and 2) that Crohn had received no valid consideration when it accepted the bill, or, in the alternative, that Crohn should have been relieved of liability anyway due to Kundamal’s breach of promised performance.

上诉的基本结论　我们认为，初审法官的认定不存在明显错误，即持票银行购买汇票后，已向出票公司提供了信贷。因此我们同意，持票银行已成为正当执票人，并因此有权就该汇票取得付款，无论承兑公司是否基于其与出票公司的协议而持有任何抗辩。因此，我们维持原判。

Because we believe that Judge Brieant's finding that Eurasbank gave credit to Kundamal when it purchased the bill of exchange was not clearly erroneous, we agree that Eurasbank became a holder in due course, and thereby was entitled to payment on the bill of exchange regardless of any defenses Crohn might have derived from its agreement with Kundamal. Consequently, we affirm the judgment.

正当执票人的条件　我们同意初审法官有关持票银行已成为正当执票人的判决。汇票义务人在对抗汇票购买人时，可以引用其有权对汇票出票人所主张的任何抗辩，除非该购买人享有正当执票人的权利（第 3.306 条）。如果执票人在取得票据时支付了价值，以善意作为，且未得到票据已过期，或已被拒付，或任何人对票据持有抗辩或票据索赔的通知，该执票人即为正当执票人［第 3.302 条（1）款］。本案当事方承认，持票银行在取得汇票时系以善意作为，且未得到任何抗辩或索赔的通知。承兑公司仅辩称，持票银行未支付价值。

We agree with Judge Brieant that Eurasbank became a holder in due course. The obligor on a bill of exchange may assert against a person who purchases the bill any defenses he may have against the bill's drawer unless the purchaser has the rights of a holder in due course. See N.Y.U.C.C. Sec. 3-306. A holder in due course is a holder who takes the instrument for value, in good faith and without notice that it is overdue or has been dishonored or of any defense against or claim to it on the part of any person. See N.Y.U.C.C. Sec. 3-302（1）. The parties do not dispute that Eurasbank took the bill in good faith and without notice of any claims or defenses. Crohn argues only that Eurasbank gave no value.

是否支付了价值 初审法官认定，持票银行在贷记出票公司账户并将该贷记用于清偿出票公司之前所欠债务（信托收据）的余额后，即属于支付了价值。该交易符合法典有关支付价值的定义中的一种情况。法典定义的相关部分规定，“执票人在下列情况下属于通过支付价值取得票据：其所取得的票据，系用于支付针对任何人持有的前存索赔，或系为该索赔设立担保，无论该索赔是否已到期”［第3.303条（b）款］。银行如果对票据取得了担保权益，亦属于支付价值（第4.209条）。银行在下列情况下取得担保权益：“票证被存入账户后，银行为票证提供了信贷，且信贷已被提取或使用。”［第4.208条（1）（a）款］

对第二个账户的借记 承兑公司辩称，持票银行虽然贷记了出票公司账户，但并没有支付价值，因为其按相同数额同时借记了出票公司另一个账户，相当于立即收回了贷记金额。第二个账户的借记入账目前还存在，且在

Judge Brieant found that Eurasbank had given value when it credited Kundamal's account and applied the credit to retire the outstanding balances on Kundamal's antecedent debts, which took the form of "trust receipts". This transaction complied with one of the Uniform Commercial Code's definitions of taking for value which states that "[a] holder takes the instrument for value ... when he takes the instrument in payment of or as security for an antecedent claim against any person whether or not the claim is due". N.Y.U.C.C. Sec. 3-303 (b). A bank can give value by taking a security interest in an instrument. See N.Y.U.C.C. Sec. 4-209. A bank has taken a security interest "in case of an item deposited in an account to the extent to which credit given for the item has been withdrawn or applied". N.Y.U.C.C. Sec. 4-208 (1) (a).

Crohn, however, argues that Eurasbank gave no value when it credited Kundamal's account because it simultaneously debited a second account in the same amount, and thereby immediately reinstated the outstanding obligations. This debit on the second account remains, and was not reversed

持票银行将第一个账户的贷记用于清偿"信托收据"欠款后，也未取消该借记。

不构成真正的借记　初审法官的结论是，目前仍然存在的借记项目只是"入账需要"，本来也许仅用于显示"流通在外的即时付款汇票的资产账目"，代表了持票银行可从承兑公司收回的资金。虽然初审法院本来还可将所有记账项目显示得更完整一些，并对其含义解释得更清楚一些，但我们认为，现有证据更多地是支持初审法官的认定，而不是否定该认定。因此，对于其认定，即持票银行已将贷记用于清偿出票公司的前存债务，我们不能说存在明显错误［引用《联邦民事诉讼法》］。

临时贷记的性质　承兑公司还辩称，由于持票银行针对前存债务的贷记只是临时贷记，因此不属于已经支付价值。持票银行的格式收款合同背面说明：双方同意，此种贷记是附条件贷记，并以银行最终收到相应数额款项为条件；如果银行未收到此种款

when Eurasbank later applied the credit to the "trust receipt" accounts.

Judge Brieant concluded that this remaining debit entry, as a "bookkeeping requirement", could have shown "an asset account for an outstanding sight draft", representing the funds Eurasbank could collect from Crohn. Although it would have been preferable for the district court to have had a more complete set of accounting entries with a more explicit explanation of their significance, we find that the evidence is more supportive than not of Judge Brieant's determination. Consequently, we cannot say that his finding that Eurasbank applied the credit to Kundamal's antecedent debts was clearly erroneous. See Fed.R.Civ.P.

Crohn also argues that Eurasbank gave no value because it applied only a provisional credit to the antecedent debts. Printed language on the reverse of the bank's Collection Order form states that ... it is understood that such credit is conditional and is subject to collection and receipt by ［the bank］ of the requisite number of

项，下述签名的客户（本案出票公司）将在银行提出要求后，就银行提供的贷记数额向银行作出补偿，再加上按约定利率计算的贷记期间的利息。

dollars; in the absence of such receipt and collection by [the bank], the undersigned [i.e. Kundamal] will, upon [the bank's] demand reimburse [the bank] for the amount so advanced plus the agreed rate of interest for the time outstanding.

初审法官认定，上述合同文字说明，持票银行在将信贷用于前存债务时，规定了附加条件。承兑公司辩称，在这种情况下，根据M诉G案的判决，本来不应将持票银行视为正当执票人，因为该案说，“根据法典，提供临时贷记不等于失去了所支付的价值”。

Judge Brieant found that such language made conditional the credit which Eurasbank applied to the antecedent debts. So, Crohn argues that, under Marine Midland Bank-New York v. Graybar Electric Co., which states that "the giving of a provisional credit is not a parting with value under the Uniform Commercial Code", Eurasbank should not have been found to be a holder in due course.

承兑公司引用的判例 M诉G案的判决，并不要求我们在本案中对持票银行作出不利判决，因为在该案中，银行可以在任何时间撤回信贷，且实际上撤回了信贷，但在本案中，只要承兑公司不就汇票违约，持票银行就没有权利撤回提供给出票公司的信贷。

The holding in Marine Midland does not require us to decide against the bank in this case, because in Marine Midland, the bank could reverse the credit at any time, and, in fact did reverse the credit, whereas, Eurasbank could not have reversed the credit given to Kundamal until Crohn had defaulted on the bill of exchange.

在M诉G案中，银行将存储在客户保险箱里的支票取出后，单方给客户账户作出贷记，

In Marine Midland, a bank withdrew a check deposited into its client's lockbox and unilaterally gave a credit to its client's account

然后单方用该贷记清偿了客户的前存债务。银行将该支票送至受票人银行收款后得知，支票的出票人（银行客户的顾客）已就该支票发出停付命令。因此，银行撤回了给客户账户的贷记，并恢复了原债务。与此同时，银行的客户陷入破产。银行因此起诉客户的顾客（支票的出票人），辩称自己在将贷记用于客户的前存债务后，自己成为支票的正当执票人。

which it then applied unilaterally by way of setoff to its client's antecedent debts. Upon forwarding the check to the drawee bank for payment, the bank learned that the client's customer had issued a stop payment on the check. The bank then reversed the credit and reinstated the debts. Meanwhile, the bank's client had filed for bankruptcy. The bank then sued the client's customer for payment and argued that it had become a holder in due course when it applied the credit to its client's antecedent debts.

在 M 诉 G 案中，由于银行有权撤回并实际上撤回了所提供的信贷，银行从未同意接受其客户之顾客的信用风险，也没有向其客户"提供"该贷记的实际效益。该案上诉法院说："基于此种分析，相比其他债权人，银行的处境并非更差。且银行系单方同意，以收回支票项下的信贷为条件，将支票项下的信贷用于清偿前存债务。因此，必须实事求是地说，银行的做法无非是试图挽回前存债务的损失。"

Because the bank in Marine Midland could and did reverse the credit, it had neither bound itself to accept the credit risk of its client's customer nor "made available" to its client the benefits of the credit. "Under this analysis the bank is in no worse position than any other creditor", the Court of Appeals observed, "and the bank's unilateral agreement to take the credit for the indebtedness, conditioned on payment of the check for which the credit was given, is recognized for what it was--an attempt to recoup its losses".

关键在于是否承担票据违约风险 与 M 诉 G 案不同的是，

Unlike the bank in Marine Midland, Eurasbank did not unilaterally apply the

本案持票银行并未单方将信贷用于清偿出票公司的前存债务。实际上，出票公司明确指示银行以该方式使用该信贷。格式收款合同背面所印制的文字，没有说持票银行有权单方在任何时间撤回贷记。该文字最多只是说，如果持票银行要追究出票公司作为汇票出票人的责任，必须以出票公司的客户出现汇票违约为前提条件。

在这种情况下，合同上述印制文字仅显示了持票银行根据法典本来就可以行使的权利［第3.413条（2）款（除非在出立汇票时规定了无追索权，否则，出票人必须对被拒付的汇票承担责任）；第3.507条（2）款（“汇票被拒付后，执票人有权立即追究出票人或背书人的责任”）］。法典上述条款是为了保护票据受让人和促进商业交易。因此，声称受让人只有首先解除转让人的义务后才能成为正当执票人的说法，完全没有道理。

持票银行承担了票据违约风

credit to Kundamal's outstanding obligations. Indeed, Kundamal had expressly instructed the bank to use the credit in that manner. The printed language on the back of the Collection Order form does not say that Eurasbank had a unilateral right to reverse the entries at any time. At best, the language suggests that Kundamal's customer's default on the bill of exchange was a condition precedent to the bank's seeking recourse against the bill's drawer, Kundamal.

In this context, the printed language merely expressed the rights which Eurasbank already would have been able to exercise under the Uniform Commercial Code. See N.Y.U.C.C. Sec. 3-413（2）（unless drawing without recourse, drawer remains liable for payment on dishonored draft）; N.Y.U.C.C. Sec. 3-507（2）（"holder has upon dishonor an immediate right of recourse against drawers or indorsers"）. Under provisions which seek to protect transferees and to encourage commercial transactions, it would make little sense if, to become a holder in due course, a transferee must discharge the transferor's obligation.

In essence, to become a holder in due

险　从本质上说，在将票据项下的信贷用于清偿前存债务时，执票人要想成为正当执票人，就必须事先同意接受相关风险，即承担票据义务人票据违约的风险。在 M 诉 G 案中，由于银行在提供信贷时已事先保留了单方撤回信贷的权利，因此，银行实际上没有同意承担其客户之顾客的违约风险。在这种情况下，在 M 诉 G 案中，没有必要向银行提供法典对正当执票人所提供的充分保护（第 3.303 条正式评论 3）。在该案中，银行一旦得知票据有可能得不到支付，完全可以撤销基于票据提供的信贷，而无须卷入票据诉讼之中。

course by applying a credit to antecedent debts, the holder must have agreed to expose itself to the credit risk of the party obligated on the instrument taken in payment of the antecedent debts. As the bank in Marine Midland, when it first extended the credits, retained the right unilaterally to reverse the credits, it had refrained from exposing itself to the credit risk of its client's customer. Thus, the position of the bank in Marine Midland did not necessitate according it full protection under the Uniform Commercial Code's provisions for a holder in due course. See Sec. 3-303 Official Comment 3. Had the bank learned that the item was not likely to be paid, it would not have had to sue on the instrument but could have rescinded the transaction at will.

形成对照的是，本案持票银行实际上已用承兑公司取代了原本由出票公司承担的债务，即视前者为偿债的主要当事方。持票银行即使得知承兑公司和出票公司之间出现交易纠纷，本来也不可能再任意撤销给出票公司的信贷，而是必须等待承兑公司的拒付，并因此承担两家公司都不付

In contrast, Eurasbank did replace Kundamal with Crohn as the primary party to whom it looked to repay the debts originally owed by Kundamal. Had Eurasbank learned that the Crohn-Kundamal deal had gone amiss, it could not have revoked the credits at will, but still would have to wait for Crohn's default, and thereby incur further risk of non-payment by either Crohn or Kundamal.

款的进一步风险。

结论 持票银行已将票据项下的信贷用于清偿前存债务，且无权任意撤回。因此，对于持票银行是否属于正当执票人，持票银行之交易的实际效果，完全相当于其提供了信贷，且接受该信贷的人"有权提用"该信贷［第4.208条（1）（b）款；第4.213条（4）款］。因此，出票公司自己有权提取该信贷，并将该信贷用于清偿"信托收据"项下的债务。

By applying a credit, which Eurasbank could not reverse at will, to reduce antecedent debts, Eurasbank's transaction had the same practical effect, on the question of its being a holder in due course, as if the bank had made the credit available for "withdrawal as of right", see N.Y.U.C.C. Sec. 4-208（1）（b）; N.Y.U.C.C. Sec. 4-213（4）, and thereby gave the right to Kundamal, itself, to draw down upon the credit and to apply the proceeds to retire the "trust receipts".

由于我们同意初审法院的判定，即持票银行已成为正当执票人，且有权从承兑公司取得票据付款，而不受制于承兑公司的抗辩（第3.305条），因此我们没必要再考虑承兑公司的抗辩是否能够成立。维持原判。

As we agree with the district court that Eurasbank became a holder in due course and is entitled to payment from Crohn regardless of Crohn's defenses, see N.Y.U.C.C. Sec. 3-305, we need not consider whether there is any merit to those defenses. Affirmed.

案例 24　本票的受让人是否有权起诉制票人?

Paul P. Piper, Jr. v. Daniel P. Goodwin et al.
派普尔诉古德温案

联邦第六巡回上诉法院 1994 年；20 F.3d 216, 23 UCC Rep.Serv.2d 466

简　介

本案涉及两张凭令付款本票的付款问题。地产公司（Rivergrove Development）出立了本票，但地产公司的若干实际控制人（Goodwin 等）在之前的另一项诉讼中被判定应承担本票制票人和背书人的责任，因此作为制票人成为本案被告。本票的原始执票人（Moore）欠了本案的本票受让人（Piper）一笔巨额债务。因此，前者根据普通法的转让（assignment）方式，将自己的全部财产都转让给了后者，包括本案的两张本票。前者转让财产时，由于之前诉讼的缘故，两张本票处于法院的掌管之下。因此，前者未能向后者直接交付两张本票，也未能在本票上作出背书。

随后，本票的受让人要求制票人支付本票。在制票人拒绝支付后，受让人提起本次诉讼。制票人辩称，受让人无权起诉，因为两张本票是凭令付款票据，因此，转让人在将本票转让或流通给受让人时，必须在本票上背书并将本票交付给受让人。但是，在转让的当时，本票在法院掌管之下，转让人既没有背书也没有交付，因此受让人不属于本票的执票人，无权要求制票人付款。

初审法院作出了受让人胜诉的判决，而上诉法院维持了该判决。上诉法院认为，受让人要取得本票项下的付款，不一定必须本身是本票的执票人。根据法典的“庇护原则”（shelter rule），只要票据的转让人有权取得票据付款，受让人就有可能继承转让人的权利，因而也有权取得付款，即使该转让只是普通法上的“转让”（assignment），而不是法典第3篇中的“转让”（transfer）或“流通”（negotiation）。在本案中，毫无争议的是，本票的转让人曾是本票的执票人。因此，即使其仅以普通法上的转让将本票转让给本案受让人，受让人也取得了转让人的全部权利，包括取得本票付款的权利。此外，上诉法院还认为，在本案中，即使根据法典第3篇的规定，本案受让人很有可能也取得了本票的转让（transfer）。原因在于，转让人在之前的相关诉讼中，是先将本票交付给了受让人的律师，然后由该律师交付给了法院保管。上诉法院认为，将本票交付给受让人律师的情况，可能已经满足了法典第3篇有关转让的要求。但无论如何，这不影响本案的判决结果。在本案中，上诉法院的判决是以诉讼当时的田纳西州旧版法典为依据的，但当时法典的正式文本已经更新。两个版本的基本原则没有本质区别，但条文编号有所不同。所以，上诉法院分别提到两者。

判　决

本案基本情况　持有两张本票的受让人（原告）基于旧版法典起诉3名制票人（被告），要求后者支付本票。初审法院基于陪审团有利于受让人的裁定，判定制票人支付本票，并加付利息和原告律师费。制票人就5个问题提起上诉。我们审阅这些问题

Pursuant to Tennessee's version of the Uniform Commercial Code, the plaintiff sued three individual defendants for collection on two promissory notes. The jury found in favor of the plaintiff and the district court entered a judgment against the defendants on the notes, together with interest and attorney fees. Five issues have been raised on appeal. After

后认定原判不存在错误，因此维持原判。

reviewing these issues, we find no error and affirm.

制票人的理由　制票人辩称，受让人提起诉讼时不是本票的执票人，因此在法律上无权寻求本票的付款。制票人引用旧版法典第 3.202 条称，两张本票均系凭令付款，因此如果要将其流通给受让人，转让人必须将本票交付给受让人，并作出背书。制票人称，关于转让人是否已将本票交付给受让人，本案证据存有疑问。但毫无疑问的是，转让人至少并未将任何一张本票背书给受让人。制票人称，由于受让人未取得本票的流通，因此不是本票的执票人，无权提起本诉讼。

The defendants argue that Piper was not a holder of the notes when he commenced this action and, thus, he had no legal right to seek their collection. Relying on Tenn. Code Sec. 3-202, the defendants contend that because both notes are payable to order, to be negotiated to Piper the notes had to have been delivered to him and endorsed by Moore. The defendants maintain that the evidence is questionable as to whether Moore delivered the notes to Piper and, at a minimum, it is clear that neither note was endorsed by Moore. Therefore, the defendants argue, because the notes were not negotiated to Piper, he is not a holder and cannot bring this action.

庇护原则　即使我们假定制票人对旧版法典第 3.202 条的解释是正确的，该解释也不能解决本案问题。本案的事实，最好根据旧版法典第 3.201 条的规定进行分析。该条规定："（1）票据的转让，使受让人取得转让人对票据的全部权利，但如果受让人本身一直参与涉及该票据的欺诈或非法活动，或其作为前执票人

Even if we were to assume the defendants' interpretation of Sec. 3-202 is correct, it does not resolve this matter. The facts of this case are better analyzed under Tenn Code Sec. 3-201, which provides: "（1） Transfer of an instrument vests in the transferee such rights as the transferor has therein, except that a transferee who has himself been a party to any fraud or illegality affecting the instrument or who as a prior

已得到票据存在抗辩或索赔的通知，他就不能通过从后来的正当执票人取得票据转让，来改善自己的地位。（2）转让票据中的担保权益，使受让人在所转让之权益的范围内，取得上述权利。（3）除非另有协议，在收取价值后转让当时非属凭票付款的票据，使受让人取得要求转让人作出无限制背书的权利，且此种权利可以强制实际履行。只有作出背书后，流通才发生效力。在此之前，不能假定受让人是所有权人。”

holder had notice of a defense or claim against it cannot improve his position by taking from a later holder in due course. （2）A transfer of a security interest in an instrument vests the foregoing rights in the transferee to the extent of the interest transferred. （3）Unless otherwise agreed any transfer for value of an instrument not then payable to bearer gives the transferee the specifically enforceable right to have the unqualified endorsement of the transferor. Negotiation takes effect only when the endorsement is made and until that time there is no presumption that the transferee is the owner."

有关庇护原则的判例 通常将法典上述规定称为“庇护原则”。在情况类似本案的其他判例中，田纳西州法院和解释过法典该项条款的其他州法院都判定，虽然不存在符合要求的票据流通，但是基于普通法，受让人可以取得转让人的权利。在M诉M案中，本票的受让人就本票未付余额起诉本票的付款人。在上诉中，付款人辩称，受让人不具有就本票提起诉讼的法律理由。法院基于旧版法典第3.201

This provision is often referred to as the “shelter rule”, and in circumstances similar to the one before us, Tennessee courts, and other courts interpreting similar provisions, have held that an assignee does have the rights of the assignor, notwithstanding the absence of a proper negotiation. In Martin v. Martin, the plaintiff, an assignee of a note, brought an action against the payors for the alleged unpaid balance of the note. On appeal, the defendants argued that the assignee did not have standing to sue on this note. The court referred to Tenn.Code Sec. 3-201 and found

条判定，由于转让本票的转让人当时不占有本票，因此转让人不可能基于票据法将本票转让或流通给该案受让人。法院承认，在该情况下，受让人不是本票的执票人。但法院同时判定，在付款人与转让人之间的基础交易中，付款人对转让人负有债务，而受让人从转让人取得了就该债务起诉的权利，因此，受让人有权起诉付款人。

that since the assignor did not have possession of the note, it could not have transferred or negotiated the note to the plaintiff. The court conceded that because of this fact, the plaintiff was not a holder of the note. Nevertheless, the court held that the plaintiff had received an assignment of a cause of action on the underlying obligation of the payors to the assignor. Thus, the court found the plaintiff could maintain this action.

庇护原则适用于本案　本案事实与M诉M案的事实相类似。当本案转让人将自己的资产转让给受让人时，转让人不占有本票，因为在之前的相关诉讼中，本票已被交由法院保管。在不占有本票的情况下，转让人无法将本票转让或流通给受让人。但是，如同M诉M案的情况，受让人就本票的诉讼权取得了普通法上的转让。因此我们判定，受让人有权提起本诉讼。

The facts before us are similar to those in Martin. When Moore assigned his assets to Piper, he did not have possession of the notes because they were with the court in which he had previously filed the related lawsuit. Without possession of the notes, Moore could not transfer or negotiate them to Piper; however, as in Martin, Piper did receive an assignment of the cause of action on the underlying notes. Therefore, we find Piper can bring this claim.

可能也构成票据法的转让　此外，相对M诉M案，本案情况对受让人更有利，因为与M诉M案不同，本案有证据表明，

Moreover, the case before us is even stronger than the one in Martin, because unlike in Martin, there is evidence that the notes themselves were transferred to Piper.

即使根据票据法，本票本身也被转让给了受让人。我们认为，本案转让人将其资产转让给受让人并将本票交付给后者律师的行为，构成了法典第3.201条庇护原则中所说的票据法转让［引用法律词典（该词典将“转让”定义为“对财产或财产权益任何形式的、直接或间接的、无条件或附条件的、自愿或非自愿的处置或剥离”）］。

We believe the assignment of Moore's assets to Piper and Moore's delivery of the notes to Piper's attorney constitutes a transfer as intended by section 3-201's shelter rule. See Black's Law Dictionary （defining transfer as “every mode, direct or indirect, absolute or conditional, voluntary or involuntary, of disposing of or parting with property or with an interest in property”）.

庇护原则的其他判例 在S诉F案中，法院需要确定受让人是否享有正当执票人的权利。法院的结论是，根据庇护原则，正当执票人的任何受让人均可取得正当执票人的全部权利，只要受让人自己没有涉及任何欺诈或非法活动，且受让人不是曾得到抗辩或索赔通知的前执票人。同样，在A诉S案中，法院评论说，庇护原则“使受让人有可能通过取代转让人的身份，来改善自己的地位。因此，只要受让人可以证明票据的转让人是执票人，受让人自己就可以主张执票人的权利”［另参见F诉A案（“受让

In Schwegmann Bank & Trust Co. v. Falkenberg, the court had to determine whether the plaintiff was entitled to holder in due course rights. The court concluded that, pursuant to the shelter rule, the transferee of a holder in due course acquires all the rights of the holder in due course as long as the transferee was not personally involved in any fraud or illegality, and the transferee was not a prior holder who had notice of a defense or claim against the instrument. Similarly, in American National Bank & Trust Co. v. St. Joseph Valley Bank, the court observed that the shelter rule “allows a transferee a possible betterment of his own position by assuming the status of his transferor. Thus, a

人要主张正当执票人的权利，不一定自己必须是正当执票人"）]；B 诉 S 案（"这些判例所明确确立的原则是，本案受让人可以基于转让人的身份获得保护，包括转让人所享有的正当执票人的身份"）。

transferee may claim the rights of a holder if he proves that his transferor was a holder". See also Fidelity Bank, Nat'l Ass'n v. Avrutick（"the transferee itself need not be a holder in due course in order to assert the rights of a holder in due course"）; B.L. Nelson and Assoc. v. Sunbelt Sav.（"The clear import of these cases is that assignees of the FSLIC are entitled to the protected status that the corporation itself enjoys, including holder in due course status"）.

与新版法典原则一致　上述判例与新版法典第 3.203 条的庇护原则是一致的。新版法典第 3.203 条正式评论 2 说，"票据转让使受让人取得转让人强制履行票据的全部权利，'包括正当执票人所享有的任何权利'。即使转让人未作背书，致使受让人未能成为执票人，受让人仍然属于第 3.301 条所述的有权强制履行票据的人，只要转让人在转让时是执票人。即使受让人不是执票人，根据新版法典第 3.203 条（b）款的规定，受让人仍然取得了转让人作为执票人的权利"。更重要的是，旧版法典第 3.201 条正

These cases are consistent with the Uniform Commercial Code's version of the shelter rule, Sec. 3-203. Comment 2 to Sec. 3-203 states that "transfer vests in the transferee any right of the transferor to enforce the instrument 'including any right as a holder in due course.' If the transferee is not a holder because the transferor did not indorse, the transferee is nevertheless a person entitled to enforce the instrument under Section 3-301 if the transferor was a holder at the time of transfer. Although the transferee is not a holder, under subsection（b）the transferee obtained the rights of the transferor as holder". More significantly, Comment 1 to Tenn.Code Sec. 3-201 states: "Any

式评论1说:“任何人对票据的转让,均构成其全部票据权利的转让。即使这些权利不能构成‘所有权’,受让人仍被视为取得了这些权利。”

结论 在本案中,毫无争议的是,对于制票人出立的本票,转让人是执票人。在转让人将本票转让给受让人后,后者取得了前者作为执票人的全部权利,包括通过诉讼取得本票付款的权利。因此我们判定,受让人有权提起本诉讼。

person who transfers an instrument transfers whatever rights he has in it. The transferee acquires those rights even though they do not amount to ‘title’.”

Here, it is undisputed that Moore was a holder of the notes made by Rivergrove Development. Because he transferred these notes to Piper, Piper obtained all of the rights that Moore had as a holder. This includes the right to bring a cause of action to recover on the notes. Accordingly, we hold that Piper can bring this claim.

案例 25　本票上的签名是代表本人还是代表公司?

First Safety Fund National Bank v. Janet M. Friel
第一安全基金国民银行诉弗莱尔案

马萨诸塞州上诉法院 1987 年；504 N.E.2d 664

简　介

本案涉及一家小型封闭式（closely-held）公司为了从银行获取贷款而出具的两张本票。两张本票的签署时间相隔大约一年。在这两张本票上，公司的总经理女士（Janet Friel）在每一张本票上都作出签名，并且都签了两次。系一次注明系以公司总经理的身份签名，另一次仅签署了总经理女士的名字，而没有其他说明。在公司破产后，银行要求总经理女士个人支付该本票，因为银行认为总经理女士是本票的共同制票人。总经理女士则认为，自己当时在本票上的签名是代表公司作出的签名，而不是共同制票人的签名，因此不应为本票承担个人责任。

本案的事实背景是，这家公司是该女士与丈夫共同拥有的家庭型公司，本来由丈夫经营和管理，而该女士则完全没有参与过管理，也没有相关的知识和经验。在丈夫由于意外事故而去世后，该女士不得不担任了公司的总经理，但日常管理工作在很大程度上依赖其丈夫的弟弟（David Friel）。随后，公司出于经营需要，两次从银行获得贷款。与银行联系和谈判的都是该女士丈夫的弟弟，但贷款文件和本票最后需要由该女士签名。对于本案的两张本票，当时已担任公司总经理的女士根据银行的要求，在本票的右下角签了两次名。显然，总经理女士没有真正理解为什么要签两次名，也不理解两个签名的区别和法律效力。这样的签名方式，应该是该女士丈夫的弟弟事先与银行商量好的，但他不愿向总经理女士作出明确解释，银行也没有作出解释。

银行起诉总经理女士后，初审法院判决，银行和总经理女士都知道后者系代表公司签署该本票，因而后者无须承担个人责任。上诉法院推翻了该判决，认定总经理女士应承担个人责任。上诉法院认为，从签名方式看，原则上总经理女士必须承担个人责任，除非她能证明，本票当事方无意让她承担个人责任。从本案证据看，不能说银行无意让总经理女士承担个人责任。事实上，对于小型封闭式公司，这可能正是银行的本意。银行的这种本意属于正常做法，无可厚非。如果说存在误解，应该只是总经理女士的单方误解，但这种误解从法律上不足以免除其个人责任。上诉法院认为，没有证据表明银行有欺诈行为，并且银行也没有义务向总经理女士解释第二个签名的效力。

判　决

签名的一般效力　根据法典规定，“除非票据清楚地显示签名系以其他身份作出，否则应将该签名视为背书”（第3.402条）。为了进一步说明这个原则，法典的正式评论说，“如果签名的身份存在模糊，则解决该问题的法律原则是，将该签名视为背书”（第3.402条正式评论）。该评

Under the Uniform Commercial Code, “Unless an instrument clearly indicates that a signature is made in some other capacity it is an endorsement” . G. L. Section 3-402. To ram home the point, the commentators to the Code say that “any ambiguity as to the capacity in which a signature is made must be resolved by a rule of law that it is an indorsement” . Comment to Section

论还解释说，“如果签名的位置在票据右下角，则显示签名人意图作为本票的制票人或汇票的出票人而签名”。在本案中，每张本票上的总经理女士的两个签名都位于本票的右下角。即使是授权代理人（如公司的总经理），如果其在票据上签署自己的名字，但票据上并未显示该签名系以代理人的身份作出，该代理人也要对票据承担个人责任［第 3.403 条（2）款］。

本案的情况　如果一个人签名时，在公司名字后面显示了授权代理人的名字和职务，该签名无疑将被视为以代理人身份作出的签名［第 3.403 条（3）款］。但本案总经理女士的问题是，她的第一个签名属于第 3.403 条（3）款的类型，即代理人的签名，而第二个签名则属于第 3.403 条（2）款的类型，即代表了个人责任的签名。实际上，如果不是为了说明个人责任，那么未注明代理人身份的第二个签名，就完全是多此一举（参见 T 诉 S 案）。

3-402 of the Uniform Commercial Code. “［A］ signature in the lower right hand corner of an instrument”, the comment explains, “indicates an intent to sign as the maker of a note or the drawer of a draft”. Both of Mrs. Friel’s signatures on each note were in the lower right hand corner. Even an authorized representative, e.g., the president of a corporation, who signs his own name to an instrument is personally obligated if the instrument does not show that the signature is made in a representative capacity. G. L. Section 3-403（2）.

To be sure, when the name of a corporation is followed by the name and office of an authorized individual, that signature is made in a representative capacity. G. L. Section 3-403（3）. Mrs. Friel’s difficulty is that one signature fits in the Section 3.403（3） category, i.e., representative capacity; the second fits in the Section 3.403（2） category; i.e., it denotes personal obligation. Indeed, were there not some such purpose, signing a second time without a modifier as to representative status would be a peculiarly empty gesture. See Tesoro Petroleum Corp. v. Schmidt.

连带责任是正常做法 对于小型且股权封闭的公司来说，并不少见的情况是，当公司借入款项时，公司本身以及公司的主要管理人员或股东都要承担连带义务。贷款人通常都需要取得此种额外的还款保证（R 诉 C 案；引用著作）。虽然在马萨诸塞州还未遇到过这种双重签名的情况，但其他州曾判定，当公司的高级管理人员作出两次签名时，即一次以代理人身份签名，而另一次没有注明代理人身份，该高管人员就要对票据承担个人责任［L 诉 P 案（第二个签名在本票背面）；P 诉 P 案；T 诉 S 案］。

Dual obligations on the parts of a corporate borrower and its principal officers or stockholders are not unusual when small, closely held corporations borrow money. Reaching by lenders for the additional credit is the norm. Rotuba Extruders, Inc. v. Ceppos. White & Summers, Uniform Commercial Code. Although the dual signature point has not arisen in the Massachusetts cases, other jurisdictions have held a corporate officer personally liable when he or she has signed twice, once in a representative capacity and once without any representative indicia. Lumbermen Associates, Inc. v. Palmer（second signature on the back of the note）. Porter v. Pfahl. Tesoro Petroleum Corp. v. Schmidt.

除非存在相反证明 但问题并非到此为止。即使一个人在本票上的签名看上去系以个人身份作出，只要该人可以证明下列事实，就无须承担个人责任：本票的直接当事方，如本案中的银行、公司和公司总经理，实际上无意让签名人承担个人责任［第 3.403 条（2）（b）款］。签名人要承担主动证明的举证责任，

That does not, however, end the inquiry. The person who signs a note in an apparent individual capacity may escape personal liability by establishing that the immediate parties to the note -- here the bank, the company, and Mrs. Friel -- had established that personal obligation was not to attach. G. L. Section 3-403（2）（b）. The burden of affirmatively showing the parties had “otherwise established” that personal

证明根据当事方的“另行约定”，对于看上去并未限制个人责任的本票签名，签名人实际并不承担个人责任（C 诉 P 案；C 诉 O 案；L 诉 M 案）。

liability would not attach to an apparently unqualified signature on a note falls upon the signer. Commonwealth Bank & Trust Co. v. Plotkin. Carlton Ford, Inc. v. Oste. Leahy v. McManus.

本票的签署过程　在本案中，根据初审法官所认定的事实和所提交的报告，上诉庭判定，银行和总经理女士均已确认，总经理女士无须承担个人责任。对此，我们希望进一步分析案件中的某些事实因素。代表本案公司提出贷款申请并进行相关谈判的，是总经理已去世丈夫的弟弟。弟弟安排并陪同总经理女士来到银行。在与银行稍加交谈之后，一位银行职员把贷款文件交给总经理女士，并告诉她签上其名字和职务，随后指着下一行，告诉她只签她的名字。对于为什么要签两次名字，总经理女士没有提出任何问题。

In the instant case the Appellate Division concluded on the basis of the report and the trial judge's findings of fact that the bank and Mrs. Friel had established she would not be personally liable. We, therefore, recite additional elements of the facts. It was David Friel who applied for the loans on behalf of the company and conducted whatever negotiations were involved. He arranged to accompany Mrs. Friel to the bank, where, after small talk, a bank officer presented prepared loan documents and instructed Mrs. Friel to sign her name and title, then pointed to the next line and told her to sign only her name. Mrs. Friel asked no questions about why she was asked to sign twice.

她看了一下贷款文件，但并没有阅读，至少没有试图真正理解。但是，即使认真阅读该文件，本来对她也没有什么真正帮助，因为她对商业、银行业务或

She glanced over but did not read the papers -- at least not in any comprehending fashion. Reading the instruments carefully would not have done her much good, as Mrs. Friel was without experience in business,

公司融资没有经验。在总经理女士签名的旁边，没有类似“共同制票人”或“保证人”这类的用词。在本票的正文中也没有任何相关文字来提醒经验不足的银行客户，说明客户在作出第二个签名时，如果不标注显示代理人身份的职务，签名人就要承担个人责任。本票上注明的付款承诺人的地址是公司的地址。贷款的款项是用于公司业务。总经理女士本人并没有打算因为该签名而对本票承担个人责任。从银行的角度看，在两张本票任何一张的签字仪式中，银行都没有警告总经理女士说，第二个签名将会给她带来个人责任。

banking, or corporate finance. There were no words such as “co-maker” or “guarantor” next to the defendant’s signature, nor was there anything in the text of the notes which would have alerted an unsophisticated bank customer that a second signature without a title indicating representative capacity would create personal liability. The address of the promisor on the notes was that of the company. Loan proceeds were for company purposes. Mrs. Friel did not intend that her signatures create personal liability on the notes. For its part, the bank at neither of the signing ceremonies warned Mrs. Friel that her second signatures created personal obligations.

不存在共同理解　从初审法官认定的上述事实中可以看到，银行与总经理女士并没有达成共同理解。如果说，票据的直接当事方已“确认”了责任限制，该词就意味着他们已达成协议。但上述情况正好相反。我们也许可以承认这个事实，即总经理女士的主观理解是，她所签署的是纯粹的公司贷款文件，但是，

What follows from the facts found by the trial judge was that the bank and Mrs. Friel had not arrived at common ground. That is the antithesis of the immediate parties to the instrument having “established” limits of liability, a word that implies an agreement. We may accept as a fact Mrs. Friel’s subjective understanding that she was signing for a purely corporate loan but, in order for her to prevail, the bank must either （1） have

如果因此而否定其个人责任，银行必须：（1）已经让她明白，银行不寻求她个人的信用支持，或（2）已经显示出银行的意图，即不会追索公司以外的财产。但是，在本案已认定的事实中或法庭报告中，没有任何证据可以支持上述任何一个结论。

given her to understand that it was not looking to her credit or （2） it must appear that the bank's intent was not to look beyond the company's assets. Neither proposition finds support in the facts found or the compendium of the evidence contained in the report.

免责需要主动证明　从上述案件材料中我们知道，总经理女士并未参与贷款条款的谈判，也没有提出过任何问题，且银行也没有以任何方式说明她需要对贷款承担个人责任。但是，所有这些都远远不能构成主动的证明，即当事方已经同意，贷款将仅由公司承担责任。如同C诉P案的情况，我们在某种程度上知道借款人的意图，但是，没有任何证据可以显示银行的意图（另参见C诉O案；N诉V案）。一名制票人在本票上签名时，即使其主观上仅以代理人的身份签署，但是，如果该主观意图没有被透露出来，就不能证明存在第3.403条（2）（b）款所要求的共同理解（参见K诉C案；R

From those sources we know that Mrs. Friel did not negotiate the terms of the loans, she asked no questions, and the bank said nothing one way or the other about requiring her to become personally obligated on the loans. All that falls well short of an affirmative showing that the parties had agreed that the corporation was to be solely liable. As in Commonwealth Bank & Trust Co. v. Plotkin, we know something about the borrower's intent, but there is no manifestation of intention on behalf of the bank. See also Carleton Ford, Inc. v. Oste； Norfolk County Trust Co. v. Vichinsky. An undisclosed intention by a maker to sign only in a representative capacity does not establish the understanding required by G. L. Section 3-403 （2）（b）. See Kuhns v. Coussement； Rotuba Extruders, Inc. v. Ceppos； Seale v.

诉C案；S诉N案；T破产案）。

银行不存在误解 在上诉庭的判决中，多数派法官的判决似乎是基于共同误解和欺诈而免除了总经理女士的责任。但是，上诉庭并未认定，银行对总经理女士的个人责任问题存在任何误解，且本来也没有任何证据可以支持这种认定。银行在相隔了一年的两个场合分别要求总经理女士作出背书，且并未要求其在担保协议上也作出第二个签名（因为此签名没有任何意义）。这都说明，签名方式是银行的既定政策。总经理女士完全有可能对第二个签名的后果存在误解，但交易当事一方的误解，不足以引用共同误解的原则，因为该原则要求双方都存在误解（C诉T案；B诉S案；L诉C案；参见M诉S案；引用《合同法重述（第2版）》；请对照D诉B案）。

单方误解的问题 在某些情况下，存在单方误解的当事方也可以要求解除合同。《合同

Nichols; In re Turner.

In its opinion, the majority of the Appellate Division appears to have relieved the defendant of liability on the basis of defenses of mutual mistake and fraud. There was, however, no finding -- nor would evidence have supported it -- that the bank was mistaken about Mrs. Friel's personal obligation. That the bank asked for her indorsement on two separate occasions, a year apart, and did not seek a second signature on the security agreement （on which it would have been of no effect） bespeaks a conscious policy. Mrs. Friel may have been mistaken as to the consequence of her second signatures but the mistake of one party to the transaction is not sufficient to invoke the principle of mutual mistake; the mistake must be shared by both parties. Century Plastic Corp. v. Tupper Corp. Berman v. Sandler. LaFleur v. C.C. Pierce Co. See Maloney v. Sargisson; Restatement （Second） of Contracts. Contrast Dover Pool & Racquet Club, Inc. v. Brooking.

There are limited circumstances in which a party may avoid a contract on the basis of a unilateral mistake: "if he does not bear

法重述（第 2 版）》说：“如果一个当事方并未承担误解的风险，并且（a）基于该误解的情况，如果继续强制履行该合同，就会导致显失公平，或（b）另一个当事方知道该误解，或其过错引起了该误解”，则合同可以被解除（引用《合同法重述（第 2 版）》；参见 C 诉 C 案）。如果一项合同“在将全部条款相加后，构成过于苛刻的交易，而法院出于良知，无法协助该合同的履行”，该合同就属于显失公平（引用《合同法重述（第 2 版）》；C 诉 C 案；C 诉 W 案）。如同我们所看到的，对于封闭持有的公司来说，主要管理人员被要求在公司本票上背书，是普通的商业做法，因此几乎不会被视为显失公平。本案证据材料并未显示银行知道或有理由知道总经理女士对第二个签名的后果缺乏了解。前面讨论过的法典第 3.402 条，已将误解的风险分配给票据的签名人（参见《合同法重述（第 2 版）》）。另外，在 A 诉 P 案中，法院认为，法律的一般原则是，

the risk of mistake... and （a） the effect of the mistake is such that enforcement of the contract would be unconscionable, or （b） the other party had reason to know of the mistake or his fault caused the mistake.” Restatement （Second） of Contracts. See Covich v. Chambers. A contract is unconscionable if “the sum total of its provisions drives too hard a bargain for a court of conscience to assist”. Restatement （Second） of Contracts. Covich v. Chambers. Campbell Soup Co. v. Wentz. As we have seen, a note of a close corporation indorsed by a principal officer is a commercial commonplace, hence scarcely unconscionable. The record does not suggest that the bank knew or had reason to know about Mrs. Friel’s ignorance of the consequences of her second signature. Section 3-402 of the Uniform Commercial Code, discussed above, places the risk of mistake on the signer of an instrument. See Restatement （Second） of Contracts. See also Allen v. Plymouth, stating the general rule that relief is not granted for a mistake about what the law is if a person is ignorant of the law or mistaken about what it prescribes.

如果一个人对法律缺乏了解，或对法律规定存在误解，法律不会就该误解向该人提供救济。

关于欺诈问题 如果要认定欺诈，必须存在重大不实陈述，或存在欺骗性半真半假的语言或行为（参见K诉A案；N诉B案）。在本案中，虽然银行没有向总经理女士解释第二个签名的后果，但这尚不足以构成欺诈（S诉W案）。在签名之前的任何时间里，银行均未与总经理女士有过任何可以使后者受到误导的交往。在两次签字仪式上，当事方均未就票据和总经理女士签名的法律效力进行过讨论。总经理女士称，一方的沉默致使另一方有合理理由得出某种结论，但本案不是这种情况（请比较R诉P案）。

银行没有提醒的义务 也许有人希望，银行贷款职员应该善于替顾客着想，因此应该向没有律师陪伴的借款人解释一下文件和签名的效力。但是，对于一项商业交易，法律没有此种要求。在本案中，我们应该说明，案件

As to fraud, it requires a material misrepresentation or, through words or conduct, the conveyance of half truths which deceive. See Kannavos v. Annino; Nei v. Burley. The failure of the bank to explain to Mrs. Friel the consequences of her second signature did not rise to fraud. Swinton v. Whitinsville Sav. Bank. There were no preliminary dealings between Mrs. Friel and the bank by which she might have been misled. On neither signing occasion did the parties discuss the legal significance of the instruments and the signatures required of Mrs. Friel. This is not a case, as the defendant argues, where silence would reasonably lead a party to a particular conclusion. Contrast Richardson Elec. Co. v. Peter Francese & Son.

One might wish that a conscientious loan officer would explain the consequences of documents and signatures to a borrower not represented by counsel, but the law, in a commercial transaction context, imposes no duty so to do. In the instant case, it should be remarked, the record does not permit us to

证据材料不允许我们作出这样的假设，即银行职员知道总经理女士在业务方面经验不足。银行职员完全有可能未意识到需要进行披露，因为其完全有可能认为，这只是一项非常普通的交易。

suppose that the bank officer was aware of the defendant's commercial naivete. The bank officer may well have felt no call to discourse on what he would have thought a quite routine transaction.

结论 我们的上述结论，与法典第 3.402 条的正式评论所表述的法典宗旨是相符的。该宗旨要求，对商业票据表面所显示之内容的含义，要作出相互一致的解释（参见 H 诉 W 案；T 破产案）。特此推翻初审法院的判决。判决银行有权就两张本票的剩余本金取得付款，再加上已经发生的利息，以及银行所支出的合理律师费。

Our conclusions are consistent with the policy expressed in the comment to G. L. Section 3-402, to give consistent meaning to what appears on the face of commercial paper. See Havatampa Corp. v. Walton Drug Co.; In re Turner. The judgment entered in the trial court is reversed. Judgment is to enter for the plaintiff for the unpaid principal amounts of the two notes, together with accrued interest, plus reasonable attorney's fees incurred by the plaintiff.

案例 26　银行处理票据时是否行使了正常谨慎?

Espresso Roma Corporation v. Bank of America
洛马公司诉美洲银行案

加利福尼亚州上诉法院 2002 年；124 Cal.Rptr.2d 549

简　介

本案原告公司是由同一名股东（Boyd）拥有的几家公司，而该股东是这些公司的总经理。公司在本案被告银行（Bank of America）持有支票账户。本案的争议涉及公司一名雇员伪造的支票。在银行支付了这些伪造的支票后，公司起诉银行，要求银行赔偿损失。

从 1996 年年底到 1999 年 4 月，公司曾雇用一名财务经理（Joseph Montanez）负责公司的财务和记账工作。该财务经理可以拿到公司空白支票，并在计算机上填写支票内容。他随后下载了公司的计算机软件并偷取了空白支票，开始在家里制作公司支票，并将支票用于个人消费。公司直到 1999 年 5 月才发现，并随后报告给银行。此时该财务经理已离开公司，不知去向。从 1997 年 10 月至 1999 年 4 月，他伪造的公司支票总额超过 33 万美元。

公司因此起诉银行，称银行应承担支付伪造支票的责任。银行基于两个理由拒绝承担责任。首先，根据法典第 4.406 条（f）款的规定，如果伪造的情况发生在一年以前而公司未能发现，则无论银行在支付支票时是否存在疏忽，银行都不再对错误付款承担责任。其次，对于一年以内的支票，根据法典第 4.406 条（d）款和（e）款的规定，如果客户未能在本应发现伪造之后的 30 天内发现并报告给银行，银行就不再承担责任，除非银行对支票作出付款时本来就存在疏忽。本案主要的争议问题是，对于一年以内的伪造支票，银行在支付时是否存在疏忽？或者说，银行是否行使了正常谨慎？

是否存在疏忽或是否行使了正常谨慎，必须根据一定的标准来判断。而这个标准，就是上诉法院花费了大量精力讨论的“合理的商业准则”。法院最终判定，本案银行在支付伪造支票时遵守了合理的商业准则，不存在疏忽，因此维持了初审法院的判决，即批准银行提出的无审判决动议并判决银行胜诉。

判　决

本案的基本情况　初审法院批准了银行的无审判决动议，并作出了银行胜诉的判决。法院认为，根据法典第 4.406 条（d）款和（e）款的规定，关于银行就支票付款并支取公司账户的行为，公司无权以无授权付款为由指控银行。我们维持原判。

The court entered judgment in favor of the Bank after it granted the Bank's motion for summary judgment on the ground that appellants were precluded by California Uniform Commercial Code section 4-406, subdivisions （d） and （e） from asserting any claims against the Bank for unauthorized payment of checks drawn on their accounts. We shall affirm the judgment.

超过一年的错误付款　银行无审判决动议的依据是法典第 4.406 条。当银行支付的支票存在涂改或无授权签名情况时，第 4.406 条对银行向客户承担的责

The Bank's motion for summary judgment was based upon section 4-406, which limits a payor bank's liability to its customer for making payment upon checks with alterations or unauthorized signatures.

任作出限制。银行主张，根据第4.406条（f）款，如果向银行报告伪造的时间，距离伪造的发生时间已超过一年，公司就完全无权再向银行索赔。根据（f）款的条文，“无论客户或银行是否行使了谨慎”，该款均适用；并且，“在将对账单或已注销票证提供给客户后，客户如果在一年内未能发现和报告票证的任何无授权签名或涂改，即无权基于该无授权或涂改向银行索赔”。

Pursuant to subdivision （f） of section 4-406, the Bank asserted that appellants were absolutely precluded from asserting forgeries processed more than one year before the forgery was reported. By its terms subdivision （f） applies, “[w] ithout regard to care or lack of care of either the customer or the bank”, and precludes “a customer who does not within one year after the statement or items are made available to the customer discover and report the customer's unauthorized signature” from asserting it against the Bank.

公司的谨慎义务 银行同时还引用了第4.406条(d)款和(e)款。这两款对客户的索赔权规定了某些前提条件。根据第4.406条（c）款的规定，对于银行向客户提供的月度对账单或已注销支票，客户有义务迅即审阅，并行使合理谨慎来发现无授权签名或涂改，并在发现此类问题后，迅即向银行报告。

The Bank also relied upon the conditional preclusion established by subdivisions （d） and （e） of section 4-406. Subdivision （c） of section 4-406 imposes a duty upon the customer promptly to review monthly statements or checks made available to the customer by the bank, to exercise reasonable care in discovering any unauthorized signature or alteration, and promptly to notify the bank of the discovery of such items.

银行的谨慎义务 根据第4.406条（d）款的规定，如果客户未能履行上述义务，且同一人针对同一账户多次伪造支票，且

Pursuant to subdivision （d）, if the customer fails to comply with these duties, when the same person has forged checks on the account, the customer is precluded

客户在首次收到载有伪造票证的月度对账单或已注销支票后本应发现该伪造并通知银行但实际未在 30 天内发现并通知银行，则对于银行的无授权付款，客户无权向银行索赔［第 4.406 条（d）（2）款］。但如果客户可以证明，银行“在支付票证时未能行使正常谨慎，且此种不谨慎对损失的发生具有助推作用”，客户仍然有权追究银行的责任［第 4.406 条（e）款；R 诉 W 案］。

from making a claim against the bank for the unauthorized payment unless the customer notified the bank no more than 30 days after the first forged item was included in the monthly statement or canceled checks, and should have been discovered. （ § 4-406（d）（2）） This preclusion is conditional because the customer may avoid its application by establishing that the bank “failed to exercise ordinary care in paying the item and that the failure contributed to ［the］ loss” （ § 4-406（e）； Roy Supply, Inc. v. Wells Fargo Bank）.

不存在可供审理的事实问题

初审法院在批准银行的无审判决动议时判定，“根据第 4.406 条（d）款和（e）款，对于支取公司账户的支票付款，公司无权以无授权付款为由向银行索赔”。法院特别判定，公司未就下述问题提出可供审理的事实：“对于从公司账户支取的支票，银行处理该支票的体系是否违反了银行自己的程序”，或是否不合理地偏离了本地银行界的惯常做法。法院还判定，公司的专家证人在证词中也未能就“银行是否未能

In its order granting summary judgment, the court held that appellants were precluded by “sections 4-406（d） and 4-406（e） from asserting claims against the ［B］ank for unauthorized payments of checks drawn on ［appellants’］ checking accounts”. The court specifically ruled that appellants failed to create a triable issue of fact as to whether “the ［B］ank’s system of processing checks for appellants’ accounts violated the ［B］ank’s procedures” or varied unreasonably from general banking usage in the area. The court also ruled that the declaration of appellant’s expert failed to create a triable issue of fact “as

行使正常谨慎”的问题提出可供审理的事实。法院还判定，银行没有义务以肉眼方式查验支票。

to whether the [B]ank failed to exercise ordinary care", and that the Bank had no duty to sight review the checks.

举证责任问题 公司辩称，“关于不存在任何可供审理之事实的问题，银行未能完成其初步举证责任”，即未能初步证明:(1)虽然银行已提供月度对账单和已注销支票，但公司未能在30天内发现伪造并向银行报告，并且(2)银行在支付票证时行使了正常谨慎(参见A诉A案；引用民事诉讼法)；因此，举证责任从未转移至公司；同时，即使举证责任已转移至公司，关于银行是否行使了正常谨慎的问题，公司专家证人的证词也已提出了可供审理的事实问题。在这种情况下，法院无权作出有利于银行的无审判决。

Appellants argue that the burden never shifted to them to create a triable issue of fact because the Bank failed to meet its "burden of production to make a prima facie showing of the nonexistence of any triable issue of fact", that (1) despite the availability of monthly statements and canceled checks, appellants failed to discover and notify the Bank of the forgery within 30 days, and (2) it exercised ordinary care in paying the item. (See Aguilar v. Atlantic Richfield Co.; Code Civ. Proc.) Appellants further contend that, even if the burden did shift to them, the declaration of their own expert created a triable issue of fact on the issue whether the bank exercised ordinary care, precluding summary judgment in the Bank's favor.

根据法典第4.406条(d)款的规定，在月度对账单或已注销支票中首次列出了伪造的票证后，如果客户未能在本应发现该伪造的30天内向银行报告，则对于银行的无授权付款，客户即

Pursuant to section 4-406, subdivision (d), the customer is precluded from making a claim against the bank for unauthorized payment unless the customer notified the bank no more than 30 days after the first forged item was included in the monthly statement

无权向银行索赔［第 4.406 条（d）（2）款；正式评论 2］。

本案的基本事实　根据公司的起诉书，伪造的支票是在 1997 年 10 月至 1999 年 5 月被提示给银行付款的。但是，直到 1999 年 5 月 15 日左右，公司才发现或报告该伪造。为了初步证明应适用法典第 4.406 条（d）款对客户的限制条件，银行提供了公司总经理的证词，即在每一次对账单关账后的很短时间内，银行就向公司提供了月度对账单和已注销支票。公司总经理作证说，他每月都收到了对账单，且其中包含了已注销支票。1999 年 5 月，当其开始怀疑有人擅自出具支票后，他查阅了银行对账单和过去的支票。在查出伪造情况后，他通知了银行。上述证据可以支持这个推论，即 1997 年 11 月的对账单，应该是首次包含了伪造支票的对账单［参见 M 诉 B 案（在该案中，伪造的支票在 1966 年 3~5 月从账户中

or canceled checks and should have been discovered. (§ 4-406 (d) (2); see also Official Comments on U. Com. Code, com. 2)

According to the complaint, the forged checks were presented for payment between October 1997 and May 1999, but appellants did not discover or report them until on or about May 15, 1999. To establish its prima facie case that the conditional issue preclusion created by section 4-406 (d) applied, the Bank presented the deposition testimony of Boyd, that it made monthly account statements and canceled checks available to appellants shortly after the closing period of each statement. Boyd testified that he received statements on a monthly basis, and they included canceled checks. When Boyd began to suspect unauthorized checks were being written and reviewed the statements and checks in May 1999, he was able to identify, and reported, the forgery. This evidence supports the inference that the first monthly statement that would have reflected the forgery by Montanez would have been in November 1997 (see Mac v. Bank of America [where forged checks cleared account between March

支出，因此法院的推论是，4~6月的对账单包含了该支票）]。虽然公司有办法发现本案的伪造情况，但是直到一年半之后，公司才发现和报告了伪造情况，远远超出了第4.406条（d）款规定的30天期限。

公司的主张和理由 公司辩称，其总经理的证词不能支持银行的主张，即银行已经按月提供了对账单和已注销支票，因为总经理还作证说，在有些情况下，对账单或已注销支票也会出现不能按时通过邮件到达的情况。不过，总经理同时承认，当出现这种情况时，他可以到银行营业处拿到对账单或其副本。因此，银行的主张，即已根据法典第4.406条（a）款向公司提供了月度对账单，与公司总经理的证词完全不矛盾。公司还辩称，银行有义务自己出示对账单和已注销支票，或由银行职员作证说银行已提供了该材料，而不能依赖公司总经理自己的承认。但此辩称不能成立，因为总经理的作证符合规则并可被采纳（引用民事诉讼法）。

and May 1966, it was inferable that statements from April through June reflected those checks]). Yet, despite having the means to discover the forgeries, more than a year and a half elapsed before appellants discovered and reported any of them, far beyond the 30 days specified in section 4-406, subdivision (d).

Appellants argue that Boyd's testimony did not support the Bank's assertion that it made monthly checks or statements available because Boyd also testified that there were some instances in which the statements or checks did not arrive through the mail in a timely fashion. Boyd, however, acknowledged that when this occurred he was able to pick up the statement or a duplicate at the branch. Nothing in Boyd's testimony contradicts the Bank's assertion that it made monthly statements available to appellants in accordance with section 4-406, subdivision (a). Nor is there any merit to appellants' assertion that the Bank was required to submit the statements and canceled checks themselves, or a declaration of a bank officer that it made them available, instead of relying upon Boyd's admission, which was competent and admissible evidence (Code Civ. Proc.).

公司还提出，银行应准确说明每一张伪造支票到底被包含在哪一个月的对账单里，因为只有这样，才能说明公司是否本应发现该伪造，并计算 30 天的通知期限。但正好相反，在类似本案这样的情况下，即所有的伪造均出自同一个人，客户（本案的公司）无权提出索赔的真正原因是，其未能在本应发现第一张伪造票证的 30 天内向银行报告［第 4.406 条（d）（2）款］。无论 1997 年 10 月之后的第一份对账单准确的是在哪一天发送给公司的，银行所提供的证据都证明，银行已经按月度向公司提供了对账单和已注销支票。尽管如此，公司直到 1999 年 5 月中旬才第一次报告了伪造的情况，远在 30 天期限过期之后。

Appellants also suggest that the Bank was required to establish, with respect to each forged check, exactly when it made the monthly statement including the forged check available, thereby providing the means by which appellants should have discovered the forgery, and triggering the 30-day notification period. To the contrary, where as here, the forgeries are all committed by the same person, it is the failure to report the first forged item within 30 days that precludes the customer from asserting the subsequent forgeries (§ 4-406（d）（2））. Regardless of the exact date the first monthly statement after October 1997 was made available to appellant, the evidence the Bank submitted established that it made statements and checks available on a monthly basis, yet the first forgery was not reported until mid-May 1999, long after the 30-day period expired.

公司应承担举证责任 由于已经初步证明，银行提供了月度对账单和已注销支票，而公司未能在 30 天内将伪造问题报告给银行，因此，除非公司能够证明，银行“在支付票证时未能行使正

Having established a prima facie case that the Bank made monthly statements and checks available, and that appellants failed to notify the Bank within 30 days, the preclusion pursuant to section 4-406, subdivision （d） applies unless the customer can establish

常谨慎，且该不谨慎对损失的发生具有助推作用”［4.406 条（e）款］，否则，就要适用第 4.406 条对公司追索权的限制。

that the bank, “failed to exercise ordinary care in paying the item and that the failure contributed to ［the］ loss”. § 4-406（e）.

银行正常谨慎的定义 法典第 3.103 条（a）（7）款对“正常谨慎”的定义是：“对于从事商业的人，‘正常谨慎’是指遵守该人所在地通行的且适用于该人商业领域的合理商业准则。如果任何银行以自动化方式处理任何票据的收款或付款，合理商业准则不要求该银行检验该票据，只要省略该检验并不违反该银行自己制定的规则，且只要该银行的规则并未不合理地偏离本篇或第 4 篇未予禁止的一般银行惯例。”

“Ordinary care” is defined by section 3-103, subdivision （a）（7） as follows: “‘Ordinary care’ in the case of a person engaged in business means observance of reasonable commercial standards, prevailing in the area in which the person is located, with respect to the business in which the person is engaged. In the case of a bank that takes an instrument for processing for collection or payment by automated means, reasonable commercial standards do not require the bank to examine the instrument if the failure to examine does not violate the bank's prescribed procedures and the bank's procedures do not vary unreasonably from general banking usage not disapproved by this Article 3 or Article 4.”

相关判例 在S诉W案中，法院基于第 4.406 条（d）款和（e）款，批准了银行的无审判决动议并作出其胜诉的判决。该法院解释说，第 4.406 条中“正常谨慎”的概念，“是以‘职业性疏忽的

As explained in Story Road Flea Market, Inc. v. Wells Fargo Bank, a case in which the court upheld a motion for summary judgment in the Bank's favor based upon section 4-406, subdivisions （d） and （e）, ordinary care as used in section 4-406 is a “ ‘professional

标准’来判断谨慎程度。这个标准的参照是银行界所使用的程序，而不考虑‘通情达理的人’在类似情况下本来会如何做”（S 诉 W 案）。该法院认为，“合理的商业准则不要求银行去查验票据，只要该省略不违反银行自己制定的程序，且银行的程序并未不合理地偏离一般银行惯例”（S 诉 W 案）。

negligence’ standard of care which looks at the procedures utilized in the banking industry rather than what a ‘reasonable person’ might have done under the circumstances”.（Id）“［R］easonable commercial standards do not require the bank to examine the instrument if the failure to examine does not violate the bank’s prescribed procedures and the bank’s procedures do not vary unreasonably from general banking usage.”（Id）

银行初步证明不存在疏忽

在本案中，银行为了支持其无审判决动议，提交了其专家证人的证词。该证词初步证明银行已行使了正常谨慎。该证人首先说明了自己的行业专家资历，随后说明，“本案银行和规模相似的银行（包括旧金山湾区内的类似银行）都属于‘批量入账’的银行”，而他本人“熟悉这些银行处理支票的设计思路和程序”。

The Bank, in support of its motion for summary judgment, presented a prima facie showing that it exercised ordinary care, through the declaration of its expert, Jack Thomas. In addition to stating his qualifications as an expert in the field, Thomas declared that he was “familiar with the check processing strategies and procedures employed by banks similarly sized to Bank of America, including those within the San Francisco Bay area, which are ‘bulk file bookkeeping’ banks”.

该证人进一步解释说，“本案银行对支票处理采用‘批量入账’方式”，也就是说，采用自动方式处理支票，而不是用肉眼

He further explained that “Bank of America is a ‘bulk file bookkeeping’ check processor”, meaning that it processes checks automatically and does not visually examine

查验每一张支票或核实其签名。该证人说，本案银行在加利福尼亚州每天处理的支票超过100万张，因此尽管其使用防伪识别装置，但该装置的设计原理无法抓住“伪造雇主支票的骗子雇员，因为只有雇主才能认出这种支票是伪造的”。

individual checks or verify signatures. Thomas declared that Bank of America processes in excess of one million checks per day in California, and although it uses fraud filters, they are not designed to "catch a crooked employee who forges his employer's checks, which only the employer would know are forged".

该证人认为，本案银行的“做法和程序，与加利福尼亚州其他采用‘批量入账’方法的银行是一致的”。该证人还“向本案银行的负责人进行过核实，即银行在处理本案争议的支票时，确实遵守了银行处理支票的程序”。该证人的结论是，“在处理本案公司的支票时，根据本案银行所在地区以及本案公司持有账户地区的通行的合理商业准则，本案银行行使了正常谨慎”。

Thomas declared that the Bank's "practices and procedures are consistent with those of all other large 'bulk file bookkeeping' banks in California". Thomas also "verified with the responsible [B]ank officer that [the Bank] followed its procedures with respect to the checks at issue in this litigation when it processed the checks". He concluded that the Bank "exercised ordinary care in processing [appellants'] checks in observance of reasonable commercial standards prevailing in the area in which Bank of America is located, and where [appellants] maintained their accounts".

公司的反驳不能成立　公司辩称，上述证词本身不足以定义“本地区”的合理商业准则［第3.103条（a）（7）款］，且证

Appellants argue that this declaration was insufficient to define the reasonable commercial standard "in the area", (§ 3-103, subd. (a) (7)) and

词未能显示，本案银行所使用的支票自动处理程序，并未不合理地偏离一般的银行惯例，因为该专家证人说，银行做法所符合的准则，是全加利福尼亚州“批量入账”银行的商业准则，且仅仅考虑了类似规模银行的做法。

failed to demonstrate that the Bank’s automated check processing did not vary unreasonably from general banking usage, because the expert stated that the Bank’s practices conformed to commercial standards for “bulk file bookkeeping” in all of California and considered only the practices of similarly sized banks.

但是，公司的上述主张，是把“全加利福尼亚州”这个提法孤立看待，并脱离了原有的上下文。该证人特别说明，他也对“旧金山湾区”类似规模的银行的做法很熟悉。因此，从整体看，证词所表达的意思是，本案银行的做法不仅符合湾区类似规模银行的做法，而且符合全加利福尼亚州类似规模银行的做法。

Appellant, however, takes the reference to the entire State of California in isolation and out of context, because the expert specifically stated that he was also familiar with the practices of similarly sized banks in the “San Francisco Bay area”. Thus, read as a whole, the expert’s declaration expressed the opinion that the Bank’s practices conformed not only with those of similarly sized banks in the Bay Area, but also with similarly sized banks in the State of California.

公司还主张，专家证词不仅要证明本案银行的做法符合本地区类似规模银行的做法，而且要证明其符合本地区所有银行的做法。这个主张对我们没有说服力。正好相反，根据法典第 3.103 条（a）（7）款的定义，正常谨慎是指“遵守该人所在地通行的，

Nor are we persuaded by appellant’s contention that it was necessary to offer expert opinion that the Bank’s practices were consistent with those of all banks in the area, not just those of similarly sized banks. To the contrary, section 3-103, subdivision（a）（7）defines ordinary care as “observance of reasonable commercial standards, prevailing

并适用于该人商业领域的合理商业准则”。这项规定的含义是,准则的合理性是基于可比业务而言的[第4.406条正式评论4(如果银行的“程序是合理的,且被本地区其他类似银行所惯常遵守”,且银行在处理争议支票时遵守了该程序,就证明银行行使了正常谨慎)]。

in the area in which the person is located, with respect to the business in which the person is engaged”, meaning the standard of reasonableness is set by comparable businesses. (See com. 4, § 4-406) [ordinary care is established if the bank's “procedure is reasonable and is commonly followed by other comparable banks in the area” and was followed by the bank in processing the checks in issue.]

在确定不同银行是否具有可比性时,规模是相关因素,因为从银行业来说,一家小型和支票数量相对较少,且与客户相熟的银行,其处理支票的合理商业程序,相对于每天处理超过100万张支票的大型银行的合理程序,肯定会有很大区别。

Size is a relevant factor in identifying comparable businesses because, in the banking context, a reasonable commercial standard for processing checks at a small bank with a relatively small volume of checks, and personal familiarity with its customers, would be quite different than what is reasonable for a large bank that processes upwards of a million checks per day.

银行履行了初步举证责任

因此,银行证人的证词已经证明,本地区具有类似规模的银行的通行的、合理的行业做法是,使用具有防伪过滤装置的自动化系统大规模处理支票,但该程序不包括肉眼查验每一张支票来核实签名。本案银行的程序符合这个标

Thomas's declaration therefore established that the reasonable industry standard prevailing in the area for similarly sized banks was to bulk process checks through an automated system that employs fraud filters, but does not include sight review of individual checks for signature verification. The Bank's procedures conformed to this

准，而这个标准与加利福尼亚州其他采用批量入账方式的银行的一般银行惯例也是一致的。本案银行在本案中也遵守了其程序。

standard, which also was consistent with general bank usage as reflected by the practices of other bulk file bookkeeping banks in California, and it followed those procedures in this case.

我们的结论是，银行证人的作证足以初步证明，本案银行行使了正常谨慎。因此，举证责任转移至公司，其需要提出本案可供审理的事实问题（S 诉 W 案）。

We conclude that Thomas's declaration was sufficient to establish a prima facie case that the Bank exercised ordinary care, thereby shifting the burden to appellant to create a triable issue of fact. （Story Road Flea Market, Inc. v. Wells Fargo Bank）

公司的相反证词　公司也提交了其专家证人的相反证词。对此，初审法院的结论是正确的，即对于本案银行是否“未能行使正常谨慎”，该证词未提出可供审理的事实问题。该证人作证说，他访问了“附近县的大型和小型银行，并询问了他们的实际做法”。这些银行是在账户营业厅决定是否就票证付款，并拥有“查验支票伪造签名”的方法，无论是使用签名卡，还是采用数字成像技术。他还作证说，对于造成透支的支票，缺乏签名的支票，或超过某个金额的支票，这些银行会手工查验。

Although appellants submitted the declaration of its own expert, John Moulton, in opposition, the trial court correctly concluded that it failed to create a triable issue of fact on the question whether the Bank "failed to exercise ordinary care". Moulton declared that he called upon "large and small banks in Alameda County to inquire of their actual practices". These banks make decisions for payment of items at the branch where the account is kept and have the "means to check signatures for forgeries" present, whether it be by signature card or digital imaging. He also declared that these banks would manually examine checks which resulted in an overdraft, were unsigned, or exceeded a certain amount.

相反证词不足以反驳银行证词 该证人证词的关键瑕疵在于，他并没有通过调查批量入账且具有类似营业规模的银行来定义适用的合理商业准则，而只是说明，大型银行和小型银行会对某些特定支票采用肉眼查验或其他处理的做法，并以该做法作为证词的基础。但是，如果不能证明本地区类似银行都会选取个别支票进行肉眼查验，则仅仅说明本案银行的系统不对个别支票进行肉眼查验或核实签名，并不足以证明存在可供审理的事实，因为第3.103条（a）（7）款规定，“合理的商业准则并不要求银行查验票据，只要省略该查验并不违反该银行自己制定的程序，且只要该银行的程序并未不合理地偏离一般的银行惯例”。

The fundamental defect in Moulton's declaration is that, instead of defining the applicable reasonable commercial standard of care by looking at comparably sized banks using bulk file bookkeeping, he bases his opinion that the standard of care requires certain checks be selected for sight review, or other special handling, upon the practices of large and small banks. Without a showing that comparable banks in the area select individual checks for sight review, the fact that the Bank's system did not select individual checks for sight review, or signature verification, is insufficient to create a material issue of fact because section 3-103, subdivision（a）（7）specifies that "reasonable commercial standards do not require the bank to examine the instrument if the failure to examine does not violate the bank's prescribed procedures and the bank's procedures do not vary unreasonably from general banking usage".

肉眼查验无法发现本案的伪造 此外，即使仅仅为讨论目的而假设，合理的商业准则确实要求本案银行制定相关规则来挑选

Moreover, assuming arguendo that reasonable commercial standards did require that the Bank have established criteria for selecting some checks for sight review,

某些支票进行肉眼查验，公司证人的证词仍然无法证明存在可供审理的事实，因为从该证词中无法推断出，此种系统的缺失，是损失发生的助推因素［第 4.406 条（e）款］。公司证人并没有说明，对于挑选某些支票进行肉眼查验的自动处理系统，除挑选透支的支票或超过某个数额的支票外，还能有什么其他的挑选标准。因此，即使假设本案银行采用了挑选某些支票进行肉眼查验的此种系统，公司证人的证词也没有提供任何依据来说明，本案中的任何无授权支票本来会被挑选出来进行肉眼查验，并因此可以更早地发现伪造情况。

Moulton's declaration still fails to create a triable issue of fact because it provides no basis to infer that the failure to have such a system contributed to the loss. （§ 4-406, subd.（e））Moulton does not specify what the criteria should be, in an automated check processing system that selects some checks for sight review, other than reviewing a check that causes an overdraft, or is in excess of some unspecified amount. Therefore, even if such a system of selection for sight review had been used by the Bank, the declaration provides no basis for inferring that any of the unauthorized checks would have been selected for sight review, resulting in earlier discovery of the forgeries.

签名卡丢失无关紧要　公司还辩称，根据其证人的证词，谨慎的标准还包括,需要有适当“方法”对签名进行核实，但在本案中，银行已经无法找到公司账户的签名卡了。但是，无论是银行自己的程序，还是合理的商业准则，都不要求银行对任何伪造支票进行肉眼查验［第 3.103 条（a）（7）款］。由于银行没有义务

Appellants also argued that, based upon Moulton's declaration, the standard of care included having the “means” available to verify signatures, and the Bank had been unable to locate the signature cards relating to appellants' accounts. However, neither the Bank's own procedures, nor reasonable commercial standards, required that the bank sight review any of the forged checks（§ 3-103, subd.（a）（7））. Absent

核实签名，且没有证据说明银行自己的程序要求对本案任何伪造支票进行肉眼查验，因此，银行无法找到账户签名卡的情况无关紧要，而签名卡的丢失本来也不可能是公司损失的助推因素［第4.406条（e）款（公司必须证明，银行未能行使正常谨慎的行为，是公司损失的助推因素）］。维持原判。

a duty to verify the signatures, or evidence that the Bank's own procedures required sight review of any of the forged checks, it is irrelevant that the Bank could not locate the signature cards, and the fact that they were missing could not have contributed to appellants' loss.（§ 4-406, subd.（e）［plaintiff must show that the bank's failure to exercise ordinary care contributed to plaintiff's loss］.）The judgment is affirmed.

案例 27　雇员的行为是否在雇佣范围之内?

Gina Chin Associates Inc. v. First Union Bank
锦清伙伴公司诉第一联盟银行案

弗吉尼亚州最高法院 2000 年；500 S.E.2d 516

简　介

本案原告是一家食品公司（Chin），在本案被告银行（First Union）持有支票账户。银行的一名柜员（Cardenas）在银行柜台从事接待客户的工作，包括接受客户存入银行的支票。柜员的哥哥有一位女朋友（Lehman），即本案中的骗子女士。骗子女士在原告食品公司担任财务工作，熟知公司的财务流程，并会使用计算机制作公司的应付款支票。骗子女士也曾在银行工作过，熟悉银行的业务流程。

骗子女士通过自己的男朋友认识了被告银行的柜员以后，说服了柜员和自己共同进行诈骗活动。骗子女士利用自己在食品公司的工作便利，伪造向公司供应商出具的付款支票和公司总经理的签名，再伪造供应商的背书，使支票向她自己付款，然后再将支票存入自己在被告银行开设的账户。每次存入的支票都是交给该柜员。该柜员在接受这些支票时，自然知道支票是伪造的。随后，骗子女士会给柜员一定的报酬。最终，诈骗活动被发现，2 人均被判刑入狱。

随后，食品公司起诉柜员的雇主银行，认为基于“雇主责任原则”(Doctrine of Respondeat Superior)，银行要对柜员故意接受伪造支票的行为承担责任。本案最主要的争议是，柜员的行为是否可被视为“雇佣范围”(scope of employment)之内的行为？如果答案是肯定的，柜员的行为就被视为银行的行为，因而柜员的欺诈就成为银行的欺诈，而银行也就无法再以食品公司自己的疏忽作为抗辩。

本案的审理经过了两次初审和两次上诉。下述判决是第二次上诉后的判决。弗吉尼亚州最高法院判定，对“雇佣范围”这个概念不能作狭隘解释。即使雇员的侵害行为明显违反了雇主规定，且明显出于雇员自己的利益，但只要相关行为在雇员的工作职责范围内(如本案柜员接受支票存入的工作)，就有可能属于雇佣范围之内。初审法院以无审判决的形式判定，柜员的行为不可能属于雇佣范围之内，并因此作出了有利于银行的判决。弗吉尼亚州最高法院推翻了该判决，认为公司已完成了雇佣关系的初步举证，因而下一个问题，即柜员的行为是否在雇佣范围之内，必须在银行进一步举证后，通过法院审理而确定，并有可能需要陪审团的裁定。

判　决

第二次初审判决　我们需要在本上诉中确定初审法院的判决是否存在错误。初审法院排除了受害公司提交的某些证据，因为法院认定，作为法律问题，银行柜员参与伪造支票存入账户的欺诈行为时，超出了雇佣范围，因此雇主银行无须对该行为承担民事责任。

In this appeal, we consider whether the trial court erred in striking the evidence at the conclusion of the plaintiff's case-in-chief by ruling, as a matter of law, that a bank teller who participated in a scheme to deposit forged checks was acting outside the scope of his employment, thus relieving his employer from civil liability for those acts.

本案的基本情况　1996 年 6 月 11 日，公司就骗子女士和银行柜员的伪造活动起诉银行，要求就公司损失取得 270,488.72 美元的赔偿。公司指控银行存在疏忽，因为后者接受了支票的存入并作出了付款，但这些支取公司账户的支票的出票人签名和受款人背书都是伪造的。公司进一步指控，对于银行柜员的刑事违法行为，银行应承担被代理人的责任。

On June 11, 1996, Chin filed a motion for judgment against First Union seeking $270,488.72 in damages resulting from the forgery scheme of Lehman and Cardenas. Chin alleged that First Union was negligent when it accepted for payment checks drawn on Chin's accounts bearing both forged signatures of the drawer and forged endorsements of the payees. Chin further alleged that First Union was vicariously liable for Cardenas' criminal acts.

第一次初审判决　初审法院上次审理时，支持了付款银行对受害公司的整体抗辩，以无审判决的形式判决银行胜诉，理由是基于公司所陈述的事实情况，法典的某些规定否定了支票的出票人起诉存款银行的权利。对于初审法院的判决，我们接受了公司的上诉，推翻了初审法院的判决，并将案件发回重审。

The trial court initially sustained First Union's demurrer to Chin's motion for judgment and entered summary judgment in favor of First Union on the ground that under the factual circumstances asserted by Chin certain provisions of the Uniform Commercial Code barred an action by the drawer of a check against the depository bank. We awarded Chin an appeal from that judgment, reversed it, and remanded the case for further proceedings.

第一次上诉判决　在第一次推翻原判并发回重审时，我们曾判定，“根据法典第 3.404 条和第 3.405 条的规定，公司的指控

In doing so, we held that "Chin's motion for judgment pled a cause of action pursuant to § § 3-404 and § 3-405 of the Uniform Commercial Code". We explained

存在法律基础”。我们解释说，根据法典的上述规定，在确定谁应对受损失的人承担责任时，应采用“疏忽程度比较原则”，原因在于，“这个过程的所有参与者在出立和处理支票时，都有义务行使正常谨慎”。

本来应该重审疏忽问题 因此，在本案具体情况下，为了最终确定疏忽的相对程度，就要将银行和公司各自雇员的行为进行比较。这属于完全应由陪审团裁定的问题。简单地说，虽然相关事实没有争议，即银行接受了伪造支票并作出付款，而公司使自己雇员有机会取得支票并伪造，但是，当时诉讼中仍然未能确定的最终问题是，是否仅是银行存在疏忽？还是银行和公司都存在疏忽？如果是后者，双方各自的疏忽程度如何？

第二次初审的情况 在重审中，初审法院于1999年7月17日进行了陪审团审理。银行提出了排除公司证据的动议，要求排除公司预计将会提出的有关银行通常惯例和做法的专

that pursuant to these statutes the concept of comparative negligence is employed to determine liability to the person sustaining the loss based upon the premise “that all participants in the process have a duty to exercise ordinary care in the drawing and handling of [checks]”.

Thus, in the context of the present case, the ultimate issue of comparative negligence, which is solely a jury issue, centers upon the conduct of First Union through its employees and that of Chin through its employees. In short, there is no dispute that while First Union accepted the forged checks for payment and Chin permitted access to its checks by its employee who forged them, the ultimate issue still undecided at that point in the proceedings was whether First Union was negligent or whether First Union and Chin were both negligent and, if so, to what comparative extent.

Upon remand, a jury trial was commenced in the trial court on July 17, 1999. After First Union prevailed on its motion in limine to exclude the anticipated testimony of Chin’s expert witness regarding established banking customs and standards, the trial

家证词。法院支持了银行的动议，理由是“本案主要是雇佣关系范围问题”。

公司的举证　公司将银行柜员、骗子女士和公司财务主管均列为证人。柜员和骗子女士详细说明了伪造支票和存入骗子女士账户的事实。柜员还作证说，自己从银行离职后，骗子女士继续在另一家银行从事伪造活动，因为柜员的哥哥在该银行担任柜员，而骗子女士在该银行也持有账户。公司财务主管则对公司未能发现伪造的情况提供了证词。公司举证结束后，法院向陪审团宣布了当事方已承认的事实，包括柜员的主管对柜员的行为并不知情的事实。

双方的主张　随后，银行要求排除公司的上述证据，称公司未能证明柜员有意接受伪造支票存入的行为系雇佣范围内的行为。银行辩称，“虽然接收这些支票也许是银行业务的一部分，因为银行业务确实包括接受支票的存入，但没有证据表明，本案

court stated “the primary issue is scope of employment”.

Cardenas, Lehman, and Donald Chin, Chin’s treasurer, were each called as witnesses for Chin. Cardenas and Lehman detailed the scheme to forge the checks and to deposit them into Lehman’s account. Cardenas further testified that after he left his employment with First Union, Lehman continued the forgery scheme using her account at another bank where Cardenas’ brother worked as a teller. Donald Chin testified concerning the failure of Chin to detect the forgery scheme. At the conclusion of Chin’s case-in-chief, the jury was read stipulations of fact, including the stipulation that Cardenas’ acts were not known to his supervisors.

First Union moved to strike Chin’s evidence, asserting that Chin had failed to establish that Cardenas was acting within the scope of his employment in knowingly accepting the forged checks for deposit. First Union argued that “although taking these checks may have been incidental to First Union’s business because it takes checks for

柜员的行为是为银行利益而为”。

作为回复，公司则引用了C诉B案和其他判例，称无须证明雇员的特定错误行为是为雇主利益而为，而是只需要证明，雇员当时所提供的服务，确属其受雇从事的服务。公司认为，其所提供的证据显示，柜员在接受伪造支票的存入时，系作为银行的雇员而作为。

初审法院未进行实质重审 初审法院在重审中判定，作为法律问题，柜员的行为“不在该雇员的授权范围之内，且根据公司提供的证据，即使从最有利于公司的角度去看，通情达理的人也不可能得出其他结论”。对于该判决，我们再次允许公司上诉。

本次上诉的程序因素 首先需要说明的是，如同下面将会显示的，本案在程序方面的状况具有重要意义。在初审法院排除了公司的证据后，本案才上诉到本院。因此，我们要在无法看到全

deposit, there was no evidence that it was in furtherance of First Union's interest".

Chin, citing Commercial Business Systems, Inc. v. BellSouth Services, Inc., and other cases, responded that the specific wrongful act by the employee need not be in furtherance of the employer's interest so long as the service that the employee was performing at the time was in the course of his employment. Chin asserted that its evidence showed that Cardenas was acting as an employee of First Union when he accepted the forged checks for deposit.

The trial court ruled as a matter of law that Cardenas' acts "were not within the scope of the employee's authority; and reasonable persons cannot differ on the conclusion reached herein based on the evidence presented by the Plaintiff, with all inferences most favorable to the Plaintiff". We awarded Chin this appeal.

Initially, we note that the procedural posture of this case, as will be demonstrated, is significant. The case is before us following the trial court's grant of the motion to strike Chin's evidence. In that posture, we are unable to review this case in consideration of

部已提交证据的情况下作出本上诉判决。此外，虽然本院在上一次上诉时曾审阅过本案，但是，关于公司对银行的指控，我们本次判决不涉及该指控最终能否成立的问题。尽管如此，基于下面说明的理由，我们推翻初审法院的判决,并再次将本案发回重审。

all the evidence that may have been produced on the issue in question. Moreover, despite our consideration of this case in the prior appeal, we are unable to reach the ultimate merits, or lack thereof, of Chin's claims against First Union. However, for the reasons that follow, we will reverse the judgment of the trial court and remand the case for further proceedings.

雇主责任的基本原则　对于一方基于“雇主责任原则”而声称另一方应承担雇主责任的问题，本院在将近 80 年前的 D 诉 M 案中曾作如下说明：如果一个人以故意和恶意方式自行作为而向另一人施加侵害，那么他自己应对该侵害承担赔偿责任。但同时，没有理由允许雇主将自己的生意交由完全无视公共利益的雇员去打理，从而使雇主逃脱其本应承担的责任。因此，对于雇员在雇佣和职责范围内以故意和恶意方式向他人施加的侵害，要求雇主和雇员必须同时承担赔偿责任，明显是正确的和公正的。雇员的侵害行为是否出于缺乏判断、性格缺陷或情绪失控，都无关紧要。并且，雇员在施加侵害

With respect to an assertion of liability based upon the doctrine of respondeat superior, this Court made the following pertinent observation almost 80 years ago in Davis v. Merrill：If a person, acting for himself, willfully and maliciously inflict an injury upon another, he is liable in damages for such injury. And there is no reason why a master should be permitted to turn his business over to servants who have no regard for the public welfare and thereby escape the responsibility which he would otherwise have to bear. It is manifestly right and just that both corporations and individuals be required to answer in damages for wanton and malicious assaults inflicted upon others by their servants, while acting within the scope of the servant's employment and duty, and it matters not whether the act of the servant is due to lack

时是否已经超出严格意义上的职责和授权范围，也无关紧要。

of judgment, the infirmity of temper, or the influence of passion, or that the servant goes beyond his strict line of duty and authority in inflicting such injury.

雇佣范围的确定 但是，几乎自从本州法院首次处理这个问题之日起，这个问题就是“令人困扰”的难题，即基于特定案件的特定事实，如何确定雇员的过错行为是否在雇佣范围之内？（参见K诉D案；A诉R案）

Almost from its first consideration by the courts of this Commonwealth, however, the determination of the issue whether the employee's wrongful act was within the scope of his employment under the facts of a particular case has proved "vexatious". See, e.g., Kidd v. De Witt; Appalachian Power Company v. Robertson.

我们曾将“雇佣范围”定义如下，一般而言，一项具有下列特征的行为属于“雇佣范围”之内:（1）该行为得到雇主明示或默示指使,或与业务有天然联系，并且（2）该行为虽然错误或不明智，但目的是促进雇主利益，或系基于某种本能或冲动，且该本能或冲动系雇员履行雇主业务之活动的自然后果（K诉W案）。

We have defined "scope of employment" in the following terms: Generally, an act is within the scope of the employment if (1) it was expressly or impliedly directed by the employer, or is naturally incident to the business, and (2) it was performed, although mistakenly or ill-advisedly, with the intent to further the employer's interest, or from some impulse or emotion that was the natural consequence of an attempt to do the employer's business Kensington Associates v. West.

应避免狭隘解释 上述定义第2段中的文字是银行在本案中所主张的主要立场。显然，本案

The language in [paragraph 2 of] this definition is the focal point of First Union's assertion in the present case. First

银行将该文字解释为，雇员的施害行为，必须是雇员为使雇主获益而施行的。第一眼看上去，该文字确实容易引起此种解释。但是，我们之前的判例并不支持通过引申方式来作出这种解释［参见 P 诉 C 案（医师与病人发生的不道德性关系有可能构成雇佣范围内的行为）；C 诉 B 案（即使雇员的行为违反了公司禁止利益冲突和禁止在签订合同时接受贿赂的政策，该行为仍有可能构成雇佣范围内的行为）］。同时，在本案中，我们也明确否定这种解释。

Union apparently interprets this language to require that the specific act which caused the injury be performed by the employee with an intent to benefit the employer. At first blush, this language is susceptible to such an interpretation. However, our prior decisions do not support that interpretation by implication, see, e.g., Plummer v. Center Psychiatrists, Ltd. （counselor engaging in unethical sexual relationship with patient was potentially acting within scope of employment）; Commercial Business Systems （employee violating company rule against self-dealing and accepting illegal bribes to award contracts was potentially acting within the scope of employment）, and we expressly reject it now.

在涉及雇员故意施行错误行为的案件中，不应对上述定义的文字进行狭隘的和字面的解读，不应将其作为法律问题自动适用于特定案件的事实。如果这样，该定义将出现明显的自相矛盾。本次诉讼以及本案银行要求排除公司证据的动议，就可以说明上述观点。当雇员故意施行错误行为并造成他人损伤时，从简单的

In cases involving a willful and wrongful act of an employee, a narrow and literal reading of the language in this definition, which would create a patent conflict within it, is not to be applied as a matter of law to the facts of a particular case. The present case and First Union’s assertions in support of its motion to strike Chin’s evidence are illustrative of the point. Where an employee commits a willful and wrongful act that results

逻辑角度看，该雇员通常不具有“促进雇主权益”的目的。也就是说，雇员通常没计划使雇主受益。

in injury to others, simple logic suggests that such employee generally does not do so “with the intent to further the employer’s interest”. That is to say, the employee generally does not intend to benefit the employer.

不能仅考虑行为动机　在本案中，如果说银行柜员为使自己获利而故意接受伪造支票的存入时，其目的并不是促进银行雇主的权益，这当然可以是一个合理结论。但从法律角度看，对于银行提出的排除公司证据的动议，上述情况本身没有解决该动议向初审法院提出的法律问题。相反，很明显，在涉及雇主责任问题时，为了正确地适用该原则，不能简单地断定，雇员故意作出的错误行为根本不可能是为了促进雇主的权益，或以某种形式使雇主受益。如果对此还存有某种疑惑，C诉B案和P诉C案已明确地解决了这个问题。

Here, it may well be reasonable to conclude that a bank teller does not intend to further the interest of his employer bank when he knowingly accepts forged checks for deposit for his own gain. However, that does not resolve the legal issue presented, as a matter of law, to the trial court upon a motion to strike the injured party’s evidence. Rather, it should be apparent that the proper application of this definition in the context of the doctrine of respondeat superior does not resolve into a simplistic determination that an employee’s willful and wrongful act was not done with the intent to further the employer’s interest or to benefit the employer in some way. Any doubt that may have existed in that regard was clearly resolved in Commercial Business Systems and in Plummer.

我们承认，在将上述定义适用于任何特定案件的事实时，如同本案一样，经常会遇到这个困

As in the present case, we recognize that the difficulty in applying this definition to the facts of a particular case frequently

难："真正需要解决的是，雇员行为是否属于雇佣范围之内这个问题，是应由法院来确定，还是属于应提交陪审团裁定的事实问题呢？"（C 诉 D 案）

arises where "[t] he real inquiry is, was the question as to whether [the employee] was acting within the scope of his employment one to be determined by the Court, or was it a question of fact to be submitted to, and determined by, the jury?" Crowell v. Duncan.

雇佣关系作为责任的初步证据　已确立的原则可为初审法院的分析提供一些指导。虽然原告需要承担举证责任，证明雇员在从事争议行为时，该行为在雇佣范围之内，但我们一贯判定，只要能证明雇佣关系的存在，就算是已初步证明了雇主的责任，尽管该初步证明可被反驳（M 诉 S 案）。因此，"在雇主与雇员的关系被证明以后，雇主就有义务证明，雇员在从事争议行为时，该行为不在雇佣范围之内。如果根据所提交的证据，该问题仍存有疑问，就应将其提交给陪审团裁定"[K 诉 W 案（其中引用 B 诉 S 案）；另参见 P 诉 C 案；T 诉 B 案]。

Settled principles guide the trial court's considerations. While the plaintiff has the burden of persuasion on the issue whether the employee was acting within the scope of his employment at the time of the act complained of, we have consistently held that proof of the employment relationship creates a prima facie rebuttable presumption of the employer's liability. McNeill v. Spindler. Thus, "[w] hen an employer-employee relationship has been established, the burden is on the [employer] to prove that the [employee] was not acting within the scope of his employment when he committed the act complained of, and if the evidence leaves the question in doubt it becomes an issue to be determined by the jury". Kensington Associates (quoting Broaddus v. Standard Drug Co.); see also Plummer; Turner v. Burford Buick Corp.

应考虑是否属于职务行为

应该承认，在有些情况下，损害是由故意侵权行为（且经常是刑事侵权行为）所引起，且雇主明显不可能认为这属于雇佣范围之内的行为，但无论如何，该行为又是在雇佣过程中实施的，甚至是基于雇佣关系所提供的便利而实施的。此时，初审法院的任务可能会格外困难。此类案件中需要考虑的因素包括，雇员在偏离雇佣范围时，是否“出于外部的、独立的和个人的动机，且系为自己的利益所为”（B 诉 S 案）。在这个问题上，我们需要将两个因素相区分。一个因素是雇员从事该行为的动机，另一个因素是雇员的服务是否在雇佣范围之内。在进行这种区分时，我们曾判定，雇员实施被指控之行为的动机，不能决定该行为是否在雇佣范围之内（C 诉 B 案；T 诉 W 案）。具有决定性的因素是，“其所从事的包含了侵权行为的服务，是否发生于公司的正常业务过程中”（D 诉 M 案；C 诉 B 案）。

Admittedly, the trial court's task may be particularly difficult in cases in which the injury is caused by an intentional, often criminal, tortious act which clearly would not have been contemplated by the employer as being within the scope of employment, but which nonetheless was performed incident to the employment and even facilitated thereby. Such cases invoke consideration of whether the employee deviated from the scope of his employment because of an "external, independent, and personal motive to do the act upon his own account". Broaddus. In that regard, we have distinguished between the motive of the employee and the relevant question whether the service performed was within the scope of employment. In making this distinction, we have held that the motive of the employee in committing the act complained of is not determinative of whether it took place within the scope of the employment relationship. Commercial Business Systems; Tri-State Coach Corp. v. Walsh. Rather, the issue is "whether the service itself, in which the tortious act was done, was within the ordinary course of such business". Davis v. Merrill; Commercial

Business Systems.

相关判例 在C诉B案中，雇员违反雇主设立的禁止利益冲突的制度，自行设立了一家企业，与那些向雇主公司提供服务的企业做生意。该雇员在公司中负责合同谈判和合同管理，而其利用自己的这种身份，将公司的业务输送给那些同意与自己个人企业合作并支付贿赂的供应商。我们判定，这些事实本身不能"得出最终结论说，雇员的行为不在雇佣范围之内"。尽管雇员的动机是追求个人利益，而不是雇主利益，但他仍然属于"在从事他被雇佣从事的工作中行使他的职权"。

In Commercial Business Systems, an employee, in violation of conflict of interest rules established by his employer, created a business to work with companies that provided services to his employer. The employee then used his position as a contract negotiator and administrator to funnel business to suppliers who agreed to work with his company and pay him illegal "kickbacks". We held that these facts did not "conclusively establish that [the employee] was not acting within the scope of his employment". Although the employee's motive was to advance his self-interest, rather than the interest of his employer, he was nonetheless "performing his duties in the execution of the services for which he was employed".

由陪审团裁定的事实问题

我们强调，在确定雇员行为是否处于雇佣范围之内时，雇员的恶意动机并非毫无关系。但是，动机只是需要考虑的因素之一。因此，除非雇员的行为仅微小地偏离了雇主业务，或该行为的偏离非常明显且不同寻常，否则，对于上述两种极端之间的情况，需

We emphasize that the employee's improper motive is not irrelevant to the issue whether the act was within the scope of employment. Rather, it is merely a factor to be considered in making that determination, and, unless the deviation from the employer's business is slight on the one hand, or marked and unusual on the other, but falls instead between those two extremes, the question

要由陪审团作出结论（M诉S案；K诉W案）。因此，我们在C诉B案中判定，“证据表明，存在需要由陪审团裁定的问题，即雇员在施行错误行为时是否处于雇佣范围之内”（另参见P诉C案）。

如果将上述原则应用到本案，则对于银行提出的排除证据的动议，初审法院需要确定，根据公司提供的证据，作为法律问题，一名通情达理的陪审员是否不可能裁定柜员和银行之间存在雇主与雇员关系？或在存在此种雇佣关系时，是否不可能裁定，柜员在从事损害公司的行为时，其行为系在雇佣范围之内？银行并不否认，公司提供的证据已明确证明，柜员和银行之间存在雇佣关系。因此，公司提供的证据，已初步证明了银行的责任。

银行的理由不能成立 但银行辩称，公司所提供的证据，正好也足以使银行完成其举证责

is for the jury. McNeill; Kensington Associates. Thus, in Commercial Business Systems, we held that “the evidence presents a jury issue whether [the employee] acted within the scope of his employment when he committed the wrongful acts”. see also Plummer.

Applying these principles, the issue presented to the trial court by First Union's motion to strike was whether the evidence presented by Chin was such that, as a matter of law, a reasonable juror could not find that an employer-employee relationship existed between Cardenas and First Union or that, although such a relationship existed, Cardenas was acting within the scope of that employment at the time of the commission of the acts which injured Chin. First Union does not contest that Chin produced clear evidence that established the necessary employment relationship between Cardenas and First Union. Accordingly, Chin's evidence established a prima facie case of First Union's liability.

First Union contends, however, that Chin's evidence was also sufficient to meet First Union's burden of production

任，即柜员的行为是否在其雇佣范围之外。此外，作为法律问题，该证据也足以否定所假定的雇主责任。对此，我们不能同意。

on the issue whether Cardenas' acts were nevertheless outside the scope of that employment and, moreover, that this evidence was sufficient to rebut the presumption of liability as a matter of law. We disagree.

银行辩称，公司的证据证明，柜员的过错行为并非“受雇主的明示或默示指使”，因为柜员的行为，包括将企业的业务支票存入个人账户，存入大额支票时未事先得到主管批准，故意接受带有伪造背书的支票的存入，都违反了银行的指示。

First Union asserts that Chin's evidence establishes that Cardenas' wrongful acts were not "expressly or impliedly directed by the employer" because he violated directives in accepting commercial checks for deposit into a personal account, in failing to obtain a manager's approval to accept high value checks for deposit, and in knowingly accepting checks for deposit with forged endorsements.

但是，银行的上述辩解不能成立。一项行为即使没有得到雇主的明示或默示指使，也有可能在雇佣范围之内。同样，一项行为即使违反了雇主的指示，也并非必然不在雇佣范围之内。实际上，如前面所说，检验的标准是“雇员所从事的包含了侵权行为的服务，是否发生于雇主的正常业务过程之中”。在本案中，很明显，银行柜员接受支票的存入，属于其在本案银行正常业务

This assertion is without merit because the act need not be expressly or impliedly directed by the employer in order for the act to occur within the scope of the employment. Similarly, an act committed in violation of an employer's direction is not always beyond the scope of the employment. Rather, as previously noted, the test is "whether the service itself, in which the tortious act was done, was within the ordinary course of" the employer's business. In this instance, it is clear that accepting checks for deposit by

过程中所提供的服务。

a bank teller is a service within the ordinary course of First Union's banking business.

银行进一步辩称，公司的证据还证明，柜员的行为完全是出于他个人和骗子女士的利益。因此，银行辩称，柜员系在雇佣范围之外作为，因为他从事该行为是出于"外部的、独立的和个人的动机。"

First Union further asserts that Chin's evidence also establishes that Cardenas was acting exclusively for his own benefit and that of Lehman. Thus, First Union contends that Cardenas was acting outside the scope of his employment because he had an "external, independent, and personal motive" to perform the act.

毫无疑问，当柜员决定参与刑事阴谋而接受伪造支票的存入时，他不是在忠实地履行他对雇主的职责和义务。柜员在参与骗子女士的计谋时系出于个人利益，并且，他的行为"性质恶劣且违反雇主规定"（C诉B案）。但是很明显，他在从事此种行为时，是在从事一名银行柜员的正常工作，即接受支票的存入。

There can be no doubt that Cardenas was not steadfast in the performance of his duties and obligations to his employer when he chose to participate in a criminal scheme to accept forged checks for deposit. Cardenas was acting out of self-interest in participating in Lehman's scheme, and his conduct was "outrageous and in violation of his employer's rules". Commercial Business Systems. Nonetheless, it is clear that in doing so he was performing a normal function of a bank teller in accepting checks for deposit.

结论 归纳而言，银行的主张，以及初审法院排除公司证据并支持银行无审判决动议的理由，明显不是由于公司未能提供

In sum, First Union's assertions, and the apparent basis of the trial court's decision to strike Chin's evidence and to award summary judgment to First Union, are premised not

足够的初步证据，证明柜员的侵害行为发生时与银行存在必要的雇佣关系，而是由于他们认为，没有足够的证据可证明争议行为属于雇佣范围之内。如同我们之前的解释，公司没有义务承担举证责任，证明柜员的行为系在雇佣范围之内；相反，公司只要证明了雇佣关系的存在，公司就有权要求法院继续审理本案，且银行必须承担举证责任，证明柜员的行为系在雇佣范围之外。

on the failure of Chin to present sufficient evidence to establish a prima facie case of the necessary employment relationship at the time of the injury to Chin, but on the failure of that evidence to prove that the acts complained of were committed within the scope of that employment. As we have explained, Chin did not have the burden of presenting evidence that Cardenas’ acts were within the scope of his employment. Rather, having established that the employment relationship existed, Chin was entitled to have the case go forward with the burden on First Union to prove that Cardenas acted outside the scope of his employment.

前面我们曾提到，本案的程序状况具有重要意义。在银行并未提供额外证据的情况下，公司提供的证据足以表明，本案存在需要由陪审团裁定的问题，即柜员的行为是否在雇佣范围之内。因此，根据现有证据，这个问题不能由初审法院作为法律问题自行决定。

The procedural posture of the case, as we noted above, is significant. Chin’s evidence, without any additional evidence offered by First Union, was sufficient to establish a jury issue whether Cardenas acted within the scope of his employment. That issue therefore, on the evidence presented, did not lend itself to a resolution as a matter of law by the trial court.

基于上述理由，我们判定，初审法院的判决是错误的，因为其支持了银行排除公司证据的动

For these reasons, we hold that the trial court erred in sustaining First Union’s motion to strike Chin’s evidence and

议，并作出了有利于银行的无审判决。我们推翻初审法院的原判，要求初审法院根据本判决意见重新审理。

awarding summary judgment to First Union. Accordingly, we will reverse the judgment of the trial court and remand the case for further proceedings consistent with the views expressed in this opinion.

案例28　付款银行是否有权引用冒名人原则?

Title Insurance Co. of Minnesota v. Comerica Bank California

明尼苏达产权保险公司诉加利福尼亚州考梅里卡银行案

加利福尼亚州上诉法院 1994 年；32 Cal.Rptr.2d 735

简　介

本案中的女士（Helen Nastor）是其当地小有名气的商人。她的儿子（Rudy Nastor）为了获得一笔钱，假冒其母亲的名义向本案金融公司（First National Mortgage Company）借款。为此，女士的儿子伪造了其母亲的授权书，其中说明女士授权其儿子代表女士借款并签署相关文件。金融公司基于该授权书，先后出立了两张以该女士为受款人的贷款资金支票。

作为两笔贷款的担保，女士的儿子同样使用该伪造的授权书，将女士的某些不动产抵押给一家保险公司（Title Insurance）。基于该不动产抵押，保险公司向金融公司提供了还贷保险。也就是说，如果金融公司在收回贷款的过程中遇到任何困难，致使贷款无法收回，保险公司将负责偿还。女士的儿子拿到贷款支票后，找了一位女性合谋人，冒充该女士将支票拿到本案的被告银行

(Comerica Bank),并在支票上伪造了该女士的签名。银行未能识别该伪造签名,因而支付了支票。

金融公司随后因未收到贷款的还款而联系了该女士,且保险公司打算拍卖作为担保物的不动产。直到此时,该女士才知道此事。由于该女士事先对此事完全不知情,且不存在任何疏忽或其他过错,因而在法律上无须承担任何责任。也就是说,既不承担贷款的还款责任,也不需要将不动产交出拍卖。由于该女士不承担任何责任,因此没有成为本诉讼的当事方。女士的儿子及其合谋人此时已没有任何剩余资金,因此没有任何赔偿能力。保险公司基于保险合同偿还了金融公司的贷款,并代位取得了金融公司的权利。随后,保险公司起诉支付了支票的本案被告银行,指控银行基于伪造背书作出了付款。

在通常情况下,如果银行基于伪造背书支付了支票,且在付款时存在疏忽,银行就要承担错误付款的责任。在本案中,银行也许确实存在疏忽,但银行提出,根据法典的“冒名人原则”(impostor rule),虽然支票的背书是伪造的,但该背书仍然可以作为支票的有效背书,因此银行有权支付该支票。也就是说,由于该支票属于本可正常支付的支票,因此根本不存在银行是否存在疏忽的问题。

初审法院支持了银行的主张,认定本案适用冒名人原则,因而保险公司不持有合法的起诉理由。保险公司上诉后,上诉法院对“冒名人原则”进行了较详细的分析,包括法典新版和旧版的不同规定(本案事件发生于旧版时期,但审理是在新版时期)。上诉法院认定,本案情况不属于冒名人原则所适用的情况,因为冒名人原则仅适用于票据出立过程中的冒名顶替。在金融公司出立支票时,虽然女士的儿子谎称自己有权代表该女士,但并没有自己冒充该女士,也没有让同谋人冒充该女士,因此,实际上不存在冒名顶替的情况。随后,在兑现支票时,虽然同谋人确实冒充了该女士,但此时已经到了支票兑现阶段,与支票的出立无关。因此,上诉法院判决,初审法院基于冒名人原则而驳回保险公司起诉的判决是错误的。

判　决

本案的基本情况　本上诉涉及“冒名人原则”的适用和范围。根据该原则，即使支票的出票人在冒名受款人的诱骗下出立支票，后者背书后的支票仍然有效［第3.404条(a)款；旧版第3.405条（1）（a）款］。本案原告保险公司称，初审法院错误适用了该原则，即错误驳回了保险公司提出的疏忽指控，而支持了被告银行的起诉在法律上不能成立的一般性抗辩。我们同意保险公司的主张，即在本案具体事实下，冒名人原则不适用，并因此推翻初审法院驳回保险公司起诉的判决。

At issue in this appeal is the applicability and scope of the “impostor rule”, which makes an indorsed check effective if the drawer was induced to issue the check by an impersonator of the payee.（Com.Code, § 3-404, subd.（a）; former Com.Code, § 3-405, subd.（1）（a）.）Plaintiff Title Insurance Company of Minnesota contends the trial court erroneously applied this rule in sustaining the demurrer of the drawee bank, respondent Comerica Bank–California（“Bank”）, to plaintiff’s complaint for negligence. We agree that the impostor rule is not applicable under the circumstances presented, and accordingly reverse the judgment of dismissal.

一般性抗辩的审理标准　在审查下级法院有关一般性抗辩的判决时，我们假设起诉书中所陈述的所有主要事实都是真实的，并在此基础上确定起诉书是否提出了有可能获得救济的有效指控（B诉C案；S诉P案）。

In reviewing an order sustaining a demurrer, we assume the truth of all material facts properly pleaded in the complaint and determine whether it states any valid claim entitling the plaintiff to relief.（B & P Development Corp. v. City of Saratoga; Serrano v. Priest）

保险公司的指控　本案保险

According to the complaint, Bank

公司在起诉书中称，付款银行有义务“设立和遵守必要、有效和合理的程序和商业做法，使银行不致违反其对存款人和客户应尽的谨慎义务。银行的义务包括，当冒名人或伪造人试图兑现支票并支取客户在银行账户中的款项时，立即通知包括本案金融公司在内的客户”。

had a duty “to establish and practice such procedures and business practices as are or may be reasonably necessary and effective to avoid a breach of any of the duties of care owed by BANK to the depositors and customers of BANK, including therein a duty to immediately inform customers such as FNMC when impostors and/or forgers attempt to cash a check drawn on such customers' accounts with BANK”.

保险公司称，付款银行违反了上述义务,因为其未能确保“付款的支票都是存款人已适当背书和提示的支票”。在冒名人试图兑现本应向本案女士付款的支票时，假如银行“抓住了”冒名人，其本来就会通知金融公司，而金融公司本来就会在发放第二笔贷款之前发现伪造的授权书。

Bank breached this duty, plaintiff alleged, by failing to ensure “that only properly endorsed and presented checks of its depositors [were] paid”. Had Bank “caught” the impostor trying to cash the check payable to Helen, it would have informed FNMC of the attempt, and FNMC would have discovered the forged power of attorney before it made the second loan.

银行引用冒名人原则 银行一般性抗辩的全部基础是，本案应适用冒名人原则。银行辩称，对于保险公司提出的疏忽指控，冒名人原则构成“绝对抗辩”。银行引用的是新版法典第3.404条（a）款。根据该款，如果在冒名人的引诱下，支票的出票人

Bank's demurrer is based entirely on the asserted applicability of the impostor rule, which, according to Bank, interposes an “absolute defense” against plaintiff's allegations of negligence. Bank relies on the current provisions of section 3-404, subdivision (a), which makes an indorsement by any person effective

出立了向冒名人付款或向“冒名人的合谋人”付款的支票，则任何人在该支票上作出的背书均为有效。在本案中，银行辩称，冒名人（冒充本案女士的人）的合谋人是女士的儿子，而冒名人向银行提示了支票并取得了付款。

保险公司的反驳　保险公司的回应是，新版法典第 3.404 条（a）款不适用，因为新版法典是 1992 年才制定的，晚于本案起诉书中所述的事件。保险公司辩称，本案应适用旧版法典第 3.405 条（1）（a）款。旧版法典的规定与新版法典的规定几乎相同，但旧版法典的适用范围不包括对代理关系的虚假陈述。在本案中，女士的儿子向金融公司虚假陈述说，自己有权作为女士的代理人，并因此获得了支票。保险公司称，根据旧版法典，本案交易不在冒名人原则的范围之内。

应以旧版法典为准　我们同意保险公司的主张，即本案的处理应受旧版法典第 3.405 条（1）（a）款的约束，因为本案事件发生于 1988 年，而当时旧版法

if an impostor had induced the issuance of the instrument to either the impostor or “a person acting in concert with the impostor”. In this case, argues Bank, Rudy was acting in concert with the impostor（the impersonator of Helen）, who presented the check to Bank for payment.

Plaintiff responds that section 3-404（a） is not applicable, because it was not enacted until 1992, after the events alleged in the complaint. Instead, plaintiff maintains, this case is controlled by former section 3-405, subdivision（1）（a）. The expression of the rule in the latter statute is substantially the same as that of the current provisions, but excluded from its reach are false representations of agency. Because Rudy obtained the check from FNMC by falsely representing that he was authorized to act as Helen’s agent, plaintiff argues the transaction at issue is outside the scope of the impostor rule.

We agree with plaintiff that former section 3-405（1）（a） governs the disposition of this case, since the events at issue took place in 1988, while that statute was still in effect. Former section 3-405（1）

典仍然有效。旧版法典第 3.405 条（1）（a）款规定："任何人以受款人名字冒名作出的背书在下列情况下有效：（a）票据系由冒名人以通信或其他方式引诱制票人或出票人按该受款人的名字出立给冒名人或其合谋人。"

（a）provided："An indorsement by any person in the name of a named payee is effective if （a） An impostor by use of the mails or otherwise has induced the maker or drawer to issue the instrument to him or his confederate in the name of the payee."

冒名人原则的适用范围　在本案具体情况下，法典上述规定不能使付款银行免于承担责任。如同加利福尼亚州一个法院在旧版法典第 3.405 条制定之前的一个判例中所解释的，只有当任何人通过冒充受款人而取得支票的出立时，冒名人原则才适用。法院说："如果出票人将支票交付给冒充受款人的冒名人，认为冒名人就是可以在支票上作出背书并兑现支票的人，则当冒名人以其所冒充的人的名字作出背书时，该背书不属于伪造。这项原则的合理之处在于，支票项下的款项，被实际支付给出票人本来确实希望向其付款的人。也许另一个人与冒名人所冒充的人重名，且该人与冒名人有某种合同关系，因此，受票人银行在向支

This section does not protect Bank from liability under the circumstances presented. As one California court explained prior to the enactment of former section 3-405, the impostor rule is applicable only when the issuance of the check has been accomplished through impersonation of the payee: "[W] here a check is delivered to an impostor as payee and the drawer believes that the impostor is the person upon whose endorsement it will be paid, the endorsement by such impostor in the name which he is using to impersonate another is not a forgery. The soundness of the rule obtains in the fact that the money has actually been paid to the person for whom it was really intended. Because another person might bear the very name assumed by the impostor and might have some contractual relationships with the impostor does not subject to a loss the drawee

票原本设想的受款人支付了支票后，不应该承担相应损失。”（S 诉 B 案；另参见 S 诉 U 案；R 诉 B 案）

bank when it has paid the check to the person intended as the payee." （Schweitzer v. Bank of America. See also Security–First Nat. Bank v. United States； Ryan v. Bank of Italy Nat. T. & S. Assn.）

该法院在 S 诉 B 案中的分析，对本案有指导作用。假设本案的金融公司（支票的出票人）系被女士的冒名人所引诱而向女士的儿子或向冒名人出立了支票，则根据冒名人原则，本案中的背书在对抗金融公司时就是有效的。此种结果的理由在于，从银行取得付款的人，正是金融公司意图使其获得付款的人。

The reasoning of the Schweitzer court directs our analysis in the present case. If FNMC （the drawer） had been induced by an impostor of Helen to issue the check either to Rudy or to the impostor, then the indorsement would be considered effective as to FNMC under the impostor rule. The rationale for this result is that Bank has paid the person whom FNMC intended to receive the money.

其他原则也导致同样结果

如果适用有关疏忽或禁止自相矛盾的法律原则，本案上述场景也会得出同样结果，即损失风险应由支票的出票人承担，因为其更有能力识破欺诈［参见 F 诉 S 案（与伪造人打交道的当事方应承担损失）；I 诉 M 案（法典规定，伪造背书所造成的损失应由最有能力防止该伪造的一方承担）；E 诉 F 案（该案将“意指受款人”理论与疏忽理论或禁

When viewed under principles of negligence or estoppel, the outcome of this scenario would be the same： the risk of loss would be shifted to the drawer of the instrument, who was in a better position to detect the fraud. （See Fireman's Fund Ins. Co. v. Security Pacific Nat. Bank ［burden of loss on party who deals with the forger］； Intelogic v. Merchants Nat. Bank ［under UCC, loss resulting from forged indorsement should fall upon party best able to prevent it］； East Gadsden Bank v. First City Nat.

止自相矛盾理论相区别)]。

冒名人原则不适用于本案 但是,本案事实并非冒名问题。在本案中,金融公司所出立的支票的受款人是女士本人,而不是自称为该女士的冒名人;金融公司本意中的支票背书人和收款人都是该女士本人,而不是被误认为该女士的人。毫无疑问,金融公司的意图,是仅与该女士进行交易。因此,冒名人原则所提供的保护理由在本案中不存在(参见E诉F案)。

代理身份的不实陈述不属于冒名顶替 一个人仅虚假陈述说自己是受款人的代理人,不足以适用冒名人原则。旧版法典第3.405条正式评论2说:"'冒名人'是指冒名顶替的情况,而不延伸至虚假陈述的情况,即当事方自称是受款人的授权代理人。因此,如果制票人或出票人小心翼翼地出立了向被代理人付款的票据,则立票人有权要求取得被代理人的背书。"在本案中,支

Bank of Gadsden [intended payee theory distinguished from negligence or estoppel theory].)

This case presents different facts, however. Here, FNMC made the check payable to the true Helen, not to an impostor representing herself as Helen. FNMC intended that Helen herself—not a person it believed to be Helen—indorse the check and receive the proceeds. There is no question that FNMC intended to deal solely with Helen. The rationale underlying the protection of the impostor rule thus does not apply here. (Cf. East Gadsden Bank v. First City Nat. Bank of Gadsden)

A person's false representation that he or she is an agent of the payee is not sufficient. Uniform Commercial Code Comment 2 to former section 3-405 notes: "'Impostor' refers to impersonation, and does not extend to a false representation that the party is the authorized agent of the payee. The maker or drawer who takes the precaution of making the instrument payable to the principal is entitled to have his indorsement." Here, Rudy obtained issuance of the check to Helen not by impersonating her, but by falsely representing

票系向女士付款，而女士的儿子在取得支票时，并非冒充该女士，而是作出虚假陈述，说自己有权代表该女士。这种行为自然具有欺诈性质，但不属于冒名顶替，因此，这种行为不属于旧版法典第 3.405 条（1）（a）款所说的通过引诱获得票据出立的情况（参见 B 诉 C 案；V 诉 M 案；W 诉 F 案；V 诉 Z 案）。

that he was authorized to act on her behalf. Although clearly fraudulent, this conduct does not constitute impersonation and thus cannot be considered an inducement to issue the instrument within the meaning of former section 3-405（1）（a）.（Cf. Broward Bank v. Commercial Bank; Valley Bank v. Monarch Inv. Co.; W.R. Grimshaw Co. v. First Nat. Bank & Tr. Co. of Tulsa; Valley Bank & Trust v. Zions First Nat. Bank）

提示支票时的冒充是不同问题　银行强调，女士的儿子系与女士的冒名人合谋作为。但是，这不影响本案结论。银行如果要获得旧版法典第 3.405 条（1）（a）款的保护，就必须提供事实证明，冒名人系通过冒名顶替而引诱金融公司出立了支票，无论是向她自己付款，还是向其同谋（女士的儿子）付款。但是，起诉书没有提出此种事实。唯一的冒名顶替是在向银行提示支票时发生的。

Bank's emphasis on the asserted fact that Rudy was acting in concert with Helen's impostor is of no consequence. To invoke the protection of former section 3-405（1）（a）Bank would have to point to facts showing that by impersonation the impostor induced FNMC to issue the check either to her or to Rudy, her confederate. The complaint alleges no such facts, however. The only impersonation that took place was in the presentation of the check to Bank.

其他判例　有些法院认为，如果在用于取得付款的票据本身之上伪造受款人的签名，这也属于冒名顶替。如在 M 诉 B 案中，

Some courts have found impersonation where the payee's signature is forged on the very documents required to obtain the money. In Minster State Bank v. Baybank

丈夫“以通信或其他方式”，在本票上伪造了他妻子的名字，而法院认为这属于冒名顶替（请比较B诉C案）。在F诉M案中，某人在取款单上伪造账户存款人的签名，导致银行出立了两张支取存款人账户的支票。同样，在I诉M案中，法院所面临的问题是，某人所伪造的受款人签名，是否直接诱使支票的出票人根据一份虚构的回租协议而出立了该支票。

Middlesex, for example, the husband engaged in imposture "by the use of mails or otherwise" by forging his wife's name to a promissory note.（Contra, Broward Bank v. Commercial Bank of Hollywood）Fidelity & D.Co. of Md. v. Manufacturers Han. Tr. Co. involved a forgery of a depositor's signature on a withdrawal order, resulting in the issuance of two checks against the depositor's account. Similarly, the court in Intelogic v. Merchants Nat. Bank, considered whether the forgery of a payee's signature directly induced the drawer to issue checks under a purported lease-back agreement.

上述判例不影响本案 在本案中，无人指控女士的儿子在贷款文件本身上伪造了女士的签名。实际情况是，女士的儿子在授权书上伪造了女士的签名，而该授权书只允许前者将自己称为后者的代理人。之后，女士的儿子利用该代理身份从金融公司取得了贷款，但表面原因是代表该女士。因此，即使假设在贷款文件上伪造受款人名字可以构成冒名顶替，本案也不属于该情况。女士儿子的伪造行为不属于冒名

In the case before us, however, there is no allegation that Rudy forged Helen's signature on the loan documents themselves. Instead, Rudy forged Helen's signature on a power of attorney, which enabled him only to represent himself as Helen's agent. Thereafter, he used that agency status to obtain the loan from FNMC, ostensibly on Helen's behalf. Thus, even assuming that forgery of a payee's signature on loan documents constitutes an imposture, that scenario did not occur here. Rudy's act of forgery was not an impersonation but only a misrepresentation

顶替，而是虚称自己有权代表女士从事业务的不实陈述。

新版法典冒名人原则不改变本案结果 本案审理即使适用目前的冒名人原则，即新版法典第 3.404 条（a）款，结果也是一样的。新版的唯一重大改变是，承认冒名人既可以冒充受款人，也可以冒充受款人的代理人。关于该修订，法典正式评论说，“根据旧版法典第 3.405 条（1）（a）款，如果冒名人冒充甲，并引诱出票人出立了向甲的指定人付款的支票，冒名人可将该支票流通。但是，如果冒名人冒充乙公司的总经理甲，且支票向乙公司的指定人付款，法典该款就不适用。目前的第 3.404 条（a）款，使冒名人在以上两种情况下都具有流通该支票的权力”。这项评论明显说明，要适用冒名人原则，仍然必须存在冒名顶替，无论恶意行为人是冒充被代理人还是代理人。恶意行为人对自己代理身份的不实陈述，不足以导致该原则的适用（参见 I 诉 M 案）。

结论 因此，我们的必然结

of his authority to do business on behalf of Helen.

The result is no different even under section 3-404（a）, the current version of the rule. The only significant change in this section is its recognition that the impostor may pretend to be either the payee or the payee's agent. As the Uniform Commercial Code Comment to the revised law notes, “Under former Section 3-405（1）（a）, if Impostor impersonated Smith and induced the drawer to draw a check to the order of Smith, Impostor could negotiate the check. If Impostor impersonated Smith, the president of Smith Corporation, and the check was payable to the order of Smith Corporation, the section did not apply. Section 3-404（a） gives Impostor the power to negotiate the check in both cases”. This comment makes it clear that impersonation is still required to invoke the impostor rule, whether the perpetrator of the deception pretends to be the principal or the agent. Misrepresentation of the perpetrator's agency status does not suffice.（See Intelogic v. Merchants Nat. Bank）

We must conclude, therefore, that the

论是，冒名人原则不适用于本案情况。女士的儿子真实地说明了自己的名字，但虚假地声称自己是女士的代理人。因此，女士的儿子没有从事冒名人原则所述的冒名顶替行为。女士的冒名人从事了冒名顶替行为，但该行为并未引诱金融公司出立支票，因为该冒名顶替是随后向银行提示支票时才发生的。因此我们判定，初审法院基于冒名人原则支持了银行的一般性抗辩的判决是错误的。

不涉及案件的实质审理 但是，不应将上述结论视为对保险公司之指控最终是否可以成立的意见。审阅一般性抗辩的标准是，“仅考虑原告之起诉在法律上是否满足起诉标准，而不涉及指控内容是否真实，或原告是否最终能够证明其指控”(Y 诉 C 案；A 诉 A 案)。因此，对于保险公司能否在所有方面均证明其对银行疏忽的指控，或能否克服银行可能提出的任何主动抗辩，或能否对抗银行可能提出的无审判决动议，我们不发表意见

impostor rule is inapplicable under these circumstances. By correctly identifying himself as Rudy but falsely representing himself to be Helen's agent Rudy did not engage in the impersonation required by the impostor rule. The impersonation by Helen's impostor cannot be said to have induced FNMC to issue the check, since it took place only afterward, when the impostor presented the check to Bank. Accordingly, we hold that the trial court incorrectly sustained Bank's demurrer based on the application of the impostor rule.

This conclusion, however, should not be construed as a comment on the merits of the complaint. A demurrer tests “only the legal sufficiency of the complaint, not the truth of its factual allegations or the plaintiff's ability to prove those allegations” (Yue v. City of Auburn; Alcorn v. Anbro Engineering, Inc.). Thus, we express no opinion whatsoever as to whether plaintiff can prove all the elements of negligence, whether it will be able to withstand any affirmative defenses that may be asserted by Bank in its answer, or whether it could successfully resist a motion for summary judgment. (See generally,

（参见 B 诉 B 案；E 诉 C 案；S 诉 F 案；旧版法典第 3.406 条）。推翻初审法院驳回原告保险公司起诉的判决。

Basch v. Bank of America； E.F. Hutton & Co. v. City National Bank； Sehremelis v. Farmers & Merchants Bank； see also former Com.Code, § 3-406.） The judgment of dismissal is reversed.

案例 29　共同融通方之间如何分担责任？

Daigle v. Chaisson
戴格尔诉查森案

路易斯安那州上诉法院 1981 年；396 So. 2d 573

简　介

本案涉及一张本票的共同融通方之间的责任关系问题。本票的制票人（本票的主义务人，Jerry Iguess）从银行（Calcasieu Marine National Bank）取得了一笔贷款，并出立了本票作为还款凭据。由于制票人的信誉不足，银行要求本案 3 名个人作为融通方在本票上作出背书签名。该 3 人为本案原告（Alvin Daigle）、原告妻子和本案被告（David Chaisson）。本案被告（共同融通方）与制票人是业务上的合作伙伴，而这笔借款也是用于该业务。但本案原告（同样为共同融通方）与该业务无任何关联，完全是为了向制票人提供信誉支持而签署本票的。

随后，制票人宣告破产，因而银行要求 3 名融通背书人支付本票。本案原告偿还了银行的贷款，并因此成为本票的执票人。本案原告随后起诉本案被告，要求后者作为共同背书人（共同融通方）分担本票的还款金额。本案的争议问题是，原告执票人是否有权要求被告共同背书人作出分担？如果有权，后者应分担多少？

法典有关融通方的规定，主要涉及融通方与受融通方之间的关系，即保证人与被保证人之间的关系，但对于本案 3 名融通方之间的关系，即各个保证人之间的关系，则缺乏相关规定。路易斯安那州上诉法院最终结合法典的规定、该州民法典的规定和该州最高法院的判例，推翻了初审法院的判决，并判定原告执票人有权从被告共同背书人获得相当于还款金额 1/3 的分担。

判　决

本案的问题　本案涉及一张本票。原告是本票的背书人和目前的执票人。被告是本票的共同背书人。前者要求后者就本票支付补偿，或作为替代方法而承担相应份额。初审法院驳回了前者对后者的起诉。前者因此上诉。在执票人作为融通方和背书人支付了本票后，本案的主要问题是：其是否可向共同背书人追索？如果可以，有权追索的金额是多少？

This is a suit on a promissory note. Plaintiff Alvin Daigle, an indorser and presently the holder of the note, seeks indemnity or, in the alternative, contribution from the defendant, David Chaisson, a co-indorser. The district court rejected plaintiff's claim against defendant. Plaintiff appeals. The principal issue is whether plaintiff, suing as an accommodation indorser who has paid the instrument, has a right of recourse against defendant, and, if so, for how much.

初审法院的判决　在完成证据提交后，初审法院判决，执票人无权要求共同背书人补偿或分担。法院的结论是，执票人必须首先追究本票制票人的责任；在此之前，无权要求共同背书人补偿。基于下述理由，我们推翻该

After the presentation of the evidence, the district court denied plaintiff any indemnity or contribution against Chaisson. In its written opinion, the court concluded that plaintiff could not obtain contribution from a co-indorser without first seeking recourse from the maker. For the reasons which follow,

判决。

融通方的定义 路易斯安那州1975年以法典取代了之前的《流通票据法》。法典规定，融通方是指“以任何身份在票据上签名，用于向票据其他当事方出借其名字的人”[第3.415条(1)款]。从本票上可以看出，本案的原告、原告妻子以及本案被告，均作为背书人签名，且3个背书的融通性质很明显，因为签名不在本票的所有权顺序之内[第3.415条(4)款]。此外，该认定也得到当事方证词的支持，即3名背书人的名字系作为向银行提供的额外担保而加在本票上。

本案背书的状况 紧邻本票的3个背书之上，有下列文字：“下述签名人特此向本案银行、银行后继者、背书人或受让人承担连带保证责任，保证本贷款到期时按时获得偿付。”3个背书位于本票背面，是横向排成一排，而不是竖向。本案原告的背书在最左面，后面依次为被告和原告妻子的背书。

we reverse.

Under the Commercial Laws, La. R.S. adopted in 1975 and repealing the former Negotiable Instruments Law, an accommodation party is "one who signs the instrument in any capacity for the purpose of lending his name to another party to it". La.R.S. 3-415 (1). From the note itself, it is apparent that Daigle, his wife and Chaisson signed the note as indorsers. The accommodation character of the three indorsements is also clear since they do not appear in the chain of title to the note. La.R.S. 3-415 (4). This finding is also supported by the testimony which reflects that the names of the three indorsers were added to the instrument as additional security for the bank.

Directly above the three indorsements on the note is found the following language: "... the undersigned hereby jointly and severally guarantee to the Calcasieu Marine National Bank of Lake Charles, its successors, indorsers or assigns, the punctual payment at maturity of said loan". The three indorsements on the reverse side of the note appear in a horizontal line rather than vertical. Plaintiff's indorsement is farthest to the left followed by that of Chaisson and then plaintiff's wife.

连带责任的含义 本案审理初期，我们将“连带”这个词解释为，3名背书人将他们自己作为一个整体与主义务人捆绑在一起。在普通法中，“连带”被视为与路易斯安那州民法中“整体”这个词具有同样含义（J诉J案；F诉S案）。此外，由于这些当事方“保证”贷款将得到按时偿还，银行有权就贷款的全部数额，直接追究每一个背书人的责任，而无须首先追究制票人的责任［第3.416条（1）款］。

Initially, we interpret the phrase “jointly and severally” to mean that the three indorsers bound themselves in solido with the principal obligor. The common law term “joint and several” has been held synonymous with our Civil Law term “in solido”. Johnson v. Jones-Journet, Ford Motor Credit Company v. Soileau. Moreover, as these parties “guaranteed” the punctual payment of the loan, the bank could proceed directly against each indorser for the whole amount without first making demand upon the maker. La.R.S. 3-416（1）.

本质上属于制票人 第3.416条正式评论说：“对付款作出保证的背书人，相当于同时作出了弃权，不仅无权再要求获得提示、拒付通知或拒付书，也无权要求首先对制票人或受票人进行追索。在背书使用了‘保证’这个措辞后，背书的性质不受影响［第3.202条（4）款］，但背书人的责任将与共同制票人的责任没有区别。”

The Official Comment to Uniform Commercial Code, Section 3-416 states: “An indorser who guarantees payment waives not only presentment, notice of dishonor and protest, but also all demand upon the maker or drawee. Words of guarantee do not affect the character of the indorsement as an indorsement ［Section 3-202（4）］; but the liability of the indorser becomes indistinguishable from that of the co-maker.”

背书人之间的责任顺序 第

The order of liability of indorsers is

3.414条（2）款则规定了不同背书人之间的责任顺序："除另有约定外，背书人依据他们作出背书的顺序相互承担责任。背书的顺序，假定为票据上显示的签名顺序。"

在本案中，也许可以基于法典第3.414条（2）款辩称，在签字横线上全部3个背书签名中，由于本案原告执票人的签名位于最左边，而被告共同背书人的签名在后，所以执票人是第一个签名人。因此，按法典上述规定，执票人无权向共同背书人追索。但是，当事方有权反驳第3.414条（2）款的假定，只要有证据表明，实际的签名顺序不同于此，或当事方对责任分担另有不同意图或约定［参见第3.415条（3）款；G诉C案］。

本案的实际情况 本案证词显示，制票人和共同背书人是共同从事焊接业务的商业伙伴。目前的贷款，是用于他们焊接工厂所购买的土地和设备。执票人作证说，仅仅是为了向制票人提供融通，他和他妻子才将自己的名

provided in La.R.S. 3-414（2） as follows: "Unless they otherwise agree, indorsers are liable to one another in the order in which they indorse, which is presumed to be the order in which their signatures appear on the instrument."

It could be argued under Section 3-414（2） that since plaintiff signed farthest to the left, followed by Chaisson, on the horizontal line on which all three indorsers signed, that plaintiff indorsed first and is precluded by this section from any recourse against Chaisson. However, the presumption of Section 3-414（2） may be rebutted by evidence which shows a different order or division of liability was intended or agreed to by the parties. See La.R.S. 3-415（3） and Gulf National Bank v. Computer Analysis, Inc.

In the instant case, the testimony shows that Jerry Iguess and David Chaisson were business partners engaged in a welding business. The present debt was incurred to purchase land and equipment for their welding shop. Plaintiff testified that his and his wife's names were supplied to the instrument only

字签在本票上。执票人作证说，自己在制票人和共同背书人的业务经营中不持有任何权益，且自己也未收到贷款的任何款项。案件证据还显示，全部 3 个背书都是同时签在本票上的。

不存在独自承担责任的本意　我们认为，本票上签名的具体情况以及上述的其他因素都说明，3 名背书人的意图并不是按照签名顺序来承担本票责任。本案所有证据都显示，没有任何一名背书人计划承担比其他任何一名背书人更大份额的责任。共同背书人对此没有提出相反主张。

因此，我们的结论是，第 3.414 条（2）款不妨碍执票人向其他背书人进行追索。但我们看到，在克服了第 3.414 条（2）款对顺序问题的假定之后，对于同样作为融通方的各个背书人，法典并没有规定他们之间如何补偿或分担。

融通方之间的责任划分　我们知道，在路易斯安那州上诉法院工作报告中，建议将第 3.415 条（5）款解释为，“向票据执票

to accommodate Iguess. Daigle testified that he had no financial interest in defendants' business, nor did he receive any of the funds borrowed. The record also shows that all three indorsements were affixed to the instrument simultaneously.

We think the circumstances surrounding the signing of the note, as well as the other factors mentioned, negate any intent on the part of the indorsers to be bound in the order in which they signed. All of the evidence in the record shows no indorser was to share a greater portion of the liability than the other co-indorser. Chaisson makes no contention to the contrary.

We thus conclude that Section 3-414（2）does not bar plaintiff from seeking recourse against his co-indorsers. We find, however, no provisions in the Commercial Laws which provide for indemnification or contribution between accommodation indorsers once the presumption of Section 3-414（2） has been overcome.

We are aware that in The Work of the Louisiana Appellate Courts, the author suggests La.R.S. 3-415（5） should be construed to mean that “An accommodation

人作出付款的融通背书人，仍然有权向票据的其他背书人和制票人追索，并就本票中所规定的律师费、其他费用和利息取得补偿”。法典第3.415条（5）款的规定是：“融通方不对受融通方承担责任。融通方如果支付了票据，有权就票据向受融通方追索。”

法典仅规定与受融通方的关系 我们的看法是，第3.415条（5）款仅约束融通方和“受融通方”之间的关系。在大多数情况下，受融通方是本票的制票人，但也有可能是本票所有权顺序中的前手背书人，或是本票另一个当事方。第3.415条（5）款所述的规则很清楚，即融通方不对受融通方承担责任，无论谁是受融通方；并且，如果融通方支付了票据，其有权就该票据向受融通方追索。我们不能将（5）款的含义解释为，如果两名或多名共同背书人均为融通方，且其中一人同意与其他人作为一个整体支付主债务（如本案的这种情况），那么，任何融通方都可以

indorser who pays the holder may still pursue the other indorsers and the maker on the instrument and recover whatever attorney's fees, costs, and interest the note provides". Section 3-415（5） reads as follows："An accommodation party is not liable to the party accommodated, and if he pays the instrument has a right of recourse on the instrument against such party."

In our view, Subsection （5） governs only the relationship between the accommodation party and the "party accommodated". The party accommodated in most cases is the maker, but it could be a prior indorser in the chain of title or another party. The rule which Section 3-415（5） makes clear is that an accommodation party is not liable to the party accommodated, whoever he be, and if an accommodation party pays the instrument he has a right of recourse on the instrument against such party, meaning the party accommodated. We cannot construe Subsection （5） as meaning that where one of two or more accommodation co-indorsers agrees to be bound in solido to pay the principal obligation, as in the present case, that one of the accommodation parties

在支付票据后，再“就票据”起诉其他融通方，要求就主债务、利息、律师费等获得补偿。

can pay the instrument and sue the other accommodation parties “on the instrument” for the principal debt, interest, attorney’s fees, etc.

法典第 3.415 条正式评论 5 可以支持我们对该款的上述解释。该评论说，“本条（5）款的目的，是改变诸如 Q 诉 V 案等之前判例的结果。这些判例判定，融通背书人在支付票据后，不能就票据起诉受融通方，因为不存在融通方可以重新获得的‘前存权利’。但是，根据保证法的一般原则，付款后的融通方代位了已收到付款的执票人的权利，因此可以就票据而行使其追索权”。

Our construction of the statute is supported by the Official Comment 5 under the U.C.C., Section 3-415 which reads as follows: “Subsection （5） is intended to change the result of such decisions as Quimby v. Varnum, which held that an accommodation indorser who paid the instrument could not maintain an action on it against the accommodated party since he had no ‘former rights’ to which he was remitted. Under ordinary principles of suretyship the accommodation party who pays is subrogated to the rights of the holder paid, and should have his recourse on the instrument.”

相关文章（引用文章）也支持我们的观点。该文章说：“法典第 3 篇与之前的《流通票据法》不同，因为法典承认，融通方无论是以制票人身份还是背书人身份在票据上签名，本质上都是保证人。法典的正式评论强调了融通方的保证人性质：‘融通方与其他类型的保证人的唯一区别就

The Comment, Suretyship Law And Negotiable Instruments Law: The Liability Of An Accommodation Party To A Negotiable Instrument In Louisiana, Loy.L.R. also supports our position: “Article 3 （of the U.C.C.）, unlike the Negotiable Instruments Law, recognizes that an accommodation party, whether he signs the instrument as a maker or as an indorser is basically a surety. The official

是，融通方的责任系票据责任，且融通方是票据另一当事方的保证人。因此，融通方的义务取决于他签名时的身份。’法典的正式评论随后讨论了融通制票人的责任，而在之前的法律中，通常不把融通制票人视为保证人。由于法典的正式评论反复将融通方称为保证人，因此，法典起草人的意图毫无疑问地是想把保证法用于定义融通方的责任，至少在一定程度上是这样。”

comments emphasize the accommodation party's suretyship nature: ‘He differs from other sureties only in that his liability is on the instrument and he is a surety for another party to it. His obligation is therefore determined by the capacity in which he signs.’ The comments continue to discuss the liability of an accommodation maker, a party not generally treated as a surety under prior law. Because the comments repeatedly refer to the accommodation party as a surety, the drafters doubtless intended suretyship law, at least to some extent, to apply in defining the liability of the accommodation party.”

融通方之间的关系应参照保证法 由于法典未打算在一般意义上触动保证法的规则，因此，法典起草者在将融通方称为保证人时，大概只是想引用相关州的保证法。但不太清楚的是，相关州的保证法到底在何种程度上可以被用来定义融通方的责任。

Because the Uniform Commercial Code does not generally purport to regulate suretyship law, the drafters in referring to the accommodation party as a surety presumably meant to refer to the state law of suretyship. What remains unclear is the extent to which state suretyship law may be used to define the liability of the accommodation party.

前面曾得出结论说，法典没有规定在多个融通背书人之间如何进行责任补偿或分担。因此，一旦克服了第3.414条（2）款关于责任顺序的假定，

Having concluded the Commercial Laws contain no provisions for indemnification or contribution amongst accommodation indorsers, once the presumption of La.R.S. 3-414（2） is overcome, we must look to

我们就必须从路易斯安那州其他法律领域来寻找适用于本案的规则。本州法典第 1.103 条规定："除非被本法特定条款排除，路易斯安那州的其他法律应予适用。"

other areas of Louisiana law which may apply to the instant case. La.R.S. 1-103 provides: "Unless displaced by the particular provisions of this title, the other laws of Louisiana shall apply."

当本案执票人和共同背书人作为融通背书人和保证人签署本票时，他们同意成为与主债务人连为一体的保证人（引用路易斯安那州民法典；C 诉 R 案）。此外，法典第 3.415 条正式评论说，"融通方永远都是保证人"。

When Daigle and Chaisson signed the note as accommodation indorsers and guarantors, they contracted to become solidary sureties for the principal debtor. La. C.C. Article 3035, C. I. T. Corporation v. Rosenstock. Moreover, the U.C.C. Official Comment to Section 3-415 states: "an accommodation party is always a surety."

民法典的规定　路易斯安那州的保证法明确承认，保证人在支付了主债务后，有权向其他共同保证人追索。本州民法典第 3058 条规定："如果多人是同一债务人和同一债务的保证人，则清偿了该债务的保证人有权按照每一个保证人的比例份额向其他保证人追索；但是，只有在该保证人被起诉且基于该诉讼清偿了该债务之后，该保证人才有权获得上述救济。"

Our Louisiana law of suretyship expressly recognizes the right of a surety who has paid the primary debt to seek recourse from other co-sureties. La.C.C. Article 3058 provides: "When several persons have been sureties for the same debtor and for the same debt, the surety who has satisfied the debt, has his remedy against the other sureties in proportion to the share of each; but this remedy takes place only, when such person has paid in consequence of a lawsuit instituted against him."

相关判例　本州最高法院近

Our Supreme Court has recently applied

期曾将有关保证人的上述原则应用于融通背书人。在A诉V案中，公司的5名股东（包括该案原告）签署了一份独立的长期有效的保证书，为公司的债务作出担保，将他们自己和公司连为“整体”。公司曾出立两张本票：第一张仅由公司签名；而第二张由5名股东签名，此外还有一位第六名股东作为融通背书人签名。在公司违约后，银行基于各位股东的保证，要求他们付款。该案原告，即提供保证的股东之一，就两张本票向银行作出清偿。随后，他起诉公司和其他5名股东。

these rules of suretyship to accommodation indorsers. In Aiavolasiti v. Versailles GardensLand Development Co., five stockholders of a corporation, including Aiavolasiti, executed a separate continuing guarantee binding themselves in solido with the corporation for the latter's debts. The corporation issued two notes, the first signed only by the corporation, while the second was signed by the five guarantors, plus a sixth stockholder as accommodation indorser. When the corporation defaulted, and the bank made demand on the stockholders under their guaranties, plaintiff, one of the guarantor stockholders, bought both notes. Then he sued the corporation and the five other stockholders.

依据本州民法典第3058条，本州最高法院判决，对于第一张本票，原告有权从其他每一名共同保证人获得原告所支付的数额的1/5，作为每名保证人本应承担的责任。对于那张有6名当事方作为融通背书人签署的本票，最高法院同样基于有关保证人的原则，判决原告有权从每一个背书人获得1/6的数额，作为每名

Relying on La.C.C. Article 3058, the Supreme Court awarded plaintiff, on the first note, contribution from each co-surety for one-fifth of the amount plaintiff paid, representing the virile share of each surety. On the note where six parties had signed as accommodation indorsers, the Supreme Court, again applying the rules of suretyship, awarded plaintiff contribution of one-sixth of the amount paid as the virile share of each

保证人本应承担的责任。在计算两张本票的补偿份额时，都将公司排除了。

本案的结论　本案事实与 A 诉 V 案中第二张本票的情况非常类似。如同该案一样，本案的融通背书人和保证人将他们自己与债务人连为“整体”。因此，对于银行来说，各个背书人就是连为整体的共同债务人。但是，在承担从属债务的各名背书人之间，如果他们并未明确约定将他们自己也连为整体，那么，他们之间的法律关系应受保证法原则的约束。在本案中，我们看不出他们有意连为整体。因此我们遵循 A 诉 V 案的原则判定，原告执票人有权根据本州民法典第 3058 条，从被告共同背书人获得后者按比例本应承担的债务份额。本案有 3 名融通背书人，因此，原告有权就其支付的债务数额，从被告获得 1/3 的款项。

针对执票人的诉讼不是必要前提　我们意识到本州民法典第 3058 条所规定的条件，即“只有在保证人被起诉且基于该诉讼

indorser. On each note, the corporation was excluded from the calculation of the virile share.

The facts in the instant case are substantially identical to those involving the second note in Aiavolasiti. As in Aiavolasiti, the accommodation indorsers and guarantors in the present case bound themselves in solido with the debtor. Thus, with respect to the bank, the indorsers were co-debtors in solido. The legal relationship between the accessory obligors, however, is governed by the rules of suretyship, absent a clear intention to be bound as solidary obligors even among themselves. We find no such intention in the present case. Following Aiavolasiti, we conclude that plaintiff is entitled to recover Chaisson’s proportionate share of the debt under La.C.C. Article 3058. There being three accommodation indorsers, plaintiff is entitled to recover from Chaisson one-third of the amount he paid in satisfaction of the debt.

We are aware of the proviso in LSA-C.C. Article 3058 that a surety can seek contribution from the other sureties only “when such person has paid in consequence

清偿了债务之后”，该保证人才有权从其他保证人获得分担。但是，最高法院在A诉V案中说：“虽然该款规定，保证人只有在被起诉且基于该诉讼清偿了债务之后，才可以要求其他保证人分担，但该规定不妨碍原告获得分担。只要共同保证人已知债务到期或已同意作出付款，则即使不是在诉讼之后才清偿该债务，也可以寻求分担(L诉W案)。在本案中，其他保证人明确知道债务已经到期，且在本案审理时未就该债务提出任何可引用的抗辩。此外，由于所有的保证人都已经与主债务人连成一个整体，因此没有理由再拖到诉讼之后（参见L案；C诉B案）。”

本案如A诉V案一样，不存在针对原告执票人的诉讼，但是，执票人所追索的共同保证人都知道债务已经到期，且他们在本案中未提出对债务的抗辩理由。此外，如同A诉V案，本案的共同保证人与主债务人已连为整体。

of a lawsuit instituted against him”. However, in Aiavolasiti, the court stated: “Although this article permits contribution only if the debt was paid in consequence of a lawsuit, this does not prevent plaintiff's recovery in the present suit. Contribution is permitted even if the debt was not paid in response to a lawsuit provided that the co-sureties had knowledge that the debt was due or consented to the payment. Leigh v. Wright. The other guarantors clearly had knowledge that the debt was due in the present case, and no possible defense was suggested at trial. Moreover, since all of the guarantors were bound in solido with the principal debtor, there is no reason to require the delay pending lawsuit. See, Louisiana Bank and Trust Co., Crowley v. Boutte.”

In the present case, as in Aiavolasiti, no case was filed against the plaintiff, but the co-surety from whom he seeks contribution knew that the debt was due and also urged no defense to the debt at trial. Moreover, in the present case, as in Aiavolasiti, the co-surety guarantors are bound in solido with the principal debtor.

基于以上所述理由，特此推翻初审法院的原判，判决原告执票人胜诉并有权从被告共同背书人获得 2511 美元的补偿。

For the reasons assigned, the judgment appealed is reversed and set aside. It is now ordered, adjudged and decreed that there be judgment herein in favor of plaintiff, Alvin Daigle, and against the defendant, David D. Chaisson, for the sum of $2511.

案例 30　银行是否有权拒付银行本票?

Hotel Riviera, Inc. v. First Natl. Bank & Trust Co. of Oklahoma City
里维尔酒店公司诉俄克拉何马市第一国民银行和信托公司案

联邦第一巡回上诉法院 1985 年；768 F.2d 1201, 41 U.C.C. Rep. Serv. 363

简　介

本案涉及一张银行本票（cashier's check）的付款争议。在本案中，一名骗子（Richard Pemberton）将两张支票存入了其持有账户的银行（First National Bank），即本案的被告银行。从两张支票的表面看，支票是该人雇主出立给两家客户的，而客户又将支票背书给了该人。但实际上，骗子系以非法手段从其雇主获得这两张支票，并伪造了受款人的背书。银行收到两张支票后，在尚未核实支票状况且未收到支票款项的情况下，即按支票的面额给骗子的账户贷记了 48 万美元。随后该骗子用该款项从银行购买了一张面额为 25 万美元的银行本票。

骗子拿到银行本票之后，立即飞往拉斯维加斯市，进入本案原告酒店的赌场内进行赌博。为了获得赌资，骗子将银行本票交给酒店换取赌场筹码。酒店本来规定所有票据必须先经过核实，但当时已是深夜，所以酒店暂时收下了该银行本票。酒店第二天早上给银行打电话核实，而此时骗子还在酒店内。银行说，受款人名字、本票金额和本票序号都正确。酒店随后将该银行本票存入自己银行。

两天后，出立银行本票的被告银行发现了骗子的诈骗行为，并随后拒付酒店持有的银行本票。酒店因此起诉银行。银行拒付的理由是，骗子存入银行的支票是伪造的，导致银行未收到支票款项，因此其出立的银行本票缺乏对价。在法典中，缺乏对价可以构成“相对抗辩”（personal defense），但不构成“绝对抗辩”（real defense）。前者可以对抗一般执票人，但不能对抗正当执票人。在本案初审中，酒店承认自己不属于正当执票人，因为该银行本票系用于支付赌债。所以，本案被告银行认为，其持有的缺乏对价的抗辩，可以用于对抗酒店。初审法院支持了银行的抗辩。

上诉法院认为，也许酒店在初审中本来无须承认自己不属于正当执票人，因为本案争议与赌债本身无关。但由于酒店已承认自己不是正当执票人，因此上诉法院只能在此基础上进行审理。总体而言，银行持有的缺乏对价的抗辩是无可置疑的，而此种抗辩可以对抗一般执票人的效力也是无可置疑的。但上诉法院认为，这个结果对酒店是不公平的。银行在未收到伪造支票的款项之前就向骗子提供款项，是造成本案状况的基础原因。虽然银行的这种做法可能符合银行界的通行做法，但毕竟这是银行自己的行为。也就是说，损失的根本原因在于银行自己的做法。并且，酒店在最终接受该银行本票前，还特意与银行进行了核实，而银行对该银行本票作出了确认。虽然这些因素都不是否定银行抗辩的法定理由，但在银行和酒店之间，毕竟酒店更加无辜，因此让酒店承担损失似乎不公平。此外，还必须考虑到商业领域对银行本票通常给予的高度信任。上诉法院最终判决，银行必须支付该银行本票。

判　决

本案的情况　本案是为了强制履行一张银行本票的付款。银行本票的立票人是作为本案被告

The underlying action was brought to enforce payment of a cashier's check issued by the appellee, First National Bank and

的银行。受款人（诈骗人）随后将银行本票背书给酒店。在酒店就本票作出付款提示时，银行拒付该本票，因为银行已经发现，本票的购买人（诈骗人）在购买该本票时，用于付款的票据是伪造的。在初审中，银行辩称，酒店不是正当执票人，因此银行有权以缺乏对价这项相对抗辩来对抗酒店。初审法院支持了银行的抗辩主张，并作出银行胜诉的判决。我们推翻原判。

Trust Company of Oklahoma City, Oklahoma（Bank）, and endorsed by the payee to the appellant, Hotel Riviera, Inc.（Hotel）. When the check was presented for payment, the Bank dishonored it having discovered the check had been paid for with forged instruments. In the trial court, the Bank argued the Hotel was not a holder in due course, thereby permitting the Bank to assert the personal defense of failure of consideration. The trial court allowed the defense, entered judgment for the Bank. We reverse.

本案的问题 对于银行本票的购买人（诈骗人）在购买本票时的欺诈行为，酒店并不知情。本案的问题是，在这种情况下，酒店作为本票的被背书人，是否受制于银行的抗辩？尽管酒店已同意自己不是正当执票人，因为转让人（诈骗人）将本票背书给酒店的目的，是支付转让人的赌博债务，但即使如此，本案仍然涉及银行本票的性质，以及是否从其他角度看酒店属于交易中的无辜当事方。

The question presented is whether the Hotel, as endorsee without knowledge of the underlying fraud of the purchaser of the cashier's check, is subject to the Bank's defense. Even though the Hotel agrees it is not a holder in due course because it accepted the endorsement of the cashier's check in satisfaction of a gambling debt, the issue turns upon the nature of a cashier's check and consideration of whether the Hotel is otherwise an innocent party to the transaction.

银行本票的性质 分析的关键在于银行本票的性质。我们注

Our analysis hinges on the nature of a cashier's check. We note that although there

意到，虽然法院判例对此类票据的认知存在一定分歧，但我们曾经说过，银行本票所代表的，是银行在出立该本票时已经作出了“承兑”（从法典对这个词的使用方式的角度看）的债务（A 诉 F 案；S 诉 C 案）。

is some judicial disparity in the perception of instruments of this genre, we have said that a cashier's check is an indebtedness of a bank which is accepted--as that term is applied by the Uniform Commercial Code （U.C.C. or Code）--upon its issuance. Anderson, Clayton & Co. v. Farmers National Bank of Cordell; State of Pennsylvania v. Curtiss National Bank of Miami Springs, Florida.

银行可对直接欺诈人提出抗辩　在绝大多数情况下，如果银行已对支票作出了承兑，就代表银行已承诺，在收到支票的提示后将会兑付该支票（法典第 3.410 条）；但是，本院和其他法院都承认，这项一般原则也有一项例外。虽然法典并未具体规定，但法院一直允许银行在下述特定情况下拒付银行本票：提示银行本票的执票人曾参与某种欺诈，且该欺诈是银行本票初始出立的原因（A 诉 F 案；T 诉 F 案；引用文章）。这个例外的基础是无可置疑的公平原则，因为不应该允许任何人通过欺诈行为而获利。但是，从未在类似本案的案件中适用过该公平原则。

Under most circumstances, acceptance by a bank constitutes a promise to honor the check upon presentment, U.C.C. Sec. 3-410; but we and other courts have recognized an exception to that general rule. Although not specifically provided in the Code, banks have been allowed to countermand cashier's checks when presented by a holder who has participated in some act of fraud which has led to or caused the original issuance of the cashier's check. Anderson, Clayton & Co. v. Farmers National Bank; TPO Inc. v. FDIC; Lawrence, Making Cashier's Checks and Other Bank Checks Cost-Effective, Minn.L.Rev. Underlying this exception is the unassailable equity that no one should profit from fraudulent acts. Yet, that equity has never been applied in the context of this case.

本案的无辜执票人 本案面临的问题是，银行本票的被背书人从未参与过银行本票购买过程中的欺诈，也不了解该欺诈，那么，其是否应代替欺诈的行为人（诈骗人）来承担该欺诈的后果？银行辩称，答案应该是肯定的，因为将本票背书给酒店系为支付赌债，致使该背书根据内华达州法律而无效（参见S诉H案）。即使仅为讨论目的而假定银行的主张可以成立，该主张在本案中也无必要，因为酒店已承认其不属于正当执票人。内华达州法典第1.030条规定，赌博债务不可强制履行，但实际上，当一项交易中的票据制票人（本案银行）并不是赌博交易的当事方时，上述法律规定是否还适用于此种交易，是存在疑问的。

The question we face here is whether the endorsee who neither participated in nor knew of the fraudulent procurement of the cashier's check should bear the burden of the fraudulent actor. The Bank argues for the affirmative because the check was endorsed in payment of a gambling debt, rendering the endorsement void under the laws of Nevada. See Sea Air Support, Inc. v. Herrmann. Assuming only for the sake of argument the contention is sound, the Hotel's concession that it is not a holder in due course moots the point. However, it is arguable whether Nev.Rev.Stat. Sec. 1.030, which makes gambling debts unenforceable, would apply to transactions in which the maker of the instrument （here the Bank） was not a party to the gambling transaction.

本票背书无关紧要 因此，关于诈骗人对本票的背书和流通，如果该行为的目的本身有任何意义，该意义也仅体现在酒店在取得本票的占有时，是否知道其中存在“瑕疵”。但是，由于酒店已经承认本票存在瑕疵，因

Thus, if the purpose for which Pemberton endorsed and negotiated the check is significant, it is significant only in relation to whether the Hotel came into possession of the check with knowledge of its “defects”. Since that point is conceded, however, we need only consider whether the Hotel can

此我们只需要考虑，在这种情况下，酒店是否仍然有权根据法典第 3 篇而要求银行支付本票。

nonetheless demand payment of the check under Article 3 of the U.C.C.

保护无辜执票人的理由　当恶意执票人要求取得付款时，应该允许受欺诈的银行提出抗辩，但我们相信，本案不存在这个问题。涉及恶意执票人时，执票人以欺诈方式取得本票出立的行为，与无辜银行所受到的损失存在关联。但是，本案不存在这种关联。

We believe the reason for allowing a defrauded bank to defend against a demand for payment made by a culpable holder does not obtain here. There is a relationship between the acts of a holder who procures the issuance of a check by fraud and the loss resultantly sustained by an innocent bank. No similar relationship exists here.

确实，酒店接受本票系用于抵消赌博债务，但酒店接受本票的行为并不是银行受到损害的原因。损害的原因是，诈骗人在存入银行的支票上伪造了背书，用该支票支付了银行本票，而银行未经核实该支票的存款，就出立了自己的银行本票。酒店没有助推该损害的发生。酒店接受诈骗人所背书之本票的行为，与银行的损失毫无关联。

It is true the Hotel accepted the check in payment of a gaming debt; yet, that acceptance was not the cause of the Bank's injury. The forged endorsements of the checks deposited by Pemberton in payment of the cashier's check, coupled with the Bank's subsequent issuance of its own check without verification of the deposit, caused the injury. The Hotel had no part in prompting that injury, and its subsequent acceptance of the endorsement by Pemberton is irrelevant to the Bank's loss.

酒店的实际情况　初审法院的结论是，银行本票的受款人（诈骗人）的欺诈行为导致本票的出

The trial court concluded that the Hotel's acceptance of the check placed the Hotel in the same position as a payee

立，而酒店在接受该本票后，就处于与受款人同等的处境。但我们认为，在银行与无辜的被背书人之间，适用这种逻辑是有问题的。特别是在本案中，酒店在无条件接受该本票和改变了自己处境之前，曾先行向银行核实了该本票的情况。

银行在出立银行本票时，即被视为已对该银行本票作出了承兑，因此，即使该本票被用于支付赌债，也不应允许银行以本票背书无效而逃避其承兑责任。这种结果，一方面不符合逻辑，另一方面也构成对法典明确意图的规避［第4.303条（1）（a）款］。

银行本票在商界的信誉 本判决并不否定内华达州法律的效力，即用于支付赌债的票据不可强制履行。本判决也并非无视这个概念，即相对抗辩可以构成抗辩。但是，本判决确实是要承认银行本票的独特性质，并维护此类票据的作用。在商业领域内，银行本票具有现金的威严（引用著作；引用文章）。从法律角度看，该威严是否经得起推敲，不

whose fraud caused the issuance of the check. We respectfully suggest the logic is faulty as between the Bank and the innocent endorsee. This is especially true when, as here, the endorsee obtains the issuing bank's verification of the check prior to its unconditional acceptance and the endorsee's change of position.

Since the cashier's check was accepted on issuance, the Bank cannot be allowed to escape the effect of its acceptance on the ground that the endorsement was nullified because it was made in payment of a gambling debt. That result is both a non sequitur and an intentional avoidance of the clear import of U.C.C. Sec. 4-303（1）（a）.

This holding does not deny the effect of Nevada law regarding the enforceability of instruments given in satisfaction of gambling debts, nor does it ignore the concept of allowing the assertion of personal defenses. It does, however, recognize the peculiar nature of a cashier's check and effects the purpose of such an instrument. In commercial circles, cashier's checks have the aura of cash. Am.Jur.2d, Banks； Lawrence. Whether that aura bears scrutiny in the law is irrelevant

是本案要讨论的问题。对本案来说，唯一重要的是，在商业领域，普遍对银行本票给予高度尊崇，因为银行本票代表了该本票之出立银行的付款承诺。

here. It is important only that there is a universal commercial reverence for cashier's checks which is the product of the issuing bank's promise of payment.

结论　虽然法典仅仅是从一般意义上规定，银行在出立本票时即已作出了承兑，但任何否定此种效力的尝试，仍然必须在逻辑上与法典所建立和依赖的流通票据法相符合。如果银行本票的购买人以欺诈方式取得本票并试图将其流通，上述逻辑关系明显是存在的，但是，在涉及未以任何方式欺诈银行的被背书人时，该逻辑就不再存在（W 诉 A 案）。简言之，缺乏对价的相对抗辩不适用于本案交易。推翻初审法院的原判，并要求改判本案原告酒店胜诉。

While the U.C.C. speaks in general terms about the acceptance of cashier's checks upon issuance, any attempt to exclude that consequence must have some logical relationship to the law of negotiation established and relied upon in the Code. While that relationship is manifest when a fraudulent purchaser attempts to negotiate a cashier's check, the logic fails in the case of an endorsee who has done nothing to cheat the issuing bank. Whitehead v. American Security and Trust Co. In short, the personal defense of failure of consideration is inapplicable to the instant transaction. The judgment of the District Court is reversed with directions to enter judgment in favor of the appellant.

担 保 交 易

案例31　受担保方是否有权引用组合文件原则?

In Re Sabol
萨博尔破产案

伊利诺伊州中区联邦破产法院 2006 年；337 B.R. 195

简　介

在本破产案中，债权人银行向破产法院登记了自己对破产债务人所持有的担保债权。债务人破产前从事录音业务，为了购买音响器材，曾向银行申请贷款，并由银行向州政府的“小企业管理局”（Small Business Administration，SBA）申请，由 SBA 为该贷款提供还款保证。在银行与债务人的贷款文件中以及在银行向 SBA 提交的贷款保证申请书中，都有担保物的描述。银行的意图是将债务人将要购买的音响器材作为担保物。银行随后还在担保交易的登记处登记了融资声明。但是，银行并未与债务人签订单独的担保协议。

破产受托人就银行登记的担保债权提出异议，认为银行与债务人没有订立担保协议，因此银行的担保权益无效。银行则认为，根据“组合文件原则”（composite document rule），将贷款项目中的所有文件放在一起，可以认为存在担保协议。破产法院认为，本案虽然存在很多文件，但实际上缺少一份既包含了债务人签名，同时又具体描述了担保物的文件。比如，本票上有债务人的签名，且印制的标准条款提到了“任何”担保物，但法院认为这个印制条款没有具体的针对性，不能与音响器材联系起来。而在向小企业管理局提交的贷款保证申请表中，虽然具体列出了担保物，但缺少债务人的签名，甚至无法证明债务人看到过这个申请表。法院认为，法典目前对担保协议的要求已经非常简单，当事方应尽量遵守，因此法院没有理由采取过于宽松的处理。最终，法院认定本案中不存在担保协议，因此银行不持有有效的担保权益。

判　决

本案的问题　在本破产清算案中，庭审完成之后，破产受托人提出主张，要求本院确认银行对破产债务人的若干音响设备所持有的担保权益是否有效。主要问题在于，银行在没有订立担保协议的情况下，是否可以依赖“组合文件原则”取得有效的担保权益？

This adversary proceeding is before the Court, after trial, on the complaint by Charles E. Covey, as Trustee of the Chapter 7 estate (“TRUSTEE”), to determine the validity of a security interest held by Morton Community Bank (“BANK”) in several items of sound equipment owned by Michael S. Sabol, one of the Debtors (“DEBTOR”). The main issue is whether the Composite Document Rule can rescue the BANK from the absence of a security agreement.

双方的理由　破产受托人声称，银行不持有法典第9篇项下的有效价款担保权益，因为不存在称为“担保协议”的独立文件，且其他文件中的文字也没有明确向银行提供担保权益。银行则基于“组合文件原则”声称，将贷

The TRUSTEE contends that the BANK does not have a valid purchase money security interest under Article 9 of the UCC, because there is no separate document captioned “Security Agreement” or any language in any other document explicitly granting a security interest. The BANK, relying on the

款申请书、本票、债务人授权和融资声明这些文件组合在一起，可以构成设立担保权益的协议。

"Composite Document Rule", contends that the loan application, the promissory note, the authorization and the financing statement, taken together, establish an agreement to create a security agreement.

担保协议的一般要求 一般而言，对债务人资产所持的财产权利的性质和范围，应适用州法（参见 B 诉 U 案）。因此，关于本案当事方是否订立了有效的担保协议的问题，应适用伊利诺伊州法律。根据该州法律，非占有性的担保权益只有在下列情况下才发生附着并可强制履行：债务人已对包含了担保物描述的担保协议作出了认证；债权人已支付价值；债务人对担保物拥有权利［法典第 9.203 条（b）（3）（A）款］。"担保协议"被定义为"设立或提供担保权益的协议"［法典第 9.102 条（73）款］。"担保权益"是指"动产或不动产附着物中担保债务之付款或履约的权益"［法典第 1.201 条（37）款］。

Generally, state law determines the nature and extent of the property rights in the debtor's assets. See, e.g., Butner v. U.S. Under Illinois law, which governs the issue of whether the parties have entered into a valid security agreement, a nonpossessory security interest does not attach and is not enforceable unless the debtor has authenticated a security agreement that contains a description of the collateral, value has been given, and the debtor has rights in the collateral. ILCS 9-203（b）（3）（A）. A "security agreement" is defined as "an agreement that creates or provides for a security interest". ILCS 9-102（73）. A "security interest" is an interest in personal property or fixtures which secures payment or performance of an obligation. ILCS 1-201（37）.

书面担保协议的作用 书面担保协议被认为具有两个作用：

The requirement of a written security agreement is said to serve two purposes:

第一，可以起到证明作用，避免就担保物问题产生争议；第二，可以起到反欺诈法作用，避免仅仅基于口头陈述而强制履行一方所称的债权（OU 破产案；OW 破产案；D 破产案）。为了设立担保权益，担保协议不需要使用特定文字或"专门用语"（K 破产案）。虽然"组合文件原则"提供了很大的宽容度，但是，仍然必须具备一定的文字表述，说明债务人具有提供担保权益的意图（N 破产案；Z 破产案）。因此，如果融资声明仅仅指明了担保物，但并没有包含任何具有"设立"意图的文字来说明债务人在所描述的担保物中设立了担保权益，该融资声明就不能代替担保协议（W 破产案；Z 破产案）。

the first being evidentiary in that it eliminates disputes as to what items are secured and the second in the nature of a statute of frauds, by precluding the enforcement of claims based only on an oral representation. In re Outboard Marine Corp.; In re Owensboro Canning Co., Inc.; In re Data Entry Service Corp. No particular words of grant or "magic words" are required to be included in a security agreement to create a security interest. In re Krause. Notwithstanding the lenity of the Composite Document Rule, there must be some language reflecting the debtor's intent to grant a security interest. In re NTA, LLC; In re Zurliene. Accordingly, a financing statement which does not contain any grant language by the debtor creating a security interest in the described collateral, but merely identifies the collateral, cannot substitute for a security agreement. In re Westpfahl; Zurllene.

组合文件原则 尽管法典要求必须存在描述了担保物且经过签名或认证的担保协议，但对于何种情况可满足该要求，有些法院采取了宽松态度。根据"组合文件原则"，可以将两份或

Notwithstanding the statutory requirement of a signed or authenticated security agreement that describes the collateral, some courts have adopted a liberal view of what suffices to meet that requirement. Under the "Composite Document Rule",

多份文件组合在一起作为担保协议［N 破产案（为了满足法典第 9.203 条对业经签名的书面协议的要求，并非一定要存在称为“担保协议”的独立的、正式的文件）］。组合文件原则是否适用，以及在何种程度上适用，属于州法问题（B 破产案）。联邦第七巡回上诉法院曾肯定某地区法院的判决，认为在分析一份转让文件是否实际上被当事方视为担保协议时，要将该交易的其他全部文件综合考虑，即使该转让文件表面上只单纯用于转让（W 诉 R 案）。

伊利诺伊州判例 本案争议应适用伊利诺伊州法律。关于是否可以使用组合文件原则来满足第 9.203 条（b）（3）（A）款对担保协议的要求，州最高法院尚未有过判例。伊利诺伊州上诉法院有关这项原则的唯一判例是 S 诉 C 案。该案涉及使用百货公司信用卡进行的一次购物。在顾客开卡时所签署的信用卡申请表上，包含了担保协议的内容。随后，顾客使用信用卡进行了多次

two or more documents in combination may qualify as a security agreement. In re Numeric Corp. (separate formal document entitled “security agreement” is not always necessary to satisfy the signed writing requirement of § 9-203). Whether and to what extent the Composite Document Rule applies is a question of state law. Matter of Bollinger Corp. The Seventh Circuit Court of Appeals has affirmed a district court’s holding that all of the documents constituting a transaction may be considered when analyzing whether an assignment, absolute on its face, was, in fact, intended as a security agreement. Wambach v. Randall.

Illinois law governs this dispute. The Illinois Supreme Court has not addressed whether the Composite Document Rule may be used to satisfy the security agreement requirement of UCC § 9-203(b)(3)(A). The only Illinois Appellate Court decision addressing the Rule is Sears, Roebuck & Co. v. Conry, a case in which a Sears credit card purchase was at issue. After having earlier opened the account by signing a credit card application that contained a security agreement, the customer made credit card

购物，并均在销售小票上签名。小票描述了相关商品，并包含了允许百货公司对所购商品持有价款担保权益的文字。百货公司每隔一段时间会更新担保协议的格式并将新格式发给持卡人，但无须持卡人签名。

关于百货公司是否已证明其对小票所列货物持有价款担保权益，该案法院判决说："在本案中，顾客签署了百货公司信用卡的销售小票。小票通过引用方式包含了担保协议，并就所购商品向百货公司提供了价款担保权益。与前面引用的判例类似，已签名的百货公司信用卡销售小票构成了伊利诺伊州法律所要求的业经签名的担保协议。"

在S诉C案中，由于销售小票本身已满足第9.203条的要求，即书面文件业经签名，描述了担保物，且在其中设立了担保权益，因此该案实际上不涉及组合文件原则。本院认为，该案对本案不适用。因此可以说，伊利诺伊州法院尚未就组合文件原则作出过肯定或否定。

purchases and signed sales tickets describing the merchandise and containing language granting Sears a purchase money security interest in the purchased goods. The form of security agreement was periodically updated by Sears by sending the cardholder the new form with no signature required.

On the issue of whether Sears proved that it retained a purchase money security interest in the goods listed on the sales receipts, the court held as follows: "In the instant case, the defendants signed Sears credit card sales receipts incorporating a security agreement by reference and granting Sears a security interest in the items purchased. By analogy with the cases cited above, the signed Sears credit card receipts satisfied the Illinois statutory requirement of a signed security agreement."

Since the sales receipts, by themselves, satisfied the requirements of § 9-203 of a signed writing describing the collateral and granting a security interest therein, Conry is not a true composite document case and, in this Court's view, has no application to the issue at bar. It thus appears that no Illinois court has approved or disapproved of the use of the Composite Document Rule.

手续已经高度简化 在法典制定之前，动产抵押的相关要求比较机械，且有时过于复杂，因此基于衡平原则和实用主义，普通法发展出了一些例外原则。但从 1962 年起，法典就担保交易的文件要求和完善方式，引入了新型的、简化的体系。由于法典已将设立担保权益的形式要求简化到不能再简单的程度，我们已经不再需要上述的衡平法例外。为了提高法典的确定性，并保持一定程度的可辨识标准，很重要的一点就是强制履行法典第 9 篇所规定的最低形式要求（参见 K 破产案）。

The pre-UCC era of chattel mortgages, and the technical and sometimes complex requirements associated therewith, fostered common law exceptions in the name of equity and pragmatism. Beginning in 1962, however, the UCC ushered in a new, simplified regime for documenting and perfecting secured transactions. Because the UCC reduces to an absolute minimum the formal requirements for the creation of a security interest, the need for those equitable exceptions no longer exists. In the interests of certainty and maintaining some identifiable standard, it is important to enforce the minimal formal requirements set forth in Article 9 of the UCC. See, In re Kevin W. Emerick Farms, Inc.

应采取严格解释方法 因此有理由认为，在解释法典对文件的形式要求时，应趋于严格而不是宽松，因为这更加符合法典为商业交易提供确定性和可靠性的总体意图。其他一些法院也对组合文件原则作出了严格解释（参见 N 破产案；Z 破产案；W 破产案；D 破产案）。

Thus, an argument can be made that strict rather than liberal interpretation of the UCC documentation requirements is more consistent with the overall purpose of the UCC to create certainty and reliability in commercial transactions. Other courts have applied the Composite Document Rule narrowly. See, In re NTA, LLC, supra; In re Zurliene; In re Westphal; In re Dean & Jean Fashions, Inc.

银行的理由 本案银行依赖

The BANK relies upon the DEBTOR'S

债务人自己的证词，证明债务人理解其通过签署贷款文件，就所购买的设备向银行提供了担保权益。此外，债务人在登记破产债权时，也将银行登记为担保债权人。银行的另一个理由是，贷款申请表上逐项列出了担保物，且本票中规定了银行对“担保物”的权利以及债务人违约时银行的权利。并且，债务人授权对融资声明进行登记，而融资声明中描述了担保物。

testimony that he understood that by signing the loan documents that he was granting the BANK a security interest in the equipment that he was going to purchase, as reflected in his treatment of the BANK as a secured creditor in his bankruptcy schedules. The BANK also relies on the itemization of collateral on the loan application, the provision in the note regarding the BANK'S rights in "collateral" and its rights upon default, the debtor's authorization and the description of the collateral in the financing statement.

申请表的问题　但是，虽然在银行向小企业管理局提交的贷款担保申请表中逐项列出了担保物，但不应允许银行将申请表中对担保物的列举，用于证明债务人提供担保权益的意愿。申请表包含了两个独立部分：一部分由债务人填写，另一部分由银行填写。担保物列在由银行填写的那一部分。该页由银行职员填写，且填写日期是债务人在贷款申请表上签名一周之后。

The BANK'S reliance on the listing of collateral under the description of loan terms on its application for the SBA guarantee reveals nothing about the DEBTOR'S intent to grant a security interest. The application consists of two separate portions: one completed by the DEBTOR and one completed by the BANK. The listing of the collateral appears on the BANK'S portion of the document. That page was completed by officers of the BANK and is dated one week after the DEBTOR'S signature on his application for the loan.

本票的问题　银行还提到了

The BANK points to the provisions

本票的条款。该条款并无任何针对性地描述了银行对担保物的权利,以及发生违约后银行的权利。根据本票中的定义,“担保物”是指“为了担保本票之付款而取得的任何财产”。在发生违约后,本票允许银行“取得任何担保物的占有”,并可“出售、出租或以其他方式处置任何担保物”。但是,本票并未指明担保物是什么。实际上,本票本身也预期另有一项担保协议。本票的总则规定,“借款人必须签署所有必要文件,以便在任何时间都符合贷款文件的要求,使贷款人可以获取、完善和维持其对担保物的留置权”。

of the note which describe, generically, the BANK'S rights in collateral and upon default. The note defines "Collateral" as "any property taken as security for payment of this Note". Upon default, the note authorizes the BANK to "take possession of any Collateral" and to "sell, lease, or otherwise dispose of any Collateral". The note does not identify the collateral. In fact, the note itself contemplates a separate security agreement. Under the heading of general provisions, the note provides that "Borrower must sign all documents necessary at any time to comply with the Loan Documents and to enable Lender to acquire, perfect, or maintain Lender's liens on Collateral".

授权条款的问题　债务人允许银行登记融资声明的授权,同样也不具有担保协议的效力。债务人所给予的授权是,“就债务人目前所寻求之贷款的任何担保权益”进行登记。银行所引用的N破产案与本案情况不同。在N破产案中,虽然当事方没有签署正式担保协议,但债务人的董事会曾授权制备法典所要求的融

The DEBTOR'S authorization for the BANK to file a financing statement is equally inefficacious. It authorizes that filing "as to any security interest in the loan . . . presently sought by the [DEBTOR]". In re Numeric Corp., relied on by the BANK, is distinguishable. In Numeric, although the parties had not signed a formal security agreement, the board of directors of the debtor authorized the preparation of a UCC financing

资声明，用于覆盖债权人对销售合同中列出的某些设备的担保权益。法院认定，董事会的决议证明，当事方已就设立担保权益达成“事实上的协议”，因此，该决议与融资声明对担保物的具体描述结合起来，可以构成担保协议。

融资声明的问题 银行的依据还包括已登记的融资声明。融资声明是法典所允许的，但债务人没有在声明上签名。银行于2001年7月18日登记了融资声明，即贷款完成交割将近两个星期之后。银行未能提供证人证明，在债务人签署授权登记融资声明的文件时，银行曾将融资声明展示给债务人。债务人作证说，当时未讨论担保权益的问题。这与银行的证词相矛盾，因为银行说，在贷款手续完成之时或之前，曾将融资声明展示给债务人。本院不能假定，在无法证明银行当时已提供了融资声明的情况下，该声明与组合文件原则的适用存在任何关系。

银行引用的判例 银行引用

statement to cover the creditor's security interest in certain equipment described in a bill of sale. Finding that the directors' resolution established "an agreement in fact" by the parties to create a security interest, the court held that the resolution, taken with the financing statement's itemization of the collateral, constituted a security agreement.

The BANK also relies on its financing statement. The financing statement, as permitted by the Revised UCC, was not signed by the DEBTOR. The financing statement was not filed by the BANK until July 18, 2001, almost two weeks after the loan was closed. No one from the BANK testified that the financing statement was presented to the DEBTOR at the time that he signed the document authorizing its filing. The DEBTOR'S testimony that a security interest was not discussed contradicts any suggestion that the financing statement was presented to the DEBTOR at or prior to the loan closing. This Court will not presume that a financing statement, not shown to be contemporaneous, has any part to play in the Composite Document Rule.

In re Data Entry Service Corp., a case

了另一个涉及小企业管理局贷款担保的判例，即D破产案，但该案的事实情况与本案不同。在该案中，债务人除了已签署本票，还签署了一项贷款协议，其中列出了第一序位抵押权项下的担保物，包括机器、设备、家具及不动产附着物、库存、应收款和一般无形财产。在文件结尾紧邻债务人签名的上方，协议说明债务人已同意协议所规定的条件。此外，还在州务卿处登记了两份包含了担保物描述的融资声明，且每份声明均有债务人的签名。法院认定，该贷款协议本身，或者该协议与已签名的融资声明一起，足以构成由小企业管理局作为受担保方的担保权益。

involving an SBA loan, relied on by the BANK, is factually distinguishable. In that case, in addition to the note, the debtor signed a Loan Agreement which listed as collateral, first liens on machinery, equipment, furniture and fixtures, inventory, accounts and general intangibles. Directly above the debtor's signature, at the end of the document, the Agreement provided that the debtor agreed to the conditions imposed. In addition, two financing statements describing the collateral were filed with the Secretary of State, each signed by the debtor. The court determined that the Loan Agreement, by itself or in conjunction with the signed financing statements, was sufficient to create a security interest in favor of the SBA.

在小企业管理局担保贷款的M破产案中，结果也基本类似。如D破产案一样，债务人签署了贷款协议。协议在"贷款条件"中列明了担保物，包括"对所有设备、库存和应收款的第一序位抵押权"。此外，在T破产案中，该案法院的判决也显示了本案银行立场的缺陷。该案法院认

A similar result was reached in In re Maddox, another SBA-guaranteed loan case. As in Data Entry, the debtor had signed a loan agreement which identified collateral under "Terms of the Loan" as a "first lien on all equipment, inventory and accounts receivable". The court's decision in In re Tracy's Flowers and Gifts, Inc., highlights the weakness of the BANK'S position.

定，虽然“最简单”的融资声明本身不能兼作“担保协议”，但该案债权人登记的融资声明中包含了额外文字，因此该声明可以构成担保协议。该文字是：“此本票由债务人目前拥有的以及未来取得的所有应收款、库存和设备担保；此留置权所担保的贷款系根据小企业管理局国家项目而提供。”

结论 本院认为，无论是将本案银行所依赖的任何文件单独审阅还是将所有文件组合审阅，都不足以证明债务人意图设立担保权益。任何一份文件中都找不到向银行提供担保权益的文字。关于银行提交给小企业管理局的申请表，没有证据表明债务人已阅读或审核其中的“贷款条款”，更不用说已同意该条款。融资声明是唯一描述了担保物的文件，但债务人没有签名，且很可能从未见过该文件。还剩下什么？只有本票中的标准印刷条款，其中提到银行对“任何担保物”的权利以及债务人对“任何担保权

Recognizing that a “bare bones” financing statement, standing alone, cannot double as a “security agreement”, the court held that the following additional language included in the creditor’s [financing statement], qualified as a security agreement: “This note is secured by all accounts, inventory and equipment now owned or hereafter acquired by [the debtor] . . . The loan secured by this lien was made under [a SBA] nationwide program.”

Whether considered alone or in combination, this Court finds that there is not sufficient evidence of the DEBTOR’S intent to create a security interest in the documents relied on by the BANK. No language conveying a security interest to the BANK is found in any of the documents. There is no evidence that the DEBTOR read or reviewed, much less agreed to, the “loan terms” contained in the BANK’S application to the SBA. The financing statement, containing the only description of collateral, is not signed by the DEBTOR and, in all likelihood, was never seen by him. What is left? Only boilerplate references in the note to the BANK’S rights in “any collateral” and in the authorization to

益”的授权。

银行向小企业管理局申请贷款担保的申请表上列出了担保物。这份申请表上假如有债务人的签名，本来应该能满足法典第9.203条规定的最低要求。但是，本案不存在经债务人签名或认证并描述了担保物（或以引用方式描述了担保物）的文件，因此，无法承认担保权益的存在。本院的看法是，如果可以适用组合文件原则，那么最合适的适用场景是，当债务人已签署或认证了包含担保物描述但未包含同意设立担保权益文字的某种文件时，根据组合文件原则，通过引用债务人签署的各项贷款文件，来证明债务人同意设立担保权益的意愿。但是，不应利用该原则来绕过法典第9.203条所明确规定的最低要求，即必须存在描述了担保物且业经签名或认证的书面文件。

应遵守法典的最低要求　本案银行也许确有设立担保权益的意图，但本院不认为上述结果对银行过于残酷。法典第9篇的主

“any security interest”.

Had the BANK’S application for SBA guarantee, which listed the collateral, been signed by the DEBTOR, the minimal requirements of § 9-203 may well have been satisfied. But without a description of the collateral in a signed or authenticated document or in a separate document incorporated by reference into a signed or authenticated document, no security interest can be recognized. This Court is of the view that the Composite Document Rule is most appropriately used, if at all, to allow the debtor’s intent to grant a security interest to be demonstrated by reference to the various loan documents where the debtor has signed or authenticated a document containing a description of the collateral that does not contain words of grant. The Rule should not be applied, however, to bypass the necessity of a signed or authenticated writing that describes the collateral, as that is the clearly stated minimum requirement of § 9-203.

Even though the BANK may have intended that there was to be a security interest, the Court does not view the result reached as unduly harsh. The primary

要目的是在商业交易中保持一致性和确定性。受担保方为设立和保护其担保权益而需要采取的步骤，已被降至了最低限度。这些步骤既简单又明确(M破产案)。因此，要求受担保方遵守这些步骤，不属于过分的要求(S破产案)。

purpose of Article 9 of the UCC was to create uniformity and certainty in commercial transactions. The steps required to be taken by secured parties to establish and protect their interests, having been reduced to a minimum, are simple and clearly laid out. In re Modafferi. It is not unreasonable to require that they be complied with. See, In re Swersky.

银行在破产程序中登记了36,967.34美元的担保债权，而破产受托人提出异议，认为银行不持有有效的担保权益。本院现已认定该担保权益无效，因此应支持受托人的异议和否定银行所称的担保债权，并将相应数额的债权视为无担保债权。

The TRUSTEE objected to the BANK'S proof of claim filed as secured in the amount of $36,967.34 on the basis that the BANK had no valid security interest. Having now obtained that determination, the objection should be allowed, the BANK should be denied any secured claim, but should be allowed an unsecured claim in the amount stated in its claim.

案例 32　融资声明中的债务人名字是否严重误导？

In Re Tringham Holdings, Inc.
特灵汉控股公司破产案

弗吉尼亚州东区联邦破产法院 2006 年；354 B.R. 363

简　介

在本破产案中，破产受托人对受担保方（Suna Bros.，Inc.）所持的担保权益提出质疑，认为在受担保方登记的融资声明中，错误地描述了债务人的名字，具有“严重误导”（seriously misleading）性质。因此，根据法典第 9 篇的规定，该融资声明不能起到完善担保权益的作用。破产法院支持了破产受托人的主张，认定受担保方的担保权益未获得完善，因此可被破产受托人撤销。

破产债务人在州政府公共档案中注册的全名是“Tringham Holdings，Inc.”。受担保方在以寄售形式将一批珠宝交给破产债务人出售后，为了完善自己对珠宝的担保权益，及时登记了法典所要求的融资声明，但融资声明将债务人的名字写成“Tringham Holdings”，而没有包括名字最后的“Inc.”。从严格的角度看，这属于融资声明对债务人名字的错误描述，但该错误是否使融资声明成为法典所说的“严重误导”，则是本案争议的问题。

法院认为，法典的要求是，如果使用债务人的正确名字对融资声明进行检索，并同时使用政府登记处的标准检索逻辑，那么，只要该检索可以找到相关的融资声明，则即使融资声明包含了错误信息，融资声明也不属于严重误导，而如果找不到该融资声明，融资声明就由于该错误而被视为严重误导。根据这个标准，本案的融资声明属于严重误导。另外的一个问题是，不仅官方的登记处提供融资声明的检索服务，还有一些其他商业公司也提供检索服务。这些商业公司可能会使用自己的检索软件。在本案中，即使使用错误的名字，商业检索服务商仍然可以找到相应的融资声明。但法院认为，在涉及融资声明的效力时，必须以官方的检索结果为准。

判　决

一般原则　如果需要通过登记融资声明使担保权益得以完善，该声明必须实质上满足法典的相关要求。一般而言，如果债务人是公司，融资声明就必须使用公司注册地公共档案中所登记的公司名字，否则融资声明无效［法典第9.503条（a）（1）款］。

Where a filed financing statement is required to perfect a security interest, it must substantially satisfy the requirements of a financing statement. Generally, the name of a corporate debtor, as indicated on the public record of the debtor's jurisdiction of organization, must be listed on the financing statement for it to be valid. Va.Code Ann. § 9-503（a）（1）.

不构成严重误导即可　只要融资声明实质上满足了法典要求，"即属于有效的融资声明，即使其存在次要错误或疏漏，除非该错误或疏漏使融资声明严重误导"［法典第9.506条（a）款］。根据法典规定，"除（c）款另有

Where the requirements are substantially satisfied, a financing statement "is effective, even if it has minor errors or omissions, unless the errors or omissions make the financing statement seriously misleading". Va.Code Ann. § 9-506（a）. By law, "［e］xcept as otherwise provided in subsection（c）, a

规定外，如果融资声明未能根据第 9.503 条（a）款充分提供债务人的名字，融资声明即属于严重误导”［第 9.506 条（h）款］。

本案的情况　在本案受担保方所登记的融资声明中，债务人名字“Tringham Holdings”无疑与弗吉尼亚州政府公共档案中所记录的该公司名字“Tringham Holdings，Inc.”有所区别。因此，除非可以得到法典第 9.506 条（c）款的豁免，否则该融资声明就属于严重误导，致使受担保方的担保权益无法获得完善。

新旧不同的检索标准　关于融资声明中的错误，法典第 9.506 条（c）款所规定的例外，代表了新版法典第 9 篇对旧版法典的修改。在 2001 年修改前的旧版法典中，弗吉尼亚州法典第 9 篇不包含相当于目前（b）款和（c）款的内容。之前，在判断融资声明是否充分时，采用的是“尽职检索人”标准。

目前的规则　关于融资声明中的错误是否构成严重误导，目前第 9.506 条（c）款的规则更

financing statement that fails sufficiently to provide the name of the debtor in accordance with § 9-503（a）is seriously misleading”. Va.Code Ann. § 9-506（h）.

There is no question in this case that the name of the debtor in the Suna financing statement, “Tringham Holdings”, was not the same corporate name as that on the public record for the state of Virginia, “Tringham Holdings, Inc.”. Therefore, unless excepted by Va.Code Ann. § 9-506（c）, the financing statement is seriously misleading and is ineffective to perfect Suna’s security interest.

The exception in subsection（c）represents a shift between the previous version of Article 9 and Revised Article 9 in dealing with errors on financing statements. Prior to the revisions enacted in 2001, Virginia’s version of Article 9 had no equivalent to subsections（b）and（c）. Instead, the governing principle for financing statement sufficiency was a diligent searcher standard.

Subsection（c）now provides a more concrete rule for determining if errors are seriously misleading, providing that: “If

加具体。该款规定："即使融资声明未能根据第 9.503 条（a）款充分提供债务人的名字，但如果基于债务人的正确名字，并使用登记处的标准检索逻辑（如果有），可以在登记处通过对记录进行检索找到该份融资声明，即不应认为所提供的名字使融资声明产生严重误导。"

a search of the records of the filing office under the debtor's correct name, using the filing office's standard search logic, if any, would disclose a financing statement that fails sufficiently to provide the name of the debtor in accordance with § 9-503（a）, the name provided does not make the financing statement seriously misleading."

对检索的要求 根据法典规定，判断一项检索是否恰当的标准是：应该使用债务人的正确名字，登记处的标准检索逻辑，以及登记处的数据库[参见第 9.506 条正式评论 2（该评论说，"根据本款的规定，一份严重误导的融资声明，即使可以通过下列方式被找到，仍属于无效：（i）使用登记处以外的检索逻辑来检索登记处的数据库；或（ii）使用登记处的标准检索逻辑来检索登记处以外的数据库"）]。

According to the statute, the appropriate standard by which to judge a search is the filing office's standard search logic for a search under the debtor's correct name, in the filing office's database. See, e.g., Va.Code Ann. § 9-506 Official Comment 2（stating that "a financing statement that is seriously misleading under this section is ineffective even if it is disclosed by（i）using a search logic other than that of the filing office to search the official records, or（ii）using the filing office's standard search logic to search a data base other than that of the filing office"）.

其他州的判例 其他州的若干判例在适用其本州法典的上述条款时都强调，在确定一份融资声明是否属于严重误导时，

Several cases in other jurisdictions, applying parallel provisions in their respective Uniform Commercial Codes, emphasize that the filing office's standard search logic is the

登记处的标准检索逻辑是决定性因素［参见 P 诉 C 案（堪萨斯州州务卿使用债务人的正确名字进行检索而未能找到相关融资声明，因此该融资声明属于严重误导）；R 诉 R 案（法院认为，旧版法典第 9 篇项下的判例法不再适用。如果使用债务人的正确名字进行检索而不能显示相关融资声明，该融资声明即属于严重误导）；A 诉 C 案（该案遵循 R 诉 R 案的先例作出判定，无论在其他非官方检索中是否可以省略债务人正确名字的尾词，法律所要求的检索标准是，通过登记处进行检索，并使用债务人的正确名字）］。很明显，在这些州进行检索时，应以登记处的标准检索逻辑为准。

governing factor in determining whether a financing statement is seriously misleading. See, Pankratz Implement Co. v. Citizens National Bank（finding a financing statement seriously misleading where the official search conducted by the Kansas secretary of state under the proper name did not reveal the financing statement）; Receivables Purchasing Co., Inc., v. R & R Directional Drilling, LLC（explaining that case law under the previous version of Article 9 was no longer applicable and finding a financing statement seriously misleading where a search under the debtor's correct name did not reveal the financing statement）; All Bus. Corp. v. Choi（following Receivables Purchasing Co. and holding that regardless of private searches done with incomplete sterns of the proper debtor name, the law required a search through the clerk's office with the correct name）. Therefore, it is clear in these jurisdictions that the filing office's standard search logic governs.

本案的检索情况　关于本案，从登记融资声明时起至本案庭审时止的这段时期内，几家商业检索服务商，包括 CS 公司、

In the time period between filing of the financing statement and the trial in this Adversary Proceeding, a number of UCC searches were performed by private search

AI公司和UC公司，都曾对本案的融资声明进行过检索，且每家公司的检索都找到了受担保方的融资声明登记。当事方没有提供证据说明，CS公司或AI公司的检索是以何种方式进行的。在审理中，受担保方的一个证人作证说，她曾使用UC公司的系统，以“Tringham Holdings”这个名字进行检索后，找到了受担保方的融资声明。

companies such as Corporation Service Company, Access Information Services, and UCC Retrievals, Inc. Each of these searches disclosed the existence of the Suna financing statement. No evidence was presented as to the underlying methodology behind the Corporation Service Company or Access Information Services, Inc., searches. At trial, a witness for Suna testified that she had conducted the search by UCC Retrievals, under the name “Tringham Holdings”. Her search disclosed the existence of the Suna financing statement.

上述证人作证说，她检索时之所以使用了“Tringham Holdings”而没有使用正确的“Tringham Holdings, Inc.”，是因为她认为“Inc.”这个尾词属于“干扰词”。此处所说的“干扰词”，是指在对融资声明电子数据库进行检索时，被去除或被忽视的词。该证人将“Inc.”视为干扰词的原因是，该词列于“公司行政人员国际协会”制定的干扰词清单中。该协会干扰词清单上还包括“Corporation”、“Corp”、“Company”、“Co.”、

Her rationale for searching under the name “Tringham Holdings” rather than the correct “Tringham Holdings, Inc.”, was that she considered the term “Inc.” to be a “noise word”. Noise words for these purposes are words that are removed or ignored in the process of performing an electronic database search for financing statements. The witness classified “Inc.” as a noise wore because it is one of such words on a list promulgated by the International Association of Corporation Administrators (IACA). Other abbreviations on the IACA “noise word” list include “Corporation”,

"Limited"和"Ltd."。

本案受担保方反复强调，这些商业检索服务商在使用"标准检索逻辑"后，找到了受担保方的融资声明。但很明显，目前法典的检索标准已不再是尽职检索人的标准检索逻辑，也不再是商业检索机构的标准检索逻辑，而是政府登记处的标准检索逻辑。

弗吉尼亚州检索逻辑　弗吉尼亚州公司管理委员会在《弗吉尼亚州行政法典》中规定了登记规则，说明了委员会进行检索时使用的标准检索逻辑。登记处基于所收到的检索名字，使用标准检索逻辑来得出检索结果。检索还有若干额外要求，包括规则第（4）款的规定："干扰词"包括但不限于"an"、"and"、"for"、"of"和"the"。其中，"the"这个词在任何情况下都应被忽视；对于其他干扰词，则除非其处于一个组织名字的起始位置，否则也应被忽视。商业组织中的某些词被改为标准缩略词：将"company"改为"co."，"corporation"改

"Corp"，"Company"，"Co."，"Limited"，and "Ltd."．

Suna repeatedly emphasizes that these private searches used "standard search logic" to disclose the Suna financing statement. The relevant standard is clearly no longer the diligent searcher's standard search logic nor a private search organization's standard search logic, but it is instead the filing office's standard search logic.

The Virginia State Corporation Commission has promulgated filing rules in Va. Admin. Code that describe the standard search logic employed by the commission when conducting a search. Search results are produced by the application of standardized search logic to the name presented to the filing officer, along with several additional requirements, including the following subsection 4： "Noise words" include, but are not limited to, "an", "and", "for", "of", and "the". The word "the" always will be disregarded and other noise words appearing anywhere except at the beginning of an organization name will be disregarded. Certain business words are modified to a standard abbreviation： company to "co.",

为“corp.”,“limited”改为“ltd.”,“incorporated”改为“inc.”(《弗吉尼亚州行政法典》)。对于“公司行政人员国际协会”制定的干扰词清单,委员会并未全部采用。

破产受托人请弗吉尼亚州公司管理委员会的一名雇员作证,解释了委员会在对与法典有关的登记进行官方检索时所使用的检索软件的编程原理。根据该雇员的解释,软件的检索逻辑会修正检索人所输入的名字,以便去除名字中的某些内容,包括标点符号、空格以及委员会规则中列出的5个干扰词。此种修正后的检索条目将和登记在案的融资声明进行匹配,而后者也曾根据同样标准进行过修正。

本案的相关证据 本案当事方没有提交证据证明,商业检索服务商的检索是基于债务人的正确名字并遵循弗吉尼亚州公司管理委员会的标准检索逻辑而进行的。在审理中,有关商业检索的唯一额外证据是,UC公司

corporation to “corp.”, limited to “ltd.”, incorporated to “inc.”. Va. Admin. Code. The State Corporation Commission has not adopted the full list of noise words promulgated by the IACA.

Plaintiff called as a witness an employee of the Virginia State Corporation Commission, who described the coding of the UCC search program utilized by the Corporation Commission in its official UCC searches. As explained by the witness, the search logic modifies a given entry by removing certain items from the name entered by a searcher, including punctuation, spaces, and the five noise words listed in the State Corporation Commission Rules. This creates a search key which is then matched to names on filed financing statements, which have likewise been modified in accordance with the same standards.

No evidence was presented to show that the private searches were conducted in accordance with the Virginia State Corporation Commission's standard search logic on the debtor's correct name. The only private search supported by additional evidence at trial was the one conducted by UCC Retrievals, Inc.

曾使用管理委员会的网站，将“Tringham Holdings, Inc.”简化为“Tringham Holdings”后进行检索。这种方式完全基于 UC 公司检索人自己的理解。她认为，“Inc.”在弗吉尼亚州属于干扰词。该检索人在输入“Tringham Holdings”之后，找到了本案受担保方的融资声明。没有证据表明，该检索人亦曾输入过“Tringham Holdings, Inc.”并找到了该融资声明。

This search was conducted using the State Corporation Commission's website, but only after the witness truncated the name, "Tringham Holdings, Inc." to "Tringham Holdings", based solely on her own belief that "Inc." was a noise word in the state of Virginia. The searcher entered "Tringham Holdings" into the search field and retrieved the Suna financing statement. No evidence was presented that the searcher ever entered "Tringham Holdings, Inc.", into the search field and recovered the Suna financing statement.

检索逻辑是否符合相关规定　受担保方试图辩称，公司管理委员会的检索逻辑存在缺陷，因为其未将“Inc.”作为干扰词予以过滤，而“公司行政人员国际协会”则将该词视为干扰词。受担保方的证人作证说，委员会正在修改干扰词清单并改变检索逻辑，以便包含“inc.”这类词。但在与本案相关的所有时间内，相关标准未将“Inc.”视为干扰词。目前搜索引擎的编码只将 5 个冠词作为干扰词进行过滤。

Suna attempts to argue that the State Corporation Commission's search logic is faulty because it does not filter out "Inc." as a noise word, even though the IACA considers it as such. According to Plaintiffs witness, the State Corporation Commission is in the process of revising its list of noise words and changing the search logic to include terms such as "inc." However, the standard in place at all times relevant to this case did not include "Inc." as a noise word; at present, the underlying search engine code filters out only five articles as noise words.

《弗吉尼亚州行政法典》

Suna makes much of the fact that noise

的登记规则说，搜索引擎所过滤的，“包括但不限于”5个冠词。受担保方认为这个表述具有很大意义。受担保方实际上是想证明，搜索引擎没有正确遵守行政法典规定的检索方法。由于搜索引擎仅过滤5个冠词，因此不是“不限于”，而是仅限于该5个词。

words in the filing rules contained at Va. Admin. Code “include, but are not limited to” the five articles filtered out by the search engine. Suna essentially argues that the search engine improperly employs the search methodology prescribed by the statute, because it in fact filters out only the five articles and thus is “limited to” those words only.

无论上述辩称在逻辑上是否能够成立，本院也无法基于行政法典的文字本身得出结论说，“Inc.”应被视为干扰词。行政法典第（4）款第3句说，“某些商业用语被修改为标准的缩略语”，而最后一个缩略语是将“incorporated”改为“inc.”（引用《弗吉尼亚州行政法典》）。如果“inc”是标准的缩略语，那么根据行政法典中公司管理委员会的标准检索逻辑以及采纳了该逻辑的搜索引擎编码，该词就不可能同时作为干扰词而被忽视。其结果很明显就是，在弗吉尼亚州的法典检索中，“Inc.”不能作为干扰词。在这方面，委员会的检索逻辑是按目

Regardless of whether this argument makes logical sense, the court cannot conclude on the basis of the statutory language that “Inc.” should be considered a noise word. The third sentence of subsection 4 says that “Certain business words are modified to a standard abbreviation ...” the last of which is “incorporated” to “inc.”. Va. Admin. Code. If “inc” is a standard abbreviation, it cannot simultaneously be a disregarded noise word according to the State Corporation Commission’s standard search logic as embodied by this statute and the search engine code utilizing it. As a result, it is clear that “Inc.” is not a noise word for purposes of a Virginia UCC search, and the State Corporation Commission’s search logic is functioning as it was presently intended to

前设计的运行方式在正常运行。

不具效力的判例　受担保方还辩称，法典第 9.503 条（c）款中有关使用登记处标准检索逻辑的文字，实际上未体现其真实含义。但是，受担保方引用的几个判例，却无法支持上述说法。对受担保方相对最有帮助的是 P 诉 Y 案。佐治亚州中区联邦地区法院在该案中判定，当事方虽然省略了债务人名字后面的“Inc.”，但不属于严重误导，因为检索“几乎必然会找到融资声明”，并且，“尽职的债权人在使用‘Benjamin S. Youngblood， Inc.’这个名字对记录进行检索时，应被视为已得到通知，即需要查询‘Benjamin Scott Youngblood’这个债务人的权益”。

但是，该判例本质上是无视佐治亚州法典的规定，因为法典要求使用登记处的标准检索逻辑。该案判决似乎是基于旧版法典第 9 篇的尽职检索人标准。此外，在佐治亚州上诉法院 2006 年判决 A 诉 C 案后，2005 年联邦地区法院 P 诉 Y 案的效力已

function in this respect.

None of the cases cited by Suna support its proposition that the language of § 9-503（c） does not mean what it says regarding the use of the filing office's standard search logic. The closest Suna comes is in its discussion of Planned Furniture Promotions, Inc. v. Youngblood, Inc., where the United States District Court for the Middle District of Georgia ruled that a party's omission of “Inc” from the end of the debtor's name was not seriously misleading because a search “would almost assuredly turn up a financing statement ...”, and “a diligent creditor searching the filing records under the name Benjamin S. Youngblood, Inc. would be put on notice to inquire into the interests of a debtor listed as Benjamin Scott Youngblood”.

This case essentially ignores the provisions of the Georgia UCC referring to the fling office's standard search logic and appears to rest on pre-revised Article 9 law dealing with the diligent searcher standard. Further, the 2006 Georgia Court of Appeals case, All Bus. Corp., calls into question the U.S. District Court's 2005 ruling in Planned

存在疑问。后者所肯定的，是佐治亚州法律中已被废除的尽职检索人原则。

结论 本院认定，P诉Y案的逻辑不适用于本案。反之，那些适用了法典直白文字并要求使用登记处标准检索逻辑的判例，对本案具有说服力。因此，如果融资声明所登记的债务人名字不正确，那么，只有在基于债务人的正确名字并使用登记处的标准检索逻辑可以找到该融资声明时，该融资声明才不属于严重误导。

使用登记处的标准检索逻辑进行检索时，确有可能导致这类情况，即融资声明中看似微小的错误，也会导致担保权益不能获得完善。但是，确保按债务人的正确名字登记融资声明，不是十分困难的事。对债权人并没有很多要求，无非就是正确地登记债务人的名字。根据法典规定，如果未能履行这个任务，很明显，担保权益的完善地位就会丧失。

在本案中，在经过弗吉尼

Furniture Promotions by reaffirming the defunct status of the diligent searcher rule under Georgia law.

This court finds the logic of Planned Furniture Promotions inapplicable to the present case and finds persuasive the number of cases that apply the plain language of the UCC, requiring a search using the filing office's standard search logic. Thus, a search using the correct debtor name under the filing office's standard search logic, must reveal the financing statement filed under the incorrect name or it will be deemed seriously misleading.

While application of the filing office's standard search logic may lead to situations where it appears that a relatively minor error in a financing statement leads to a security interest becoming unperfected, it is not that difficult to ensure that a financing statement is filed with the correct name of the debtor. Little more is asked of a creditor than to accurately record the debtor's name, and according to the statute, failure to perform this action clearly dooms the perfected status of a security interest.

The official search certified by the State

亚州公司管理委员会认证的官方检索中，在输入“Tringham Holdings, Inc.”这个正确名字后，不能检索到受担保方的融资声明。在唯一基于债务人的正确名字并使用委员会实际采用的标准检索逻辑的检索中，无法找到受担保方的融资声明。因此本院必须认定，该融资声明属于严重误导，不足以完善受担保方对担保物的担保权益。

Corporation Commission, under the correct name, “Tringham Holdings, Inc.”, fails to disclose the Suna financing statement. Thus, the only search which used the correct name under the standard search logic actually employed by the State Corporation Commission did not disclose the Suna financing statement. As a result, the court must conclude that the financing statement is seriously misleading and is insufficient to perfect Suna’s security interest in the collateral.

案例 33　担保物的错误描述是否影响担保权益的效力？

In Re Product Design and Fabrication, Inc.
产品设计和制造公司破产案

艾奥瓦州北区联邦破产法院 1994 年；182 B.R. 803

简　介

在本破产案中，破产受托人根据联邦《破产法》和法典的相关规定，对于受担保方（Michelosen）在破产发生前的一段时间内基于 3 项贷款而对破产债务人（PDF）的设备所取得的担保权益，请求破产法院认定担保权益无效。在债务人破产之前，受担保方共向债务人提供了 3 项贷款，数额分别为 10 万美元、5 万美元和 10 万美元。债务人为了取得贷款，将自己的机器设备抵押给受担保方。在抵押之前，债务人请资产评估师（Hilpipre）对这些机器设备进行了估值。根据评估报告，机器设备的价值为 314,434 美元。评估报告没有包括债务人的库存。

基于该评估报告，债务人与受担保方达成融资安排。1992 年 6 月 30 日，双方签署了第一份融资协议，规定由受担保方提供 10 万美元贷款，并以评估报告中的机器设备作为担保物。随后，债务人的律师根据上述融资协议准备了担保协议。在该协议中，担保物种类一栏中有多种选择，包括“设备”和“库存”。律师本应在“设备”一栏打钩，但出于疏忽而选择了“库存”。在担保协议有关担保物的条款中，规定担保物列于协议的“附件 A”（资产评估报告）。但是，债务人出于大意或疏忽，没有将附件 A 附在自己持有的那份担保协议后面。1992 年 7 月 23 日，双方签署了基本相同的第二份融资协议，由受担保方向债务人再提供 5 万美元的贷款。1992 年 8 月 1 日，双方签署了第三份融资协议，由受担保方再提供 10 万美元的贷款。这份协议“取代和整合”了之前的两份融资协议，并把贷款数额改为 3 次贷款的总额，即 25 万美元。第三份融资协议中列出的担保物仍然为机器设备。为使上述担保权益获得完善，受担保方于 1992 年 8 月 7 日登记了融资声明，其中所列的担保物是“设备”。

1992 年 8 月 14 日，债务人申请破产。破产受托人出售了债务人的全部财产，包括机器设备和库存。受担保方在破产程序中主张对债务人的机器设备持有完善的担保权益，并要求以出售机器设备的收入来清偿债务人所欠的贷款。破产受托人则主张，担保协议对担保物的描述是“库存”，而融资声明所列的担保物是“设备”，两者存在矛盾，因此受担保方对债务人的机器设备未取得完善的担保权益。此外，债务人向受担保方提供的担保权益属于《破产法》中的“优惠转让”（preferential transfer），属于可被撤销的转让，因此担保权益无效。这是破产法院在本案中需要解决的两个主要问题。

关于第一个问题，如果在债务人提出破产时，受担保方不持有完善的担保权益，就无须再考虑第二个问题，因为根据《破产法》的规定，破产受托人有权撤销在破产发生时任何尚未获得完善的担保权益。受担保方就 3 项贷款签署了必要文件，并根据法典第 9 篇的规定登记了融资声明。但问题在于，由于当事方的疏忽，担保协议在描述担保物时，错误地选择了“库存”而不是“设备”，而在融资协议和融资声明中，担保物则是“设备”。此外，本来应该把包含设备清单的评估报告作为附件附在担保协议后面，但当事方因疏忽而未将其附在协议后面，因此无法看到担保物的具体描述。基于以上两个问题，破产受托人主张，债务人和受担保方之间不存在有效的担保协议，因此担保权益没有发生附着，更不可能获得完善。法院最终认定，基于对案件全部事实的分析，当事方无疑意图在设备中设立担保权益，且对附件 A 的内容均所有了解。因此，担保协议的笔误和附件A的缺乏，不影响担保协议的效力。因此，受担保方对债务人的设备持有完善的担保权益。

第二个问题是，如果受担保方持有的是完善担保权益，破产受托人是否仍有权撤销该担保权益？这涉及《破产法》中优惠转让的问题。虽然这不是法典而是《破产法》的问题，但直接影响完善担保权益的效力。根据《破产法》的规定，优惠转让不包括同时发生的价值交换，而仅指对"前存债务"(antecedent debt)的清偿。同时发生的价值交换不导致债务人资产的减少，因此不损害其他债权人的权益。而如果债务人用现有财产去清偿前存债务，就有可能损害其他债权人。

在本案中，受担保方向债务人提供的3项贷款，构成了《破产法》所说的"债务"，因为贷款是债务人所承担的债务。受担保方就该贷款对债务人的设备所取得的担保权益，构成了将债务人资产转给受担保方的"转让"，因为在债务人破产时，其他债权人无权获得这部分财产。《破产法》所说的"前存"债务，是指贷款(债务)的发生时间早于担保权益(转让)的发生时间。因此，为了确定本案中是否存在因前存债务而引起的转让，就必须确定贷款和担保权益两者发生的准确时间。法院分析后认定，前两项贷款构成优惠转让，而最后一项贷款不构成优惠转让。因此，破产受托人有权撤销受担保方对前两项贷款的担保权益，但无权撤销最后一项贷款的担保权益。

判　决

当事方的主张　破产受托人提出两项主张。首先，由于"担保协议"所描述的担保物是库存，而不是机器或设备，因此受担保方未对债务人的设备取得担保权益，无权对设备出售后的收益提出主张。其次，破产受托人称，

The trustee's complaint makes two claims. First, that because the "security agreement" described inventory, not machinery or equipment, Michelosen did not obtain a security interest in PDF's equipment and, therefore, may make no claim to the proceeds of sale. Second, the trustee argues

即使受担保方对债务人的机器和设备取得了担保权益，但对于该担保权益涉及的 3 笔贷款中的两笔，该担保权益的完善也可被撤销，因为其属于《破产法》中的优惠转让。受担保方辩称，其对机器和设备出售后的收益持有不可撤销的完善担保权益。

that even if Michelosen obtained security interests in debtor's machinery and equipment, the perfections of the interests, as it relates to two of the three loans, are avoidable as preferential transfers under ［Bankruptcy Code］. Michelosen contends that he has unavoidable perfected security interests in the proceeds of the sale of machinery and equipment.

是否在设备中设立了担保权益　第一个问题是，债务人是否向受担保方提供了设备的担保权益？为使担保权益发生附着，债务人必须签署“描述了担保物”的担保协议［法典第 9.203 条（1）（a）款］。检验担保物描述是否充分的标准，是看该描述是否合理指明了担保物（F 诉 S 案；法典第 9.110 条）。描述必须起到应起的作用；必须“使人能够辨识所描述的对象”(F 诉 W 案）。

The first issue is whether PDF gave Michelosen a security interest in its equipment. In order for a security interest to attach, the debtor must sign a security agreement “which contains a description of the collateral”. Iowa Code § 9-203（1）（a）. The test of sufficiency of a collateral description is that of reasonable identification. First State Bank v. Shirley Ag Service, Inc.; Iowa Code § 9-110. The description must do the job assigned to it; it must “make possible the identification of the thing described”. First State Bank of Nora Springs v. Waychus.

错误描述和缺少附件　本案的担保协议为格式文件，其对担保物作出如下描述：“债务人目前拥有的和未来取得的库存。附件 A 为该担保物目前的清单，

The form Security Agreement describes the collateral as: “All of Debtor's inventory now owned or hereafter acquired［,］ an inventory of which is attached hereto as Exhibit ‘A’ and by this reference made

并构成本协议的组成部分。”破产受托人辩称，法院在解释该协议对担保物的描述时,应忽视“库存”这个词之后的部分，因为协议的附件A(评估人的评估报告)显然没有附在债务人所保存的那份担保协议后面。而本案第30项证据(担保协议)虽然有债务人总经理的原始签名，但文件上没有订书机的订书孔。

a part hereof.” The trustee argues that in interpreting the contract's description of collateral the court should stop reading after the word “inventory”. Apparently, Exhibit A, the Hilpipre appraisal, was not attached to the Security Agreement document in PDF's files. Exhibit 30, which bears an original signature by Janey, did not have staple holes.

附件缺失的问题 本院认为，在确定受担保方是否对设备持有担保权益时，上述事实不具有重要意义。债务人的律师准备了一式两份的用于签字的担保协议，因此协议应该有两份正本。即使评估报告同时也没有被订在第30项证据的另一份正本上，致使担保协议表面上因缺乏附件而不完整，但是，以引用方式将附件A结合进担保协议的做法，已经说明了当事方的意图，即协议的完整表述是包含了该附件A的。担保协议是用于满足反欺诈法，而不是向第三方作出通知(F诉S案)。

The court believes this fact is not significant for purposes of whether Michelosen had a security interest in equipment. Downer prepared two Security Agreements for signature so there would be duplicate originals. Even if no counterpart of Exhibit 30 had the appraisal stapled to it, the Security Agreement on its face would be incomplete without the exhibit. Incorporation of Exhibit A by reference shows that the complete expression of the agreement includes the exhibit. A security agreement serves a statute of frauds function rather than notice to third parties. Shirley Ag Service.

当事方已知附件内容 担保

The parties to the Security Agreement

协议的当事方当时已知协议所指的担保物是什么。在担保协议签字的当时，附件 A 是已经存在的并可辨识的文件。附件中的内容是贷款得以发放的基础之一。债务人和受担保方都有评估报告的副本。担保协议的各项文件是债务人准备的，而债务人的首席财务官将整套文件都发给了受担保方。

knew what the collateral was. Exhibit A was an identifiable document in existence at the time the Security Agreement was executed. The information on the exhibit was part of the inducement for the loan. Both PDF and Michelosen had copies of the appraisal. PDF prepared the Security Agreement documents, and Rank sent a complete set of the documents to Michelosen.

可通过引用方式包含附件

可以通过引用其他可辨识的文件，对担保物作出描述并将其纳入协议［N 破产案（规定了“见附件”的担保协议，被视为对担保物作出了合理描述）；A 破产案中的 N 诉 P 案（本票具有设立担保权益的效力，因为其规定，担保物“见发货单”）；M 诉 S 案（担保协议通过附件描述了担保物）］。

Collateral may be described by means of incorporation by reference to other identifiable documents. In re Nickerson & Nickerson, Inc. （security agreement referring to “attached schedules” reasonably identified collateral）; Nolden v. Plant Reclamation（In re Amex-Protein Development Corp.）（note referencing collateral “as per invoices” created security interest）; Mitchell v. Shepherd Mall State Bank （security agreement used attached exhibit to describe collateral）.

破产受托人引用的 M 破产案并不导致与上述相反的结论。法院在该案中认定，担保协议明确无误地提供了对机器、设备、家具和不动产附着物的担保权

The case Matter of Martin Grinding & Machine Works, Inc., cited by the trustee, is not to the contrary. In Martin Grinding, the court found the security agreement unambiguously gave a security interest in

益。法院只是没有采纳那些将担保物进一步扩大至库存和应收款的外部证据(M 破产案)。

缺少附件无关紧要 在本案中,债务人签署的担保协议中包含了用打字机增加的文字,而该文字明确将附件 A 作为担保协议对担保物的描述的一部分。本院因此认定,协议对担保物的描述包含了评估报告中所列的全部项目。

错误描述担保物的问题 但是,评估报告所列出的项目都是债务人的机器和设备,而没有包括任何库存。在法典中,"库存"与"设备"是互不兼容的两个类别[第9.109条(2)款和(4)款;正式评论2]。因此,担保物的描述存在模糊之处,因为协议中的"库存",与评估报告中对项目类别的定性不符。模糊之处在于,当事方到底意图在某种程度上以"库存"这个词来修改评估报告中的担保物清单,还是打算就评估报告列出的全部财产设立担保权益?

machinery, equipment, furniture and fixtures. The court did not allow extrinsic evidence to enlarge the security interest to include inventory and accounts receivable. Id.

The additional typewritten language on the face of the Security Agreement executed by PDF expressly incorporates Exhibit A into the description of collateral. Therefore, the court finds that the description of collateral includes all items listed on the Hilpipre appraisal.

The items on the appraisal are PDF's machinery and equipment. There is no inventory on the list. The terms "inventory" and "equipment" are mutually exclusive. Iowa Code § 9-109(2) and (4) and Official Comment 2. Thus, the collateral description is ambiguous because the term "inventory" is inconsistent with the classification of items in the appraisal. The ambiguity is whether the parties intended the term "inventory" to modify the list in some way or whether the parties intended to give a security interest in all items on the appraisal.

通过其他证据确认当事方的意图　当合同条款存在模糊之处时，可以使用外部证据来证明当事方的意图（A 诉 A 案）。在破产受托人引用的 S 破产案中的 A 诉 S 案中，法院认为当事方的意图“无关紧要”，因为法院认定担保协议是完整而明确无误的。但在本案中，在债务人签署的担保协议中，对担保物的描述确有模糊之处。因此，本院将参考其他证据来确定当事方的意图。

Extrinsic evidence is admissible to discover the intent of the parties to a contract when its terms are ambiguous. Anderson v. Aspelmeier, Fisch, Power, Warner & Engberg. In American State Bank v. Swearingen （In re Swearingen）, cited by the trustee, the court stated that the parties' intent was “immaterial” because the court found the security agreement complete and unambiguous. Because the Security Agreement signed by PDF is ambiguous in its description of collateral, the court will consider other evidence to determine the parties' intent.

债务人总经理作证说，债务人无意在库存中设立担保权益，而是意图在评估报告中所列的各项财产中设立担保权益。担保协议中提到了 1992 年 6 月 30 日的融资协议，而这与债务人总经理的证词一致。融资协议显示，当事方的意图是，以评估报告中列出的机器和设备作为贷款的担保。本院的结论是，担保协议是在评估报告中列出的债务人的机器和设备中设立了担保权益。

Janey testified that PDF did not intend to create a security interest in inventory. Its intent was to give a security interest in all items listed in the appraisal. The Security Agreement's reference to the June 30, 1992, Financing Agreement is consistent with Janey's testimony. The Financing Agreement shows that the parties intended to secure the loan with PDF's machinery and equipment as listed on the Hilpipre appraisal. The court concludes that the Security Agreement creates a security interest in PDF's machinery and equipment included in the Hilpipre appraisal.

汽车不构成有效担保物　评

The Hilpipre appraisal included vehicles.

估报告还包含了汽车。这些汽车也属于债务人的设备，但在所有这些汽车的产权证书上，都未注明受担保方的担保权益。本院认定，受担保方对构成设备且具有产权证书的汽车不持有完善的担保权益[参见法典第9.302条(3)(b)款]。破产受托人有权根据《破产法》的规定，撤销向受担保方所转让的汽车中的担保权益。但是，对于可以通过登记使担保权益获得完善的全部机器和设备，受担保方均通过1992年8月7日登记的融资声明获得了完善的担保权益。本院无须就评估报告中特定财产是否已获得完善进行逐一认定。

A notation of a security interest in favor of Michelosen was not placed on the titles of any motor vehicles which were PDF's equipment. The court finds and concludes that Michelosen did not have a perfected security interest in titled motor vehicles which were equipment. See Iowa Code § 9-302(3)(b). The transfer of the security interest in vehicles to Michelosen is avoidable by the trustee pursuant to [Bankruptcy Code]. However, the financing statement filed August 7, 1992 gave Michelosen a perfected security interest in the machinery and equipment perfectible by filing. It is unnecessary for the court to make findings regarding perfection as to particular items on the appraisal.

融资协议本身已构成担保协议 本院还判定，3份融资协议中的任何一份本身都足以构成担保协议，并使受担保方对债务人的机器和设备取得担保权益。所有的融资协议均由债务人签署，并均包含了对担保物的描述[法典第9.203条(1)(a)款]。当事方的意图是为贷款提供担保。在表达设立担保权益的意图

The court also concludes that each Financing Agreement, standing alone, is sufficient to constitute a security agreement giving Michelosen a security interest in PDF's machinery and equipment. The Financing Agreements are signed by the debtor and contain a description of the collateral. Iowa Code § 9-203(1)(a). The parties intended to make a secured loan. Specific "words of grant" are not necessary to

时，无须使用任何特定的“设立”文字（B 破产案中的 B 诉 B 案）。本案融资协议的各项文件，足以证明“设立或提供担保权益”的意图［法典第 9.105 条（1）（L）款］。

是否可参考担保协议以外的文件　破产受托人还主张，由于本案已有“担保协议”，因此法院不能再将其他文件视为担保协议。受托人引用了 L 破产案中的 R 诉 P 案来支持其主张。在 L 破产案中，债务人签署了两份担保协议，覆盖了“应收款、合同权利……以及与前述相关或由其产生的一般无形财产”。在签署该担保协议之前，当事方曾签署了一份覆盖债务人“全部财产”的承诺书。

但是，L 破产案无法支持受托人有关法院不能认定存在多项担保协议的主张，因为该案本身就有两份有效的担保协议。每一份担保协议都包含了“非一体化条款”，保留了债权人在之前协议中的权利。在本案中，债务人的担保协议包含了“非弃权条

show an intention to create a security interest. Bossingham v. Bloomington Production Credit Association （In re Bossingham）. The Financing Agreement documents show an intent to “create or provide for a security interest”. Iowa Code § 9-105（1）（L）.

The trustee cites Royal Bank & Trust Co. v. Pereira （In re Lady Madonna Industries, Inc.）, for the proposition that the existence of the “Security Agreement” prevents the court from considering other documents as security agreements. In Lady Madonna, the debtors had signed two security agreements covering “accounts receivable, contract rights ... and general intangibles relating thereto or arising therefrom”. Prior to signing the security agreements, the parties had executed a commitment letter covering “all assets” of Lady Madonna Industries.

The Lady Madonna case does not stand for the proposition that a court cannot consider multiple security agreements because the case itself involved two valid security agreements. Each security agreement contained a “non-merger clause” which preserved the creditor’s rights under previous agreements. PDF’s Security Agreement contains a

款”，保留了受担保方在之前协议中的权利。在本案最后的申辩中，受托人的律师也承认，几份融资协议本身就满足了法典对担保协议的要求。在L破产案中，法院认定，承诺书本身不足以构成担保协议，因此不允许债权人使用该承诺书来扩大其担保权益的范围。该案的法院说：“在某些案件中，各项贷款合同文件对担保物的描述存在矛盾，因此需要考虑担保权益的覆盖范围。这些案件通常都判定，如果存在一份表面上已经很完整的担保协议，则法院将不会引用其他文件来扩大担保权益的范围，除非担保协议本身提及其他文件。”

"non-waiver clause" that preserves Michelosen's rights under prior agreements. In closing argument, counsel for the trustee conceded that, standing alone, the Financing Agreements would meet the requirements of a security agreement. The court in Lady Madonna found that the commitment letter alone did not qualify as a security agreement and would not permit the creditor to use the letter to expand its security interest. The court stated: "[c] ases considering the extent of a security interest where there is a conflict in the collateral descriptions in the loan documents have generally held that where there is a security agreement complete on its face, the courts will not refer to other documents to expand the scope of the security interest unless the security agreement itself refers to those other documents."

本案两类文件可以相互补充 因此，L破产案与本案有所区别，因为在本案中，债务人的融资协议与担保协议对担保物的描述并不冲突，且融资协议本身满足了法典对担保协议的要求，且担保协议本身也提到了融资协议。本院判定，债务人通过融资

The Lady Madonna case is distinguishable, therefore, because the collateral description in PDF's Financing Agreement does not conflict with the Security Agreement, the Financing Agreement alone meets the requirements of a security agreement, and the Security Agreement refers on its face to the Financing Agreement. The court

协议以及担保协议这两类文件，共同就自己的设备向受担保方提供了担保权益。

concludes that PDF gave Michelosen a security interest in its equipment under the Financing Agreements as well as the Security Agreement.

优惠转让的问题 下一个问题是，向受担保方所作的转让，是否构成了《破产法》第 547 条（b）款所述的可撤销的优惠转让？当事方承认，转让发生在破产申请之前 90 天内，且当时债务人已失去清偿能力；并且，受担保方通过该转让所获得的清偿，大于债务人清算时受担保方本可获得的清偿。问题在于，向受担保方所作的转让，是否系基于前存债务？为了回答这个问题，本院必须确定转让发生的时间节点。

The next issue is whether the transfers to Michelosen constituted avoidable preferential transfers under 11 U.S.C. § 547（b）. The parties agree that the transfers were made to Michelosen within 90 days before the petition filing date while PDF was insolvent, and that the transfers would enable Michelosen to receive more than he would receive in a Chapter 7 distribution if the transfers had not been made. The issue is whether the transfers to Michelosen were on account of an antecedent debt, which requires the court to determine when the transfers were made.

担保权益的发生时间 涉及优惠转让时，应根据《破产法》第 547 条（e）款的规定来确定转让发生的时间节点。本案所涉及的转让，是担保权益的设立［《破产法》第 101 条（58）款（“转让”包括保留所有权并以此作为担保权益）］。根据《破产法》第 547 条（e）款，如果担保权益

For the purposes of preference law, 11 U.S.C. § 547（e） determines the time at which a transfer is deemed to have been made. The transfers at issue are the creation of security interests. 11 U.S.C. § 101（58）（“transfer” includes retention of title as a security interest）. Under § 547（e）, if a security interest is perfected pre-petition, such a transfer is made：（A） at the time such

系在破产申请之前获得完善，则转让被视为在下列时间发生:（A）转让在转让人和受让人之间发生效力的时间，只要转让在当时或之后10天内获得完善；或（B）转让获得完善的时间，只要转让在该10天之后获得完善［《破产法》第547条（e）（2）（A）款和（B）款］。

transfer takes effect between the transferor and the transferee, if such transfer is perfected at, or within 10 days after, such time; ［or］（B） at the time such transfer is perfected, if such transfer is perfected after such 10 days. 11 U.S.C. § 547（e）（2）（A） and （B）.

财产转让的完善时间，应根据州法来确定（B诉A案）。由于《破产法》未对转让的生效时间作出定义，因此，这个问题亦应根据州法来确定［J诉F案（在不与《破产法》冲突的情况下，财产权利的问题应根据州法确定）］。

State law determines when a transfer of property is perfected. Bergquist v. Anderson-Greenwood Aviation Corp. The Bankruptcy Code does not define when a transfer takes effect; that issue is also governed by state law. Johnson v. First National Bank of Montevideo, Minnesota （in the absence of conflict with bankruptcy law, state law governs questions of property rights）.

附着是担保权益的发生时间 在当事方已满足担保权益发生附着的各项条件后，担保权益在债务人和债权人之间发生效力［法典第9.203条（1）款］。本院的结论是，担保权益根据州法发生附着后，《破产法》第547条（e）（2）款所述的具有设立担保权益效力的转让，即在

A security interest is enforceable between the debtor and creditor when the parties meet the requirements for attachment. Iowa Code § 9-203（1）. The court concludes that a transfer creating a security interest takes effect between a debtor-transferor and the creditor-transferee under § 547（e）（2） when the security interest attaches under state law. Under Iowa law, a security interest attaches

债务人（转让人）与债权人（受让人）之间发生效力。根据艾奥瓦州法律，担保权益在下列情况下发生附着：（1）债务人已签署包含担保物描述的担保协议；（2）已支付价值；（3）债务人对担保物拥有权利［法典第9.203条（1）款］。在将附着日期和完善日期进行比较后，法院即可确定《破产法》第547条（e）（2）款所述之转让的发生时间。

when：（1）the debtor has signed a security agreement which contains a description of the collateral;（2）value has been given; and（3）the debtor has rights in the collateral. Iowa Code § 9-203（1）. After comparing the date of attachment and the date of perfection, the court can then determine the time of transfer under 11 U.S.C. § 547（e）（2）.

受担保方支付价值的时间

毫无争议的是，在提供3项贷款之前，债务人已对担保物（列在评估报告中的设备）拥有权利。本院必须确定的是，受担保方何时支付了价值，以及债务人何时签署了包含担保物描述的担保协议。有关支付价值的要求，关注点在于债权人支付价值的时间，而不在于债务人收到价值的时间［法典第9.203条（1）（b）款；P诉T案］。“价值”的定义也包括“有约束力的贷款承诺”或“任何足以支持简式合同的对价”［法典第1.201条（44）（a）款和（d）款］。

It is undisputed that PDF had rights in the collateral, the equipment listed on the Hilpipre appraisal, prior to the three loans. The court must decide when Michelosen gave value and when PDF signed a security agreement describing the collateral. The requirement that value be given focuses on what the creditor has given, rather than on what the debtor has received. Iowa Code § 9-203（1）（b）; Putnam Realty, Inc. v. Terminal Moving & Storage Co., Inc. Value is defined to include "a binding commitment to extend credit" or "any consideration sufficient to support a simple contract". Iowa Code § 1-201（44）（a）and（d）.

根据上述定义，受担保方在签署每一份融资协议的时间支付了价值，因为其在协议中承诺提供额外贷款［P诉T案（受担保方的贷款承诺就等于支付价值，并构成足以支持简式合同的对价）；S诉F案（银行在签署包含贷款承诺的本票时支付价值；支付价值不是在第二天出立支票时才发生）］。因此，在本案中，债务人从受担保方收到支票的日期不具有决定意义，而支票随后的兑付日期更不具有该意义。受担保方支付价值的时间是3份融资协议的签署日期，即1992年的6月30日、7月23日和8月1日。

Under this definition, Michelosen gave value at the time each Financing Agreement was signed by promising to lend additional funds. Terminal Moving & Storage（secured party gave value by promise to extend credit, consideration sufficient to support a simple contract）; State Bank & Trust Co. of Beeville v. First National Bank of Beeville（bank gave value when it signed a note, committing itself to lend, not the next day when it wrote a check）. Thus, the dates PDF received checks from Michelosen are not determinative, much less the dates the checks were later honored. Michelosen gave value on the dates of the three Financing Agreements: June 30, 1992, July 23, 1992, and August 1, 1992.

转让的发生时间 如前所述，在本案中，担保协议和融资协议两者均构成可强制履行的担保协议。本院将根据第一份足以对3项贷款任何一项均有效力的文件来确定债务人签署担保协议的时间。对于10万美元的第一项贷款，当事方于1992年6月30日签署了担保协议，即第一份融资协议的签署日期，因此受

As discussed above, both the Security Agreement and the Financing Agreements qualify as enforceable security agreements. The court will use the first document effective as to each of the three loans to determine when PDF signed a security agreement. The parties signed a security agreement as to the first loan of $100,000 on June 30, 1992, the date of the first Financing Agreement. Michelosen gave value on that date. PDF had an interest in the

担保方被视为于该日支付了价值。债务人在该日之前已对设备拥有权益。因此，第一项担保权益于1992年6月30日发生附着，并于8月7日获得完善，即超过该日期10天之后。根据《破产法》第547条（e）款，与第一项贷款相连的转让，于1992年8月7日发生。

equipment prior to that time. The security interest attached on June 30, 1992 and was perfected August 7, 1992, more than ten days after that date. Therefore, under § 547（e）, the transfer in connection with the first loan took place on August 7, 1992.

对第二项贷款也采用同样的分析方法。第二份融资协议的签署日期为1992年7月23日。受担保方当日支付了价值，而债务人当日签署了担保协议。完善也发生在1992年8月7日，即超过上述日期10日之后。因此，与第二项贷款相连的转让，于1992年8月7日发生。

The analysis is similar for the second loan. Michelosen gave value and PDF signed a security agreement on the date of the second Financing Agreement, July 23, 1992. Perfection took place on August 7, 1992, more than ten days after that date. The transfer in connection with the second loan also took place August 7, 1992.

到第三项贷款发生之前，债务人已经签署了包含未来贷款的担保协议。“担保协议”的签署最迟发生于1992年7月28日，即债务人的律师将担保协议的文件送交给受担保方的日期。受担保方于8月1日承诺提供额外的10万美元贷款，因此系于该日支付价值。因此，第三次转让于

By the time of the third loan, PDF had already signed a security agreement covering future advances. The Security Agreement was signed, at the latest, by July 28, 1992, the date Rank sent Michelosen the security agreement documents. Michelosen gave value on August 1, 1992, by promising to loan an additional $100,000. The third transfer was effective between the parties August 1. Because the

8月1日在当事方之间生效。由于该转让在10天内获得完善，因此转让被视为发生于1992年8月1日。

transfer was perfected less than ten days later, the third transfer is deemed to have taken place on August 1, 1992.

前存债务的认定 在确定了转让的各个日期后，本院即可进一步确定，根据《破产法》第547条（b）（2）款，各次转让是否系为支付前存债务？债务的产生时间，是债务人每次签署融资协议的时间 [《破产法》第101条（12）款（“债务”是指对一项索赔而承担的责任）；第101条（5）款（“索赔”的定义）]。

Having established the dates of transfer, the court can determine whether the transfers were made on account of antecedent debt under § 547（b）（2）. Debt was created at the time each Financing Agreement was executed by PDF. See 11 U.S.C. § § 101（12）（“debt” means liability on a claim）and 101（5）（defining “claim”）.

结论 在本案中，前两项转让构成了《破产法》中的优惠转让，因为两次转让都发生在1992年8月7日，并分别用于6月30日和7月23日产生的债务。与10万美元额外贷款相连的第三项转让不构成优惠转让，因为债务于1992年8月1日发生，而转让也于该日发生。第三份融资协议规定其“取代并整合”前两份贷款协议，但这份协议不改变前两项贷款的优惠转让性质。虽然根据法典第1.201条（44）

The first two transfers were preferences because the date of each transfer was August 7, 1992 for debt incurred June 30 and July 23, respectively. The third transfer was not a preference as to the additional $100,000 loan because the debt arose on August 1, 1992, the same date as the transfer. The third Financing Agreement, which “superseded and consolidated” the first two loan agreements, did not affect the preferential status of the first two loans. Although a security interest given for pre-existing debt is given for value under Iowa Code § 1-201（44）（b）, the third （b）款，用于支付前存债务的担保权益亦构成价值的支付，但第三份融资协议不改变前两项贷款的债务发生时间。因此，该两项贷款仍被视为用于前存债务。

Financing Agreement did not affect the date the debt arose as to the first two loans. The transfer as to those loans was still on account of antecedent debt.

在本案中，受担保方未提出主动抗辩。破产受托人承认，如果受担保方在 10 天之内使设备中的担保权益获得完善，该担保权益就不属于可撤销转让。本院希望说明，本案结果不是基于《破产法》第 547 条（c）（3）款中 10 天期限的要求，因为该款仅适用于价款担保权益。与第三项贷款相连的转让本来也不构成优惠转让，是因为考虑到了贷款的发生时间和担保权益的完善时间。因此，对于破产受托人所主张的撤销，受担保方没必要提出任何主动抗辩。

Michelosen did not plead an affirmative defense. The trustee concedes that if Michelosen perfected a security interest in equipment within ten days, it is not an avoidable transfer. The court notes that this result is not because of the ten-day requirement in 11 U.S.C. § 547（c）（3）, which applies only to purchase money security interests. The transfer as to the third loan was not a preference in the first instance because of the timing of both the loan and the perfection of the security interest. It is unnecessary to show an affirmative defense to prevent the trustee's avoidance.

基于上述理由，本院判定，破产受托人有权撤销前两项贷款。关于第三项贷款，受担保方对设备的收益，持有价值 10 万美元的不可撤销的完善担保权益。

Therefore, judgment shall enter in favor of the trustee as to the first two loans. As to the third loan, Michelosen has an unavoidable perfected security interest in proceeds of equipment in the amount of $100,000.

案例34　哪些因素决定了受担保方对担保物的权利？

In the Matter of Lammot duPont Copeland, Jr.
考普兰破产案

联邦第三巡回上诉法院1976年；531 F.2d 1195, 18 UCC Rep.Serv. 833

简　介

在本破产案中，破产债务人（Copeland）在破产之前曾为两家公司提供个人保证，以便后者可以从本案受担保方（Pension Benefit）取得贷款。作为该保证的担保，债务人同意将自己的某些股票作为担保物。为此，债务人、受担保方和托管公司（Wilmington Trust）3方订立了“托管协议”（escrow agreement），规定由托管公司作为托管代理人持有该股票，并在债务人违约时将股票交付受担保方，以便受担保方出售或作其他处置。

几年后，获得贷款的两家公司违约。受担保方随后通知债务人和托管公司，要求托管公司根据托管协议将股票交付给受担保方。债务人没有回复，并随后提出破产申请。破产程序开始之后，债务人同意交出股票，因此托管公司将股票交给受担保方。在债务人进入重组程序后，债务人代表破产财产提出要求，要求受担保方退回股票，或在出售股票后，将股票收益中超出欠款数额的部分退还给债务人。

本案经破产法院和联邦地区法院审理后进入本上诉程序。上诉法院判决书的下述部分主要涉及两个问题。

第一个问题是，受担保方对股票的担保权益是否发生了附着并获得了完善？如果没有发生附着或没有获得完善，则受担保方的担保权益在破产程序中就是无效的，其对股票的权利就不能对抗破产重组程序中代表破产财产起诉的债务人。也就是说，债务人就有权收回股票，并将其并入破产财产，而受担保方只能作为无担保债权人参与破产程序。上诉法院认定，在破产申请生效的当时，担保权益已经发生附着并获得完善。

第二个问题是，即使担保权益是完善的，受担保方随后对股票的处理，是否符合法典第9篇的规定？在本案中，受担保方从托管公司取得股票的交付后，将股票登记在自己名下，并一直保留股票而未出售。同时，由于股票价值随着破产程序的进行而上涨，受担保方和债务人就这部分上涨价值的归属也产生争议。上诉法院认定，由于债务人已经拒绝了受担保方保留股票的建议，因此受担保方随后对股票的留持，违反了法典对担保物处置的规定。因此，受担保方对股票的完善担保权益，必须受制于债务人根据法典规定而对担保物享有的权利。

判　决

地区法院有关附着问题的判决　债务人首先辩称，受担保方对股票的担保权益未获得完善，因为在债务人申请破产重组之日，即1970年10月20日，该担保权益尚未发生附着。但地区法院作出相反判决。

Copeland first argues that Pension Benefit's security interest was unperfected because it had not attached as of October 20, 1970, the date on which debtor filed his Chapter XI petition. The district court determined to the contrary.

附着和完善的条件　法典第9.303条规定，“在担保权益发生

Section 9-303 provides that a "security interest is perfected when it has attached and

附着后，且在获得完善之必要步骤均已完成后，担保权益获得完善”。根据第9.204条的规定，如果存在可供担保权益附着的担保协议，支付了价值，且债务人对担保物拥有权利，担保权益即发生附着。“除非另有明确协议推迟附着的发生时间”，否则，担保权益在上述所有条件满足后立即发生附着［第9.204条（1）款］。

when all of the applicable steps required for perfection have been taken”. Attachment occurs under § 9-204 when there is an agreement that the security interest attach, value is given, and the debtor has rights in the collateral. A security interest attaches immediately upon the happening of these events “unless explicit agreement postpones the time of attaching”. § 9-204（1）.

质押协议的规定 当质押协议于1967年签订时，有关附着的上述条件即已满足，但债务人声称，当事方明确同意推迟了附着的时间。为了支持该说法，债务人引用了质押协议第8条。该条规定：“如果出质人在履行本协议任何条款时出现违约，或如果本票中所述的贷款还款出现违约，且该违约持续达到15天，则受质人有权通过挂号信件，在向出质人给予15天的通知后，要求托管公司立即将其作为托管人所持有的所有股票以及股票授权文件交付给受质人，或交付给受质人可能指定的任何其他人。

Although the aforementioned prerequisites to attachment had been fulfilled on the date the pledge agreement was executed in 1967, Copeland contends that the parties explicitly agreed to postpone the time of attachment. In support of this contention, he relies upon paragraph 8 of the pledge agreement which states: “In the event there is a default by the Pledgor in the performance of any of the terms of this Agreement, or if there is a default in the payment of the loan as provided in the note and if such default continues for a period of fifteen days, the Pledgee shall have the right, upon fifteen days’ notice, sent by registered mail to the Pledgor, to call upon The Wilmington

交付之后，受质人有权以自己所能采纳的任何方式和所能获得的任何价格，出售股票的部分或全部，而无须就股票价格可能发生的任何下跌承担责任，也无须获得出质人的进一步同意。如果股票以任何正常方式公开出售，则受质人有权购买该股票的部分或全部。对于出售后获得的收益，受质人有权保留相当于贷款尚未支付的全部本金和利息的数额，再加上出售股票所实际产生的费用，然后将余额支付给出质人。如果出售所获得的收益不足以支付贷款的全部本金和利息以及出售股票的费用，出质人将继续对不足部分承担责任。”

Trust Company to forthwith deliver all of the stock and stock powers which it is holding as security hereunder to Pledgee, or such other party as Pledgee may designate, and thereupon, without any liability for any diminution in price which may have occurred, and without further consent by the Pledgor, the said Pledgee may sell all or part of the said stock in such manner and for such price or prices as the said Pledgee may be able to obtain. At any bona fide public sale, the Pledgee shall be free to purchase all or any part of the pledged stock. Out of the proceeds of any sale, the Pledgee shall retain an amount equal to the entire unpaid principal and interest then due on the loan plus the amount of the actual expenses of the sale and shall pay the balance to the Pledgor. In the event that the proceeds of any sale are insufficient to cover the entire unpaid principal and interest of the loan plus the expenses of the sale, the Pledgor shall be liable for any deficiency."

债务人的理由 债务人辩称，根据协议的上述规定，在下列所有条件均已满足之前，受担保方的担保权益不可能发生附着：（1）债务人已违约；

Copeland argues that by the terms of this paragraph, Pension Benefit's security interest did not attach until each of the following events had occurred:（1）the debtor had defaulted;（2）default had continued for

（2）违约已持续15天；（3）受担保方已提前15天使用挂号信发出通知；（4）已向托管公司提出交付股票和授权文件的适当要求；（5）股票及授权文件已被交付给受担保方。由于股票是在1970年12月1日才被交付给受担保方的，因此债务人称，在1970年10月20日破产日这个关键日期，担保权益尚未发生附着，因此也尚未获得完善。

对协议文字的解读 债务人主张，协议第8条的相关文字推迟了附着发生的时间，但我们认为，该文字仅规定了违约时有序强制履行担保权益的程序。可以理解，债务人希望尽最大可能来保护自己的股票，防止受担保方过于匆忙地提前出售并兑现该股票。实际上，除去与本案无关的一些例外，法典第9.501条特别规定，关于发生违约时受担保方的权利和义务，当事方有权自行约定。协议第8条无非是就债务人所质押的价值不菲的股票，尽量保护债务人的权益，避免受担

fifteen days; （3） fifteen days written notice by registered mail had been sent to the debtor by Pension Benefit; （4） proper demand had been made upon Wilmington Trust to deliver the stock and stock powers; and （5） the stock and stock powers had been delivered to Pension Benefit. Since the stock was not turned over to Pension Benefit until December 1, 1970, he maintains that the security interest had not attached, and consequently, was not perfected, on the pivotal date of bankruptcy, October 20, 1970.

We believe that the relevant language of paragraph 8 which debtor urges postpones the date of attachment merely establishes an orderly procedure for enforcement of the security interest upon default. It is understandable that debtor would seek to protect his stock to the fullest extent possible from hasty and premature foreclosure attempts by Pension Benefit. Indeed, § 9-501 of the Code, with exceptions not here relevant, specifically recognizes the right of parties to a security agreement to agree among themselves as to the duties and responsibilities of a secured party when default occurs. To read paragraph 8 as anything other than an attempt

保方在理由不足的情况下声称存在违约，并作出不适当的强制履行。如果不以此种方式解读该条款，就会扭曲当事方所设想的交易的性质，并使受担保方为还贷所设立的担保权益失去意义。

to safeguard debtor's interest in the valuable pledged stock against unwarranted claims of default and improper attempts to enforce the security interest would distort the nature of the transaction envisioned by the parties and would render Pension Benefit's security for repayment of the loan largely meaningless.

之所以这样说，是因为如果作其他解读，受担保方在股票中的权益，将次于任何在受担保方之后但在债务人破产之前对股票取得完善担保权益的债权人，而这显然不是质押协议任何一个当事方所设想的情况。因此，我们的结论是，质押协议的目的不是推迟受担保方担保权益的附着时间，而是为了保护债务人对股票的权益，以便在受担保方声称存在违约时，避免受担保方不当取得股票占有。

We say this because Pension Benefit's interest in the stock would be subordinate to any intervening creditors who had obtained and perfected a security interest in the stock after Pension Benefit but before bankruptcy, a result clearly not intended by either party. We therefore conclude that the pledge agreement was not intended to delay the date of attachment of Pension Benefit's security interest, but rather was designed to protect debtor's interest in the stock from improper attempts by Pension Benefit to obtain its possession in the event there was a claim of default.

债务人引用的判例　债务人为了支持其对质押协议的解释而引用了两个判例，但这两个判例不能改变我们的结论。第一个判例是 P 破产案中的 D 诉 W 案。该案与本案明显不同，因此只需

Our conclusion is not altered by the two cases which debtor argues support his proffered interpretation of the pledge agreement. The first--In re Portland Newspaper Publishing Co., Inc., DuBay v. Williams, --is sufficiently dissimilar as

简单说明。虽然该案初审裁判官的判决似乎包含了可在某种程度上支持本案债务人立场的文字，但该案的联邦上诉法院是基于其他理由而维持了该判决。上诉法院认定，当事方未能有效地在未来应收款中设立担保权益，因此不再讨论当事方是否有效地推迟了担保权益附着时间的问题。

to warrant only brief mention. While the opinion by the referee in that case contains language which would appear to lend some support to debtor's position, the circuit court affirmed on alternate grounds. Since it found that no security interest had been created in future accounts receivable, the court did not reach the question of whether the parties had effectively agreed to postpone the time of attachment.

协议的文字区别体现了不同意愿 本案债务人所主要依赖的判例，是有关股票买卖的 D 破产案。在该案中，股票买卖交易是通过同时签署 3 份文件而完成的，即购买协议、本票和托管协议。为了担保股票价款的支付，购买协议在股票中设立了担保权益，而股票则由买方交给托管代理人保管。购买协议第 1（b）（3）款包含了下列文字：“如果买方就本票项下之本金或利息的付款出现违约，且买方未能在收到卖方的违约通知后 5 天内纠正该违约，则托管代理人在收到卖方的通知后，应将股票证书交付给卖方；交付之后，卖方对股票

The primary case relied upon by debtor is In re Dolly Madison Industries, Inc. That case involved a sale of stock which was accomplished by means of the simultaneous execution of a purchase agreement, promissory note and escrow agreement. In order to secure payment of the purchase price of the stock, the purchase agreement created a security interest in the stock which was placed by the purchaser in escrow. Paragraph 1（b）（3） of the purchase agreement contained the following provision： “In the event that AFL shall be in default in the payment of principal or interest under its promissory note . . . and if said default shall not be cured within five days after receipt by AFL of notice thereof from seller, then the escrow

证书所代表之股份所享有的权利和义务，将如同宾夕法尼亚州当时有效的法典第 9 篇项下持有担保物的受担保方所享有的权利和义务。”

agent, upon notice thereof from seller, shall deliver the certificates to seller, whereupon seller's rights and obligations in and to the shares represented by the certificates ... shall be those of a secured party holding collateral under the provisions of Article Ⅸ of the Uniform Commercial Code as in effect in the Commonwealth of Pennsylvania."

该案初审法院判定，协议中的黑体文字部分，显示了当事方根据法典第 9.204 条（1）款而推迟附着时间的意愿，即推迟至付款违约问题最终未得到补救的时间。本院当时维持了地区法院的判决。

The district court held that the ［bold］ portion of the agreement manifested the parties' intention to delay attachment of the security interest, pursuant to § 9-204（1）, until the event of an uncured default in payment. This Court affirmed the district court's decision.

本案协议文字的区别　本案债务人称，D 破产案中的购买协议，是本案质押协议第 8 条“在功能上、事实上和法律上的同一版本”。他声称，两份协议都规定，只要违约未得到纠正，且债权人作出适当通知和要求，就应该将股票交付给担保债权人。但是，债务人在试图将 D 破产案协议等同于本案协议时，忽略了两者之间的明显差别。D 破产案担保协议与本案协议不同的是，前者

Copeland contends that the purchase agreement in Dolly Madison is the 'functional, factual and legal equivalent' of paragraph 8 of the pledge agreement in the instant case. Both provide, he asserts, that upon an uncured default and appropriate notice and demand, the stock is to be delivered to the secured creditor. In seeking to analogize the agreement in Dolly Madison to the one in the case before us, the debtor ignores the obvious differences between the two provisions. The security agreement in Dolly Madison, unlike

专门规定，在出现违约、发出通知以及向债权人交付股票之后，“卖方对股票证书所代表之股份所享有的权利和义务，将如同法典第9篇项下持有担保物的受担保方所享有的权利和义务”。这必然意味着，只有在发生违约之后，且在购买协议规定的其他前提条件满足之后，卖方才有可能取得完善担保权益受担保方的地位。

the agreement in the instant case, specifically provides that in the event of default, notice, and delivery of the stock to the creditor, “the seller's rights and obligations in and to the shares represented by the certificates ... shall be those of a secured party holding collateral under the provisions of Article Ⅸ of the Uniform Commercial Code...”. By necessary implication, the seller achieves the status of a secured party with a perfected security interest only after default and the fulfillment of the other preconditions specified in the purchase agreement.

本院认为，与D破产案购买协议的文字形成对照的是，本案质押协议的第8条没有明示或默示地推迟担保权益发生附着或获得完善的时间。反之，对于受担保方何时可以取得完善担保权益受担保方的地位，该条完全没有提及。在当事方未根据法典第9.204条（1）款而明确约定推迟附着发生时间的情况下，我们不想推断说，当事方的意图是改变担保权益根据法典规定发生附着和获得完善的正常过程。正相反，本案证据充分支持初审法院的结

In contrast to the language of that agreement, paragraph 8 of the pledge agreement in the case sub judice neither explicitly nor implicitly postpones the attachment or perfection of the security interest. Rather, it is completely silent as to the time at which Pension Benefit achieves the status of a secured creditor with a perfected security interest. Absent an explicit agreement to postpone the time of attachment, as required by § 9-204（1）, we are reluctant to infer that the parties intended to alter the normal sequence of events by which a security interest attaches and becomes perfected under

论，即当事方的意图是使担保权益立即生效。因此，如同初审法院一样，我们判定，受担保方的担保权益于 1967 年 7 月签署质押和托管协议时发生附着。

the Code. To the contrary, the evidence fully supports the district court's conclusion that the parties intended the security interest to become effective immediately. We therefore hold, as did the district court, that Pension Benefit's security interest attached in July, 1967, upon the execution of the pledge and escrow agreements.

担保权益是否获得完善 债务人随后引用法典第 9.304 条（1）款和第 9.305 条而辩称，即使假设担保权益已发生附着，该担保权益在破产当日也尚未适当获得完善。第 9.304 条规定，对于第 9.105 条（1）（g）款和第 8.102 条所定义的票据（如本案公司股票），只有受担保方占有票据，其中的担保权益才可获得完善。第 9.305 条对该规则作出修改，允许受担保方通过其保管人占有票据而使担保权益获得完善。

Relying on § 9-304（1） and § 9-305, Copeland next argues that even assuming the security interest had attached, it was not properly perfected on the date of bankruptcy. Section 9-304 provides that a security interest in instruments, defined in § 9-105（1）（g） and § 8-102 to include corporate securities such as the Christiana stock, can only be perfected by the secured party's taking possession. Section 9-305 modifies this rule by permitting a secured party to perfect his security interest through the possession of his bailee.

受担保方是否占有股票 法典第 9.305 条相关部分规定："信用证和信用工具［第 5.116 条（2）（a）款］、货物、票据、流通所有权凭证或动产契据中的担保权益，可以通过受担保方占有担

Section 9-305 states in pertinent part: "A security interest in letters of credit and advices of credit （subsection （2）（a） of Section 5-116）, goods, instruments, negotiable documents or chattel paper may be perfected by the secured party's taking possession of the

保物而获得完善。除由所有权凭证所覆盖的货物外，如果此种担保物由其他保管人占有，则从该保管人收到有关受担保方对担保物之权益的通知时起，受担保方被视为占有担保物。”

债务人主张，受担保方的担保权益不因托管公司占有股票而获得完善，因为托管公司是债务人和受担保方双方的代理人。债务人主张，上述情况与第9.305条中“收到通知的保管人”的要求不符,达不到所需的占有程度。他主张，为了满足法典该条的要求，必须由受担保方独立控制的代理人占有。

托管和质押的区别无关紧要 债务人为了支持其主张，花费了很大精力来说明当事方之间的关系在普通法中本来具有的性质。他辩称，由于托管公司系为债务人和受担保方双方持有股票，因此，该安排必须被视为托管，而不能被视为已完成的质押，因为后者需要由受质人或受其绝对支配或控制的代理人取得

collateral. If such collateral other than goods covered by a negotiable document is held by a bailee, the secured party is deemed to have possession from the time the bailee receives notification of the secured party's interest. . .”

Debtor maintains that Pension Benefit's security interest was not perfected by Wilmington Trust's possession of the stock because Wilmington Trust was the agent of both parties. He asserts that this position is inconsistent with the degree of possession needed to perfect under the “bailee with notice” provision of § 9-305. To satisfy the requirement of this section, he urges, possession must be maintained by an agent under the sole control of the secured party.

In support of this contention, debtor places considerable emphasis upon what would have been the nature of the relationship between the parties at common law. Since the stock was held by Wilmington Trust as agent for both parties, he argues that the arrangement must be characterized as an escrow, rather than a perfected pledge which requires possession by the pledgee or an agent under his absolute dominion and control.

占有。通过引用D破产案，债务人进一步强调，托管和质押在法律上不可能同时存在。债务人强调，由于受质人或其代理人没有取得占有，因而本案交易不构成普通法中的质押；并且，法典采纳了普通法中有关质押的原则，要求受质人或受其绝对控制的代理人取得担保物占有；基于上述原因，根据法典第9.304条和第9.305条的规定，受担保方的担保权益至破产之日尚未获得完善。

初审法院承认，托管公司属于普通法中的托管代理人，因此，从完成质押的角度看，托管公司不可能成为受担保方的代理人。尽管如此，初审法院仍判定，法典第9.305条允许通过向保管人作出通知来完善担保权益，而该要求在本案中已满足，因此担保权益已获得完善。债务人辩称，法典第9.305条对质押采纳了普通法的严格要求。但初审法院拒绝了该主张。法院判定，如果接受该主张，就会否定当事方为贷款设定担保物以对抗第三方债权

Citing In re Dolly Madison Industries, Inc., he further stresses that the simultaneous existence of an escrow and a pledge is a legal impossibility. Since the transaction fails as a common law pledge for lack of possession by the pledgee or his agent, and since the Code, he asserts, has incorporated the requirement of the common law pledge that the pledgee or an agent under his absolute control maintain possession of the collateral, Pension Benefit's security interest was unperfected under § 9-304 and § 9-305 on the date of bankruptcy.

Although concluding that Wilmington Trust was an escrow agent at common law and hence incapable of becoming Pension Benefit's agent for the purpose of perfecting the pledge, the district court held that the provision of § 9-305 permitting perfection by a "bailee with notice" had been satisfied, and that the security interest was consequently perfected under the Code. The court rejected debtor's argument that § 9-305 had incorporated the restrictive possession requirement of the common law pledge, finding that an acceptance of this proposition would frustrate the parties'

人的意愿，会否定质押法与法典的公共政策考虑，还会不适当地限制托管机制的使用。

intent to collateralize the loan as against third party creditors, would be in disregard of the policy considerations underlying both the law of pledge and the Code, and would unduly restrict the use of the escrow device.

我们认为，实际上没必要考虑当事方的普通法权利，因为我们相信，法典第 9.305 条的文字和宗旨已可支持初审法院的结论，即 1967 年 7 月把股票交给托管公司后，受担保方的担保权益就已获得完善。确实，法典没有完全排除普通法（第 1.103 条），也没有废除现存的其他担保工具（第 9.102 条正式评论 2），但第 9 篇通过为各种担保方式建立统一制度，简化了法典制定之前的融资担保制度。法典用单一的"担保权益"概念，取代了之前各种担保工具中已过时的区分方法［第 9.102 条；第 1.201 条（37）款］，并为担保权益的设立和完善制定了一套统一规则，用于规制"在动产和不动产附着物中（包括货物、所有权凭证、票据等）设立担保权益的任何交易（无论交易采用何种形式）"

We find it unnecessary to consider the parties' rights at common law because we believe that the language and policy underlying § 9-305 support the district court's conclusion that Pension Benefit's security interest was perfected upon delivery of the stock to Wilmington Trust in July, 1967. While it is true that the Code does not wholly displace the common law, § 1-103, nor abolish existing security devices, Official Comment 2, § 9-102, Article 9 simplifies pre-Code secured financing by providing for the unitary treatment of all security arrangements. It eliminates many of the antiquated distinctions between various security devices in favor of a single "security interest", § § 9-102, 1-201（37）, and a single set of rules regarding creation and perfection, designed to govern "any transaction（regardless of its form）which is intended to create a security interest in personal property or fixtures including goods,

（第 9.102 条）。

由于本案任何一方均不否认，质押和托管协议的目的是在股票中设立法典所述的担保权益，因此我们认为，债务人所强调的普通法中有关质押和托管的区别，并没有特别意义。这些概念所涉及的唯一问题是，根据法典第 9.305 条的规定，托管公司取得股票占有后，受担保方的担保权益是否已经获得完善？

托管代理人的占有具有通知作用　所以，我们现在讨论上述问题。从历史角度，在法典制定之前，债权人或第三方占有担保物的作用，是向潜在债权人发出通知，宣示占有人对担保物可能持有的权益。对于之前由债权人占有而起到的通知作用，法典仍予以保留。根据法典的规定，可以通过登记融资声明而向未来贷款人作出通知（第 9.302 条）；或取决于担保物的性质，也可以通过受担保方或其代理人占有担保物而作出通知（第 9.304 条；

documents, instruments . . ." § 9-102.

Since neither party denies that the pledge and escrow agreements were intended to create a security interest in the stock within the meaning of the Uniform Commercial Code, we attach no particular significance to the common law distinctions between the pledge and the escrow which debtor stresses, except insofar as they bear on the question of whether Pension Benefit's security interest was properly perfected under § 9-305 of the Code through Wilmington Trust's possession of the stock.

It is to that question which we now turn. Historically and prior to the Code, possession of collateral by a creditor or third party has served to impart notice to prospective creditors of the possessor's possible interest therein. The Code carries forward the notice function which the creditor's possession formerly provided. Notice to future lenders is furnished under the Code by a filed financing statement, § 9-302, or by the possession of the property subject to the security interest by a secured party or his agent, § § 9-304, 9-305, depending upon the nature of the collateral.

第 9.305 条）。

当法典要求通过受担保方或其保管人占有担保物而获得担保权益的完善时，很明显，如果占有人是债务人或与债务人有紧密关系的人，则对于债务人财产上可能存在的抵押，该占有不足以向潜在债权人作出警示（参见 B 破产案）。因此，法典第 9.305 条正式评论 2 说："受担保方可以自己取得或由代理人取得占有，但很明显，债务人或由债务人控制的人没有资格作为受担保方的此种代理人。"

Where the Code requires perfection by possession of the secured party or his bailee, it is clear that possession by the debtor or an individual closely associated with the debtor is not sufficient to alert prospective creditors of the possibility that the debtor's property is encumbered. See, In re Black Watch Farms, Inc. Thus, Official Comment 2 to § 9-305 states: "Possession may be by the secured party himself or by an agent on his behalf: it is of course clear, however, that the debtor or a person controlled by him cannot qualify as such an agent for the secured party. . ."

但是，从法典上述评论或第 9.305 条的政策目标中，并不能得出债务人希望我们得出的结论，即占有担保物的人必须是由受担保方独自管理或控制的人。反之，我们相信，只要占有人不是债务人控制的第三方管理人，且该占有足以向潜在贷款人宣示担保物中可能存在的完善担保权益，法典第 9.305 条所述的"收到通知的保管人"的通知目的就算实现了。

It does not follow from this statement or from the policy underlying § 9-305, however, that possession of the collateral must be by an individual under the sole dominion and control of the secured party, as debtor urges us to hold. Rather, we believe that possession by a third party bailee, who is not controlled by the debtor, which adequately informs potential lenders of the possible existence of a perfected security interest satisfies the notice function underlying the "bailee with notice" provision of § 9-305.

在本案中，托管公司根据质

In the case presently before us, the

押和托管两项协议占有担保物。无论托管公司系作为托管代理人还是质押持有人而持有该股票，托管公司占有股票而债务人不占有股票的情况，都明显地向未来债权人宣告，债务人不对股票拥有不受限制的所有权和其他权益。托管公司作为一家独立的、公司化经营的实体，不可能被自动视为债务人自己一家的工具或代理人。因此，该占有不存在误导债权人的风险。

collateral was held by Wilmington Trust pursuant to the terms of both the pledge and escrow agreements. Regardless of whether Wilmington Trust retained the stock as an escrow agent or as a pledge holder, its possession and the debtor's lack of possession clearly signaled future creditors that debtor's ownership of and interest in the stock were not unrestricted. As an independent, institutional entity, Wilmington Trust could not be regarded automatically as an instrumentality or agent of the debtor alone. There was consequently no danger that creditors would be misled by its possession.

所有权无关紧要　虽然债务人仍然保留了股票注册所有权人的身份，并有权就股票进行表决和取得收益，但这不能改变我们的认定。在涉及担保交易当事方的权利和义务时，担保物所有权的归属无关紧要（法典第 9.202 条；B 诉 R 案）。

The fact that debtor remained owner of record and was empowered to vote the shares and receive current income does not compel a different finding. The location of title to collateral is immaterial with respect to the rights and obligations of the parties to a security transaction. § 9-202; Barney v. Rigby Loan & Investment Co.

之前判例不能否定本案结论　在 D 破产案中，本院以无审判决维持了地区法院的判决，但该判决不会导致本案得出不同结论。在该案中，破产裁判官驳

Nor do we believe our summary affirmance of the district court's decision in In re Dolly Madison Industries, Inc. dictates a contrary conclusion. In reversing a decision by the referee denying the trustee's application

回了破产受托人收回担保物的请求。地区法院推翻了破产裁判官的判决，因为地区法院认定，担保协议已将案件中一名债权人所主张的担保权益的附着时间推迟至破产日期之后。作为其判决的支持，地区法院说明，在付款完成或违约发生之前，当事方将担保物置于托管代理人中立管辖的行为，体现了他们推迟附着发生时间的意愿。虽然法院说明，托管和质押在法律上不可能同时存在，但是，该说明仅仅是为了强调，当事方之所以刻意选择托管方式而不是质押方式，目的是推迟附着的发生时间。

for a turnover order, the district court in Dolly Madison rested its decision on a finding that the security agreement postponed the attachment of the security interest asserted by a creditor of the bankrupt until after bankruptcy. In support of this decision, the court noted that the parties had evidenced their intent to delay attachment by placing the collateral in the neutral custody of an escrow agent pending payment or default. Statements by the court indicating that the simultaneous existence of an escrow and a pledge is a legal impossibility were merely intended to underscore the parties' deliberate choice of the escrow device rather than a pledge in order to assure that attachment would be postponed.

由于地区法院已认定当事方专门通过协议推迟了附着时间，因此没有必要再确定附着后的担保权益是否已获得完善。因此，即使判决中存在相关表述，即以托管方式持有担保物并不足以构成第 9.305 条意义上的占有，因此不能使债权人的担保权益获得完善，该表述也仅仅是不具约束力的附加看法。

Since the district court found that attachment had been delayed by specific agreement of the parties, it was not called upon to determine whether an attached security interest had been perfected. Hence, any statements suggesting that the placement of collateral in escrow precludes a creditor from perfecting his security interest for lack of sufficient possession under § 9-305 are mere uncontrolling dicta.

有关担保权益效力的结论

Having found that Wilmington

在认定托管公司对股票的占有构成了对潜在债权人的必要通知之后，我们的结论是，托管公司属于第 9.305 条所述的“收到通知的保管人”，因此，其对股票的占有，使受担保方的担保权益获得完善。因此，担保权益的完善时间是 1967 年 7 月，也就是将股票交给托管公司并就受担保方在股票中的担保权益作出通知的时间，早于破产日期 3 年多。因此，地区法院的判决是正确的，即判定作为破产经管人的债务人对股票的权益次于受担保方的权益，并驳回前者收回股票的申请。

Trust's possession of the stock afforded the requisite notice to prospective creditors, we conclude that it was a "bailee with notice" within the meaning of § 9-305 and that its possession therefore perfected Pension Benefit's security interest. Hence, perfection occurred in July, 1967, more than three years in advance of bankruptcy, on the date the stock was delivered to Wilmington Trust with notification of Pension Benefit's interest therein. For this reason, the district court correctly concluded that debtor's interest in the stock as debtor-in-possession was subordinate to that of Pension Benefit and properly denied debtor's application for a turnover order.

受担保方保留股票余额的问题　我们现在讨论受担保方提出的上诉问题。为了理解这个问题，首先需要说明一下之前发生的情况。在债务人就贷款发生违约之后，托管公司于 1970 年 12 月 1 日将股票交付给受担保方。在交付当时，股票的市场价值低于贷款的未偿余额。由于这个原因，在申报破产债权时，受担保方以无担保债权人的身份提交了修改

We now turn to the appeal of Pension Benefit. A brief synopsis of the events preceding this appeal is necessary to an understanding of the issues raised. When the Christiana stock was surrendered by Wilmington Trust to Pension Benefit on December 1, 1970, following Copeland's default on the loan, its then market value was less than the amount remaining due on the loan. For this reason, Pension Benefit filed an amended proof of claim as an unsecured

后的债权登记。这显然是为了追索不足部分。此外，由于股票之前已由债务人作出空白背书，因此受担保方将股票登记在自己或自己指定人名下，且随后一直持有股票。

creditor, apparently seeking to recover the deficiency. In addition, it registered the stock, which had been indorsed in blank by the debtor, in its own name or the name of its nominee, and has at all times since the date of transfer retained the stock.

在受担保方提交了修改后的债权登记一年半之后，债务人就该登记提出异议。此外，由于此时股票已经增值，债务人同时提起反诉，要求法院：禁止该股票的出售；根据《破产法》第 57h 条评估股票的价值；确定受担保方的债权总额；指令受担保方在贷款偿还之后，将股票的所剩余额交还给债务人。受担保方则要求驳回债务人的上述主张，称该反诉缺乏法律依据，并称根据禁止自相矛盾原则，债务人因耽延过久而无权提出反诉。

A year and a half after Pension Benefit filed its amended claim, debtor filed an objection to the claim, and since the value of the stock had appreciated, simultaneously filed a counterclaim praying for injunctive relief, an evaluation of the stock pursuant to § 57h of the Bankruptcy Act, a determination of the total amount of Pension Benefit's claim, and an accounting by Pension Benefit for any surplus which might exist after satisfaction of the claim. Pension Benefit filed a motion to dismiss, contending that the counterclaim failed to state a claim upon which relief could be granted and that the debtor was barred by estoppel and laches from asserting the counterclaim.

破产裁判官部分地支持了债务人的反诉主张，同意就股票价值组织评估，并要求受担保方在出售股票前向破产法院提出申请。但对于债务人的另一项主张，

The referee partially granted the relief requested in debtor's counterclaim by scheduling an evaluation proceeding and by requiring Pension Benefit to make application to the bankruptcy court prior to any proposed

即当股票价值超出贷款余额时，受担保方须将余额交还债务人，破产裁判官当时专门说明，不就该问题作出决定。在地区法院维持了破产裁判官的判决后，受担保方修改其请求后提出上诉。

sale of the stock. It specifically declined to rule at that time on debtor's prayer for an accounting in the event the value of the stock were found to exceed Pension Benefit's claim. Following the district court's affirmance of the referee's order, Pension Benefit perfected this appeal.

受担保方的异议　受担保方对地区法院判决的全部异议可归纳为一点，即受担保方于取得股票交付的日期（1970 年 12 月 1 日）就取得了股票的独家权利。受担保方辩称，股票交付之后，债务人对股票不再享有任何主张或权益，因此无权追索股票所增加的价值。

Underlying each of the Pension Benefit's objections to the order of the district court is its contention that its exclusive right to the stock became vested on December 1, 1970, the date the stock was delivered to it. Thereafter, it argues, the debtor had no further claim to or interest in the stock and was therefore precluded from seeking to recover its surplus value.

受担保方在答辩书中承认，其对股票的权益受制于“担保交易法的规定，即债权人有义务将担保物的剩余价值交还债务人，并以商业上合理的方式出售或以其他方式处置其所持有的担保物”。但受担保方强调，由于股票市场低迷，因此其对股票的留持属于“商业上合理的处置”，并符合法典第 9 篇的规定。受担保方称，基于上述原因，破产裁

Pension Benefit concedes in its brief that its own interest in the stock was subject to "the requirements of the secured transactions law concerning the obligation of the creditor to return any excess value to the debtor and also to sell or otherwise dispose of the collateral coming into its hands in a commercially reasonable manner. . .". It stresses, however, that its retention of the stock was a "commercially reasonable disposition" in light of the depressed market

判官和地区法院均没有权力干扰受担保方对股票的所有权，没有权力批准债务人所要求的反诉救济。债务人则辩称，其仅仅是在行使法典第9.507条（1）款所提供的权利，也就是要求受担保方对股票作出处置，并根据法典第9.504条的规定将余额交还自己。

and consequently in compliance with the requirements of Article 9 of the Code. For this reason, Pension Benefit contends that the referee and the district court lacked the authority to interfere with its ownership rights in the stock and to award the affirmative relief requested by the debtor. Debtor, on the other hand, argues that he is merely invoking his rights under § 9-507（1） and seeking to require Pension Benefit to dispose of the stock and account for any surplus, as required by § 9-504 of the Uniform Commercial Code.

处置担保物的方式 受担保方所提之主张的效力，部分地取决于对法典第9篇违约条款的正确解释和适用，因此我们必须先看一下这些条款。法典第9篇除允许受担保方在债务人违约时就其债权寻求法院判决外，并通过司法程序强制履行其担保权益［法典第9.501条（1）款］，还提供了违约后强制履行担保权益的两种替代方式。首先，受担保方可以“出售、出租或以其他方式处置”担保物。此时，受担保方有义务将收益的剩余部分交还债务人，或者有权要求债务人

Since the validity of Pension Benefit's contention depends, in part, upon the proper interpretation and application of the default provisions of Article 9, we must first examine those provisions. In addition to permitting a secured party, in the event of default, to reduce his claim to judgment and to enforce the security interest by any available judicial procedure, § 9-501（1）, Article 9 of the Code establishes two alternative methods of enforcing a security interest upon default. First, a secured party may "sell, lease or otherwise dispose of" collateral, in which case he must account to the debtor for any surplus or hold the debtor liable for any

就不足部分承担责任（法典第 9.504 条）。其次，受担保方可用书面形式，建议由自己保留担保物，作为债务的充分清偿［法典第 9.505 条（2）款］。但是，如果债务人在 30 天内对此种建议作出书面拒绝，受担保方就必须按第一种方式处理［法典第 9.505 条（2）款］。

deficiency. § 9-504. Second, a secured party may make a written proposal to retain the collateral in full satisfaction of the obligation. § 9-505（2）. If the debtor objects to this proposal in writing within thirty days, however, the secured party must proceed in accordance with the first alternative. § 9-505（2）.

未能正确处置担保物的后果　法典第 9.507 条规定了受担保方未能遵守上述条款的后果。该条相关部分规定："如果已证明受担保方在处置担保物的过程中未能遵守本章规定，法院可按适当条款和条件，指令作出处置或指令停止处置。如果处置已经完成，则债务人，或有权获得处置通知的其他人，或在处置前受担保方已就其担保权益获得通知的其他人，有权就受担保方未能遵守本章条款而使自己受到的损失，向受担保方索赔。"

The consequences of a secured party's failure to comply with these provisions are outlined in § 9-507 which provides in pertinent part："If it is established that the secured party is not proceeding in accordance with the provisions of this Part disposition may be ordered or restrained on appropriate terms and conditions. If the disposition has occurred the debtor or any person entitled to notification or whose security interest has been made known to the secured party prior to the disposition has a right to recover from the secured party any loss caused by a failure to comply with the provisions of this Part. . ."

本案的实际情况　在 1973 年 3 月 13 日之前，受担保方既没有出售股票，也没有向债务人发出通知，建议由自己根据第

Prior to March 13, 1973, Pension Benefit neither sold the stock nor served notice upon the debtor that it proposed to retain the stock in full satisfaction of its claim pursuant to

9.505条（2）款的规定保留股票，作为债务的充分清偿。通知耽延至3月13日，且在30天内被债务人以正常方式拒绝。因此，受担保方有义务根据第9.504条“出售、出租或以其他方式处置”股票，且受担保方的此义务不得由债务人弃权。

§ 9-505（2）. Its belated proposal to that effect on March 13 was properly rejected by debtor within thirty days. § 9-505（2）. Pension Benefit was therefore obligated to “sell, lease or otherwise dispose of” the stock under § 9-504. Its duty to proceed in accordance with that section could not be waived.

保留是否构成处置 受担保方坦率承认未按法典第9.504条所述将股票公开出售或出租，但同时辩称，仅在自己账册上作出登记，显示股票已出售给自己，或显示已在公开市场出售该股票且同时再买回，就足以构成第9.504条所述的出售。虽然法典允许受担保方在公开买卖中购买担保物，且当担保物属于“通常在公认市场上买卖的类型”时（如本案情况），也允许在私下买卖中购买［法典第9.504条（3）款］，但本案事实上不存在此种公开或私下购买。因此，我们无须以虚拟方式分析受担保方本来有权采用的替代方式，以及该方式是否本来可以满足法典的要求。

Pension Benefit properly concedes that the stock was not publicly sold or leased within the meaning of § 9-504. It argues, however, that a mere entry on its books recording the sale of stock to itself, or a sale and simultaneous purchase of the stock on the open market, would have satisfied the sale requirement of that section. While the Code permits a secured party to purchase collateral at a public sale and where, as here, it “is of a type customarily sold in a recognized market”, at a private sale as well, § 9-504（3）, no such sale--public or private--was in fact conducted. We therefore need not consider the available alternatives which Pension Benefit hypothetically could have pursued and which would have satisfied the sale requirement of the Code.

自行登记是否构成处置 作

Pension Benefit argues in the alternative

为替代理由，受担保方辩称，将股票登记在自己名下或自己指定人名下，就相当于根据第 9.504 条，以唯一“商业上合理”的方式“处置”了股票。虽然法典确实要求受担保方以商业上合理的方式作出处置［法典第 9.504 条；第 9.507 条（2）款］，但这项义务不能排除第 9.504 条和第 9.505 条的具体要求。根据这两条的要求，在本案这种情况下，即在债务人反对受担保方以保留担保物作为债务清偿方式的情况下，受担保方必须“出售、出租或以其他方式处置”担保物。因此，在判断受担保方的行为是否属于商业上合理之前，我们必须首先判断，受担保方保留股票和转移所有权的行为，是否构成了担保物的处置。

that by registering the stock in its own name or the name of its nominee, it has “disposed” of the stock under § 9-504 in the only “commercially reasonable” manner. While it is true that the Code requires secured creditors to proceed in a commercially reasonable manner, § § 9-504, 9-507（2）, this obligation does not displace the specific provisions of § 9-504 and § 9-505 which require a secured party to “sell, lease or otherwise dispose of” collateral, if, as here, the debtor properly objects to the secured party’s proposal to retain the collateral in satisfaction of his claim. Before determining the commercial reasonableness of Pension Benefit’s behavior, we must therefore first determine whether its retention of the stock and transfer of title constituted a disposition of the collateral.

其他处置方式的含义 在未出售或出租担保物的情况下，第 9.504 条（1）款允许受担保方以“其他方式处置”担保物。但这个措辞有些模糊，且当事方未能引用任何相关判例来说明其含义。结合第 9.504 条其他各款而

No cases have been cited to us concerning the meaning of the somewhat obscure language of § 9-504（1） permitting a secured party to “otherwise dispose of” collateral in the absence of a disposition by sale or lease. However, our examination of that provision, together with the other

审阅该款之后，我们认为，该款并非像受担保方所主张的那样，目的是适用于无所不包的情形。例如，第9.504条(3)款规定，“担保物的处置，可以在公开或私下程序中进行，也可以通过一项合同或多项合同进行”。这项条款说明，对担保物的处置，需要受担保方作出某种主动行为。

subsections of § 9-504, indicates that it was not intended to have the sweeping application which Pension Benefit urges. For example, § 9-504 (3) states that "(d) isposition of the collateral may be by public or private proceedings and may be made by way of one or more contracts". This subsection suggests that a disposition of the collateral requires some sort of affirmative action or conduct on the part of the secured party.

有关担保交易法的一位权威评论家说：“担保物的出售，无论是现在、过去还是将来，都是默认的正常程序。因此，为什么法典第9.504条不仅允许通过出售来处置担保物，而且还允许出租或‘其他方式’(在出售和出租之外，无法想象所谓的‘其他’到底包括什么)？”(引用著作)。

A leading commentator on the law of secured transactions has stated: "Sale of collateral is, always has been and always will be the normal default procedure. Why then does § 9-504 authorize disposition not only by sale, but by lease or 'otherwise' (although exactly what 'otherwise' includes in addition to sales and leases defeats the imagination)?" G. Gilmore, Security Interests in Personal Property.

处置需要采取主动行为 无论“以其他方式处置”的修饰文字到底意图包含什么，我们的结论是，仅仅保留担保物并不属于该款所设想的处置方式。任何相反的结论，都会抹杀法典对受担保方保留担保物和处置担保物的

Whatever import the modifying language "or otherwise dispose of" is intended to have, we conclude that the mere retention of collateral is not the type of disposition which this provision contemplates. A contrary conclusion would obliterate the distinction which the Code draws between the

后果所作的区分。同时，就会允许受担保方通过保留担保物而实现第 9.504 条所说的处置，并就价值的不足部分再进行追索。如果认可此种行为属于“商业上合理”，就会与法典目标相悖，因为法典规定，以有效方式保留担保物后，基础义务即被完全解除［法典第 9.502 条（2）款；第 9.505 条正式评论 1］。

consequences of a secured party's retaining and disposing of collateral. It would permit a secured party to dispose of collateral under § 9-504 by retaining it and in addition, to claim a deficiency. To sanction this course of conduct as "commercially reasonable" would contravene the Code's mandate that an effective election to retain the collateral results in a complete discharge of the underlying obligation. § 9-502（2）; Official Comment 1, § 9-505.

关于处置问题的结论 无论是在债务人对受担保方保留股票的建议作出拒绝之前，还是在拒绝之后，受担保方均未“出售、出租或以其他方式处置”担保物。因此，受担保方未遵守法典第 9 篇违约条款所规定的义务。因此，受担保方对股票的权利，受制于债务人基于法典第 9.507 条（1）款所享有的追索权。但我们必须强调，关于债务人所寻求的具体救济（取得股票的多余价值）是否适当，我们在本上诉中不作决定，因为这需要由破产法院作为初审问题作出判定。

Since Pension Benefit did not "sell, lease or otherwise dispose of" the collateral, either before or after debtor's objection to its proposed retention of the stock, it failed to comply with the duties imposed upon it as a secured creditor by the default provisions of Article 9. Its interest in the stock was therefore not immune from debtor's claim for statutory relief pursuant to § 9-507（1）. We emphasize, however, that we do not decide whether the specific relief which debtor requests, i.e., an accounting for the surplus value of the stock, is appropriate. That determination must be made by the bankruptcy court in the first instance.

受担保方认为，自己作为担

There is no merit to Pension Benefit's

保债权人，对股票享有“不受约束”的权利，而此种权利“已经生效”，因此，破产法院无权干扰该权利。受担保方的该主张不能成立。我们维持地区法院有关驳回债务人收回股票之主张的判决。同时，我们维持地区法院有关驳回受担保方对债务人反诉之抗辩的无审判决。此外，我们推翻地区法院有关受担保方在出售或处置股票之前必须向破产法院提出申请的判决，但当事方的其他权利不受影响。

claim that the bankruptcy court is barred from interfering with its so-called “vested” right as a secured creditor to the “unfettered” use of the stock. The order of the district court denying debtor’s application for a turnover order will be affirmed. Insofar as the order of the district court denies Pension Benefit’s motion to dismiss debtor’s counterclaim and awards debtor partial summary judgment, it will be affirmed. Insofar as the order of the district court requires Pension Benefit to make application to the bankruptcy court prior to any proposed sale or disposition of the stock, it will be vacated without prejudice.

案例 35　价款担保权益可以延及后得财产吗？

In Re Smith
史密斯破产案

密苏里州西区联邦破产法院 1983 年；29 B.R. 690

简　介

在本破产案中，两名债权人对破产债务人所持牛群的出售收入发生争议。一个债权人是农业管理局（FmHA），另一个债权人是银行。债务人于 1976 年向银行申请贷款，并与银行订立了担保协议，规定银行对债务人“目前拥有的和随后取得的全部家畜”取得担保权益。债务人当时实际上不拥有任何家畜。银行随后向债务人提供了少量贷款，但债务人未用该贷款购买家畜。银行随即通过登记融资声明，使担保权益获得完善。1981 年 6 月至 1982 年 1 月，债务人又从银行取得一些贷款。银行于 1981 年 8 月针对 1976 年的融资声明登记了续期声明，将融资声明的有效期从 1981 年再延长 5 年。

在上述期间内，债务人于 1979 年 3 月从农业管理局取得贷款。双方订立了担保协议。担保协议将债务人的“牛和猪”列为担保物。农业管理局登记了融资声明，其中将债务人的家畜、家畜收益以及债务人随后取得的财产列为担保物。债务人使用农业管理局的贷款购买了牛和猪。农业管理局曾于 1981 年

9月初检索融资声明登记，未看到银行的续期声明。1981年9月28日，农业管理局在并未提供新贷款的情况下，又与债务人订立了一份担保协议，同样将牛和猪作为担保物。对于这份担保协议，当事方没有登记融资声明。

1982年3月，债务人发生违约，农业管理局收走了债务人的牛（当时债务人已不持有任何猪），并将牛的出售款用于偿还贷款。随后，债务人申请破产。银行在得知农业管理局拿走了牛群出售的收益后，对该收益提出主张，因此产生了本诉讼。在本案中，银行和农业管理局都对债务人的牛群持有完善担保权益。银行的担保权益因首先于1976年登记而获得完善，并因1981年的续期声明而保持完善。农业管理局的担保权益随后于1979年获得完善，但农业管理局认为，自己提供的贷款实际用于债务人所购买的牛，因此自己的担保权益属于价款担保权益，具有优先权。

本案的关键在于确认农业管理局对担保物的“价款担保权益”（purchase money security interest）。法院认定，债务人从事农业经营，因此根据法典的定义，其持有的牛不属于“库存”（inventory），而对于库存以外的担保物，受担保方无须事先通知其他权益人即可取得价款担保权益。因此，农业管理局对于债务人的牛持有价款担保权益，并因此享有优先权。双方争议的另一个问题是，对于大牛所生的小牛，农业管理局是否也持有价款担保权益？根据法典规定，担保物的可分辨“收益”（pcoceeds，如本案中的小牛）仍然属于担保物，但法典没有明确规定，该担保物是否仍然可以保持价款担保物的属性。法院认为，价款担保权益是一种特殊的优先权，应尽量加以严格解释。由于农业管理局的贷款并未用于取得小牛，因此农业管理局对小牛的担保权益不属于价款担保权益。因此，银行作为首先登记融资声明的一方，对小牛享有优先权。

判　决

库存和非库存中价款担保权益的优先权　法典第9.312条

Section 9-312 R.S.Mo. deals with “[p]riorities among conflicting security interests

就“同一担保物中冲突担保权益的优先顺序”作出规定。该条相关部分规定：“……（3）库存担保物中的价款担保权益，优于同一担保物中的冲突担保权益，只要：（a）在债务人取得担保物占有时，价款担保权益获得完善；并且（b）当价款担保权益的持有人已知其他受担保方对库存持有担保权益时，或当其他受担保方已就同类库存登记了融资声明时，该其他受担保方已就价款担保权益收到了通知……”法典该条还规定，“（4）涉及非库存担保物中的价款担保权益时，只要在债务人取得担保物的占有时或在取得占有后的 10 天内价款担保权益获得完善，该价款担保权益即优于同一担保物中的冲突担保权益”。

in the same collateral”. The section provides, in part, that “. . .（3） A purchase money security interest in inventory collateral has priority over a conflicting security interest in the same collateral if （a） the purchase money security interest is perfected at the time the debtor receives possession of the collateral; and （b） any secured party whose security interest is known to the holder of the purchase money security interest or who, prior . . . had filed a financing statement covering the same . . . type of inventory, has received notification of the purchase money security interest . . .”. [The section also provides that:] “（4） A purchase money security interest in collateral other than inventory has priority over a conflicting security interest in the same collateral if the purchase money security interest is perfected at the time the debtor receives possession of the collateral or within ten days thereafter.”

农产品不属于库存　根据法典第 9.109 条（3）款的分类，“货物如果是农业经营中使用的家畜，就属于‘农产品’；并且，货物如果是农产品，就既不属于设备也不属于库存”。法典正式

Section 9-109（3） classifies goods as “‘[f] arm products’ if they are... livestock...used...in farming operations... If goods are farm products they are neither equipment nor inventory”. The statutory comment notes that “4. Goods are ‘farm

评论说，“4. 只有当债务人从事农业经营时，处于其占有下的货物才属于‘农产品’。一群家畜中的任何牲畜，无论是通过购买取得，还是通过自然增殖取得，都属于农产品”。

products' only if they are in the possession of a debtor engaged in farming operations. Animals in a herd of livestock are covered whether they are acquired by purchase or result from natural increase".

价款担保权益已获得完善

本案证据显示，农业管理局在向债务人提供贷款前登记了融资声明。债务人使用该贷款中的很大一部分购买了猪和牛。该采购系在贷款发放之后两个月之内发生。因此，农业管理局的价款担保权益在债务人收到担保物时获得完善。

The evidence shows that FmHA filed its financing statement prior to the funds being paid to debtor. Debtor used a substantial part of the money to purchase pigs and cattle. The purchases were made within two months of the advance. The purchase money security interest therefore was perfected when debtors received the collateral.

非库存的优先原则 在本案全部相关时间内，债务人均从事农业经营，因此，根据法典第9.109条（3）款的定义，其牲畜不属于“库存”。此时，债权人之间的优先顺序，应根据第9.312条（4）款予以确定。根据该款，即使其他债权人已就同类担保物先行登记了融资声明，且担保协议覆盖后得财产，后手提供贷款并取得价款担保权益的受担保方，亦无须通知该债权人，而仍

Debtors were engaged in farming at all times herein set out and Section 9-109（3） excludes, therefore, these animals from the definition of inventory. The question of priority of creditors consequently is determined by reference to Section 9-312（4）. That section does not require notice to a creditor holding a prior filing in the same product with an after acquired clause and allows the creditor making a purchase money advance to have priority over the creditor holding "after acquired" rights. Thus, in

可享有优于该“后得财产”债权人的权利。因此，在 1979 年 5 月，对于债务人所购买的牛，农业管理局享有优于银行的权利。

May of 1979, FmHA had a priority in the purchased cattle over the claim of the Bank.

1981 年的协议 银行在其陈述书中承认，在 1981 年 9 月 27 日之前，农业管理局对担保物持有价款担保权益。但银行辩称，1981 年 9 月 28 日的担保协议否定了农业管理局的此种身份，使其仅对前存债务持有担保协议，并因此使银行恢复至因首先登记融资声明而取得的优先地位。但是，没有证据显示，作为订立 1981 年 9 月之担保协议的交换，农业管理局放弃了第一份担保协议或融资声明登记，或提供了新的贷款。对于 1981 年的担保协议，没有登记融资声明。

In its brief the Bank concedes that FmHA had a purchase money security interest in the collateral until September 27, 1981. The Bank argues that the security agreement dated September 28, 1981, destroyed that status and gave FmHA a security interest for an antecedent debt, thus restoring the Bank to its first filed priority status. There is no evidence that FmHA released its first security agreement or UCC filing or advanced new funds in return for execution of this September, 1981 security agreement. No financing statement was filed in connection with the 1981 security agreement.

该协议不影响本案结果 对于为什么订立 1981 年的协议，不存在任何解释性证词。看上去似乎是因为，农业管理局的代理人在检索担保权益的登记后发现或认为，银行的担保权益已到期，因此农业管理局订立了该担保协议。也有可能是为了描述当时所

There was no testimony explaining the 1981 agreement. It would appear that it was taken after the FmHA agent ran a lien search and discovered, or so it seemed, that the Bank lien had expired. The 1981 agreement may have been taken to identify the then existing security. There are a number of reasons why execution of the 1981 security agreement is

存在的担保物而订立了该协议。但基于多项理由，1981 年担保协议的订立无关紧要。银行在此之前已经登记了续期声明，且法院也作出此种认定。尽管农业管理局未发现该声明，或登记处可能未将该声明入档，但银行不承担其后果。银行在某些方面继续享有受担保方的身份。对于债务人购买的牛，虽然银行首先作出了登记，但农业管理局的价款担保权益享有优先权；并且，即使银行的登记已过期，农业管理局也无须采取任何行动来保持自己的优先权。

immaterial. The Bank had filed a continuation statement and the Court so finds. The Bank is not charged with FmHA's failure to discover such a filing or the apparent failure of the Recorder to index or file. The Bank continued to occupy a secured position in some respects. Nonetheless, as to the purchased cattle, FmHA's purchase money position was a priority without regard to the prior Bank filing and needed no subsequent action to maintain that priority even if the Bank's filing had lapsed.

本院的结论是，在没有其他因素时，1981 年协议的签署对本案没有影响。1979 年协议是完善的，且未被随后的协议修改。法典第 9.108 条不适用。在本案中，当 1981 年协议订立时，受担保方没有提供贷款，没有承担义务，没有放弃特定的担保权益，也没有支付价值（请比较 P 破产案）。

The Court concludes that execution of the 1981 security agreement, without more, is of no significance. The 1979 agreement was perfected and not altered by the subsequent agreement. Section 9-108 does not apply. In this instance the secured party made no advance, incurred no obligation, released no specific security interest and gave no value when the 1981 agreement was executed. Compare Matter of Peska Assoc. Inc.

小牛中担保权益的性质　银行还辩称，与购买的牛不同，对

The Bank also contends that the FmHA security agreement loses its purchase money

于增殖的牛来说，农业管理局的担保协议已失去价款性质和相应的优先权。增殖的牛不等于购买的牛。这些牛属于一般意义上的“后得”担保物。农业管理局的担保协议也包含了随后增加的担保物。因此需要回答的问题是，如果大牛属于价款担保权益的担保物，大牛生下的小牛是否仍然属于价款担保权益的担保物?

character and priority as to cattle produced from those purchased. Calves which are bred are not purchased. They are “after acquired” in a general sense. The FmHA security agreement also covers all increased. The question then is whether cattle bred from security for a purchase money security interest are themselves purchase money security.

法典缺乏明确规定　根据法典第 9.107 条的定义，价款担保权益是指“任何人通过提供贷款而支付价值后所取得的担保权益，且该价值系为使债务人取得对担保物的权利或使用，只要该价值确实用于此目的”。在本案中，毫无疑问，债务人使用农业管理局的贷款购买了大牛，且债务人自己因此获益。通过牛的自然增殖过程，该贷款最终也使债务人从小牛(价款担保物的产物)获益。

Section 9-107 defines a purchase money security interest as one “taken by a person who by making advances . . . gives value to enable the debtor to acquire rights in or the use of collateral if such value is in fact so used”. Here there is no question that debtors used the FmHA advance to purchase cattle which they used for their benefit. The advance ultimately, through a natural process, also enabled debtors to have the use of calves, i.e., the products of the purchase money collateral.

根据法典的相关规定，包括有关添附物的第 9.314 条和有关混合物或加工物的第 9.315 条，即使担保物的形态发生变化，其

The Uniform Commercial Code enables a security interest to follow collateral even if it is transformed. See Section 9-314, as to rules concerning accessions and Section 9-315, as

中的担保权益仍然存在。法典的这些规定虽然保留了担保权益，但并没有解决我们的问题，即该担保权益是否仍然保留了价款担保权益的地位？但是，有明显迹象表明，价款担保权益的地位没有改变。例如，第9.315条(1)(b)款规定，覆盖货物的融资声明，“在货物经过制造、加工或组装后，仍然覆盖随后产生的产品”。在H诉L案中，法院判定，当库存设有价款担保权益时，如果出售旧库存后收取了货款，并用该货款购买了新库存，则新库存中的担保权益仍将保持价款担保权益的性质。

to rules concerning commingled or processed goods. But these statutes, while preserving a security interest, do not resolve the issue as to whether the interest retains its purchase money character but there is clear suggestion that the character remains unchanged. See, for example, Section 9-315 (1) (b) which provides that a financing statement covering goods "also covers the product into which the goods have been manufactured, processed or assembled". See also Holzman v. L.H.J. Enterprises, Inc., where the Court held that inventory purchased from the sale of inventory subject to a purchase money security interest retained the character of purchase money security.

应对价款担保权益作严格解释 价款担保权益是登记优先原则的例外。根据该例外，债权人如果使债务人取得特定财产，该债权人可就该财产取得担保权益。虽然担保物的形态有可能变化（如制造后的变化），但担保物通常不会自行增加，而牛是可以的。在通常情况下，只要保持原始担保物的完好，或能追溯其收益，就可以维持原有价款担保

The purchase money security interest as an exception to the rules of priority of filing allows the creditor to have a security interest in identified collateral which it enabled the debtor to obtain. While such collateral may be transformed, as through manufacturing, it does not expand through its own effort. Cattle do. The purchase money security interest is maintained by keeping the collateral intact or tracing the proceeds. Cattle as collateral expand by natural process.

权益。但是，作为担保物的牛可以通过自然过程增殖。

相关判例　在 I 破产案中，争议问题是租赁的种牛所获得的后代。法院判定，种牛后代中的担保权益不属于价款担保权益，因为债权人向债务人提供的仅仅是“种牛的权利和使用权”，而不包括种牛的后代。法院认为，法典第 9.204 条显示，由于在担保协议订立时，债务人对尚未怀胎的种牛的后代不拥有权利，因此担保权益无法附着于该后代，因而债权人对该尚未怀胎的种牛的后代也不享有权利。

In a case styled In re Ingram, the Court held a security interest in progeny of leased cattle was not a purchase money security interest because the creditor only enabled the debtor to acquire “rights in and use of the breeder stock” and not the progeny. The suggestion in Section 9-204 is that since the debtor had no rights in unconceived progeny at the time the security agreement was executed, no security interest could attach and therefore the creditor acquired no rights in such unconceived animals.

结论　价款担保权益的优先权，是优先权一般原则的例外。因此，尽管其对牛群的适用比较模糊，但仍应对该例外进行严格解释（请比较 I 诉 F 案）。在进行严格解释时必须记住的是，即使是牛群的自然增殖，也需要借助一些外部帮助，而此种帮助中的某些因素并非来自价款受担保方。

The purchase money security interest priority is an exception to the general rule and should be construed narrowly even though the application to a cattle situation is inexact. Compare Index Store Fixture Co. v. Farmer’s Trust Co. It must be remembered, in support of a narrow reading, that even the natural process of herd growth does not proceed without assistance not provided by the purchase money creditor.

假设本案证据显示，价款担保物中的一部分被出售后，用货

The result could be different if the evidence showed that some part of the

款购买了新的牲畜，那么结论可能会不一样，但本案并非这种情况。同样，如果仅仅是用小牛取代了死亡的大牛，结论可能也会不一样，但本案同样不属于这种情况。在本案中，虽然牛的数量减少了，但没有证据表明，牛的衰亡是减少的原因。

purchase money collateral was sold and new animals purchased, but that is not the case here. Similarly this could be a variation if the calves only replaced cattle that had died. Again, while the herd has diminished here, there is no evidence that diminution occurred from the aging process.

因此，本院的结论是，价款担保权益不适用于本案的小牛。农业管理局有权获得的是，在断赎时保存了价款担保物性质的那些牛的出售收益；银行有权获得的，则是所有其他牛的销售收入。证据显示，债务人使用农业管理局的贷款购买了19头牛和20只猪。农业管理局在断赎中出售了13头牛和7头小牛。在断赎当时，债务人已没有任何猪了。关于其他牛的下落，已无相关证据。出售价格并没有在每头牲畜之间分别计算，但是看上去，所有的牛都是使用贷款购买的。因此，本院要求当事方首先自己协商如何分配，然后再告诉法院是否需要再次庭审来解决分配问题。特此判决。

The Court concludes, therefore, that the purchase money security interest does not apply to the calves. FmHA is entitled to the proceeds of the sale of those cattle which retained purchase money character at the time of foreclosure but the Bank is entitled to the proceeds from the sale of any others. The evidence shows that debtors purchased 19 cows and 20 pigs with the FmHA loan. FmHA sold 13 cows and 7 calves. Debtors owned no pigs at the time of the foreclosure. There is no evidence as to disposition of the other cows. The sale price was not allocated among the animals, although it appears that all of the cows could have been part of the purchase money herd. The parties are directed to confer and to advise the Court whether a further hearing would be necessary to resolve the issue of allocation. So Ordered.

案例36　受担保方对担保物的应收款是否持有价款担保权益?

Mbank Alamo National Association v. Raytheon Medical Systems
埃姆银行全国联合会诉雷神医疗系统公司案

联邦第五巡回上诉法院 1989 年；886 F.2d 1449, 10 U.C.C. Rep. Serv. 2d 35

简　介

本案债务人（Howe）是医疗设备经销商，于 1983 年 1 月分别与本案银行（MBank）和化工公司（DuPont）订立了贷款和担保协议，规定将债务人当时持有和未来产生的库存和应收款作为担保物。银行和化工公司随即先后登记了融资声明，使上述担保权益获得完善。

债务人随后又与本案供应商（Raytheon）订立了协议，规定供应商以赊销方式向债务人提供 X 光设备，并对该设备持有价款担保权益。协议还规定，债务人在将设备出售给自己的客户后，应将所获得的应收款（设备销售货款）转让给供应商，使供应商可以直接从债务人的客户收到设备货款。债务人每次将设备的应收款转让给供应商后，供应商即针对该特定应收款登记融资声明。1983 年 7 月至 1984 年 12 月，转让给供应商的应收款约 85 万美元。

在银行和化工公司得知供应商收走了债务人获得的应收款后，以供应商非法侵占财产为由起诉供应商。银行和化工公司的理由是，银行和化工公司针对债务人应收款而登记的融资声明，早于供应商登记的融资声明，因此对于债务人从客户获得的应收款，银行和化工公司享有优先权，而供应商无权收走。供应商则认为，由于自己对X光设备持有价款担保权益，因此自己对出售该设备后的应收款也持有价款担保权益，并因此对应收款享有优先权。

初审法院和上诉法院均认定，供应商虽然对X光设备持有价款担保权益，但不对债务人销售该设备后所取得的应收款持有价款担保权益。法院认为，X光设备本质上属于债务人的库存，而法典对待库存的规定与其他种类的担保物有所不同。从价款担保权益的角度看，如果是其他担保物，价款担保权益会继续存在于担保物的收益，但如果是库存，价款担保权益将不会继续存在于库存的应收款，除非受担保方单独就该应收款作出登记。在本案中，虽然受担保方确实在收到应收款转让后登记了融资声明，但该登记晚于银行和化工公司针对应收款所作的登记。因此，根据首先登记的优先权一般原则，银行和化工公司对X光设备出售后的应收款享有优先权，而供应商必须将所收到的应收款返还给银行和化工公司。

判　决

供应商的主张和初审判决　除声称对应收款持有价款担保权益外，供应商还声称，即使自己对应收款不持有价款担保权益，银行也已放弃其对应收款的担保权益。初审法院批准了银行和化工公司的无审判决动议，认定供应商对应收款不持有价款担保权益，且所称的银行弃权不存在依据。

In addition to its contention that it had a PMSI in the accounts receivable, Raytheon claimed that even if it did not have a PMSI in those accounts, MBank waived its security interest in the accounts. The district court granted MBank's and DuPont's motions for summary judgment, deciding that Raytheon had no PMSI in the accounts receivable and that Raytheon had not raised an issue of MBank's alleged waiver.

根据一般原则，首先登记的完善担保权益享有优先权，而其他担保权益则依登记顺序而顺次享有权利［法典第 9.312 条（e）款］。价款担保权益是“首先登记”原则的例外。此种权益优于其他完善担保权益，而不考虑登记的时间顺序［法典第 9.312 条（c）款和（d）款］。初审法院认定，供应商不享有价款担保权益这项例外；根据法典第 9.312 条（e）（1）款的规定，银行因首先登记而享有优先权；化工公司因登记在后而享有第二优先权。

The general rule provides that the first perfected security interest to be filed has priority and other perfected interests stand in line in the order in which they were filed. See Sec. 9.312（e）. PMSIs are excepted from the first-to-file rule and take priority over other perfected security interests regardless of the filing sequence. Sec. 9.312（c），（d）. The district court found that Raytheon did not fall within the PMSI exception, that MBank had priority as the first to file, under Sec. 9.312（e）（1）, and that DuPont takes second priority since it filed next.

供应商声称，初审法院判决错误，因为法院不承认供应商就应收款享有法典第 9.312 条（d）款所述的收款享有价款担保权益。该款规定，“除库存外，其他担保物中的价款担保权益优于同一担保物或其收益中的冲突担保权益，只要在债务人取得担保物占有时或其后 20 天内，价款担保权益获得完善”。

Raytheon claims the district court erred by not recognizing its priority in the accounts receivable as a PMSI under Sec. 9.312（d）. Section 9.312（d） provides that “［a］ purchase money security interest in collateral other than inventory has priority over a conflicting security interest in the same collateral or its proceeds if the purchase money security interest is perfected at the time the debtor receives possession of the collateral or within 20 days thereafter”.

价款担保权益的定义　首要问题是，供应商必须证明自

As a threshold matter, Raytheon must establish that it meets the statutory definition

己的权益符合法典对价款担保权益的定义。供应商声称，根据第9.107条（2）款的定义，自己符合法典的要求。法典该款规定，“价款担保权益”是指任何人在下列情况下取得的担保权益……（2）通过提供贷款或承担债务而支付了价值，使债务人取得对担保物的权利或使用，但该价值必须确被用于该目的。为了满足上述要求，供应商必须证明:（1）自己已支付价值;（2）该价值使债务人对应收款取得权利;（3）该应收款符合法典对担保物的定义。

任何足以支持简式合同的对价，均能满足价值的要求［参见T诉F案；法典第1.201条（44）（d）款］。为讨论的目的，假定供应商已支付价值，因为其已向债务人提供信贷，使债务人承诺将应收款转让给自己（T诉F案），但即使如此，供应商也未能满足上述另外两个要求。

价值必须用于担保物　债权人为了获得价款担保权益，其所

of a PMSI. Raytheon contends that it fits the statutory requirements of a PMSI under Sec. 9.107（2）, which provides: A security interest is a “purchase money security interest” to the extent that it is...（2） taken by a person who by making advances or incurring an obligation gives value to enable the debtor to acquire rights in or the use of collateral if such value is in fact so used. To meet these requirements Raytheon must show:（1） that it gave value;（2） that the value given enabled Howe to acquire rights in the accounts receivable; and （3） that the accounts receivable qualify as collateral within the meaning of the statute.

The value requirement is satisfied by any consideration sufficient to support a simple contract. See Thet Mah and Assoc. v. First Bank of North Dakota; Sec. 1.201（44）（d）. Assuming arguendo that Raytheon gave value by extending credit to Howe in exchange for Howe's promise to assign the accounts receivable to Raytheon, see Thet Mah, Raytheon has failed to satisfy the other two requirements.

To create a PMSI, the value must be given in a manner that enables the debtor

支付的价值必须使债务人对担保物取得权益。如果债务人使用债权人的贷款购买特定物品，上述要求即获得满足[参见I诉O案；D破产案（价款担保权益附着于所实际购买的物品）；引用文章（价款担保权益的优先权，仅限于“用于取得可分辨的特定物品的那部分贷款”）]。

to acquire interest in the collateral. This is accomplished when a debtor uses an extension of credit or loan money to purchase a specific item. See Ingram v. Ozark Prod. Credit Assoc.; In re Dillon（PMSI lien attaches to item actually purchased）; Jackson & Kronman, Secured Financing and Priorities Among Creditors, Yale L.J.（PMSI priority limited “to loans that can be traced to identifiable, discrete items of property”）.

价值未用于应收款　本案涉及的担保物是应收款。为了尽量将自己的权益压入价款担保权益的模子，供应商对本案交易作出如下描述：“供应商同意就自己出售给债务人的设备向债务人提供信贷，使债务人有可能再出售给下家客户，并取得该出售合同的应收款权利；在供应商提供信贷并交付设备后，该收款权利发展成为应收款担保物的权利。”但我们认为，供应商的上述说法过于勉强。我们只有完全无视该交易的真实本质，才有可能接受该说法。

The collateral at issue here is the accounts receivable. In an attempt to force its interest into the PMSI mold, Raytheon has characterized the transaction as follows: “Raytheon, by agreeing to extend credit on its equipment, enabled Howe X-Ray to enter into subsequent contracts of sale with its customers, thereby acquiring rights in the contract accounts which, upon the specific advance and delivery of equipment, blossomed into a right to the collateral accounts receivable.” Raytheon, however, cannot force this transaction to fit. To accept this characterization, we would have to close our eyes to the true nature of the transaction.

供应商的主张本质上是说，供应商以信贷方式向债务人提供

Raytheon, in essence, is claiming that it advanced x-ray machines to Howe on

了X光设备，而该设备使债务人能够从客户购买应收款。但是，这不符合我们对本案商业交易实际情况的理解。虽然如同供应商所主张，理论上也许有可能通过提供资金来购买应收款，从而对应收款取得价款担保权益（参见N诉L案；引用文章），但不可能通过提供X光设备而实现这个目的。

credit, which then enabled Howe to purchase accounts receivable from its customers. This, however, does not comport with our view of commercial reality. While, as Raytheon suggests, it may be theoretically possible to create a PMSI in accounts receivable by advancing funds for their purchase, see Northwestern Nat'l Bank Southwest v. Lectro Systems; Gilmore, The Purchase Money Priority, Harv.L.Rev., the same cannot be done by advancing x-ray machines.

我们认为，本案交易分为两个步骤。首先，供应商向债务人赊销设备，供后者用于零售；其次，债务人出售设备后，将应收款转让给供应商。供应商提供的信贷，使债务人对设备取得权益，但未对应收款取得权益。因此，从法典角度看，供应商提供的信贷未使债务人对应收款（担保物）取得权益。

We view this as a two-step transaction in which Raytheon first advanced machines to Howe for retail sale and, once these machines were sold, Howe then assigned the accounts receivable to Raytheon. Through the credit advance, Howe acquired an interest in the machines, not the accounts receivable. Raytheon's credit advance, therefore, did not enable Howe to acquire an interest in the accounts receivable, as collateral within the meaning of the statute.

与法典本意不符　此外，供应商通过对本案交易作出其自己的定义而试图获得的价款担保权益的优先地位，并不是法典起草者本来设想的情况。价款担保权

Additionally, in its characterization of the transaction, Raytheon is attempting to benefit from the PMSI's preferred status in a manner that was not contemplated by the U.C.C. drafters. PMSIs provide an avenue for heavily

益的本意是，当债务人已债务缠身，致使曾提供过贷款的债权人不愿再提供更多贷款时，债务人仍有可能通过设立价款担保权益的方式就特定货物获得贷款（引用文章）。由于价款担保权益的持有人可对所购买的特定货物取得优先权，因此，贷款人有一定动力在特定交易中提供信贷或贷款。但是，法典对价款担保权益持有人之优先权的范围有特定限制。

burdened debtors to obtain credit for specific goods when creditors who have previously loaned money to the debtor may be unwilling to advance additional funds. Jackson & Kronman, Secured Financing and Priorities Among Creditors, Yale L.J. By giving a PMSI holder a priority interest in the specific goods purchased, there is some incentive for a lender to advance funds or credit for the specific transaction. The scope of a PMSI holder's preferred interest, however, is specifically limited by the Code.

库存的特殊性　根据法典第9.312条（c）款的规定，库存中的价款担保权益局限于该库存本身，或局限于"在库存被交付给买方之时或之前所收到的可分辨现金收益"。法典起草者说明，一般而言，就库存提供的融资，主要是看重库存所带来的应收款、动产契据或其他收益（法典第9.312条1972年修订理由评论4）。

Under Sec. 9.312（c）, a PMSI in inventory is limited to that inventory or to "identifiable cash proceeds received on or before the delivery of the inventory to a buyer..." . The drafters noted that general financing of an inventory business is based primarily on accounts resulting from inventory, chattel paper and other proceeds. Sec. 9.312, Official U.C.C. Reasons for 1972 Change comment（4）.

考虑到"应收款融资在经济活动中比带来应收款之库存的融资更重要，且理想的规则是使应收款融资的法律地位明确化"（上述评论4），法典起草者专

Reasoning that "［a］ccounts financing is more important in the economy than the financing of the kinds of inventory that produce accounts, and ［that］ the desirable rule is one which makes accounts financing

门将出售库存的应收款排除在价款担保权益保护范围之外。因此，即使库存中存在价款担保权益，且持有人对库存出售后的应收款提出主张，针对债务人应收款而在先登记的融资声明亦具有优先效力。

certain as to its legal position”, id., they specifically excluded accounts resulting from the sale of inventory from the protections of a PMSI. Thus, financing statements that are filed on a debtor’s accounts take precedence over any subsequent claim to accounts as proceeds of a PMSI in inventory.

此外，有些贷款人会周期性提供贷款，并以之后取得的库存作为担保物。为了保护他们，价款担保权益持有人要享有优先权，必须事先向其他受担保方作出通知[法典第9.312条（c）（2）款；正式评论3]。

Additionally, to protect lenders who make periodic advances against incoming inventory, the PMSI holder is required to notify other secured parties before it can take priority. Sec. 9.312（c）（2）; Official U.C.C. Comment 3.

其他担保物的价款担保权益 当担保物不是库存时，优先权规则有所不同。根据法典第9.312条（d）款，除库存外，其他担保物中的价款担保权益，使权益持有人不仅对担保物享有优先权，还对其收益享有优先权，无论是否存在应收款。对收益的权利之所以存在差异，是因为当事方对不同担保物的期待值不同。

The priority scheme, however, differs in the context of collateral other than inventory. Under Sec. 9.312（d）, a PMSI in collateral other than inventory entitles the holder to a superior interest in both the collateral and its proceeds regardless of any intervening accounts. The differing entitlement to proceeds is due to differences in the expectations of the parties with respect to the collateral involved.

不属于库存的其他担保物，通常是指商业活动中使用的设备（参见1972年修订理由评论4；

Collateral other than inventory generally refers to equipment used in the course of business. See Official U.C.C. Reasons for

引用文章）。与库存不同，对于其他担保物来说，“一般不会期待将担保物出售并收到出售收益，因此，法典起草者认为，对原始担保物持有价款担保权益的当事方，应该对担保物的收益也享有相同的权利”（参见法典第 9.312 条 1972 年修订理由评论 3）。

1972 Change comment（4）; Gilmore, The Purchase Money Priority, Harv.L.Rev. Since, unlike inventory, "it is not ordinarily expected that the collateral will be sold and that proceeds will result, [the drafters found it] appropriate to give the party having a purchase money security interest in the original collateral an equivalent priority in its proceeds". Sec. 9.312, Official U.C.C. Reasons for 1972 Change comment（3）.

本案的设备是库存　本案债务人的主要业务是出售库存，包括出售供应商提供的 X 光设备［参见法典第 9.109 条（4）款］。债务人获得的应收款属于机器的销售收益。银行和化工公司预期债务人的库存会产生应收款，并基于该预期而对应收款取得担保权益。假如我们接受供应商的辩称，即其对债务人应收款持有价款担保权益，那就相当于我们同意，供应商对库存的收益也享有优先权，而这直接与法典起草者的明确意图相冲突。并且，就相当于供应商可以成功绕开第 9.312 条（c）（2）款对通知的要求。

Howe's business primarily involved the sale of inventory, which included the Raytheon x-ray machines. See Sec. 9.109（4）. The accounts receivable are proceeds resulting from the sale of the machines. MBank and DuPont took security interests in the accounts receivable, in accordance with their expectation that sale of the inventory would generate the accounts. If we were to accept Raytheon's argument that it holds a PMSI in Howe's accounts receivable, we would be giving Raytheon a priority interest in the proceeds of inventory, in direct contravention to the express intent of the drafters. Additionally, Raytheon would have successfully avoided the notice requirements of Sec. 9.312（c）（2）.

供应商的理由 但供应商辩称，价款担保权益的内在立法理由，实际上倾向承认供应商对债务人应收款的优先权。供应商认为，除其所提供的融资外，债务人没有其他融资来源，因此，“银行和化工公司均受益于该融资安排，因为供应商的信贷使债务人得以在市场上生存并偿还债务”。供应商还称，如果将法典解释为，供应商这类债权人的担保权益仅限于还款承诺和对库存的价款担保权益，那么，对于债务缠身的类似债务人，“信贷的宝贵来源”将出现“枯竭”，因为债务人的应收款早已先期设立了留置权，因此债务违约的风险过于巨大。

Raytheon argues, however, that the policies underlying PMSIs actually favor recognizing Raytheon's priority interest in Howe's accounts. It points out that Howe could find no other source of financing besides Raytheon and that "MBank and DuPont benefited by the financing arrangements because the extension of [credit] by Raytheon helped Howe X-ray stay in business thereby servicing its debts". Raytheon also contends that if the Code is interpreted to limit the security interests of creditors, such as Raytheon, to a mere promise of repayment and the grant of a PMSI in inventory, a "valuable source of credit" to similarly encumbered debtors would "dry up". This is because the risk of default is too great in the face of prior liens on the debtor's accounts.

法典的考虑 但是，法典本身已回答了上述问题。法典起草者显然已充分意识到，如果价款担保权益持有人的优先权不能延伸至库存的应收款，贷款人提供库存融资的动力就会降低（法典第9.312条1972年修订理由评论8）。但法典起草者仍未扩大价款担保权益的保护范围，而只

The Code itself, however, answers this argument. The drafters were apparently well aware that the failure to extend a PMSI holder's priority status to the resulting accounts would provide less incentive for inventory financiers to provide credit. See Sec. 9.312, 1972 Official U.C.C. Comment 8. Yet, they did not extend the protections of a PMSI and merely noted that "[m] any

是说明，“对于提供库存融资的很多当事方，只要库存本身的担保权益获得最优先保护，他们就已经很满足。他们已经知道，其他人会基于库存出售后的应收款提供融资，因此自己对库存的优先权不会延伸到应收款”（上述修订理由评论 8）。法典起草者对该问题的承认，以及对应收款融资的偏袒保护，说明法典起草者对于融资“枯竭”的问题并不太担心。

parties financing inventory are quite content to protect their first security interest in the inventory itself, realizing that when inventory is sold, someone else will be financing the accounts and the priority for inventory will not run forward to the accounts”. Id. The drafter’s recognition of the problem and the statutory favoring of accounts financing demonstrate that the drafters were not overly concerned that this source of financing would “dry up”.

保护供应商的其他方法　此外，如果供应商希望确保自己的收款，也还有其他解决方法。供应商除可根据第 9.312 条（c）（2）款的通知程序对库存本身取得价款担保权益外，还可专门针对其 X 光设备的应收款，与银行和化工公司订立后者债权的降位协议。此外，供应商也可直接将设备出售给债务人的客户，由客户直接向供应商付款，而债务人可获得销售佣金。假设供应商采用了上述两种方法之一，本来无须绕开法典有关通知和登记的规定。

Additionally, Raytheon had alternative means of securing its right to receive payment. Besides obtaining a PMSI in the inventory by complying with the Sec. 9.312（c）（2）notice requirements, it could have entered subordination agreements with MBank and DuPont on the specific accounts resulting from the sale of Raytheon’s x-ray machines. It also could have sold the machines to Howe’s customers who would have paid Raytheon directly, with Howe receiving a commission on the sale. If Raytheon had followed either of these courses, it would not have subverted the notice and filing requirements of the Code.

结论　由于本案交易超出了法典所设想的价款担保权益的范围，因此，我们拒绝“扩大价款担保权益的特殊保护范围，以便不破坏法典的基本宗旨，即保证商业交易的可预期性”（M诉I案）。由于供应商对债务人的应收款不持有价款担保权益，因此本案应适用“首先登记”的优先权原则（参见F诉F案）。作为最后登记融资声明的一方，供应商的权益次于银行和化工公司的权益。维持对银行和化工公司的胜诉判决。

As this transaction goes beyond that contemplated by the PMSI provisions, we decline “to expand the scope of special protection afforded a purchase money security interest, lest in so doing we defeat the underlying purposes of the Code： to bring predictability to commercial transactions”. Mark Prod. U.S., Inc. v. Interfirst Bank Houston, N.A. Since Raytheon did not have a PMSI in Howe’s accounts receivable, the first-to-file priority rules govern. See Ford Motor Credit Co. v. First State Bank of Smithville. As the last to file, Raytheon’s interest is subordinate to those of MBank and DuPont. The judgments for MBank and DuPont are AFFIRMED.

案例37　受担保方是否对租赁协议项下的设备持有完善担保权益?

In the Matter of Leasing Consultants, Inc.
租赁咨询公司破产案

联邦第二巡回上诉法院 1973 年；486 F.2d 367, 13 UCC Rep.Serv. 189

简　介

在本破产案中，作为受担保方的银行对破产债务人（Leasing）在一项租赁协议项下的租金和设备提出主张，但代表破产财产的破产受托人要求破产法院驳回银行的主张。破产债务人是一家位于纽约州的公司，在破产前从事工程设备出租业务，曾作为出租方与位于新泽西州的承租方（Plastimetrix）订立租赁协议，将出租方所拥有的位于新泽西州的工程设备出租给承租方。

随后，债务人为了从本案银行取得贷款而与银行订立了担保协议，将租赁协议作为担保物抵押给银行。租赁协议主要代表了债务人（出租方）的两项权利：一项是收取租金的权利，另一项是在租赁协议终止后收回租赁设备的权利。在下述判决中，法院将后一项权利称为"可回转权益"（reversionary interest）。所谓"可回转"，是指租赁协议到期后，设备可以回转至作为出租方的债务人。银行取得租赁协议的抵押后，一方面实际占有了租赁协议的相关文件，另一方面在债务人（出租方）的所在地纽约州登记了融资声明。

在债务人（出租方）破产后，破产受托人对银行主张的担保权益提出异议。关于租金问题，破产法院确认了银行的权利，认定租赁协议属于“动产契据”（chattel paper），而动产契据的适当登记地为债务人的所在地纽约州。因此，在纽约州登记的融资声明使银行对动产契据的担保权益获得完善。对于这项判决，破产受托人不持异议。

关于“可回转权益”问题，破产法院支持了破产受托人的主张，认定租赁协议本身和协议项下的设备是相互独立的担保物。租赁协议是动产契据，而协议项下的设备是货物。对于货物来说，需要在货物所在地新泽西州进行登记，而银行没有在该州登记。也就是说，银行在对租赁协议中的担保权益取得完善后，不等于对租赁协议项下所出租的设备中的担保权益也取得完善。也就是说，虽然这是一项交易，但其中涉及两项相互独立的登记。学者有时将此称为“双重完善”（double perfection）问题。在联邦地区法院维持了破产法院有关“可回转权益”未获得完善的判决后，银行提起上诉。

上诉法院认为，假如债务人与承租方之间的租赁协议是真实的租赁交易，而不是伪装成租赁的担保交易，那么地区法院的判决就是正确的，因为在这种情况下，设备的所有权没有发生转移，仍然属于债务人，因此设备本质上是独立于租赁协议的债务人的另一项财产，需要根据法典的一般规定，在设备的所在地新泽西州进行登记，而本案银行没有作出这种登记，因此对设备不持有完善的担保权益。但是，假如租赁协议本质上是担保协议，则设备的所有权即已转移至承租方，因而债务人已不再享有任何“可回转权益”，因为设备不能再回到债务人了。在这种情况下，由于该设备此前已被银行从承租方收回并拍卖，因此本案破产受托人无权再代表债务人的破产财产向银行追索该设备或其收益。

上诉法院认为，破产法院和地区法院没有解决的一个问题是，租赁协议到底是否属于真实的租赁交易，因为地区法院只是基于某些证据，“假定”该协议为真实租赁交易。上诉法院因此判决将案件发回地区法院重审，以便确定租赁协议的真实性质，并在此基础上进一步解决银行和破产受托人之间对设备的权利争议。

判　决

本案问题和下级法院判决　基于破产受托人和银行均认可的事实，双方同意本案仅涉及法典第 9 篇解释的一个法律问题。该问题的准确描述是：“银行取得租赁协议的转让后，为使该协议中以及协议项下由债务人出租给承租方的设备中的担保权益获得完善，是否必须向新泽西州州务卿登记针对债务人的融资声明？”破产法院对此作出肯定答复，并指令银行将其收到的 60,000 美元及其利息交还给破产受托人。银行上诉后，地区法院维持了破产法院的判决。

Under stipulated facts the Trustee and Bank agreed that the question presented was solely one of law-involving the construction of Article 9 of the Uniform Commercial Code-and that the precise issue was: “Was the Bank required to file a financing statement against the Bankrupt with the Secretary of State of New Jersey in order to perfect a security interest in the leases assigned to it and the equipment leased thereunder by the Bankrupt to Plastimetrix?” The Referee answered in the affirmative and ordered the Bank to turn over the $60,000, with interest, to the Trustee. On review the district court affirmed.

法典的目的和对担保物的分类　如地区法院所承认的，有关“担保交易”的法典第 9 篇的目的是，“提供简单和单一的框架，使现今大量存在的担保融资交易能够以更低成本和更高确定性进行”（法典第 9.101 条正式评论）。

As the district court recognized, the aim of Article 9 of the Uniform Commercial Code, relating to “Secured Transactions”, is “to provide a simple and unified structure within which the immense variety of present-day secured financing transactions can go forward with less cost and with greater certainty”.

为此，对于不同形式的担保，法典该篇的起草者删除了它们仅存于形式上的区别。但是，基于担保物的财产种类不同而形成的一些区别，仍被法典起草者保留下来。

Uniform Commercial Code, Sec. 9-101, Official Comment. The drafters of this article eliminated many distinctions among security devices based on form alone. On the other hand, distinctions based on the type of property constituting the collateral were retained.

租赁协议被假定为真实租赁 基于当事方律师对事实的确认，地区法院假定债务人（出租方)和承租方之间的协议属于“真实租赁协议”，而不是“附条件销售协议”或其他仅用于设立担保的工具。因此，地区法院认定，银行“对下列两项财产取得了担保权益：租赁协议项下收取租金的权利，以及租赁协议项下之设备的可回转权益”。

Based on the stipulation of counsel, the court assumed that the agreements between Leasing and Plastimetrix were “true leases” and not “conditional sales agreements” or devices intended to create only a security interest. Accordingly the court found that the Bank acquired “a security interest in both the right to receive rental payments under the lease and in the reversionary interest in the underlying equipment”.

租赁协议属于动产契据 地区法院还判定，且当事方也同意，租赁协议本身属于“动产契据”［法典第9.105条（1）（b）款］。并且，银行对该动产契据的担保权益，已经通过在纽约州登记融资声明并取得租赁协议的占有而获得完善［法典第9.304条（1）款；第9.305条；第9.102条（1）款］。

The court held, and the parties agree, that the leases themselves were “chattel papers” （U.C.C. Sec. 9-105（1）（b）） and that the Bank’s security interest in the chattel paper was perfected by filing financing statements in New York and taking possession of the leases. U.C.C. Sec. 9-304(1), 9-305, and 9-102(1).

设备需要在新泽西州登记 地区法院进一步判定，“相比而言，机器本身则构成位于新泽西州的‘设备’。因此，为使担保权益获得完善，必须满足新泽西州的要求”。地区法院判定，由于银行未能完善机器中的“可回转权益”，破产受托人“作为法典第 9.301 条（3）款所定义的留置权债权人，其基于法典第 9.301 条（1）（b）款所拥有的权利，优于未完善的担保权益”。

动产契据和设备的区别 为了强调动产契据项下的权利和机器中的可回转权益两者的区别，地区法院引用了里威教授的解释：“在个别情况下，在担保协议的购买人和租赁协议的购买人之间，前者可能比后者有优势。如果后者购买的是设备租赁协议，则购买人所取得的只是转让人对设备租赁协议的权益。购买人如果希望对协议项下的设备本身也取得权益，就必须对设备取得担保权益并使其获得完善。”（引用文章）

地区法院的结论是，“租赁

The court held further: “By contrast, the machines themselves constituted ‘equipment’ located in New Jersey and hence, for perfection purposes, came within the scope of the New Jersey requirements.” The Bank having failed to perfect its interest in the reversion in New Jersey, the court concluded that the Trustee “-a lien creditor within the meaning of Uniform Commercial Code Sec. 9-301（3）-has priority over an unperfected security interest under Sec. 9-301（1）（b）”.

Emphasizing the distinction between rights under the chattel paper and the reversionary interest in the equipment, the court quoted from Professor Levie as follows: “In one situation the purchaser of a security agreement may have an advantage over the purchaser of a lease. Where ［he］ purchases equipment leases, he takes only an assignor’s interest in the equipment lease itself. If ［he］ wishes to be secured by an interest in the goods as well, he must obtain a security interest * * ［in the goods］ and perfect it.” Levie, Security Interests in Chattel Paper, Yale L.J.

The district court concluded: “The

协议所代表的权利，与设备中可回转权益所代表的权利，两者存在真实区别，且该区别有逻辑和判例的支持。如果忽视该区别，将无助于维护法典的清晰性和统一性，并有可能误导第三方债权人。对于类似本案银行这样处境的当事方来说，最简单的解决方法，就是在设备所在州根据该州法律对设备的可回转权益进行登记。”

distinction between the rights represented by the lease and those represented by the reversionary interest in the equipment is a real one, supported by logic and precedent. To ignore the distinction contributes neither to clarity nor uniformity under the Uniform Commercial Code. Moreover, it may mislead third party creditors. The simple solution for a bank in the situation of petitioner is to file notices as to its interest in the reversion in accordance with the law of the state where the equipment is located."

银行的理由 银行辩称：（1）无论将租赁协议视为“真实租赁”还是担保交易，在纽约州（出租方和动产契据所在州）对担保协议的登记，均可覆盖出租方（债务人）的全部权益，包括对租金的权益，和对无论位于何处的设备的权益，而无须单独就设备作出登记；或（2）作为替代理由，如果认为存在“真实租赁”和担保交易的区别，那么银行有权要求举行庭审，以确定租赁协议到底是“真实租赁”，还是以租赁形式掩盖的设备担保权益；并且（3）无论上述哪一

Bank contends that (1) whether the leases be considered "true leases" or security devices, the filing of the security interest in New York (where lessor and the chattel paper were located) covered all of the lessor's rights in the rentals and related equipment wherever located, without a separate filing against the equipment; or (2) alternatively, if a distinction is recognized between a "true lease" and a security device, appellant is entitled to an evidentiary hearing to determine whether the instruments were "true leases" or security interests in the equipment through the device of a lease; and (3) in any event, Leasing

种情况，对于出租给承租方的设备，出租方（债务人）实际上已不持有“可回转”权益。

in fact had no “reversionary” interest in the property leased to Plastimetrix.

银行主张，在纽约州对租赁协议文件进行登记并取得实际占有，将足以覆盖位于新泽西州的租赁设备。银行的理由是，债务人（出租方）的“可回转权益”是“无形权益，因此该权益的所在地就是债务人的住所地纽约州，而不是新泽西州”。假如设备中的可回转权益真的属于“一般无形财产”，则在纽约州州务卿办公处和债务人营业地所在县登记后，银行对设备的担保权益本来确实可以获得完善［纽约州法典第 9.103 条（2）款；第 9.401 条（1）（c）款］。

In contending that the filing and physical possession of the lease instruments in New York were sufficient to cover the leased equipment located in New Jersey, appellant argues that the “reversionary interest” of Leasing is “an intangible interest, sited at Leasing's domicile in New York, and not in New Jersey”. If the reversionary interest in the equipment were characterized as a “general intangible”, the Bank's security interest in the equipment would have been perfected when it filed with the New York Department of State and in the county in which Leasing had a place of business. N.Y.U.C.C. Secs. 9-103（2）, 9-401（1）（c）.

可回转权益是对货物的权益　但是，法典政策不支持上述解释。我们同意地区法院的结论，即可回转权益属于对“货物”的权益，而不是对无形财产的权益。因此，为了完善可回转权益中的担保权益，必须在设备所在的新泽西州登记融资声明［新泽西州法典第 9.102 条（1）款；第 9.302

The policies of the Code, however, militate against such an interpretation. We agree with the district court that the reversionary interest is an interest in “goods” rather than an interest in intangibles, and that to perfect the security interest in the reversionary interest in the equipment it was necessary to file a financing statement in New Jersey where the equipment was located.

条；第 9.401 条（1）（c）款］。

本案的租赁财产本身明显属于“货物”，因此我们的结论与地区法院一样，即未来可回转权益同样属于货物权益，无论其代表的担保物是“设备”还是“库存”。法典起草者对担保物的分类，主要基于相关担保物的性质或使用，而不是担保物在特定时间节点的所有权状况。很重要的因素是，第 9.106 条正式评论对“一般无形财产”的举例，都是内在性质为无形的财产种类。法典若干条款和正式评论也说明，即使“货物”被出租，货物中的担保权益仍为货物权益［参见法典第 9.103 条（2）款；第 9.109 条（4）款和正式评论 3；第 9.304 条（3）款；纽约法典第 9.109 条；引用著作］。因此我们的结论是，如果租赁文件构成“真实租赁”，则租赁设备中的担保权益并未获得完善，因为银行未在新泽西州登记融资声明。

两者的区别对本案有关键意

N.J.Stat.Anno. 9-102（1）, 9-302, 9-401（1）（c）.

Obviously the leased property itself is “goods”. We conclude, as did the district court, that the future reversionary interest is likewise an interest in goods, whether it represents “equipment” or “inventory” collateral. The drafters of the Code classified collateral mainly according to the nature or use of the underlying entity, rather than the character of its ownership at any given time. Significantly, the examples of “general intangibles” given in the Official Comment to Sec. 9-106 are all types of property that are inherently intangible. And several Code sections and comments suggest that a collateral interest in “goods” remains such even when the goods are leased. See Secs. 9-103（2）; 9-109（4） and Official Comment 3; 9-304（3）; N.Y.U.C.C. 9-109, Practice Commentary. We conclude accordingly that if the instruments were “true leases”, the security interest in the leased equipment was not perfected because of the failure of the Bank to file financing statements in New Jersey.

In view of our holding that under a true

义　由于我们已经认定，如果租赁协议属于真实租赁，就必须在新泽西州登记，因此，确认租赁协议到底是"真实租赁"还是担保协议，对本案具有关键意义。如果协议是真实租赁，债务人(出租方)就是设备的所有权人。如果协议是伪装后的担保协议，承租方就是所有权人，因而在纽约州进行登记并占有协议文件，就可以使银行的担保权益获得保护。

lease the filing of a financing statement in New Jersey would be required, the determination of whether the lease instruments were "true leases" or security agreements is critical. If the agreements were true leases, Leasing was the owner of the equipment. If they were disguised security agreements, Plastimetrix was the owner, and the filing and possession of the agreements in New York would protect the security interest of the Bank.

是否为真实租赁需要进一步审理　地区法院假定本案出租方和承租方之间的协议事实上属于"真实租赁"的依据，是审理中银行与破产受托人对相关事实的下列书面确认："在本案所有相关时间节点，债务人都拥有租赁设备，但其所有权受制于本确认文件之附件所列的银行的追索权和其他权益。"

In assuming that the agreements between the lessor and lessee were in fact "true leases" the district court relied upon a provision in a stipulation of the parties that, "At all times relevant hereto the Bankrupt [Leasing] owned the leased equipment, subject to the claims and interests of the Bank thereto and therein as appears from the exhibits attached to the stipulation".

但是，上述书面确认是在案件被提交给破产法院之前作出的；并且，当事方当时似乎没有意识到，真实租赁与担保交易的区别将对本案判决结果具有关键

This stipulation was made prior to submission of the petition to the Referee in Bankruptcy and apparently before the parties were aware that the distinction between a true lease and a security device would be crucial

影响。情况完全有可能像银行所辩称的那样，即银行和破产受托人仅约定，“相对银行而言”，而不是相对承租方而言，债务人(出租方)在“受制于银行权利”的情况下，是设备的所有权人。并且，对于债务人与承租方之间的协议，无论是银行还是破产受托人，都缺乏真实、完整和确切的了解，也不一定参与了协议性质的确认。

破产受托人主张，案件证据可以支持租赁协议是“真实租赁”这个结论。破产受托人的依据是租赁协议、当事方的事实确认书以及地区法院基于该确认书所作的“假定”。破产受托人辩称，租赁协议是否为真实租赁的问题，是在本上诉中第一次提出，因此必须基于本院目前已有证据来决定。但是，银行在答复该说法时，引用了银行在初审中提交给地区法院的陈述书，其中说：“如果法院确认该区别具有决定意义，则法院不能仅从声明和补充声明中来确认承租方的租赁协议到底是伪装成租赁的担保交易

to a determination of this case. It may well be, as appellant argues, that the Bank and Trustee had simply agreed that Leasing was the owner of the equipment, “vis-a-vis the Bank [and not vis-a-vis Plastimetrix], subject to the rights of the Bank”, and that, “Neither the Bank nor the Trustee knew all of the real, complete, underlying agreements between Leasing and Plastimetrix”, necessarily involved in determining the nature of the agreements.

In contending that the record supports the conclusion that the agreements were “true leases”, appellee relies upon the lease agreements, stipulation of the parties, and the “assumption” of the district court based upon the stipulation. Appellee then argues that the question of whether the agreements were true leases was first raised on appeal and that the case must be decided on the record now before the court. In its reply brief, however, appellant quotes from the brief it submitted to the district court, reading in part: “If this Court concludes the distinction is determinative, it cannot be determined from the Statement and Supplemental Statement, whether the Plastimetrix leases are leases

还是真实租赁。”

W 破产案的法院说，“是否意图将一项租赁作为担保交易，需要根据每个案件的具体事实确定”[法典第 1.201 条（37）款]。在确认该问题时，法院有权适当地考虑“租赁协议本身的内容，以及租赁协议以外的因素”（W 破产案）。

我们的结论是，本案应被发回地区法院重审，通过听证和审理来确定，租赁文件到底是“真实租赁”，还是伪装成租赁的担保交易。

intended as security devices （hence security agreements） or are true leases.”

“Whether a lease is intended as security is to be determined by the facts of each case...” U.C.C. Sec. 1-201（37）. In making this determination the court may properly consider “factors outside of the lease as well as the contents of the lease itself...”. In Re Walter Willis, Inc.

We conclude that the case should be remanded for a determination by the district court, following an evidentiary hearing, whether the lease instruments were in fact “true leases” or lease devices intended as security.

案例 38　对前手权益的知情是否影响担保权益的效力？

Lawrence Shallcross v. Community State Bank and Trust Co.
谢考斯诉社区州民银行和信托公司案

新泽西州高等法院 1981 年；434 A.2d 671

简　介

本案涉及两个受担保方对同一担保物的争夺。一个受担保方是剪床的卖方（Shallcross），另一个受担保方是向买方提供贷款的银行。卖方通过附条件销售协议向买方（Dunphey）出售一台剪床。协议规定，买方将分期付款，且在货款完全付清之前，卖方将保留剪床的所有权。一段时间之后，银行向买方提供贷款，并与买方订立了担保协议，将剪床列为担保物之一。银行随后通过登记融资声明使担保权益获得完善。在买方违反贷款协议后，银行将剪床出售。卖方在得知剪床被出售后，认为自己是剪床的所有权人，指控银行侵占自己财产。银行则认为自己对剪床持有完善的担保权益并享有优先权，要求法院以无审判决的形式驳回卖方的起诉。

本案主要涉及 3 个问题。第一个问题是，卖方对剪床的“所有权”是否可以对抗银行的完善担保权益？根据法典规定，法典第 9 篇的优先权规则不考虑所有权，所以，尽管卖方认为自己保留了剪床的所有权，但实际上所保留的该所有权不能对抗银行。第二个问题是，卖方是否持有价款担保权益？附条件销售合同实际上属于担保交易，因此可以认为卖方对剪床持有价款担保权益，因为该担保权益所担保的是剪床的价款。卖方认为，在这种情况下，自己的权益优于银行首先获得完善的权益。但法院认定，即使是价款担保权益，卖方也需要在一定期间内使其获得完善，但在本案中，卖方的权益实际上没有获得完善，属于未完善的价款担保权益，因此无法对抗银行的完善的权益。第三个问题是，如果银行在提供贷款和取得担保权益的完善时，已经知道卖方对剪床持有前手权益，那么银行的优先权是否受到影响？法典对此没有作出明确规定，但法院最终认定，此种知情不影响银行的优先权。

判　决

优先权的一般规则　法典第 9 篇就冲突担保权益的评估和优先顺序的确定提供了基本框架。第 9.312 条（5）款相关部分规定，如果不涉及该条其他各款所规制的情况［包括不能根据该条（3）款和（4）款享有特别优先权的价款担保权益］，则同一担保物中冲突担保权益之间的优先顺序，应按下列方式确定：（a）如果两项担保权益均以登记方式获得完善，应按登记的时间顺序确定，无论哪项担保权益首先根据第 9.204 条（1）款发生附着，也无论附着发生于登

Article 9 lays out the framework upon which competing security interests can be evaluated and priorities established. In this regard, N.J.S.A. 9-312（5） provides in relevant part that: In all cases not governed by other rules stated in this section（including cases of purchase money security interests which do not qualify for the special priorities set forth in subsections （3） and （4） of this section）, priority between conflicting security interests in the same collateral shall be determined as follows:（a） in the order of filing if both are perfected by filing, regardless of which security interest attaches first under 9-204（1） and whether it attaches

记之前还是之后。

银行首先获得完善 本案银行无疑首先登记了融资声明，因此早于卖方使自己的担保权益获得了完善。但卖方称，基于若干理由，不应按法典的上述条款确定当事方之间的优先顺序。下面对其理由逐一讨论。

保留所有权的问题 首先，卖方辩称，自己保留了对剪床的所有权，而该事实使第9篇的“首先登记”的规定不适用。但是，法典第9.202条清晰无误地规定：“无论担保物的所有权属于受担保方还是债务人，本篇有关权利、义务和救济的所有条款均适用。”因此从表面看来，第9.312条（5）款可以适用于本案交易，而保留所有权的方法不足以对抗在所有权转移之前已获得完善的担保权益（B诉P案；参见G诉H案）。

价款担保权益的问题 其次，卖方也不能依赖法典有关价款担保权益的条款来对抗银行的

before or after filing...

Here, it is undisputed that the bank filed first in time and therefore perfected its security interest prior to Shallcross. Shallcross maintains that this provision does not establish the relative positions of the parties, for several reasons which will be discussed serially.

First, Shallcross argues that he retained title to the shear and that that fact rendered the "first in time" provision of Article 9 inapplicable. However, N.J.S.A. 9-202 provides clearly and unequivocally that: "Each provision of this Chapter with regard to rights, obligations and remedies applies whether title to collateral is in the secured party or in the debtor." On its face, then, N.J.S.A. 9-312（5） applies to this transaction and the retention of title device is not sufficient to defeat a security interest perfected prior to the transfer of title. Brandywine Lanes, Inc. v. Pittsburgh Nat'l. Bank; see George W. Ultch Lumber Co. v. Hall Plastering, Inc.

Nor can Shallcross rely on the rules governing purchase money security interests in order to defeat the bank's claim. A purchase

主张。本质上，价款担保权益属于附条件销售交易，即卖方对担保物保留担保权益，用于担保价款的支付。涉及价款担保权益时，优先权规则分为两类：一类涉及以库存作为担保物的情况，另一类涉及非库存担保物。对于这两类中的任何一类，卖方的主张都不能成立。

money security interest is, in essence, a conditional sale in which the seller retains an interest in the collateral to secure payment of the purchase price. The rule as to priorities in the face of a purchase money security interest is divided into two categories: that governing inventory collateral and that governing interests in collateral other than inventory. Under neither of these provisions can Shallcross succeed in his claim.

关于上述问题，法典第9.312条（3）款规定："库存担保物中的价款担保权益，优于同一担保物中的冲突担保权益，只要：（a）在债务人取得担保物占有时，价款担保权益获得完善；并且（b）当价款担保权益持有人已知其他受担保方持有担保权益时，或在该持有人登记价款担保权益之日前，其他受担保方已就同样或同类库存作出登记时，只要在债务人取得价款担保权益担保物的占有之前，该其他受担保方收到该价款担保权益持有人之权益的通知；并且（c）上述通知说明，发出通知的人对债务人的库存已经取得或预计取得价

In this respect, N.J.S.A. 9-312（3）provides that："A purchase money security interest in inventory collateral has priority over a conflicting security interest in the same collateral if （a） the purchase money security interest is perfected at the time the debtor receives possession of the collateral; and （b） any secured party whose security interest is known to the holder of the purchase money security interest or who, prior to the date of the filing made by the holder of the purchase money security interest, had filed a financing statement covering the same items or type of inventory, has received notification of the purchase money security interest before the debtor receives possession of the collateral covered by the purchase money security

款担保权益，并对库存的项目或种类作出描述。”

interest; and (c) such notification states that the person giving the notice has or expects to acquire a purchase money security interest in the inventory of the debtor, describing such inventory by item or type.”

法典第9.312条(4)款进一步对非库存担保物作出规定：“涉及非库存担保物中的价款担保权益时，只要在债务人取得担保物的占有时或在取得占有后的10日内价款担保权益获得完善，该价款担保权益即优于同一担保物中的冲突担保权益。”

N.J.S.A. 9-312 (4) goes on to provide in the case of noninventory collateral that: “A purchase money security interest in collateral other than inventory has priority over a conflicting security interest in the same collateral if the purchase money security interest is perfected at the time the debtor receives possession of the collateral or within ten days thereafter.”

卖方的权益未获得完善 在本案中，无论担保物是否被视为库存，卖方都不享有价款担保权益的特别优先权，因为在买方取得担保物的占有之时或其后10日内，卖方的担保权益并未获得完善。法院一直都严格执行法典为此所规定的时间限制，因为如果不严格执行，时间限制就会变得毫无意义（S诉K案；N诉P案；N诉M案）。

So that whether the collateral is viewed as inventory or otherwise, since Shallcross did not perfect at the time Dunphey received possession of the collateral or within ten days thereof, the special priority afforded a purchase money security interest is unavailable to him. The time restrictions in the code in this connection have been strictly adhered to by the courts and to hold otherwise would render them meaningless. Sherman Cty. Bank v. Kallhoff; North Platte State Bank v. Production Credit Ass’n; National Cash Register Co. v. Mishkin’s 125th Street, Inc.

应该说明的是，卖方就此还提出，在出具销售确认单之前，不应认为已经取得第 9.312 条所说的担保物的“占有”。但该主张得不到法律支持。但是，即使为讨论目的而假定存在法律支持，无论如何卖方仍然不享有价款担保权益，因为他甚至在出具销售确认单之时或在其后 10 日内，也没有使担保权益获得完善。

It should be noted in this regard that Shallcross has also suggested that Dunphey should not be considered to have “received possession” of the collateral within the meaning of N.J.S.A. 9-312 until the bill of sale was executed. There is no authority for this view. But even assuming for the purpose of this argument that there were, since Shallcross did not even perfect at the time of the execution of the bill of sale or within ten days thereof, the special priority would not be available to him in any event.

后手权益人的知情问题　因此，卖方的权利必须根据法典第 9.312 条（5）款的优先权一般原则来确定。如前面所提到的，法典明确规定，如果两项冲突的担保权益均已通过登记获得完善，则优先顺序应根据登记时间来确定。为了对抗法典的该项规定，卖方提出，银行由于事先已经知道卖方对担保物的前手权益，因此不能享有优先权。从事实角度看，卖方的主张是，银行在向买方提供贷款前，已知卖方对剪床持有权益，因此系在受制于卖方权益的情况下接受了剪床作为担

Shallcross must therefore proceed under the general priority rules of N.J.S.A. 9-312（5）. As has previously been noted, that statute clearly provides that the priority is to be determined by the order of filing when both security interests are perfected by filing. In order to avoid the effect of the statute, Shallcross has suggested that the bank’s knowledge of his prior interest in the collateral prevents the bank from obtaining a priority. Factually, Shallcross asserts that the bank knew of his interest in the shear before it loaned Dunphey the money and accordingly took the shear as collateral subject to his interest. In support of this position, Shallcross

保物。卖方为了支持该主张而声称，当银行代表来买方车间检查该车间和设备时，卖方也在场，并亲自听到买方告诉该代表说，自己就该剪床欠卖方的钱。

claims that he was present in Dunphey's shop when a representative of the bank came to inspect the shop and equipment, and that he personally heard Dunphey inform the representative that he still owed Shallcross money on the shear.

关于上述问题，新泽西州没有相关判例，但在审阅法典规定、其他州判例以及新泽西州法典的正式评论后，我们的结论是，法典优先权条款不受对前手权益知情的影响。

Although no New Jersey court has yet to pass on this issue, a review of the statute, decisions from other jurisdictions and the Official Code Comments adopted by New Jersey leads to the conclusion that knowledge of a prior interest does not affect the priority provisions of the act.

法典文字不涉及知情问题

首先应该说明的是，法典第9.312条（5）款的文字没有显示，了解前手权益或得到通知就会否定该款所设立的优先顺序。法典该条不存在通知条款这个事实，具有特别重要的意义，因为在法典某些其他条款中，法典起草者认为，有必要加入知情条款或通知条款。例子之一是法典第9.301条（1）（a）款。该款涉及未完善担保权益和留置权债权人之间的优先顺序，即“除（2）款另有规定外，未完善的担保权益受制

First, it should be noted that there is no suggestion in the language of N.J.S.A. 9-312（5） that knowledge or notice of a prior interest is a bar to the invocation of the priorities established therein. The absence of a notice provision in this section of the act is particularly significant since the drafters of the act saw fit to specifically include knowledge or notice provisions in other sections of it. One such example is N.J.S.A. 9-301（1）（a）, dealing with the priority between an unperfected security interest and a lien creditor：“Except as otherwise provided in subsection （2）, an unperfected security

于……（b）留置权债权人的权利，只要该人在成为留置权债权人之前，不知道该担保权益，且该担保权益尚未获得完善”。

interest is subordinate to the rights of ...（b）a person who becomes a lien creditor without knowledge of the security interest and before it is perfected.”

显然，法典起草者已设想到，对另一项权益的了解，在某些情况下会阻碍后手权益取得优先权。因此，假如法典起草者打算使知情成为第 9.312 条（5）款中的因素，他们本来会专门如此规定。甚至在有关库存价款担保权益的第 9.312 条（3）款中也有通知条款，但在（5）款中却没有。因此很显然，第 9.312 条（5）款中未就“知情”或“通知”作出规定是有意为之。因此，不能认为该款已默示包含通知条款。此结论也符合相关判例的倾向（F 诉 A 案；S 破产案；N 诉 D 案；M 诉 N 案；B 诉 H 案；N 诉 M 案）。

Obviously, the drafters contemplated that, in certain cases, knowledge of another interest would bar the subsequent interest from obtaining priority. Had they intended that this be an element of N.J.S.A. 9-312（5）, they would have specifically provided so. Even in N.J.S.A. 9-312（3）, which governs a purchase money security interest in inventory collateral, there is a notice provision. There is, however, no such provision in clause （5）. Hence, it seemed clear that the failure to set forth a “knowledge” or “notice” provision in 9-312（5） was intentional and that such a provision is not to be implied. This conclusion is consistent with the weight of decisional authority. First Nat’l Bank and Trust Co. v. Atlas Credit Corp.; In re Smith; National Bank of Sarasota v. Dugger; Madison Nat’l Bank v. Newrath; Bloom v. Hilty; Noble Co. v. Mack Financial Corp.

相关判例　其他州的主要相关判例是 S 破产案。在该案中，

The leading out-of-state case on the subject is In re Smith, where the court

法院对上述问题进行了大量讨论。在该案中，买方购买了一辆汽车，并与经销商签署了附条件销售合同。该合同随后被转让给银行。当事方没有登记融资声明。几个月之后，信贷公司向买方提供了贷款，而买方签署了以汽车为担保物的动产抵押合同，并登记了融资声明。信贷公司当时实际知道，银行已对汽车持有未完善的担保权益。法院判决，基于多项理由，事先知情无关紧要。这些理由对本案也同样适用。

discussed these issues at length. There, Smith purchased an automobile, and a conditional sales contract was executed by the dealer and subsequently assigned to the First National Bank of Minneapolis. No financing statement was filed. A few months later Community Credit Co. lent Smith money and Smith executed a chattel mortgage on the automobile and a financing statement was filed. Community Credit Corp. had actual knowledge of the unperfected security interest held by First National in the automobile. The court concluded that prior knowledge was irrelevant for several reasons equally applicable here.

判例的分析 首先，该案法院谈到登记系统的尊严。这是基尔莫教授在他有关动产担保的著作中提到的一个问题(引用著作)。该案法院说:“理想的情况是使担保权益尽快获得完善。因此，如果受担保方不登记，就要自行承担风险，即自己的权益会次于来得更晚但更勤快的当事方。应该指出的是，从通知其他当事方的角度看，登记具有特殊作用。因此我们同意，如果后手

First, the court discussed the integrity of the filing system, a point raised by Professor Gillmore in his treatise, Security Interests in Personal Property. The court commented:
“It is desirable that perfection of interests take place promptly. It is appropriate then to provide that a secured party who fails to file runs the risk of subordination to a later but more diligent party. In this regard it should be pointed out that filing is of particular importance with respect to notice to other parties. It is agreed that where the later party

当事方实际上已就前手的权益得到通知，就不再依赖登记方式来通知该当事方。但是，从这个角度分析问题过于狭隘。有些当事方可能会基于系统的登记状况而提供贷款，并订立有关担保物的担保协议。假如此时出现争议，他们可以打败前手的未完善担保权益，但从另一个角度讲，他们也许根本就不想陷入争议。也就是说，他们的预期，不是出现争议时可以最终获胜，而是根本不存在可以引起争议的前手权益，无论其是否已获得完善。要保护对登记系统的此种预期，唯一方法是尽快使所有担保权益获得完善。”

其次，该案法院还承认，“知情”这个标准涉及证据问题。知情是主观标准，相对于登记日期等客观标准，主观状态的证明困难得多（S 破产案）。最后，该案法院还分析了法典的正式评论，认为其支持这个观点，即“知情”不属于这个问题中需要考虑的因素。

has actual notice there is no need to rely upon a filing to notify him of a prior interest. The problem, however, cannot be analyzed in this narrow context. Some parties may rely on the record in extending credit and obtaining a security agreement in collateral. Although they will prevail over the unperfected prior interest in time if a dispute arises, it is entirely possible that they wanted to avoid the dispute altogether. In other words, they may not have relied in ultimately prevailing in the event of a dispute but they may have relied on the complete absence of a prior interest perfected or otherwise out of which a dispute could arise. The only way this kind of record expectation can be protected is by prompt, perfection of all security interests."

In conjunction with this, the Smith court also recognized the evidentiary problems created by a knowledge requirement, which is subjective and is much more difficult to establish than an objective criterion such as the date of filing. Id. Finally, the court in Smith analyzed the Official Comments accompanying the Code and determined that they supported the view that knowledge is not an element for consideration in this connection.

法典正式评论的举例 第9.312条的正式评论包含若干举例，说明如何解决该条（5）款的优先顺序争议。这些举例与S破产案的结论一致。最相关的是第二个举例。两个人均就同一担保物提供非价款性质的贷款。债务人占有担保物。在第二人提供贷款时，两者的担保权益均未获得完善。此时，首先（通过占有担保物或作出登记）使担保权益获得完善的人享有优先权。并且，在完善该权益的当时，是否知道另一人权益的存在，对结果没有影响。

The official comments to § 9-312 contain several examples which illustrate the resolution of priority disputes under clause （5）. These examples comport with the conclusion in Smith. Example 2 is perhaps closest in point. A & B non-purchase money advances against the same collateral. The collateral is in the debtor's possession and neither interest is perfected when the second advance is made. Whichever secured party first perfects his interest （by taking possession of the collateral or by filing） takes priority and it makes no difference whether he knows of the other interests at the time he perfects his own.

上述举例的文字很清楚，即无论受担保方在完善自己的权益时是否知道另一项权益的存在，结果都一样。该举例和法典制度的要点，都是鼓励尽快使担保权益获得完善，并以此作为确定优先顺序的清晰无误的方法，避免打开诉讼的“闸门”。目的就是如此单纯。

The language of this example is clear — it makes no difference whether the secured party knows of the other's interest at the time he perfects his own. The point of the example and the statutory scheme itself is to encourage the prompt perfection of security interests as an unequivocal method of establishing priorities with certainty and without opening the flood gates of litigation, no more or no less.

结论 不应将上述解释的任

Nothing in this interpretation can be

何部分视为与法典第 1.203 条的善意要求相冲突。本案没有证据显示，银行存在引诱、恶意或不公行为。因此，没有理由以“禁止自相矛盾”这类原则来阻止银行的优先权主张。这并不等于说，第 9.312 条（5）款的优先顺序在任何情况下都不可能受到恶意因素的影响，而只是说，本案不属于这种情况。基于以上理由，批准银行申请的无审判决动议。

considered to controvert the good faith requirement of N.J.S.A. 1-203. For this record is devoid of any evidence to show a leading on, bad faith or inequitable conduct on the part of the bank which would justify what in essence is estoppel against the assertion of a priority. This is not to say that the priorities established under N.J.S.A. 9-312（5） would never be affected by a showing of bad faith. That is simply not the question presented here. For the foregoing reasons the motion for summary judgment is hereby granted.

案例39 受担保方是否对担保物的收益享有完善担保权益?

Howarth v. Universal CIT Credit Corporation
豪沃斯诉环球斯特信贷公司案

宾夕法尼亚州西区联邦地区法院 1962 年；203 F. Supp. 279

简 介

本案原告（Howarth）是债务人（Spohn）破产案中的破产受托人，代表破产财产起诉信贷公司（UCIT），要求信贷公司退还某些财产，因为这些财产是信贷公司在债务人破产之前 4 个月内从债务人取走的。但是，如果信贷公司对这些财产持有完善担保权益，破产受托人就无权追回该财产。所以，本案的争议焦点是，在债务人破产之日，信贷公司是否对争议财产持有完善担保权益?

法院将争议财产根据不同情况分为 7 项:（1）银行存款;（2）股票;（3）应收款;（4）11 辆旧车；（5）17 辆旧车；（6）42 辆旧车；（7）汽车零件和配件。之后，法院根据当事方所订立的协议和所登记的融资声明，分别分析了信贷公司是否对这些财产持有完善担保权益。在本案审理时，法典第 9 篇已将担保交易整合成单一形式，但在案件交易的当时，当事方仍然使用了早期的担保形式，包括下述判决中提到的“信托收据”（trust receipt）。在本案中，信贷公司给身为汽车经销商的债务人提供贷款，而债务人则向信贷公司出具“信托收据”，表明经销商系以信托受托人的身份，代表信贷公司持有汽车并进行销售，并代表信贷公司持有销售后的货款。根据信托法，这意味着与汽车有关的一切权利本质上都属于信贷公司。信托收据大体上相当于法典第 9 篇所说的担保协议。

根据法院对争议财产的分析，对于前 3 项财产，由于不能证明它们属于出售担保物之后获得的可分辨收益，因此信贷公司不对这些财产持有完善担保权益，而破产受托人则有权收回该财产。第（4）项至第（6）项财产是旧车，有些是直接使用信贷公司贷款取得的，有些是债务人出售新车时，按以旧换新方式收回的。按以旧换新方式收回的旧车，属于新车的收益。信贷公司所登记的融资声明，已经包含了旧车以及新车出售后的收益。因此，信贷公司本来对这些旧车持有完善担保权益。但破产受托人提出，宾夕法尼亚州的《机动车法》规定，无论是新车还是旧车，留置权都必须注明在汽车产权证书上，否则留置权无效。债务人收回的这些旧车虽然带有原所有权人的产权证书，但并未将信贷公司的担保权益进行标注。破产受托人因此主张，信贷公司的担保权益未获得完善。法院综合分析法典第 9 篇和《机动车法》的相关规定后认定，当旧车由经销商持有时，无须将担保权益标注在产权证书上。因此，信贷公司的担保权益有效。

判 决

银行存款 债务人在银行账户中存有 6734.21 美元。信贷公司曾获得法院 75,000 美元的胜诉判决，因此法院查封该存款后，将其转给了信贷公司。但是，该银行存款的查封是在债务人破产前 4 个月内，且当时债务人已处于无力清偿状态，因此该查封无

Spohn's bank account in the Peoples First National Bank & Trust Company in the sum of $6734.21 was garnisheed and transferred to UCIT pursuant to a writ of attachment execution issued on a judgment in favor of UCIT in the sum of $75,000. The lien against the bank cash obtained by the attachment within four months of bankruptcy

效(引用《破产法》)。

不能确定存款的来源 债务人银行账户不在信贷公司控制之下，且存款来源未能确定。显然，信贷公司未能证明，银行账户存款的任何部分源于其担保权益所覆盖之担保物的出售收益。信贷公司辩称，存款必然源于担保物的此种出售收益。但这属于缺乏根据的假设，因为全部存款均有可能来自债务人的服务收入，或债务人普通股股票的出售收入，或债务人获得的贷款。

本院不能假设银行存款的来源。信贷公司要承担举证责任，证明进入银行账户的存款是债务人处置担保物后所取得的现金收益。但信贷公司未能举证。债务人在破产程序开始前 10 日内收到该现金并将其存入账户［参见法典第 9.306 条（2）款］，且该现金不属于出售或处置任何担保物后所收到的可分辨现金。因此，该现金不受制于信贷公司的担保权益，并可由代表无担保债权人的破产受托人追索。我们

and while Spohn was insolvent is null and void. Bankruptcy Act.

Spohn's bank account was not under the control of UCIT, and the source of this money has not been identified. Apparently UCIT has not been able to trace any of the money in the bank to proceeds from the sales of collateral on which it held a security interest. The defendant argues that the money must have come from the sale of property in which it had a security interest. This is an unwarranted assumption for all of it could have come from services rendered, sale of Spohn's common stock, or loans to Spohn.

The court may not assume the source of the money in the bank. The burden is upon UCIT to trace cash proceeds received by Spohn from the disposition of secured collateral into the bank deposits. This it has not done. This cash was received by Spohn, the debtor, and deposited more than 10 days prior to the bankruptcy proceeding (cf. U.C.C. § 9-306（2））; it is not identifiable cash proceeds received from the sale or disposition of any collateral. Thus it is free from any security interest of UCIT and is subject to the claims of general creditors represented by

判定，信贷公司对银行存款现金所作的查封属于可撤销的优惠清偿。因此，破产受托人有权追回这 6734.21 美元。

the plaintiff-trustee. We hold the bank cash garnisheed by UCIT is a voidable preference and the plaintiff-trustee is entitled to recover $6734.21.

股票　债务人在破产前 4 个月内，将 20 股福特汽车公司股票转让给信贷公司。信贷公司出售股票后获得 869.42 美元。无法确定债务人之前购买该股票的资金源于何处，因此该股票不属于“可分辨收益”。我们判定，向信贷公司作出的此项转让，是可撤销的优惠清偿，因此破产受托人有权追回 869.42 美元。

The sum of $869.42 was realized from the sale of 20 shares of Ford Motor Company common stock transferred to UCIT within four months of Spohn's bankruptcy. There is no tracing to indicate where the money came from to enable Spohn to purchase these shares. The stock is not “identifiable proceeds”. We hold that the transfer to defendant is a voidable preference and that the plaintiff-trustee is entitled to recover $869.42.

应收款　债务人以现金和支票形式，从客户收回应收款共计 10,847.75 美元，并在破产之前 4 个月内将此款转让给信贷公司。在这笔款项中，已确认 1100 美元系出售两辆新车的现金收益，而信贷公司对该车辆持有完善担保权益。其余 9747.75 美元则存在争议。款项源于出售汽车、配件和服务的现金收入，但已混合在一起。

Spohn collected customers receivables by cash and checks in the sum of $10,847.75 and transferred this amount to UCIT within four months of bankruptcy. Of this sum $1100.00 was identified as cash proceeds from the sale of two new vehicles on which UCIT held a perfected security interest, leaving in dispute the sum of $9747.75. This remainder comprises commingled cash proceeds arising from the sale of motor vehicles, parts and services.

无法对已混合的应收款进行辨别　从当事方的事实确认书和

From the Stipulated Facts and Exhibit L, it cannot be ascertained whether any of

本案L附件中，无法确认信贷公司是否对文件中所列的收入项目持有完善担保权益。L附件仅显示了这些收入项目的付款人姓名、付款数额以及将款项转给信贷公司的日期。此外，即使我们假定，这些款项中有一部分款项确实源于汽车配件和汽车的销售，我们仍然无法确认是否有任何款项来自债务人所提供的服务。由于信贷公司对提供服务所带来的收益不持有担保权益，其无权获得有可能来自服务的收益。

the articles sold were covered by a perfected security interest in favor of UCIT. Exhibit L gives only the name of the person owing the account, the amount paid, and the date the money was transferred to UCIT. Moreover, even if it were to be assumed that some of the accounts arose from the sale of parts and vehicles, it still could not be ascertained whether or not any portion of any account arose from services performed by Spohn. As UCIT did not hold a security interest in proceeds received from the sale of services, it is not entitled to retain proceeds which may have come from this source.

此外，我们对法典的理解是，破产程序中涉及混合后的现金收益时，只有收益系破产前10日内收到的担保物收益，受担保方才有权获得该收益。基于以上原因，我们判定，破产受托人有权收回9747.75美元。

Furthermore, as we understand the Uniform Commercial Code, in insolvency proceedings the secured creditor is only entitled to commingled cash when it is received as proceeds of collateral within ten days of the filing of the petition. For these reasons, we hold that the plaintiff-trustee is entitled to $9747.75.

直接提供贷款的11辆旧车

本案的旧车信托收据证明，信贷公司为这11辆旧车的取得提供了贷款。对于债务人持有并用于出售的旧车，信贷公司基于

These 11 used vehicles were financed by UCIT as is evidenced by used car Trust Receipts. UCIT obtained a security interest in these used vehicles held by Spohn for resale by virtue of the Agreement for

批发融资协议而取得了担保权益。该协议所覆盖的担保物包括新车和旧车，也包括旧车信托收据。当事方通过在州务卿办公处和债务人营业地 AL 县登记处登记融资声明，使该担保权益获得了完善。

产权证书标注问题　破产受托人辩称，要对旧车取得完善担保权益，唯一方法是根据宾夕法尼亚州《机动车法》的规定，在每辆车的产权证书上对留置权作出注明。我们不同意这个说法。

《机动车法》的一般规定　确实，在本案所涉及的旧车批发交易当时，宾夕法尼亚州的《机动车法》“明确规定了在机动车中设立留置权的方法”。该法要求，必须在汽车产权证书上注明留置权或他项权利（M 诉 C 案）。但尽管如此，应该可以肯定地说，涉及用于批发的新车时，为新车提供贷款的融资公司，可以通过在州务卿办公处和经销商营业地所在县的登记处登记融资声明，对该新车取得完善担保权益［法典第 9.302 条（1）款；第 9.401

Wholesale Financing, covering new and used merchandise, and the used car Trust Receipts. This security interest was perfected by filing Financing Statements in the offices of the Secretary of the Commonwealth and the Prothonotary of Allegheny County where Spohn did business.

The plaintiff-trustee argues that the only way to obtain a perfected security interest in used motor vehicles is by noting the lien on the title certificate of each car pursuant to the Pennsylvania Motor Vehicle Code. We do not agree.

It is true that the Motor Vehicle Code in effect during the wholesale transactions involved in this litigation "clearly established a method of creating liens on motor vehicles" by showing a lien or encumbrance on the certificate of title. Mellon National Bank & Trust Company v. Cabin. Notwithstanding, it seems certain that a finance company which advances money for wholesale financing of new cars can perfect a valid security interest therein by filing a financing statement in the offices of the Secretary of the Commonwealth and the Prothonotary of the County in which the dealer does business. U.C.C.

条(1)(a)款；S诉G案；T诉A案；参见G诉W案］。我们的理解是，这是因为《机动车法》规定，像本案债务人这样的经销商，“在新车被售出之前，无须就销售中的新车取得产权证书”。

§ § 9-302(1), 9-401(1)(a); Sterling Acceptance Co. v. Grimes; Taylor Motor Rental, Inc. v. Associates Discount Corp; cf. Girard Trust Corn Exchange Bank v. Warren Lepley Ford, Inc. As we see it, this is because the Motor Vehicle Code provides that a dealer, such as Spohn, “need not obtain certificate of title for new motor vehicles... until and before sale thereof”.

旧车的产权证书问题 同样,《机动车法》的另一项条款规定，旧车经销商“无须申领产权证书”，但应在获得旧车后的10日内通知政府交通部门。因此，我们的看法是，类似本案信贷公司这样的从事批发融资的公司，在根据法典第9.302条(1)款和第9.401条(1)(a)款登记融资声明后，可以就旧车取得完善担保权益。

Likewise, [another provision] of the Motor Vehicle Code provided that a dealer in used cars “shall not be required to apply for a certificate of title” but shall notify the Department of the acquisition of the vehicle within ten days. Therefore, it is our opinion that a company such as UCIT engaged in wholesale financing may perfect a valid security interest in used cars by filing a financing statement pursuant to § § 9-302 (1) and 9-401(1)(a) of the U.C.C.

新车和旧车应同等对待 由于《机动车法》的上述两项相关条款非常类似，我们想象不出有什么合理理由可以说明，为什么从事批发融资的债权人不能使用对新车取得完善担保权益的同样方法，来取得对旧车的完善担保

In view of the similarity of [two provisions] of the Motor Vehicle Code, we cannot perceive any good reason why a lender engaged in wholesale financing cannot perfect a valid security interest in used cars by the same method he employs to perfect a valid security interest in new cars.

权益。

法典宗旨　法典是在包含了上述条款的《机动车法》之后而制定的，而法典所述的基本宗旨可以支持我们的上述结论。法典的基本宗旨是："（a）简化和更新管辖商业交易的法律规则，并为商业交易提供更高的精确性和确定性；（b）保留商业交易的灵活性，并鼓励通过习惯、惯例和当事方协议，不断扩展商业做法和机制。"[法典第 1.102 条（2）款]

登记是更加方便和有效的方法　此外，我们认为，对于经销商的潜在债权人来说，上述解释可以简化债权人保护自己的方法。如果债权人希望查验经销商的新车抵押状况，他们必须在州务卿办公处和县登记处检索登记文件，而在进行此种检索时，他们也可以同时看到库存旧车的抵押状况。这个方法显然更方便、更有效。否则，债权人为了保护自己，就不得不检查经销商库存中每一辆旧车的产权证书，而根据《机动车法》的规定，经销商

Our conclusion finds support in the underlying purposes and policies of the U.C.C., enacted subsequent to these sections of the Motor Vehicle Code, which are: "（a） to simplify and modernize and develop greater precision and certainty in the rules of law governing commercial transactions; （b） to preserve flexibility in commercial transactions and to encourage continued expansion of commercial practices and mechanisms through custom, usage and agreement of the parties." Section 1-102（2）.

In addition we think it simplifies the means whereby a dealer's prospective creditors may protect themselves. A creditor who must search the records in the offices of the Secretary of the Commonwealth and the Prothonotary of the County for notice of encumbrances on new cars in a dealer's inventory at the same time will get notice of encumbrances on the used cars in his inventory. This method seems to be much more convenient and effective than if the creditor in order to protect himself should be forced to demand an inspection of the dealer's title certificate to each used car in his

本来就无须就库存旧车取得产权证书。

inventory, — a certificate which the dealer is not required to obtain under the Motor Vehicle Code.

旧车证书标注的不合理之处

此外，如果认可破产受托人的主张，则类似本案信贷公司这样的从事旧车批发融资的贷款人，就只能要求经销商对其收购的每一辆旧车都取得产权证书，并将贷款人的担保权益注明在产权证书上，而这与《机动车法》对经销商的豁免是矛盾的。并且，该程序将在旧车的所有权链条中增加一个所有权人(非系使用人的经销商)，从而降低了旧车的价值。我们不认为这是立法机构的意图，即从事旧车批发融资的贷款人为了取得有效的抵押权，必须经历这种费力、费时和费钱的程序，而为新车提供贷款的贷款人，则可简单地通过登记适当的融资声明使担保权益获得完善。

Moreover, if the plaintiff-trustee's contention prevails, a lender such as UCIT who engages in wholesale financing of used cars would be compelled to insist that a dealer obtain a new certificate of title for each used car acquired, contrary to the exemption stated in the Motor Vehicle Code, and show the finance company's encumbrance thereon. This procedure would add a non-using owner, i. e., the dealer, to the chain of title, thereby decreasing the value of the used car. We do not think the Legislature intended to subject those engaged in wholesale financing of used cars to such troublesome, time-consuming and costly procedure to obtain a valid lien, when those engaged in financing new cars can perfect a valid security interest by simply filing the appropriate financing statements.

学者的立场　一位学者认为：“根据法典，从事机动车批发交易的适当程序是向州务卿办公处进行登记。”(引用著作)。另一位学者也作出类似表述：

In Tanner, Pennsylvania Business Law Under the Uniform Commercial Code, it is stated：“Under the Commercial Code, filing with the Secretary of the Commonwealth is the proper procedure for wholesale transactions in

“如果银行向机动车制造商、改装商或经销商提供贷款，且以新车或旧车作为担保物，则应登记融资声明。如果车辆是新车，则原本就未曾颁发可供银行标注担保权益的产权证书（引用《机动车法》）。如果是旧车，旧车的原所有权人会将产权证书交给借款人（经销商）持有，但借款人在将旧车重新售出前，无须取得新的产权证书（引用《机动车法》），因此，不要求银行将担保权益标注在产权证书上。在这种情况下，登记融资声明是银行唯一可以对此种旧车取得完善担保权益的方法。”（引用著作）

motor vehicles.” A similar statement appears in Pennsylvania Banks and the Uniform Commercial Code: “If a bank is lending money to a motor vehicle manufacturer, jobber or dealer on the security of new or used vehicles, the filing of a financing statement will be necessary. If the vehicles are new no certificate of title will have been issued on which the bank's security interest could be indicated [V.C.]. If they are used vehicles the borrower will hold the certificate of title of the former owner, assigned to the borrower, but he will not be required to obtain a new certificate of title until he resells the vehicle [V.C.], and hence there is no requirement that the bank's security interest be indicated on the certificate. The filing of a financing statement, therefore, is the only way in which the bank can obtain a perfected security interest in such vehicles.”

买方没有风险　破产受托人还辩称，为了保护旧车的买方（从经销商的库存中购买旧车的人），使其不受制于融资公司的留置权，应该要求经销商为库存中每一辆旧车取得产权证书，并将融资公司的留置权标注在证书

The plaintiff-trustee also argues that to protect buyers of used cars in a dealer's inventory from liens in favor of a finance company, the dealer should be required to obtain a title certificate for each used car in his inventory, despite the exemption in the Motor Vehicle Code, and show the finance

上，即使《机动车法》已免除此种要求。但是，法典第9.307条(1)款已对此种买方提供了保护，因此其并不受制于车辆中的完善担保权益。即使买方实际知道批发融资协议的存在，他们也仍然受到保护（参见S诉G案）。

company's lien thereon. However, § 9-307（1） of the U.C.C. protects such buyers and they take the cars free of perfected security interests, and this is so even if the buyers have actual knowledge of the wholesale security agreement. Cf. Sterling Acceptance Co. v. Grimes.

额外收益问题 最后，破产受托人称，信贷公司只对11辆旧车提供了6340美元的贷款，但最终通过出售这些旧车获得了7805美元，因此破产受托人有权收回超出的1465美元。

Finally, the plaintiff-trustee contends that because UCIT had advanced only $6340.00 on these 11 used cars, he is entitled to the excess amount of $1465.00 received when UCIT sold this collateral for $7805.00.

批发融资协议规定："在贷款全部清偿之前，我们（债务人）作为信托受托人，将单独持有全部销售收益，而你们（信贷公司）是信托受益人。"本院认为，针对债务人欠信贷公司的全部债务，该协议已覆盖了出售任何担保物所获得的任何收益，使信贷公司对全部收益享有担保权益。同时，该担保权益通过登记融资声明已获得完善。融资声明规定："本声明覆盖的收益"包括"财产出售后获得的现金"。由于债务人尚有未偿债务，因此

The Agreement for Wholesale Financing provides: "Until payment in full, we ［Spohn］ will hold all proceeds separately and in trust for you ［UCIT］." In our opinion, this agreement creates a security interest in all proceeds arising from the sale of any collateral for the entire debt owing to UCIT by Spohn. The security interest in all proceeds was perfected by filing the Financing Statement, which specifies: "The following proceeds are also covered", inter alia, "cash taken in the sale... of the property...". Since there is a remainder due on the Spohn debt, we hold that UCIT is entitled to retain all the

我们判定，信贷公司有权保留 11 辆旧车的全部出售收益。

money it received from the sale of the 11 used cars.

以信托身份取得的 17 辆旧车　这 17 辆旧车是债务人在出售 17 辆新车时，按以旧换新方式，为冲抵部分货款而收购的。基于批发融资协议、新车信托收据和融资声明，信贷公司对出售的每一辆新车均持有完善担保权益。债务人以信托受托人身份出售了该 17 辆新车。

These 17 used vehicles were taken in trade by Spohn toward the purchase price of 17 new vehicles. On each of the new vehicles sold, UCIT held a perfected security interest by virtue of the Agreement for Wholesale Financing, new car Trust Receipts, and Financing Statement. The 17 new vehicles were sold out of trust by Spohn.

属于新车的可分辨收益　如前面曾指出的，根据批发融资协议、信托收据和融资声明，信贷公司对出售担保物后所获得的收益持有完善担保权益。融资声明规定："本声明还覆盖下列收益……（b）按以旧换新方式取得的商品。"上述的其他文件实质上也规定，信贷公司对"以旧换新所获得的财产"持有担保权益。因此，这些以旧换新获得的旧车是融资声明所覆盖的可分辨收益［法典第 9.306 条（1）（a）款］。

As heretofore pointed out, pursuant to the Agreement for Wholesale Financing, the Trust Receipts, and the Financing Statement, UCIT had a perfected security interest in the proceeds arising from the sale of collateral. The Financing Statement provided: "The following proceeds are also covered ...（b）merchandise taken in trade." The other mentioned documents provided in substance that UCIT was to have a security interest in "trade-ins". Thus, these used vehicles taken in trade were identifiable proceeds covered by the Financing Statement. U.C.C. § 9-306（1）（a）.

产权证书标注问题　破产受托人称，根据《机动车法》，对

The plaintiff-trustee contends that according to the Motor Vehicle Code no lien

于"以旧换新所获得的财产",必须将留置权标注在产权证书上,否则不能取得留置权。本院认为,对于信贷公司这样从事新车和旧车批发融资的贷款人,如果经销商为出售目的而持有汽车,且贷款人已对新车和其收益取得了担保权益,则其可以根据第9.302条(1)款,通过登记融资声明使其对新车之出售收益的担保权益获得完善。并且,基于《机动车法》的规定,经销商无须就每一辆以旧换新的旧车取得产权证书并标注留置权。我们判定,本案信贷公司有权保留出售17辆旧车的收益。

推定以信托身份取得的42辆旧车 这42辆旧车是出售新车时按以旧换新方式收购的,而新车是由信贷公司基于批发融资协议和信托收据而提供融资的。因此,这些旧车也必须被视为可分辨收益。如前所述,信贷公司已通过登记融资声明,使收益中的担保权益获得完善。

推定认为存在信托关系 当事方未确认债务人系以信托身份

can be obtained on a "trade-in" unless the lien is noted on the title certificate. It is the opinion of the court that a finance company such as UCIT engaging in wholesale financing of new and used vehicles held for resale by a dealer, and having obtained a security interest in new vehicles and the proceeds thereof, may perfect its security interest in the proceeds by filing in compliance with § 9-302(1) of the U.C.C., and, in view of [relevant provision] of the Motor Vehicle Code, need not require the dealer to procure title certificates for each "trade-in" on which to show its lien. We hold that UCIT is entitled to retain the money received from the sale of the 17 used vehicles.

These 42 used vehicles were taken in trade for new vehicles, which had been financed by UCIT, under the terms of the Agreement for Wholesale Financing and the Trust Receipts. These vehicles must also be regarded as identifiable proceeds in which, as previously shown, UCIT had perfected a security interest by filing the Financing Statement.

It was not stipulated that the new vehicles were sold out of trust by Spohn.

出售这些新车。但我们对相关担保协议的解释是，信贷公司在全部收益中都设立了担保权益；在债务人欠信贷公司的债务全部清偿前，此种收益应包括这 42 辆以旧换新的旧车。如前所述，批发融资协议规定，在全部欠款还清之前，债务人将以信托身份代表信贷公司单独持有全部收益。同样，信托收据规定，在债务人失去清偿能力时，信贷公司有权宣布债务人的全部余债均提前到期；还规定信贷公司“可以要求债务人以现金向信贷公司支付担保物的销售收入。支付完成前，债务人将以信托身份代表信贷公司单独持有该收入”。在债务人将旧车转让给信贷公司时，就信贷公司贷款的全部车辆，债务人欠信贷公司的债务超过 400,000 美元。因此我们认为，这 42 辆旧车是信贷公司有权获得的收益，因此信贷公司有权保留出售这些旧车所获的款项。

However, as we interpret the pertinent security agreements, UCIT created a security interest in all proceeds, which would include these 42 “trade-ins”, until all the indebtedness due by Spohn to UCIT was paid. As heretofore quoted, the Agreement for Wholesale Financing provided that until payment in full, Spohn would hold all proceeds separately and in trust for UCIT. Likewise, the Trust Receipts, after providing that UCIT could accelerate all indebtedness then owing to it by Spohn in the event of insolvency, further provided that UCIT “may require the respective amount on any chattel to be paid to it in cash. Until such payment we [Spohn] will hold all proceeds of sale separately and in trust for Universal C.I.T.”. Since Spohn owed UCIT upwards of $400,000 on all the chattels which it had financed at the time of the transfers, we think these 42 used cars were proceeds to which UCIT is entitled. We hold that UCIT is entitled to retain the money received from the sale of the 42 used vehicles.

汽车零件和配件　债务人所签署的动产抵押和贷款协议，在债务人当时拥有和随后可能取得

The Chattel Mortgage and Loan Agreement executed by Spohn created a security interest in Spohn’s inventory of all

的全部库存零件和配件中设立了担保权益。该动产抵押特别包括了“我们现在拥有以及未来可能取得的全部库存零件和配件”，并规定可以对其进行展示和出售。

parts and accessories now owned or which may hereafter be acquired. The Chattel Mortgage specifically covered "our complete inventory of all parts and accessories now owned or which may hereafter be acquired", and provided for their display and sale.

信贷公司通过登记融资声明完善了该担保权益。融资声明覆盖了新车、旧车、卡车、拖拉机和拖车的“替换零件和配件”。当事方似乎已确认，已登记的融资声明包含了动产抵押协议中所描述的担保物。即使不存在该确认，我们也不同意破产受托人的主张，即融资声明的描述不足以完善这些零件和配件中的担保权益。

The security interest was perfected when UCIT filed a Financing Statement covering "replacement parts and accessories" for new and used motor vehicles, trucks, tractors and trailers. It seems to be stipulated that the Financing Statement was filed as to items described in the Chattel Mortgage. Even if the stipulation is disregarded, we cannot agree with plaintiff-trustee's argument that the description in the Financing Statement is insufficient to perfect a security interest in these items.

描述的充分性问题 法典第9.402条(1)款规定:“融资声明如果指明了其所覆盖的担保物的类型，即属于充分。”法典第9.110条规定:“为本篇目的，任何描述，无论是否具体，只要合理指明所描述的对象，即为充分。”我们认定，担保协议和融资声明均合理指明了债务人库存

U.C.C. § 9-402 (1) provides: "A financing statement is sufficient if it...contains a statement indicating the types...of property covered." U.C.C. § 9-110 provides: "For the purposes of this Article any description is sufficient whether or not it is specific if it reasonably identifies the thing described." We find that the security agreements and the Financing Statement reasonably identify

中的汽车零件和配件，且融资声明的描述足以构成对潜在债权人的通知（N 诉 C 案）。因此，信贷公司有权保留出售这些物品所获的款项。

the motor parts and accessories in Spohn's inventory, and that the description in the Financing Statement is sufficient to give notice to potential creditors. National-Dime Bank of Shamokin v. Cleveland Brothers Equipment Co., Inc. Therefore, UCIT is entitled to retain the money received from the sale of these items.

结论　本院判决，破产受托人有权获得的数额为 17,351.38 美元。

Judgment should be entered in favor of the plaintiff-trustee in the amount of $17,351.38.

案例40　买方在哪个时间节点成为正常业务中的买方?

In Re Havens Steel Co.
栖息地钢铁公司破产案

密苏里州西区联邦破产法院 2004 年；317 B.R. 75

简　介

在本破产案中，破产债务人(Havens Steel)是一家钢材供应和施工公司。债务人破产后，本案买方（Austin）和银行（Commerce）就债务人提供给买方的一批钢材产生争议。银行曾向债务人提供过贷款，并就债务人的库存钢材和收益等取得了完善的担保权益。随后，债务人与买方订立了一份供应和施工合同（下述判决中所说的“项目合同”，即“Subcontract”），规定由债务人为买方的一家印刷厂提供建设和施工服务（下述判决中所说的“项目”，即“Project”）。该合同的内容既包括提供钢材和其他相关材料，也包括设计、制造和施工等。债务人和买方同意，该合同的主要性质是提供服务而不是出售货物，因此合同不受法典第2篇的管辖。也就是说，从该合同的角度，本案买方实际上是接受服务的一方，而不是购买货物的买方，但是，由于本案争议仅涉及该合同项下的货物，因此法院将接收货物的一方视为买方。

当债务人宣告破产时，与买方订立的合同项目正在施工。当时，债务人计划用于买方项目的一些钢材，分别位于 3 个地方：（1）由债务人占有且正在加工的一批钢材，而买方尚未就这批钢材付款；（2）放置在债务人渥太华工厂的一批钢材，且买方已就其中的部分钢材支付了货款；（3）位于买方项目工地的一批钢材，而买方占有该钢材并已支付了部分货款。所有这些钢材均已被确定用于项目，因此本案当事方承认，这些钢材均已特定化。根据项目合同，买方应根据项目进展分期付款。债务人可以向买方提交付款申请书，要求取得阶段性的付款。买方的上述付款就是根据上述程序作出的。

在债务人破产之后，银行主张有权收回上述钢材，认为自己对钢材持有完善担保权益，而买方对钢材不持有任何担保权益。但买方则认为，自己虽然不持有担保权益，但属于该钢材的“正常业务中的买方”（buyer in ordinary course of business），因而不受制于银行对钢材的完善担保权益。根据法典的规定，在债务人将货物出售给正常业务中的买方之后，受担保方持有的完善担保权益不能对抗该买方。所以，本案的争议集中在两个问题上。第一，对于各批钢材来说，本案买方是否属于正常业务中的买方？第二，从具体时间节点看，本案买方到底何时成为正常业务中的买方？或者说，在债务人破产之日，买方是否已经成为正常业务中的买方？

法院对上述 3 批钢材分别进行了分析。关于第一批钢材，即处于债务人占有之下且买方尚未付款的钢材，买方既未付款，也未取得钢材的占有，因此明显尚未成为正常业务中的买方。因此，银行的完善担保权益对这批钢材具有效力。关于第二批钢材，法院认定，对于买方已付款的那部分钢材，买方属于正常业务中的买方，尽管买方不完全符合法典第 2 篇对正常业务中的买方的定义；但对于买方未付款的那部分钢材，银行则享有优先权。关于第三批钢材，由于买方已取得钢材的占有，因此无论是否已付款，买方对该批钢材都享有优先权。法院的分析是围绕法典对正常业务中的买方的具体要求而进行的，其中主要涉及占有问题和所有权转移问题。

判　决

本案的问题和法典基本原则　对于本案的问题，即“贷款人对卖方库存持有的担保权益何时终止”，应以法典第9篇为起点寻求答案。具体而言，是法典第9.201条和第9.315条。第9.201条规定，担保协议对担保物购买人具有效力。第9.315条规定，“担保物被出售、出租、许可、交换或作其他处置后，其中的担保权益继续存在，除非受担保方允许担保物在处置后不受制于该担保权益”。

正常业务中的买方不受制约　法典第9.201条和第9.315条的正式评论均说明，这些条款的基本原则是，在担保物被出售后，受担保方在担保物中的权益继续存在，除非受担保方同意放弃担保权益，或除非第9篇任何其他条款允许担保物的取得方不受制于其中的担保权益。两项正式评论均提到有关“正常业务中的买方”的第9.320条。这也是本案

The starting point for our answer to the question posed "When does a lender's security interest in a seller's inventory terminate?" is UCC Revised Article 9, and more particularly, UCC § § 9-201 and 9-315. Section 9-201 provides that a security agreement is effective against purchasers of collateral and § 9-315 provides that "a security interest ... continues in collateral notwithstanding sale, lease, license, exchange, or other disposition thereof unless the secured party authorized the disposition free of the security interest...".

The Official Comments to both § § 9-201 and 9-315 explain that these code sections contain the general rule that a secured party's interest in collateral continues upon the sale of the collateral unless the secured party consents to the release of its security interest or one of the provisions in Article 9 under which a party takes free and clear of the security interest applies. Both comments list § 9-320, the "buyer in ordinary course", the code section relied upon by Austin as an

买方所依赖的例外之一。

example of such an exception.

银行提出的所有权问题　但在讨论银行是否已同意担保物可在不受制于其担保权益的情况下被出售，或法典第 9.320 条是否适用于本案任何钢材的出售之前，非常有必要提一下法典第 9.201 条和第 9.315 条对银行主要辩称的影响。银行辩称，决定买方是否不受制于贷款人在担保物中担保权益的关键，在于所有权的转移，而无须考虑买方是否为法典第 9.320 条所述的正常业务中的买方。

However, before moving on to our discussion of whether Commerce consented to the sale of its collateral free of its security interest or whether § 9-320 applies to any of the steel at issue here, it is important to note the effect § § 9-201 and 9-315 have on Commerce's primary argument that the transfer of title determines when a buyer takes collateral free of a lender's security interest, without regard to the buyer's BIOC status under § 9-320.

所有权问题原则上无关紧要　根据法典第 9.201 条和第 9.315 条，对于存在担保权益的货物，买方可以取得所购货物的所有权，只是所有权将受制于贷款人在货物中的担保权益；但正常业务中的买方不受此限。看上去，银行似乎忘记了担保交易的上述基本原则，因为银行太急于划定其优先权最终让位于买方的时间节点，并希望尽可能将该时间节点推迟至钢材用于项目的时间。很难想象像本案银行这样的大型

Under § 9-201 and § 9-315 a buyer (other than a buyer in ordinary course) of goods subject to a security interest takes title to the goods purchased, but that title is subject to the lender's security interest. It seems that Commerce may have lost sight of this fundamental rule of secured transactions in its zeal to fix the point in time when its security interest finally ceded priority to Austin at the last possible moment, i.e., upon the steel's incorporation into the project. It is hard to imagine, though, that Commerce, a major lending institution, does not routinely

贷款机构在一般情况下会不持有这个立场，即买方在购买了银行的担保物后，除非合同或法典另有允许，否则，其所取得的所有权要继续受制于银行的担保权益。但是，银行在这个问题上的前述辩称，确实与该立场和法律规定直接冲突，因此必须被驳回。

本案的两个具体问题 本案所应考虑的正确问题是，银行是否已同意担保物的出售可以不受制于其担保权益？或买方是否属于正常业务中的买方？

银行是否已经同意的问题 关于在债务人出售银行担保物当时，银行是否已表示了同意的问题，当事方未提供任何肯定或否定的证据。但是，当事方共同提交的作为案件附件的债务人和银行之间的担保协议，规定了在何种条件下债务人有权出售担保物，且之后担保物不再受制于银行的担保权益。具体而言，该协议规定，“承诺人（债务人）只要不存在本协议项下的违约，即可出售库存，但必须在正常业务中出售，且只能出售给正常业务

take the position that a buyer who purchases Commerce's collateral, sold without contractual or statutory authorization, takes title to the collateral subject to Commerce's continuing security interest. However, Commerce's argument on this point is directly contrary to that position and the law and, will therefore, be disregarded.

The proper inquiry is whether Commerce consented to the sale of its collateral free of its security interest or whether Austin qualified as a buyer in ordinary course.

The parties did not offer any evidence of Commerce's contemporaneous consent (or lack thereof) to the Debtor's sale of Commerce's collateral, but the security agreement between the Debtor and Commerce submitted as a joint exhibit sets forth the conditions upon which the Debtor has authority to sell Commerce's collateral free and clear of Commerce's security interest. Specifically, it provides that, "while Grantor (the Debtor) is not in default under this Agreement, Grantor may sell Inventory, but only in the ordinary course of its business and only to buyers in the ordinary course of

中的买方”。

因此，根据上述协议条款，买方必须证明，债务人在向买方“出售”库存的当天，债务人不存在违约，且买方属于正常业务中的买方。由于我们在下文中已经判定，买方属于正常业务中的买方，因此我们无须再讨论“出售”这个词如何适用于本案的问题，债务人在出售当天是否处于违约状态的问题，以及银行是否同意了担保物出售的问题。但是，我们必须说明的是，虽然担保协议很可能是银行的固定格式文件，但该协议却否定了银行在庭审时所持的立场，即法典第9.320条不适用于本案的项目合同。

法典对正常业务中的买方的定义　法典第9.320条规定，“正常业务中的买方不受制于其卖方在担保物中设立的担保权益，即使担保权益已获得完善，且买方当时知道担保权益的存在”。第9.320条的正式评论3提到了第1.201条有关正常业务中的买方的定义。该定义的相关部分规定，“正常业务中的买方”是指

business”.

Thus, under this provision Austin would have to show that the Debtor was not in default on the date the Debtor “sold” the inventory to Austin and that Austin qualifies as a buyer in the ordinary course of business. In light of our ruling below regarding Austin's status as a buyer in the ordinary course of business, we do not need to address how the term “sell” applies here, whether the Debtor was in default on the date of the sale, and ultimately, whether Commerce consented to the sale of its collateral; however, we do note that the security agreement, presumably a Commerce form document, belies Commerce's position at trial that § 9-320 does not apply to the Subcontract.

Section 9-320 provides that “a buyer in ordinary course of business takes free of a security interest created by the buyer's seller, even if the security interest is perfected and the buyer knows of its existence”. Official Comment 3 to § 9-320 references § 1-201 for the definition of buyer in ordinary course of business, which, in turn, provides in pertinent part: “Buyer in ordinary course of business” means a person that buys goods

以善意买进货物的人，且该人不知道该销售侵犯了另一人对货物的权利，并以正常方式向从事该类货物销售的卖方买进。如果卖方向任何人作出的销售符合卖方行业的通常或惯常做法，或符合卖方自己的通常或惯常做法，买方即属于以正常方式买进货物。买方只有根据法典第2篇取得货物的占有，或有权追索货物，才有可能成为正常业务中的买方。

in good faith, without knowledge that the sale violates the rights of another person in the goods, and in the ordinary course from a person in the business of selling goods of that kind. A person buys goods in the ordinary course if the sale to the person comports with the usual or customary practices in the kind of business in which the seller is engaged or with the seller's own usual or customary practices. Only a buyer that takes possession of the goods or has a right to recover the goods from the seller under Article 2 may be a buyer in ordinary course of business.

本案买方的状况 根据上述定义，我们认定，对于本案买方已占有的全部钢材，买方属于正常业务中的买方；对于位于渥太华工厂且买方已付款的那部分钢材，买方亦属于正常业务中的买方。

Under this definition, we find that Austin qualifies as a BIOC of all of the steel in its possession, and with regard to the steel located at the Ottawa Plant, Austin is a BIOC of the steel for which it had paid.

其他条件均已满足 法典第1.201条要求买方在买进货物时，必须“以善意买进，且不知道该销售侵犯了另一人对货物的权利，并以正常方式向从事该类货物销售的卖方买进”。这项要求可以轻松得到满足。善意，是指“相关行为或交易中的事实上的

Section 1-201's requirement that Austin buys goods "in good faith, without knowledge that the sale violates the rights of another person in the goods, and in the ordinary course from a person... in the business of selling goods of that kind", is easily dispatched. Good faith in this context means "honesty in fact in the conduct or

诚实”（法典第 1.201 条）。在本案中，无人指控买方与债务人交易时存在不诚实行为，也不存在任何有关不诚实行为的证据。当事方在审理中已承认，上述定义中的其他因素也不存在问题。

时间节点问题　但问题在于，法典并没有说明，在一项交易中，买方到底在哪个时间节点成为正常业务中的买方。因此，这个问题明显需要进行更多的分析。特别是，本院未找到处理过这个问题的密苏里州或堪萨斯州判例。

特定化和所有权转移　关于正常业务中的买方这个尊崇地位何时降临至买方，至少有 5 个潜在的时间节点：订立合同；货物特定化；所有权转移；交付货物；接受货物。但通常认为，真正的时间节点只有两个，即货物特定化和所有权转移。在本案中，对于应以哪个节点为准，毫不奇怪的是，当事方无法达成一致。

银行认为应以所有权为基准　如果认为银行在一定程度上承认，正常业务中的买方是本案的问题之一，那么银行所主张的

transaction concerned”, UCC § 1-201, and there has been no allegation or evidence introduced that Austin was dishonest in its conduct in the transactions with the Debtor. The parties stipulated to the existence of the rest of these elements.

In contrast, because the UCC does not identify the point in a transaction when a buyer attains BIOC status, this element requires considerably more analysis, especially since the Court has not found any dispositive cases from Missouri or Kansas on this issue.

There are at least five potential points at which the ascendancy to the honored role of BIOC can be fixed—upon contracting, upon identification of the goods, upon transfer of title, upon delivery, or upon acceptance of the goods—but only transfer of title and identification have received serious consideration. And, not surprisingly, the parties do not agree on which event controls.

To the extent that Commerce recognizes that BIOC status is an issue here, it advocates using title as the watershed, and as mentioned above, Commerce contends that title did not

立场是，应将所有权作为该身份的“分水岭”。上面提到，银行主张，只有钢材用于项目后，所有权才发生转移(而买方则主张，钢材付款后就取得货物所有权)。反之，买方则辩称，在货物被特定于合同项下时，买方即成为正常业务中的买方。本案当事方承认，全部相关钢材均已特定化。

pass until the steel was incorporated into the project. (Austin maintains that it took title to the steel when it paid for the steel.) Austin, on the other hand, argues that a buyer attains BIOC status when goods are identified to a contract, and the parties have stipulated that all of the steel at issue had been identified.

银行(以及赞成以所有权为决定因素的判例)认为，只有买卖已经发生，买方才能成为正常业务中的买方，而根据法典第2.106条的定义，“买卖”是指所有权从卖方转移至买方，用于换取价款。因此，银行的推理是，购买人只有取得货物所有权之后，才能成为正常业务中的买方。基于4个原因，本院不同意采纳此种立场。

Commerce's position—as well as the position of the cases favoring title as the determining factor—is that a sale must have taken place in order for a purchaser to be a BIOC, and "sale" is defined in UCC Article 2 (§ 2-106) as the passing of title from the seller to the buyer for a price. Therefore, Commerce reasons, a purchaser cannot be a BIOC until it obtains title to goods. The Court declines to adopt this position for four reasons.

银行的主张不能成立 首先，本院认为，银行错误地解释了法典。法典并没有专门要求“买卖”(代以“买卖合同”也同样可行)必须已经发生。并且，即使法典第1.201条暗含了“买卖”的要求，引用第2篇对“买

First, the Court believes that it misconstrues the statute. The statute does not specifically require that a sale has taken place (interposing "contract for sale" would be equally sensible), and to the extent that § 1-201 implicitly requires a sale, the reference to Article 2's definition of sale is unwarranted

卖”的定义也缺乏道理，因为法典第 2 篇已明确淡化了所有权的重要性。也许更重要的是，法典其他条文已对第 2 篇作出了具体的交叉引用。根据制定法解释原则，如果法典某项条款交叉引用了法典第 2 篇，那么，没有提到第 2 篇的其他条款就不应引用第 2 篇。

in light of Article 2's express de-emphasis of the importance of title, and perhaps more importantly, the existence of a specific cross-reference to Article 2 in another part of the statute. Rules of statutory construction dictate that the cross-reference to Article 2 in one section militates against a reference to Article 2 where it is not mentioned.

其次，从法典角度看，将特定化作为基准更合理。法典第 1.201 条的要求之一是（下文将更详细讨论），正常业务中的买方必须占有货物，或“有权根据第 2 篇从卖方索取货物”。所引用的法典这段文字，是指买方根据第 2.502 条从破产卖方索取货物的救济，以及根据第 2.716 条通过“实际履行”取回货物的权利。审阅法典这些条款后可以看到，买方索取货物的权利，取决于特定化，而不取决于所有权（参见法典第 2.502 条；第 2.716 条）。

Second, identification makes more sense in the context of the statute. One of the requirements of § 1-201 （discussed in greater detail below） is that a BIOC either has possession of the goods or has "the right to recover the goods from the seller under Article 2". The quoted section of the statute is understood to refer to a buyer's remedy to recover goods from an insolvent seller under § 2-502 or a buyer's right to replevin or specific performance under § 2-716. A review of these provisions reveals that identification, rather than title, is key to the buyer's right to recover goods. See UCC § § 2-502, 2-716.

再次，判例法的趋势是，明显不再将所有权转移作为买方是否已成为正常业务中的买方的判断标准。在 D 诉 B 案推翻了 C

Third, there is an apparent trend in the case law away from transfer of title as the point at which BIOC status is attained. After Daniel, the case that overruled Chrysler （the

诉A案(以所有权作为基准的经典判例)之后,我们没有看到其他判例判定,只有在所有权转移之后,买方才能成为正常业务中的买方。

seminal case advocating the use of title), there are apparently no cases holding that BIOC status is attained upon the transfer of title.

最后,我们希望说明,从公共政策角度看,以特定化而不是所有权为基准,可以促进法典第9篇的基本宗旨,即保护无辜买方并将损失风险留给受担保方,因为后者有能力通过管控和检测库存来保护自己,并且也许有较强的承受损失的能力。

Finally, from a policy standpoint we note that using identification rather than passage of title advances Article 9's policy of protecting innocent buyers and places the risk of loss on the secured party who has the ability to protect itself by requiring various inventory controls and reports and who may be in a better position to absorb the loss.

应以特定化为标准 因此,本院的结论是,在货物被特定于合同项下之时,买方成为正常业务中的买方。在本案中,当事方已经承认,全部钢材均已特定于项目合同。

Therefore, the Court concludes that a buyer attains BIOC status at the time goods are identified to a contract, and in this case, the parties stipulated that all of the steel had been identified to the Subcontract.

占有或有权追索货物的问题 我们前面已认定,买方在本案交易中所达到的处境,使买方已有可能成为正常业务中的买方。因此,相对任何特定钢材而言,买方是否实际上已成为正常业务中的买方,将取决于其是否满足法典第1.201条的最后一个

Having determined that Austin had reached the point in the transaction when it could qualify for BIOC status, whether Austin actually attained BIOC status with regard to particular steel turns on the final test set forth in § 1-201, which limits BIOC status to buyers who "take possession of the goods or [have] a right to recover the goods from

条件，即买方必须“取得货物的占有，或有权根据第 2 篇从卖方索取货物”。对于放置在项目场地的 402,305 磅钢材（价值 154,485.12 美元），买方已取得实际占有，并已成为正常业务中的买方，因此无须进一步讨论。

the seller under Article 2”. Because Austin had physical possession of the 402,305 pounds of steel （worth $154,485.12） located at the Project site, no further discussion is necessary； Austin was a BIOC with regard to that steel.

普通法中的追索也可适用 对于本案起诉之日位于渥太华工厂的大部分钢材，买方也是正常业务中的买方，但法典对该部分钢材的适用并非直截了当。第一眼看上去，对于在起诉当日尚由债务人占有的这批钢材，买方不属于法典所说的正常业务中的买方，因为买方不实际占有该钢材，并且也没有权利根据法典第 2 篇追索该钢材，因为项目合同不属于法典第 2 篇范围内的合同。

Austin was also a BIOC of most of the steel at the Ottawa Plant as of the petition date, but the application of the statute with regard to that steel is not as straightforward. At first blush, the statute appears to preclude Austin from being a BIOC of the steel in the Debtor’s possession on the petition date because Austin did not have physical possession of that steel and Austin did not have the right to recover it under Article 2, inasmuch as the Subcontract was not covered by Article 2.

法典的立法本意 但是，在比较了法典第 1.201 条的新旧版本之后，以及在分析了旧版判例和新版第 1.201 条正式评论之后，我们认定，只要当事方能证明，其有权根据普通法（相对于法典第 2 篇）“追索”货物，且法典的其他条件也得到满足，

However, upon comparison of the revised § 1-201 to its predecessor statute and a consideration of cases applying the predecessor statute and of the official comment to revised § 1-201, we find that a party that can establish a common law（versus an Article 2-based） “right to recover” may qualify as a BIOC, assuming the other

该当事方就有可能成为正常业务中的买方。

立法历史 旧版法典第1.201条不要求正常业务中的买方必须占有货物或有权根据第2篇向卖方追索货物。适用旧版法典第1.201条的判例也没有这个要求。审阅了适用旧版法典第1.201条的判例后可以看到，之所以将“有权追索”这个要求加入新版法典第1.201条，最有可能的原因是，关于正常业务中的买方，大多数诉讼都涉及货物的追索，即当卖方贷款人对货物持有担保权益时，买方追索或被追索货物。在这种诉讼中，证明对货物的占有权，是追索的一个关键因素（参见F诉E案）。

有关追索权的结论 在考虑了“有权追索”的上述来源后，本院不认为法典第1.201条增加此种要求的目的是将法典项下的救济仅限于法典第2篇的买方。本院的此种解释，也可以得到新版法典第1.201条正式评论9的支持。该评论说，根据法典第1.201条（9）款倒数第二句，如

requirements of the statute are met.

The former UCC § 1-201 did not contain the requirement that a BIOC have possession of or the right to recover the good from the seller under Article 2. Nor did the cases applying former § 1-201. Based on a review of the cases applying former § 1-201, the incorporation of the “right to recover” requirement into revised § 1-201 is most likely a function of the fact that BIOC litigation most often arises in the context of a replevin action brought by or against the buyer of goods in which the seller’s lender has a security interest, and establishing a right to possession is a fundamental element of a replevin action. See First Nat. Bank of Steeleville v. ERB Equipment Co., Inc.

In light of the origins of the “right to recover” requirement, the Court does not believe that the embodiment of that requirement into § 1-201 was intended to limit recourse under the statute to only Article 2 buyers. Official Comment 9 to Revised § 1-201 further supports this interpretation, stating: The penultimate sentence ［of § 1-201（9）］ prevents a buyer that does not

果相对于卖方，买方无权占有货物，则买方就不能成为正常业务中的买方。关于买方何时有权占有货物，应参见法典第 2.502 条和第 2.716 条。但是，如果所涉及的情况是卖方直接将货物交付给买方的下家客户或受赠人，则该倒数第二句无意妨碍买方成为正常业务中的买方。法典此项要求所关心的问题是，在对抗卖方时，买方（或从买方取得货物的下家）是否有权占有货物（新版法典第 1.201 条正式评论 9）。

have the right to possession as against the seller from being a buyer in ordinary course of business. Concerning when a buyer obtains possessory rights, see Sections 2-502 and 2-716. However, the penultimate sentence is not intended to affect a buyer's status as a buyer in ordinary course of business in cases involving delivery by the seller to a person buying from the buyer or a donee from the buyer. The requirement relates to whether as against the seller the buyer or one taking through the buyer has possessory rights. Official Comment 9, Revised § 1-201.

法典上述正式评论说明，第 2 篇新增加的要求只具有参考价值，而不是为了将法典仅限于第 2 篇范围内的合同。因此，本院相信，如果任何当事方在不引用第 2 篇的情况下，可以证明其对货物拥有可对抗卖方的占有权，则该当事方也可以成为法典所述的正常业务中的买方。本院认定，对于放置在渥太华工厂且已被特定于本案项目的钢材，买方拥有此种占有权。

This Comment suggests that the inclusion of the Article 2 "requirement" was for referential value rather than for purposes of restricting the statute to Article 2 contracts. Therefore, the Court believes that a party that establishes its possessory rights over goods as against the seller, without reference to Article 2, also qualifies as a BIOC under this portion of the statute. The Court finds that Austin had such a right with respect to the steel located at the Ottawa Plant and which had been identified for the Project.

普通法中的追索权　普通法至少提供了两种诉讼理由，使本

There are at least two common law causes of action which would give rise to

案买方有权追索货物。毫不意外的是，这些普通法的权利，类似法典第2篇向货物购买人提供的权利。在本案中，根据取回理论［法典第2.716条（3）款］，对于已付款的货物，买方有追索权。同时，买方还享有实际履行的衡平法权利［法典第2.716条（1）款和（2）款］，即对于债务人占有之下的全部钢材，买方有权取得交付；但是，对于尚未付款的钢材，买方有义务支付货款。

Austin's right to recover. And it is no surprise that these parallel similar rights were granted by Article 2 to purchasers of goods. Under a replevin theory （UCC § 2-716（3））, Austin had a right to recover the goods for which it had paid, and Austin had an equitable right to specific performance（UCC § 2-716（1） and （2）） for delivery of all of the steel in the Debtor's possession, although Austin would have to pay for any steel for which payment was owing.

银行被假定不当占有钢材

在密苏里州普通法中，希望成功行使取回权的当事方必须证明其有权占有相关财产，且被告在缺乏授权的情况下控制了财产，且被告因此剥夺了原告占有财产的权利（F诉E案）。但是，在法典第1.201条的假设举例中，以及在本案问题已设定的环境中，普通法的后两项要求无法适用。原因在于，假设本案债务人未发生破产且法院未命令设立分隔账户，则银行本来很可能已经行使了其担保债权人的权利，并取得

To prevail on a replevin claim under Missouri common law, a party must establish that it is entitled to possession of the property, that the defendant has exercised unauthorized control over the property, and that the defendant deprived plaintiff of its right to possession. First Nat. Bank of Steeleville. In the context of the hypothetical posed by § 1-201, and the artificial circumstances in which this issue has arisen, the second two requirements are inapplicable. For in the absence of the Debtor's bankruptcy filing and the Court's order creating the segregated account, Commerce likely would have

了库存的占有或控制。在本案中，必须假定该行为本来会发生，而该行为的后果是，银行本来会取得相关钢材的占有或控制，而买方则会失去钢材。因此，本案买方为证明其有权取回钢材，就仅仅需要证明自己对钢材的占有享有优先权。而本院认定，买方确实享有该优先权，因为买方已为钢材支付了货款。因此（如下文将要讨论的），买方对钢材拥有所有权［参见 S 诉 S 案（对于取回权诉讼来说，所有权虽然不是必要因素，但可用于证明对货物的占有权）；F 诉 B 案］。

付款与所有权的关系　基于当事方已承认的事实和买方所提供的证据，本院前面已认定，对于放置在渥太华工厂的部分钢材，买方已支付 447,260.08 美元。但对于买方为钢材所作的此种付款的效力，当事方存在分歧。买方声称，根据项目合同，该钢材的所有权"至迟在付款之时"转移至买方，而银行则辩称，付款时所有权并未转移，而只有当钢材被用于最终项目时，所有权才

exercised its right as a secured creditor and taken possession or control of the inventory. The effect of that conduct, which must be implied here, would be that Commerce would have been in possession or control of the steel to the exclusion of Austin. Therefore, all that is required here to establish a right to replevin is Austin's superior possessory right to the steel, and the Court finds that Austin has that right because it paid for the steel and, therefore （as discussed below）, held title to the steel. See, e.g., Strothkamp v. St. John's Community Bank, Inc. （title may establish right to possession, although it is not crucial to a replevin action）； Fawley v. Bailey.

Based on the Stipulation and the evidence submitted by Austin, the Court found （above） that Austin paid for $447,260.08 of the steel located at the Ottawa Plant. The parties did not agree, however, as to the effect of Austin's payment for that steel. Austin contends that under the Subcontract title to the steel passed "no later than payment", whereas Commerce argues that title did not pass upon payment, but, rather, title to the steel passed upon incorporation of the steel into the final project. Although the parties

发生转移。虽然当事方为此问题花费了大量时间进行辩论，但本院认为这个问题很容易解决。

合同已规定付款时所有权转移 对于法典第2篇范围之外的合同，所有权在当事方约定的时间转移，而合同是当事方意图的最好证明（M诉M案）。本案当事方有关所有权转移的意图，在项目合同中有明确表述。合同第8.2.1条规定：“供应商（债务人）担保，对于付款申请书所列出的所有工程内容，所有权至迟在付款之时转移至业主（买方）。”为了证明这个本来清晰的条款实际上不够清晰，银行引用了项目合同另一项条款（第8.2.1.3条）。该条规定，“付款申请书不得包含有关下列工程内容的付款请求：尚未被用于工程的材料和设备”。银行辩称，所有权并未在付款之时转移至买方，因为在债务人的付款申请书中，包含了尚未被“用于”工程的钢材。本院不认为银行有权解释一份其并不属于当事方的合同。此外，本院还认为银行的解

spent considerable time debating this point, the Court dispatches it easily.

Under a non-Article 2 contract, title passes at the time agreed upon by the parties, and a contract is the best evidence of the parties' intent. Miller v. Municipal Electric Lighting & Power Co. In this case, the Subcontract provides a clear indication of the parties' intent regarding the passage of title. Paragraph 8.2.1 states: “the Subcontractor (the Debtor) warrants that title to all Work covered by an Application for Payment will pass to the Owner no later than the time of payment.” Commerce attempts to muddy the clarity of this provision by pointing to another provision in the Subcontract (paragraph 8.2.1.3) which states that “[payment] applications shall not include request for payments of amounts on account of materials and equipment not yet incorporated into the Work”, and then arguing that title did not pass to Austin upon payment because it applied for payment on account of steel not yet “incorporated” into the project. Aside from questioning Commerce's standing to interpret a contract to which it was not a party,

释过于牵强，且不合逻辑。

银行的主张不能成立 首先，如同买方在回复银行审前陈述书时曾指出的，银行错误地解释了项目合同第 8.2.1.3 条中“用于”这个词，且完全无视“项目内容”这个词的定义对于“用于”这个词的效力。银行辩称，必须按直白和通常方式来理解“用于”这个词的含义；而根据这种方式，这个词在第 8.2.1 条中是指，债务人无权就尚未实际用于项目的工程内容提出付款申请。

本院同意，应使用直白和通常方式来理解“用于”这个词的含义，而该含义就是，将某种因素结合进另一种已存因素，使两者成为不可分割的整体。银行解释说，“用于”是与“项目”、“建筑”或“结构”这些词相关联的。但实际情况并非如此，因为“用于”系与“工程内容”相关联并被后者限定。“工程内容”是已被定义的词汇，指“项目文件所规定的建设和服务，无论已经全部完成还是部分完成，并且

the Court finds Commerce's interpretation strained and illogical.

First, as Austin pointed out in its response to Commerce's pre-trial brief, Commerce misconstrues the Subcontract's use of the word “incorporate” in paragraph 8.2.1.3 and completely ignores the effect of the defined term “Work” as it relates to “incorporate”. Commerce argues that “incorporate” must be given its plain, ordinary meaning, and that doing so in the context of paragraph 8.2.1 means that the Debtor cannot apply for payment for work not physically incorporated into the Project.

The Court agrees that “incorporate” should be given its plain, ordinary meaning, ie., to unite or work into something already existent so as to form an indistinguishable whole. But “incorporate” is not modified by “Project”, “building”, or “structure” as Commerce's interpretation suggests; rather, “incorporate” is linked to and modified by a defined term, “Work”, which means “the construction and services required by the Subcontract Documents, whether completed or partially completed, and includes all labor, materials, equipment and services provided

包括供应商(债务人)为履行其义务而已经提供或将要提供的所有人工、材料、设备和服务”(项目合同第1.1.6条)。因此,项目合同第8.2.1条清晰无误地规定,对于债务人已经提供的货物或服务,在“工程内容”被实际用于项目之前,债务人就可申请付款。实际上,“工程内容”的定义已专门考虑到了此种付款申请。

其次,对于项目合同,即使我们采纳银行的解释,银行所主张的结果也不合逻辑。所有权转移至买方的时间,仍然不迟于付款时间,即使付款系用于债务人尚无权申请付款的货物。也就是说,即使债务人过早地就尚未被用于项目的货物申请付款,且(假定)此种申请构成违约,只要买方实际上已经作出付款(无论付款的对错),那么,根据合同第8.2.2条的规定,就不能阻止所有权发生转移。因此,本院认定,根据债务人与买方之间的项目合同,对于本诉讼开始前已经付款的所有钢材,买方均

or to be provided by the Subcontractor (the Debtor) to fulfill the Subcontractor's obligations". (Subcontract paragraph 1.1.6) Thus, paragraph 8.2.1 provides unambiguously that the Debtor can apply for payment for goods or services performed before that "work" is actually incorporated into the Project; in fact, the definition of "Work" specifically contemplates such an application.

Second, the result suggested by Commerce does not flow even if we adopt Commerce's interpretation of the Subcontract. Title would still pass to Austin no later than payment, even if the payment was for goods for which the Debtor was not yet entitled to apply for payment. In other words, the Debtor's (hypothetical) breach of the contract by prematurely applying for the payment of goods not yet incorporated into the Project does not prevent paragraph 8.2.2 from transferring title of the goods for which payment (rightly or wrongly) was made. Therefore, the Court finds that under the Subcontract between the Debtor and Austin, Austin held title to all of the steel for which

取得了所有权，并因此有权取回该钢材。

买方有权获得实际履行　根据密苏里州法律，如果法律不能向原告提供充分救济，且合同是公平和清晰的，则作为权利问题，原告有权获得实际履行［L 破产案（其中引用 M 诉 C 案）］。相对于动产买卖，实际履行更多地应用于不动产买卖，但只要货物具有独特性，或难于从其他地方获得，实际履行就属于货物买卖的适当救济［L 破产案；B 诉 V 案（法院指令汽车经销商就出售汽车的买卖合同作出实际履行，因为当时新车极难买到）］。

在本案中，部分钢材是专门采购的，部分钢材是根据买方规格定制的，法律无法提供充分救济，因此有理由判决实际履行。本院认定，本案当事方对钢材价值的确认，已证明合同是公平和清晰的。虽然在提起诉讼之日，位于渥太华工厂的某些钢材还没有达到可交付的状态，但这不妨碍买方取回该货物的权利，因为当事方对钢材价值的确认，已经

payment was made as of the petition date, and thereby had the right to replevin that steel.

Under Missouri law, a plaintiff is entitled to specific performance as a matter of right if there is no adequate remedy at law and the contract is fair and plain. In re Laclede Gas Co. v. Amoco Oil Co. （citing Miller v. Coffeen）. Although specific performance relating to the sale of personal property is less common than for real estate, specific performance is appropriate when the goods are unique or difficult to obtain elsewhere. Id; Boeving v. Vandover （ordering an auto dealer to specifically perform on a contract for the sale of a car at a time when new cars were extremely difficult to obtain）.

In this case, specific performance is warranted because there is no adequate remedy at law, inasmuch as the steel at issue had either been custom-ordered or fabricated to Austin's specifications, and the Court finds that the contract was fair and plain, as evidenced by the parties' stipulation to the values of the steel at issue. That some of the steel at the Ottawa Plant may not have been ready for delivery as of the petition date is not a barrier to Austin's recovery here because the

考虑到尚未交付且仅部分完成了制造的钢材的较低价值。

values to which the parties stipulated account for the lesser value of the undelivered, partially fabricated steel.

简言之,本院重申以上认定,即虽然法典第1.201条要求正常业务中的买方必须有权根据第2篇追索货物,但该条也同时暗含了根据第2篇以外其他法律追索货物的权利。根据普通法中取回货物的权利,或取得实际履行的权利,买方有权追索已付款但尚未取得交付的钢材。

In short, the Court reiterates its findings in this section that § 1-201's requirement that a BIOC have a right to recover the goods under UCC Article 2 encompasses the right to recover goods under non-Article 2 law, and Austin had a right to recover the undelivered steel for which Austin paid under either a common law replevin or specific performance theory.

买方已取得推定占有 从另一角度看,买方也已满足了法典第1.201条的要求,即买方必须"取得货物的占有,或有权根据第2篇追索货物",因为对于已付款但尚未获得交付的钢材,买方取得了"推定占有"。根据本院的解释,法典所说的"占有"包含了"推定占有"。

Austin also fulfills § 1-201's requirement that Austin "take possession of the goods or [have] a right to recover the goods from the seller under Article 2", because Austin had "constructive possession" of the paid-for, undelivered steel, and the Court interprets "possession" as used in the statute to include "constructive possession".

推定占有的概念 推定占有的概念被应用于很多场合。这个概念承认,在有些情况下,即使没有取得实际的、物理意义上的占有,但由于相关人占有该物品的权利或能力足够强大,因

Constructive possession is a concept, used in a variety of contexts, which recognizes that there are circumstances under which the right or ability to possess an object is strong enough to give rise to the legal effect of "possession" in the absence of actual

此法律承认，该情况已产生等同于“占有”的法律效力［参见 V 诉 F 案（该案讨论了取得仓单交付后的推定占有）；E 诉 A 案（该案承认，在取回权诉讼中，被告如果控制货物并有能力交付货物，即被视为推定占有原告的货物）；另参见 S 诉 C 案（该案对不同情况作出区别。当一个人自身携带毒品，或可轻易获取并严密控制毒品时，就属于“实际占有”，而当其有权力和意愿在特定时间对毒品行使所有权或控制时，无论是直接行使还是通过其他人行使，都属于“推定占有”）］。因此，本院认定，为满足法典第 1.201 条所述的要求，买方在为钢材作出付款并取得所有权后，即对钢材取得了足够程度的占有权，使其就该钢材取得了推定占有。

physical possession. See, e.g., Vogelsang's Adm' r v. Fisher (discussing constructive possession conferred upon delivery of a warehouse receipt); Emory v. Arnold (acknowledging that action in replevin will lie against defendant in constructive possession of plaintiffs goods if defendant has control over and ability to deliver those goods). See also, State v. Chavez (drawing distinction between "actual possession" of an illegal substance, where the person has the substance on his person or within his easy reach and convenient control, and "constructive possession", where a person has the power and intention at a given time to exercise dominion or control over the substance either directly or through another person or persons). Accordingly, the Court finds that Austin's possessory rights, arising from Austin's payment for and title to the steel, were sufficiently strong to imbue Austin with constructive possession of the steel, in the context of § 1-201.

法典支持推定占有的解释

本院的上述解释，即法典第 1.201 条所要求的“占有”也包含推定占有，可以得到法典的支持。因

The Court interpretation of "possession", as used in § 1-201, to encompass constructive possession is supported by the fact that the UCC does not define possession and the

为，一方面，法典未对“占有”作出定义；另一方面，法典第9.313条正式评论3说，在法典中，“占有”不要求实际占有。尽管该正式评论未具体使用“推定占有”这个词，但其意在说明，在当事方并不实际占有担保物时，应根据代理法的原则来确定该当事方是否可被视为推定占有担保物。

suggestion in the Official Comment to § 9-313 that “possession” in the code does not require actual possession. Official Comment 3 states that agency principles should be applied to determine whether a party not in actual possession of collateral should be considered to have constructive possession of it, although the comment does not use that specific term.

例如，对于某些担保物（如票式证券），只有取得占有，才能使其中的担保权益获得完善，但法典规定，如果受担保方的代理人占有担保物，担保权益仍然可以获得完善。法典上述正式评论还继续说，如果债务人所控制的其他人持有担保物，则即使表面上该人系为受担保方的利益持有担保物，法院仍可认定，也许债务人应被视为持有担保物（并导致担保权益不能获得完善）［参见怀特教授和萨莫斯教授的著作（其中讨论了第9篇范围内担保权益的完善问题）］。

So, for example, a secured creditor may have a perfected security interest in certain collateral, e.g., a certificated security, for which possession is necessary to perfect, if the secured creditor’s agent is in possession of the collateral. The Comment goes on to say that a court could find that the debtor may have possession of the collateral （thereby defeating perfection）, if the collateral is possessed by a person in control of the debtor, even if that person holds the collateral for the ostensible benefit of the secured creditor. See also, J. White & R. Summers, Handbook of the Law under the Uniform Commercial Code （discussing perfection by possession under Article 9）.

由于法典正式评论对“占有”

Thus, in light of the flexible definition

这个词的定义持灵活态度，本院认定，即使货物的卖方在货款已全额支付且所有权已转移至买方后仍然留持货物，视买方已取得法典第 1.201 条所述的占有，应属适当。

of possession contemplated by the Official Comment, the Court finds it appropriate to apply that term, as it is used in § 1-201, to the situation where a seller of goods retains the goods after full payment for those goods and the transfer of title to the buyer.

此外，在本案中适用推定占有原则，还可以促进法典第 1.201 条（和第 9.320 条）所明显体现出的目的，即通过赋予正常业务中的买方这个地位的方式，来保护无辜买方［参见 C 诉 A 案（法院说，“如果买卖已经发生，且买方已经取得货物的所有权，就不能仅因为买方尚未取得货物占有而不承认其为正常业务中的买方”）］。

Further, the decision to apply constructive possession principles here also advances the apparent goal of § 1-201 （and § 9-320）, which is to provide BIOC protection to innocent buyers. See Chrysler Corp. v. Adamatic （“It seems clear that, if there is a sale and the buyer has obtained title to the goods, his status as a buyer in ordinary course will not be defeated merely because he has not taken possession”）.

因此，本院认定，对于放置在渥太华工厂的钢材，买方就其已付款的那部分钢材，取得了该钢材的推定占有，且此种占有满足了法典第 1.201 条有关正常业务中的买方必须占有货物的要求。

Thus, the Court finds that with regard to the steel located at the Debtor's Ottawa Plant and for which Austin had paid, Austin had constructive possession of that steel and such possession satisfies § 1-201's requirement that a BIOC have possession of the goods.

结论 归纳而言，基于以上说明的原因，本院认定，在提起本诉讼之日，关于银行在已特定

In sum, for the reasons stated above, the Court finds that Commerce's security interest in the steel identified to the Austin project as

于买方项目的钢材中所持的担保权益，在买方成为法典第 9.320 条所述的正常业务中的买方后，该担保权益即行终止。本院进一步认定，对于买方占有下的价值 154,485.12 美元的钢材，以及买方已付款且放置在债务人渥太华工厂的价值 384,017.08 美元的钢材，买方属于正常业务中的买方。因此，对于争议中的 732,283.56 美元的钢材，买方就其中总计 538,502.20 美元的钢材享有优于银行的权益。

of the petition date terminated to the extent Austin qualifies as a buyer in ordinary course of business under UCC § 9-320. The Court further finds that Austin qualifies as a buyer in ordinary course of business with regard to the $154,485.12 worth of steel in Austin's possession and the $384,017.08 worth of steel for which Austin had paid, and which was located at the Debtor's Ottawa Plant. Thus, in total, Austin has an interest superior to Commerce in $538,502.20 of the $732,283.56 of steel at issue.

案例 41　应收款的转让是否属于担保交易?

In Re Tri-County Materials, Inc.
三县材料公司破产案

伊利诺伊州中区联邦地区法院 1990 年；114 B.R. 160

简　介

在本破产案中，破产债务人（Tri-County）在破产前经营沙石矿。本案买方（Ladd）是工程公司，因工程需要，与债务人订立了购买沙石的合同。债务人为了向买方供应沙石，需要添加工程设备，因此与本案出租方（KMB）订立了租赁设备的合同。租赁合同规定，为了向出租方支付设备的租赁费，债务人将买方未来应向债务人支付的沙石货款转让给出租方。债务人和出租方随后将租赁合同的这项条款通知了买方，要求买方在购买沙石后，向债务人核实设备应付的租赁费，然后将相应数额的沙石货款直接支付给出租方。这项安排相当于债务人把未来应收款的一部分转让给了出租方。

随后，债务人宣布破产。截至破产日，债务人尚欠出租方 30,484 美元。同时，买方尚欠债务人较大一笔沙石货款。在破产程序中，出租方基于与债务人之间的包含了应收款转让条款的租赁合同，要求买方向出租方支付债务人尚未付清的设备租赁费。债务人此时已成为破产财产的经管人（debtor in possession），并代表破产财产对出租方的主张提出异议，认为债务人向出租方转让应收款的安排属于担保交易。根据法典第 9.302 条（1）（e）款的规定，在此种转让中，出租方相当于受担保方，并且，除非此种转让属于债务人应收款非“重要部分”（significant part）的转让，否则只有在登记融资声明后，才能使出租方的担保权益获得完善，而在本案中，当事方未登记融资声明。

在法典第 9 篇中，应收款的转让被推定视为担保交易。因此，当事方即使实际上只是转让应收款，也要按第 9 篇的规定登记融资声明，否则受让方的权利可能得不到法律承认。但法典规定了一项例外，即如果所转让的应收款不构成债务人应收款的“重要部分”，就无须对该转让进行登记。在本案中，当事方并没有登记，因此，如果所转让的是应收款的“重要部分”，那么出租方的担保权益就并未获得完善，因而可被债务人撤销。在这种情况下，出租方只能作为无担保债权人参与破产程序的分配。

法典本身没有对“重要部分”作出定义。最终，联邦地区法院认定，“重要部分”有两个标准：一个是百分比标准，另一个是“偶然”标准，而两个标准都必须同时达到。在本案中，所转让的应收款占总应收款的比例较低，因此从这个角度看，所转让的应收款不是“重要部分”。但是，虽然此次转让是孤立的，但并不是“偶然”的，因此未能满足第二个标准。由于本案的转让未能同时达到两个标准，地区法院维持了破产法院的判决，即本案所转让的应收款是“重要部分”，因此，由于当事方未进行登记，因此出租方所取得的担保权益未获得完善，在破产程序中无效，致使出租方只能作为无担保债权人参与破产程序的分配。

判　决

破产法院的判决　破产法院判决，设备出租方对于买方欠债务人的款项，不持有有效的担保

Pending before the Court is an appeal and cross-appeal of the bankruptcy court's decision that KMB, Inc. did not have a valid

权益。当事方提起上诉。基于以下说明的原因，本院维持破产法院的判决。

出租方的主张 债务人申请破产时，欠出租方共计 30,484 美元。出租方称，在债务人欠出租方的数额限度内，债务人已将买方欠债务人的应付款转让给出租方。因此，出租方对买方的应付款持有担保权益。

应收款转让的例外 法典第 9.302 条规定：“（1）为使担保权益获得完善，必须登记融资声明，但下列情况除外……（e）应收款的转让，只要该转让无论单独计算，还是与向同一受让人的其他转让合并计算，均不构成转让人未结应收款的重要部分。”

出租方认为不构成重要部分的理由 出租方主张，其有权根据法典第 9.302 条（1）（e）款主张权利，因为自己日常业务不包括应收款融资，所以本案交易属于偶然和孤立的交易。同时，债务人欠出租方的款项，仅占债务人有权从买方收取的 250,000

security interest in funds owing to the Debtor. For the reasons stated below, the bankruptcy court is affirmed.

Tri-County owed KMB $30,484 at the time of filing bankruptcy. KMB claims that, because Tri-County assigned its right to receive payments from Ladd to the extent that it owed money to KMB, it had a security interest in the money owed to Tri-County.

Ill.Rev.Stat. § 9-302 provides: “（1） a financing statement must be filed to perfect all security interests except the following ... （e） an assignment of accounts which does not alone or in conjunction with other assignments to the same assignee transfer a significant part of the outstanding accounts of the assignor.”

KMB takes the position that it is entitled to rely on § 9-302（1）（e） because it is not regularly engaged in accounts receivable financing, thus making this a casual and isolated transaction, and because the amount which Tri-County owed to KMB, when compared to the $250,000 which Tri-County was entitled to receive from Ladd was a mere

美元中的12%。因此，该应收款的转让不属于其应收款重要部分的转让。债务人辩称，出租方未能满足法典两项要求中的任何一项，因此不对买方的应付款持有完善担保权益。

12%, thus making it an insignificant transfer. Tri-County argues that because KMB fails to meet either test it did not have a perfected security interest in the Ladd account.

两个标准 主张享有法典第9.302条（1）（e）款所述例外的当事方，对法典该款的适用性承担举证责任（参见C诉U案）。虽然法典没有对"重要部分"作出定义，但判例法发展出两个标准。

The burden of proving the applicability of § 9-302（1）（e） rests on the party asserting the exception. See, Consolidated Film Industries v. United States. Although the Code does not define "significant part", case law has developed two tests.

第一个标准是百分比标准。其关注点在于所转让的部分在未结应收款的整体中的占比（B破产案；S诉C案）。第二个标准是"偶然或孤立"标准。这是法典第9.302条正式评论5所建议的标准。该评论说："本条（1）（e）款所述例外的目的在于，对于偶然或孤立的转让，法典不会在交易完成后再将其视为无效。应收款的某些法律过于宽泛，致使所有的应收款转让都必须进行法律所规定的登记，而无论转让的性质或目的。对于一些没有任何当事方会想到登记的转让，

The first test is referred to as the percentage test. This test focuses on the size of the assignment in relation to the size of outstanding accounts. In re B. Hollis Knight Co.; Standard Lumber Company v. Chamber Frames, Inc. The second test is the "casual or isolated" test. This test is suggested by the language of Comment 5 to UCC § 9-302 which states that: "The purpose of the subsection （1）（e） exemptions is to save from ex post facto invalidation casual or isolated assignments: some accounts receivable statutes have been so broadly drafted that all assignments, whatever their character or purpose, fall within their

法律仍可能会因缺乏登记而认定转让无效。这类转让，就是本条（1）（e）款所述的例外。一个人如果经常接受债务人应收款的转让，那就应该进行登记。”

filing provisions. Under such statute many assignments which no one would think of filing may be subject to invalidation. The subsection （1）（e） exemptions go to that type of assignment. Any person who regularly takes assignments of any debtor's accounts should file.”

在确定一项转让是否为偶然或孤立时，需要考虑交易的整体事实。如果交易不属于惯常商业融资活动的一部分，则根据这个标准，就无须进行登记。这个标准的理由大概在于，如果债务人应收款的转让属于日常业务的一部分，要求担保债权人登记就是合理要求；反之，对于偶然或孤立的交易，登记可能就是不合理要求。

The totality of circumstances surrounding the transaction determines whether an assignment was casual or isolated. If the transaction was not part of a regular course of commercial financing then under this test filing is not required. The rationale appears to be the reasonableness of requiring a secured creditor to file if assignment of debtor's accounts is a regular part of business and the corresponding unreasonableness of a filing requirement for casual or isolated transactions.

应同时满足两个标准　关于是否必须同时满足上述两个标准后才能适用法典的例外，还是满足其中任何一个标准即可，不存在权威判例。本案的破产法院认可 B 破产案的判决，即两个标准都必须得到满足，而本院也认可该原则。法典的文字特别规定，转让必须是未结应收款的非重要

There is no authoritative determination of whether both tests must be met in order to claim the exemption or whether either by itself is sufficient. The bankruptcy court agreed with the Hollis Knight court which held that both tests must be met. This Court agrees with that assessment. The statutory language specifically requires that the assignment be an insignificant part of the outstanding account.

部分。因此，每项转让都至少需要满足这个标准。如果一项转让是未结应收款的重要部分，那么即使可证明其是偶然或孤立的，也不能享有例外，因为不符合法典的明确规定。反之，考虑到法典正式评论有关此种例外的目的，则即使转让是未结应收款并不重要的一部分，但如果是转让给惯常从事融资业务的债权人，此种应收款也不应享有例外。基于法典该条的文字和目的，要求两项标准都必须得到满足是合乎逻辑的。

Thus, at the very least, this test must be met in every instance. A showing of a casual or isolated assignment of a significant part of outstanding accounts would not be entitled to the exemption given this clear statutory requirement. On the other hand, given the comments to the UCC regarding the purpose of this exemption, in a case involving the transfer of an insignificant part of outstanding accounts to a creditor whose regular business is financing, such accounts should not fall within this exemption. Thus it is a logical result of the language and purpose of this section to require that both tests be met.

所转让的应收款占比较低

在法典中，应收款是指“因出售或出租货物或因提供服务而获得的收取付款的权利，无论该权利是否通过己方履约已赚取”（法典第 9.106 条）。本案债务人的破产债务登记表显示，在提出破产重组申请时，债务人有 10 项应收款，其中远超其他各项的最大一项，就是应从本案买方收取的 250,000 万美元。根据向出租方所作之转让的规定，出租方可

Under the UCC, an account is “any right to payment for goods sold or leased or for services rendered which is not evidenced by an instrument or chattel paper, whether or not it has been earned by performance” . Ill. Rev.Stat. § 9-106. The Debtor’s bankruptcy schedules indicate that Tri-County had ten accounts at the time of the Chapter 11 filing, of which the largest by far was the Ladd contract for $250,000. The assignment to KMB permitted KMB to: “request that the Ladd Construction Company...make any and

"要求买方将其欠债务人的款项的部分或全部支付给出租方"。

all payments to [Tri-County]."

显然，债务人未将买方的全部应付款都转让给出租方，而只是转让了债务人欠出租方的那部分款项。在当事方订立转让协议时，预估的设备租金总额为 30,000 美元，而最终的实际数额为 30,484 美元。因此，即使假定买方应付的款项是债务人的唯一应收款，转让的数额也只占债务人总应收款的大约 12%。

It is thus clear that the assignment was not of the entire Ladd account but only of that portion of the account necessary to cover the balance due to KMB. At the time the parties entered into the Agreement, the total rental amount was estimated at $30,000; the actual figure turned out to be $30,484. The ratio of the amount assigned to the total account, even assuming that the Ladd contract was the only account, is approximately 12%.

虽然在重要部分和非重要部分之间不存在明确界限，但 12% 的比例无疑偏向非重要部分［参见 S 诉 C 案（16% 属于非重要部分）］。因此，与本案破产法院的认定相反，上述第一个标准实际上已满足。破产法院之所以认定为不满足，是假定债务人已将买方的全部应付款均转让给出租方，但这项假定没有证据支持。

Although there is no bright line marking the division between significant and insignificant, the 12% figure is surely on the "insignificant" side. See, Standard Lumber Co. v. Chamber Frames, Inc. (16% insignificant). Thus, the first test, contrary to what the bankruptcy court found, has been satisfied. The bankruptcy court based its finding on the assumption that Tri-County had assigned the entire Ladd account to KMB, an assumption that is not supported by the record.

不属于偶然交易　案件证据还毫无争议地显示，出租方的业

The record also shows without contradiction that KMB was not in the business of

务不包括接受合同的转让，且本案转让交易的任何一方从未进行过这类交易。破产法院认定，尽管这次转让具有“孤立”性质，但该转让属于“典型的担保交易”，因此不属于可以免于登记的“偶然和孤立”的那类例外。

accepting contract assignments, nor had either party to the assignment engaged in such a transaction at other times. The bankruptcy court found that despite the “isolated” nature of this assignment, it was “a classic secured transaction”, and thus failed to fall within the “casual and isolated” exception to the filing requirement.

本院同意破产法院的认定。这不是那类“偶然”交易，不属于通情达理的当事方未能意识到登记之重要性的交易。相反，双方均为公司，并就该交易订立了正式书面协议，还向买方发送了协议的通知。出租方的其他行为，也体现了当事方对该交易的重视程度。这正是法典所要求的通过登记来取得完善权益的那类交易。

This Court agrees with that assessment. This is not the type of “casual” transaction in which reasonable parties would fail to see the importance of filing. Rather, it was evidenced by a formal, written agreement between two corporations; notice of the agreement was sent to Ladd, and other conduct engaged in by KMB indicates the degree of formality attached to it. This is the type of transaction for which the UCC requires filing in order to perfect.

结论 由于出租方未能使其担保权益获得完善，本院维持破产法院的原判。

Because KMB failed to perfect its security interest, this Court affirms the bankruptcy court’s ruling.

案例 42　受担保方是否对新债务人的后得财产持有完善担保权益？

Retail Marketing Co. v. Core-Mark Mid-Continent, Inc.
零售经销公司诉考马克中陆公司案

联邦第十巡回上诉法院 1995 年；50 F.3d 1520, 26 U.C.C. Rep. Serv. 2d 563

简　介

本案破产债务人（MAKO）在破产前经营连锁便利店。出于经营需要，破产债务人之前曾从本案融资方（Coremark）取得融资，并将其当时持有的以及随后取得的（after-acquired）全部库存，以及库存的任何收益，均作为担保物提供给融资方。融资方登记了融资声明，其中列出了上述担保物，并将破产债务人列为债务人。

破产债务人随后进入破产重组程序。根据破产重组计划，本案收购方（RMC）收购了破产债务人便利店的部分库存，并接手了便利店的经营。重组计划规定，对于收购方所收购的库存，融资方原来持有的担保权益将继续保持有效。收购方为此另行签署了本票和担保协议，承认了融资方原有的担保权益。重组完成之后，融资方没有登记新的融资声明。收购方接手便利店后，将原有库存逐渐售出，并用所得货款购进了新库存。随后，收购方也宣告破产。

在收购方的破产程序中，融资方和收购方发生争议并引起本诉讼。双方都同意，对于收购方从破产债务人所实际收购的那些库存（旧库存），融资方继续持有完善担保权益。双方的争议在于，对于该库存售出后，收购方用其收益再度取得的库存（新库存），融资方是否仍然持有完善担保权益。融资方认为，由于其对旧库存持有完善担保权益，且担保协议覆盖了后得财产，因此融资方对该库存的后得财产（新库存）也持有完善担保权益。收购方认为，对于新库存，由于债务人已经更换，因此融资方必须登记新的融资声明，而由于其并未登记，因此其对新库存的担保权益没有获得完善。

根据法典的一般规定，担保物被转让后，其中的担保权益继续存在；并且，如果原来的担保权益是完善的，则担保权益将继续保持完善。因此，担保物被转让后，受担保方通常无须登记新的融资声明。但在本案中，当事方争议的主要问题是，法典所说的“被转让的担保物”到底是指什么？是仅指旧库存，还是也包括新库存？由于原有的担保协议包含了后得财产，因此，从某种意义上可以说，由于担保物中已包含了后得财产，因此，“被转让的担保物”自然也同时包含旧库存和新库存。

上诉法院的分析主要集中于法典第 9.402 条（7）款第三句的解释。对于法典的这项条款，不同法院的解释存在分歧，但本案上诉法院认为，破产债务人转让给收购方的担保物，仅包括其实际转让的旧库存，而不包括收购方随后取得的新库存。在转让完成之后，债务人发生变化，从原有的破产债务人转化为收购方这个新债务人。根据法典规定，在债务人发生变化后，受担保方需要登记新的融资声明。据此，上诉法院判决，融资方由于没有针对新债务人（收购方）登记新融资声明，因此对新库存的担保权益没有获得完善。

判　决

破产法院的判决　破产法院驳回了收购方的主张并否决了其

The bankruptcy court rejected this argument and denied the motion. In so

动议。法院的判决依据是法典第 9.402 条（7）款。该款相关部分规定，“如果债务人将担保物转让，已登记的融资声明对被转让的担保物继续有效，即使受担保方知道或同意该转让”。根据这项规定，破产法院的结论是，“担保物”一词也包括后得财产，并因此判定，融资方已登记的且覆盖了破产债务人担保物的融资声明仍然有效，并使融资方在收购方的后得库存中的担保权益保持有效，而“无须以收购方名字重新进行登记”。

holding, the bankruptcy court relied on Okla. Stat.Ann. Sec. 9-402（7）, which provides in pertinent part that “［a］ filed financing statement remains effective with respect to collateral transferred by the debtor even though the secured party knows of or consents to the transfer”. Under this provision, the bankruptcy court concluded that the term “collateral” encompassed after-acquired property. Thus, the court held that Coremark's financing statement covering the MAKO collateral remained effective and served to perfect its security interest in RMC's after-acquired inventory “without the necessity of refiling a financing statement in ［RMC's］ name”.

地区法院的判决　收购方上诉后，地区法院推翻了破产法院的判决。具体而言，地区法院判定，根据法典第 9.402 条（7）款，融资方的融资声明只对破产债务人根据重组计划所实际转让的担保物继续有效。因此，地区法院的结论是，对于收购方随后取得的后得库存，融资方的担保权益未获得完善，因为融资方没有重新登记将收购方列为债务人的融

RMC appealed to the district court which reversed the bankruptcy court's holding. Specifically, the district court held that under Sec. 9-402（7）, Coremark's financing statement remained effective only as to the collateral actually transferred by MAKO under the bankruptcy plan. Thus, the district court concluded that Coremark's security interest in RMC's after-acquired inventory was unperfected because Coremark failed to file a new financing statement naming RMC

资声明。因此，地区法院作出了有利于收购方的无审判决，而融资方提起本上诉。

as the debtor. Consequently, the district court granted summary judgment in favor of RMC. This appeal followed.

融资方的主张 在本上诉中，融资方辩称，地区法院无审判决收购方胜诉是错误的。具体而言，融资方主张，根据法典第9.402条（7）款，将破产债务人列为债务人的已登记融资声明，可使融资方在收购方的后得库存中的担保权益获得完善。在本上诉中，我们将彻底重新审查地区法院的无审判决（E诉J案）。

On appeal, Coremark argues the district court erred in granting summary judgment in favor of RMC. Specifically, Coremark contends that under Sec. 9-402（7）, the financing statement it filed naming MAKO as the debtor served to perfect its security interest in RMC's after-acquired inventory. We review the district court's grant of summary judgment de novo. Eaton v. Jarvis Products Corp.

本案问题受州法管辖 根据《破产法》(引用《破产法》)，破产程序开始后，重组计划中的经管债务人（本案中的收购方）可作为虚拟留置权债权人而主张该债权人的权利。留置权债权人的权利由州法确定（M破产案中的W诉U案）。根据俄克拉何马州法律，留置权债权人的权利优于未完善受担保方的权利[法典第9.301条(1)(b)(3)款]。因此，在破产程序中，如果债权人的担保权益未获得完善，该债权人即“被视为无担保债权人，

Pursuant to 11 U. S. C. Sec. 544（a）（1）, a debtor-in-possession （RMC in this case） may assert the rights of a hypothetical lien creditor once it files a bankruptcy petition. The rights of a lien creditor are determined by state law. Woodson v. Utica Square Nat'l Bank of Tulsa （In re McClain）. Under Oklahoma law, a lien creditor has priority over an unperfected, secured creditor. Okla.Stat.Ann. 9-301(1)(b)（3）. Thus, in a bankruptcy proceeding, if the creditor's security interest is not perfected, the creditor "stands as [a] general unsecured creditor who must defer to the

并受制于破产受托人的权利”（C 破产案中的 J 诉 S 案，其中引用 M 破产案）。

trustee”. Jones v. Small Business Admin.（In re Cohutta Mills, Inc., quoting In re Merts Equipment Co.）

担保权益获得完善的原则 根据俄克拉何马州法律，受担保方使担保权益获得完善的条件之一是填写并登记融资声明。其中应描述担保权益所涉及的担保物，并列出债务人的名字［法典第 9.302 条（1）款］。融资声明登记之后，担保权益即获得完善（法典第 9.303 条），并使受担保方免受同一担保物中冲突权益的威胁（法典第 9.312 条）。

Under Oklahoma law, a secured creditor perfects a security interest in part by preparing and filing a financing statement describing the collateral subject to the security interest and naming the debtor. Okla.Stat.Ann. 9-302（1）. Once a financing statement is filed, the security interest becomes perfected. Sec. 9-303, protecting the secured party against conflicting interests in the same collateral. Sec. 9-312.

法典第 9.402 条规定了融资声明初始登记和后续修订的形式要求。该条（7）款规定，在某些特定情况下，受担保方有义务重新登记融资声明。关于债务人的名字，只要融资声明列出了债务人的个人、合伙或公司名字，则无论是否还添加了商号或各位合伙人的名字，融资声明对债务人的描述都被视为充分。

Section 9-402 covers the formal requisites of the initial filing and subsequent amendment of a financing statement. Subsection（7）addresses a secured party’s duty to refile a financing statement in certain enumerated instances. A financing statement sufficiently shows the name of the debtor if it gives the individual, partnership or corporate name of the debtor, whether or not it adds other trade names or the names of partners.

债务人变化后需要重新登记 当债务人的名字发生较大

Where the debtor so changes his name, or in the case of an organization, its name,

变化时，或当债务人系组织时，如果其名字、识别特征或公司结构发生较大变化，致使已登记的融资声明具有严重误导性质，那么，对于债务人在该变化4个月之后取得的担保物，原登记不再具有使担保物中担保权益保持完善的效力，除非在该4个月期限到期之前，重新登记适当的融资声明。对于被债务人转让的担保物，原登记的融资声明则继续有效，即使受担保方知道或同意该转让[法典第9.402条(7)款]。

identity, or corporate structure that a filed financing statement becomes seriously misleading, the filing is not effective to perfect a security interest in collateral acquired by the debtor more than four (4) months after the change, unless a new appropriate financing statement is filed before the expiration of that time. A filed financing statement remains effective with respect to collateral transferred by the debtor even though the secured party knows of or consents to the transfer. Okla. Stat.Ann. Sec. 9-402(7).

上述第9.402条(7)款的第二句规定，受担保方有义务在某些特定情况下重新登记融资声明，例如，"'新'债务人成为债务人的后继公司，并导致债务人的识别特征或结构发生变化"(B破产案中的B诉F案，其中引用了B诉C案)。形成对照的是，第9.402条(7)款的第三句仅适用于"担保物被善意地转让给与转让人无关的第三方"这类情况(B诉C案)。

Under this section, the second sentence addresses a secured creditor's obligation to refile a financing statement in instances where there has been a "change in the identity or structure of the debtor in which the 'new' debtor is a successor enterprise of the original debtor". Bluegrass Ford-Mercury, Inc. v. Farmers Nat'l Bank of Cynthiana. (In re Bluegrass Ford-Mercury, Inc., citing Bank of the West v. Commercial Credit Fin. Serv.) In contrast, the third sentence applies only to those instances where there has been a "bona fide transfer [of collateral] to third parties unrelated to the transferor". Bank of the West.

本案的关键问题　将上述原则应用于本案后，当事方同意，与本案事实相吻合的唯一法典条款，是第9.402条(7)款的第三句。根据该句的规定，当事方同意，对于破产债务人根据重组计划向收购方实际转让的担保物，融资方的担保权益继续保持完善。但是，当事方对于下述问题持不同意见：在破产债务人完成转让后，如果收购方又取得新担保物，那么，将破产债务人列为债务人的融资声明是否仍能使融资方的担保权益获得完善？因此，本上诉中我们必须解决的核心问题是，根据法典第9.402条（7）款最后一句，对于破产债务人完成转让后收购方新获得的担保物，融资方的融资声明是否可使其担保权益保持完善？

Applying these principles to the instant case, the parties agree that the only provision applicable to the facts before us is the third sentence of Sec. 9-402（7）. Under this provision, the parties agree that Coremark's security interest remained perfected in the collateral actually transferred to RMC under the MAKO plan. The parties disagree, however, as to whether the financing statement naming MAKO as the debtor operated to perfect Coremark's security interest in collateral acquired by RMC after the MAKO transfer. Thus, the central issue we must resolve in this appeal is whether under the last sentence of Sec. 9-402（7）, Coremark's financing statement perfected its security interest in collateral acquired by RMC after the MAKO transfer.

对融资方有利的判例　不同法院曾对法典第9.402条（7）款作出过解释，但结论并不一致。例如，在T破产案中，银行向几名个人债务人提供贷款，并以不动产附着物、设备、库存和后得财产作为担保物。为使担

Courts which have addressed the scope of Sec. 9-402（7） have reached differing conclusions. For example, in In re Taylorville Eisner Agency, a bank made a loan to individual debtors secured by fixtures, equipment, inventory, and after-acquired property. In order to perfect its

保权益获得完善，银行登记了融资声明，并将全部个人列为债务人。在签署本票和担保协议的同一天，这些个人将担保物转让给他们之前已设立的一个公司，且该公司承担了向银行偿还贷款的义务。银行没有登记将该公司列为债务人的新融资声明。被转让的担保物成为公司库存。公司将该库存出售后，用后得财产更新了库存。再后，公司宣布破产。该案破产受托人引用第 9.402 条（7）款最后一句辩称，由于银行没有登记将公司列为新债务人的新融资声明，因此，对于公司随后取得的库存，银行不持有完善担保权益。

security interest, the bank filed a financing statement naming the individuals as debtors. On the same day as the note and security agreement were signed, the individual debtors transferred the collateral to a corporation they had previously formed and the corporation assumed the bank loan. The bank did not file a new financing statement naming the corporation as the new debtor. After selling the inventory which had been transferred and replacing it with after-acquired inventory, the corporation declared bankruptcy. Relying on the last sentence of Sec. 9-402（7）, the trustee argued that because the bank had not filed a new financing statement naming the corporation as the new debtor, the bank did not have a perfected security interest in the corporation's after-acquired inventory.

审理该案的地区法院不同意上述主张，并在判决书中说："该款最后一句提到被债务人转让的担保物，但这必然是指设有第 9.105 条（1）（c）款所定义之担保权益的财产。因此，在本案中，担保权益既覆盖现有的不动产附着物和设备，也覆盖后得的库存和商品。第 9.402 条（7）

The district court disagreed, stating in pertinent part："[T] he final sentence speaks of collateral transferred by the debtor, which must mean the property subject to the security interest as defined in UCC Sec. 9-105（1）（c）. In this case the security interest covered existing fixtures and equipment as well as acquired inventory and merchandise. The third sentence of subsection 7 is clear

款第三句的意思很明显，即对于被债务人转让的担保物，无论受担保方是否知道或同意，已登记的融资声明都继续有效。而被转让的担保物，也必然包括后得财产。”因此，该法院判定，银行为了维持其对后得财产的完善担保权益，无须登记将公司列为新债务人的新融资声明。

that the filed statement remains effective with respect to collateral transferred by the debtor regardless of the knowledge or consent of the secured party. This also means collateral which is after-acquired property." Consequently, the district court held that the bank did not have to file a new financing statement naming the corporation as the new debtor in order to retain its perfected security interest in after-acquired property.

相反的判例　但在B诉F案中，联邦第六巡回上诉法院却得出不同结论。在该案中，银行向一家汽车经销商提供贷款，并通过登记融资声明完善了银行的担保权益。融资声明将该经销商列为债务人，并覆盖了其“全部库存新车和展示车”。该经销商的资产随后被出售给个人，而该个人又将资产出售给一家无利益关系的新公司。银行没有登记将新公司列为债务人的新融资声明。新公司随后宣布破产。

The Sixth Circuit reached a contrary result in Bluegrass. In Bluegrass, a bank made a loan to Bluegrass-Ford, a car dealership. The bank perfected its security interest by filing a financing statement which covered “all new cars and demonstrators in the inventory of Bluegrass Ford, Inc.” . The assets of the dealership were subsequently sold to an individual who then transferred the assets to a new, unrelated corporate entity called Bluegrass Ford-Mercury, Inc. The bank did not file a new financing statement naming Bluegrass Ford-Mercury as the new debtor. The new dealership subsequently filed bankruptcy.

在该案上诉程序中，银行辩称，以旧经销商名字登记的融资

On appeal, the bank argued that the financing statement filed in the name of

声明，使新公司后得库存中的担保权益也获得完善。第六巡回法院拒绝了该主张。法院认为，法典第 9.402 条（7）款最后一句只适用于“债务人所转让的担保物”。法院随后判定，该文字不包含“作为受让人的债务人（新公司）当时尚未取得的财产”。因此，法院的结论是，银行原来以旧经销商名字登记的融资声明，不能使新公司的后得库存中的担保权益获得完善。

Bluegrass Ford perfected its security interest in the after-acquired inventory of Bluegrass Ford-Mercury. The Sixth Circuit rejected this argument. The court noted that the last sentence of Sec. 9-402（7） applies only “to collateral transferred by the debtor”. The court then held that this language did not “encompass collateral not yet acquired by the transferee debtor”. Consequently, the court concluded that the bank's financing statement originally filed in the name of Bluegrass Ford did not perfect its security interest in Bluegrass Ford-Mercury's after-acquired inventory.

其他判例 遵循联邦第六巡回上诉法院的判决，其他一些法院也判定，根据第 9.402 条（7）款，该款所说的“债务人所转让的担保物”不包括后得财产（参见 C 破产案），因此，受担保方只有登记新的融资声明，列出原债务人的第三方受让人的名字，才能对该受让人的后得财产取得完善担保权益［参见 M 破产案中的 S 诉 A 案（法院同意破产受托人的主张，即银行有义务登记一份修订的融资声明。只

In accordance with the Sixth Circuit, other courts have concluded that pursuant to Sec. 9-402（7）, after-acquired property cannot constitute “collateral transferred by the debtor”, see In re Cohutta Mills, and that a creditor perfects a security interest in after-acquired property of the debtor's transferee by filing a new financing statement in the name of the debtor's third party transferee. See Steinberg v. American Nat'l Bank & Trust Co. of Chicago（In re Meyer-Midway, Inc.）（“The Court agrees with the Trustee that the Bank would be obligated to file a

有这样，才能使银行对于新的担保物，或对于银行希望根据后得财产条款而获得保护的担保物取得完善的担保权益）；C 诉 S 案；引用文章（“对于受让人所取得的新财产，如果要完善其中的担保权益，受担保方必须登记一份由受让人签名的新的融资声明，或者必须取得新财产的占有”）]。

revised financing statement to be perfected in new collateral or collateral intended to secure the Bank under the after-acquired property clause”）； Citizens Savings Bank v. Sac City State Bank； see also William M. Burke, The Duty to Refile Under Section 9-402（7）of the Revised Article 9, Bus.Law. （“In order to perfect any security interest in the new property acquired by the transferee, the secured creditor must either file a financing statement signed by the transferee or take possession of the new property”）.

结论　我们的结论是，第六巡回上诉法院的分析是正确的。如同该法院所说，根据第 9.402 条（7）款，已登记的融资声明仅对“债务人所转让的担保物”继续有效。受让人将原有担保物转让后再购买的新库存，不可能被视为“债务人所转让的”财产（C 破产案）。因此，在担保物转让之前以转让人名字登记的融资声明，不能使受担保方对受让人的后得财产的担保权益获得完善（参见 B 诉 F 案；M 破产案）。

We conclude the Sixth Circuit's reasoning is correct. As the court noted, under Sec. 9-402（7） a filed financing statement remains effective only as “to collateral transferred by the debtor”. Inventory purchased by the transferee after the transfer cannot constitute property “transferred by the debtor”. In re Cohutta Mills. Thus, a financing statement filed prior to a transfer of collateral in the name of the transferor does not serve to perfect a security interest in the transferee's after-acquired property. See Bluegrass； In re Meyer-Midway.

将上述分析应用于本案后，我们的结论是，本案融资方所登

Applying this reasoning to the instant case, we conclude the financing statement

记的将破产债务人列为债务人的融资声明，不能使融资方对收购方的后得库存的担保权益获得完善。因此，融资方本应登记新的融资声明,将收购方列为债务人。由于融资方未能这样做，其对收购方后得库存的担保权益处于未完善状态。

Coremark filed in the name of MAKO did not perfect its security interest in RMC's after-acquired inventory. Rather, in order to perfect its security interest in RMC's after-acquired property, Coremark should have filed a new financing statement naming RMC as the debtor. Because Coremark failed to do so, its security interest in RMC's after-acquired inventory remained unperfected.

融资方的另一个理由不能成立 融资方辩称，上述结果直接与破产债务人重组计划的明文规定相冲突，因为该计划规定，融资方的留置权将“根据其原有条款继续保持充分效力”。融资方辩称，根据重组计划的该规定，融资方无须以收购方的名字登记融资声明，而仍可对收购方的后得库存取得完善担保权益。我们不同意该主张。

Coremark contends this result would contravene the express provisions of the MAKO bankruptcy plan which provided that Coremark's lien would "continue in full force and effect in accordance with [its] terms". Coremark contends this provision of the bankruptcy plan relieved it from the requirement of filing a financing statement in the name of RMC to perfect its security interest in RMC's after-acquired inventory. We disagree.

重组计划规定，融资方的留置权将继续存在于“收购方根据重组计划所收购”的资产中。如上文所述，此种被收购的资产，是指破产债务人转让给收购方的库存。因此，根据重组计划的明文规定，融资方的留置权仅针对

The plan provided that Coremark's lien would continue as to assets "to be acquired by RMC pursuant to [the] Plan". As noted above, the assets to be acquired consisted of the inventory transferred by MAKO to RMC. Consequently, under the express terms of the plan, Coremark's lien remained perfected only

收购方基于重组计划所收购的财产而保持完善。因此，与融资方的声称正相反，破产重组计划没有免除融资方重新作出登记的义务，即融资方必须在新融资声明中将收购方列为债务人后，才能对其后得库存取得完善担保权益。维持地区法院的判决。

as to property acquired by RMC under the MAKO plan. Thus, contrary to its assertions otherwise, the MAKO plan did not relieve Coremark of the requirement that it file a financing statement naming RMC as the debtor in order to perfect its security interest in RMC's after-acquired inventory. Affirmed.

案例 43　如何适用最低区间余额原则中的比例原则?

Bombardier Capital, Inc. v. Key Bank of Maine
庞巴迪资本公司诉缅因凯易银行案

缅因州最高法院 1994 年；639 A.2d 1065

简　介

本案涉及两个当事方对同一银行账户内资金的争议。该银行账户的持有人是已经破产的本案债务人（Sherlock Homes）。债务人之前曾分别从账户所在银行（Key Bank）和另一家金融公司（Bombardier Capital）获得贷款，并分别与两个债权人订立了担保协议，以债务人库存的预制活动房屋及其全部收益作为担保物。银行和金融公司都通过登记融资声明使各自的担保权益获得完善。债务人出售库存后所获得的现金收益，被存入该银行账户。

债务人在出售了两栋由金融公司提供贷款的活动房屋后，向金融公司出立了两张支票。随后，银行从债务人账户的情况中看到债务人财务状况不佳。当时，虽然账户内有足够资金支付该两张支票，但银行没有支付，而是先从账户内提取了全部资金，用于偿付债务人欠银行的担保贷款。债务人随后宣告破产。由于债务人没有足够资金偿还金融公司的贷款，金融公司起诉银行，认为银行从账户内划走资金的做法，属于对金融公司财产的侵占。

在本案中，银行和金融公司都对账户内资金持有完善担保权益，因为两者都对债务人的库存和收益持有担保权益，而该资金属于出售库存后的收益。通常而言，如果两个受担保方争夺同一担保物（如本案账户内的资金），两者之间的优先顺序需要根据法典有关优先权的一般原则（首先登记或完善，“first to file or perfect”）来确定，或根据法典的某些特殊原则（如有关价款担保权益的原则）来确定。但在本案中，账户内的资金来源不同，且已完全混合而无法分辨。并且，账户里既有债务人自己的资金，也有属于两个受担保方的资金（出售库存后的收益）。在这种情况下，法典没有提供具体的区分方法来确定哪些资金归债务人，哪些资金归受担保方；对于归属于两个受担保方的那部分资金，法典也没有说如何在两者之间分配。

对于这个问题，法院传统上借用衡平法中的“最低区间余额原则”（lowest intermediate balance rule）来解决，而不再适用法典中的任何优先权原则。最低区间余额原则源于信托法。根据该原则，如果受托人将自己的资金和自己掌管的受益人资金相混合，混合资金的剩余部分原则上被视为受益人的资金。如果有两个受益人，则两个受益人应按比例分享。在本案中，虽然可以认为有两个受益人（银行和金融公司），但初审法院认为，两者不应按比例分享，因为银行属于有过错的一方，即明知融资公司也对账户资金持有担保权益，但仍然利用自己掌管账户的便利，而自行划走了账户内的全部资金。缅因州最高法院判定，虽然银行存在一定过错，但似乎不足以推翻按比例分配的原则，因此两者仍应按比例分享。

判　决

初审法院的判决　初审法院以无审判决的形式判决金融公司胜诉。银行提起上诉。初审法院的认定是，银行侵占了金融

Defendant Key Bank of Maine（the “Bank”）appeals from a summary judgment entered in favor of plaintiff Bombardier Capital, Inc.（“Bombardier”） in the

公司的资金，应向金融公司赔偿45,073.84美元。

本案问题和上诉结论 双方均对存入支票账户的资金持有担保权益，而该资金已与账户内其他资金混合。本案问题是，银行作出错误抵销后，应如何计算金融公司的损失？银行认为，初审法院的判决存在错误，因为法院拒绝按比例适用“最低区间余额原则”。我们同意银行的主张，因此推翻原判并发回重审，要求按22,884.19美元计算金融公司的损失。

初审法院的计算 基于双方不存在争议的事实，初审法院判决，作为法律问题，金融公司对收益的担保权益可以追溯至支票账户内的资金。由于账户余额已低于金融公司追索的收益数额，初审法院判定，金融公司可获得45,073.84美元，相当于账户的最低期间余额21,793.84美元，再加上23,280美元。后者是金融公司持有权益之库存的后续销售收益，并在银行行使抵销权之

Superior Court. The court ruled that the Bank converted Bombardier's funds and assessed damages of $45,073.84.

Both parties have a security interest in proceeds deposited in a commingled checking account. At issue is the measure of Bombardier's damages for a wrongful setoff by the Bank. The Bank contends that the court erred by refusing to apply the "lowest intermediate balance rule" on a pro rata basis. We agree with the Bank, and we vacate and remand for the entry of a judgment for Bombardier in the amount of $22,884.19.

Based on [the] undisputed facts, the Superior Court held as a matter of law that Bombardier's security interest in proceeds was traceable to funds in the checking account. Because the account balance had fallen below the amount of proceeds claimed by Bombardier, the court awarded $45,073.84, a sum equal to the lowest intermediate balance, $21,793.84, plus $23,280 of proceeds from later sales of Bombardier inventory deposited before the Bank exercised its setoff. The Bank appeals.

前被存入账户。银行提起上诉。

银行认为应适用比例原则 银行承认侵占了属于金融公司的某些财产，但辩称，金融公司有权获得的赔偿是 22,778.78 美元，而不是初审法院判定的 45,073.84 美元。银行声称，初审法院的错误在于，其考虑了银行的行为，但没有按比例适用最低区间余额原则。

The Bank acknowledges that it converted some of Bombardier's property. It argues, however, that Bombardier is entitled to only $22,778.78 in damages, not the $45,073.84 awarded by the Superior Court. The Bank contends that the court erred by considering the Bank's conduct and by failing to apply the lowest intermediate balance rule pro rata.

本案的实际情况 双方均对债务人的部分库存持有担保权益。双方的担保权益均继续存在于担保物的"任何可分辨收益"中［法典第 9.306 条（2）款］。担保物出售后被存入债务人账户的任何收益，都应当用于担保当事方所提供的贷款。如果我们分别看每个当事方的情况，则金融公司对 59,843.53 美元的收益享有担保权益，而银行对 88,906.17 美元的收益享有担保权益。但问题在于，账户余额已不足以偿付两个当事方的全部贷款。因此，为了计算银行因侵占行为而应向金融公司支付的赔偿数额，法院必须从账户余额中分

Both parties had a security interest in a portion of Sherlock's inventory. Both security interests "continued in any identifiable proceeds" of the secured collateral. M.R.S.A. § 9-306（2）. Any proceeds from the sale of collateral deposited in Sherlock's account rightfully secure the debt owed to the secured party. If we consider each party separately, Bombardier would have a security interest in $59,843.53 of proceeds, and the Bank would have a security interest in $88,906.17 in proceeds. The problem arises because the account balance was insufficient to satisfy both debts. Therefore, in order to award damages for conversion, the court was required to trace that portion of the account balance identifiable as Bombardier proceeds.

辨出属于金融公司的收益。

可分辨收益 法典没有对“可分辨收益”作出定义，也没有说明账户内的混合资金应如何划分。事实上，如果指望从法典内寻找这个问题的答案，“就如同向斯芬克斯寻求答案”（引用文章）。因此，基于衡平法中有关信托和返还的原则，大多数法院均适用衡平法中的“最低区间余额原则”［参见 H 诉 B 案；引用《信托法重述》（第 2 版）］。

The Uniform Commercial Code neither defines “identifiable proceeds” nor suggests how to allocate proceeds in a commingled account. In fact, turning to the Code for guidance on this issue is “like seeking advice of the Sphinx”. Robert H. Skilton, The Secured Party’s Rights, S.Ill.U.L.J. Instead the majority of courts have applied by analogy the “lowest intermediate balance rule” found in the equitable law governing trusts and restitution. See, e.g., Harley-Davidson Motor Co. v. Bank of New England; Restatement (Second) of Trusts.

最低区间余额原则 但是，采用衡平处理方法的信托法，目的是保护无辜的受益人，因而无法直接解决本案担保交易所引起的问题（引用文章）。在信托法中，如果受托人将自己的资金与受益人的资金相混合，且受托人随后提取资金并将其花费，就要适用最低区间余额原则（引用《信托法重述》）。例如，受托人为受益人持有 1000 美元，并随后将该 1000 美元与自己资金混合后一起存入银行。受托人随

Trust law, however, with its equitable solutions designed to protect innocent beneficiaries, does not directly address the issue presented by this secured transaction problem. Secured Party’s Rights. Trust law applies the lowest intermediate balance rule when, after commingling the beneficiary’s money with her own, the trustee draws out funds and dissipates them. Restatement. For example, T is trustee for B of $1000. T deposits B’s money together with $1000 of her own money in a bank. T then withdraws all but $500 and spends it. T later deposits $1000

后提取了账户中的大部分资金并花费殆尽，只剩下 500 美元。此时，受益人有权获得 500 美元，即最低区间余额（引用《信托法重述》）。

of her own money back into the account. B is entitled to $500, the lowest intermediate balance. Restatement.

多个受益人的比例原则　但是，如果不止一个受益人对混合资金账户持有权益，就要按比例适用上述原则（引用《信托法重述》）。根据比例原则，如果受托人为受益人甲持有 1000 美元，并为受益人乙持有 2000 美元，并将全部资金存入受托人个人账户，然后提取并花费了账户内大部分资金，只剩 1500 美元。此时，根据按比例最低区间余额原则，甲有权获得 500 美元，乙有权获得 1000 美元。根据该原则，任何一个受益人都不能获得最低区间余额的全部，而只能按比例分配。

When more than one beneficiary has an interest in a commingled account, however, the rule is applied pro rata. Restatement. Under this formulation, T deposits the $1000 he holds in trust for B along with $2000 he holds in trust for B2 in T's personal account. T then withdraws and spends all but $1500. The lowest intermediate balance is prorated so that B is entitled to $500 and B2 is entitled to $1000. Id. Under this rule, neither beneficiary receives the full lowest intermediate balance, but each recovers her proportionate share of the lowest intermediate balance.

对本案的适用　将上述原则应用于本案后，假设金融公司是唯一的受担保方，那么，金融公司本来有权获得的数额是：两张支票被提示收款之前账户内的最低区间余额，再加上随后存入的

Applying these rules to the instant case, if Bombardier were the only secured creditor it would be entitled to the lowest intermediate balance before the checks were presented for payment, plus any proceeds identifiable to Bombardier deposited after that time. Using

归属于金融公司的可分辨收益。根据此种原则，初审法院得出的数额为45,073.84美元。

this rule the Superior Court arrived at a figure of $45,073.84.

但是，本案实际上有两个受担保方。如果承认两者的担保权益都有效，就需要持续地对账户余额按比例分配。也就是说，每次出现账户余额不足以偿付两者全部贷款的情况时，就要按比例计算。附件A显示了适当计算后的数额。

Here, however, there are two secured creditors. Recognition of both security interests requires continuous prorating of the account balance. Each time the balance falls below the amount necessary to satisfy both debts, it must be prorated. Appendix A documents the appropriate calculations.

至11月14日当日，账户内的收益为88,906.17美元。将这个数额按每个债权人有权获得的比例分配后，金融公司有权获得的可分辨收益为22,884.19美元，银行有权获得的为66,021.98美元。也就是说，由于银行有权获得66,021.98美元，因此，银行仅侵占了最低期间余额的剩余部分。基于此种分析，金融公司的损失数额为22,884.19美元。

As of November 14, the account contained proceeds totalling $88,906.17. Prorating this amount by the proportion each creditor was entitled to receive yields $22,884.19 in identifiable proceeds traceable to Bombardier and $66,021.98 traceable to the Bank. Because the Bank was entitled to $66,021.98, it converted only the remaining portion of the lowest intermediate balance. Under this analysis, Bombardier's damages equal $22,884.19.

银行过错的问题 金融公司辩称，不应按比例适用最低区间余额原则，因为如此适用的假设是双方都同等无辜。金融公司提出的这个主张显示，在从信托法

Bombardier argues that it is improper to apply the lowest intermediate balance rule pro rata because such an application assumes that the parties are equally innocent. Bombardier's argument points up the difficulties involved

借用相关概念来解决受担保方之间的法律争议时存在一定困难。在信托法中，按比例分配原则将受托人视为过错方，并假定两个受益人都同等无辜（引用《信托法重述》）。但在本案中，金融公司辩称，两个受益人并非同等无辜。银行对账户作出的抵销属于错误行为，因为当时其已知道金融公司也对账户资金持有担保权益。因此，金融公司请求本院判定，维持初审法院对最低区间余额原则的适用。

关于如何分析类似本案银行的做法，存在一些判例。在B诉F案中，被告银行知道原告债权人对账户资金持有担保权益，但仍在取得债务人同意后，将账户内的大部分资金用于偿还债务人对银行所欠的无担保债务。这样做之后，账户内余额不足以偿付原告债权人的贷款。法院判定，原告债权人对账户资金享有优先权，因此有权根据最低区间余额原则，取得账户中的可分辨收益。法院没有将账户内的可分辨收益在原告和被告之间按比例分配，

in borrowing concepts from trust law to solve legal conflicts between secured parties. In the context of trusts, the pro rata rule identifies the trustee as a wrongdoer and assumes that both beneficiaries are equally innocent. Restatement. Here, Bombardier argues, the parties are not equally innocent because the Bank acted wrongfully in setting off the account knowing that Bombardier also had a security interest in funds in the account. Therefore, Bombardier urges us to uphold the Superior Court's application of the lowest intermediate balance rule.

There is authority for considering a bank's behavior in situations similar to that presented here. In Brown & Williamson Tobacco Corp. v. First Nat' l Bank of Blue Island, the defendant bank, knowing that the plaintiff creditor had a security interest in the funds, obtained authorization from the debtor to use most of its account balance to satisfy an unsecured bank loan. That action drained the account of sufficient funds to satisfy plaintiff's loan. The court held that plaintiff had a priority interest and was entitled to the proceeds identifiable using the lowest intermediate balance rule. The identifiable

因为法院认为被告干扰了原告的有效担保权益，妨碍了原告对其权益的行使。法院认为，“被告必须为其行为付出代价。否则，法院就支持了错误的一方”。

funds were not prorated between plaintiff and defendant because defendant had interfered with plaintiff's valid security interest and prevented plaintiff from enjoying that interest. "Defendant must pay the price for its action. Otherwise [the court] would be placing roses around the wrong horse".

但在B诉F案中，被告银行对账户内的资金不持有担保权益。也就是说，本来就没有理由适用比例原则。在另一个判例中，法院判定，对资金进行追溯的方法，要受制于“法院适用衡平原则的自由裁量权”[I破产案中（资金被混合后，法院可以行使自由裁量权，并可以适用最低区间余额原则来追溯收益）]。但是，至少有两个法院认为，如果当事方不是同等无辜，则适当的救济是，过错更多的一方应承担举证责任，来证明其对账户资金的权利（参见A案；C诉S案）。在本案中，对于根据比例原则银行有权获得的收益数额，银行已经作出了证明。

In Brown, however, the defendant bank asserted no security interest in the funds, which meant that there was no basis on which to apply the pro rata rule. Another court has held that tracing rules are subject to "the equitable discretion of the court". In re Intermountain Porta Storage, Inc. (where funds are commingled, court may exercise discretion and apply lowest intermediate balance rule to trace proceeds). At least two courts, however, have stated that, when the parties are not equally innocent, the proper remedy is simply to place the burden of proof on the party less innocent to demonstrate its interest in the account. See Ex parte Alabama Mobile Homes, Inc.; C.O. Funk & Sons, Inc. v. Sullivan Equipment, Inc. Here, the Bank has identified the amount of proceeds traceable to it under the pro rata rule.

在本案中，我们认定，法律

In this instance, we determine that the

可以借用衡平原则，但无须全盘照搬。如果一方侵占另一方的财产，另一方有权取得相当于侵占发生时的财产价值的赔偿。在本案中，如果判决金融公司可以获得超出其比例份额的赔偿，将使金融公司获得一笔横财。本院推翻原判并发回重审，指令作出金融公司有权获得 22,884.19 美元赔偿的判决。

law borrows a concept from equity without adopting the entire panoply of equitable principles. Conversion entitles a party to damages equaling the value of its property at the time of the conversion, and to award Bombardier anything more than its pro rata share would result in a windfall. The entry is： Judgment vacated. Remanded for the entry of a judgment in favor of plaintiff in the amount of $22,884.19.

案例44　账户资金混合后哪些是受担保方的应得收益？

Universal CIT Credit Corp. v. Farmers Bank of Portageville
环球斯特信贷公司诉波特镇种植主银行案

密苏里州东区联邦地区法院 1973 年；358 F. Supp. 317

简　介

本案涉及信贷公司（CIT）与银行（Farmers Bank）之间就一笔账户资金产生的争议。在本案中，破产债务人（Ryan）在破产前经营一家汽车销售公司。出于经营需要，债务人与信贷公司达成“库存融资”（floor plan financing）的安排。根据这项安排，信贷公司向债务人提供贷款，并对债务人的所有库存汽车及其收益持有担保权益。信贷公司通过登记融资声明使担保权益获得了完善。债务人在本案银行设有个人账户，用于债务人的所有日常资金往来。汽车销售后的货款，也被债务人存入这个账户。因此，从信贷公司的角度，账户内的一部分资金是汽车担保物的收益。债务人和信贷公司的合作关系随后出现问题。信贷公司通知债务人将终止双方合作，并不再提供新的贷款。

由于没有其他融资来源，债务人预感自己将很快陷入破产。此时，债务人账户内尚有一定资金。债务人之前曾从银行取得无担保贷款，尚欠银行 12,000 美元。债务人与银行关系较好，因此希望先用账户内的资金归还银行贷款。为此，1970 年 1 月 15 日下午 3 时过后，债务人联系了银行的一名职员，告诉他信贷公司将自己逼入破产境地，因此自己想先把银行的贷款还了，而不再顾及信贷公司的贷款。当时银行已结束当天的营业，但银行职员还是从账户内划走了债务人所欠的 12,000 美元。信贷公司于次日要求兑现债务人之前开出的支票，但账户内已没有足够资金。随后，债务人宣告破产。信贷公司因而起诉银行，认为银行侵占了本属于信贷公司的资金。

在本案中，银行是债务人的无担保债权人，而信贷公司是担保债权人。对于账户内的资金，只要属于出售汽车后的可分辨收益，信贷公司就持有担保权益。但在本案中，账户混合了各种资金，已经无法再分辨。因此，法院只能根据信托法中的衡平原则，基于“最低期间余额原则”，来确定账户内到底有多少剩余资金应归属于信贷公司。由于账户在一段时间内多次存入和提取资金，因此必须根据每一次进出分别计算，并且要考虑进入的资金是否应归属于信贷公司。

本案另一个问题是，银行是否有权从账户内划走资金，用于偿还债务人欠银行的贷款？根据一般原则，即使受担保方对账户内资金持有担保权益，但如果账户内资金被支出，例如，像本案中这样被用于偿还银行的贷款，受担保方不一定再有权进行追索。但在本案中，法院认为，银行的做法不在“正常业务过程中”（ordinary course of business），因此，尽管银行的债权本来是真实的，且债务人在通常情况下可将账户资金用于偿还银行贷款，但在本案情况下，银行不享有获得该付款的权利。另外，法院认为，可能也存在一些其他理由，致使银行无权自行作出抵销。

判　决

本案基本情况　当事方不存在争议的事实是，信贷公司对债务人的 6 辆汽车及其收益持有一

It is not disputed that plaintiff had a continuously perfected security interest in six automobiles and their proceeds. See

直处于完善状态的担保权益［参见法典第9.306条（3）款］。债务人分别将这些汽车出售，并将每一辆车的货款存入银行支票账户。在作出这些存款之前或同时，其他资金也被存入这个账户。同时，在出售第一辆车和最后一辆车之间的这段时间，从这个账户开具了多张支票。

信贷公司的主张 信贷公司基于法典第9.306条（2）款声称，银行没有权利于1970年1月15日从该账户中支取12,000美元。法典该条规定："除本篇另有规定外，担保物被债务人出售、出租或以其他方式处置后，其中的担保权益继续存在，除非受担保方在担保协议中或以其他方式同意债务人的处置；并且，担保权益还继续存在于债务人所收到的可分辨收益中，包括所收到的任何款项。"

银行的主张 银行辩称，出售6辆汽车所获得的收益，不属于法典第9.306条（2）款所述的"可分辨"收益。银行辩称，当这些收益被存入债务人账户并

§ 9-306（3）V.A.M.S. Ryan sold separately each of these automobiles and deposited the amount received on each sale in his checking account at the defendant bank. Funds from other sources were deposited in the checking account prior to and contemporaneously with such deposits. Numerous checks were issued on the account between the time of the first and last sale.

Plaintiff contends that the defendant bank was not entitled to debit Ryan's checking account in the amount of $12,000 on January 15, 1970, relying upon Section 9-306（2）, which provides: "Except where this article otherwise provides, a security interest continues in collateral notwithstanding sale, exchange or other disposition thereof by the debtor unless his action was authorized by the secured party in the security agreement or otherwise, and also continues in any identifiable proceeds including collections received by the debtor."

Defendant contends that the proceeds from the sales of the six automobiles were not "identifiable" within the meaning of § 9-306（2）. Defendant argues that when the proceeds were deposited and thereby

因此与账户中其他资金混合之后，并当超出存入资金数额的大笔资金被随后从该账户中提取之后，汽车的收益就完全丧失了可辨性。

可分辨的标准　密苏里州尚无任何判例曾对法典上述规定中所使用的“可分辨”一词作出定义。法典第 1.103 条规定，除非被法典任何特定条款所排除，其他具有补充作用的法律原则都继续适用于商业合同。基于法典第 1.103 条，本院认定，如果管辖本案交易的州法认为本案收益可以追溯，该收益即属于“可分辨”。在某些类似的情况下，密苏里州曾认可某些判例中所采纳的方法，即基于推定信托而从混合资金中追溯特定资金（P 诉 P 案）。因此，根据密苏里州法律，虽然销售 6 辆汽车的货款已和其他资金混合，且随后从混合后的资金中又提取了资金，但仅此事实本身，不足以使该收益成为不可分辨的收益。

信托法原则　如 P 诉 P 案法院所说：“如果违反自己义务

commingled with other funds in Ryan’s account and thereafter substantial withdrawals were made exceeding the amount of the deposited proceeds, the proceeds completely lost their identity.

No Missouri case defines the term “identifiable” as used in this section. It is provided in § 1-103 that all supplemental bodies of law continue to apply to commercial contracts except insofar as displaced by the particular provisions of the Uniform Commercial Code. Applying § 1-103, this court concludes that proceeds are “identifiable” if they can be traced in accordance with the state law governing the transaction. Missouri has recognized in an analogous situation suits to impose a constructive trust that special funds may be traced into commingled funds. Perry v. Perry. The mere fact that the proceeds from the sales of the six automobiles were commingled with other funds and subsequent withdrawals were made from the commingled account does not render the proceeds unidentifiable under Missouri law.

As the court said in Perry v. Perry: “where a defaulting trustee has first

的受托人先将受托资金与自己资金相混合，然后再从混合后的资金中取款，用于清偿自己的债务，那就应假定，其所提取的是自己放入混合资金中的那部分资金，‘而不是受托资金’。因此，剩下的全部资金都是他以受托人身份承担责任的受托资金。”（L诉L案；C诉C案）

commingled the trust funds with his own and then paid them out in satisfaction of his own debts, it will be presumed that the payment was made from his own contribution to the commingled fund, ‘and not out of the trust money,’ so that whatever is left is the money for which he is accountable in his fiduciary capacity. Lolordo v. Lacy; Cross v. Cross.”

银行借记账户的权利 但是，在对收益进行溯源之前，有必要先确定另一个问题，即在本案事实背景下，假定债务人的支票账户包含了出售6辆汽车的收益，那么，银行是否仍然有权借记该账户？法典第9.306条正式评论2（c）说：“如果现金收益被存入债务人的支票账户，且在债务人的业务过程中被支出，则毫无疑问，即使该账户的资金是受担保方的收益，收到款项的人也可以不受制于受担保方的权利。但这里所说的，是正常情况下的付款或转账。在适当情况下，如果存在欺诈性转让，则相关法律无疑会允许受担保方从非正常受让人追回该收益，或从与债务

Before tracing the proceeds, it is necessary to decide whether under the circumstances in this case the defendant bank was entitled to debit Ryan’s checking account if the account contained proceeds from the sales of the six automobiles. Comment 2（c） to § 9-306 provides: “Where cash proceeds are covered into the debtor’s checking account and paid out in the operation of the debtor’s business, recipients of the funds of course take free of any claim which the secured party may have in them as proceeds. What has been said relates to payments and transfers in ordinary course. The law of fraudulent conveyances would no doubt in appropriate cases support recovery of proceeds by a secured party from a transferee out of ordinary course or otherwise

人合谋欺诈受担保方的受让人追回该收益。”

欺诈问题　关于这个问题，密苏里州没有相关判例。但是，密苏里州长期以来都承认，欺诈性转让的标志之一，是正常业务过程以外的交易（B 诉 B 案）。在密苏里州，“欺诈问题如同其他事实问题一样，都可以通过背景证据来证明。并且，有些情况一直都被视为带有欺诈的表象或标志。有时，多项情况中的单独一项可能不足以证明欺诈，但有可能构成欺诈的假定，特别是当同时存在欺诈的多项表象时”（B 诉 B 案）。

银行借记不在正常业务过程之中　在本案中，债务人告诉银行的一位职员说，信贷公司已经终止了库存贷款项目，而自己希望能保证银行贷款的安全。债务人要求该职员借记自己的账户。当该职员建议由债务人出立一张向银行付款的支票时，债务人表示，自己希望银行以借记方式支取自己的账户，并且还告诉该职员，他已经给信贷公司出立了若

in collusion with the debtor to defraud the secured party.”

There are no Missouri cases on point. However, Missouri has long recognized that one indicia of a fraudulent conveyance is a transaction outside the usual course of doing business. Bank of New Cambria v. Briggs. In Missouri, “fraud, like any other fact, may be established by circumstantial evidence [and] [t] here are circumstances which have come to be recognized as indicia or badges of fraud, one of which circumstances alone may not prove fraud, but may warrant an inference of fraud, especially where there is a concurrence of several indicia of fraud”. Id.

Ryan told Saalwaechter that plaintiff had revoked the floor plan and that he wanted the bank to be safe on its loan. Ryan asked Saalwaechter to debit his account. When Saalwaechter suggested that Ryan write a check to the bank, Ryan indicated that he preferred the bank run a debit against the account and further informed Saalwaechter that he had issued checks to plaintiff and wished to keep plaintiff from collecting on the checks. All of these events, including the debit

干支票，但不想让信贷公司收到该支票的款项。所有这些情况，包括对债务人账户的借记，在债务人于 1970 年 1 月 15 日关闭业务之后都显露出来。这些事实明显说明，对债务人账户的借记，不是发生在正常业务过程中。如上所说，密苏里州没有直接涉及这个问题的判例，但本院的结论是，在本案的情况下，密苏里州法院不会允许银行保留不在正常业务过程中通过借记而取得的款项，并以这种方法来挫败信贷公司对 6 辆汽车的可分辨收益的担保权益。

to Ryan's account, transpired after the close of business on January 15, 1970. These facts clearly show that the debit of Ryan's account was not in the ordinary course of business. Although, as indicated above, there are no Missouri cases directly on point, this court concludes that the Missouri courts would not, under these circumstances, permit the defendant bank to retain the amount debited outside the usual course of business and thereby defeat the security interest of plaintiff in the identifiable proceeds of the sale of the six automobiles.

银行进行询问的义务 有关银行抵销权的法律也支持上述结论。作为一般原则，一般的存款账户均受制于银行的抵销权［F 诉 J 案（该案遵循了 A 诉 J 案的先例）］。上述一般原则的一个例外是，如果银行“已了解到足够多的事实，知道其他人对账户持有权益时，银行就有义务对账户的信托性质进行了解”，而没有权利作出抵销［N 诉 T 案（该案遵循了 B 诉 M 案的先例）］。

Support for this conclusion is also found in the law governing a bank's right of set-off. As a general rule an account constituting a general deposit is subject to the bank's right of set-off. First National Bank of Clinton v. Julian, following Adelstein v. Jefferson Bank & Trust Company. An exception to that general rule is that a bank is not entitled to a set-off where it has "sufficient knowledge of facts relating to the interests of others in the account as to put the bank on inquiry to ascertain the trust character of the account".

N 诉 T 案说明，可以使用间接证据来证明银行对存款之“信托性质”的了解，也可以使用其他证据，只要能够证明，银行已经掌握了足够多的信息，因此有义务对存款的信托性质进行询问。

在本案中，银行知道债务人与信贷公司存在库存融资关系，也知道债务人向信贷公司出立了若干支票但并不想让信贷公司获得付款。同时，债务人坚持要求银行借记其账户，且银行在营业时间结束后与债务人进行了沟通。所有上述情况，足以使银行有义务就债务人账户全部或部分资金可能具有的信托性质进行询问。

银行抵销权的效力　此外，即使本案银行不了解上述事实，其是否有权作出抵销仍然存在疑问。在 A 诉 F 案中，被告银行对一个债务人的账户作出了部分抵销，而一位持有连续完善担保权益的受担保方对该账户资金持

Northern Ins. Co. v. Traders Gate City National Bank, following Brown v. Maguire's Real Estate Agency. The Northern Insurance Company case indicates that the bank's knowledge of the “trust character” of a deposit can be shown by indirect evidence or by showing that the bank would have sufficient information to put it on inquiry as to the trust character of the deposit.

The bank's knowledge that Ryan had floor plan financing with plaintiff, that Ryan had issued checks to plaintiff which Ryan did not want collected by plaintiff, and Ryan's insistence that the bank run a debit against his account, coupled with the communication of such facts after banking hours, were sufficient to put the bank on inquiry as to the possible trust character of all or part of the funds deposited in Ryan's account.

Moreover, it is disputable whether the bank, even absent knowledge of the above facts, would be entitled to a set-off. In Associates Discount Corp. v. Fidelity Union Trust Company, a bank set off part of an account of one of its debtors which contained proceeds in which another party

有权益，因为账户资金包含了其担保物的收益。银行引用了法典第9.104条（i）款。该款规定：“本篇不适用于（i）任何抵销权。”银行辩称，自己因此有权作出抵销。但作为回复，该案法院认为：“法典这项规定不可能意味着，一名无担保债权人，如本案对争议资金持有债权的银行，在自己有机会进行抵销时，有权简单地抓住这个机会来挫败一项完善担保权益。法典该条仅仅说明，一名债权人即使不持有担保权益，也有可能享有抵销权。”

在该案中，银行声称，如果银行实际上并不知道账户资金中存在担保权益，银行就有权作出抵销。银行引用了新泽西州采纳法典之前的一些判例。该案法院回复说：“但是，这些判例即使适用于本案，也要受制于立法机构更高的权威性。立法机构通过采纳法典，使受担保方对出售担保物后的可分辨收益继续享有担保权益。”［法典第9.306条（2）款；A诉F案］

held a continuously perfected security interest. The defendant relied on § 9-104（i）, which provides：“［T］his Chapter does not apply...（i） to any right of set-off.” In response to the defendant's argument that it was entitled to the right of set-off, the court said：“This section, however, cannot mean that a general creditor, as the bank is here with respect to the funds in question, may abrogate a perfected security interest simply by having a right to an opportunity for a set-off. All this section means is that a right of set-off may exist in a creditor who does not have a security interest.”

The bank then contended that it was entitled to a set-off in the account in the absence of actual knowledge on its part that the funds in the account were subject to a security interest. The defendant relied on cases decided prior to the adoption of the Uniform Commercial Code in New Jersey. In response, the court said：“However, these cases, if applicable, are subject to the superior authority of the Legislature which, by enacting the Uniform Commercial Code, continued a plaintiff's security interest in the identifiable proceeds of sales of the collateral. N.J.S.A.

9-306（2）." Id.

最低期间余额原则　本院最后一项任务是，确认 6 辆汽车出售后的收益去向，以便确定银行于 1970 年 1 月 15 日银行营业结束后对债务人账户的借记是否侵占了该收益。如上所述，P 诉 P 案说明了法律的一般原则，即如果资金已混合，则在进行资金溯源时必须假定，所支出的任何款项，均不源于其他人持有合法权益的资金。这项原则通常称为“最低期间余额”原则。

This court's final task is to trace the proceeds of the sales of the six automobiles to determine if they were taken by the bank when it debited Ryan's account after the close of business on January 15, 1970. As indicated above, Perry v. Perry, stated the general rule that in tracing commingled funds it is presumed that any payments made were from other than the funds in which another had a legally recognized interest. This is commonly referred to as the "lowest intermediate balance" rule.

剩余资金被假定属于受益人　《信托法重述（第 2 版）》第 202 条的评论 j 的相关部分说：“如果受托人在银行同一账户中存入信托资金和自有资金，随后从存款中提取资金并花费了所提取的资金，随后又将自有资金存入账户，则受益人对账户内存款所享有的衡平留置权，在通常情况下不得超出存款的最低区间余额。”上述评论 j 所提供的第 20 个举例说明如下：“甲作为受托人持有乙的 1000 美元。甲将此款项以及自有的 1000 美元存入

Restatement of Trusts, Second, § 202, Comment j provides in pertinent part: "Where the trustee deposits in a single account in a bank trust funds and his individual funds, and makes withdrawals from the deposit and dissipates the money so withdrawn, and subsequently makes additional deposits of his individual funds in the account, the beneficiary cannot ordinarily enforce an equitable lien upon the deposit for a sum greater than the lowest intermediate balance of the deposit." Illustration 20 to Comment j is as follows: "A is trustee for B of $1000. He deposits this money together with $1000

银行。甲提取并花费了 1500 美元。甲随后又将自有的 1000 美元存入账户。乙对账户持有 500 美元的留置权，即这个期间内的最低余额。”

of his own in a bank. He draws out $1500 and dissipates it. He later deposits $1000 of his own in the account. B is entitled to a lien on the account for $500, the lowest intermediate balance.”

新存入资金的归属 本案情况在一个方面与上述评论 j 以及举例中所说的情况有所不同。本案中具有“信托性质”的资金存入，不是只有 1 次，而是分别有 6 次，且有将近 1 个月的跨度；且在这个期间内，多次向账户存入和从账户提取数额较大的其他资金。

The situation in the instant case differs from Comment j and the Illustration in one respect. We have not one, but six, separate deposits of funds of a “trust character” spanning a period of nearly a month, during which time a substantial number of withdrawals and deposits of other funds were made in the account.

《信托法重述（第 2 版）》第 202 条的评论 m 说：“如果受托人将信托资金存入其个人银行账户，且随后提取资金并花费了所提取的资金，且随后再向该账户存入自有资金，并显示出要归还其所提取的信托资金的意愿，则受益人对账户内存款的留置权，将不限于最低区间余额。如果信托资金和自有资金均被存入受托人以信托名义设立的账户，而不是受托人以个人名义设立的账户，且受托人从账户中提取了

Comment m to the Restatement of Trusts, Second, § 202 provides：“Where the trustee deposits trust funds in his individual account in a bank, and makes withdrawals from the deposit and dissipates the money so withdrawn, and subsequently makes additional deposits of his individual funds in the account, manifesting an intention to make restitution of the trust funds withdrawn, the beneficiary’s lien upon the deposit is not limited to the lowest intermediate balance. Where the deposit of trust funds and of his individual funds was in an account in the

超出其自有资金的数额，且随后再存入其自有资金，则受益人对账户存款的留置权，将不限于最低区间余额，因为新的存款将被视为对之前所提取的信托资金的归还。”

name of the trustee as such, and not in his individual account, and he withdraws more than the amount of his individual funds, and subsequently deposits his individual funds in the account, the beneficiary's lien upon the deposit is not limited to the lowest intermediate balance since the new deposit will be treated as made by way of restitution of the trust funds previously withdrawn."

新存入的资金不属于信贷公司　因此，受托人随后存入信托账户的资金，被假定系用于归还原来提取的资金（P 诉 P 案）。但是，受托人随后存入其自有账户的资金则不存在此种假定，除非受托人“显示出归还的意愿”。在本案中，不存在证明此种意愿的证据。因此，如果债务人随后存入自有账户的资金，与 6 辆汽车的出售收益无关，所存入的该资金就不能被视为对之前提取的信托资金的归还。但是，6 辆汽车中每一辆出售后所存入账户的资金，将被视为对信托资金的增加，因此将适用最低区间余额原则。

Thus, individual funds subsequently deposited to a trust account by the trustee are presumed to be by way of restitution. Perry v. Perry. Subsequent deposits by the trustee to his own account, on the other hand, are not so treated unless the trustee "manifests an intention to make restitution". No such manifestation of intent was shown in this case. Therefore, subsequent deposits of funds not relating to the proceeds from the sales of the six automobiles in Ryan's individual account will not be treated as made by way of restitution of trust funds previously withdrawn. However, each deposit of the proceeds of the sales of the six automobiles will be treated as additions to the trust fund, and the lowest intermediate balance theory will be followed.

结论 本院查验债务人的账户记录后认定，在银行1970年1月15日通过借记账户而支取12,000美元之前，基于信贷公司所持有的持续完善的担保权益，信贷公司有权获得的可分辨收益数额为11,429.11美元。在作出12,000美元借记之前，账户内经调整后的余额为15,823.35美元。从该数额中减去账户余存的“收益”（11,429.11美元），则银行有权借记的金额为4394.24美元。因此，信贷公司有权从银行追回银行超额借记的7605.76美元。这个数额被确定为信贷公司持有完善担保权益之担保物的收益。特此判决。

The court has examined the banking records of the Ryan account and finds that the identifiable proceeds in which plaintiff held a continuously perfected security interest on January 15, 1970 prior to the bank's $12,000 debit entry was $11,429.11. The pro forma balance prior to the $12,000.00 debit entry was $15,823.35. Subtracting from this amount the "proceeds" remaining in the account ($11,429.11), the amount which the bank was entitled to debit was $4394.24. Accordingly, plaintiff is entitled to recover from the bank the excess amount debited, or $7605.76. That amount is identified as proceeds in which plaintiff had a perfected security interest. So ordered.

案例 45　受担保方是否已放弃担保协议项下的权利?

National Livestock Credit Corp. v. Schultz
国民畜牧信贷公司诉舒尔茨案

俄克拉何马州民事上诉法院 1982 年；653 P.2d 1243

简　介

本案原告信贷公司（National Livestock）多年向一家养牛场（Schultz，本案农场主和被告之一）提供养牛场经营所需的贷款。信贷公司对农场主的牛群和全部收益持有完善的担保权益。根据双方的担保协议，农场主售牛时，无须事先取得信贷公司的书面同意，但必须要求买方在货款支票上将农场主和信贷公司列为共同受款人，并将支票直接交付给信贷公司，用于偿还信贷公司的贷款。农场主从未遵守过这个规定，一直都是要求买方向自己付款，然后自己随后再支付给信贷公司。对于农场主违反担保协议的做法，信贷公司从未提出过异议，因为农场主最终还是将售牛款转给了信贷公司，因此信贷公司并未受到任何损失。

若干年之后，信贷公司计划转变业务经营方向，因此告知农场主不再提供新贷款，并要求农场主在一定时间内偿还全部贷款余额。为此，农场主需要将全部库存的牛都售出。随后，农场主以不同方式将剩余的牛出售给若干买方（同被列为本案被告）。同以前一样，买方将支票交付给农场主，而没有交付给信贷公司。农场主此时还欠很多饲料供应商的钱，因此多次将售牛的货款用于支付供应商，而没有支付给信贷公司。信贷公司得知后，起诉农场主和牛的买方，认为农场主违反担保协议，并要求买方向信贷公司支付购牛的货款。由于买方实际上已向农场主支付过货款，因而自然拒绝再次支付。但是，由于某些原因，这些买方不能被视为正常业务中的买方，因而根据法典规定，他们所购买的牛要继续受制于信贷公司的担保权益。由于此时农场主已宣告破产，因此信贷公司的诉讼主要是针对这些买方。

这些买方承认，根据法典的一般规定，如果农场主的出售未得到信贷公司的授权，且买方不属于正常业务中的买方，则即使买方已经取得所购的牛并已向农场主支付过货款，信贷公司的担保权益仍然有效。但是，买方的抗辩理由是，虽然农场主的出售方式违反了担保协议，但信贷公司多年默许了农场主的做法，因而构成对担保协议相关条款的弃权。买方的另一个理由是，信贷公司的“履约过程”（course of performance），也就是其在担保协议履行过程中的实际做法，构成了对协议明示条款的修改，因此农场主的出售不违反修改后的协议。信贷公司认为，履约过程是法典第2篇中的概念，不能被用于第9篇中的担保交易，但这个说法未被法院接受。最终，法院认定信贷公司的担保权益对本案买方不再具有效力。

判　决

本案的问题　本上诉的主要问题是：担保协议规定了牛群担保物的出售条件，以保护受担保方的完善担保权益，但受担保方的行为长期与该条件不符，因此是否应认为其已放弃该条件？次

The major question raised by this appeal is whether the terms of a cattle security agreement regarding sale of the cattle, designed for perfected lender's protection, were waived by the creditor's long-term course of conduct inconsistent with the

要问题是：在针对牛群买方的侵占行为诉讼中，基于禁止自相矛盾原则的损害性依赖理论，是否应认为受担保方无权否认其已同意出售牛群？就此两个问题，初审法院均判决信贷公司败诉。我们维持原判。

信贷公司的主张　信贷公司长篇陈述中所列出的各项理由，可以归结为一点：本案的担保协议仅受法典第 1 篇（总则）和第 9 篇（担保交易）管辖，因此，初审法院的判决是错误的，因为其认定，可以引用法典第 2 篇规定的履约过程和弃权条款，来反驳担保协议的明示条款。信贷公司进一步辩称，信贷公司与本案各买方之间不存在任何相关交易，因此不能将禁止自相矛盾原则适用于信贷公司，并用该原则来阻止信贷公司对牛群所主张的担保权益。我们在下述讨论中将维持初审法院有关弃权问题的判决，因而没有必要再讨论信贷公司提出的损害性依赖理论。

其他法律原则的效力　信贷公司承认，并且不能不承认，法

protective provisions. A secondary issue is whether a secured party is estopped to deny authorization of the sale in a suit for conversion against the buyer based upon a detrimental reliance theory. The trial court resolved both issues against the loan company. We affirm.

The arguments raised by National in its voluminous brief boil down to this： only the provisions of general Article One of the Uniform Commercial Code and of secured transactions Article Nine govern security agreements, and therefore, the trial court erred in finding that the course of performance and waiver provisions of Article Two can be invoked to undermine express terms of a security agreement. It further argues there were no transactions between National and defendant packing companies that could act to estop National from asserting its security interest in the cattle. Since we affirm the trial court's order as to the waiver issue, it becomes unnecessary to address the detrimental reliance theory.

National concedes, as it must, that the uniform code expressly provides that its

典明确规定，法典条款应由其他法律原则和衡平原则加以补充，除非这些原则被法典特定条款排除（法典第1.103条）。法典同时还明确规定，为了促进法典的基本宗旨，应灵活地解释和适用法典。法典的基本宗旨之一就是，“使商业做法能够通过惯例、实践和当事方协议不断发展”[法典第1.102条（1）款和（2）（b）款]。

provisions shall be supplemented by principles of law and equity unless these principles have been displaced by particular provisions of the act. O.S. § 1-103. The code, too, explicitly provides that it is to be liberally construed and applied to promote its underlying purposes and policies, one of which is "to permit the continued expansion of commercial practices through custom, usage and agreement of the parties". O.S. § 1-102（1）&（2）（b）.

处置担保物后的一般原则

适用于本案的主要法典条款，是法典第9.306条。该条相关部分规定：“（2）除本篇另有规定外，担保物被出售、交换或以其他方式处置后，担保权益继续存在于担保物中，除非受担保方在担保协议中或以其他方式同意该处置；并且，担保权益还存在于任何可分辨收益中，包括债务人所收到的付款。”

The principal code provision having application to the present appeal is O.S. § 9-306, which provides in part: "（2）Except where this Article otherwise provides, a security interest continues in collateral, notwithstanding sale, exchange or other disposition thereof, unless the disposition was authorized by the secured party in the security agreement or otherwise, and also continues in any identifiable proceeds including collections received by the debtor."

很明显，根据法典规定，如果受担保方未同意担保物的出售，则对于买方已取得的担保物，以及债务人出售担保物后所收到的收益，受担保方继续持有担保

Clearly, the statute continues the secured party's security interest both in the collateral in the hands of a buyer as well as the proceeds received by the borrower from the unauthorized sale of the collateral.

权益。但是，如果受担保方“在担保协议中或以其他方式”同意该出售，担保权益将会丧失。

The security interest can be lost, however, and is lost if the sale is authorized by the secured party in the "security agreement or otherwise".

信贷公司的辩称　初审法院认定,本案中没有争议的事实是，信贷公司之前的行为，以及在本案中有关牛群出售的行为，已构成对合同权利的放弃。但信贷公司认为，虽然自己不否认相关事实，但不同意法院的结论，因为不应将弃权原则适用于法典范围内的担保协议。具体而言，信贷公司称，初审法院本来无权将法典第 2 篇中的某个概念适用于第 9 篇范围内的交易。信贷公司在提出上述主张时，假定初审法院判决时所依据的唯一法典条文是第 2.208 条。

The trial court found the undisputed facts to be that National's prior conduct and its actions in regard to the sales at issue here constituted a waiver of its contractual rights. While National does not deny the facts are undisputed, it does disagree with the court's conclusion on the ground that the doctrine of waiver cannot be applied to a U.C.C. security agreement. More specifically National contends that the court impermissibly applied an Article Two concept to an Article Nine transaction, and in advancing this thesis it assumes that the only statutory basis for the decision is O.S. § 2-208.

其他法律原则的适用　我们认为，信贷公司错误地理解了初审法院的判决依据，错误地理解了法典各项独立条款之间的相互影响，并错误地理解了其他具有补充效力的法律原则和衡平原则对商业交易的影响。法典第 1 篇包含了另一项适用于法典通篇的

We think National misapprehends the basis of the trial court's decision and the effect the separate articles of the uniform code have on one another as well as the effect supplemental principles of law and equity have on commercial transactions. Another provision in Article One, which is applicable to all sections of the code, amply supports

条款，而该条款可以充分支持初审法院的结论。至少曾有一个法院正确地指出，法典第1篇的各项定义（第1.201条）自动成为法典每一篇的组成部分。因此，任何“担保协议”，首先必然是法典第1.201条所定义的“协议”。根据法典的定义，协议是指“当事方的实际约定。此种约定应通过当事方使用的语言确定，或通过其他客观情况，包括本法所规定的（第2.208条）履约过程推定”。因此，协议必然包含担保协议。所以，某种履约过程，可以构成对担保协议中某个明示条款的弃权。

the trial court's legal conclusions. As at least one court has quite correctly pointed out, the definitions in Article One （O.S. § 1-201） are automatically made a part of each article in the code and thus a "security agreement" must first be an "agreement" as defined in § 1-201. And, since an agreement is defined by the code as "the bargain of the parties in fact as found in their language or by implication from other circumstances including ... course of performance as provided in this Act（Section ... 2-208）," this has to include security agreements. Therefore, a certain course of performance can result in the waiver of an express term in a security agreement.

支持弃权结论的另一个理由 其次，法典还提供了支持弃权理论的另一个理由。根据法典第9.306条（2）款，如果对于担保物的处置，受担保方“在担保协议中或以其他方式”给予了授权，担保权益就将不复存在。不能简单地将这项规定中的黑体部分视为多余。实际上，其中的“或”这个连词，使“其他方式”至少与担保协议明示条款具有同

There is yet another U.C.C. basis for the invocation of the waiver theory. Section 9-306（2） contemplates extinguishment of a security interest if disposition of collateral is authorized by a secured party "in the security agreement or otherwise". The ［bold］ language cannot be considered as mere surplusage and, in fact, the connective "or" gives it at least as much substantive value as the express terms of a security agreement. National's course of conduct certainly

等的实质价值。信贷公司的行为方式，无疑必须被视为以“其他方式”作出的出售授权，并因此导致本案买方在取得牛群后，不受制于信贷公司的担保权益。

has to be considered as an “otherwise” authorization of the sale that resulted in defendant purchasers taking the cattle free from National’s security interest.

衡平原则的适用　最后，除去法典各篇和各条之间的相互联系，前面还提到，在确定当事方权利时，法典第 1.103 条和第 1.102 条还允许使用其他法律原则和衡平原则对法典进行补充。法典的这两项条款，不仅要求法院要看当事方使用的文字，还要分析他们的行为，以确定他们实际达成了何种协议，以及何种结果是最公平的。基于本案实际情况，我们无疑应该适用长期遵循的这项衡平原则：“如果两个人都是无辜的，但其中一人必须承担第三人行为所造成的损失，那么，致使该第三人有机会造成损失的那个人，就必须承担该损失。”（P 诉 J 案）。

Finally, apart from the interconnections among the various articles and sections of the code, the previously mentioned § § 1-103 and 1-102, which allow for supplementation of the code with principles of law and equity in determining rights of the parties, require the court to look not only at the words used by the parties but to analyze their conduct as well in determining what agreement they actually made and what the equities should be. Certainly the facts of this case lend themselves to the application of one time honored maxim of equity: “Where one of two innocent persons must suffer by the act of a third, he who has enabled such third person to occasion the loss must suffer.” Pettis v. Johnston.

在本案中，我们假定信贷公司是无辜的当事方，但是，在养牛业务的状况恶化后，信贷公司没有采取措施来改变之前经营顺

Assuming National is an innocent party, it made no effort to alter the customary financial practices of prosperous times after the cattle business turned sour. This “business

利时所形成的资金安排。此种“平安无事”的态度，使农场主有机会不正当地使用争议资金。因此，从衡平角度看，应该由信贷公司承担损失。维持原判。

as usual” attitude made it possible for Schultz to misapply the funds in question and, therefore, from an equitable standpoint National should bear the loss. Affirmed.